OHIO COUNTY PUBLIC LIBRARY

murach's
ASP.NET 4.5
web programming
with C# 2012

Mary Delamater

Anne Boehm

DCLC

OHIO COUNTY PUBLIC LIBRARY
WHEELING. W. VA. 26003

TRAINING & REFERENCE

murach's
ASP.NET 4.5
web programming
with C# 2012

Mary Delamater

Anne Boehm

005.2762
DeLa
2012

MIKE MURACH & ASSOCIATES, INC.

4340 N. Knoll Ave. • Fresno, CA 93722

www.murach.com • murachbooks@murach.com

DEC 1 1 2014

1270294924

Authors:	Mary Delamater
	Anne Boehm
Editor:	Mike Murach
Cover design:	Zylka Design
Production:	Maria Spera

Books for .NET developers

Murach's C# 2012

Murach's ASP.NET 4.5 Web Programming with C# 2012

Murach's ADO.NET Database Programming with C#

Murach's Visual Basic 2012

Murach's ASP.NET 4.5 Web Programming with VB 2012

Murach's ADO.NET Database Programming with VB

Books for open-source web developers

Murach's HTML5 and CSS3

Murach's JavaScript and jQuery

Murach's JavaScript and DOM Scripting

Murach's PHP and MySQL

Books for Java programmers

Murach's Java Programming

Murach's Java Servlets and JSP (2nd Ed.)

Murach's Android Programming

Books for database programmers

Murach's SQL Server 2012 for Developers

Murach's MySQL

Murach's Oracle SQL and PL/SQL

For more on Murach books, please visit us at www.murach.com

© 2013, Mike Murach & Associates, Inc.
All rights reserved.

Printed in the United States of America

10 9 8 7 6 5 4 3 2 1
ISBN: 978-1-890774-75-2

Contents

Expanded contents

Chapter 5   How to test and debug ASP.NET applications

Section 2   ASP.NET essentials

Chapter 6   How to use the standard server controls

Section 3   ASP.NET database programming

Chapter 12   An introduction to database programming

Chapter 17   How to use object data sources with ADO.NET

Section 4   Finishing an ASP.NET application

Chapter 18   How to secure a web site

Section 5 Going to the next level

Introduction

ASP.NET is one of the primary technologies for developing web applications today. Together with Microsoft's Visual Studio, it provides a host of productivity features that you let you quickly build professional e-commerce applications.

Because this book assumes that you already know the basics of C#, it gets you off to a fast start with ASP.NET. In fact, by the end of chapter 5, you'll know how to use ASP.NET and Visual Studio to develop and test multi-page database applications. You'll also know how to integrate HTML5 and CSS3 into your ASP.NET applications.

But this is much more than a beginning book. By the time you're done, you'll have all the skills you need for developing e-commerce web applications at a professional level. You'll also find that this book does double duty as the best on-the-job reference book that money can buy.

What this book does

To be more specific about what this book presents, here is a brief description of each of its sections:

- Section 1 is designed to get you off to a fast start. It shows you how to use Visual Studio and ASP.NET to develop both one-page and multi-page Web Forms applications that get data from a database. It shows you how to integrate HTML5 and CSS into your web applications. It even shows you how to test and debug your web applications, a part of the job that many books treat too lightly or too late. At that point, you're ready for rapid progress in the sections that follow.

- Section 2 presents the other skills that you're likely to use in every ASP.NET application that you develop. That includes how to use the server controls and validation controls, as well as how to use state, cookies, and URL encoding to control the operation of an application. It also includes how to use master pages, themes, site navigation, ASP.NET routing, and friendly URLs to create user-friendly web sites.

- In section 3, you'll learn how to use the data access features of ASP.NET. That includes using SQL data sources, which reduce the amount of data access code that you need to write for an application. It includes bound controls that are designed to work with data sources, including the GridView, DetailsView, FormView, ListView, and DataPager controls.

And it includes object data sources, which make it easier to build 3-layer applications that separate the presentation code from the data access code.

- Section 4 presents the skills that you need for finishing an e-commerce application. Here, you'll learn how to secure data transmissions between client and server, how to authenticate and authorize users, how to use email, how to prevent problems caused by Back button refreshes, and how to deploy your applications. At this point, you've learned everything you need to know to develop and deploy e-commerce web applications.

- Then, section 5 shows you how to take your applications to another level. First, you'll learn how to use ASP.NET Ajax to build rich Internet applications (RIAs). Then, you'll learn how to create and consume WCF and Web API services. Last, you'll be introduced to ASP.NET MVC, which is completely different than developing web applications with Web Forms, but does a better job of separating the presentation, business, and database code.

To get the most from this book, we recommend that you start by reading the first section from start to finish. But after that, you can skip to any of the other sections to get the information that you need, whenever you need it. Since this book has been carefully designed to work that way, you won't miss anything by skipping around.

Why you'll learn faster and better with this book

Like all our books, this one has features that you won't find in competing books. That's why we believe you'll learn faster and better with our book than with any other. Here are some of those features.

- Because section 1 presents a complete subset of ASP.NET in just 5 chapters, you're ready for productive work much faster than you are when you use competing books. This section also uses a self-paced approach that lets experienced programmers move more quickly and beginners work at a pace that's right for them.

- Because the next 3 sections present all of the other skills that you need for developing e-commerce web applications, you can go from beginner to professional in a single book.

- If you page through this book, you'll see that all of the information is presented in "paired pages," with the essential syntax, guidelines, and examples on the right page and the perspective and extra explanation on the left page. This helps you learn faster by reading less...and this is the ideal reference format when you need to refresh your memory about how to do something.

- To make sure that you learn ASP.NET as thoroughly as possible, all of its features are presented in the context of complete applications. These applications include the web forms, the aspx code, and the C# code. As we see it, the best way to learn ASP.NET is to study applications like these, even though you won't find them in most competing books.

What software you need

To develop ASP.NET applications, you can use any of the full editions of Visual Studio 2012. These editions come with everything you need, including Visual Studio, C# 2012, a built-in web server called IIS Express that's ideal for testing ASP.NET applications on your own computer, and a scaled-back version of SQL Server called SQL Server Express LocalDB.

For a no-cost alternative to the commercial packages, you can download Visual Studio Express 2012 for Web from Microsoft's web site. It too provides all of the items listed above, it's a terrific product for learning how to develop ASP.NET applications, and both the applications and the skills that you develop with it will work with any of the full editions of Visual Studio. For information about installing these products, please refer to appendix A.

How our downloadable files can help you learn

If you go to our web site at www.murach.com, you can download all the files that you need for getting the most from this book. These files include:

- all of the applications in this book
- the starting code for the exercises at the ends of the chapters
- the solutions to the chapter exercises

These files let you test, review, and copy the application code. In addition, if you have any problems with the exercises, the solutions are there to help you over the learning blocks. Even when you've come up with a solution that works, our solution may show you a more elegant way to handle a problem. Here again, appendix A shows you how to download and install these files.

3 companion books for ASP.NET programmers

As you read this book, you may discover that your C# skills aren't as strong as they ought to be. In that case, we recommend that you get a copy of *Murach's C# 2012*. It will get you up-to-speed with the language. It will show you how to work with the most useful .NET classes. And as a bonus, it will show you how to develop Windows Forms applications.

The second companion is *Murach's SQL Server for Developers*. To start, it shows you how to write SQL statements in all their variations so you can code the right statements for your data sources. This often gives you the option of having Microsoft SQL Server do more, which simplifies your application code. Beyond that, this book shows you how to design and implement databases and how to use features like stored procedures.

Another book that we recommend is *Murach's ADO.NET Database Programming with C#*. This book shows you how to write the ADO.NET code that you need for using object data sources in your applications. It gives you insight into what ADO.NET is doing as you use SQL data sources. And it shows you how to work with XML, create reports, and use LINQ and the Entity Framework.

2 books for every web developer

Although chapter 3 presents a subset of the HTML and CSS skills that you need for ASP.NET programming, every web developer should have a full set of these skills. For that, we recommend *Murach's HTML5 and CSS3*. Beyond that, every web programmer should know how to use JavaScript and jQuery for client-side programming. For that, we recommend *Murach's JavaScript and jQuery*.

If you're new to these subjects, these books will get you started fast. If you have experience with these subjects, these books make it easy for you to learn new skills whenever you need them. And after you've used these books for training, they become the best on-the-job references you've ever used.

Support materials for trainers and instructors

If you're a corporate trainer or a college instructor who would like to use this book for a course, we offer an Instructor's CD that includes: (1) a complete set of PowerPoint slides that you can use to review and reinforce the content of the book; (2) instructional objectives that describe the skills a student should have upon completion of each chapter; (3) test banks that test mastery of those skills; (4) extra chapter exercises and projects that prove mastery; and (5) solutions to the extra exercises and projects.

To learn more about this Instructor's CD and to find out how to get it, please go to our web site at www.murach.com and click on the Trainers or Instructors link. Or, if you prefer, you can call Kelly at 1-800-221-5528 or send an email to kelly@murach.com.

Please let us know how this book works for you

This is the fifth edition of our ASP.NET book. For each edition, we've added the new features of ASP.NET, but we've also tried to improve the content and structure of the book. This time, with help from a new author, we've tried to improve both the technical excellence and educational effectiveness of every chapter in this book.

Now that we're done, we hope that we've succeeded in making this edition our best one ever. So, if you have any comments, we would appreciate hearing from you. If you like our book, please tell a friend. And good luck with your web programming.

Anne Boehm, Author
anne@murach.com

Mary Delamater, Author
mary@techknowsolve.com

Section 1

The essence of ASP.NET programming

This section presents the essential skills for designing, coding, and testing ASP.NET web applications. After chapter 1 introduces you to the concepts and terms that you need to know for ASP.NET programming, chapter 2 shows you how to develop a one-page web application with ASP.NET. That includes designing the form for the application and writing the C# code that makes it work, and that gets you off to a fast start.

Next, chapter 3 shows you the right way to use HTML5 and CSS3 with an ASP.NET application, and chapter 4 shows you how to develop a two-page Shopping Cart application that gets product data from a database. At that point, you'll know how to build multi-page applications. Then, chapter 5 shows you how test and debug ASP.NET applications.

When you finish all five chapters, you'll be able to develop real-world applications of your own. You'll have a solid understanding of how ASP.NET works. You'll be ready for rapid progress as you read any of the other sections of the book...and you can read those sections in whatever sequence you prefer.

1

An introduction to ASP.NET programming

This chapter introduces you to the basic concepts of web programming and ASP.NET. Here, you'll learn how web applications work and what software you need for developing ASP.NET web applications. You'll also see how the HTML code for a web form is coordinated with the C# code that makes the web form work the way you want it to. When you finish this chapter, you'll have the background that you need for learning how to develop ASP.NET web applications with Visual Studio 2012.

An introduction to web applications

A *web application* consists of a set of *web pages* that are generated in response to user requests. The Internet has many different types of web applications, such as search engines, online stores, auctions, news sites, social sites, and games.

Two pages of a Shopping Cart application

Figure 1-1 shows two pages of an ASP.NET web application. In this case, the application is for an online store that lets users purchase Halloween products, including costumes, masks, and decorations. In chapter 4, you'll learn how to build this application.

The first web page in this figure is used to display information about the products that are available from the Halloween store. To select a product, you use the drop-down list that's below the banner at the top of the page. Then, the page displays information about the product including a photo, short and long descriptions, and the product's price. The application gets the data for these pages from a database.

If you enter a quantity in the text box near the bottom of the page and click the Add to Cart button, the second page in this figure is displayed. This page lists the contents of your shopping cart and provides several buttons that let you remove items from the cart, clear the cart, return to the previous page to continue shopping, or proceed to a checkout page.

Of course, the complete Halloween Superstore application also contains other pages. For example, if you click the Check Out button in the second page, you're taken to a page that lets you enter the information for completing the order. As you go through this book, you'll learn how to add other pages to this application.

The Order page of a Shopping Cart application

The Cart page of a Shopping Cart application

Figure 1-1   Two pages of a Shopping Cart application

The components of a web application

The diagram in figure 1-2 shows that web applications consist of *clients* and a *web server*. The clients are the computers, tablets, and mobile devices that use the web applications. They access the web pages through programs known as *web browsers*. The web server holds the files that make up the pages of a web application.

A *network* is a system that allows clients and servers to communicate. The *Internet* is a large network that consists of many smaller networks. In a diagram like the one in this figure, the "cloud" represents the network or Internet that connects the clients and servers.

Networks can be categorized by size. A *local area network* (*LAN*) is a small network of computers that are near each other and can communicate with each other over short distances. Computers in a LAN are typically in the same building or adjacent buildings. This type of network is often called an *intranet*, and it can run web applications that are used throughout a company.

In contrast, a *wide area network* (*WAN*) consists of multiple LANs that have been connected. To pass information from one client to another, a router determines which network is closest to the destination and sends the information over that network. A WAN can be owned privately by one company or it can be shared by multiple companies.

An *Internet service provider* (*ISP*) is a company that owns a WAN that is connected to the Internet. An ISP leases access to its network to companies that need to be connected to the Internet. When you develop production web applications, you will often implement them through an ISP.

To access a web page from a browser, you can type a *URL* (*Uniform Resource Locator*) into the browser's address area and press Enter. The URL starts with the *protocol*, which is usually HTTP. It is followed by the *domain name* and the folder or directory *path* to the file that is requested. If the file name is omitted in the URL, the web server looks for a default file in the specified directory. The default files usually include index.html, index.htm, default.html, and default.htm.

The components of a web application

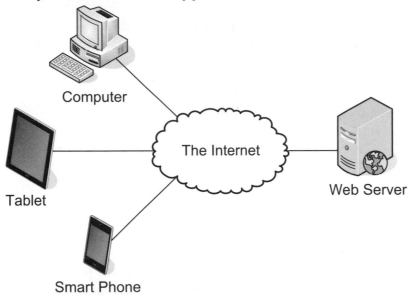

The components of an HTTP URL

Description

- A web application consists of clients, a web server, and a network.

- The *clients* use programs known as *web browsers* to request web pages from the web server. Today, the clients can be computers, smart phones, or tablets.

- The *web server* returns the pages that are requested to the browser.

- A *network* connects the clients to the web server.

- To request a page from a web server, the user can type the address of a web page, called a *URL*, or *Uniform Resource Locator*, into the browser's address area and then press the Enter key.

- A URL consists of the *protocol* (usually, HTTP), *domain name*, *path*, and file name. If you omit the file name, the web server will look for a file named index.html, index.htm, default.html, or default.htm.

- An *intranet* is a *local area network* (or *LAN*) that connects computers that are near each other, usually within the same building.

- The *Internet* is a network that consists of many *wide area networks* (*WANs*), and each of those consists of two or more LANs. Today, the Internet is often referred to as "the Cloud", which implies that you don't have to understand how it works.

- An *Internet service provider* (*ISP*) owns a WAN that is connected to the Internet.

Figure 1-2   The components of a web application

How static web pages are processed

A *static web page* like the one in figure 1-3 is a web page that doesn't change each time it is requested. This type of web page is sent directly from the web server to the web browser when the browser requests it. You can spot static pages in a web browser by looking at the extension in the address bar. If the extension is .htm or .html, the page is a static web page.

The diagram in this figure shows how a web server processes a request for a static web page. This process begins when a client requests a web page in a web browser. To do that, the user can either enter the URL of the page in the browser's address bar or click a link in the current page that specifies the next page to load.

In either case, the web browser builds a request for the web page and sends it to the web server. This request, known as an *HTTP request*, is formatted using the *HyperText Transfer Protocol* (HTTP), which lets the web server know which file is being requested.

When the web server receives the HTTP request, it retrieves the requested file from the disk drive. This file contains the *HTML* (*HyperText Markup Language*) for the requested page. Then, the web server sends the HTML back to the browser as part of an *HTTP response*.

When the browser receives the HTTP response, it *renders* (translates) the HTML into a web page that is displayed in the browser. Then, the user can view the content. If the user requests another page, either by clicking a link or entering another URL into the browser's address bar, the process begins again.

A static web page

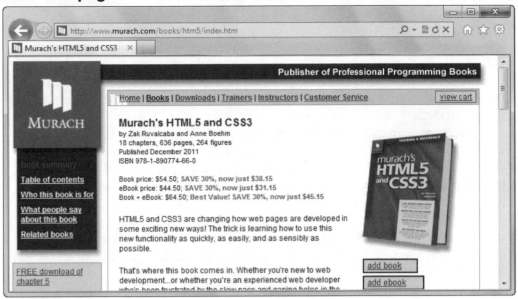

How a web server processes a static web page

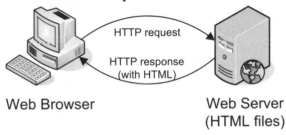

Web Browser   Web Server
                               (HTML files)

Description

- *Hypertext Markup Language* (*HTML*) is used to design the pages of a web application.

- A *static web page* is built from an *HTML document* that's stored on the web server and doesn't change. The file names for static web pages usually have .htm or .html extensions.

- When the user requests a static web page, the browser sends an *HTTP request* to the web server that includes the name of the file that's being requested.

- When the web server receives the request, it retrieves the HTML for the web page and sends it back to the browser as part of an *HTTP response*.

- When the browser receives the HTTP response, it *renders* the HTML into a web page that is displayed in the browser.

Figure 1-3   How static web pages are processed

How dynamic web pages are processed

A *dynamic web page* like the one in figure 1-4 is a page that's created by a program on an *application server*. This program uses the data that's sent with the HTTP request to generate the HTML that's returned to the server. In this example, the HTTP request included the product code. Then, the program retrieved the data for that product from a *database server*, including the path to the photo for the product.

The diagram in this figure shows how a web server processes a dynamic web page. The process begins when the user requests a page in a web browser. To do that, the user can click a link that specifies the dynamic page to load or click a button that submits a form that contains the data that the dynamic page should process.

In either case, the web browser builds an HTTP request and sends it to the web server. This request includes whatever data the application needs for processing the request. If, for example, the user has entered data into a form, that data will be included in the HTTP request.

When the web server receives the HTTP request, the server examines the file extension of the requested web page to identify the application server that should process the request. The web server then forwards the request to that application server.

Next, the application server retrieves the appropriate program. It also loads any form data that the user submitted. Then, it executes the program. As the program executes, it generates the HTML for the web page. If necessary, the program will also request data from a database server and use that data as part of the web page it is generating.

When the program is finished, the application server sends the dynamically generated HTML back to the web server. Then, the web server sends the HTML back to the browser in an HTTP response.

When the web browser receives the HTTP response, it renders the HTML and displays the web page. Note, however, that the web browser has no way to tell whether the HTML in the HTTP response was for a static page or a dynamic page. It just renders the HTML.

When the page is displayed, the user can view the content. Then, when the user requests another page, the process begins again. The process that begins with the user requesting a web page and ends with the server sending a response back to the client is called a *round trip*.

When you build ASP.NET applications, *Internet Information Services (IIS)* is used for the web server, and ASP.NET is used for the application server. You're also likely to use Microsoft's SQL Server for the *DBMS (database management system)*.

A dynamic web page

How a web server processes a dynamic web page

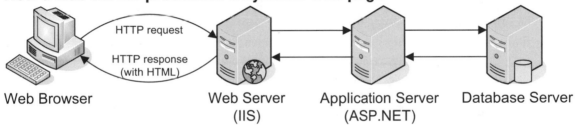

Web Browser   Web Server   Application Server   Database Server
                        (IIS)   (ASP.NET)

Description

- A *dynamic web page* is a web page that's generated by a program running on a server.
- When a web server receives a request for a dynamic web page, it looks up the extension of the requested file and passes the request to the appropriate *application server* for processing.
- When the application server receives the request, it runs the appropriate program. Often, this program uses data that's sent in the HTTP request to get related data from a *database management system* (*DBMS*) running on a *database server*.
- When the application server finishes processing the data, it generates the HTML for a web page and returns it to the web server. Then, the web server returns the HTML to the web browser as part of an HTTP response.
- The process that starts when a client requests a page and ends when the page is returned to the browser is called a *round trip*.
- When you build ASP.NET applications, *Internet Information Services* (*IIS*) is used for the web server and ASP.NET is used for the application server.

Figure 1-4   How dynamic web pages are processed

An introduction to ASP.NET development

In the topics that follow, you'll be introduced to the five ways to develop ASP.NET applications, the three types of development environments you can work in, and more.

Five ways to develop ASP.NET applications

Figure 1-5 summarizes the five ways that you can develop ASP.NET applications when you use Visual Studio 2012. That is likely to be four more than you need.

ASP.NET *Web Forms* were introduced in 2002. They were a replacement for *ASP (Active Server Pages)*, which is now called *Classic ASP*. In contrast to ASP, ASP.NET Web Forms let you work with a design model like the one for Windows Forms.

The primary focus of ASP.NET is *Rapid Application Development (RAD)*. ASP.NET accomplishes this by letting web developers work with server controls on a design surface. Then, ASP.NET converts the server controls to HTML. Today, 70% or more of ASP.NET development is done with Web Forms, and that's how you'll learn to develop web applications in this book.

In recent years, though, Microsoft added ASP.NET MVC to its web development offerings. It provides a way to implement the *Model-View-Controller (MVC)* pattern that offers improved separation of concerns and unit testing.

Separation of concerns refers to breaking an application into components so each one deals with a single concern. For example, one component can be responsible for communicating with the database, another for presenting information to users, and so on. This enables code reuse, limits the number of places a change needs to be made, and lets more than one person work on an application at the same time.

Unit testing refers to a process in which blocks of code are used to test whether other blocks of code do what they're supposed to do. This leads to more thorough testing because the unit tests can be run each time a change is made to the code.

Because the benefits of ASP.NET MVC are compelling, about 30% of ASP.NET web development is done with MVC. On the other hand, MVC development is more difficult than Web Forms development, and MVC isn't designed for Rapid Application Development. As a result, MVC is used primarily for large, commercial applications that are developed by teams, and Web Forms are used for most other applications.

The other three ways to develop ASP.NET applications that are presented in this figure have limited use. That's why they aren't presented in this book.

The two main ASP.NET technologies

- ASP.NET Web Forms
- ASP.NET MVC

Three other ASP.NET technologies

- ASP.NET Web Pages with Razor
- ASP.NET Dynamic Data Entities
- ASP.NET Reports Web Site

What the technologies do

ASP.NET	Description
Web Forms	A development environment similar to Windows Forms, with controls on a design surface. Its focus is on Rapid Application Development (RAD).
MVC	A development environment similar to PHP or classic ASP. It uses the Model-View-Controller (MVC) design pattern and the Razor templating engine for in-line data binding. Its focus is on separation of concerns and unit testing, and it gives the developer complete control over the HTML.
Web Pages with Razor	A version of Web Forms that uses the Razor templating engine for in-line data binding without having to use the MVC design pattern. It is used in simple scenarios.
Dynamic Data Entities	A version of Web Forms that uses Entity Framework and Routing to dynamically generate data-driven web sites. It is used in simple scenarios.
Reports Web Site	A Web Forms site that includes a report.

Description

- Microsoft has developed several ASP.NET technologies over the years. The two most popular are ASP.NET Web Forms and ASP.NET MVC.

- *Web Forms* is the oldest and most established technology. It provides for *RAD* (*Rapid Application Development*) by letting developers build web pages by working with controls on a design surface.

- *MVC* (*Model-View-Controller*) is relatively new to the .NET family. It addresses perceived weaknesses in Web Forms, such as inadequate *separation of concerns* and the difficulty of *unit testing*.

- Web Pages with Razor, Dynamic Data Entities, and Reports Web Sites are recent additions to ASP.NET. Each has a narrow area of applicability.

- Because 70% or more of ASP.NET web development is done with Web Forms, that's what this book shows you how to do.

- Because most of the other 30% of ASP.NET web development is done with MVC, the last chapter in this book introduces that approach. Then, you can decide whether it is something that you need to learn for the work that you do.

Figure 1-5   Five ways to develop ASP.NET applications

Three environments for developing ASP.NET applications

Figure 1-6 shows three development environments for ASP.NET applications. In a standalone environment, a single computer serves as both the client and the server. In an intranet environment, the clients are connected to the server over an intranet. And in an Internet environment, the clients are connected to the server over an Internet.

In all three environments, the clients need an operating system like Windows 7 or 8 that supports ASP.NET 4.5 development, the .NET Framework 4.5, and Visual Studio 2012. Since the .NET Framework 4.5 comes with Windows 7 and 8 and also with Visual Studio 2012, you don't need to install it separately.

For the server, you need to install IIS as the application server and a database management system like SQL Server. In a standalone environment, you're likely to use IIS Express and SQL Server Express LocalDB, which come with Visual Studio 2012. But in an intranet or Internet environment, you're likely to use a full version of IIS and SQL Server.

In an intranet environment, the server also requires either *FPSE* (*FrontPage Server Extensions*) or *WebDAV* (*Web-based Distributed Authoring and Versioning*), depending on which version of IIS the server uses. FPSE and WebDAV provide the services that Visual Studio 2012 uses to communicate with the web site on the server. Normally, though, you don't have to worry about this because the network manager sets this up.

In an Internet environment, the server also requires an *FTP server*, which is used to copy the files in a web site between the client computer and the server. The FTP server uses *File Transfer Protocol* (*FTP*) to perform the copy operations, and IIS can be configured to act as an FTP server as well as a web server. Here again, you usually don't have to worry about this because the server manager sets this up.

The table in this figure shows that Visual Studio 2012 is available in several editions. Most professional developers will work with either Professional or Premium. But large development teams may use Ultimate, which includes features that provide for specialized development roles such as architects, developers, and testers.

A free alternative is Visual Studio Express 2012 for Web. This edition is designed for individual developers, students, and hobbyists, and almost everything that you'll learn in this book will work with the Express edition. Whenever something doesn't work or works differently in the Express edition, the related figure will note the differences.

If you're learning on your own, you will most likely work in a standalone environment using Visual Studio 2012 Express for Web, IIS Express, and SQL Server Express LocalDB, which are all free. If you're working in a computer lab for a course, you will most likely work in an intranet environment, but it could also be an Internet environment. To install the client software that you'll need for any of these environments, you can follow the procedures in appendix A.

Standalone development

Windows 7 or later
.NET Framework 4.5
Visual Studio 2012
IIS Express
SQL Server

Intranet development

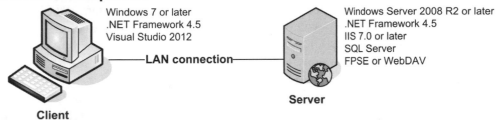

Windows 7 or later
.NET Framework 4.5
Visual Studio 2012

——LAN connection——

Windows Server 2008 R2 or later
.NET Framework 4.5
IIS 7.0 or later
SQL Server
FPSE or WebDAV

Client

Server

Internet development

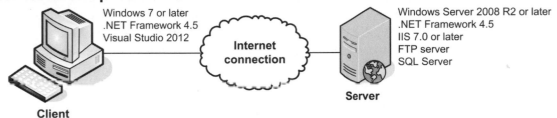

Windows 7 or later
.NET Framework 4.5
Visual Studio 2012

**Internet
connection**

Windows Server 2008 R2 or later
.NET Framework 4.5
IIS 7.0 or later
FTP server
SQL Server

Client

Server

The four editions of Visual Studio 2012

Edition	Description
Visual Studio Express 2012 for Web	Free edition for web development in Visual Basic or C#.
Visual Studio Professional 2012	Lets you build Windows, web, mobile, and Office apps.
Visual Studio Premium 2012	For individuals or teams, it includes basic tools for testing, database deployment, and change and lifecycle management.
Visual Studio Ultimate 2012	For teams, it includes full testing, modeling, database, and lifecycle management tools.

Description

- When you use standalone development, a single computer serves as client and server.
- When you use intranet development, a client communicates with a server over a *local area network (LAN)*. For this, the server requires either *FPSE (FrontPage Server Extensions)* or *WebDAV (Web-based Distributed Authoring and Versioning)*.
- When you use Internet development, a client communicates with a server over the Internet. For this, the server requires an *FTP server*. The FTP server uses *File Transfer Protocol (FTP)* to transfer files between the client computer and the server.

Figure 1-6   Three environments for developing ASP.NET applications

The components of the .NET Framework

Because you should have a basic understanding of what the *.NET Framework* does as you develop applications, figure 1-7 summarizes its major components. As you can see, this framework is divided into two main components, the .NET Framework Class Library and the Common Language Runtime, and these components provide a common set of services for applications written in .NET languages like Visual Basic or C#.

The *.NET Framework Class Library* consists of *classes* that provide many of the functions that you need for developing .NET applications. For instance, the ASP.NET classes are used for developing ASP.NET web applications, and the Windows Forms classes are used for developing standard Windows applications. The other .NET classes let you work with databases, manage security, access files, and perform many other functions.

The *Common Language Runtime*, or *CLR*, provides the services that are needed for executing any application that's developed with one of the .NET languages. This is possible because all of the .NET languages *compile* to a common *Intermediate Language* (or *IL*), which is stored in an *assembly*.

The CLR also provides the Common Type System that defines the data types that are used by all the .NET languages. That way, you can use the same data types no matter which .NET language you're using to develop your applications.

The .NET Framework

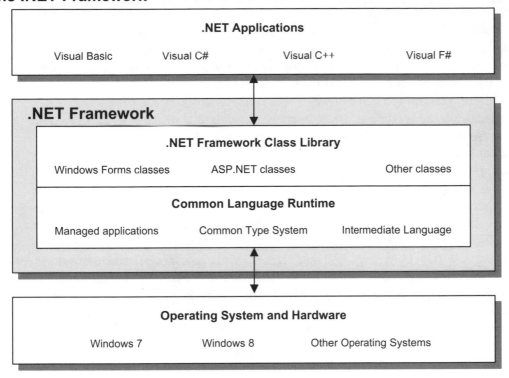

Description

- .NET applications work by using services of the *.NET Framework*. The .NET Framework, in turn, accesses the operating system and computer hardware.

- The .NET Framework consists of two main components: the .NET Framework Class Library and the Common Language Runtime.

- The *.NET Framework Class Library* provides pre-written code in the form of classes that are available to all of the .NET programming languages.

- The *Common Language Runtime*, or *CLR*, manages the execution of .NET programs by coordinating essential functions such as memory management and security.

- The Common Type System is a component of the CLR that ensures that all .NET applications use the same data types regardless of what programming languages are used.

- All .NET programs are *compiled* into *Microsoft Intermediate Language* (*MSIL*) or just *Intermediate Language* (*IL*), which is stored in an *assembly*. This assembly is then run by the CLR.

Figure 1-7   The components of the .NET Framework

How state is handled in ASP.NET applications

Although it hasn't been mentioned yet, a web application ends after it generates a web page. That means that any data maintained by the application, such as variables or control properties, is lost. In other words, HTTP doesn't maintain the *state* of the application. This is illustrated in figure 1-8.

Here, you can see that a browser on a client requests a page from a web server. After the server processes the request and returns the page to the browser, it drops the connection. Then, if the browser makes additional requests, the server has no way to associate the browser with its previous requests. Because of that, HTTP is known as a *stateless protocol*.

Although HTTP doesn't maintain state, ASP.NET provides several ways to do that, as summarized in this figure. First, you can use *view state* to maintain the values of server control properties. For example, you can use view state to preserve the values of the items in a drop-down list. Because ASP.NET implements view state by default, you don't need to write any special code to use it.

Second, you can use *session state* to maintain data between executions of an application. To make this work, ASP.NET creates a *session state object* that is kept on the server whenever a user starts a new session. This session object contains a unique *session ID*, and this ID is sent back and forth between the server and the browser each time the user requests a page. Then, when the server receives a new request from a user, it can retrieve the right session object for that user. In the code for your web forms, you can add data items to the session object so their previous values are available each time a web form is executed.

Third, you can use an *application state object* to save *application state* data, which applies to all of the users of an application. For example, you can use application state to maintain global counters or to maintain a list of the users who are currently logged on to an application.

Fourth, you can use *server-side caching* to save data. This is similar to application state in that the data saved in the cache applies to all users of an application. However, caching is more flexible than application state because you have control over how long the data is retained.

Last, you can use the *profile* feature to keep track of user data. Although a profile is similar to a session state object, it persists between user sessions because it is stored in a database. Because profiles are used infrequently, they aren't presented in this book, but you will learn how to use the other four ways to handle state.

Why state is difficult to track in a web application

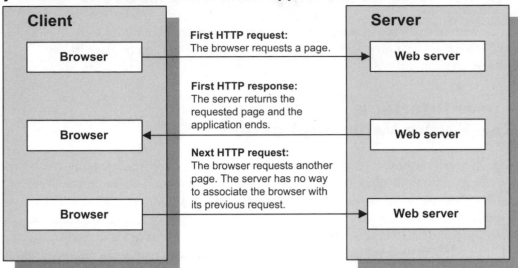

Concepts

- *State* refers to the current status of the properties, variables, and other data maintained by an application for a single user. The application must maintain a separate state for each user currently accessing the application.

- HTTP is a *stateless protocol*. That means that it doesn't keep track of state between round trips. Once a browser makes a request and receives a response, the application terminates and its state is lost.

Five ASP.NET features for maintaining state

Feature	Description
View state	Implemented by default, so no special coding is required. See chapter 2.
Session state	Uses a session state object that is created when a user starts a new session. The values in this object are available until the session ends. See chapter 4.
Application state	Uses an application state object that is created when an application starts. The values of this object are available to all users of the application until the application ends. See chapter 8.
Server-side caching	Like application state, the values in a server-side cache can be shared across an application. Unlike application state, a cache item is maintained only until its expiration time is reached. See chapter 8.
Profiles	One profile can be maintained for each user of an application. The data in a profile is stored in a database and maintained from one user session to another.

Description

- ASP.NET provides five ways to deal with the stateless protocol of a web application. The two that you'll use the most are *view state* and *session state*.

Figure 1-8   How state is handled in ASP.NET applications

How an ASP.NET application works

With that as background, you're ready to learn more about how an ASP.NET application works. That's why this topic presents a one-page Future Value application.

The user interface
for the Future Value application

Figure 1-9 presents the user interface for a one-page application called the Future Value application. In ASP.NET, pages like this are called *web forms*. To make these pages work, each form contains ASP.NET *server controls* that let the user interact with the page. For instance, this page contains these server controls: a drop-down list, two text boxes, a label that displays the future value, and two buttons. It also uses validation controls that check the user entries for validity.

To use the Future Value application, the user selects a monthly investment amount from the drop-down list, enters data into the two text boxes, and clicks the Calculate button. Then, if the data is valid, the future value is displayed. Otherwise, error messages are displayed below the buttons. To clear the controls, the user can click the Clear button.

The processing for the Calculate and Clear buttons is done on the server. That means that when either button is clicked, the form is submitted to the server, the C# code on the server processes the data in the form, and the form is returned to the browser. In other words, clicking either button leads to a round trip.

For example, when the Calculate button is clicked, the C# code on the server calculates the future value, and the form is returned to the browser with the future value displayed. That's a round trip. Similarly, when the Clear button is clicked, the C# code on the server resets the value in the drop-down list to 50 and clears the text boxes and the Future Value label. Then, the form is returned to the browser. That's also a round trip.

In some cases, though, the form isn't submitted to the browser when the Calculate button is clicked. That happens when JavaScript is enabled in the user's browser and one or more entries are invalid. Then, the JavaScript code that has been generated from the validation controls runs in the browser, detects the invalid entries, and displays appropriate error messages...without submitting the form to the server. That saves a round trip.

What if JavaScript isn't enabled in the user's browser? Then, the form is submitted to the server, and the server checks the entries for validity. That too is done by the code that's generated by the validation controls. In this example, that means a round trip occurs each time the user clicks the Calculate button if Java-Script is disabled. Fortunately, though, most browsers have JavaScript enabled.

The Future Value application after the user clicks the Calculate button

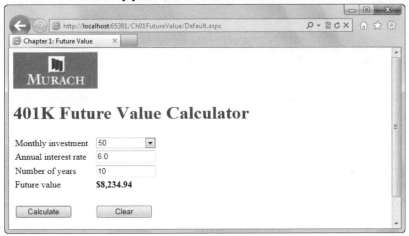

The Future Value application with error messages displayed

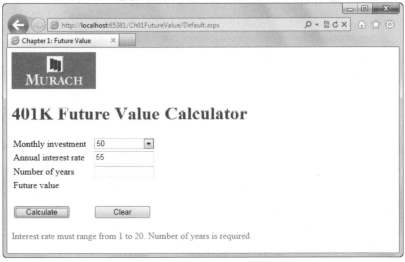

Description

- To calculate the Future Value of a monthly investment, the user selects a value in the drop-down list, enters values into the two text boxes, and clicks the Calculate button.

- If JavaScript is enabled in the browser, it is used to check the user's entries for validity. If the entries are valid, the form is submitted to the server, the future value is calculated, and the page is returned to the browser with the future value displayed. If the entries are invalid, error messages are displayed by the JavaScript and the form isn't submitted.

- If the user clicks on the Clear button, the form is submitted to the server, the drop-down list is reset to 50, the text boxes are cleared, and the page is returned to the browser.

- If JavaScript isn't enabled in the browser, the page is always submitted when the user clicks the Calculate button and the server does the validity checking.

Figure 1-9   The Future Value application

The files used by the Future Value application

Figure 1-10 presents the Future Value form as it appears in the Web Forms Designer that you use when you develop web forms with Visual Studio 2012. In chapter 2, you'll learn how to use this Designer, but for now just try to get the big picture of how this form works.

If you look closely at the Designer window in the middle of Visual Studio, you can see the table that's used for this form. You can also see the server controls: the drop-down list that's used to select a monthly investment amount, text boxes for interest rate and number of years, a label for displaying the result of the future value calculation, and Calculate and Clear buttons.

If you look at the Solution Explorer to the right of the Designer window, you can see the folders and files that this application requires. These are summarized in the table in this figure.

The first two files in the table are for the web form. The file with aspx as the extension (Default.aspx) contains the code that represents the design of the form. This code consists of standard HTML code plus asp tags that define the server controls. We refer to this as *aspx code*, because the file that contains the code has the aspx extension.

The file with aspx.cs as the extension (Default.aspx.cs) contains the C# code that controls the operation of the form. The cs file extension indicates that it is a C# file. This is called a *code-behind file* because it provides the code behind the web form.

The third file in the table in this figure is the web.config file. It contains configuration information like which version of the .NET Framework is being used.

The fourth file is the jpg file for the logo that's displayed at the top of the form. This file is in the Images folder that's shown in the Solution Explorer.

These four files and the Images folder are all that this one-page application requires. However, two other folders are often used for Web Forms applications. An App_Code folder is used for user classes, and an App_Data folder is used for databases or files. You'll see these used in the Shopping Cart application in chapter 4.

Before I go on, you should realize that the aspx and C# code for a web form doesn't have to be in separate files. However, by keeping the aspx and C# code in separate files, you separate the presentation elements of a page from its C# coding. This is one way that ASP.NET Web Forms provides for separation of concerns.

The Future Value form in Design view of Visual Studio 2012

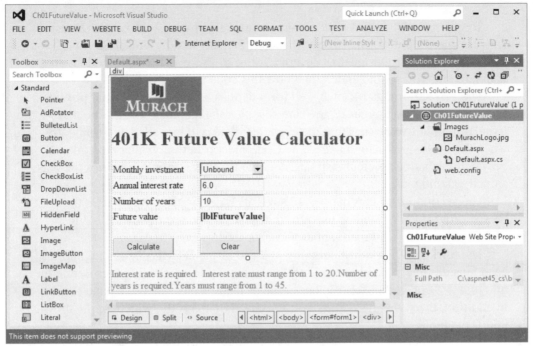

The files in the Future Value application

Folder	File	Description
(root)	Default.aspx	The aspx file for the default page.
(root)	Default.aspx.cs	The code-behind file for the default page.
(root)	web.config	An XML file that contains configuration data for the application like which .NET Framework is being used.
Images	MurachLogo.jpg	The logo image for the form.

Description

- For each web form in an application, ASP.NET 4.5 keeps two files. The file with the aspx extension holds the HTML code and the asp tags for the server controls. The file with the aspx.cs extension is the *code-behind file* that contains the C# code for the form.

- When you use Visual Studio to build an ASP.NET application, the name of the first form is Default.aspx and its code-behind file is Default.aspx.cs.

- Every ASP.NET application also includes a web.config file with configuration data.

- The Future Value application also contains a folder named Images that contains the jpg file for the logo that's displayed at the top of the page.

- Two other folders that you'll find in many ASP.NET applications are an App_Code folder for user classes, and an App_Data folder for databases or files.

Figure 1-10   The Future Value application in Visual Studio 2012

The aspx code for the Default form

To give you some idea of how aspx code works, figure 1-11 shows the aspx code for the Default form. Most of this code is generated by Visual Studio as you use the Web Forms Designer to design a form, so you don't have to code it all yourself. But you should understand how this code works.

The first set of tags for each web form defines a *page directive* that provides four attributes. The Language attribute says that the language is C#. The Auto-EventWireup attribute says that the event handlers will be called automatically when the events occur for a page. The CodeFile attribute says that the code-behind file is named Default.aspx.cs. And the Inherits attribute specifies the class named _Default.

The second set of tags defines a DOCTYPE declaration, which tells the browser that HTML5 will be used for this page. If you aren't already using HTML5, you can learn more about it in chapter 3.

The html tags mark the beginning and end of the HTML document, and the head tags define the head section for the document. Here, the title tags define the title that is displayed in the title bar or tab of the browser when the page is run. In addition, the style tags define the styles used by the page, which aren't shown in this example.

The content of the web page itself is defined within the div tags, which are within the body and form tags. Notice that the first form tag includes a Runat attribute that's assigned a value of "server." That indicates that the form will be processed on the server by ASP.NET. This attribute is required for all ASP.NET web forms and all ASP.NET server controls.

The asp tags within the div tags define the server controls that appear on the page. Since these controls include the Runat attribute with a value of "server," they will be processed on the server by ASP.NET. The last phase of this processing is generating the HTML for the controls so the page can be displayed by a browser.

The asp code for the Calculate and Clear buttons includes an OnClick attribute. This attribute names the event handler that's executed when the user clicks the button and the form is posted back to the server.

The asp code for the Clear button includes a CausesValidation attribute. This attribute tells the page whether to fire the validation event used by the validation controls. Setting this attribute to false for the Clear button means that the data validation controls will do their work when you click Calculate, but not when you click Clear.

Within the form, an HTML table is used to format the server controls. Here, the first four rows include the server controls that accept the user entries and display the future value. The fifth row provides vertical spacing. And the last row includes the Calculate and Clear button controls.

After the table are four field validator controls that aren't shown. These are server controls that provide the validity checking and display the error messages, both in the browser with JavaScript and on the server with C#. In the next chapter, you'll learn how to build this web form with its controls.

The aspx file for the Default form (Default.aspx)

```
<%@ Page Language="C#" AutoEventWireup="true" CodeFile="Default.aspx.cs"
Inherits="_Default" %>

<!DOCTYPE html>

<html xmlns="http://www.w3.org/1999/xhtml">
<head id="Head1" runat="server">
    <title>Chapter 1: Future Value</title>
    <style><!-- CSS code for the generated styles --></style>
</head>
<body>
    <form id="form1" runat="server">
    <div>
        <img alt="Murach" class="style1" src="Images/MurachLogo.jpg"  /><br />
        <h1 style="color: #0000FF">401K Future Value Calculator</h1>
        <table class="style2">
            <tr>
                <td class="style3">Monthly investment</td>
                <td><asp:DropDownList ID="ddlMonthlyInvestment"
                    runat="server" Width="106px"></asp:DropDownList></td>
            </tr>
            <tr>
                <td class="style3">Annual interest rate</td>
                <td><asp:TextBox ID="txtInterestRate" runat="server"
                        Width="100px">6.0</asp:TextBox></td>
            </tr>
            <tr>
                <td class="style3">Number of years</td>
                <td><asp:TextBox ID="txtYears" runat="server"
                        Width="100px">10</asp:TextBox></td>
            </tr>
            <tr>
                <td class="style3">Future value</td>
                <td><asp:Label ID="lblFutureValue" runat="server"
                        Font-Bold="True"></asp:Label></td>
            </tr>
            <tr>
                <td class="style3"> </td>
                <td> </td>
            </tr>
            <tr>
                <td class="style3"><asp:Button ID="btnCalculate"
                    runat="server" Text="Calculate" Width="100px"
                        OnClick="btnCalculate_Click" /></td>
                <td><asp:Button ID="btnClear" runat="server"
                        Text="Clear" Width="100px" OnClick="btnClear_Click"
                        CausesValidation="false" /></td>
            </tr>
        </table>
        <br />
        <!-- aspx code for the field validators -->
    </div>
    </form>
</body>
</html>
```

Figure 1-11   The aspx code for the Default form of the Future Value application

The C# code for the Default form

To give you some idea of how the C# code for a form works, figure 1-12 presents the code-behind file for the Default form. Here, I've highlighted the code that's specific to ASP.NET. The other code is standard C# code.

The first highlighted line is a class declaration. Usually, a form class will have the same name as the form, but ASP.NET uses _Default (with a leading underscore) as the class name for the Default form.

Because the class declaration uses the partial keyword, this is a partial class that must be combined with another partial class when it's compiled. In fact, the code in this partial C# class is combined with the compiled code in its aspx file. The rest of this class declaration indicates that this class inherits the System.Web.UI.Page class, which is the .NET class that provides the basic functionality of ASP.NET pages.

Each time this web form is requested, ASP.NET initializes it and raises the Load event, which is handled by the Page_Load method. You will often see a page property called IsPostBack used in the Page_Load method to determine whether or not a page is being posted back. If the value is false, the page is being loaded for the first time.

In this figure, the Page_Load method checks the IsPostBack property to see if this is the first page load. If it is, the code executes a loop that puts a range of dollar amounts into the drop-down list for monthly investment. Otherwise, nothing is done by this method.

Another page property that you will often use is called IsValid. This property indicates whether the page's validation controls detect invalid data in the server controls when the Calculate button is clicked. This property is used in the btnCalculate_Click method that is executed when the user clicks on the Calculate button, which starts a postback.

The btnCalculate_Click method starts by checking the IsValid property to see if the data is valid. If it is, this method retrieves the values from the server controls, converts them to the proper data types, and sends them to the CalculateFutureValue method for processing. When that method returns the future value, the btnCalculate_Click method formats the result as currency and puts it in the future value label. Then, the form is returned to the browser.

The btnClear_Click method is executed when the user clicks on the Clear button. This too starts a postback. Then, after the Page_Load method is executed, the btnClear_Click method clears the server controls by setting the index of the drop-down list to 0 and setting the text box and label properties to empty strings.

Since this book assumes that you already know how to use C#, you should be able to follow the C# code in this figure. The new points to note are (1) the Page_Load method is executed each time the page is requested, (2) the IsPostBack property tells whether a page is being requested for the first time, and (3) the IsValid property tells whether the validator controls have detected invalid data.

The code-behind file for the Default form (Default.aspx.cs)

```csharp
using System;
using System.Web;
using System.Web.UI;
using System.Web.UI.WebControls;

public partial class _Default : System.Web.UI.Page
{
    protected void Page_Load(object sender, EventArgs e)
    {
        if (!IsPostBack)
            for (int i = 50; i <= 500; i += 50)
                ddlMonthlyInvestment.Items.Add(i.ToString());
    }

    protected void btnCalculate_Click(object sender, EventArgs e)
    {
        if (IsValid)
        {
            int monthlyInvestment = Convert.ToInt32(
                    ddlMonthlyInvestment.SelectedValue);
            decimal yearlyInterestRate = Convert.ToDecimal(
                    txtInterestRate.Text);
            int years = Convert.ToInt32(
                    txtYears.Text);

            decimal futureValue = this.CalculateFutureValue(
                    monthlyInvestment, yearlyInterestRate, years);

            lblFutureValue.Text = futureValue.ToString("c");
        }
    }

    protected decimal CalculateFutureValue(int monthlyInvestment,
    decimal yearlyInterestRate, int years)
    {
        int months = years * 12;
        decimal monthlyInterestRate = yearlyInterestRate / 12 / 100;
        decimal futureValue = 0;

        for (int i = 0; i < months; i++)
        {
            futureValue = (futureValue + monthlyInvestment)
                * (1 + monthlyInterestRate);
        }
        return futureValue;
    }

    protected void btnClear_Click(object sender, EventArgs e)
    {
        ddlMonthlyInvestment.SelectedIndex = 0;
        txtInterestRate.Text = "";
        txtYears.Text = "";
        lblFutureValue.Text = "";
    }
}
```

Figure 1-12   The C# code for the Default form of the Future Value application

Perspective

Now that you've read this chapter, you should have a general understanding of how ASP.NET applications work and what software you need for developing these applications. With that as background, you're ready to learn how to develop ASP.NET applications of your own. You'll start that process in the next chapter.

Terms

web application	Web Forms
web page	ASP (Active Server Pages)
client	classic ASP
web browser	RAD (Rapid Application
web server	Development)
network	MVC (Model-View-Controller)
intranet	separation of concerns
LAN (local area network)	unit testing
Internet	FPSE (FrontPage Server Extensions)
WAN (wide area network)	WebDAV (Web-based Distributed
ISP (Internet service provider)	Authoring and Viewing)
URL (Uniform Resource Locator)	FTP server
protocol	FTP (File Transfer Protocol)
domain name	.NET Framework
path	.NET Framework Class Library
static web page	CLR (Common Language Runtime)
HTML (Hypertext Markup Language)	IL (Intermediate Language)
HTTP request	compile
HTTP (HyperText Transfer Protocol)	assembly
HTTP response	state
render HTML in the browser	stateless protocol
dynamic web page	view state
application server	session state
database server	web form
DBMS (database management	server control
system)	aspx code
round trip	code-behind file
IIS (Internet Information Services)	page directive

Summary

- A *web application* consists of a set of *web pages* that are run by clients, a web server, and a network. *Clients* use *web browsers* to request web pages from the web server. The *web server* returns the requested pages.

- A *local area network* (*LAN*) connects computers that are near to each other. This is often called an *intranet*. In contrast, the *Internet* consists of many *wide area networks* (*WANs*).

- One way to access a web page is to type a *URL* (*Uniform Resource Locator*) into the address area of a browser and press Enter. A URL consists of the *protocol* (usually, HTTP), *domain name*, *path*, and file name.

- To request a web page, the web browser sends an *HTTP request* to the web server. Then, the web server gets the HTML for the requested page and sends it back to the browser in an *HTTP response*. Last, the browser *renders* the HTML into a web page.

- A *static web page* is a page that is the same each time it's retrieved. In contrast, the HTML for a *dynamic web page* is generated by a server-side program, so its HTML can change from one request to another. Either way, HTML is returned to the browser.

- For ASP.NET applications, the web server is usually *Internet Information Services* (*IIS*) and ASP.NET is the application server. The web server also requires a *database management system* (*DBMS*) like SQL Server.

- Today, the most popular way to develop ASP.NET applications is to use *Web Forms*. It encourages *Rapid Application Development* (*RAD*), and it accounts for about 70% of ASP.NET development.

- The other popular way to develop ASP.NET applications is to use ASP.NET *MVC* (*Model-View-Controller*). It provides better *separation of concerns* and *unit testing*, and it accounts for about 30% of ASP.NET development.

- To develop ASP.NET applications on your own computer, you need Windows 7 or later, Microsoft .NET Framework 4.5, Visual Studio 2012, IIS Express, a DBMS like SQL Server Express LocalDB, and one or more browsers.

- When you develop ASP.NET applications on an intranet or the Internet, IIS is on the web server and the DBMS is on the web server or a database server so the client doesn't need them.

- The *.NET Framework* provides the services that ASP.NET applications use to access the operating system and computer hardware. Its main components are the *Class Library* and the *Common Language Runtime* (*CLR*).

- HTTP is called a *stateless protocol* because it doesn't keep track of the data (state) between *round trips*. However, ASP.NET provides five ways to keep track of state including *view state* and *session state*.

- The pages in an ASP.NET application are called *web forms*. They contain *server controls* like drop-down lists, text boxes, labels, and buttons.

- Each page in an ASP.NET application consists of an aspx file for the HTML and server controls and an aspx.cs file for the C# in the *code-behind file*.

- Before a web form can be run, its aspx and C# files are compiled into an *assembly* that consists of *Intermediate Language* (*IL*) that is run by the CLR.

Before you do the exercises for this book...

Before you do the exercises for this book, you should install the software that's required for this book as well as the downloadable applications for this book. Appendix A shows how to do that.

Exercise 1-1   Use your web browser to run the Future Value application

In this exercise, you'll run the Future Value application. This will test whether you've successfully installed the software and applications for this book.

Start Visual Studio and open the Future Value application

1. Start Visual Studio.

2. Use the FILE→Open→Web Site command (or the FILE→Open Web Site command if you're using Visual Studio Express) to open the web site at this location:

   `C:\aspnet45_cs\Ex01FutureValue`

   In the dialog box that's displayed, just navigate to the Ex01FutureValue folder and click the Open button.

Run the Future Value application

3. Press F5 to run the application. That should display the Future Value form in Visual Studio's default web browser.

4. Without changing the values that are displayed, click the Calculate button. This starts a postback that returns the page with the result of the calculation.

5. Click the Clear button to clear the values from the text box controls.

6. Click the Calculate button again. Then, note the error messages that are displayed. These messages were generated by the validation controls.

7. Click the Clear button again. Note that the error messages go away. That's because the Clear button has its CausesValidation attribute set to false.

8. Select an investment amount from the drop-down list, enter an annual interest rate greater than 20 and a number of years greater than 45. Then, click the Calculate button to see the error messages that are displayed.

9. Change the interest rate to 5 and the number of years to 30. Then, Click the Calculate button to see that the future value is displayed, which means the entries were valid.

10. Experiment on your own if you like. When you're through, use the FILE→Close Solution command to close the web site, and click on the No button when the ensuing dialog box asks whether you want to save a file. Then, close Visual Studio.

2

How to develop a one-page web application

In the last chapter, you were introduced to the basic concepts of web programming and ASP.NET. Now, this chapter shows you how to use Visual Studio to develop the Future Value application that you reviewed in the last chapter. If you've used Visual Studio to develop Windows applications, you'll see that you develop ASP.NET applications in much the same way. As a result, you should be able to move quickly through this chapter.

How to work with ASP.NET web sites

This chapter starts by presenting some basic skills for working with ASP.NET applications. Once you're comfortable with those skills, you'll be ready to learn how to build your first ASP.NET application.

How to start a new web site

In the web development world, the terms *web site*, *web application*, and *web project* are often used interchangeably. When you use Visual Studio 2012, though, these terms have specific meanings.

In ASP.NET, a *web project* is either an *ASP.NET Web Forms Site* (often called a *web site*) or an *ASP.NET Web Forms Application* (often called a *web application*). Both of these project types can be used for simple display web sites or interactive web applications. The difference is in how the projects are configured, compiled, and deployed. The first table in figure 2-1 lists the main differences between the two project types.

Because Web Forms Applications are pre-compiled and deployed as a single assembly, they can perform better and protect your code from being seen. Because Web Forms Sites are deployed as individual files and compile when requested, they can be easier to work with and easier to change. In this book, all of the applications are Web Forms Sites, but the forms development and C# coding are the same with either project type.

To start a new Web Forms Site, you use the dialog box shown in this figure. Here, you select the language you want to use, the type of web site you want to create, and the location for the web site. You also select the template that you want to use.

For this book, all the web sites use the ASP.NET Empty Web Site template. When you use this template, the starting web site contains only a web.config file, which stores information about the web site. For professional web sites, though, you may want to use the ASP.NET Web Forms Site template.

To specify the location of the web site, the Web Location drop-down list gives you three options. The simplest option is to create a *file-system web site*. This type of web site can be in any folder on your local disk, or in a folder on a shared network drive. By default, Visual Studio will run a file-system web site using the IIS Express web server.

The second option, HTTP, lets you create a web site that runs under IIS on your local computer or on a computer that can be accessed over a local area network. The third option, FTP, lets you create a web site on a remote server by uploading it to that server using FTP.

The dialog box in this figure specifies a file-system web site named Ch02FutureValue that will be in the aspnet45_cs folder on the C: drive of the computer. Then, when the OK button is clicked, Visual Studio creates the folder named Ch02FutureValue and puts the web.config file for the web site in that folder. It also creates a solution file in the default folder for those files, and a site named Ch02FutureValue on the IIS Express web server.

The New Web Site dialog box

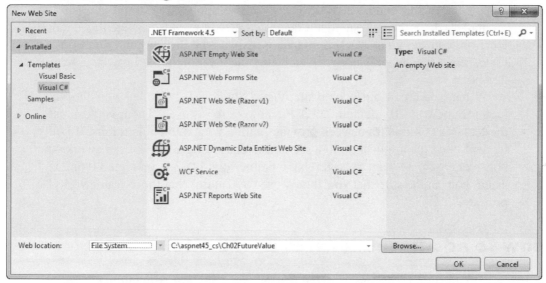

Web Forms Site vs. Web Forms Application

Feature	Site	Application
Project Files	None	One or more
Compilation	At run time	Pre-compiled to single assembly
Class file location	App_Code folder	Anywhere in folder structure
How to start (VS)	FILE→New→Web Site	FILE→New→Project
How to start (VS Express)	FILE→New Web Site	FILE→New Project

Three web location options for ASP.NET web sites

Option	Description
File System	A web site created on your local computer or in a shared folder on a network.
HTTP	A web site created under the control of an IIS web server.
FTP	A web site created on a remote hosting server.

Description

- In ASP.NET, a *web project* is either a *Web Forms site* (*web site*) or a *Web Forms application* (*web application*).

- To create a new web site, use the commands shown in the first table above. Note the slight variation in the commands for the Express edition of Visual Studio.

- When you create a new web site, Visual Studio creates a solution folder and file for the web site in the default location for solution files, which is Visual Studio 2012/ Projects in your My Documents folder. It also creates a web site on the IIS Express web server.

- By default, new web sites use .NET Framework 4.5, but the drop-down list at the top of the dialog box lets you change that.

Figure 2-1   How to start a new web site

By default, Visual Studio 2012 creates a solution file for your web site in My Documents\Visual Studio 2012\Projects. This solution file is stored in this folder no matter where the web site itself is located. If you want to change this default location, you can go to TOOLS→Options, expand the Projects and Solutions node, select the General category, and enter the location in the Projects Location text box.

When you create a new web site, Visual Studio 2012 also lets you choose a target framework. By default, .NET Framework 4.5 is used. Then, you can use the features that this framework provides within your web applications. If you'll be deploying the application to a server that doesn't have .NET Framework 4.5, however, you may want to target .NET Framework 4.0, 3.5, or even 3.0 or 2.0. Then, you can be sure that you'll only use the features that those frameworks provide.

How to add a web form to a web site

If you start a web site from the ASP.NET Empty Web Site template, you'll need to add a *web form* to the web site. To do that, you can use the Add New Item dialog box shown in figure 2-2. From this dialog box, you select the Web Form template. Then, you enter the name you want to use for the new form and click the Add button to add it to your web site.

When you add a new web form, be sure that the language setting is Visual C# and that the Place Code in Separate File box is checked. These settings are easy to overlook, but difficult to change manually if they're set wrong when you create the page. Also, be sure to enter a name for the form unless you want the default name, Default.aspx, to be used.

If you select the Place Code in Separate File box, two files are added to your project. For instance, files named Default.aspx and Default.aspx.cs were added to the project in this figure. The Default.aspx file will be used for the HTML and ASP code that defines the form, and the Default.aspx.cs file will be used for the C# code that determines how the form works. After the files are added to the project, Visual Studio displays the aspx file for the web form.

Another way to add a web form is to use the Add Web Form command in the shortcut menu for the project. When you choose this command, the dialog box that's displayed only lets you specify the name for the form. Then, the form that's created uses C# by default, and the code for the form is placed in a separate file, which is usually what you want.

To add an existing web form from another web site to your web site, you can use the second procedure in this figure. You might want to do that if you need to create a form that's similar to a form in another web site. When you add the aspx file for a form, the code-behind file is added too. Then, you can modify the aspx and C# code so the form works the way you want it to in your new web site.

The Add New Item dialog box for adding a new web form

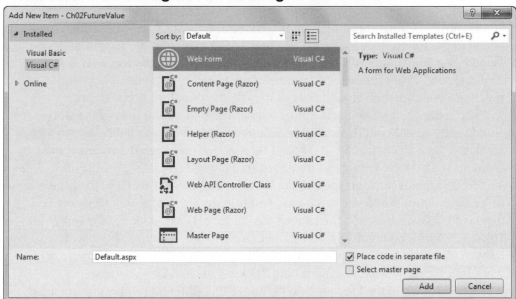

Two ways to open the Add New Item dialog box

- Right-click the project in the Solution Explorer, and choose Add→Add New Item from the shortcut menu.
- Click on the project in the Solution Explorer to select it, and then choose the WEBSITE→Add New Item command.

How to add a new web form to a project

- In the Add New Item dialog box, select the Web Form template, enter a name for the form or leave it as Default.aspx, check the Place Code in Separate File box, and click the Add button.
- Choose Add→Web Form from the shortcut menu for the project. Then, enter a name for the form in the dialog box that's displayed and click the OK button.

How to add an existing web form to a project

- In the Solution Explorer, right-click the project and choose Add→Add Existing Item. Then, locate the form you want to add, select it, and click the Add button.

Description

- If there's a *web form* in another application that is like one that you're going to develop, you can copy that form into your web site. That copies both the web form and the code-behind file. Then, you can modify the aspx code and C# code so the form works the way you want it to.
- The drop-down list above the list of templates lets you change the order of the templates. The two buttons let you choose whether the templates are displayed as small icons or medium icons.

Figure 2-2   How to add a web form to a web site

How to work with the Visual Studio IDE

Figure 2-3 shows the Visual Studio IDE after a form named Default has been added to the Future Value web site. If you've used Visual Studio for building Windows applications, you should already be familiar with the *Toolbox*, *Solution Explorer*, and *Properties window*, as well as the Standard toolbar. They work much the same for web applications as they do for Windows applications.

For instance, the Solution Explorer shows the folders and files of the web site. In the example in this figure, the Solution Explorer shows the collapsed web form and the web.config file. To expand the web form and see the code-behind file, you click on the arrowhead to the left of the web form.

To design a web form, you use the *Web Forms Designer* that's in the center of Visual Studio. When you add a new web form to a web site, this Designer is displayed in *Source view*, which shows the starting HTML code for the form. However, you'll do much of the design in *Design view*, which you can switch to by clicking on the Design button at the bottom of the Designer. You can also work in *Split view*, which includes both Source view and Design view.

As you work in the Designer, you'll notice that different toolbars are enabled depending on what view you're working in. In Source view, for example, the Standard and HTML Source Editing toolbars are enabled. In Design view, the Standard and Formatting toolbars are enabled. This is typical of the way Visual Studio works.

As you build a web site, you can close, hide, or size the windows that are displayed. You'll see some examples of this as you progress through this chapter, and this figure presents several techniques that you can use for working with the windows.

After you've designed a web form, you'll need to switch to the Code Editor, which will replace the Designer in the center of the screen. Then, you can write the C# code in the code-behind file for the form. One way to switch to the Code Editor is to double-click on the code-behind file in the Solution Explorer. You'll learn more about that in a moment.

As you work with Visual Studio, you'll see that it often provides several ways to do the same task. Some, of course, are more efficient than others, and we'll try to show you the best techniques as you progress through this book. Often, though, how you work is a matter of personal preference, so we encourage you to review and experiment with the toolbar buttons, the buttons at the top of the Solution Explorer, the tabs at the top of the Web Forms Designer or Code Editor, the shortcut menus that you get by right-clicking on an object, and so on.

For instance, to see which toolbars are displayed, you can right-click in the toolbar area, which displays a list of all of the toolbars with the active ones checked. You can then check one of the toolbars to activate it. Or, to see what toolbar buttons or controls are available, you can hover the mouse over a button or control. That also works for the buttons at the tops of windows like the Solution Explorer.

Visual Studio with the Designer in Source view and three other windows

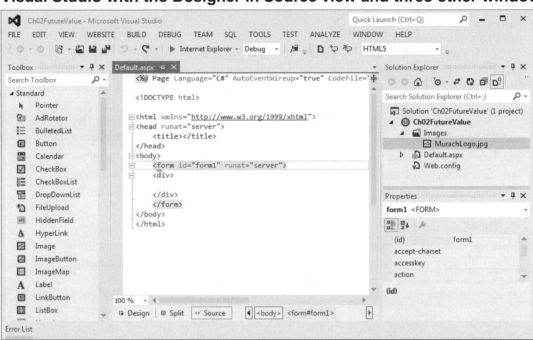

How to work with views and windows

- To change the Web Forms Designer from one view to another, click on the Design, Split, or Source button at the bottom of the Designer window.

- To hide a window, click on its Auto Hide button, which is a pin icon. Then, the window is shown as a tab at the side of the screen. To display the window again, move the mouse pointer over the tab or click on it. To restore the window, display it and click on the Auto Hide button.

- To size a window, place the mouse pointer over one of its boundaries and drag it.

- To close a window, click on the close button in its upper right corner. To redisplay it, select it from the View menu.

Description

- The primary window for designing web forms with Visual Studio is the *Web Forms Designer*, or just *Designer*, that's in the middle of the IDE.

- The three supporting windows are the *Toolbox*, the *Solution Explorer*, and the *Properties window*.

- Visual Studio often provides several different ways to do the same task. In this book, we'll try to show you the techniques that work the best.

Figure 2-3   How to work with the Visual Studio IDE

How to add folders and files to a web site

Right after you start a new web site, it makes sense to add any other folders or files that the application is going to require. To do that, you can use the shortcut menus for the project or its folders in the Solution Explorer as shown in figure 2-4. As you can see, this menu provides a New Folder command as well as an Existing Item command.

For the Future Value application, I first added a folder named Images. To do that, I right-clicked on the project at the top of the Solution Explorer, chose Add and then the New Folder command, and entered the name for the folder. Then, I added an image file named MurachLogo.jpg to the Images folder. To do that, I right-clicked on the folder, chose Add and then Existing Item, and selected the file from the dialog box that was displayed.

Those are the only other folders and files that are needed for the Future Value application, but often you'll need others. For instance, the application in chapter 4 requires three existing business classes, a database, and a number of image files.

The Future Value project as a new folder is being added

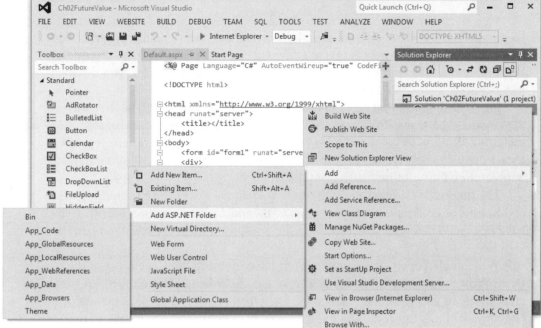

How to add a folder to a web site

- To add a standard folder, right-click on the project or folder you want to add the folder to in the Solution Explorer and choose Add→New Folder. Then, type a name for the folder in the dialog box that's displayed and press Enter.
- To add a special ASP.NET folder, right-click on the project in the Solution Explorer and choose Add→Add ASP.NET Folder. Then, select the folder from the list that's displayed.

How to add an existing item to a web site

- In the Solution Explorer, right-click on the project or folder that you want to add an existing item to. Then, select Add→Existing Item and respond to the dialog box.

Description

- When you create a new web form, Visual Studio generates the starting HTML for the form and displays it in Source view of the Web Forms Designer.
- Before you start designing the first web form of the application, you can use the Solution Explorer to add any other folders or files to the web site.

Figure 2-4   How to add folders and files to a web site

How to open or close an IIS Express web site

Web sites created in Visual Studio 2012 use *IIS Express* by default. To open them, you can use their solution files. In contrast, web sites created in earlier versions of Visual Studio or sites that are downloaded from another location use the *development server* that's part of Visual Studio. To open these sites, you use their file locations.

Figure 2-5 shows two ways to open an IIS Express web site. The first way is to display the Open Project dialog box. This box lists all of your projects, including Windows Forms and Web Forms Application projects. Then, you can locate the web site's folder, double-click the folder to reveal the solution file, and double-click the solution file to open the web site.

The other way to open an IIS Express web site is to use the Recent Projects and Solutions command to display a list of the most recent solution files that you have opened. Then, you select the web site's solution file and click it to open the web site.

You can also open sites from the Start Page by using the Recent list or the Open Project link. The items in the Recent list are links to solution files, so clicking them will open their web sites. The Open Project link opens the dialog box shown in this figure. If you know that you are going to be working on the same web site for a while, you can pin it to the Recent list on the Start Page by clicking on the pin icon for it. Then, it will be available each time you open Visual Studio.

With that as background, here's a caution. Although it might seem like you should open a web site by using the Open Web Site command rather than the Open Project command, that will create another solution file with another name. Yes, everything will still work, because a web site can have multiple solution files pointing to it. But that isn't a good practice.

To close a project, you use the Close Solution command. After you close a project for the first time, you'll be able to find it in the Recent list on the Start Page and also in the list of projects that you see when you use the Recent Projects and Solutions command.

The Open Project dialog box

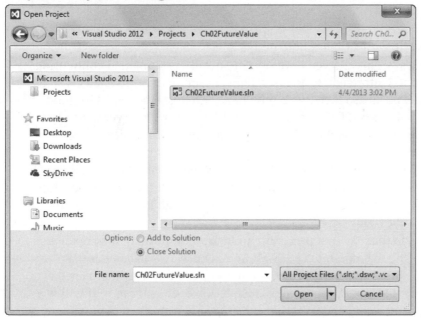

Two ways to display the Open Project dialog box

- Use the FILE→Open→Project/Solutions command (or the FILE→Open Project command for VS Express).
- Use the FILE→Recent Projects and Solutions command.

How to complete the Open Project dialog box

- Locate the web site folder and double-click it to display the solution file. Then, double-click the solution file.

How to close a solution

- Use the FILE→Close Solution command.

How to open projects from the Start Page

- Click the link for a project in the Recent list, or click the Open Project link to display the Open Project dialog box.
- To pin a web site to the Recent list so it stays there, hover the mouse over the web site name and click the pin icon.

Description

- The Open Project dialog box displays the folders for all the solutions in the default solution location, which is Visual Studio 2012\Projects in the My Documents folder.
- The Recent list and the Open Project command are also available from the Start Page that's displayed when you start Visual Studio.

Figure 2-5   How to open or close an IIS Express web site

How to convert a file-system web site to IIS Express

Previous versions of Visual Studio used a development server to host ASP.NET web sites. This allowed developers to avoid installing and configuring the IIS web server. Unfortunately, the development server didn't work as well as IIS for testing a web site so there were problems with this approach. The good news is that Visual Studio 2012 uses the new IIS Express web server instead of the development server, and IIS Express gets installed along with any of the Visual Studio editions.

The trouble is that web sites created in earlier versions of Visual Studio or web sites downloaded or moved from another location, will use the old development server by default. As a result, you will need to change the web.config files for those sites so they will use IIS Express.

To help you do that, the first procedure in figure 2-6 shows how to open a file-system web site that doesn't use IIS Express. One way you can tell that it isn't using IIS Express is that the project in the Solution Explorer includes the entire path for the file, not just its name. Then, if you open and run it, it will use the old development server and work like a file-system web site in a previous version of Visual Studio.

It's better, though, to convert a file-system web site to IIS Express using the second procedure in this figure. You will know that you have successfully converted to IIS Express when the project name no longer includes the path. You will also be able to see your project in the list of IIS Express sites in the Open Web Site dialog box when you click on Local IIS. However, you shouldn't open a web site that way.

The Open Web Site dialog box

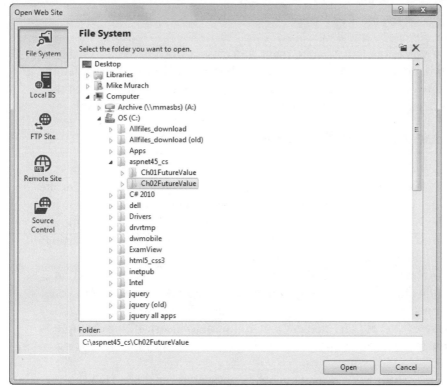

How to open a web site that doesn't use IIS Express

- Use FILE→Open→Web Site (or FILE→Open Web Site for VS Express) to display the Open Web Site dialog box. Then, click on File System, navigate to the folder for the web site, and click the Open button.

How to switch a web site to the IIS Express web server

- In the Solution Explorer, right-click the project and choose Use IIS Express. Then, follow the instructions in the message boxes that follow.

- You will know that you have been successful when the Solution Explorer displays just the project's name, rather than the entire file path.

How to see the IIS Express web sites

- In the Open Web Site dialog box, click on Local IIS.

Discussion

- When you create a new web site, Visual Studio 2012 uses the *IIS Express* web server.

- When you open a web site developed with a previous version of Visual Studio or on another computer like one of our downloadable applications, Visual Studio uses its *development server*, not IIS Express. Then, you can convert the web site to IIS Express.

Figure 2-6   How to convert a file-system web site to IIS Express

How to use Visual Studio to build a web form

Now that you know how to start, open, and close a web site, you're ready to learn how to build a web page with HTML, web server controls, and validation controls. If any of this seems confusing as you read about it, the exercise at the end of this chapter will show you that all of the skills are quite manageable.

How to enter the HTML for a web form

Figure 2-7 presents the primary ways to add HTML to a web form. For many HTML elements, the easiest way to add them is to type the HTML for the elements directly into the source code, taking full advantage of *IntelliSense*. In this figure, for example, you can see how IntelliSense provides a *snippet* for an h1 element. Just remember to press the Tab key twice to insert both the starting and ending tag for an element.

For some elements, though, it's better to insert a snippet using the second technique in this figure. To do that, you move the insertion point to where you want the snippet, right-click to display a menu, select Insert Snippet, select HTML, and select the HTML element that you want to insert. If, for example, you insert the snippet for an img element, the HTML includes the src and alt attributes.

This figure also shows how you can add an img element to the HTML by dragging the image from the Solution Explorer and dropping it wherever you want it. If you drop it in Design view, the Accessibility Properties dialog box is displayed. And that makes it easy to enter the Alternate Text property, which gets converted to an alt attribute in the HTML.

Whether or not you use the Accessibility Properties dialog box, the alt attribute should always be coded for an img element because it improves accessibility. Specifically, this attribute is used by screen readers to describe an image for the visually impaired. If an image is used for decorative purposes only, the value of this attribute should be an empty string ("").

In contrast, the Long Description property in the Accessibility Properties dialog box gets converted to the longdesc attribute. However, that attribute isn't supported by HTML5 or any modern browser. As a result, you should ignore it and leave it blank.

Usually, you'll want to make a few adjustments and additions to the HTML right after the form is added to the web site. For instance, you'll want to enter a title for the form in the title element that's in the head section. That's the title that's displayed in the title bar or tab of the browser when the form is run. You'll also want to add an h1 element to the form that describes what the page does.

After making the HTML entries, you can use either Source view or Design view to add web server controls to the form. If you work in Design view, though, you'll want to switch back to Source view from time to time. That way, you can review the source code that has been added, make sure the code is in the right location, and make adjustments to the source code.

The Future Value form in Split view after an img element has been added

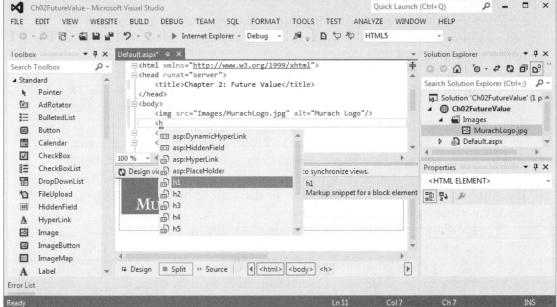

How to add HTML elements to a form

- Enter the code for the element in Source view. As you work, Visual Studio's *IntelliSense* will help you enter *snippets*, tags, attributes. To add a snippet, press the Tab key twice.

- To insert a snippet for an HTML element without using IntelliSense, move the insertion point to where you want the snippet. Then, right-click, select Insert Snippet, select HTML, and select the element that you want inserted.

Two ways to add an img element to a form

- Insert a snippet for the element. That includes the src and alt attributes, but you have to add the values.

- Drag the image from the Solution Explorer to the Designer. This inserts an img element with a valid src attribute. In Design view, the Accessibility Properties dialog box is also displayed.

How to add and remove comments

- To add a comment at the insertion point, click the Comment button in the HTML Source Editing toolbar, or press Ctrl+K and then Ctrl+C. If you select lines of code before you do this, the lines will be *commented out*.

- To remove a comment, move the insertion point into it and click the Uncomment button, or press Ctrl+K and then Ctrl+U. If you select lines of code that have been commented out before you do this, they will be uncommented.

How to synchronize the views when you're working in Split view

- Save the file or click on the message that's displayed between the views.

Figure 2-7   How to enter the HTML for a web form

How to add a table to a form

By default, forms use *flow layout*. This means that the text and controls you add to a form are positioned from left to right and from top to bottom. Because of that, the position of the controls can change when the form is displayed depending on the size of the browser window and the resolution of the display.

Usually, though, you will want more control than flow layout provides. One way to get that control is to use a table, which you'll learn about now. Another way is to use CSS, which you'll learn about in the next chapter.

Figure 2-8 shows how to add a table to a form in Design view. In this case, a table of six rows and two columns has already been added to the form, but the Insert Table dialog box is displayed to show what the settings are for that table. Usually, you can keep the dialog box entries that simple, because you can easily adjust the table once it's on the form.

The easiest way to resize a row or column is to drag it by its border. To change the width of a column, drag it by its right border. To change the height of a row, drag it by its bottom border. You can also change the height and width of the entire table by selecting the table and then dragging it by its handles.

You can also format a table in Design view by selecting one or more rows or columns and then using the commands in the TABLE menu or the shortcut menu that's displayed when you right-click the selection. These commands let you add, delete, or resize rows or columns. They also let you merge the cells in a row or column. If, for example, you want a control in one row to span two columns, you can merge the cells in that row.

Note that when you make some of these changes, Visual Studio adds classes to the HTML elements as well as a style element in the head section of the form that contains the rule sets for the classes. You'll see this when you review the aspx code for the Future Value form.

How to add text to the cells of a table

In figure 2-8, you can see that text has been entered into the cells in the first four rows of the first column of the table. To do that, you just type the text into the cells. Then, you can format the text by selecting it and using the controls in the Formatting toolbar or the commands in the Format menu. If, for example, you want to bold the four text entries, you can select the four cells that contain the text and click on the Bold button in the Formatting toolbar.

The Future Value form with a table that has been inserted into it

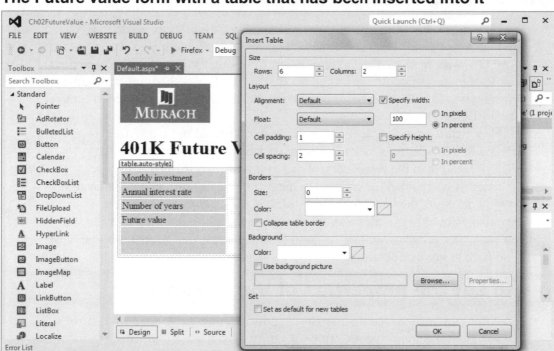

How to add a table to a form

- Use the TABLE→Insert Table command to display the Insert Table dialog box. Then, set the number of rows and columns that you want in the table, set any other options that you want, and click OK.

How to format a table after it has been added to a form

- To resize a row, drag it by its bottom border. To resize a column, drag it by its right border. To resize the entire table, select the table and then drag one of its handles.
- To select rows, columns or cells, drag the mouse over them or hold the Ctrl key down as you click on the cells. To add, delete, size, or merge selected rows or columns, use the commands in the TABLE menu or the shortcut menu.

How to add text to a table and format it

- To add text to a table, type the text into the cells of the table.
- To format the text, select it and use the controls in the Formatting toolbar or the commands in the Format menu.

Description

- To control the alignment of the text and controls on a web form, you can use tables.
- Some of the formatting that you apply to tables, rows, and columns is saved in CSS rule sets in a style element in the head section of the HTML.

Figure 2-8   How to add a table to a form and add text to the table's cells

How to add web server controls to a form

Figure 2-9 shows how to add *web server controls* to a form. To do that, you can just drag a control from the Standard group of the Toolbox and drop it on the form. Or, you can move the cursor to where you want a control inserted and then double-click on the control in the Toolbox. This works whether you're placing a control within a cell of a table or outside of a table, and whether you're in Source view or Design view.

Here again, you can add a web server control to a form by inserting a snippet. But this time, after you select the Insert Snippet command, you select ASP.NET and then the server control that you want to add.

Once you've added the controls to the form, you can resize them in Design view by dragging the handles on their sides. If the controls are in a table, you may also want to resize the columns or rows of the table. But keep in mind that you can resize a cell as well as the control within a cell, and sometimes you have to do both to get the formatting the way you want it.

How to set the properties of the controls

After you have placed the controls on a form, you need to set each control's *properties* so the control looks and works the way you want it to. To set those properties, you can work in the Properties window as shown in this figure. To display the properties for a control, just click on it in Design or Source view.

In the Properties window, you select a property by clicking it. Then, a brief description of that property is displayed at the bottom of the window. To change a property setting, you change the entry to the right of the property name by typing a new value or choosing a new value from a drop-down list. In some cases, a button with an ellipsis (…) on it will appear when you click on a property. Then, you can click the button to display a dialog box that helps you set the property.

Some properties are displayed in groups. In that case, a + symbol appears next to the group name. To expand the properties in the group, just click the + symbol, which then changes to a – symbol.

To display properties alphabetically or by category, you can click the appropriate button at the top of the Properties window. At first, you may want to display the properties by category so you have an idea of what the different properties do. Once you become more familiar with the properties, though, you may be able to find the ones you're looking for faster if you display them alphabetically.

Another way to set properties for some controls is to use the control's *smart tag menu*. In this figure, for example, you can see the smart tag menu for the drop-down list. Because smart tag menus help you set common properties, they're displayed automatically when you drag a control to a form in Design view. Later, you can display the smart tag menu of a control by hovering the mouse pointer over it until its smart tag appears and then clicking on that tag.

As you work with properties, you'll find that many are set the way you want by default. In addition, some properties such as Height and Width are set as you size and position the controls in Design view. As a result, you usually only need to change a few properties for each control.

The Future Value form after six server controls have been added to it

How to add a web server control to a web form

- Drag the control from the Standard group in the Toolbox to the form or to a cell in a table on the form. Or, move the cursor to where you want the control in either Source or Design view, and double-click on the control in the Toolbox to place it there.

- To insert a snippet for a server control in Source view, move the insertion point to where you want the snippet. Then, right-click, select Insert Snippet, select ASP.NET, and select the control that you want inserted.

How to set the properties for a control

- Select a control by clicking on it, and all of its properties are displayed in the Properties window. Then, you can select a property in this window and set its value.

- To change the Height and Width properties, drag one of the handles on a control. This also changes the Height and Width in the Properties window.

- To sort the properties in the Properties window by category or alphabetically, click on one of the buttons at the top of the window. To expand or collapse the list of properties in a group, click on the + or – symbol for the group.

- To display a smart tag menu for a control in Design view, select the control and click the Smart Tag icon on the right of the control. In Source view, click in the aspx code for the control and hover over the line that appears under the <asp> tag to reveal the smart tag icon and then click on it.

Description

- Many *web server controls* have *smart tag menus* that provide options for performing common tasks and setting common *properties*.

Figure 2-9   How to add web server controls to a form and set their properties

Common properties for web server controls

The first table in figure 2-10 presents the properties for web server controls that you're most likely to use as you develop web forms. If you've worked with Windows controls, you'll notice that many of the properties of the web server controls provide similar functionality. For example, you use the ID property to identify a control that you need to refer to in your C# code, and you can use the Text property to set what's displayed in or on the control.

In contrast, the AutoPostBack, CausesValidation, EnableViewState, and Runat properties are unique to web server controls. As you should already know, the Runat property just indicates that the control must be processed by the web server. The other three properties are more interesting.

The AutoPostBack property determines whether the page is posted back to the server when the user changes the value of the control. Note that this property is only available with certain controls, such as drop-down lists, check boxes, and radio buttons. Also note that this property isn't available with button controls. That's because button controls always either post a page back to the server or display another page.

The CausesValidation property is available for button controls and determines whether the validation controls are activated when the user clicks the button. This lets the browser check for valid data before the page is posted back to the server. You'll learn more about validation controls in a moment.

The EnableViewState property determines whether a server control retains its property settings from one posting to the next. For that to happen, the EnableViewState property for both the form and the control must be set to True. Since that's normally the way you want this property set, True is the default.

The second table in this figure lists four more properties that are commonly used with drop-down lists and list boxes. For instance, you can use the Items collection to add, insert, and remove ListItem objects, and you can use the Selected-Value property to retrieve the value of the currently selected item. Although you can set these properties at design time, they are often set by the C# code in the code-behind file. You'll learn more about these properties when you review the code-behind file for the Future Value form.

Common web server control properties

Property	Description
AutoPostBack	Determines whether the page is posted back to the server when the value of the control changes. Available with controls like check boxes, text boxes, and lists. The default value is False.
CausesValidation	Determines whether the validation specified by the validation controls is done when a button control is clicked. The default value is True.
EnableViewState	Determines whether the control maintains its view state between HTTP requests. The default value is True.
Enabled	Determines whether the control is functional. The default value is True.
Height	The height of the control.
ID	The name that's used to refer to the control.
Runat	Indicates that the control will be processed on the server by ASP.NET.
TabIndex	Determines the order in which the controls on the form receive the focus when the Tab key is pressed.
Text	The text that's displayed in the control.
ToolTip	The text that's displayed when the user hovers the mouse over the control.
Visible	Determines whether a control is displayed or hidden.
Width	The width of the control.

Common properties of drop-down list and list box controls

Property	Description
Items	The collection of ListItem objects that represents the items in the control. Although you can set the values for these list items at design time, you normally use code to add, insert, and remove the items in a drop-down list or list box.
SelectedItem	The ListItem object for the currently selected item.
SelectedIndex	The index of the currently selected item starting from zero. If no item is selected in a list box, the value of this property is -1.
SelectedValue	The value of the currently selected item.

Note

- When buttons are clicked, they always post back to the server or display other pages. That's why they don't have AutoPostBack properties.

Figure 2-10   Common properties for web server controls

How to add validation controls to a form

A *validation control* is a type of ASP.NET control that's used to validate input data. The topics that follow introduce you to the validation controls and show you how to use two of them. Then, in chapter 7, you can learn how to use all of these controls.

An introduction to the validation controls

Figure 2-11 shows the Validation group in the Toolbox. It offers five controls that can be called *validators*. These are the controls that you use to check that the user has entered valid data. You can use the last control in this group, the validation summary control, to display all the errors that have been detected by the validators on the form.

To add a validation control to a web form, you can use the same techniques that you use to add a server control. Before you can access the validation controls in the Toolbox, though, you need to open the Validation group by clicking on the arrowhead to its left. You can also add a validation control to a form by inserting a snippet.

In this example, four validators have been added to the form: two required field validators and two range validators. In this case, the controls have been added below the table so ASP.NET will use flow layout to position the controls. However, these controls could have been added to a third column of the table. Although these controls don't show when the form is displayed, the messages in their ErrorMessage properties are displayed if errors are detected.

Validation tests are typically done on the client before the page is posted to the server. That way, a round trip to the server isn't required to display error messages if invalid data is detected.

In most cases, client-side validation is done when the focus leaves an input control that has validators associated with it. That can happen when the user presses the Tab key to move to the next control or clicks another control to move the focus to that control. Validation is also done when the user clicks on a button that has its CausesValidation property set to True.

To perform client-side validation, a browser must have JavaScript enabled. Because most browsers enable it, validation is usually done on the client. However, validation is always done on the server too when a page is submitted. ASP.NET does this validation after it initializes the page.

When ASP.NET performs the validation tests on the server, it sets the IsValid property of each validator to indicate whether the test was successful. Then, after all the validators are tested, it sets the IsValid property of the page to indicate whether all the tests were valid. This is the property that's usually tested by the C# code when the page is posted to the server. You'll see how this works when you review the code-behind file for this form.

The validation controls on the Future Value form

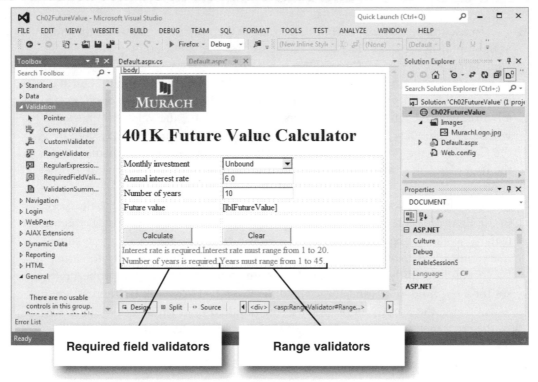

Required field validators   **Range validators**

How to add a validator to a web form

- In either Design or Source view, move the insertion point to where you want the validator and double-click on the validator in the Validation group in the Toolbox. Or, drag the validator from the Toolbox to where you want it.

- In Source view, right-click, select Insert Snippet, select ASP.NET, and select the validator control that you want to insert.

How to set the properties for a validation control

- In either Design or Source view, use the Properties window.

- In Source view, enter the properties for the validator with help from IntelliSense.

Description

- You can use *validation controls* to test user entries and produce error messages. The validation is typically done when the focus leaves the control that's being validated and also when the user clicks on a button that has its CausesValidation property set to True.

- Each validation control is associated with a specific server control, but you can associate more than one validation control with the same server control.

- If the user's browser has JavaScript enabled, the validation controls work by running JavaScript in the browser. Then, if the validation fails, the page isn't posted back to the server, which saves a round trip. If the browser doesn't have JavaScript enabled, the validation is done on the server.

Figure 2-11   An introduction to the validation controls

How to use the required field validator

To use the *required field validator*, you set the properties shown in the table at the top of figure 2-12. These are the properties that are used by all the validators.

To start, you associate the validation control with a specific input control on the form through its ControlToValidate property. Then, when the user clicks on a button whose CausesValidation property is set to True, the validator checks whether a value has been entered into the input control. If not, the message in the ErrorMessage property is displayed. The error message is also displayed if the user clears the value in the input control and then moves the focus to another control.

The Display property of the validation control determines how the message in the ErrorMessage property is displayed. When you use flow layout, Dynamic usually works the best for this property. However, if you use a validation summary control, as explained in chapter 7, you can change this property to None.

If you look at the aspx code in this figure, you can see how the properties are set for a required field validator that validates the text box with txtInterestRate as its ID. Here, the ForeColor property of the required field validator is set to "Red" so the error message will be displayed in that color. In the next chapter, you'll learn how to use CSS to get the same result.

How to use the range validator

The *range validator* lets you set the valid range for an input value. To use this control, you set the properties in the first table in this figure, plus the properties in the second table. In particular, you set the minimum and maximum values for an input value.

The aspx code in this figure also shows how the properties are set for the range validator for the text box with txtInterestRate as its ID. For this to work correctly, you must set the Type property to the type of data that you're testing. Because the interest rate entry can have decimal positions, for example, the Type property for its range validator is set to Double. In contrast, because a year entry should be a whole number, the Type property for its range validator should be set to Integer.

Common validation control properties

Property	Description
ControlToValidate	The ID of the control to be validated.
Display	Determines how an error message is displayed. Specify Static to allocate space for the message in the page layout, Dynamic to have the space allocated when an error occurs, or None to display the errors in a validation summary control.
ErrorMessage	The message that's displayed in the validation control when the validation fails.

Additional properties of a range validator

Property	Description
MaximumValue	The maximum value that the control can contain.
MinimumValue	The minimum value that the control can contain.
Type	The data type to use for range checking (String, Integer, Double, Date, or Currency).

The aspx code for a RequiredFieldValidator control

```
<asp:RequiredFieldValidator ID="RequiredFieldValidator1" runat="server"
    ControlToValidate="txtInterestRate" Display="Dynamic"
    ErrorMessage="Interest rate is required." ForeColor="Red">
</asp:RequiredFieldValidator>
```

The aspx code for a RangeValidator control

```
<asp:RangeValidator ID="RangeValidator1" runat="server"
    ControlToValidate="txtInterestRate" Display="Dynamic"
    ErrorMessage="Interest rate must range from 1 to 20."
    MaximumValue="20" MinimumValue="1" Type="Double" ForeColor="Red">
</asp:RangeValidator>
```

Description

- The *required field validator* is typically used with text box controls, but can also be used with list controls.

- The *range validator* tests whether a user entry falls within a valid range.

- If the user doesn't enter a value into a control that a range validator is associated with, the range validation test passes. Because of that, you should also provide a required field validator if a value is required.

Figure 2-12   How to use the required field and range validators

How to work with unobtrusive validation

ASP.NET 4.5 has a new feature called *unobtrusive validation* that you need to be aware of. This feature controls how the client-side validation of the validation controls is done. Figure 2-13 shows the two settings for unobtrusive validation that a web site can have.

A setting of Webforms means that unobtrusive validation is enabled and ASP.NET will use jQuery for validation. *jQuery* is a JavaScript library that provides for cross-browser compatibility and reduces the amount of JavaScript that an ASP.NET application requires. A setting of None means that unobtrusive validation is disabled and ASP.NET will do the validation the way it was done in previous versions, which is to use script elements within the HTML to supply the JavaScript for the validation.

The benefit of using unobtrusive validation is that it reduces the amount of JavaScript that has to be generated. That's why ASP.NET 4.5 enables unobtrusive validation by default.

The problem with this is that if you start a web site from the Empty Web Site template, unobtrusive validation is enabled but the jQuery library and configuration needed to use it are not there. This means that if you try to use a validation control, you will get an error. There are two ways to fix this.

One way is to add the components that are required by unobtrusive validation. To do that, you can use NuGet, which is a Visual Studio feature that makes it easy to add third-party and open-source packages to an application. You'll learn more about NuGet later, but this figure shows how to use NuGet to install the package that provides everything you need to make unobtrusive validation work in your web site.

The other alternative is to disable unobtrusive validation. To do that for one page, you can set the UnobtrusiveValidationMode property to None in the Load event handler for the page, as shown in this figure. To do that for all pages in a web site, you can add an appSettings element like the one in this figure to the web.config file.

Two values for the UnobtrusiveValidationMode setting

Value	Description
Webforms	Uses the jQuery library for the validation that's done by the validation controls.
None	Uses the older method of generating the JavaScript code for the validation controls and including it within script elements in the HTML for the page.

The Manage NuGet Packages dialog box

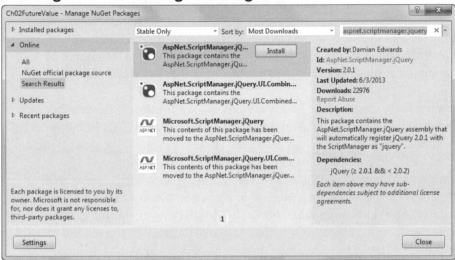

How to install the NuGet package for jQuery validation

- Right-click on the project and select Manage NuGet Packages. In the left panel of the dialog box that appears, click on NuGet Official Package Source. Next, use the box in the upper right to search for AspNet.ScriptManager.jQuery. Then, click on the Install button.

A Load event handler that turns off unobtrusive validation for a page

```
protected void Page_Load(object sender, EventArgs e) {
    UnobtrusiveValidationMode =
        System.Web.UI.UnobtrusiveValidationMode.None;
}
```

A web.config setting that turns off unobtrusive validation for a site

```
<appSettings>
    <add key="ValidationSettings:UnobtrusiveValidationMode" value="None"/>
</appSettings>
```

Description

- ASP.NET 4.5 provides a new option called *unobtrusive validation*. When it is enabled, a JavaScript library named *jQuery* is used to do the validation that's specified.
- Unobtrusive validation is on by default when you start a new web site from the Empty Web Site Template. So if you're using the validation controls, you either need to turn unobtrusive validation off or install the NuGet package for jQuery validation.

Figure 2-13 How to work with unobtrusive validation

The aspx code for the Future Value form

Figure 2-14 presents the aspx code for the Future Value form. To help you see how the code relates to the form in the browser, this figure starts with the form displayed in Internet Explorer. Here, you can see that the title in the browser tab is the same as the title in the title element in the head section of the HTML.

After the title element, you can see a style element that includes two CSS rule sets. You can also see class attributes in the table and td elements that refer to these rule sets. In the next chapter, you'll learn how this works, but for now realize that ASP.NET does this automatically when you use the Designer to format the elements on a page, even though this isn't the best way to handle this formatting.

Within the body element, the first two elements are for the image and the h1 heading. You can see how these are rendered in the browser. This is followed by a form element that contains a div element. These form and div elements are generated by ASP.NET when you add a new form to a web site.

Within the div element is a table that contains six tr elements, one for each row. Within each of these elements are two td elements, one for each column. That's the way the HTML for a table works. In the first td element for each of the first four rows, you can see the text that has been entered. In the second td element for each of these rows, a server control has been added. For instance, the control in the first row is a drop-down list, and the control in the second row is a text box. You can see how this table is rendered in the browser.

For each control, the ID property is used to give the control an identifier that's easy to refer to. Here, ddl is used as a prefix for a drop-down list and txt is used as a prefix for a text box. That makes it easy to tell what type of control an identifier refers to. These identifiers are followed by names that clearly identify the controls. Within those names, the first letter of each word is capitalized, which makes the names easier to read. This is the naming convention that's used throughout this book and the one that we recommend for your own use.

The design of the Future Value form

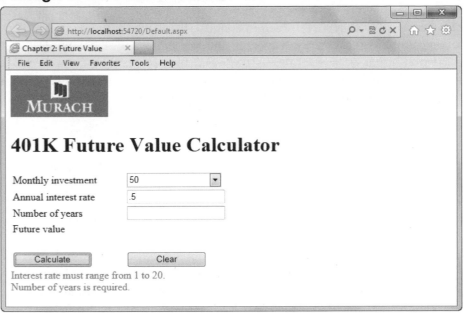

The aspx code for the Future Value form

```
<%@ Page Language="C#" AutoEventWireup="true" CodeFile="Default.aspx.cs"
Inherits="_Default" %>

<!DOCTYPE html>

<html xmlns="http://www.w3.org/1999/xhtml">
<head runat="server">
    <title>Chapter 2: Future Value</title>
    <style type="text/css">
        .auto-style1 {
            width: 100%;
        }
        .auto-style2 {
            width: 172px;
        }
    </style>
</head>
<body>
    <img src="Images/MurachLogo.jpg" alt="Murach Logo"/>
    <h1>401K Future Value Calculator</h1>
    <form id="form1" runat="server">
    <div>
        <table class="auto-style1">
            <tr>
                <td class="auto-style2">Monthly investment</td>
                <td><asp:DropDownList ID="ddlMonthlyInvestment"
                        runat="server" Height="22px" Width="147px">
                    </asp:DropDownList></td>
            </tr>
```

Figure 2-14   The aspx code for the Future Value form (part 1 of 2)

In the code for the first text box control, you can see that the Text attribute has been set to a value of 6.0. That is the interest rate that will be displayed when the form is first displayed in the browser. In contrast, the value for the second text box control is coded between the opening and closing tags for the control. These are two different ways to set the starting value for a control.

In the code for the fifth row of the table, you can see that ASP.NET has put a non-breaking space ( ) in the cell for each column. It does that for all of the empty cells in a table.

In the sixth row, you can see the aspx code for the Calculate and Clear buttons. Here, each of the buttons has an OnClick property that points to the C# code in the code-behind file that will be run when the button is clicked. The Clear button also contains a CausesValidation property, which is set to False. This property tells the page not to do validation when the button is clicked. Because the default value of the CausesValidation property is True for buttons, this property doesn't need to be set for the Calculate button.

This table is followed by the code for the validation controls. Because these controls are outside the table, their placement will be determined by flow layout. To have some control over this layout, a break element (<br />) is coded after the two interest rate validators. That means the error messages for the interest rate will be displayed on one line, and the messages for the years will be on another line. However, the Display property for these validators has been set to Dynamic, which means that space will be allocated for them only when it is needed.

The aspx code for the Future Value form (continued)

```
        <tr>
            <td class="auto-style2">Annual interest rate</td>
            <td><asp:TextBox ID="txtInterestRate" runat="server"
                Text="6.0"></asp:TextBox></td>
        </tr>
        <tr>
            <td class="auto-style2">Number of years</td>
            <td>
                <asp:TextBox ID="txtYears" runat="server">10
                </asp:TextBox></td>
        </tr>
        <tr>
            <td>Future value</td>
            <td><asp:Label ID="lblFutureValue" runat="server"
                Font-Bold="True"></asp:Label></td>
        </tr>
        <tr>
            <td class="auto-style2"> </td>
            <td> </td>
        </tr>
        <tr>
            <td class="auto-style2">
                <asp:Button ID="btnCalculate" runat="server"
                    Text="Calculate" Width="122px"
                    OnClick="btnCalculate_Click" /></td>
            <td>
                <asp:Button ID="btnClear" runat="server" Text="Clear"
                    Width="123px" CausesValidation="False"
                    OnClick="btnClear_Click" /></td>
        </tr>
    </table>
    <asp:RequiredFieldValidator ID="RequiredFieldValidator1"
        runat="server" ErrorMessage="Interest rate is required."
        ControlToValidate="txtInterestRate" Display="Dynamic"
        ForeColor="Red">
    </asp:RequiredFieldValidator>
    <asp:RangeValidator ID="RangeValidator1" runat="server"
        ErrorMessage="Interest rate must range from 1 to 20."
        ControlToValidate="txtInterestRate"
        Display="Dynamic" ForeColor="Red" Type="Double"
        MaximumValue="20" MinimumValue="1">
    </asp:RangeValidator><br />
    <asp:RequiredFieldValidator ID="RequiredFieldValidator2"
        runat="server" ErrorMessage="Number of years is required."
        ControlToValidate="txtYears" Display="Dynamic" ForeColor="Red">
    </asp:RequiredFieldValidator>
    <asp:RangeValidator ID="RangeValidator2" runat="server"
        ErrorMessage="Years must range from 1 to 45."
        ControlToValidate="txtYears" Type="Integer" Display="Dynamic"
        ForeColor="Red" MaximumValue="45" MinimumValue="1">
    </asp:RangeValidator>
    </div>
    </form>
</body>
</html>
```

Figure 2-14   The aspx code for the Future Value form (part 2 of 2)

How to add C# code to a form

To add the functionality required by a web form, you add C# code to its code-behind file. This code responds to the events that the user initiates on the form. This code also responds to events that occur as a form is processed.

How to use the Code Editor

Figure 2-15 shows how to use the *Code Editor* to enter and edit C# code, starting with three ways to start an event handler. If, for example, you double-click outside the body of the form in Design view, an event handler for the Load event of the page is started. Or, if you double-click a control, an event handler for the default event of the control is started. If you double-click on a button control, for example, an event handler for the Click event of that control is created. Then, you can enter the code that you want to be executed within the braces of the event handler.

To create event handlers for other control events, you can use the Events button at the top of the Properties window. When you click this button, a list of all the events for the control that's currently selected is displayed. Then, you can double-click on any event to generate an event handler for that event.

When Visual Studio generates an event handler for a control, it also adds the appropriate event attribute to the aspx code for that control. In the aspx code, for example, you saw the OnClick event attributes that were generated for the Calculate and Clear buttons on the Future Value form. This is how events are wired to event handlers in ASP.NET.

You can also code methods other than event handlers by entering the code for the method directly into the Code Editor window. Then, you can call those methods from the event handlers for the form.

As you enter C# code, be sure to take advantage of the snippets that ASP.NET offers. If, for example, you insert the snippet for a for loop, all of the code that you need for that structure is inserted into the code-behind file. Then, you can modify that code to suit your requirements. As you work, the Code Editor also provides IntelliSense that makes it easier to enter code.

When you test a web form, you may want to *comment out* portions of code by putting those portions of code within C# comments. Then, because comments are ignored, you can test the form to see whether those statements were the cause of a problem. Later, you can uncomment those lines of code and test again.

The Code Editor for a web form

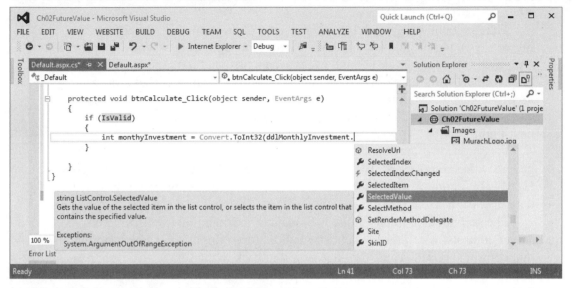

Three ways to start an event handler

- In the Designer, double-click outside the body of a web form to start an event handler for the Load event of the page.

- Double-click on a control in the Designer to start an event handler for the default event of that control.

- Select a control in the Designer, click the Events button in the Properties window (the button with the lightning bolt), and double-click the event you want.

How to insert a code snippet

- Move the insertion point to where you want the snippet. Right-click, select Insert Snippet, select Visual C#, and select the snippet.

How to comment out a portion of code

- Select the lines of code that you want to comment out. Then, click on the Comment button in the Text Editor toolbar or press Ctrl+K, Ctrl+C. To uncomment the lines, select them and click the Uncomment button or press Ctrl+K, Ctrl+U.

Description

- An *event handler* is a C# method that is executed when an event occurs, and Visual Studio will generate the starting code for an event handler.

- The *Code Editor* includes editing features such as IntelliSense, automatic indentation, snippets, and syntax checking.

- If syntax errors are detected, they are underlined with a wavy line.

- To enter a method other than an event handler, you type the method from scratch.

Figure 2-15   How to use the Code Editor to enter and edit C# code

How to use page and control events

The first table in figure 2-16 presents some of the common events for working with web pages. The Init and Load events of a page occur whenever a page is requested from the server. The Init event occurs first, and it's used by ASP.NET to restore the view state of the page and its controls. Because of that, you don't usually create an event handler for this event. Instead, you add any initialization code to the event handler for the Load event. You'll see how this works in the next figure.

In contrast, the PreRender event is raised after all the control events for the page have been processed. It's the last event to occur before a page is rendered to HTML. In section 2, you'll see how this event can be useful when working with data in session state.

The second table in this figure lists some of the common events for web server controls. When the user clicks a button, for example, the Click event of that control is raised. Then, the page is posted back to the server, the event handlers for the Init and Load events of the page are executed, followed by the event handler for the Click event of the control that was clicked.

The TextChanged event occurs when the user changes the value in a text box. In contrast, the CheckedChanged event occurs when the user clicks a radio button or checks a check box, and the SelectedIndexChanged event occurs when the user selects an item from a list.

If you want the event handler for one of these events to be executed immediately when the event occurs, you can set the AutoPostBack property of the control to True. Then, the event handler will be executed after the Init and Load event handlers for the page. If you don't set the AutoPostBack property to True, the event is still raised, but the event handler isn't executed until another user action causes the page to be posted to the server. Then, the event handlers for the Init and Load events of the page are executed, followed by the event handlers for the control events in the order they were raised.

In this figure, you can see the event handler for the Click event of the Clear button on the Future Value form. This event handler resets the value in the drop-down list to the first value in the list by setting the SelectedIndex property of the control to 0. This handler also resets the text boxes and label to empty strings. Note that the name of this event handler is btnClear_Click, which is the ID of the button followed by an underscore and the name of the event. If you look back at the aspx code, you'll see that this is the same name that's in the OnClick event property that ASP.NET adds to the control when it generates the event handler.

Common ASP.NET page events

Event	Method name	Occurs when...
Init	Page_Init	A page is requested from the server. This event is raised before the view state of the page controls has been restored.
Load	Page_Load	A page is requested from the server, after all controls have been initialized and view state has been restored. This is the event you typically use to perform initialization operations such as retrieving data and initializing form controls.
PreRender	Page_PreRender	All the control events for the page have been processed but before the HTML that will be sent back to the browser is generated.

Common ASP.NET control events

Event	Occurs when...
Click	The user clicks a button, link button, or image button control.
TextChanged	The user changes the value in a text box.
CheckedChanged	The user selects a radio button in a group of radio buttons or selects or unselects a check box.
SelectedIndexChanged	The user selects an item from a drop-down list or a list box.

Code for the Click event of the btnClear button

```
protected void btnClear_Click(object sender, EventArgs e)
{
    ddlMonthlyInvestment.SelectedIndex = 0;
    txtInterestRate.Text = "";
    txtYears.Text = "";
    lblFutureValue.Text = "";
}
```

Description

- All of the events handlers for an ASP.NET web page and its server controls are executed on the server. Because of that, a page must be posted back to the server before its events can be handled.

- When a page is posted back to the server, the Init and Load events are always raised so any event handlers for those events are run first. Then, the event handlers for any control events that were raised are executed in the order in which they were raised.

Figure 2-16   How to use page and control events in your C# code

The C# code for the Future Value form

Figure 2-17 presents the C# code for the code-behind file of the Future Value form. It consists of three event handlers that handle the Load event for the page and the Click events of the Calculate and Clear buttons. This code also includes a method named CalculateFutureValue that is called by the event handler for the Click event of the Calculate button.

In this code, the highlighted properties are the ones that are commonly tested in the code for web forms. The first one is the IsPostBack property that's used in the Page_Load method. If it is True, it means that the page is being posted back from the user. If it is False, it means that the page is being requested by the user for the first time.

As a result, the statements within the if statement in the Page_Load method are only executed if the page is being requested for the first time. In that case, the values 50 through 500 are added to the drop-down list by using the Add method of the Items collection for the list. For all subsequent requests by that user, the IsPostBack property will be True so the values aren't added to the drop-down list. Instead, the values are restored from view state.

The other page property that's commonly tested is the IsValid property. It's useful when the user's browser doesn't support the client-side scripts for the validation controls. In that case, the application has to rely on the validation that's always done on the server. Then, if IsValid is True, it means that all of the input data is valid. But if IsValid is False, it means that one or more controls contain invalid input data so the processing shouldn't be done.

In the btnCalculate_Click method, you can see how the IsValid test is used. If it isn't True, the processing isn't done. But otherwise, this method uses the SelectedValue property of the drop-down list to get the value of the selected item, which represents the investment amount. Then, it uses the Text properties of the text boxes to get the years and interest rate values. After it gets these values, it converts them to their data types (integer and decimal). Last, it calls the CalculateFutureValue method to calculate the future value, uses the ToString method to convert the future value to a string with currency format, and puts the formatted value in the label of the form. When this method ends, the web form is sent back to the user's browser.

With the exception of the IsPostBack and IsValid properties and the statement at the beginning of the Page_Load event handler that turns off unobtrusive validation, this is all standard C# code. Because of that, you shouldn't have any trouble following it. But if you do, you can quickly upgrade your C# skills by getting our latest C# book.

The C# code for the Future Value form

```csharp
using System;
using System.Collections.Generic;
using System.Linq;
using System.Web;
using System.Web.UI;
using System.Web.UI.WebControls;

public partial class _Default : System.Web.UI.Page
{
    protected void Page_Load(object sender, EventArgs e)
    {
        UnobtrusiveValidationMode =
            System.Web.UI.UnobtrusiveValidationMode.None;
        if (!IsPostBack)
            for (int i = 50; i <= 500; i += 50)
            {
                ddlMonthlyInvestment.Items.Add(i.ToString());
            }
    }
    protected void btnCalculate_Click(object sender, EventArgs e)
    {
        if (IsValid)
        {
            int monthlyInvestment =
                Convert.ToInt32(ddlMonthlyInvestment.SelectedValue);
            decimal yearlyInterestRate =
                Convert.ToDecimal(txtInterestRate.Text);
            int years = Convert.ToInt32(txtYears.Text);
            decimal futureValue =
                this.CalculateFutureValue(monthlyInvestment,
                    yearlyInterestRate, years);
            lblFutureValue.Text = futureValue.ToString("c");
        }
    }
    protected decimal CalculateFutureValue(int monthlyInvestment,
        decimal yearlyInterestRate, int years)
    {
        int months = years * 12;
        decimal monthlyInterestRate = yearlyInterestRate / 12 / 100;
        decimal futureValue = 0;
        for (int i = 0; i < months; i++)
        {
            futureValue = futureValue + monthlyInvestment
                        * (1 + monthlyInterestRate);
        }
        return futureValue;
    }
    protected void btnClear_Click(object sender, EventArgs e)
    {
        ddlMonthlyInvestment.SelectedIndex = 0;
        txtInterestRate.Text = "";
        txtYears.Text = "";
        lblFutureValue.Text = "";
    }
}
```

Figure 2-17   The C# code for the Future Value form

How to test a web application

After you design the forms and develop the C# code for a web application, you need to test it to be sure it works properly. Then, if you discover any errors, you need to find the errors, correct them, and test again. For now, you'll just learn how to test a web site with IIS Express. But in chapter 5, you'll learn more about testing and debugging.

How to run an IIS Express web site

To run a web site that uses IIS Express, you can use one of the techniques in figure 2-18. Before Visual Studio runs the web site, though, it compiles the aspx and C# code for the web forms. Then, if the web forms compile without errors, Visual Studio runs the web site using IIS Express and displays the starting page of the web site in your default browser. At that point, you can test the application to make sure that it works the way you want it to.

However, if any errors are detected as part of the compilation, Visual Studio opens the Error List window and displays the errors. These can consist of *syntax errors* that have to be corrected as well as warning messages. In this figure, just one error message and no warning messages are displayed.

To fix an error, you can double-click on it in the Error List window. This moves the cursor to the line of code that caused the error in the Code Editor. By moving from the Error List window to the Code Editor for all of the messages, you should be able to find the coding problems and fix them.

Keep in mind, though, that the error may not be in the statement in the line of code that causes the problem. For instance, the message in this example says that monthlyInvestment doesn't exist, but the problem is that this variable was spelled differently when it was declared. To fix that, you need to fix the declaration.

After you fix all of the compilation errors and run the application in the browser, you should be aware that an *exception* may occur. That happens when ASP.NET can't execute one of the statements in the C# code, even though it compiled without error. Then, if the exception isn't handled by the application, ASP.NET switches to the Code Editor window and highlights the statement that caused the exception. At that point, you can stop the application by clicking on the Stop Debugging button in the Debug toolbar or using the DEBUG→Stop Debugging command. Then, you can fix the problem and test again.

In addition to testing whether the web site runs without error, you should also test to see that it displays correctly in different browsers. Visual Studio makes it easy to change the default browsers for this purpose by providing a drop-down browser list. After you use that list to change the default browser, you can click on the browser name or press F5 to run the web site in that browser.

Visual Studio with the Error List window and browser list displayed

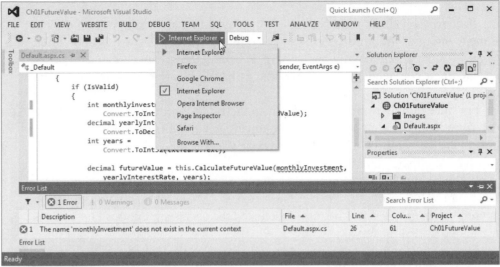

How to run an application

- To run an application in the default browser, press F5 or click on the browser name in the Standard toolbar.

- To change the default browser, select a browser from the drop-down browser list.

- The first time you run an ASP.NET application, a dialog box will appear asking whether you want to modify the web.config file to enable debugging. Click OK.

How to stop an application

- Click the Close button in the upper right corner of the browser. For some browsers like Internet Explorer, that will stop the application in Visual Studio.

- In Visual Studio, click the Stop Debugging button in the Debug toolbar or press Shift+F5. This also stops an application when an exception occurs.

How to fix syntax errors and exceptions

- To go to the statement that caused a syntax error, double-click on the error in the Error List window. That will give you a clue to the cause of the error.

- When an exception occurs, the application is interrupted and the statement that caused the error is displayed in Visual Studio. Then, you can stop the application and debug it.

Description

- Each time you modify and run an application, the aspx code and C# code is compiled. If any errors are detected, a dialog box asks whether you want to continue by running the last successful build. If you click No, the application isn't run and an Error List is displayed.

- If a statement can't be executed when the application is run, even though it compiles successfully, an *exception* will occur. Then, you need to debug the problem.

Figure 2-18   How to run a web site with IIS Express

How to view the HTML that's sent to the browser

To view the HTML for a page that's displayed in a browser, you can use one of the techniques in figure 2-19. Though you won't need to view this code often, it gives you a better idea of what's going on behind the scenes. It can also be helpful when you need to see exactly how ASP.NET has rendered the aspx code to HTML.

For the example in this figure, I copied the HTML code for the Future Value web form from the web browser into Notepad++. Then, I formatted the code to make it easier to follow. In contrast, the code that's displayed in the web browser isn't formatted so it's harder to review.

In this example, you can see some of the HTML that has been rendered for the Future Value form after the user has selected a value from the drop-down list, entered values into the text boxes, and clicked the Calculate button. This code is instructive in several ways.

First, note that this code doesn't include any asp. That's because the asp has been converted to HTML. For instance, the asp for the drop-down list in the first row of the table has been converted to an HTML select element that contains one option element for each value in the list.

Second, note that view state data is stored in a hidden input field named _VIEWSTATE. However, the value of this field is encrypted so you can't read it. Because the data in view state is passed to and from the browser automatically, you don't have to handle the passing of this data in your code.

Third, note that the values that the user entered are included in the HTML. For instance, the value in the drop-down list is 250, and the value in the first text box is 5.5. This illustrates that you don't need view state to save the information that's entered by the user. Instead, view state is used to maintain the state of properties that have been set by code. For example, it's used to maintain the values that are loaded into the drop-down list the first time the user requests the form.

Fourth, note the script element that comes right after the view state data. Although I've replaced the JavaScript code that it contained with a comment, this is one of several script elements that were generated for this form. They provide the JavaScript code for validating the data in the browser.

Fifth, note that the HTML for a label server control is a span element, not a label element as you might expect. If you were able to scroll down, you would also see that the error messages for the validation controls are displayed in span elements. As you will see in the next chapter, you sometimes need to know how a server control is rendered in HTML if you want to apply CSS formatting to it, and reviewing the source code is one way to find out.

Keep in mind that this HTML is generated automatically by ASP.NET, so you usually don't have to worry about it. You just develop the application by using Visual Studio, and the rest of the work is done for you. Sometimes, though, reviewing the source code can help you solve a debugging problem.

Some of the HTML for the Future Value form after a post back

```
<form method="post" action="Default.aspx" onsubmit="javascript:return WebForm_OnSubmit();" id="form1">
<div class="aspNetHidden">
    <input type="hidden" name="__VIEWSTATE" id="__VIEWSTATE"
        value="/wEPDwUKMTM5ODY2MzgxOQ9kFgICAw9kFgQCAQ8QZA8WCmYCAQICAgMCBAIFAgYCBwIIAgkWChAFAFAjUwBQI1MGcQB
</div>
<script type="text/javascript">
    // One of several script elements that contain JavaScript code
</script>
    <div>
        <img alt="Murach" class="style1" src="Images/MurachLogo.jpg"  /><br />
        <h1>401K Future Value Calculator</h1>
        <table class="style2">
            <tr>
                <td class="style3">Monthly investment</td>
                <td><select name="ddlMonthlyInvestment" id="ddlMonthlyInvestment" style="width:106px;">
                        <option value="50">50</option>
                        <option value="100">100</option>
                        <option value="150">150</option>
                        <option value="200">200</option>
                        <option selected="selected" value="250">250</option>
                        <option value="300">300</option>
                        <option value="350">350</option>
                        <option value="400">400</option>
                        <option value="450">450</option>
                        <option value="500">500</option>
                    </select></td>
            </tr>
            <tr>
                <td class="style3">Annual interest rate</td>
                <td><input name="txtInterestRate" type="number" value="5.5"
                        id="txtInterestRate" style="width:100px;" /></td>
            </tr>
            <tr>
                <td class="style3">Number of years</td>
                <td><input name="txtYears" type="number" value="20"
                        id="txtYears" style="width:100px;" /></td>
            </tr>
            <tr>
                <td class="style3">Future value</td>
                <td><span id="lblFutureValue" style="font-weight:bold;">$109,406.01</span></td>
            </tr>
            <tr>
                <td class="style3"> </td>
                <td> </td>
            </tr>
```

How to view the HTML for a page in a browser

- Select the View→Source command from the browser's menu or right-click on the web page and select the View Source command from the shortcut menu.

Description

- When an ASP.NET page is requested by a browser, ASP.NET generates the HTML for the page and returns that HTML to the browser.

- View state data is stored in a hidden input field within the HTML. This data is encrypted so you can't read it.

- If the page contains validation controls, the HTML for the page contains script elements that include the JavaScript that does the validation.

- Values that the user enters into a page are returned to the browser as part of the HTML.

Figure 2-19   How to review the HTML that's sent to the browser

Perspective

The purpose of this chapter has been to teach you the basic skills for creating a one-page ASP.NET application with Visual Studio. If you've already used Visual Studio and C# to develop Windows applications, you shouldn't have any trouble mastering these skills. You just need to get used to using the properties and events for web server controls and validation controls.

As you will see in the next chapter, though, you should also have a solid set of HTML and CSS skills. That way, you can separate the content for a web page (the HTML) from its formatting (the CSS), and that makes it easier to develop and maintain the pages of a web site.

Terms

web project	flow layout
Web Forms site	IntelliSense
web site	snippet
Web Forms application	web server control
web application	smart tag menu
web form	property
Web Forms Designer	validation control
Designer	validator
Toolbox	required field validator
Solution Explorer	range validator
Properties window	unobtrusive validation
Source view	jQuery
Design view	event handler
Split view	Code Editor
IIS Express	syntax error
development server	exception

Summary

- When you use ASP.NET, a *web project* is either a *Web Forms site* (or just *web site*) or a *Web Forms application* (or just *web application*).

- When you use Visual Studio to design *web forms*, the primary window is the *Web Forms Designer* (or just *Designer*). It is supported by the *Toolbox*, the *Solution Explorer*, and the *Properties window*.

- When you run a web site developed with a previous version of Visual Studio or developed on another system, Visual Studio will use the *development server* by default. However, you can change that so Visual Studio will use *IIS Express*.

- When you use the Designer to build a web form, you can work in *Source view*, *Design view*, or *Split view*.

- In Source view, *IntelliSense* and *snippets* help you enter the tags and attributes for HTML elements and web server controls. In Design view, the Toolbox makes it easy to add web server controls to a form and the Properties window helps you set the *properties* for the controls.

- ASP.NET provides *validation controls* that provide for both client-side and server-side data validation. For client-side validation, JavaScript must be enabled in the user's browser, but most browsers have it enabled.

- When *unobtrusive validation* is used for a web site, ASP.NET will use a JavaScript library called *jQuery* for the validation. That option is on by default when you start a new web site.

- Visual Studio provides a Code Editor with IntelliSense and snippets that makes it easier to enter the C# statements for the event handlers and other methods that a web site requires.

- Three of the page events that can trigger an event handler are the Init, Load, and PreRender events. The first two are raised when a page is posted back to the server. The last one is raised right before the HTML is generated for a page.

- Four of the server control events that can trigger an event handler are the Click event for a button, the TextChanged event for a text box, the CheckedChanged event for a check box or radio button, and the SelectedIndexChanged event for a list.

- The IsPostBack property of a page can be used to tell whether a page is being posted back from a browser or loaded for the first time. The IsValid property of a page can be used to tell whether the validation controls have found that all of the entries are valid.

- If you try to run a web form that has *syntax errors* in the C# code, Visual Studio stops compiling the assembly and displays the errors in an Error List window.

- An *exception* occurs when ASP.NET can't execute one of the statements in the C# code, even though it compiles without error. Then, you need to stop the application, find the cause of the exception, and fix it.

- If you view the source code while a page is displayed in a browser, you can see the hidden fields that are used for view state, the scripts that are used for data validation, and the HTML that's generated for the server controls.

Before you do the exercises for this book...

If you haven't already done so, you need to install the software that's required for this book as well as the downloadable applications. Appendix A shows how to do that.

Exercise 2-1   Build the Future Value application

This exercise guides you through the development of the Future Value application that's presented in this chapter. This will give you a chance to experiment with the many features that Visual Studio offers.

Start, close, and open the web site and use IIS Express for it

1. Start Visual Studio. If the Start Page is displayed, click its close button to close this page.

2. Start an empty file-system web site as shown in figure 2-1. It should be named Ex02FutureValue and stored in the C:\aspnet45_cs directory.

3. Add a web form as shown in figure 2-2 using the default name. Be sure that the Place Code in Separate File option is checked.

4. Add a folder named Images to your project and add the MurachLogo.jpg file to it using the techniques in figure 2-4. The jpg file is in the C:\aspnet45_cs directory, but you'll have to change the file type to Image Files or All Files (*.*) to see this file.

5. Close the web site using the technique in figure 2-5. Then, open the web site again using the Open Project dialog box that's shown in this figure. This shows that a solution file has been created for this web site.

6. Use FILE→Open→Web Site (or FILE→Open Web Site for VS Express) to display the Open Web Site dialog box. Then, click on Local IIS to see that the web site is an IIS Express web site.

Use the Web Forms Designer to build the form

7. Open the Default.aspx web form and switch to Source view. Type "Chapter 2: Future Value" in the title element in the head section of the HTML.

8. Move the cursor to the end of the opening body tag and press the Enter key to create a new line. Next, drag the Murach logo file from the Images folder in the Solution Explorer to the new line. That should create an img element with a properly coded src attribute. Now, add an alt attribute to this element with "Murach Logo" as its value, and switch to Design view to see the changes.

9. Switch to Source view, place the insertion point after the img element, and add an h1 element that has "401K Future Value Calculator" as its content.

10. Switch to Design view to see this change. Then, run the form in the default browser by pressing the F5. That automatically saves the changes to the Default.aspx file. When the dialog box asks whether you want to modify the

web.config file to enable debugging, click the OK button. After your form is displayed in the default brower, close the browser. If your default browser is Internet Explorer, this should stop the application.

11. Return to Visual Studio. If the Toolbox isn't available, that means the web form is still running. So, click the Stop Debugging button in the Debug toolbar to stop the application.

12. In Design view, use the techniques in figure 2-8 to add a table that provides for six rows and two columns to the div element. Next, add the text shown in the first four rows to the first column of the table. Then, drag the right boundary of the first column to reduce its width as shown in this figure.

13. Switch to Source view to see the HTML for the table. Note that a style element has been added to the head section and class attributes have been added to the table element and some of the td elements. This HTML was generated when you reduced the width of the first column by dragging its boundary. Note too that non-breaking space characters ( ) have been generated for the empty td elements.

14. Switch to Design view and use the techniques in figure 2-9 to add the drop-down list, text boxes, label, and buttons shown in that figure to the table. Then, adjust the size of the list, text box, and buttons, but not the label, so the table looks the way you want it to.

15. Use the techniques of figure 2-9 and the summary in figure 2-10 to set the ID and Text properties of the controls. For the Clear button, also set the CausesValidation property to False.

16. Press F5 to run the application, and check the web form to make sure it looks the way it's supposed to. Then, switch to Visual Studio and click the Stop Debugging button in the Debug toolbar.

Add the validation controls

17. In Source view or Design view, add the validation controls for the text boxes as shown in figures 2-11 and 2-12.

18. In Design view, double-click outside the body of the web form to start an event handler for the Load event of the page in the code-behind file for the form. Then, turn off unobtrusive validation by adding the statement in the Load event handler shown in figure 2-13. IntelliSense makes this easy.

19. Press F5 to run the application. Then, test the field validators by leaving fields blank or entering invalid data. The validation will be done when the focus leaves a text box or when you click on the Calculate button.

20. Stop the application. Then, if necessary, fix any problems and test again. If, for example, validation is done when you click the Clear button, you can fix that by setting its CausesValidation property to False.

Add the C# code and test as you go

21. Double-click outside of the body of the form to switch to the Code Editor. That will take you to the Load event handler that you started earlier.

22. Finish the code for the Load event handler as shown in figure 2-17, taking full advantage of the IntelliSense that's provided. Then, press F5 to compile and test this event handler. If any syntax errors are detected, use the techniques in this figure to fix them.

23. Switch back to Design view, and double-click on the Clear button to start an event handler for the Click event of that button. Then, enter the code for this event handler as shown in figure 2-17, and test again.

24. Enter the code for the CalculateFutureValue method that's shown in figure 2-17. When you're ready to add the for loop, right-click, select Visual C# from the shortcut menu, and select the for snippet. Then, finish the coding for this method.

25. Switch back to Design view, and double-click on the Calculate button to start an event handler for the Click event of that button. Next, enter the code for this event handler, but be sure to use the snippet for the if statement. This method should call the CalculateFutureValue method as in figure 2-17. Then, test this code.

26. If necessary, fix any design or coding problems that remain. When you're through, the application should work the way you want it to.

Do more testing and experimenting

27. Set the EnableViewState property of the drop-down list to False, and test the application to see what happens. When an exception occurs, stop the application and reset the property.

28. Set the EnableClientScript property for all four validators to False so the validation will only be done on the server. Then, test the application to make sure that the validation still works. When you're through testing, end the application and reset these properties.

29. Run the application again, and use the technique in figure 2-19 to review the HTML that's sent to the browser. There, you can see the HTML that's generated for the web form, the input elements with the "hidden" type that are used for view state, and the script elements that contain the JavaScript that's used for client-side validation.

30. When you're through experimenting, close the project. Then, close Visual Studio.

3

How to use HTML5 and CSS3 with ASP.NET applications

In chapter 2, you learned how to build the Future Value application without worrying about the HTML or CSS that was generated by Visual Studio. But there is a right way to use the HTML and CSS for a web application. Specifically, the HTML should provide the content and structure for a web page, and the CSS should provide the formatting. That separates the concerns, and that's what you'll learn how to do in this chapter.

The Future Value application with CSS formatting

Figure 3-1 presents another version of the Future Value application that you learned to develop in the last chapter. This time, a table isn't used to align the labels and server controls. Instead, CSS is used for all of the formatting including the alignment. This separates the formatting (the CSS) from the content (the HTML), and that's a best practice for today's web sites.

The user interface

In this figure, you can see that the user interface doesn't look exactly like the one in the last chapter. Instead, the form is centered on the screen with a black border around it, and the error messages are displayed to the right of the server controls that get the entries. In this example, the user has entered 33 for the annual interest rate, and the error message says the rate must range from 1 to 20.

The HTML that's generated for a new form

When you create a new form with Visual Studio, it generates the code that's shown in the first example in this figure. Then, the second example shows how you can modify the generated code.

Here, the DOCTYPE declaration at the top of the page says that HTML5 will be used for the HTML document (or page). If you're familiar with the declarations for earlier versions of HTML, you know that they were far more complicated than that.

This declaration is followed by the html element that includes all of the other elements for the page. Within its opening tag, you can see the xmlns attribute that was generated by ASP.NET. Although this attribute isn't necessary when you use HTML5, it doesn't hurt anything. So, you can either leave it the way it is or delete it, whichever you prefer.

In the head element, you should code a value in the title element that will be displayed in the browser's title bar or tab when the application is run. In the browser in this figure, you can see the contents of the title element in the tab for the application.

When you use an external style sheet for the CSS that will format a page, you also code a link element within the head element. This link element identifies the external style sheet that will be used. More about that in a moment.

Last, you can usually delete the div tags that are generated by ASP.NET because they aren't needed within a form element. Besides that, you should use the HTML5 semantic elements instead of div elements to show the structure of a document.

The user interface for the Future Value application

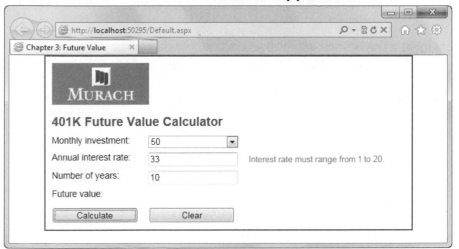

The HTML that's generated for a new form

```
<!DOCTYPE html>
<html xmlns="http://www.w3.org/1999/xhtml">
<head runat="server">
    <title></title>
</head>
<body>
    <form id="form1" runat="server">
    <div>

    </div>
    </form>
</body>
</html>
```

The HTML after it has been modified for this application

```
<!DOCTYPE html>
<html xmlns="http://www.w3.org/1999/xhtml">
<head runat="server">
    <title>Chapter 3: Future Value</title>
    <link href="Styles.css" rel="stylesheet">
</head>
<body>
    <form id="form1" runat="server">

    </form>
</body>
</html>
```

Description

- The DOCTYPE element indicates that HTML5 will be used for the document.
- The title element specifies the name that will be shown in the browser's title bar or tab.
- The link element references the external style sheet that contains the CSS for the page.

Figure 3-1   The user interface and starting HTML for the Future Value application

The aspx code for the application

Figure 3-2 presents the aspx code for this version of the Future Value application. It includes a header element for the header of the document and a section element for all of the other content of the document. These are HTML5 semantic elements.

The header element contains one standard HTML img element. It displays the logo at the top of the page. The section element starts with a standard HTML h1 element that displays the heading right below the logo.

Within the form element, you can see four standard label elements. They precede and identify the four server controls: the drop-down list, the two text boxes, and the label control that will display the result. The last two server controls are button controls for the Calculate and Clear buttons.

After each of the server controls for the text boxes, you can see two validators. The first is a required field validator. The second is a range validator. Because these validators come right after the text boxes that they validate, CSS can be used to align them so they are displayed to the right of the boxes that they relate to.

Using the techniques that you learned in the last chapter, you should be able to create a page like this without much trouble. But at that point, the layout of the page will be a mess. Then, you have to create the external style sheet and the styles that will format the page.

As you will see in a moment, you can use id or class attributes to select the elements that you want to format with CSS. That's why the CssClass attributes have been added to the code in this figure. For instance, the drop-down list and the two text boxes have been coded with the CssClass attribute set to "entry". Similarly, the four validators have their CssClass attributes set to "validator", and the two buttons have their CssClass attributes set to "button". When the form is rendered, these attributes are converted to HTML class attributes that you can use for formatting with CSS.

When you start using CSS to format your pages, you may not know which controls you need to set ID or CssClass attributes for. That's okay, though, because you can switch back and forth between the style sheet and the Designer. Then, after you get more familiar with the use of CSS, you'll have a better idea of how to set the ids and classes before you create the styles in the external style sheet.

The aspx code for the body of the Future Value application

```
<body>
    <header>
        <img id="logo" alt="Murach Logo" src="Images/MurachLogo.jpg" />
    </header>
    <section>
        <h1>401K Future Value Calculator</h1>
        <form id="form1" runat="server">
            <label>Monthly investment:</label>
            <asp:DropDownList ID="ddlMonthlyInvestment" runat="server"
                CssClass="entry"></asp:DropDownList><br />
            <label>Annual interest rate:</label>
            <asp:TextBox ID="txtInterestRate" runat="server"
                CssClass="entry">6.0</asp:TextBox>
                <asp:RequiredFieldValidator ID="RequiredFieldValidator1"
                    runat="server" CssClass="validator"
                    ErrorMessage="Interest rate is required."
                    ControlToValidate="txtInterestRate"
                    Display="Dynamic">
                </asp:RequiredFieldValidator>
                <asp:RangeValidator ID="RangeValidator1" runat="server"
                    CssClass="validator"
                    ControlToValidate="txtInterestRate" Display="Dynamic"
                    ErrorMessage="Interest rate must range from 1 to 20."
                    MaximumValue="20" MinimumValue="1"
                    Type="Double">
                </asp:RangeValidator><br />
            <label>Number of years:</label>
            <asp:TextBox ID="txtYears" runat="server"
                CssClass="entry">10</asp:TextBox>
                <asp:RequiredFieldValidator ID="RequiredFieldValidator2"
                    runat="server" CssClass="validator"
                    ControlToValidate="txtYears" Display="Dynamic"
                    ErrorMessage="Number of years is required.">
                </asp:RequiredFieldValidator>
                <asp:RangeValidator ID="RangeValidator2" runat="server"
                    CssClass="validator" ControlToValidate="txtYears"
                    Display="Dynamic"
                    ErrorMessage="Years must range from 1 to 45."
                    MaximumValue="45"
                    MinimumValue="1" Type="Integer">
                </asp:RangeValidator><br />
            <label>Future value:</label>
            <asp:Label ID="lblFutureValue" runat="server" Text="">
            </asp:Label><br />
            <asp:Button ID="btnCalculate" runat="server" Text="Calculate"
                CssClass="button" OnClick="btnCalculate_Click" />
            <asp:Button ID="btnClear" runat="server" Text="Clear"
                CssClass="button" OnClick="btnClear_Click"
                CausesValidation="False" />
        </form>
    </section>
</body>
</html>
```

Figure 3-2   The aspx code when CSS is used for the formatting

The CSS style sheet for the application

Figure 3-3 presents the CSS style sheet for the Future Value application. If you're new to *CSS* (*Cascading Style Sheets*), you just need to understand what each of the rule sets in this figure apply to because you're going to learn more about CSS in a moment.

For instance, the first three rule sets apply to the HTML body, h1, and label elements. In this case, the names before the braces { } are just the names of the HTML elements.

The next three rule sets are for the elements with class attributes equal to entry, validator, and button. Note that these names are preceded by dots (periods) to indicate that they are class names.

The last three rules sets are for elements with the id attributes that are specified. For instance, the first rule set is for the element with an id attribute equal to ddlMonthlyInvestment. In the style sheet, the ids are preceded by the pound sign (#) to indicate that they are ids.

As you learn more about CSS, you can refer back to this page to see how the CSS leads to the formatting shown in figure 3-1. For instance, the width property in the rule set for the body says that the body should be 550 pixels wide. The margin property says the body should have no top or bottom margin, but it should be centered horizontally in the browser (auto). And the border property says that the body should have a solid blue border that's 2 pixels wide.

The external style sheet for the Future Value application

```css
/* The styles for the elements */
body {
    font-family: Arial, Helvetica, sans-serif;
    font-size: 85%;
    width: 550px;
    margin: 0 auto;
    padding: 10px;
    background-color: white;
    border: 2px solid #0000FF;
}
h1 {
    font-size: 140%;
    color: #0000FF;
    padding: 0;
    margin-bottom: .5em;
}
label {
    float: left;
    width: 10em;
}
/* the styles for classes */
.entry {
    margin-left: 1em;
    margin-bottom: .5em;
    width: 10em;
}
.validator {
    font-size: 95%;
    color: red;
    margin-left: 1em;
}
.button {
    margin-top: 1em;
    width: 10em;
}
/* The styles for the server controls */
#ddlMonthlyInvestment {
    width: 10.5em;
}
#lblFutureValue {
    font-weight: bold;
    margin-left: 1em;
}
#btnClear {
    margin-left: 1em;
}
```

Figure 3-3   The CSS for the Future Value application

The HTML and CSS skills that you need

Although this book assumes that you are already familiar with HTML and CSS, the next six topics present a quick review of the HTML and CSS skills that you need for developing web applications. If you don't already have these skills, we recommend *Murach's HTML5 and CSS3* as a companion to this book.

How to code HTML elements

Figure 3-4 shows how to code *HTML elements* like those in the table within an *HTML document*. To start, each HTML element is coded within a *tag* that starts with an opening bracket (<) and ends with a closing bracket (>). For example, <h1>, <p>, and <br> are all HTML tags.

Most HTML elements are made up of three parts. The *start tag* marks the start of the element. It consists of the element name (such as h1) plus one or more optional *attributes* (such as id or class) that provide additional information for the tag. After the start tag is the *content*, which is the text or other data that makes up the element. After the content is the *end tag* that marks the end of the element. The end tag consists of a slash followed by the element's name.

Not all HTML elements have content and end tags, though. For instance, the <br> and <img> elements don't have closing tags. These can be referred to as *self-closing tags*.

Most attributes are coded with an attribute name, an equals sign, and a value in quotation marks, as shown in the second group of examples in this figure. Here, for example, the <a> element has an href attribute that provides the URL that the link should go to when it is clicked, as well as a title attribute that provides the content for the link.

Boolean attributes, however, can be coded with just the name of the attribute. For instance, the checked attribute for the input element in the second group indicates that the checked attribute is "on", so the check box that this element represents will be checked. If a Boolean attribute isn't coded, the attribute is considered to be "off".

You can also code *comments* within an HTML document as shown in the second last example in this figure. That way, you can describe sections of code that might be confusing. You can also use comments to *comment out* a portion of HTML code. That way, the code is ignored when the web page is displayed in a browser. That can be useful when testing a web page.

If you want to code a space within a line that the web browser doesn't ignore, you can use   (for non-breaking space) as shown in the last example in this figure. This is just one of the many *character entities* that you can use to display special characters in HTML, and Visual Studio automatically puts these characters into the empty cells of each row when it generates a table. Note that each character entity starts with an ampersand (&) and ends with a semicolon (;).

In the table at the top of this figure, you can see that some of the elements are *block elements* and some are *inline elements*. The difference is that by default

Common HTML elements

Element	Type	Defines
h1	Block	A level-1 heading with content in bold at 200% of the base font size.
h2	Block	A level-2 heading with content in bold at 150% of the base font size.
p	Block	A paragraph at 100% of the base font size.
img	Block	An image that will be displayed on the page.
form	Block	A form that can be submitted to the web server for processing.
a	Inline	A link that goes to another page or a location on the current page when clicked.
input	Inline	A control on a form like a text box or button.
label	Inline	A label that identifies a control on a form.
br		A line break that starts a new line.

How to code HTML elements

Two block elements with opening and closing tags

```
<h1>Halloween SuperStore</h1>
<p>Here is a list of links:</p>
```

Two self-closing tags

```
<br>
<img src="logo.gif" alt="Murach Logo">
```

How to code the attributes for HTML elements

How to code an opening tag with attributes

```
<a href="contact.html" title="Click to Contact Us" class="nav_link">
```

How to code a Boolean attribute

```
<input type="checkbox" name="mailList" checked>
```

How to code an HTML comment

```
<!-- The text in a comment is ignored -->
```

How to code a character entity for a space

```
<td> </td>
```

Description

- An *HTML document* contains *HTML elements* that specify the content of a web page.
- By default, *block elements* are displayed on new lines, but *inline elements* flow to the right of the elements that precede it.
- An *attribute* consists of an attribute name, an equals sign, and a value in quotation marks. But to show that a Boolean attribute is on, you can code just the name of the attribute.
- *Comments* can be used to describe or *comment out* portions of HTML code.
- *Character entities* provide for special characters, like a non-breaking space ( ).

Figure 3-4   Basic rules for coding HTML elements

block elements are displayed on their own lines. In contrast, inline elements flow to the right of preceding elements and don't start new lines. As a result, you need to use a br element after an inline element if you want to start a new line after it.

When you use HTML5, you can use the syntax for either of its predecessors: HTML or XHTML. In this figure, the examples are for HTML, which has a less rigid syntax. For instance, these self-closing tags have the HTML syntax:

```
<br>
<img src="logo.gif" alt="Murach Logo">
```

And these have the XHTML syntax:

```
<br />
<img src="logo.gif" alt="Murach Logo"/>
```

For consistency, you might want to use XHTML syntax because that's what Visual Studio generates. But the code works either way. We do, however, recommend that you use lowercase for all HTML code, even though HTML5 allows mixed cases.

Incidentally, you may have noticed in the first two chapters that we refer to HTML elements by the name used in the opening tag. For instance, we refer to h1 and img elements. To prevent misreading, though, we enclose one-letter element names in brackets. As a result, we refer to <a> elements and <p> elements. That will continue throughout this book.

How to use the HTML5 semantic elements

By default, Visual Studio uses HTML5 when you create a new web page, and figure 3-5 presents the *HTML5 semantic elements* that improve the structure of an HTML page. By using them, you improve the *search engine optimization (SEO)* of your web pages, at least in some search engines. So, if you aren't already using them, you should start soon.

Besides SEO improvements, the semantic elements make it easier to apply CSS to these elements because you don't have to code id attributes that are used by the CSS. Instead, you can apply the CSS to the elements themselves. You'll learn more about this in a moment.

Be aware, however, that older browsers won't recognize the HTML5 semantic elements, which means that you won't be able to use CSS to apply formatting to them. So, if you want your CSS to work in older browsers, you need to code a script element in the head section of the HTML document that provides a *JavaScript shiv*. You also need to use CSS to identify the semantic elements as block elements. In a moment, you'll learn how to do both.

The primary HTML5 semantic elements

Element	Contents
header	The header for a page.
section	A generic section of a document that doesn't indicate the type of content.
article	A composition like an article in the paper.
nav	A section of a page that contains links to other pages or placeholders.
aside	A section of a page like a sidebar that is related to the content that's near it.
figure	An image, table, or other component that's treated as a figure.
footer	The footer for a page.

A page that's structured with header, section, and footer elements

```
<body>
    <header>
        <h1>San Joaquin Valley Town Hall</h1>
    </header>
    <section>
        <p>Welcome to San Joaquin Valley Town Hall. We have some
            fascinating speakers for you this season!</p>
    </section>
    <footer>
        <p>&copy; San Joaquin Valley Town Hall.</p>
    </footer>
</body>
```

The page displayed in a web browser

San Joaquin Valley Town Hall

Welcome to San Joaquin Valley Town Hall. We have some fascinating speakers for you this season!

© San Joaquin Valley Town Hall.

Description

- HTML5 provides new *semantic elements* that you should use to structure the contents of a web page. Using these elements can be referred to as *HTML5 semantics*.

- All of the HTML5 elements in this figure are supported by the modern browsers. They will also work on older browsers if you use the workarounds in figure 3-10.

- Two benefits that you get from using the semantic elements are (1) simplified HTML and CSS, and (2) improved *search engine optimization (SEO)*.

Figure 3-5   How to use the HTML5 semantic elements

How to use the div and span elements with HTML5

If you've been using HTML for a while, you are certainly familiar with the div element. It has traditionally been used to divide an HTML document into divisions that are identified by id attributes, as shown in the first example of figure 3-6. Then, CSS can use the ids to apply formatting to the divisions.

But now that HTML5 is available, div elements shouldn't be used to structure a document. Instead, they should only be used when the HTML5 semantic elements aren't appropriate and no structure is implied. If, for example, you want to group a series of elements so you can apply CSS to them, you can put them within a div element. But that doesn't affect the structure of the content that's implied by the HTML5 elements.

Note too that div elements are often used in JavaScript applications. If, for example, a section element contains three h2 elements with each followed by a div element, JavaScript can be used to display or hide a div element whenever the heading that precedes it is clicked. Here again, this doesn't affect the structure of the content that's implied by the HTML5 elements.

Similarly, span elements have historically been used to identify portions of text that can be formatted by CSS. By today's standards, though, it's better to use elements that indicate the contents of the elements, like the cite, code, and <q> elements.

But here again, span elements are often used in JavaScript applications. This is illustrated by the second example in this figure. Here, span elements are used to display the error messages for invalid entries.

Similarly, ASP.NET generates span elements for the messages that are displayed by its validators. ASP.NET also generates span elements for its label server controls. This is illustrated by the third example in this figure.

The div and span elements

Element	Description
div	A block element that provides a container for other elements.
span	An inline element that lets you identify text that can be formatted with CSS.

The way div elements were used before HTML5

```
<div id="header">
    <h1>San Joaquin Valley Town Hall</h1>
</div>
<div id="contents">
    <p>Welcome to San Joaquin Valley Town Hall. We have some
        fascinating speakers for you this season!</p>
</div>
<div id="footer">
    <p>&copy; San Joaquin Valley Town Hall.</p>
</div>
```

Span elements in the HTML for a JavaScript application

```
<label for="email_address1">Email Address:</label>
<input type="text" id="email_address1" name="email_address1">
<span id="email_address1_error">*</span><br>

<label for="email_address2">Re-enter Email Address:</label>
<input type="text" id="email_address2" name="email_address2">
<span id="email_address2_error">*</span><br>
```

Span elements generated by ASP.NET for two validators and a label control

```
<label>Number of years:</label>
<input name="txtYears" type="text" value="10" id="txtYears" class="entry" />
    <span id="RequiredFieldValidator2" class="validator"
        style="display:none;">Number of years is required.</span>
    <span id="RangeValidator2" class="validator"
        style="display:none;">Years must range from 1 to 45.</span><br />
<label>Future value:</label>
<span id="lblFutureValue"></span><br />
```

Description

- Before HTML5, div elements were used to organize the content within the body of a document. Then, the ids for these div elements were used to apply CSS formatting to the elements.

- Today, HTML5 semantic elements should replace most div elements. That makes the structure of a page more apparent.

- Before HTML5, span elements were used to identify portions of text that you could apply formatting to. Today, a better practice is to use elements that identify the contents, like the cite, code, and <q> elements.

- Be aware, however, that ASP.NET generates span elements for validators and also for label server controls.

Figure 3-6   How to use the div and span elements with HTML5

How to provide CSS styles for an HTML page

Figure 3-7 shows the three ways that CSS styles can be provided for an HTML page. The first way is to code a link element in the head section of an HTML document that specifies a file that contains the CSS for the page. This file is referred to as an *external style sheet*, and it's a best practice to provide styles in this way. That separates the HTML from the CSS.

The second way is to code a style element in the head section that contains the CSS for the page. This can be referred to as *embedded styles*. The benefit of using embedded styles is that you don't have to switch back and forth between HTML and CSS files as you develop a page. Overall, though, it's better to use external style sheets because that makes it easier to use them for more than one web page.

The third way to provide styles is to code style attributes within HTML elements. This can be referred to as *inline styles*. But then, there's no separation between the HTML and the CSS.

When you develop a web page as in chapter 2, Visual Studio generates both embedded and inline styles. But as you've seen in figures 3-2 and 3-3, it's better to put all of the styles for a page in an external style sheet. For some web forms, it also makes sense to use two or more external style sheets for a single page, as illustrated by the last example in this figure.

When you provide external styles, embedded styles, and inline styles, the inline styles override the embedded styles, which override the external styles. If, for example, all three types of styles set the font color for h1 elements, the inline style will be the one that's used. Similarly, if two external style sheets are used for a page, the styles in the second style sheet override the ones in the first sheet.

When you provide the styles for a web page in an external style sheet, you need to *attach* the style sheet to the page. To do that, you code a link element in the head section of the HTML that points to the style sheet, as shown by the examples in this figure. This figure also shows two ways to generate the link element for an external style sheet with Visual Studio.

Three ways to provide styles

Use an external style sheet by coding a link element in the head section

```
<link rel="stylesheet" href="styles/main.css">
```

Embed the styles in the head section

```
<style>
    body {
        font-family: Arial, Helvetica, sans-serif;
        font-size: 87.5%; }
    h1 { font-size: 250%; }
</style>
```

Use the style attribute of an element to provide inline styles

```
<span style="color: red; font-size: 14pt;">Warning!</span>
```

The sequence in which styles are applied

- Styles from an external style sheet
- Embedded styles
- Inline styles

A head element that includes two external style sheets

```
<head>
    <title>The Halloween Store</title>
    <link rel="stylesheet" href="main.css">
    <link rel="stylesheet" href="order.css">
</head>
```

The sequence in which styles are applied

- From the first external style sheet to the last

How to generate a link element for an external style sheet

- To generate a link element in Source view, drag the style sheet from the Solution Explorer into the head element for the page.
- To generate a link element in Design view, choose the FORMAT→Attach Style Sheet command and select the style sheet from the Select Style Sheet dialog box.

Description

- It's a best practice to use *external style sheets* because that leads to better separation of concerns. Specifically, you separate the content for a page (HTML) from its formatting (CSS).
- Using external style sheets also makes it easy to use the same styles for two or more pages. In contrast, If you use *embedded styles* or *inline styles*, you have to copy the styles to other documents before you can use them again.
- If more than one rule for the same property is applied to the same element, the last rule overrides the earlier rules.

Figure 3-7   Three ways to provide CSS styles for an HTML page

How to code the basic CSS selectors

Figure 3-8 shows how to code the basic CSS *selectors* for applying styles to HTML elements. To start, this figure shows the body of an HTML document that contains a section and a footer element. Here, the h1 element is assigned an id of "first_heading", and the two <p> elements in this section have class attributes with the value "blue". Also, the <p> element in the footer has a class attribute with two values: "blue" and "right". This means that this element is assigned to two classes.

The three rule sets in the first group of examples are *type* (or *element*) *selectors*. To code a type selector, you just code the name of the element. As a result, the first rule set in this group selects the body element. The second rule set selects the section element. And the third rule set selects all <p> elements.

In these examples, the first rule set changes the font for the body element, and all of the elements within the body inherit this change. This rule set also sets the width of the body and centers it in the browser. Then, the second rule set puts a border around the section element and puts some padding inside the section. Last, the rule set for the paragraphs sets the margins for the sides of the paragraphs in this sequence: top, right, bottom, and left. That's why the paragraphs in the section are indented.

The two rule sets in the second group of examples use *class selectors* to select HTML elements by class. To do that, the selector is a period (.) followed by the class name. As a result, the first rule set selects all elements that have been assigned to the "blue" class, which are all three <p> elements. The second rule set selects any elements that have been assigned to the "right" class. That is the paragraph in the footer division. Here, the first rule set sets the color of the font to blue and the second rule set aligns the paragraph on the right.

The rule set in the last example uses an *id selector* to select an element by its id. To do that, the selector is a pound sign (#) followed by the id value that uniquely identifies an element. As a result, this rule set selects the h1 element that has an id of "first_heading". Then, its rule set sets the margins for the heading.

One of the key points here is that a class attribute can have the same value for more than one element on a page. Then, if you code a selector for that class, it will be used to format all the elements in that class. In contrast, since the id for an element must be unique, an id selector can only be used to format a single element.

Another key point is that a more specific style overrides a less specific style. For instance, an id selector is more specific than a class selector, and a class selector is more specific than a type selector. That means that a style for an id selector will override the same style for a class selector, which will override the same style for a type selector. Beyond that, the rules in a rule set flow from top to bottom. So, if you've set multiple rules for a property of an element, the last one will override the previous ones.

As you may know, there are many other types of selectors that you can use with CSS. But the ones in this figure will get you started with CSS. They are also the only ones that are used by the applications in this book.

HTML that can be selected by element type, class, or id

```
<body>
    <section>
        <h1 id="first_heading">The Speaker Lineup</h1>
        <p class="blue">October 19: Jeffrey Toobin</p>
        <p class="blue">November 16: Andrew Ross Sorkin</p>
    </section>
    <footer>
        <p class="blue right">Copyright SJV Town Hall</p>
    </footer>
</body>
```

CSS rule sets that select by element type, class, and id

Three rule sets with type selectors

```
body {
    font-family: Arial, Helvetica, sans-serif;
    width: 400px;
    margin: 1em auto; }
section {
    border: 2px solid black;
    padding: 1em; }
p { margin: .25em 0 .25em 3em; }
```

Two rule sets with class selectors

```
.blue { color: blue; }
.right { text-align: right; }
```

One rule set with an id selector

```
#first_heading { margin: 0 1em .25em; }
```

The elements displayed in a browser

The Speaker Lineup

October 19: Jeffrey Toobin
November 16: Andrew Ross Sorkin

Copyright SJV Town Hall

Description

- You code a selector for all elements of a specific type by naming the element. This is referred to as a *type* or *element selector*.

- You code a selector for an element with a class attribute by coding a period followed by the class name. Then, the rule set applies to all elements with that class name. This is known as a *class selector*.

- You code an id selector for an element with an id attribute by coding a pound sign (#) followed by the id value. This is known as an *id selector*.

Figure 3-8   How to code the basic CSS selectors

How to code CSS rule sets and comments

CSS code consists of *rule sets* that are applied to HTML elements by their selectors. This is illustrated by the six rule sets in figure 3-9. As you can see, each rule set consists of a selector, a set of braces { }, and one or more *rules* within the braces. Within each rule, there's the name for a *property*, a colon, the value or values for the property, and an ending semicolon.

Now, to give you a better idea of how CSS works, here's a quick description of the rule sets in this figure. Remember, though, that this book is about ASP.NET, not CSS, so it isn't going to try to teach you how to use the dozens of properties that CSS provides. For that, you'll need our HTML5 and CSS3 book.

The first rule set consists of seven rules. The first rule specifies the font to be used for the body of the document, and all the elements within the body inherit that font. The second rule specifies that the base font for the application should be 85% of the default font size for the user's browser. If you refer back to figure 3-4, you can see that a <p> element will be 100% of that base font size, and an h1 element will be 200% of that size.

The third rule for the body of the document sets its width to 550 pixels. Then, the fourth rule specifies no margin on the top or bottom of the body, and an automatic margin to the left and right of the body. The automatic margins are what centers the body in a browser window.

The fifth rule for the body provides 10 pixels of padding within the body. Then, the last two rules for the body say that the background color should be white and the body should have a solid border around it that's two pixels wide and blue (#0000FF). In figure 3-1, you can see the padding at the top, left, and bottom of the body, and you can see the border around it.

The second rule set is for all h1 elements. It sets the font size to 140% of the base font, the color to blue, the padding to 0, and the bottom margin to .5 em. Since an *em* is a unit of measure that's roughly equal to the width of a capital M in the font that's being used, it varies based on the font size that's used for an element. In this case, that .5 em margin provides the space after the heading that separates it from the labels and controls that follow it.

The third rule set applies to all of the label elements on the page. Here, the first rule floats the labels to the left. That means that the control that follows each label will flow to the right of it. Also, since validators become HTML span elements, they will flow to the right of the controls. Then, the second rule sets the width of each label to 10 ems. That provides the alignment for the four labels and controls without using a table.

The fourth rule set applies to all elements that have their class attributes set to "entry". That includes the drop-down list and the two text boxes below it. The three rules for this rule set provide a left and bottom margin and set the width for those controls.

The fifth rule set is for the control that has ddlMonthlyInvestment as its id attribute, which is the drop-down list. This rule set sets the width of the control to 10.5 ems. But look, that control has already been formatted by the rule set for

Some of the styles in the external style sheet in figure 3-3

```css
/* The styles for the elements */
body {
    font-family: Arial, Helvetica, sans-serif;
    font-size: 85%;
    width: 550px;
    margin: 0 auto;
    padding: 10px;
    background-color: white;
    border: 2px solid #0000FF;
}
h1 {
    font-size: 140%;
    color: #0000FF;
    padding: 0;
    margin-bottom: .5em;
}
label {
    float: left;
    width: 10em;
}
/* the styles for classes */
.entry {
    margin-left: 1em;
    margin-bottom: .5em;
    width: 10em;
}
/* The styles for the server controls */
#ddlMonthlyInvestment {
    width: 10.5em;
}
#lblFutureValue {
    font-weight: bold;
    margin-left: 1em;
}
```

Description

- A CSS *rule set* consists of a selector and one or more rules within braces. In Visual Studio, a rule set is called a *style rule*.

- A CSS *selector* consists of the identifiers that are coded at the beginning of the rule set. If more than one selector is coded for a rule set, the selectors are separated by commas.

- A CSS *rule* consists of a *property*, a colon, a *value*, and a semicolon. Although the semicolon for the last declaration in a block is optional, it's a best practice to code it.

- To make your code easier to read, you can use spaces, indentation, and blank lines within a rule set.

- CSS *comments* begin with the characters /* and end with the characters */. A CSS comment can be coded on a single line, or it can span multiple lines.

Figure 3-9   How to code CSS rule sets and comments

the "entry" class, which set its width to 10. However, since an id selector is more specific than a class selector, the second rule overrides the first rule so the width is set to 10.5 ems.

The last rule set is for the control with lblFutureValue as its id. That's the label control that is used to display the Future Value result when the user clicks the Calculate button. This rule set provides a left margin for the label and sets the text in the label to bold.

How to ensure cross-browser compatibility

If you want your web site to be used by as many visitors as possible, you need to make sure that your web pages are compatible with as many browsers as possible. That's known as *cross-browser compatibility*. That means you should test your applications on as many browsers as possible, including the five browsers summarized in figure 3-10.

The table in this figure shows the current release numbers of these browsers and their rating for HTML5 support. To get an updated version of this information, you can go to the URL shown in this figure. This web site will also rate the browser that you're using when you access it.

In general, Internet Explorer (IE) gives web developers the most problems because it's the least standard. In contrast, the other four browsers generally support the same features so if a web page runs on one of them, it will also run on the others. The other four browsers also provide for automatic updates, but IE typically hasn't done that.

To provide for old browsers that don't support the HTML5 semantic elements, you need to use the two workarounds shown in this figure. The first one is to include a script element that runs a *JavaScript shiv* that tells the browser that the semantic elements are being used. The script element in this example gets the shiv from a Google web site, but it is also available from other sites. It consists of just one line of code for each of the semantic elements, so it loads fast and runs quickly.

However, before you can start using CSS to format the semantic elements in older browsers, you also need to code the CSS rule set that's shown as the second workaround. This rule set tells older browsers that the semantic elements are block elements. Otherwise, the browsers might treat them as inline elements.

Because this is a book on ASP.NET, not HTML5, these workarounds aren't shown in any of the applications in this book. You just need to be aware that you still need to use these workarounds for production applications that use the semantic elements.

For this book, you should test all of your applications on Internet Explorer as well as one other browser, like Chrome or Firefox. That will be an adequate test of browser compatibility. In contrast, you should test production applications on all five of the browsers, including the older versions of these browsers that are still in use.

The current browsers and their HTML5 ratings (perfect score is 500)

Browser	Release	HTML5 Test Rating
Google Chrome	27	463
Opera	12	419
Mozilla Firefox	22	410
Apple Safari	6	378
Internet Explorer	10	320

The web site for these ratings

`http://www.html5test.com`

Guidelines for cross-browser compatibility

- Test your web pages on all of the major browsers, including all of the older versions of these browsers that are still commonly used.

- Use the HTML5 features that are supported by all of the modern browsers, especially the HTML5 semantic elements. But use the two workarounds that follow so these applications will run on the older browsers too.

The two workarounds for using the HTML5 semantic elements

The JavaScript shiv that lets older browsers know about the elements

```
<script src="http://html5shiv.googlecode.com/svn/trunk/html5.js"></script>
```

The CSS rule set that sets the eight semantic elements to block elements

```
article, aside, figure, figcaption, footer, header, nav, section {
    display: block;
}
```

Description

- Today, there are still differences in the way that different browsers handle HTML and CSS, and especially HTML5 and CSS3.

- As a developer, though, you want your web pages to work on as many different web browsers as possible. This is referred to as *cross-browser compatibility*.

- To provide for cross-browser compatibility, you need to test your applications on all of the browsers that your users might use.

- In general, Internet Explorer gives web developers the most problems because it is the least standard and hasn't provided for automatic updates.

- Eventually, all browsers will support HTML5 and CSS3 so the workarounds won't be necessary.

Figure 3-10   How to ensure cross-browser compatibility

Visual Studio features for working with HTML

In the last chapter, you learned the basic techniques for entering and editing the HTML for a form. Now, you'll learn about the enhanced features that Visual Studio offers for working with HTML.

How to use the features for entering HTML

Figure 3-11 shows some of the advanced IntelliSense features for working with HTML. In particular, *snippets* of code are offered as you enter the start of a tag in Source view of the Designer. For instance, the first example shows that the snippet for the link element is offered when you enter the letter *l*, Then, if you press the Tab key twice, the snippet is added to the source code. In this case, that's a complete link element with the href attribute ready for your entry.

The second example shows how the smart indent feature works. If you press the Enter key when the insertion point is in the content area of an element, the ending tag is dropped down two lines and the cursor is indented in the middle line ready for your content entry.

This figure also summarizes three other features that help you enter the HTML for a form. If you experiment with these features, you'll quickly see what a big help Visual Studio is.

IntelliSense as an HTML element is entered in Source view

IntelliSense options including snippets are displayed as you start a tag

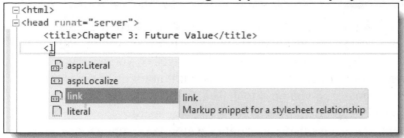

Press the Tab key twice to enter the snippet for the tag

```
☐ <html>
☐ <head runat="server">
      <title>Chapter 3: Future Value</title>
      <link href="#" rel="stylesheet" />
```

The smart indent feature

If you press the Enter key when the cursor is in the content area...

```
☐ <body>
      <header>|</header>
```

...the ending tag is dropped down two lines with the cursor where you want it

Other Video Studio features for entering HTML

- If you change the starting tag for an element, the ending tag will be automatically changed too.
- If you enter the opening tag followed by the letters that are capitalized in the name of a control, like <cb for the asp:CheckBox control, IntelliSense will list the control.
- When you start the entry of an attribute, IntelliSense lists the attributes that apply to the HTML element.

Description

- Visual Studio provides many features that make it relatively easy to enter HTML code, including IntelliSense and *snippets*.

Figure 3-11   How to use the Visual Studio features for entering HTML

How to add the attributes for the WAI-ARIA accessibility standards

The *accessibility* of a web site refers to the qualities that make it accessible to as many users as possible, especially disabled users. For instance, visually-impaired users may not be able to read text that's in images so you need to provide other alternatives for them. Similarly, users with motor disabilities may not be able to use the mouse, so you need to make sure that all of the content and features of your web site can be accessed through the keyboard.

To a large extent, this means that you should develop your applications so the content of your web site is still usable if images aren't used and the mouse and JavaScript are disabled. A side benefit of doing that is that your site will also be more accessible to search engines, which rely primarily on the text portions of your pages.

Beyond that, you can adhere to the WAI-ARIA specification for the World Wide Web Consortium (W3C), which makes rich Internet applications even more accessible to the disabled. As figure 3-12 shows, Visual Studio 2012 provides IntelliSense features that support these recommendations. Here, the first example shows how IntelliSense lists the WAI-ARIA values for the role attribute that tells a user what role an HTML element plays on the form. The second example shows how IntelliSense lists the ARIA attributes for an HTML element.

Because this is a book on ASP.NET, not accessibility, these features aren't shown in the applications for this book. For most professional web sites, though, you should provide a high level of accessibility. To help you learn more about accessibility, this figure lists three sources of information.

IntelliSense with a list of WAI-ARIA values for the role attribute

IntelliSense with a list of ARIA attributes for an HTML element

Types of disabilities

- Visual
- Hearing
- Motor
- Cognitive

Information sources

- The WebAIM web site provides a good starting point for learning about accessibility at http://www.webaim.org.
- The World Wide Web Consortium (W3C) provides a full set of accessibility guidelines at http://www.w3.org/TR/WCAG.
- W3C also provides a specification called WAI-ARIA (Web Accessibility Initiative—Accessible Rich Internet Applications) that shows how to make rich internet applications more accessible to the disabled at http://www.w3.org/TR/wai-aria.

Description

- *Accessibility* refers to the qualities that make a web site accessible to users, especially disabled users.
- The IntelliSense for Visual Studio 2012 supports the WAI-ARIA attributes for accessibility.

Figure 3-12   How Visual Studio provides for the WAI-ARIA accessibility standards

Visual Studio features for working with CSS

Next, you'll learn how to use the Visual Studio features for working with CSS. Some of these are especially useful if you don't have much experience with CSS.

How to create and edit an external style sheet

Figure 3-13 starts by showing how to create an external style sheet that is added to the project folder. Then, if you haven't already done so, you can add a link element to the head section of the HTML that points to the external style sheet. To do that, you can use one of the techniques in figure 3-7 or just enter the link element into the aspx source code.

To enter and edit rule sets in the external style sheet, you first open it in the Editor window. Then, you can go to work. As you work, IntelliSense will help you by listing properties, values, and snippets. In this figure, for example, IntelliSense shows the options that make it easy to select the solid value for the second parameter in the rule for the border property.

As you enter the selector for a rule set, you may realize that you haven't set up the id or class attribute that you need for a style. Or, you may not remember the id or class attribute that you used. In either case, you can switch to the aspx code for the form and add the attribute or get the information that you need.

To see the changes that your CSS has made to a page, you can switch to Design view for the page or pages that your CSS affects. If Design view doesn't clearly show the changes that you made, you can test the form in one or more browsers. That's the sure way to know how your CSS is working.

As you work with styles, you may want to add comments or you may want to comment out one or more rule sets or rules. To do that, you can use the techniques in this figure. This makes working with comments much easier, and the keystrokes work the same with HTML code.

Visual Studio 2012 also provides *hierarchical indentation* if you code relational selectors, like parent, child, and sibling selectors. If, for example, you provide a rule set for nav elements followed by a rule set for ul elements that are children of nav elements, the second rule set will be indented to show this hierarchical structure. For the applications in this book, though, relational selectors aren't needed so you won't see this indentation.

If you want to see a summary of the selectors for the rule sets you've created, you can open the CSS Outline window as shown in this figure. Then, you can expand the Elements, Classes, and Element IDs groups to see the selectors for the styles in your style sheet. If you click on one of the selectors, the insertion point will jump to the selector for that rule set in the style sheet.

If your CSS skills are strong, this may be all you need to know to create effective style sheets. Otherwise, the Visual Studio features that are presented next are likely to be useful.

An external style sheet in Visual Studio

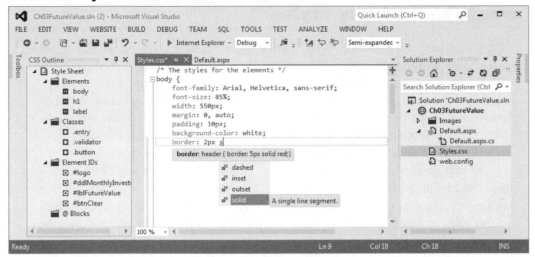

How to create an external style sheet

- Right-click on the project in the Solution Explorer. Then, choose the Add→Style Sheet command, type the name for the new style sheet, and click OK.

How to enter and edit the styles for an external style sheet

- Open the style sheet in the Editor, and enter the styles into the style sheet.

- If necessary, modify the aspx code so it provides the ids and class names that you need for the selectors in the style sheet.

- After you enter a rule set or a series of rule sets, switch to Design view to see whether the styles are working the way you want them to. Or, test the form in a browser.

How to comment out and uncomment one or more rules

- Press Ctrl+K, Ctrl+C to comment out selected rules, or Ctrl+K, Ctrl+U to uncomment them. Or, click the Comment or Uncomment button in the Style Sheet toolbar.

How to use the CSS Outline window

- Use the VIEW→Other Windows→Document Outline command to open this window. Then, to navigate to a rule set in the style sheet, click on its selector in this window.

Description

- If you know how to use CSS, the easiest way to develop a style sheet is to enter and edit the code in the Style Sheet editor.

- As you enter CSS code, Visual Studio provides IntelliSense and snippets, including support for CSS3 and vendor-specific properties (like -moz- and -webkit- properties).

- By default, if you use relational selectors like parent, child, and sibling selectors, Visual Studio displays the rule sets with *hierarchical indentation*.

Figure 3-13   How to create and edit an external style sheet

How to use Visual Studio to create and modify styles

To simplify the task of creating style rules, you can use the New Style dialog box shown in figure 3-14. To access it, you can use either of the techniques in this figure. Then, you can select an element, id, or class from the Selector drop-down list that will be used as the selector for the rule set. You can choose Existing Style Sheet from the Define In drop-down list. And you can browse to the style sheet you want to use by clicking the Browse button. In this example, the rule set will be added to an external style sheet named Styles.css.

At that point, you can set the rules for the rule set. To help you do that, the New Style dialog box provides a list of style categories. Then, when you click on a category, the controls in the dialog box change so it's easy for you to apply all of the rules in that category. For instance, the dialog box in this figure shows the properties in the Box category, which include the padding and margin properties. Here, the padding has been set to 10 pixels for all four sides of the body, the top and bottom margins have been set to 0 pixels, the right margin has been set to "auto", and the left margin is being set to auto.

As you select style properties, a preview of the style is shown at the bottom of the dialog box. Here, you can see that the body has a border around it, which was set in the Border category. Although this illustration doesn't show the padding and margin settings, the Description area below the preview lists all of the rules in the rule set. When you've set all the properties for a rule set, you can click the OK button to create it.

Modifying a style is similar, except that you access the Modify Style dialog box in the way that's shown in this figure and the controls at the top of the New Style dialog box aren't in the Modify Style dialog box. In that dialog box, though, you select a category and use the controls to set any of the properties in that category, just as you do in the Add Style dialog box.

If your CSS skills aren't that strong, the New Style and Modify Style dialog boxes make it easier to enter and edit the styles for a selector. By clicking the categories, you can see all of the properties that can be applied to a selection so you don't have to remember them. Then, you can use the controls for each property to set values that are valid. Although this may take longer than entering rules from memory, it makes creating and modifying styles relatively foolproof.

The New Style dialog box

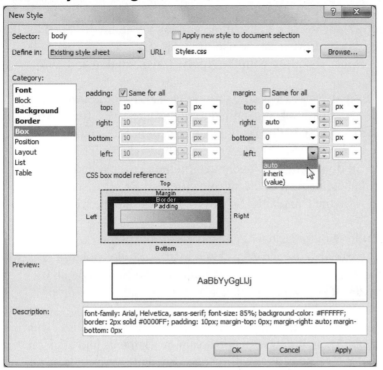

How to create a new style

- From Design view, open the New Style dialog box by choosing the FORMAT→New Style command or by selecting Apply New Style from the Target Rule drop-down list in the Formatting toolbar. You can also open this dialog box from the Apply Styles window in the next figure.

- In the New Style dialog box, enter or select the Selector for the style, select Existing Style Sheet from the Define In list, and use the Browse button for the URL entry to find the style sheet you want the new style to be placed in.

- To specify the rules for the style, select a Category and set the values for the properties in that category. Then, continue with any of the other categories.

How to modify a style

- In the Editor for a style sheet, right-click in a style and select Build Style or click on the Build Style button in the Style Sheet toolbar. You can also open this dialog box from the Apply Styles window in the next figure.

- In the Modify Style dialog box, select a category and set or reset the values for the properties in that category. Then, continue with any of the other categories.

Description

- The New Style and Modify Style dialog boxes let you set all the rules for a style. This can make it easier if your knowledge of properties is limited.

Figure 3-14   How to use Visual Studio to create and modify styles

How to use the Apply Styles window

This chapter ends by showing how to use three windows that are designed for working with styles. Each of these can be useful in some circumstances. So, here's a quick tour of them, starting with the Apply Styles window in figure 3-15.

In this example, the Apply Styles window shows the styles for the external style sheet named Styles.css that has been applied to the Future Value form. Note that the Apply Styles window is only displayed when a form is open in one of the Designer views, and the Apply Styles window only shows the styles for class and id selectors. However, if you click on an element in the Designer and a rule set has been set up for that element type, the selector for the rule set is shown at the bottom of the window in the Contextual Selectors section, like the h1 selector in this example.

When the Apply Styles window is open, you can move the pointer over a style to see its rules. You can also use the drop-down list for a style to start a new style or modify the style. Those are easy ways to open the New Style and Modify Style dialog boxes. If you want to delete a style, you can use the drop-down list for that too.

As the Apply Styles window implies, you can also use it to apply styles. This works best for class styles. Then, if you select one or more elements and click on a style for a class, Visual Studio adds the required class attribute to the selected elements.

If you're using one external style sheet for all styles, the Apply Styles window will look the way it does in this figure. But if you're using more than one external style sheet, embedded styles, or inline styles, those styles will also be shown in the Apply Styles window. That makes it easy to delete the styles that you don't want.

The Apply Styles window

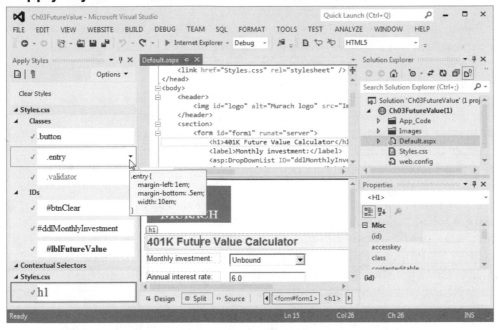

How to display the Apply Styles window

- In any of the Designer views, use the VIEW→Apply Styles command.

How to use the Apply Styles window

- To view the properties for a style, just point to the style in the Apply Styles window.

- To apply a class style to one or more elements, select the elements and click on the style in the Apply Styles window. That adds the appropriate class attribute to the HTML for the elements.

- To apply one or more class styles to a single element, select the element, hold down the Ctrl key, and click on the styles that you want to apply in the Apply Styles window. Repeat this process to remove one or more classes from an element.

- To start a new style, click the New Style button in the Apply Styles toolbar. Or, select any style and choose New Style from its drop-down list.

- To modify an existing style, select it and choose Modify Style from its drop-down list.

- To delete a style, select it and choose Delete Style from its drop-down list.

- To remove all class and inline styles for selected elements, click Clear Styles. This removes the class and style attributes from the elements.

Description

- The Apply Styles window lets you work with the styles defined in external style sheets as well as embedded styles and inline styles. It lists the styles for class and id selectors.

- The Apply Styles window has a toolbar that lets you create a new style, attach a style sheet to the current page, or control how the styles are displayed in the window.

Figure 3-15   How to use the Apply Styles window to work with styles

How to use the CSS Properties window

Figure 3-16 presents the CSS Properties window. This window makes it easy to analyze the styles that have been applied to an element in the Designer. This is useful when the styles for an element aren't working the way you want them to. This window also makes it easy to modify a style.

The CSS Properties window is divided into two panes. When you select an element in Design view, the Applied Rules pane lists the rule sets that have been applied to the element. In addition, the CSS Properties pane lists all of the properties that can be applied to the element. Then, if you click on the Summary button at the top of the window, only those properties that have been applied to the element are displayed.

In this figure, for example, the drop-down list is selected in the Designer, and the Applied Rules pane shows that the rule sets for the body element, the "entry" class, and the ddlMonthlyInvestment id have been applied to it. In addition, the CSS Properties pane shows the properties that have been applied to the element. These properties are grouped by the same categories that are used in the New Style and Modify Style dialog boxes.

In this case, the font-family and font-size properties are set by the rule set for the body. The margin-bottom, margin-left, and width properties are set by the rule set for the "entry" class. And the width property is set again by the rule set for the id. But since an id selector is more specific than a class selector, the second width property overrides the first, which is indicated by the line through the first width property.

To use this window to modify a style, you can select the rule set in the Applied Rules pane to display the style properties in the CSS Properties pane. Then, you can click on a property to select it and change the value of the property in the column to its right. Because of the use of categories, this is similar to modifying the style in the Modify Style dialog box.

The CSS Properties window

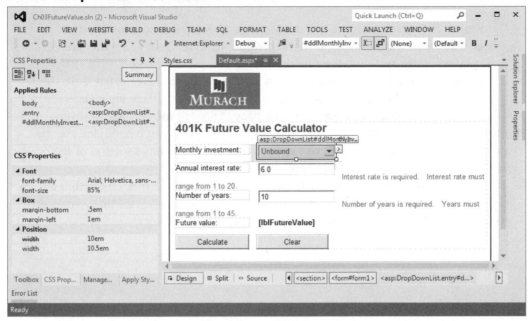

How to display the CSS Properties window

- In any of the Designer views, use the VIEW→CSS Properties command.

How to use the CSS Properties window

- To review the properties for an element, select it and click the Summary button. Then, the Applied Rules pane shows all of the rule sets that have been applied to the element, and the CSS Properties pane shows all of the rules that have been applied. If a rule has been overridden, it is crossed out in the CSS Properties pane.

- To modify the styles for an element in the Designer, select it. Or, to modify the styles for an existing rule set, select it in the Applied Rules pane. Then, in the CSS Properties pane, click on a property and change the value in the column to the right of it.

- To sort the properties by category, alphabetically, or by the properties that have been applied, use the buttons in the toolbar for this window.

Description

- The CSS Properties window can be used to review the styles applied to a selected element. It can also be used to modify styles.

- This window is especially useful for analyzing the styles for a selected element when more than one rule set applies to it. Then, you can see the sequence in which the rules are applied, and any rules that are overridden are crossed out.

Figure 3-16   How to use the CSS Properties window to work with styles

How to use the Manage Styles window

Figure 3-17 shows how to use the Manage Styles window. This window is useful when you want to move a rule set from one style sheet to another. To do that, you just drag and drop the rule set.

In the example in this figure, you can see the styles in the external style sheet named Styles.css. You can also see one style in the Current Page style sheet, which is the embedded style sheet for the page. Then, to move the style from the embedded style sheet to the external style sheet, you drag it to Styles.css and drop it there. That doesn't remove the style element in the head section of the HTML, but it does leave that element empty.

You can also use this window to change the sequence of rule sets within a style sheet by dragging and dropping them. But before you can do that, you need to use the Options list to set the display to Categorize by Order.

The Manage Styles window

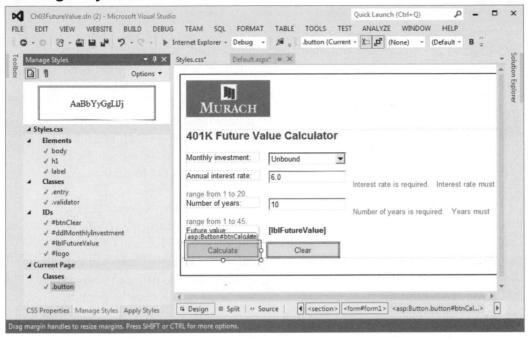

How to display the Manage Styles window

- In any of the Designer views, use the VIEW→Manage Styles command.

How to use the Manage Styles window

- To move a style from one style sheet to another, drag and drop it on the style sheet name or "Current Page".

- To change the order of the styles in the style sheet, select Categorize by Order from the drop-down Options list in the Manage Styles toolbar. Then, drag and drop a style in its new location.

- To display the properties of a style in the Manage Styles window, point to it.

- To show the preview for a style, select it in the Manage Styles window. If the preview isn't displayed, select Display Selected Style Preview from the drop-down Options list.

Description

- The Manage Styles window provides a convenient way to move the styles used by a page from one style sheet to another. That includes the styles in both embedded and external style sheets.

- All styles in an external style sheet appear under the name of that style sheet.

- All styles in an embedded style sheet appear under the Current Page heading, but only when a control that uses an embedded style is selected in the Designer.

Figure 3-17   How to use the Manage Styles window to work with styles

Perspective

Now that you've completed this chapter, you know the right way to use HTML and CSS in a Web Forms application. That means using HTML for the content and structure of a page and using CSS in an external style sheet for all of the formatting. That separates the content and structure of each page from its formatting. And that makes it easier to create and maintain a web page.

Because this book is about ASP.NET programming, not HTML and CSS, this chapter has presented only what you need to know about HTML and CSS for this book. As you will see, all of the applications in this book use simple HTML and CSS, and the programming is the same whether the formatting is simple or complex.

Of course, there's a lot more to HTML and CSS than what's presented in this chapter. So if you want to learn more, we recommend *Murach's HTML5 and CSS3*. Its first six chapters are a crash course in the HTML5 and CSS3 skills that every web developer should have, and those skills will help you get the most from the Visual Studio features for working with HTML and CSS. After you read those chapters, our HTML5 and CSS3 book becomes your best on-the-job reference.

Terms

CSS (Cascading Style Sheets)	external style sheet
HTML document	attach a style sheet
HTML element	embedded styles
tag	inline style
start tag	CSS selector
attribute	element (or type) selector
content (HTML)	class selector
end tag	id selector
self-closing tag	rule set
comment	style rule
comment out	rule
character entity	property
block element	em
inline element	cross-browser compatibility
HTML5 semantic elements	JavaScript shiv
HTML5 semantics	snippet
SEO (search engine optimization)	accessibility
style sheet	hierarchical indentation

Summary

- A best practice today is to use HTML for the content and structure of a web page and CSS for formatting the page. To do that, you use *external style sheets* to provide the CSS for your pages.

- To *attach* an external style sheet to a web page, you code a link element in the head section of the *HTML document* for the page. That element points to the location of the style sheet.

- By default, *block elements* in HTML are displayed on their own lines in browsers. In contrast, *inline elements* flow into the spaces above them and don't start new lines.

- The *HTML5 semantic elements* include the header, section, nav, aside, and footer elements. Using them makes it easier to apply CSS and also improves *SEO (search engine optimization)* in some search engines.

- Now that the HTML5 semantic elements are available, a div element should only be used when there isn't an appropriate semantic element for the purpose.

- ASP.NET generates span elements for validators as well as label controls. These are inline elements that usually flow to the right of preceding inline elements.

- *Embedded styles* are coded in a style element in the head section of an HTML document, which provides some separation between HTML elements and their styles. But *inline styles* are coded as attributes in the HTML elements themselves.

- The basic *CSS selectors* are *type* (or *element*) *selectors*, *class selectors*, and *id selectors*. Those are the ones that are used in the applications for this book.

- When you use CSS, you need to understand the order in which styles override other styles. For instance, more specific styles override less specific styles, and the last style that's applied overrides previous styles.

- A CSS *rule set* consists of one or more *rules*, and each rule consists of a *property* name and values. In ASP.NET, rule sets are referred to as *style rules*.

- To assure *cross-browser compatibility*, you need to test your web applications in all of the browsers that are likely to access your application.

- To make sure the HTML5 semantic elements work in older browsers, you need to add a script element for a *JavaScript shiv* to the head section of the HTML document. You also need to provide a CSS rule set that sets the semantic elements to block elements.

- Visual Studio provides features for working with HTML that include Intelli-Sense, snippets, and support for the WAI-ARIA *accessibility* specification.

- Visual Studio provides features for working with CSS that include Intelli-Sense, snippets, and the Apply Styles, CSS Properties, and Manage Styles windows.

Exercise 3-1   Develop the Future Value application with an external style sheet

In this exercise, you'll develop the Future Value application with an external style sheet used for all formatting. This will make you work with HTML and CSS.

Open the Future Value web site and convert it to IIS Express

1. Open the Ex03FutureValue web site in the c:aspnet45_cs folder. It already contains a web form named Default.aspx, a code-behind file for the form that's just like the one in chapter 2, and a folder named Images that contains an image file named MurachLogo.jpg.

2. Use the procedure in figure 2-6 of the last chapter to convert this web site to IIS Express.

3. Open the Default.aspx file and note that the form already contains the labels and controls needed by the Future Value application, but it doesn't contain an HTML table for layout and it doesn't contain any styling information.

4. View the form in Design view to see that the labels and controls flow to the right of the elements that precede them. This is because the labels and controls are inline elements and ASP.NET uses flow layout by default.

5. Run the application in a browser and click on the buttons to see that the application works, even though the formatting is a mess.

Begin styling the form

6. Put a br element (<br />) after the drop-down list, each text box, and the label server control (not the HTML label elements). Then, view the form to see that each label starts on a new line followed by its control.

7. Set the CssClass attributes for the drop-down list and the text boxes to "entry".

Create and attach an external style sheet

8. Using figure 3-13 as a guide, add a style sheet to the project named Styles.css, and add the rule set for the body selector that's shown in 3-3. If an option like Helvetica isn't available through IntelliSense, type it in. For the background color use "white", and for the border color use "blue".

9. Using figure 3-7 as a guide, drag the style sheet from the Solution Explorer and drop it into the head section of the HTML for the form. That should generate a link element that attaches the style sheet to the form. Then, run the form to make sure that the style sheet has been attached properly and the form is centered in the browser with a blue border around it.

10. Using figure 3-14 as a guide, use the New Style dialog box to add the h1 rule set in figure 3-3. To do that, you need to use the Font and Box categories. Then, note the changes in Design view.

11. Use the same technique to add the style for the label elements that's shown in figure 3-3. You'll find the width property in the Position category, and the float property in the Layout category.

12. Using whichever technique you prefer, add the rule sets for the "entry" class selector that's shown in figure 3-3. Then, note the changes in Design view as the formatting starts to take shape.

Create and test the rest of the styles

13. Add the rule set for the "button" class that's in figure 3-3 to the style sheet, and check that change in Design view. Oops! The CssClass attributes for the buttons haven't been set yet.

14. Use the Designer to set the CssClass attributes for the buttons and note that "button" is available from the drop-down list because that class is already in the style sheet. Then, check the change in Design view.

15. Add the three rule sets for the id selectors in figure 3-3. After each one, check the changes in Design view.

16. Test the form in one or more browsers. It should look the way it is in figure 3-1. If it doesn't, fix the problems.

Add the validation controls and their CSS

17. Add required field validators like those in figure 3-2 after the TextBox controls. But be sure that each validator comes after the TextBox control and before the br element that follows it. (You don't need to add the range validators.)

18. Add the rule set for a new "validator" class to the style sheet as in figure 3-3. Then, add the required CssClass attributes to the validator controls. One way to do that is to use the Apply Styles window as in figure 3-15.

19. Open the code-behind file for the form and notice that unobtrusive validation has been turned off, as shown in figure 2-13.

20. Test the application. It should work the way it did in chapter 2. The only difference should be in the formatting.

Experiment with some of the Visual Studio features

21. Using figure 3-14 as a guide, use the Modify Style dialog box to go through all of the settings in the rule set for the body element. Then, modify the rule set for the body element so its border is double.

22. Using figure 3-16 as a guide, use the CSS Properties window to review the properties for the DropDownList control. Note that the first width property has been crossed out because it has been overridden by the second width property.

23. Using figure 3-17 as a guide, use the Manage Styles window to review the styles for the web form. As you do that, experiment with the settings in the drop-down list in the toolbar.

24. When you're through experimenting, close the web site.

4

How to develop
a multi-page web site

In chapter 2, you learned how to develop a simple, one-page web site. Then, in chapter 3, you learned how to use HTML and CSS with any web site. Now, you'll how to develop a multi-page web site, which requires several new skills, including how to use session state and how to get the data for a web form from a database.

Introduction to the Shopping Cart application

In this chapter, you'll learn to build two pages of a Shopping Cart application. This application gets product data from a database, stores data in session state, and uses three business classes. So even though this is application is simple, you're going to learn a lot about developing web applications with ASP.NET and C#.

The two pages the Shopping Cart application

Figure 4-1 shows the two pages of the Shopping Cart application. The Order page, named Order.aspx, includes a drop-down list from which the user can select a product. The product names in this list are retrieved from an SQL Server database via an SqlDataSource control, or just data source. Then, since the Auto-PostBack property of the drop-down list is set to True, the page is posted back to the server.

On the server, the code-behind file for the Order page gets the data for the selected product from the data source, which has retrieved the data for all of the products from the SQL Server database. Then, the data for the selected product is displayed in several labels, and the ImageUrl property of the Image control on the right of the page is set to the URL for the image.

Once a product is selected, the user can enter a quantity and click the Add to Cart button. However, validation controls make sure that the entry is an integer that ranges from 1 to 500. If the entry is valid, the code-behind file for the Order page updates a list that represents the user's shopping cart. Because this list must be updated each time a product is added to the cart, the list that represents the shopping cart is saved in a session state object so it is available throughout the user's session. Then, the code behind file passes control to the Cart page.

The code-behind file for the Cart page gets the list for the cart from the session state object and displays the page shown in this figure. Then, the user can click the Remove Item button to remove the selected item or the Empty Cart button to remove all of the items. In either case, the code-behind file for the Cart page updates the cart list for the session state object and redisplays the page.

On the Cart page, the user can also click the Continue Shopping button to return to the Order page or the Check Out button to go to a page that gets the data for completing the purchase. In this case, though, the checkout page hasn't been implemented yet so a message to that effect is displayed when the user clicks the Check Out button.

The Order page

The Cart page

Figure 4-1   The two pages of the Shopping Cart application

The files and folders used by the Shopping Cart application

Figure 4-2 summarizes the files and folders used by the Shopping Cart application. By default, Visual Studio places new web form files and their code-behind files in the application's root folder, but other files are placed in special folders. The first table in this figure lists the most commonly used special folders. Besides these folders, though, you can create your own folders. For example, it's common to create an Images folder to store any image files used by the application.

The App_Code, App_Data, App_Themes, and Bin folders are used for certain types of files required by the application. For instance, class files (other than the class files for web pages) are stored in the App_Code folder, and any database files used by the application are stored in the App_Data folder. In contrast, the App_Themes folder is used to store any theme data, which you'll learn more about in section 2. And the Bin folder is used to store any compiled assemblies, such as *class libraries*, that are used by the application.

The second table in this figure lists the specific files and folders that make up the Shopping Cart application. As you can see, the App_Code folder contains three class files named CartItem.cs, CartItemList.cs, and Product.cs that define the CartItem, CartItemList, and Product classes required by the application. And the App_Data folder contains an SQL Server database file named Halloween.mdf.

The Shopping Cart application also includes folders named Images and Styles. The Styles folder contains the CSS files for the web site. The Images folder includes just one image file, banner.jpg, which provides the banner that's displayed at the top of each page. However, this folder also includes a subfolder named Products, which includes a separate image file for each product in the Products table of the database. Then, because the name of the file for each product is retrieved from the SQL Server database, the application can display the correct image for each product.

Finally, the root folder for the application contains two files for each of the application's web pages: one for the page itself, the other for the code-behind file. The root folder also contains a web.config file that is added automatically when you create an application.

The Solution Explorer for the Shopping Cart application

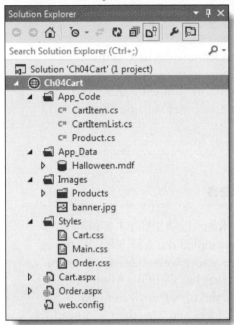

Special folders used in ASP.NET 4.5

Folder	Description
App_Code	Non-page class files that are compiled together to create a single assembly.
App_Data	Database files used by the application.
App_Themes	Themes used by the application.
Bin	Compiled code used by the application, including class libraries.

Files in the Shopping Cart application

Folder	File	Description
App_Code	CartItem.cs	A class that represents an item in the shopping cart.
App_Code	CartItemList.cs	A class that represents the shopping cart.
App_Code	Product.cs	A class that represents a product.
App_Data	Halloween.mdf	The Halloween database file.
Images	banner.jpg	An image file that displays at the top of each page.
Images\Products	(multiple)	Contains an image file for each product in the database.
Styles	(multiple)	The CSS files used to style the web pages.
(root)	Cart.aspx	The aspx file for the Cart page.
(root)	Cart.aspx.cs	The code-behind file for the Cart page.
(root)	Order.aspx	The aspx file for the Order page.
(root)	Order.aspx.cs	The code-behind file for the Order page.
(root)	web.config	The application configuration file.

Figure 4-2   The files and folders used by the Shopping Cart application

How to work with multi-page web sites

To create a multi-page web site, you need to learn some new skills like how to change the starting page for a web site, how to transfer from one form to another, and how to add classes to your site. Before you learn these skills, though, you'll learn how to create a web site that includes starting folders and files.

How to create a web site that has starting folders and files

All of the web sites in this book are started from the ASP.NET Empty Web Site template. However, there is another template called the ASP.NET Web Site template that you should be aware of. When you start a web site from this template, it generates a multi-page web application that has Default, About, Contact, Register, and Login pages, including the folders and files shown in figure 4-3.

Although this template produces far more folders and files than you need for most web sites, it is a useful source of ideas and code. If you run this application, you can see how it works. Then, you can study the code for its pages to see how they are implemented. Note, however, that much of this code won't make sense until you get further into this book. For instance, you won't understand the App_Code and App_Data folders and files until you complete this chapter. And you won't understand the Site.master file until you read chapter 9.

One feature of Visual Studio that's illustrated by the folders and files of this template is the use of NuGet packages. NuGet is a Visual Studio feature that makes it easy to install the third-party libraries and tools that are in the NuGet Gallery. The NuGet Gallery is the central package repository for the Microsoft development community and is hosted by CodePlex. Codeplex, in turn, is an open source development community hosted by Microsoft. You can see what's in the NuGet Gallery by using the WEBSITE→Manage NuGet Packages command in Visual Studio or by going to http://nuget.org.

When you install a NuGet package using the Manage NuGet Packages command, NuGet adds the folders and files for the package to your solution plus any required references and any required changes to your web.config file. Later, if you decide to uninstall the package, NuGet removes the folders and files and undoes any changes it made.

In figure 2-13 of chapter 2, you learned how to install a NuGet package called AspNet.ScriptManager.jQuery that provides for unobtrusive validation. If you open the packages.config file in a site that's created by the Web Site template, you'll see that this NuGet package is installed by default, along with several other packages. The packages.config file also shows the other NuGet packages that Microsoft thinks you might need for your web site.

A web site created from the ASP.NET Web Site template

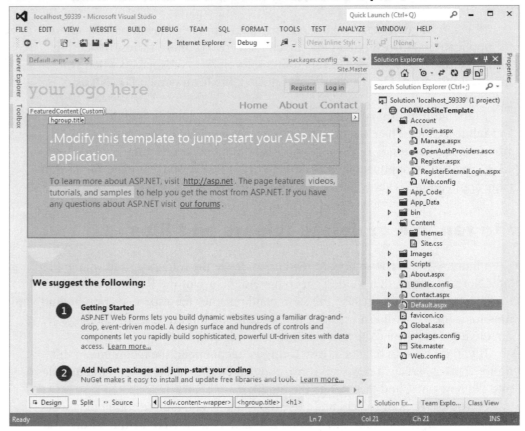

Some of the folders and files created by the Web Site template

Folder	File	Description.
Content	(multiple)	CSS files for themes, including jQuery UI CSS files.
Scripts	(multiple)	JavaScript, jQuery, and jQuery UI files.
(root)	Global.asax	A file for working with application objects.
(root)	packages.config	Config file for NuGet packages.
(root)	Site.master	The master page for the web site.

Description

- When you start a web site from the ASP.NET Web Site template, you get an application that provides Default, About, and Contact web pages, plus Register and Login pages. Then, you can modify these files to jump start your own application or just study them to see how they work.

- Besides the files for the web pages, this template provides other folders and files that are a useful source of code and ideas. As you progress through this book, you'll learn more about many of these files.

Figure 4-3   How to create a web site with starting folders and files

How to change the starting page for a web site

If a web site consists of a single form, that form is displayed when you run the application. However, if a web site contains two or more forms, the current form (the one that's selected in the Solution Explorer) is displayed when you run the application. Or, if a form isn't selected, the form named Default.aspx is displayed.

But what if a form isn't selected and the web site doesn't contain a Default.aspx file? Then, the browser displays a directory listing in the browser when the application is run. So, to make sure that the correct page is displayed when you run an application, you should always set the starting page for a multi-page application, as shown in figure 4-4.

How to rename or delete folders and files

Figure 4-4 also shows how to rename or delete the folders and files in a web site. Note, however, that we don't recommend the use of the Rename command for web forms. That's because this command renames the aspx and code-behind files for a form, but doesn't change the name of the Inherits class in the page directive for the form. And that can lead to errors later on.

If you do have to rename a web form, we recommend the technique in this figure. That is, create a new web form, copy and paste the code from the old files into the new ones, and then delete the old files.

For other types of folders and files, the Rename and Delete commands work well. However, if you think that you might need a file or web form later on, you can use the Exclude from Project command instead of the Delete command. That doesn't actually delete the file, and you can restore it by using the Include in Project command.

The menu for changing the starting page, renaming files, and deleting files

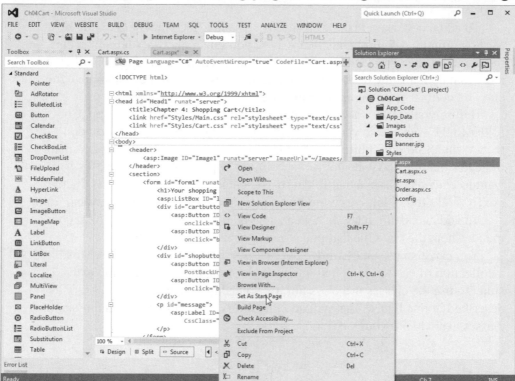

How to change the starting page for a web site

- Right-click on the aspx file and select Set As Start Page from the shortcut menu.

How to rename a web form

- Create a web form with the new name. Next, copy and paste the aspx and C# code from the old web form into the new one, but don't include the page directive for the old aspx file. Then, delete the old form.

How to rename a single file

- Right-click on the file, select Rename from the shortcut menu, and change the name.

How to delete a file from the web site

- Right-click on the file and select Delete from the shortcut menu. If the file is an aspx file, that will delete both the aspx file and its code-behind file from the web site.

- Another alternative is to select Exclude from Project from the shortcut menu for the file.

Description

- By default, the starting page for an ASP.NET web site is Default.aspx. If that isn't the page that you want the site started with, you need to change the starting page.

- Warning: If you use the Rename command to rename a web form, the file names are changed, but the name of the Inherits class in the page directive isn't changed.

Figure 4-4   How to change the starting page and rename or delete folders and files

How to add a class to a web site

To add a new class to the web site, you use the Add New Item dialog box, as shown figure 4-5. From this dialog box, you select the Class template, enter the name for the class, and click the Add button. Then, Visual Studio will create a file that contains the declaration for the new class, and you can complete the class by coding its properties and methods.

Before you create a new class, you'll typically add the special App_Code folder to the web site so you can add the class to that folder. But if you don't do that, Visual Studio will display a dialog box when you create a new class that indicates that the class should be placed in an App_Code folder and asks if you want to place the class in that folder. If you click the Yes button in this dialog box, Visual Studio will create the App_Code folder and place the new class in it.

To add an existing class to a web site, you use the Add Existing Item command. Then, the class file that you select is copied to your web site.

You can also use an existing class that is stored in a *class library*. This is a collection of classes compiled into a single assembly with a .dll file extension. To use the classes in a class library, you add a reference to the library as described in this figure. That will add the library to the Bin folder and make its classes available to your web site.

The dialog box for adding a new class to the App_Code folder

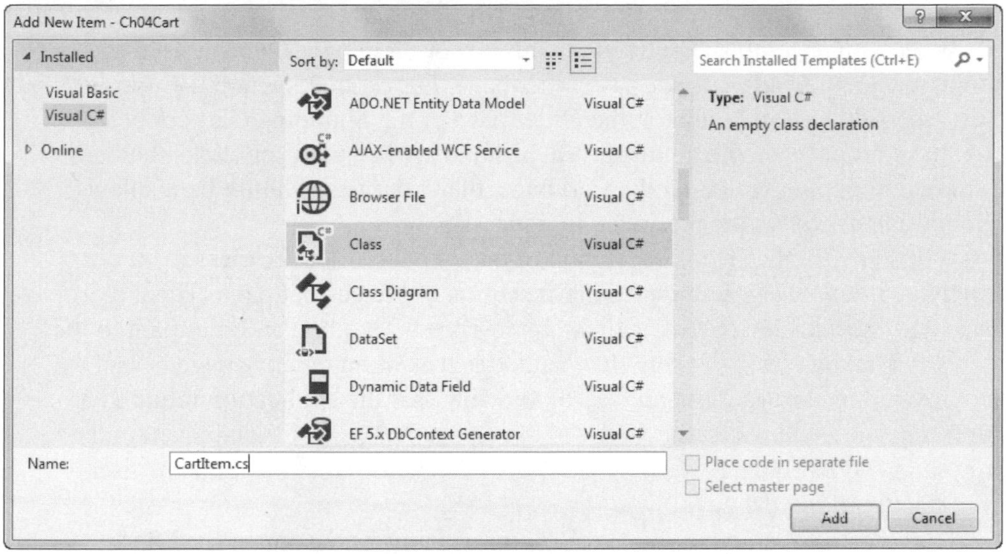

Two ways to open the Add New Item dialog box

- Right-click the App_Code folder in the Solution Explorer, and then choose Add→Add New Item from the shortcut menu.
- Click on the App_Code folder in the Solution Explorer to select it, and then choose the WEBSITE→Add New Item command.

How to add a new class to a web site

- From the Add New Item dialog box, select the Class template, name the class, and click the Add button. Then, Visual Studio will create the file with the declaration for the class.
- If you try to add a class directly to the project instead of to the App_Code folder, Visual Studio will warn you that the class should be placed in the App_Code folder and ask you if you'd like to place the class in this folder. If you click the Yes button, Visual Studio will create the App_Code folder and place the class in this folder.

How to add an existing class to a web site

- To add a class from another project to a web site, right-click the App_Code folder in the Solution Explorer and select Add→Existing Item. Then, locate the class file you want to add, select it, and click the Add button. The file is copied to your project.

How to use a class that's part of a class library

- Right-click the project in the Solution Explorer and select Add Reference from the shortcut menu. Click the Browse tab in the dialog box that's displayed, and then locate and select the dll file for the class library you want to use. The class library is added to the project's Bin folder, which is created if it doesn't already exist. To use the classes in the class library without qualification, add a using statement for the class library.

Figure 4-5   How to add a class to a web site

How to redirect or transfer to another page

When you develop an application with two or more pages, you'll need to know how to go from one page to another page. For example, when the user clicks the Add to Cart button on the Order page of the Shopping Cart application, the Cart page should be displayed. Similarly, when the user clicks the Continue Shopping button on the Cart page, the Order page should be displayed. Three ways to do that are presented in figure 4-6.

When you use the Transfer method of the HttpServerUtility class, ASP.NET immediately terminates the execution of the current page. Then, it loads and executes the page specified on the Transfer method and returns it to the browser. The drawback to using this method is that when the new page is sent to the browser, the browser has no way of knowing that the application returned a different page. As a result, the URL for the original page is still displayed in the browser's address box. This can be confusing to the user and prevents the user from bookmarking the page.

The Redirect method of the HttpResponse class works somewhat differently. When this method is executed, it sends a special message called an *HTTP redirect message* back to the browser. This message causes the browser to send a new HTTP request to the server to request the new page. Then, the server processes the page and sends it back to the browser. Although this requires an extra round trip, the user friendliness of this method usually outweighs the small performance gain that you get when you use the Transfer method.

Unlike the Transfer and Redirect methods, the RedirectPermanent method is typically used when a page is physically moved or renamed within a web site. Suppose, for example, that you create a web site that includes a page named Products.aspx that's stored in the project folder. But later, you decide to create a subfolder named Customer, and you move the Products page to this folder. Then, you can use the RedirectPermanent method as in the third example in this figure to redirect to the page. The main advantage of using this method is that search engines will store the new URL. That way, if the page is requested at the old location, it can be displayed from its new location.

The Transfer method of the HttpServerUtility class

Method	Description
`Transfer(URL)`	Terminates the execution of the current page and transfers control to the page at the specified URL.

The Redirect and RedirectPermanent methods of the HttpResponse class

Method	Description
`Redirect(URL)`	Redirects the client to the specified URL and terminates the execution of the current page.
`RedirectPermanent(URL)`	Permanently redirects to the specified URL and terminates the execution of the current page.

Code that transfers control to another page

```
Server.Transfer("Cart.aspx");
```

Code that redirects the client to another page

```
Response.Redirect("Cart.aspx");
```

Code that permanently redirects the client to another page

```
Response.RedirectPermanent("Customer/Products.aspx");
```

Description

- The Transfer method is a member of the HttpServerUtility class, which contains helper methods for processing web requests. To refer to this class, you use the Server property of the page.

- The Redirect and RedirectPermanent methods are members of the HttpResponse class, which contains information about the response. To refer to this class, you use the Response property of the page.

- When you use the Transfer method, the current page is terminated and a new page is processed in its place. This processing is efficient because it takes place on the server, but the URL in the browser's address bar isn't updated.

- When you use the Redirect method, the server sends a special message to the browser called an *HTTP redirect message*. Then, the browser sends an HTTP request to the server that requests the new page. This requires an extra round trip, but the URL for the current page is shown in the browser's address bar.

- If you change the name or location of a page, you can use the RedirectPermanent method to identify the new URL for the page. Then, search engines will store that URL and use it to display the page when they receive a request for the old URL.

Figure 4-6   How to redirect or transfer to another page

How to use cross-page posting

A fourth way to transfer to a different web page is to use *cross-page posting* as described in figure 4-7. To use cross-page posting, you specify the URL of another page in the PostBackUrl property of a button control. Then, when the user clicks the button, an HTTP Post message that contains the URL specified by the PostBackUrl property is sent back to the server. As a result, the page with that URL is loaded and executed instead of the page that was originally displayed.

For example, the Go to Cart button on the Order page uses cross-page posting to go to the Cart page. As a result, the PostBackUrl property of this button is set to Cart.aspx as shown in this figure. Then, when the user clicks the Go to Cart button, ASP.NET loads and executes the Cart.aspx page instead of the Order.aspx page.

Notice that the URL in the PostBackUrl property of this control starts with a tilde (~) operator. This operator is added automatically when you set the PostBackUrl property from the Properties window, and you'll learn more about it in the next topic.

If the user enters data into one or more controls on a page that uses cross-page posting, you can use the PreviousPage property to retrieve the data entered by the user. Usually, you'll do this in the page's Load event. As the example in this figure shows, you should first check to make sure that the PreviousPage property refers to a valid object. If it doesn't, it means that either the page isn't being loaded as the result of a cross-page posting, or the request came from another web site. In either case, no previous page is available.

If the PreviousPage property refers to a valid object, there are two ways you can use it to retrieve data from the previous page. First, you can use the FindControl method to find a control on the previous page. Because this method returns an object, you'll need to cast it to the appropriate control before you can work with its properties. For example, the code in this figure finds a text box on the previous page, casts it to a text box, and then uses its Text property to retrieve the data that the text box contains.

The other alternative is to use *custom properties* as in the third example in this figure. This requires code in two more places. First, you must add a custom property in the code-behind file of the previous page. Second, you must add a PreviousPageType directive at the top of the aspx file of the new page, just below the Page directive. Once these two pieces of code are in place, the custom property is available from the PreviousPage object, as shown.

Because of the extra programming that's required to retrieve data entered by the user, cross-page posting is best used when no user input needs to be processed. For instance, since no data needs to be processed when the user clicks the Go to Cart button on the Order page, cross-page posting is used instead of the Response.Redirect or Server.Transfer method. However, the Response.Redirect method is used for the Add to Cart button on the Order page so the selected product and the quantity entered by the user can be easily retrieved.

The PostBackUrl property of the Button control

Property	Description
PostBackUrl	Specifies the URL of the page that should be requested when the user clicks the button.

Members of the Page class used with cross-page posting

Property	Description
PreviousPage	Returns a Page object that represents the previous page.
Method	**Description**
FindControl(id)	Returns a Control object with the specified id. You must cast the Control object to a specific control before you can work with it.

The aspx code for a button that posts to a different page

```
<asp:Button ID="btnCart" runat="server" Text="Go to Cart"
    CausesValidation="False" PostBackUrl="~/Cart.aspx" />
```

How to use the FindControl method to get data from another page

```
if (PreviousPage != null) {
    TextBox txtQuantity =
            (TextBox) PreviousPage.FindControl("txtQuantity");
    lblQuantity.Text = txtQuantity.Text;
}
```

How to use a custom property to get data from a previous page

Code that sets a property in the previous page

```
public string QuantityText {
    get { return this.txtQuantity.Text; }
}
```

A PreviousPageType directive in the new page

```
<%@ PreviousPageType VirtualPath="~/Order.aspx" %>
```

Code in the new page that gets the value from the property

```
if (PreviousPage != null)
    lblQuantity.Text = PreviousPage.QuantityText;
```

Description

- *Cross-page posting* lets you use the PostBackUrl property of a button to specify the page that should be requested when the user clicks the button.

- When you post to another page, the previous page is available via the PreviousPage property. Then, you use the FindControl method or custom properties to retrieve data entered by the user.

- If you use *custom properties*, you must set the PreviousPageType directive right below the Page directive at the top of the aspx file.

Figure 4-7   How to use cross-page posting

How to code absolute and relative URLs

In chapter 1, you learned about the basic components of an *absolute URL*, which includes the domain name of the web site. When coded within a Transfer or Redirect method, an absolute URL lets you display a page at another web site. For example, the first two statements in figure 4-8 display a page at the web site with the domain name www.murach.com. The first statement displays a page named Default.aspx in the root directory of the web site. The second statement displays a page named Search.aspx in the Books directory of the web site.

To display a page within the same web site, you can use a *relative URL*. This type of URL specifies the location of the page relative to the directory that contains the current page. This is illustrated by the third and fourth statements in this figure. The third statement displays a page that's stored in the same directory as the current page. The fourth statement displays a page in the Login subdirectory of the directory that contains the current page.

The next two statements show how you can use a relative URL to navigate up the directory structure from the current directory. To navigate up one directory, you code two periods followed by a slash as shown in the fifth statement. To navigate up two directories, you code two periods and a slash followed by two more periods and a slash as shown in the sixth statement. To navigate up additional directories, you code two periods and a slash for each directory.

To navigate to the root directory for the host, you code a slash as shown in the seventh statement. You can also navigate to a directory within the root directory by coding the path for that directory after the slash, as shown in the eighth statement.

In addition to coding URLs on Transfer, Redirect, and RedirectPermanent methods, you can code them for the attributes of some server controls. This is illustrated by the last two examples in this figure. The next to last example shows how you might set the PostBackUrl attribute of a button control. And the last example shows how you might set the ImageUrl attribute of an image control.

Notice that both of these URLs start with a tilde (~) operator. This operator causes the URL to be based on the root directory of the web site. For example, the Cart.aspx file in the first URL is located in the root directory, and the banner.jpg file in the second URL is located in the Images subdirectory of the root directory.

Keep in mind, though, that the tilde operator only works on the server. For example, it will work in the Response.Redirect method or in the ImageUrl property of an Image server control, but it won't work in the src property of an HTML img element unless the img element has a runat="server" attribute.

Although you can use relative URLs in examples like these, it's easier to maintain URLs that use the tilde operator when you move pages or files from one folder to another. That's because it's easier to maintain a URL that's relative to the root directory of the web site than it is to maintain a URL that's relative to another page. For that reason, you should use the tilde operator whenever you code a URL for an attribute of a server control.

Examples of absolute and relative URLs

Statements that use absolute URLs

```
Response.Redirect("http://www.murach.com/Default.aspx");

Response.Redirect("http://www.murach.com/Books/Search.aspx");
```

Statements that use relative URLs that are based on the current directory

```
Response.Redirect("Checkout.aspx");

Response.Redirect("Login/Register.aspx");
```

Statements that use relative URLs that navigate up the directory structure

```
Response.Redirect("../Register.aspx");

Response.Redirect("../../Register.aspx");

Response.Redirect("/Register.aspx");

Response.Redirect("/Login/Register.aspx");
```

Server control attributes that use URLs that are based on the root directory of the current web site

```
PostBackUrl="~/Cart.aspx"

ImageUrl="~/Images/banner.jpg"
```

Description

- When you code an *absolute URL*, you code the complete URL including the domain name for the site. Absolute URLs let you display pages at other web sites.

- When you code a *relative URL*, you base it on the current directory, which is the directory that contains the current page.

- To go to the root directory for the host, you code a slash. Then, you can code one or more directories after the slash.

- To go up one level from the current directory, you code two periods and a slash. To go up two levels, you code two periods and a slash followed by two more periods and a slash. And so on.

- If you're specifying a URL for the attribute of a server control, you can use the web application root operator (~) to base the URL on the root of the web site.

Figure 4-8   How to code absolute and relative URLs

How to create and use data sources

To connect to a database and work with its data, you can use an ASP.NET control called a *data source*. To illustrate how this works, the following topics show you how to work with a data source control called SqlDataSource. This control can be used to retrieve data from an SQL database file, such as a Microsoft SQL Server database file.

How to create an SQL data source

ASP.NET provides several data source controls in the Data group of the Toolbox, including the SqlDataSource control. Figure 4-9 shows how to create this type of data source.

If you are going to use the SQL data source to connect to a local database file, you must first create a database and add it to the App_Data folder of the web site. For example, the Shopping Cart application for this chapter has an SQL Server database file named Halloween.mdf in the App_Data folder.

Since the data source isn't displayed on the page when the application is run, it doesn't matter where you place it on the page. However, if the data source is going to be bound to a control, it makes sense to place it near that control.

After you add the SQL data source to the page, a smart tag menu is available. Click it and then choose the Configure Data Source command to bring up the first page of the Configure Data Source wizard, which is shown in this figure. From this dialog box, select the database file you want to use for the data source.

Once you've selected the data source, you must configure the data source as described in the next figure. Then, you can bind it to the drop-down list as described in the figure after that.

The first page of the Configure Data Source wizard

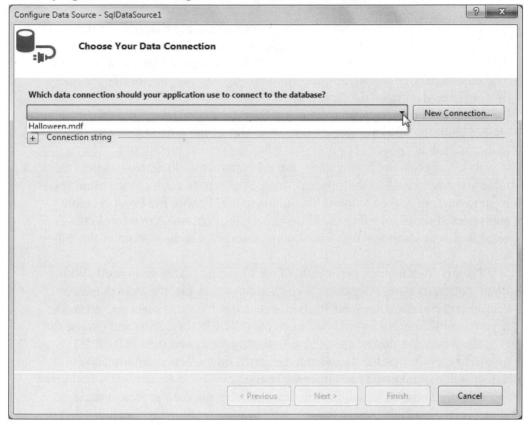

How to create an SQL data source

1. In the Web Forms Designer, open the Data group of the Toolbox and drag the Sql-DataSource control to the form in either Design or Source view.

2. Select Configure Data Source from the smart tag menu for the data source, which displays the Configure Data Source dialog box shown above.

3. From the drop-down list, select the database file or connection string that you want to use, and click Next.

4. If this is the first time you're connecting to the database file, a dialog box asks whether you want to save the connection to the application configuration file. Then, leave the Yes box checked, enter a name for the connection, and click Next.

5. Complete the Configure Data Source wizard as described in the next figure.

Description

- Before you create a *data source* for a local database file, you must add the database file to the App_Data folder.

- Data source controls are visible in the Designer, but don't show when the web site runs.

Figure 4-9   How to create an SQL data source

How to configure an SQL data source

The previous figure showed you how to complete the first page of the Configure Data Source wizard by selecting the SQL database file to use. Figure 4-10 shows you how to complete the rest of the Configure Data Source wizard. The second page of the wizard, shown in this figure, lets you specify the query that retrieves data from the database.

To create a query, you can code an SQL Select statement. Or, you can choose columns from a single table or view and let the wizard generate the Select statement for you. For now, we'll use the second technique.

To select columns from a table, use the Name drop-down list to select the table you want to select the columns from. Then, check each of the columns you want to retrieve in the Columns list. In this figure, I chose the Products table and selected six of its columns. As you check the columns, the wizard creates an SQL Select statement that's shown in the text box at the bottom of the dialog box.

The first two buttons to the right of the Columns list let you specify additional options for selecting data. If you want to select just the rows that meet certain criteria, click the WHERE button and specify the criteria you want. Or, if you want to specify a sort order, click the ORDER BY button and choose the columns you want the data sorted by. In this figure, I used the ORDER BY button to specify that the data should be sorted on the Name column, so the Select statement includes an Order By clause.

When you finish specifying the data you want the data source to retrieve, click Next. This takes you to the last page of the wizard, which includes a Test Query button. If you click this button, the wizard retrieves the data that you have specified. You can then look over this data to make sure it's what you expected. If it isn't, click the Previous button and adjust the query. If it is, click Finish.

The second page of the Configure Data Source wizard

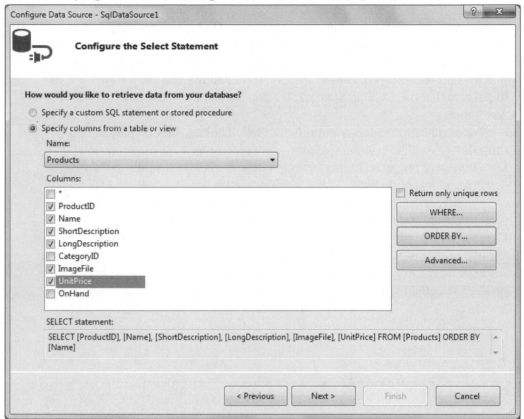

The aspx code for an SQL data source control

```
<asp:SqlDataSource ID="SqlDataSource1" runat="server"
    ConnectionString='<%$ ConnectionStrings:HalloweenConnectionString %>'
    SelectCommand="SELECT [ProductID], [Name], [ShortDescription],
        [LongDescription], [ImageFile], [UnitPrice]
        FROM [Products] ORDER BY [Name]">
</asp:SqlDataSource>
```

Description

- The Configure Data Source wizard lets you create a query using SQL. You can enter the Select statement for the query directly, or you can let the wizard construct the Select statement from your selections.

- You can click the WHERE button to specify one or more conditions that will be used to select the records.

- You can click the ORDER BY button to specify a sort order for the records.

- You can click the Advanced button to include Insert, Update, and Delete statements for the data source.

- When you click the Next button, you are asked whether you want to preview the data that's going to be returned by the data source. To do that, click Test Query.

Figure 4-10   How to configure an SQL data source

How to bind a drop-down list to a data source

Once you've created a data source, you can *bind* it to a drop-down list, as shown in figure 4-11. To start, select the Choose Data Source command from the smart tag menu for the drop-down list. Then, when the Data Source Configuration Wizard is displayed, choose the data source in the first drop-down list. In this figure, I chose SqlDataSource1, the data source that was created in the previous figures.

Next, select the column that provides the data you want displayed in the drop-down list. The column that you select here is used for the drop-down list's DataTextField property. In this figure, I chose the Name column so the drop-down list displays the name of each product in the data source.

Finally, select the column that you want to use as the value of the item selected by the user. The column you select here is used for the list's DataValueField property, and the value of that column can be retrieved by using the list's SelectedValue property. In this figure, I selected the ProductID column. As a result, the program can use the SelectedValue property to get the ID of the product selected by the user.

The Data Source Configuration Wizard dialog box

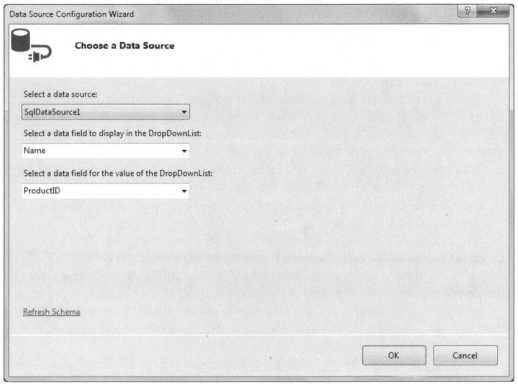

The aspx code for a drop-down list that's bound to a data source

```
<asp:DropDownList ID="ddlProducts" runat="server"
    AutoPostBack="True" DataSourceID="SqlDataSource1"
    DataTextField="Name" DataValueField="ProductID">
</asp:DropDownList>
```

Attributes for binding a drop-down list

Attribute	Description
DataSourceID	The ID of the data source that the drop-down list should be bound to.
DataTextField	The name of the data source field that should be displayed in the drop-down list.
DataValueField	The name of the data source field whose value should be returned by the SelectedValue property of the drop-down list.

Description

- You can *bind* a drop-down list to a data source so the list automatically displays data retrieved by the data source.

- You can use the Data Source Configuration Wizard dialog box to configure the data binding for a drop-down list. To display this dialog box, select the Choose Data Source command from the list's smart tag menu.

- Alternatively, you can use the Properties window or edit the aspx code directly to set the data binding attributes for a drop-down list.

Figure 4-11   How to bind a drop-down list to a data source

How to use C# code to get data from a data source

For the Shopping Cart application to work, it must retrieve the data for the product selected by the user from the drop-down list. Although there are several ways to do that, none of them are easy.

One way is to create a second data source that queries the database again to retrieve the data for the selected product, and then use a special type of ASP.NET server control called a DetailsView control that is bound to this second data source. You'll learn how to do that in section 3.

Another way is to write code that retrieves the product data from the existing SQL data source. That's the technique that the Shopping Cart application uses. However, to make this work, you must use the classes, methods, and properties that are summarized in figure 4-12.

The example in this figure shows how to retrieve data from a row that matches the ProductID value returned by the SelectedValue property of the drop-down list. First, you use the Select method of the SqlDataSource class with the Empty argument to retrieve all of the rows specified by the data source from the underlying SQL database. Then, because the return type of this method is IEnumerable, you must cast the returned object to a DataView object so you can use the methods of that class.

Once you have the rows in a DataView object, you can use the RowFilter property to filter the rows so only the row selected by the user is available. To do that, you build a filter expression that lists the column name and value. For example, ProductID='jar01' filters the data view so only the row whose ProductID column contains jar01 is included. The second statement in this figure creates a filter expression for the ID of the product the user selected.

Once you've filtered the DataView object so only the selected row is available, you can use two indexes to retrieve the data for a column. The first index identifies the only row that has been selected, so its value is 0, and this row is returned as a DataRowView object. Then, you can specify the index of the column you want to retrieve from the row, either as a string that provides the column name or as the index position of the column. In this example, column names are used for the columns that need to be retrieved. (Although using an index value is a little more efficient, specifying the column name makes the code more understandable.)

Once you establish the row and column index for each value, all that remains is to cast this value to the appropriate type. In this example, all of the columns except the UnitPrice column are cast to strings using their ToString methods, and the UnitPrice column is cast to a decimal type.

In this example, the values that are retrieved from the data source are stored in local variables. Later in this chapter, though, you will see similar code that retrieves these values and stores them in a Product object.

The Select method of the SqlDataSource class

Method	Description
Select(selectOptions)	Returns an IEnumerable object that contains the rows retrieved from the underlying database. To get all the rows, the selectOptions parameter should be DataSourceSelectArguments.Empty.

Members of the DataView class for retrieving rows

Property	Description
RowFilter	A string that is used to filter the rows retrieved from the database.

Indexer	Description
[index]	Returns a DataRowView object for the row at the specified index position.

Members of the DataRowView class for retrieving columns

Indexer	Description
[index]	Returns the value of the column at the specified index position as an object.
[name]	Returns the value of the column with the specified name as an object.

Code that gets product information for the selected product

```
DataView productsTable = (DataView)
    SqlDataSource1.Select(DataSourceSelectArguments.Empty);
productsTable.RowFilter =
    "ProductID = '" + ddlProducts.SelectedValue + "'";
DataRowView row = (DataRowView) productsTable[0];

string id = row["ProductID"].ToString();
string name = row["Name"].ToString();
string shortDesc = row["ShortDescription"].ToString();
string longDesc = row["LongDescription"].ToString();
decimal price = (decimal)row["UnitPrice"];
string imgFile = row["ImageFile"].ToString();
```

Description

- The Select method of the SqlDataSource class returns an IEnumerable object that contains the rows retrieved from the database. To work with these rows, you must cast the IEnumerable object to a DataView object.

- The RowFilter property of the DataView class lets you filter rows in the data view based on a criteria string.

- You can use the indexer of the DataView class to return a specific row as a DataRowView object. Then, you can use the indexer of the DataRowView class to return the value of a specified column. The indexer for the column can be an integer that represents the column's position in the row or a string that represents the name of the column.

- The DataView and DataRowView classes are stored in the System.Data namespace.

Figure 4-12   How to use C# code to get data from a data source

How to use session state

In chapter 1, you learned that HTTP is a stateless protocol. You also learned that ASP.NET uses *session state* to keep track of each user session and that you can use session state to maintain program values across executions of an application. Now, you'll learn how to use session state.

How session state works

Figure 4-13 shows how session state solves the problem of state management for ASP.NET applications. As you can see, session state tracks individual user sessions by creating a *session state object* for each user's session. This object contains a *session ID* that uniquely identifies the session. This session ID is passed back to the browser along with the HTTP response. Then, if the browser makes another request, the session ID is included in the request so ASP.NET can identify the session. ASP.NET then matches the session with the session state object that was previously saved.

By default, ASP.NET sends the session ID to the browser as a *cookie*. Then, when the browser sends another request to the server, it automatically includes the cookie that contains the session ID with the request. In section 2, you'll learn more about how cookies work. You'll also learn how to implement session state by including the session ID in the URL for a page instead of in a cookie.

Although ASP.NET automatically uses session state to track user sessions, you can also use it to store your own data across executions of an application. This figure lists three typical reasons for doing that. First, you can use session state to maintain information about the user. After a user logs in to an application, for example, you can use the login information to retrieve information about the user from a file or a database. Then, you can store that information in the session state object so it's available each time the application is executed.

Second, you can use session state to save objects that the user is working with. To illustrate, consider a maintenance application that lets the user change customer records. In that case, you can save the customer record that's currently being modified in the session state object so it's available the next time the application is executed.

Third, you can use session state to keep track of the operation a user is currently performing. For example, if a maintenance application lets the user add or change customer records, you can save an item in the session state object that indicates if the user is currently adding or changing a record. That way, the application can determine how to proceed each time it's executed.

How ASP.NET maintains the state of a session

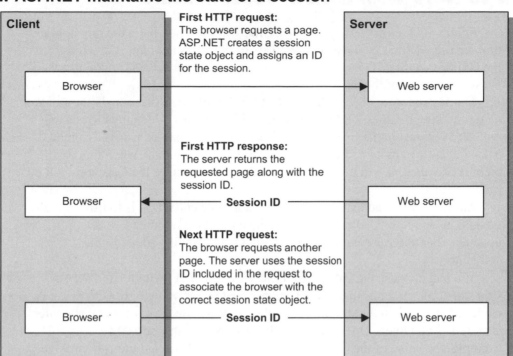

Typical uses for session state

- **To keep information about the user**, such as the user's name or whether the user has registered.
- **To save objects the user is working with**, such as a shopping cart or a customer record.
- **To keep track of pending operations**, such as what steps the user has completed while placing an order.

Description

- ASP.NET uses *session state* to track the state of each user of an application. To do that, it creates a *session state object*.
- The session state object includes a *session ID* that's sent back to the browser as a *cookie*. Then, the browser automatically returns the session ID cookie to the server with each request so the server can associate the browser with an existing session state object.
- If you want your application to work on browsers that don't support cookies, you can configure ASP.NET to encode the session ID in the URL for each page of the application. You'll learn more about this in chapter 8.
- You can use the session state object to store and retrieve items across executions of an application.

Figure 4-13   How session state works

How to work with data in session state

Figure 4-14 shows how you can use the session state object to store application data. To do that, you use the members of this object, which is created from the HttpSessionState class. To access this object from a web form, you use the Session property of the page.

The session state object contains a collection of items that consist of the item names and their values. One way to add an item to this collection is to use the indexer as shown in the first example. Here, an object named cart is assigned to a session state item named Cart. If the Cart item doesn't exist when this statement is executed, it will be created. Otherwise, the value of the Cart item will be updated.

Another way to add an item to the session state collection is to use the Add method, as in the second example. Here again, if the item already exists, it's updated when the Add method is executed. Otherwise, it's added to the collection.

You can also use the indexer to retrieve the value of an item from the session state collection, as in the third example. Here, the value of the Cart item is retrieved and assigned to the cart variable. Since the value of a session state item is stored as an Object type, you typically cast it to the appropriate type. In this example, the value of the Cart item is cast to a SortedList and the cart variable that it's assigned to is defined as a SortedList.

Because the session state object uses valuable server memory, you should avoid using it to store large items. Or, if you must store large items in session state, you should remove the items as soon as you're done with them. To do that, you use the Remove method as in the fourth example in this figure.

The first four examples in this figure use the Session property of the page to access the session state object. Because Session is a property of the System.Web.UI.Page class, however, you can only use this property from a class that inherits the System.Web.UI.Page class. In other words, you can only use it from a code-behind file for a page.

To access session state from a class that doesn't inherit the System.Web.UI.Page class, such as a database or business class, you use the Session property of the HttpContext object for the current request. To get this HttpContext object, you use the Current property of the HttpContext class as illustrated in the last example in this figure.

Common members of the HttpSessionState class

Property	Description
`SessionID`	The unique ID of the session.
`Count`	The number of items in the session state collection.

Indexer	Description
`[name]`	The value of the session state item with the specified name.

Method	Description
`Add(name, value)`	Adds an item to the session state collection.
`Clear()`	Removes all items from the session state collection.
`Remove(name)`	Removes the item with the specified name from the session state collection.

A statement that adds or updates a session state item

```
Session["Cart"] = cart;
```

Another way to add or update a session state item

```
Session.Add("Cart", cart);
```

A statement that retrieves the value of a session state item

```
SortedList cart = (SortedList) Session["Cart"];
```

A statement that removes an item from session state

```
Session.Remove("Cart");
```

A statement that retrieves the value of a session state item from a class that doesn't inherit System.Web.UI.Page

```
SortedList cart = (SortedList) HttpContext.Current.Session["Cart"];
```

Description

- The session state object is created from the HttpSessionState class, which defines a collection of session state items.
- To access the session state object from the code-behind file for a web form, use the Session property of the page.
- To access the session state object from a class other than the code-behind file for a web form, use the Current property of the HttpContext class to get the HttpContext object for the current request. This object contains information about the HTTP request. Then, you can use its Session property to get the session state object.
- By default, session state objects are maintained in server memory. As a result, you should avoid storing large items in session state.

Figure 4-14   How to use session state for storing and retrieving data

The business classes of the Shopping Cart application

Now that you've learned the basic skills for developing a multi-form application, you're ready to see all the aspx and C# code for the Shopping Cart application that's shown in figure 4-1. This starts with the C# code for the business classes.

The members of the three business classes

Figure 4-15 summarizes the members of the three business classes used by the Shopping Cart application. As you can see, the Product class is a simple class that contains only properties. An object created from this kind of class is sometimes referred to as a *Data Transfer Object*, or *DTO*. As its name implies, a DTO is used primarily to store and transfer data. Product objects are used to transfer data between the Order page and the business classes.

The CartItem class contains a Product property, which is a Product object, and a Quantity property, which is an int. It also contains an overloaded constructor, which lets you either create an empty CartItem object or populate its Product and Quantity properties on creation. In contrast to the Product class, the CartItem class contains methods as well as properties. Its first method adds to the Quantity property. Its second method returns a string containing quantity and product information, formatted in a single line. Although a CartItem object is also used to transfer data, it isn't a DTO because it has additional functionality.

The CartItemList class is a container class. In effect, it is the shopping cart. An object created from this class stores and keeps track of CartItem objects. It contains an internal list to store CartItem objects, a read-only property to display the number of CartItem objects it contains, indexers to set a CartItem object by index and to get a CartItem object by index or product ID, and methods to add and remove CartItem objects and to clear the entire CartItemList object.

The CartItemList class also contains a static method called GetCart that retrieves a CartItemList object from the session state object if one is there. Otherwise, this method creates a CartItemList object and adds it to the session state object.

Common members of the Product class

Property	Description
ProductID	Gets and sets the ID of a Product.
Name	Gets and sets the name of a Product.
ShortDescription	Gets and sets the short description of a Product.
LongDescription	Gets and sets the long description of a Product.
UnitPrice	Gets and sets the unit price of a Product.
ImageFile	Gets and sets the name of the image file for a Product.

Common members of the CartItem class

Constructor	Description
CartItem()	Creates a CartItem.
CartItem(product, quantity)	Creates a CartItem for the specified product and quantity.
Property	**Description**
Product	Gets and sets the Product of a CartItem.
Quantity	Gets and sets the quantity of a CartItem.
Method	**Description**
AddQuantity(quantity)	Adds the quantity that's passed to it to the quantity for a CartItem. Only called when the item is already in the cart.
Display()	Returns a string with CartItem data formatted so it can be displayed in one line of the list box on the Cart page.

Common members of the CartItemList class

Constructor	Description
CartItemList()	Creates a CartItemList.
Property	**Description**
Count	Gets the number of items in the CartItemList.
Indexer	**Description**
[index]	Gets and sets a CartItem using the index that's passed to it.
[id]	Gets a CartItem using the product ID that's passed to it. If the product isn't found, it returns null.
Method	**Description**
GetCart()	Gets the CartItemList from or creates it in session state.
AddItem(product, quantity)	Adds a CartItem to the CartItemList.
RemoveAt(index)	Removes the CartItem at the index from the CartItemList.
Clear()	Removes all CartItem objects from the CartItemList.

Figure 4-15   The members of the classes used by the Shopping Cart application

The code for the Product class

Now that you have a general idea of what the members of three business classes do, you can study the code for these classes. To start, figure 4-16 shows the C# code for the Product class. This class represents a product that the user can order from the Shopping Cart application. It has a property for each of the columns in the Products table in the SQL Server database except CategoryID and OnHand.

The code for the CartItem class

Figure 4-16 also shows the code for the CartItem class, which represents one item in the shopping cart. After the parameterless constructor, the next constructor for this class accepts two parameters that are used to initialize the Product and Quantity properties. These properties hold the Product object and quantity for the cart item.

The CartItem class also includes two methods. The first one, AddQuantity, is used to add the quantity that's passed to it to the cart item. This method is called when the user adds a quantity to the cart for a product that's already in the cart. The second one, Display, returns a string that formats the data in a cart item so it can be displayed in one line of the list box on the Cart page.

There are two features of this C# code worth mentioning. First, the CartItem class and the Product class are defined using auto-implemented properties. This is because the properties don't do anything but store and retrieve the values passed to them. Usually, this is all you will need when working with properties. Sometimes, though, you will want to do something with the property value, like run some data validation code or use it in a calculation. When that is the case, you will need to use private fields that are accessible through standard properties.

Second, the Display method of the CartItem class uses the Format method of the String class to create its return value. Here, the values in the last three parameters of this method are plugged into the literal that's specified by the first parameter. Using the Format method for this type of formatting is recommended over the traditional method of combining string literals and values with plus (+) signs, because it performs better and is less error prone.

The code for the Product class

```
public class Product
{
    public string ProductID { get; set; }
    public string Name { get; set; }
    public string ShortDescription { get; set; }
    public string LongDescription { get; set; }
    public decimal UnitPrice { get; set; }
    public string ImageFile { get; set; }
}
```

The code for the CartItem class

```
public class CartItem
{
    //constructors that create an empty CartItem object or one with values
    public CartItem() {}
    public CartItem(Product product, int quantity)
    {
        this.Product = product;
        this.Quantity = quantity;
    }

    //public properties for a CartItem object
    public Product Product { get; set; }
    public int Quantity { get; set; }

    //method that adds the quantity to the current quantity
    public void AddQuantity(int quantity)
    {
        this.Quantity += quantity;
    }

    //method that formats an item's name, quantity and price in one line
    public string Display()
    {
        string displayString = string.Format("{0} ({1} at {2} each)",
            Product.Name, Quantity.ToString(),
            Product.UnitPrice.ToString("c"));
        return displayString;
    }
}
```

Description

- The Product class represents a product.

- The CartItem class represents a product that the user has added to the shopping cart plus the quantity ordered.

- The Product and CartItem classes are defined with auto-implemented properties. However, if you need to do more than just store the property values, you need to use private fields that are accessible through standard properties.

- The Display method uses the Format method of the string object to format the item's properties in a single line that can be used in the Cart.

Figure 4-16   The code for the Product and CartItem classes

The code for the CartItemList class

Figure 4-17 shows the code for the CartItemList class, which represents a list of CartItem objects. This list is defined in a private field named cartItems at the beginning of the class. Then, the constructor for this class initializes this field with a new List<CartItem> object.

Next, the Count property is a read-only property that returns a count of the items in the list. It's followed by an overloaded indexer. The first indexer gets and sets a cart item in the list using the index that's passed to it. This indexer is used to get the items in the cart when they're displayed in the list box on the Cart page.

The second indexer is a read-only indexer that gets a cart item using the product ID that's passed to it. This indexer is used to determine if a product is already in the cart. If a product with the specified ID isn't found, this indexer returns a null value. This second indexer uses a *LINQ extension method* named FirstOrDefault and a *lambda expression* to retrieve the value from the cart. The FirstOrDefault method returns a null value if a product with the specified ID isn't found.

The first method, GetCart, gets the CartItemList object that's stored in a session state item named "Cart". Then, it checks to see if that object is equal to null. If it is, it means that a cart hasn't yet been created for the current user. Then, a new CartItemList object is created and added to session state. Either way, the CartItemList object is returned to the calling program.

You should notice two things about this method. First, it's a static method. That makes sense because it simply retrieves the CartItemList object that's stored in session state. It doesn't work with the current CartItemList object. Second, because this code isn't in a code-behind file, you can't use the Session property of the page to refer to the session state object. Instead, you have to refer to the session state object through the HttpContext object for the current request.

The next method, AddItem, adds a new cart item to the cart item list. It accepts a Product object and quantity as parameters. Then, it creates a CartItem object from these values and adds the cart item to the cart item list.

The last two methods, RemoveAt and Clear, should be easy to understand. The RemoveAt method removes the cart item at the given index from the list of cart items. And the Clear method removes all the cart items from the list.

Notice that the methods that add and remove items from the cart don't refer to session state directly. That's because session state is an object. So when you retrieve the cart from session state, you store it in a reference type variable. Then, when you use that variable to add and remove items from the cart, the session state object is updated automatically. This will make more sense when you see the code for the Order and Cart pages.

The code for the CartItemList class

```
using System;
using System.Collections.Generic;
using System.Web;
using System.Linq;

public class CartItemList
{
    //internal list of items and the constructor that instantiates it
    private List<CartItem> cartItems;
    public CartItemList() {
        cartItems = new List<CartItem>();
    }

    //read-only property that returns the number of items in the internal list
    public int Count {
        get { return cartItems.Count; }
    }

    //indexers that locate items in the internal list by index or product id
    public CartItem this[int index] {
        get { return cartItems[index]; }
        set { cartItems[index] = value; }
    }
    public CartItem this[string id]        {
        get {
            return cartItems.FirstOrDefault(c => c.Product.ProductID == id);
        }
    }

    //static method to get the cart object from session state
    public static CartItemList GetCart() {
        CartItemList cart = (CartItemList)HttpContext.Current.Session["Cart"];
        if (cart == null)
            HttpContext.Current.Session["Cart"] = new CartItemList();
        return (CartItemList) HttpContext.Current.Session["Cart"];
    }

    //methods that add, remove and clear items in the internal list
    public void AddItem(Product product, int quantity) {
        CartItem c = new CartItem(product, quantity);
        cartItems.Add(c);
    }
    public void RemoveAt(int index) {
        cartItems.RemoveAt(index);
    }
    public void Clear() {
        cartItems.Clear();
    }
}
```

Description

- The second indexer uses the FirstOrDefault *LINQ extension method* of IEnumerable and a *lamba expression* to retrieve an item. This requires a System.Linq using statement.

Figure 4-17   The code for the CartItemList class

The web forms of the Shopping Cart application

This chapter ends by presenting the aspx and C# code for the Order and Cart pages. If you've followed everything to this point, you shouldn't need much explanation. But the code is described in detail in case you need that.

The aspx code for the Order page

Figure 4-18 shows the aspx code for the Order page, which is shown in its rendered form in figure 4-1. This code includes HTML5 semantic elements like the header and section elements, and it is formatted by the two external style sheets that are in the Styles folder. This is consistent with the recommendations of chapter 3.

The header element defines an image that's used for the banner. The section element defines the page's form, and within the form are the HTML elements and server controls that make up the main section of the page.

To start, there is a label with the text "Please select a product", a drop-down list named ddlProducts, and the SQL data source that the drop-down list is bound to. Here, the AutoPostBack attribute for the drop-down list is set to True so the page will be posted back to the server when the user selects a product. In addition, the DataSourceID, DataTextField, and DataValueField attributes specify how the drop-down list is bound to the SQL data source.

This is followed by a div element with an ID of productData. This element starts with four label controls that will display the product information like name, short description, and long description. This is followed by a label for the Quantity entry and a text box control for receiving the entry. That is followed by two validation controls that will test the entry to make that it's there and that it ranges from 1 to 500.

The div element ends with two button controls. Here, the OnClick attribute for the first button names the event handler that will be executed when the button is clicked. In contrast, the btnCart button uses the PostBackUrl property to indicate that the Cart.aspx page should be requested when the button is clicked. Since its CausesValidation attribute is set to False, the validation controls for the txtQuantity text box won't be executed when the Go to Cart button is clicked.

Finally, just under the productData div, there is an Image server control. This control displays the image associated with the specified product. The CSS in the external style sheet for this page causes this image to flow to the right of the div element that contains the labels, text boxes, and buttons.

Note that the page uses HTML img and label elements as well as Image and Label server controls. How do you know which to use? You should use HTML elements for items that don't change, like logo images and descriptive labels. You should use server controls for items that will be changed by the code-behind C# code, like the descriptions, price, and image for each product.

The aspx file for the Order page (Order.aspx)

```
<%@ Page Language="C#" AutoEventWireup="true" CodeFile="Order.aspx.cs"
    Inherits="Order" %>

<!DOCTYPE html>
<html xmlns="http://www.w3.org/1999/xhtml">
<head id="Head1" runat="server">
    <title>Chapter 4: Shopping Cart</title>
    <link href="Styles/Main.css" rel="stylesheet" />
    <link href="Styles/Order.css" rel="stylesheet" />
</head>
<body>
    <header>
        <img src="Images/banner.jpg" alt="Halloween Store" />
    </header>
    <section>
    <form id="form1" runat="server">
        <label>Please select a product </label>
        <asp:DropDownList ID="ddlProducts" runat="server"
            AutoPostBack="True" DataSourceID="SqlDataSource1"
            DataTextField="Name" DataValueField="ProductID">
        </asp:DropDownList>
        <asp:SqlDataSource ID="SqlDataSource1" runat="server"
         ConnectionString='<%$ ConnectionStrings:HalloweenConnectionString %>'
         SelectCommand="SELECT [ProductID], [Name], [ShortDescription],
                [LongDescription], [ImageFile], [UnitPrice]
                FROM [Products] ORDER BY [Name]">
        </asp:SqlDataSource>
        <div id="productData">
            <asp:Label ID="lblName" runat="server"></asp:Label>
            <asp:Label ID="lblShortDescription" runat="server"></asp:Label>
            <asp:Label ID="lblLongDescription" runat="server"></asp:Label>
            <asp:Label ID="lblUnitPrice" runat="server"></asp:Label>
            <label id="lblQuantity">Quantity </label>
            <asp:TextBox ID="txtQuantity" runat="server"></asp:TextBox>
                <asp:RequiredFieldValidator ID="RequiredFieldValidator1"
                    CssClass="validator" runat="server"
                    ControlToValidate="txtQuantity" Display="Dynamic"
                    ErrorMessage="Quantity is a required field.">
                </asp:RequiredFieldValidator>
                <asp:RangeValidator ID="RangeValidator1"
                    CssClass="validator" runat="server"
                    ControlToValidate="txtQuantity" Display="Dynamic"
                    ErrorMessage="Quantity must range from 1 to 500."
                    MaximumValue="500" MinimumValue="1" Type="Integer">
                </asp:RangeValidator><br />
            <asp:Button ID="btnAdd" runat="server" Text="Add to Cart"
                OnClick="btnAdd_Click" />
            <asp:Button ID="btnCart" runat="server" Text="Go to Cart"
                PostBackUrl="~/Cart.aspx" CausesValidation="False" />
        </div>
        <asp:Image ID="imgProduct" runat="server" />
    </form>
    </section>
</body>
</html>
```

Figure 4-18   The aspx code for the Order page

The C# code for the Order page

Figure 4-19 presents the code for the Order page's code-behind file, Order.aspx.cs. This code starts by declaring a class-level variable that will hold a Product object that represents the item that the user has selected from the drop-down list. This variable is assigned a Product object by the second statement in the Page_Load method, which gets the Product object by calling the GetSelectedProduct method.

The Page_Load method starts by calling the DataBind method of the drop-down list if the page is being loaded for the first time (IsPostBack isn't True). This method binds the drop-down list to the SQL data source, which causes the data source to retrieve the data specified in its SelectCommand property.

Then, the Page_Load method calls the GetSelectedProduct method, which is coded in this file. This method gets the data for the selected product from the SQL data source and returns a Product object. That object is stored in the selectedProduct variable, which is available to all of the methods in this class.

Finally, the Page_Load method formats the labels and the image control to display the data for the selected product. At that point, the Order page is sent back to the user's browser.

For many applications, you don't need to call the DataBind method in the Page_Load method when you use data binding. Instead, you let ASP.NET automatically bind any data-bound controls. Unfortunately, this automatic data binding doesn't occur until after the Page_Load method has been executed. In this case, because the GetSelectedProduct method won't work unless the drop-down list has already been bound, the application calls the DataBind method to force the data binding to occur earlier than it normally would.

If the user clicks the Add to Cart button, the btnAdd_Click method is executed. After checking that the page is valid, this method calls the GetCart method of the CartItemList class to get the cart that's stored in session state. Remember that if a cart doesn't already exist in session state, this method creates a new CartItemList object and stores it in session state. Also remember that GetCart is a static method, so you call it from the class rather than an object created from the class.

Next, this method determines whether the cart already contains an item for the selected product. To do that, it uses the indexer of the CartItemList object to get the CartItem object with the product ID of the product. If an item isn't found with this product ID, the AddItem method of the CartItemList object is called to add an item with the selected product and quantity to the list. In contrast, if an item is found with the product ID, the AddQuantity method of the CartItem object is called to add the quantity to the item. Finally, this method uses Response.Redirect to go to the Cart.aspx page.

The code-behind file for the Order page (Order.aspx.cs)

```csharp
using System;
using System.Web.UI;
using System.Data;
public partial class Order : System.Web.UI.Page
{
    private Product selectedProduct;

    protected void Page_Load(object sender, EventArgs e) {
        //bind drop-down list on first load
        //get and show product on every load
        if (!IsPostBack) ddlProducts.DataBind();
        selectedProduct = this.GetSelectedProduct();
        lblName.Text = selectedProduct.Name;
        lblShortDescription.Text = selectedProduct.ShortDescription;
        lblLongDescription.Text = selectedProduct.LongDescription;
        lblUnitPrice.Text = selectedProduct.UnitPrice.ToString("c") + " each";
        imgProduct.ImageUrl = "Images/Products/" + selectedProduct.ImageFile;
    }
    private Product GetSelectedProduct() {
        //get row from SqlDataSource based on value in dropdown list
        DataView productsTable = (DataView)
            SqlDataSource1.Select(DataSourceSelectArguments.Empty);
        productsTable.RowFilter = string.Format("ProductID = '{0}'",
            ddlProducts.SelectedValue);
        DataRowView row = (DataRowView)productsTable[0];

        //create a new product object and load with data from row
        Product p = new Product();
        p.ProductID = row["ProductID"].ToString();
        p.Name = row["Name"].ToString();
        p.ShortDescription = row["ShortDescription"].ToString();
        p.LongDescription = row["LongDescription"].ToString();
        p.UnitPrice = (decimal)row["UnitPrice"];
        p.ImageFile = row["ImageFile"].ToString();
        return p;
    }
    protected void btnAdd_Click(object sender, EventArgs e) {
        if (Page.IsValid) {
            //get cart from session state and selected item from cart
            CartItemList cart = CartItemList.GetCart();
            CartItem cartItem = cart[selectedProduct.ProductID];

            //if item isn't in cart, add it; otherwise, increase its quantity
            if (cartItem == null) {
                cart.AddItem(selectedProduct,
                            Convert.ToInt32(txtQuantity.Text));
            }
            else {
                cartItem.AddQuantity(Convert.ToInt32(txtQuantity.Text));
            }
            Response.Redirect("Cart.aspx");
        }
    }
}
```

Figure 4-19   The C# code for the Order page

The aspx code for the Cart page

Figure 4-20 shows the aspx code for the second page of the Shopping Cart application, Cart.aspx, which is rendered in figure 4-1. Here, the shopping cart is displayed in a ListBox control, and the CSS in the external style sheet for this page causes the Remove and Empty buttons to flow to the right of the list box.

These two buttons, as well as the CheckOut button, use an OnClick attribute to name the event handler that's executed when the button is clicked. In contrast, the Continue button uses the PostBackUrl attribute to return to the Order.aspx page. All four buttons are styled by a CSS rule set for the button class.

The lblMessage label is used to display messages to the user. Notice here that the EnableViewState property of this label is set to False. That way, the value of this label isn't maintained between HTTP requests. So if an error message is displayed in this label, it won't be displayed the next time the page is displayed.

The aspx file for the Cart page (Cart.aspx)

```
<%@ Page Language="C#" AutoEventWireup="true" CodeFile="Cart.aspx.cs"
    Inherits="Cart" %>

<!DOCTYPE html>
<html xmlns="http://www.w3.org/1999/xhtml">
<head id="Head1" runat="server">
    <title>Chapter 4: Shopping Cart</title>
    <link href="Styles/Main.css" rel="stylesheet" type="text/css" />
    <link href="Styles/Cart.css" rel="stylesheet" type="text/css" />
</head>
<body>
    <header>
        <img src="Images/banner.jpg" alt="Halloween Store" />
    </header>
    <section>
        <form id="form1" runat="server">
            <h1>Your shopping cart</h1>
            <asp:ListBox ID="lstCart" runat="server"></asp:ListBox>
            <div id="cartbuttons">
                <asp:Button ID="btnRemove" runat="server" Text="Remove Item"
                    OnClick="btnRemove_Click" CssClass="button" /><br />
                <asp:Button ID="btnEmpty" runat="server" Text="Empty Cart"
                    OnClick="btnEmpty_Click" CssClass="button" />
            </div>
            <div id="shopbuttons">
                <asp:Button ID="btnContinue" runat="server"
                    PostBackUrl="~/Order.aspx" Text="Continue Shopping"
                    CssClass="button" />
                <asp:Button ID="btnCheckOut" runat="server" Text="Check Out"
                    OnClick="btnCheckOut_Click" CssClass="button" />
            </div>
            <p id="message">
                <asp:Label ID="lblMessage" runat="server"
                    EnableViewState="False"></asp:Label>
            </p>
        </form>
    </section>
</body>
</html>
```

Description

- The Cart.aspx page uses a list box to display the shopping cart.
- The lblMessage server control has its EnableViewState property set to False so messages set by the C# code will clear when the page posts back.
- The btnContinue button uses cross-page posting to post back to the Order.aspx page. The other buttons post back to the Cart page, where the event handler specified by the OnClick attribute of the button is executed.

Figure 4-20   The aspx code for the Cart page

The C# code for the Cart page

Figure 4-21 presents the code-behind file for the Cart page. This code starts by declaring a class-level variable that will hold the CartItemList object for the shopping cart. Then, each time the page is loaded, the Page_Load method calls the GetCart method of the CartItemList class to retrieve the shopping cart from session state and store it in this variable.

If the page is being loaded for the first time, the Page_Load method also calls the DisplayCart method. This method starts by clearing the list box that will display the shopping cart items. Then, it uses a for loop to add an item to the list box for each item in the shopping cart list. Notice that this statement uses the Count property of the CartItemList object to get the number of CartItem objects in the cart, and the Display method of the CartItem objects to get the strings to display in the list box control.

If the user clicks the Remove Item button, the btnRemove_Click method is executed. This method begins by making sure that the cart contains at least one item and that an item in the shopping cart list box is selected. If so, the RemoveAt method of the CartItemList object is used to delete the selected item from the shopping cart. Then, the DisplayCart method is called to refresh the items in the list box.

If the user clicks the Empty Cart button, the btnEmpty_Click method is executed. This method calls the Clear method of the CartItemList object to clear the shopping cart. Then, it calls the Clear method of the Items collection of the list box to clear that list.

Please note, though, that instead of using the Clear method to clear the list box, this method could call the DisplayCart method. Similarly, the btnRemove_Click method could use the Remove method of the Items collection of the list box to remove the item at the selected index instead of calling the DisplayCart method. This just shows that there is usually more than one way that methods like these can be coded.

Also note that the Cart page doesn't contain a method for the Click event of the Continue Shopping button. That's because this button uses the PostBackUrl property to post directly to the Order.aspx page. As a result, the Cart page isn't executed if the user clicks the Continue Shopping button.

The code-behind file for the Cart page (Cart.aspx.cs)

```csharp
// using statements go here
public partial class Cart : System.Web.UI.Page
{
    private CartItemList cart;

    protected void Page_Load(object sender, EventArgs e)
    {
        //retrieve cart object from session state on every post back
        cart = CartItemList.GetCart();

        //on initial page load, add cart items to list control
        if (!IsPostBack)
            this.DisplayCart();
    }

    protected void btnRemove_Click(object sender, EventArgs e)
    {
        //if cart contains items and user has selected an item...
        if (cart.Count > 0) {
            if (lstCart.SelectedIndex > -1) {

                //remove selected item from cart and re-add cart items
                cart.RemoveAt(lstCart.SelectedIndex);
                this.DisplayCart();
            }
            else { //if no item is selected, notify user
                lblMessage.Text = "Please select an item to remove.";
            }
        }
    }

    private void DisplayCart()
    {
        //remove all current items from list control
        lstCart.Items.Clear();

        //loop through cart and add each item's Display value to the control
        for (int i = 0; i < cart.Count; i++) {
            lstCart.Items.Add(this.cart[i].Display());
        }
    }

    protected void btnEmpty_Click(object sender, EventArgs e)
    {
        //if cart has items, clear both cart and list control
        if (cart.Count > 0) {
            cart.Clear();
            lstCart.Items.Clear();
        }
    }

    protected void btnCheckOut_Click(object sender, EventArgs e) {
        lblMessage.Text = "Sorry, that function hasn't been implemented yet.";
    }
}
```

Figure 4-21   The C# code for the Cart page

Perspective

The purpose of this chapter has been to get you started with the development of multi-page web applications. Now, if this chapter has worked, you should be able to develop multi-page applications of your own. Yes, there's a lot more to learn, but you should be off to a good start.

Frankly, though, much of the C# code in the Shopping Cart application is difficult, even in a simple application like this one. So if your experience with C# is limited, you may have trouble understanding some of the code. You may also have trouble writing the same type of code for your new applications.

If that's the case, we recommend that you get our latest C# book. It will quickly get you up to speed with the C# language. It will show you how to use dozens of the .NET classes, like the List<T> class. It will show you how to develop object-oriented Windows applications. It is a terrific on-the-job reference. And it is the perfect companion to this book, which assumes that you already know C#.

Terms

NuGet package
class library
HTTP redirect message
cross-page posting
custom property
absolute URL
relative URL
data source
bind a data source
session state
session state object
session ID
cookie
Data Transfer Object (DTO)
LINQ extension method
lambda expression

Summary

- In an ASP.NET web site, the App_Code folder is used for non-page classes, and the App_Data folder is used for database files.

- When you start a new web site from the ASP.NET Web Site template instead of the Empty Web Site template, many folders and files are included. These can be a source of ideas for the new web site as well as other web sites.

- By default, the starting page for a web site is the Default.aspx page, but you can change that to whichever page you want.

- If your web site needs to use classes that are part of a *class library*, you can add the class library assembly to the Bin folder of the web site.

- In the code-behind file for a web form, you can use the Transfer method to go to another page without going back to the browser. Or, you can use the Redirect method to send an *HTTP redirect message* to the browser that causes the browser to request the new page.

- With *cross-page posting*, the PostBackUrl property of a button specifies the page that's requested when the user clicks the button. Then, you can use the PreviousPage property along with the FindControl method or *custom properties* to get the data from the previous page.

- To identify the page that control should be transferred to, you can use an *absolute* or a *relative URL*.

- In an ASP.NET web site, a *data source* can be used to get the data from specific rows and columns of a database like an SQL Server database. Then, you can *bind* the data source to a control like a drop-down list. You can also use C# to get data from a data source.

- ASP.NET uses *session state* to create a *session state object* for each user of an application. This object can be used to store data that's used across the pages of an application.

- To make session state work, ASP.NET creates a *session ID* that's sent to the browser as a *cookie*. Then, the browser returns this ID to the server with each request so the server can associate the user with the right session state object.

Exercise 4-1   Build the Shopping Cart application

This exercise guides you through the process of building a Shopping Cart application like the one that's presented in this chapter. To save time, though, you'll start from a web site that has the folders and files for the images, database, non-page classes, and style sheets needed by the application.

Open the web site and review its folders and files

1. Open the web site named Ex04Cart in the C:\aspnet45_cs directory. Then, change this web site to IIS Express.

2. Run the application to see that a Directory Listing is displayed in the browser, which means the starting page hasn't been set. Then, stop the application, and set the starting page to the Order form.

3. Run the application again. When the Order page is displayed, click on the Go to Cart button to go to the Cart page. Note that both forms have all of the controls that are required, but only the Go to Cart button works.

4. Stop the application, return to Visual Studio, and review the folders and files. Note that the App_Code folder contains the three class files that this web site uses, the App_Data folder contains an SQL Server database (Halloween.mdf), and the Styles folder contains three style sheets that format the controls on the two forms. Note also that the aspx files for the web forms include all of the controls including the validation controls, but their code-behind files don't contain any methods.

5. Open the web.config file and note that unobtrusive validation has been turned off for the entire web site by using the third method shown in figure 2-13 of chapter 2.

Build out the Order page

6. Open the Order form in Source view.

7. Add an SqlDataSource control right after the code for the drop-down list, and configure the data source to get product data from the Halloween database as shown in figures 4-9 and 4-10. Use HalloweenConnectionString as the name of the connection string for the database, and click on the Test Query button in the last step to see the data that's returned by the data source.

8. Switch to Design view and display the smart tag menu for the drop-down list. Then, set Enable AutoPostBack to True, and bind the drop-down list to the data source as described in figure 4-11. If necessary, click the Refresh Schema link so you can see the field names in the drop-down lists of the dialog box.

9. Run the application to see how the drop-down list works. Now, you should be able to select a product from the list. Although the page will post back when you do that, nothing will happen.

Add the C# code for the Order form

As you enter the C# code for the Order form, be sure to take full advantage of the IntelliSense and snippets that Visual Studio provides.

10. In Design view, double-click outside the body of the Order form to switch to the code-behind file in the Code Editor and start an event handler for the Load event. Then, add a class-level declaration for a Product object before the Load event handler, as shown in figure 4-19. This is the object that's defined by the Product class in the App_Code folder.

11. Before coding the Load event handler, enter the GetSelectedProduct method that's shown in figure 4-19. This should be coded right after the code for the Load event handler. The GetSelectedProduct method gets the data for the product that's selected in the drop-down list. Then, it instantiates a new Product object. Last, it puts the database data for the product in the properties of the Product object, and it returns that Product object. After you code this method, be sure to add a using statement for the System.Data namespace.

12. Enter the code for the Load event handler that binds the SQL data source to the drop-down list the first time the page is requested. After that, add the code that displays the data and image for the selected product in the Order form each time the page is requested. To do that, use the GetSelectedProduct method that you just entered.

13. Run the application to test the code. Now, when you select a product from the list, the appropriate data for the product should be displayed on the page.

14. In Design view, double-click on the Add to Cart button to open the Code Editor and start an event handler for the Click event of that button. Then, add code to the event handler so it adds the selected product to the session object. To do that, you can use the GetCart and AddItem methods of the CartItemList class, the indexer of the CartItemList class, and the AddQuantity method of the CartItem class, as shown in figure 4-19.

Build out the Cart page and add its C# code

15. Open the aspx file for the Cart page in Design view, and set the PostBackUrl property of the Continue Shopping button so it displays the Order page. Now, test that change to make sure this button works correctly.

16. In Design view, double-click outside the body of the page to start a Load event handler and switch to the Code Editor. But before you code the Load event handler, code the DisplayCart method that's called by the event handler. It is shown in figure 4-21. Here, lstCart refers to the list box that's on the form.

17. Before the Load event handler, declare a class-level CartItemList variable that can be accessed by all the methods for this form. Then, code the Load event handler. Within this event handler, you can use the GetCart method of the CartItemList class to get the cart from session state, and you can use the DisplayCart method to display the cart items in the list box, as shown in figure 4-21.

18. Run the application to test this code. Now, when you select a product on the Order page, enter a quantity, and click the Add to Cart button, the application should add the item to the cart and display it in the Cart page.

19. Add the event handlers for the Click events of the Remove, Empty, and Check Out buttons. To start the event handler for each button, switch to Design view and double-click on the button. Then, add the code for the event handlers as shown in figure 4-21.

Test everything and experiment

20. At this point, the entire application should work correctly. If it doesn't, find the problem and fix it.

21. If you want to experiment with any aspect of this application, do that now. For instance, add the total price (quantity times unit price) for each item in the cart so each line in the cart looks like this:

```
Austin Powers (2 @ $79.99 each = $159.98)
```

22. When you're through experimenting, close the solution.

5

How to test and debug ASP.NET applications

If you've done much programming, you know that testing and debugging are often the most difficult and time-consuming phase of program development. Fortunately, Visual Studio includes an integrated debugger that can help you locate and correct even the most obscure bugs. And ASP.NET includes a trace feature that displays useful information as your ASP.NET pages execute.

In this chapter, you'll learn how to use both of these debugging tools. You'll also learn how to test an application to determine if it works properly in multiple browsers at the same time. And you'll learn how to use the Page Inspector to analyze the HTML and CSS for a page.

How to test an ASP.NET web site

When you *test* a web site or application, you try to make it fail. In other words, the goal of testing is to find all of the errors. When you *debug* an application, you find the cause of all of the errors that you've found and fix them.

To test an ASP.NET application, you typically start by running it from Visual Studio in the default browser. Then, you test the application with other web browsers to make sure it works right in all of them, even if they're all using the same application at the same time.

How to test a web site

Unless you've changed it, Windows uses Internet Explorer as its default browser. Figure 5-1 presents six different ways you can run a web application with the default browser. Three of these techniques start the debugger so you can use its features to debug any problems that might arise. The other three don't start the debugger.

The first time you run a web application using one of the first three techniques, Visual Studio displays a dialog box indicating that debugging isn't enabled in the web.config file. From this dialog box, you can choose to enable debugging, or you can choose to run the application without debugging. In most cases, you'll enable debugging so you can use the debugger with your application.

All of the techniques in this figure except the View in Browser command start the application and display the application's designated start page. However, the View in Browser command displays the selected page. For example, if you right-click the Cart page and choose View in Browser, the Cart page will be displayed. This command is useful if you want to test a page without having to navigate to it from the designated start page.

Once you've thoroughly tested an application with your default browser, you'll want to test it for *browser incompatibilities*. To do that, you need to run your application in all of the common browsers to make sure it looks and works the same in all of them. To do that, you can use the techniques in this figure. You can either change the default browser that Visual Studio uses, or you can use the Browse With dialog box to temporarily change the browser.

The Browse With dialog box

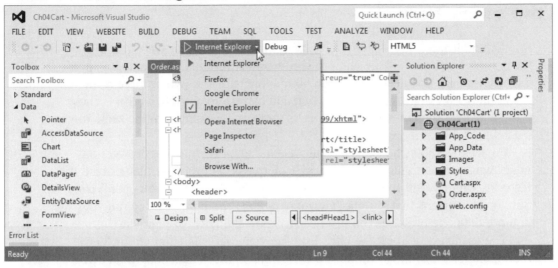

How to run an application in the default browser with debugging

- Click the browser name in the Standard toolbar, press F5, or choose the DEBUG→Start Debugging command.

How to run an application without debugging

- Press Ctrl+F5, choose DEBUG→Start Without Debugging, or right-click a page in the Solution Explorer and choose View in Browser.

How to stop an application that's run with debugging

- Press Shift+F5, click the Stop Debugging button in the Debug toolbar, or choose DEBUG→Stop Debugging.

How to run an application in a different browser

- If you want to change the default browser, click on the down arrow to the right of the browser name in the Standard toolbar, as shown above. Then, run the application.
- If you want to run an application in a different browser without changing the default, click on Browse With in the drop-down list or Browse With in the shortcut menu for a form. Then, in the Browse With dialog box, select the browser you want to use and click the Browse button to run the application without debugging.

Description

- If you run an application with debugging, you can use Visual Studio's built-in debugger to find and correct program errors.

Figure 5-1   How to test a web site

How to test a web site in two or more browsers at the same time

As you learned in chapter 3, you always need to test your web sites in all of the common browsers to prevent browser incompatibilities. For database applications, though, you also need to test your applications in two or more browsers at the same time. That way, you can find and correct concurrency errors. Those errors can occur when two different users try to make changes to the same row in a database table at the same time.

Figure 5-2 shows how to run your web site in more than one browser on your own computer when you're using IIS Express. This is possible because IIS Express, which hosts your web site, automatically starts when you open Visual Studio. This means that as long as Visual Studio is running, you can run your site in more than one browser. You just need to know the URL of your site.

The easiest way to get the URL is to run your web site from within Visual Studio using one of the methods in the previous figure. Then, copy the URL from the browser's address bar and paste it into one or more additional browsers. This is illustrated by the Internet Explorer and Firefox browsers in this figure. In this example, Internet Explorer was opened by Visual Studio so the Visual Studio debugger can be used to debug any errors that occur. Then, the Firefox browser was opened separately and the URL was copied from Internet Explorer into the Firefox address bar.

The Cart application running in two browsers at the same time

How test a web site in two or more browsers with IIS Express

- IIS Express automatically starts when you start Visual Studio 2012. Then, you can open your web site in multiple browsers by opening new browsers and copying the URL from your default browser into the address bars of the other browsers.

Description

- When you run an application in two or more browser windows simultaneously, you can test whether the application handles concurrency errors properly.

- If you open one of the browsers that's testing an application from within Visual Studio, you can use the debugger to help you debug.

Figure 5-2   How to test a web site in two or more browsers at the same time

How to use the Exception Assistant

As you test an ASP.NET application, you may encounter runtime errors that prevent an application from executing. When that happens, an *exception* is thrown. Often, you can write code that anticipates these exceptions, catches them, and processes them appropriately. If an exception isn't caught, however, the application enters break mode and the Exception Assistant displays a dialog box like the one in figure 5-3.

As you can see, the Exception Assistant dialog box indicates the type of exception that occurred and points to the statement that caused the error. In many cases, this information is enough to determine what caused the error and what should be done to correct it. For example, the Exception Assistant dialog box in this figure indicates that the input string isn't in a correct format, and that the problem was encountered in this line of code for the Order page:

```
cart.AddItem(selectedProduct,
             Convert.ToInt32(txtQuantity.Text));
```

Based on that information, you can assume that the Text property of the txtQuantity control contains a value that can't be converted to an integer, since the AddItem method of the cart object accepts an integer as its second parameter. This could happen if the application didn't check that the user entered an integer value into this control. (To allow this error to occur, I disabled the range validator for the Quantity text box on the Order page.)

Many of the exceptions you'll encounter will be system exceptions like the one shown here. These exceptions apply to general system operations such as arithmetic operations and the execution of methods. If your applications use ADO.NET, you can also encounter ADO.NET and data provider exceptions. If, for example, the connection string for a database is invalid, a data provider exception will occur. And if you try to add a row to a data table with a key that already exists, an ADO.NET error will occur. More about this in section 3.

In some cases, you won't be able to determine the cause of an error just by analyzing the information in the Exception Assistant dialog box. Then, to get more information about the possible cause of an exception, you can use the list of troubleshooting tips in the dialog box. The items in this list are links that display additional information in a Help window. You can also use the other links in this dialog box to search for more help online, to display the content of the exception object, and to copy the details of the exception to the clipboard. If you still can't determine the cause of an error, you can use the Visual Studio debugger to help you locate the problem.

The Exception Assistant dialog box

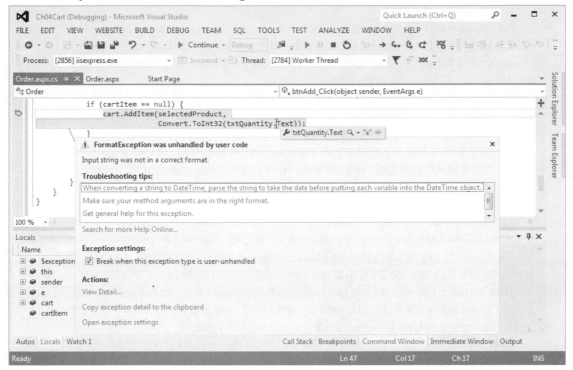

Description

- If you run an application with debugging and an *exception* occurs, the application enters break mode and the Exception Assistant displays a dialog box like the one above.

- The Exception Assistant provides the name and description of the exception, and it points to the statement in the program that caused the error. It also includes a list of troubleshooting tips that you can click on to display more information.

- The information provided by the Exception Assistant is often all you need to determine the cause of an error. If not, you can close this window and then use the debugging techniques presented in this chapter to determine the cause.

- If you continue program execution after an exception occurs, ASP.NET terminates the application and sends a Server Error page to the browser. This page is also displayed if you run an application without debugging. It provides the name of the application, a description of the exception, and the line in the program that caused the error.

Figure 5-3   How to use the Exception Assistant

How to use the Page Inspector

When you test an application, you of course test to make sure all of the C# code and all of the operations work correctly. But you also test to make sure that the pages are formatted correctly in all browsers. If they aren't, you need to fix the HTML or CSS code so they are.

To help you fix problems like that, ASP.NET provides the Page Inspector that's shown in figure 5-4. When you run an application in the Page Inspector, the pages are rendered within Visual Studio, and you can actually test the application there. But whenever you want to inspect the aspx, HTML, and CSS code for a control, you can click on the Inspect button and then move the mouse pointer over the control.

This is illustrated by the example in this figure. Here, the ListBox control is highlighted after the user has added one item to the cart. Then, in the HTML window below the Cart page, you can see the HTML that has been generated for the list box: one select element that contains one option element. In the CSS window, you can see the CSS that has been applied to the list box. And in the window to the right of the Cart page, you can see the aspx code for the list box. Since the related code is highlighted in the HTML and aspx windows, it's easy to see the relationships between the aspx and HTML code.

One of the best uses for the Page Inspector is to see the HTML that's generated for a server control. That's easier than running the application in the browser and viewing the source code there. In the case of the list box, for example, you may decide that you want to add margins or padding to the items that it contains by applying CSS to its option elements.

To make the Page Inspector especially useful, you can add and modify code while the Page Inspector is running and see the changes right away. If, for example, you add a style to the style sheet for a page, the change will be shown in the Page Inspector right away. You can also check or uncheck boxes in the CSS window to see the effect of turning a style on or off.

The best way to master the Page Inspector is to experiment with it. You may also want to search for one of the several training videos that show how to use it on the Internet. Although you won't need to use the Page Inspector often, it occasionally comes in handy.

The Cart page for the Shopping Cart application in the Page Inspector

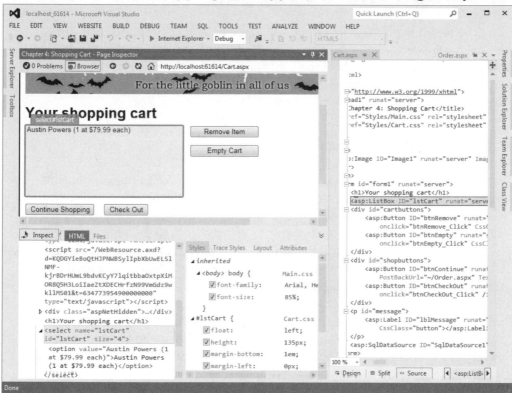

How to run an application with the Page Inspector

- In the Solution Explorer, right-click on a project or page and select View in Page Inspector from the shortcut menu. Or, you can select Page Inspector from the drop-down browser list in the Standard toolbar.

How to inspect the controls on a web page

- Click on the Inspect button in the Page Inspector. Then, move the mouse pointer over any control to see the aspx code for it, the HTML that's generated for it, and the CSS that's applied to it.

Description

- The Page Inspector lets you view the HTML that's generated for the controls on a form. This is easier than running the application in a browser and viewing its source code. The Page Inspector also shows the CSS that's used to format each HTML element.

- When you use the Page Inspector, you can test the application by entering values and using the controls. Then, you can see how your operations affect the HTML.

- If you change the aspx or CSS code, the changes are immediately reflected in the Page Inspector. You can also check or uncheck a CSS rule to see its effect on the page.

Figure 5-4   How to use the Page Inspector

How to use the debugger

The topics that follow introduce you to the basic techniques for using the Visual Studio *debugger* to debug an ASP.NET application. Note that these techniques are almost identical to the techniques you use to debug a Windows application. If you've debugged Windows applications, then, you shouldn't have any trouble debugging web applications.

How to use breakpoints

Figure 5-5 shows how to use *breakpoints* in an ASP.NET application. Note that you can set a breakpoint before you run an application or as an application is executing. Remember, though, that an application ends after it generates a page. So if you switch from the browser to Visual Studio to set a breakpoint, the breakpoint won't be taken until the next time the page is executed. If you want a breakpoint to be taken the first time a page is executed, then, you'll need to set the breakpoint before you run the application.

After you set a breakpoint and run the application, the application enters *break mode* before it executes the statement that contains the breakpoint. In this illustration, for example, the application will enter break mode before it executes the statement that caused the exception in the last figure to occur. Then, you can use the debugging features to debug the application.

In some cases, you may want to set more than one breakpoint. You can do that either before you begin the execution of the application or while the application is in break mode. Then, when you run the application, it will stop at the first breakpoint. And when you continue execution, the application will execute up to the next breakpoint.

Once you set a breakpoint, it remains active until you remove it. In fact, it remains active even after you close the project. If you want to remove a breakpoint, you can use one of the techniques presented in this figure.

You can also work with breakpoints from the Breakpoints window. To disable a breakpoint, for example, you can remove the check mark in front of the breakpoint. Then, the breakpoint isn't taken until you enable it again. You can also move to a breakpoint in the Code Editor window by selecting the breakpoint in the Breakpoints window and then clicking on the Go To Source Code button at the top of this window, or by right-clicking on the breakpoint in the Breakpoints window and choosing Go To Source Code from the shortcut menu.

If you experiment with the Breakpoints window, you'll see that it also provides other features like labeling groups of breakpoints, filtering breakpoints, and setting break conditions and hit counts. But these features are more than you'll need for most applications.

If you're using Visual Studio Express for Web, you'll see that it supports most, but not all, of the debugging features described in this chapter. For instance, the Breakpoints window isn't available with the Express Edition, and that edition only provides one Watch window.

The Order page with a breakpoint

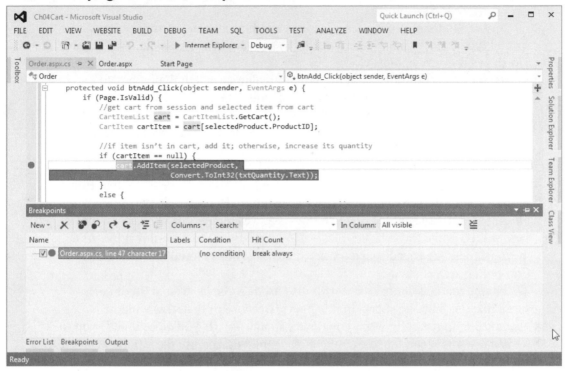

How to set and clear breakpoints

- To set a breakpoint, click in the margin indicator bar to the left of the statement at which you want the break to occur. The statement will be highlighted and a breakpoint indicator (a large dot) will appear in the margin. You can set a breakpoint before you run an application or while you're debugging the application.

- To remove a breakpoint, click the breakpoint indicator. To remove all breakpoints at once, use the DEBUG→Delete All Breakpoints command.

- To disable all breakpoints, use the DEBUG→Disable All Breakpoints command. You can later enable the breakpoints by using the DEBUG→Enable All Breakpoints command.

- To display the Breakpoints window, use the DEBUG→Windows→Breakpoints command. Then, you can use this window to go to, delete, enable, disable, label, or filter breakpoints.

Description

- When ASP.NET encounters a *breakpoint*, it enters *break mode* before it executes the statement on which the breakpoint is set. Note, however, that can't set breakpoints on blank lines.

Figure 5-5   How to use breakpoints

How to use tracepoints

Visual Studio also provides a feature called *tracepoints*. A tracepoint is a special type of breakpoint that performs an action when it's encountered. Figure 5-6 shows how tracepoints work.

To set a tracepoint, you use the When Breakpoint Is Hit dialog box to indicate what you want to do when the tracepoint is "hit." In most cases, you'll use the Print a Message option to display a message in the Output window. This message can include variable values and other expressions as well as special keywords.

For example, the message shown here will include the value of the SelectedValue property of the ddlProducts control. You can see the output from this tracepoint in the Output window in this figure. Here, the first tracepoint message was displayed the first time the page was requested. The second message was displayed when a product was selected from the drop-down list. And the third message was displayed when a quantity was entered and the Add to Cart button was clicked.

Notice that the Output window is also used to display Visual Studio messages like the first one shown in this figure. Because of that, this window is displayed automatically when you run an application. If you close it and want to reopen it without running the application again, you can use the VIEW→Output command.

By default, program execution continues after the tracepoint action is performed. If that's not what you want, you can remove the check mark from the Continue Execution option. Then, the program will enter break mode when the tracepoint action is complete.

After you set a tracepoint on a statement, the statement will be highlighted and a breakpoint indicator will appear in the margin. If program execution will continue after the tracepoint action is performed, the indicator will appear as a large diamond. But if the program will enter break mode, the standard breakpoint indicator is used.

Tracepoints are useful in situations where a standard breakpoint would be cumbersome, like in the execution of a loop. For example, suppose you have a loop that does 100 iterations, and an exception occurs in the middle somewhere. Imagine how tedious it would be to manually continue execution until you get to the error. In contrast, a tracepoint will give you a report of the loop's execution with just one click of the Start Debugging button.

The Order page with a tracepoint and the dialog box used to set it

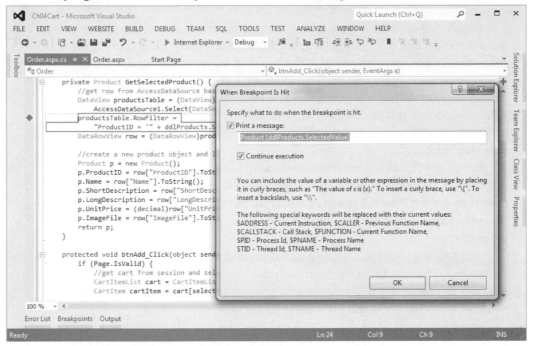

Output from the tracepoint in the Output window

Description

- A *tracepoint* is a special type of breakpoint that lets you perform an action. When ASP.NET encounters a tracepoint, it performs the action. Then, it continues execution if the Continue Execution option is checked or enters break mode if it isn't.

- You typically use tracepoints to print messages to the Output window. A message can include text, values, and special keywords.

- To set a tracepoint, right-click on a statement and choose Breakpoint→Insert Tracepoint. Then, complete the When Breakpoint Is Hit dialog box and click OK. You can also convert an existing breakpoint to a tracepoint by right-clicking on its indicator and choosing When Hit.

- If program execution will continue after the tracepoint action is performed, the tracepoint will be marked with a large diamond as shown above. Otherwise, it will be marked like any other breakpoint.

Figure 5-6   How to use tracepoints

How to work in break mode

Figure 5-7 shows the Order page in break mode. In this mode, the next statement to be executed is highlighted. Then, you can use the debugging information that's available to try to determine the cause of an exception or a logical error.

A great way to get information about what your code is doing is to use *data tips*. A data tip displays the current value of a variable or property when you hover the mouse pointer over it. You can also see the values of the members of an array, structure, or object by placing the mouse pointer over the plus sign in a data tip.

For example, this figure shows a data tip for a CartItem object, which displays its Product and Quantity properties. Since the mouse pointer is over the plus sign for the Product property, its member values are visible. You can see all this information, just by hovering the mouse pointer over variables and properties.

You can also see the values of variables and properties in the debugging windows in the bottom of the Visual Studio window. For example, the Locals window is visible in this figure. You'll learn more about the Locals window and some of the other debugging windows in a minute.

Once you're in break mode, you can use a variety of commands to control the execution of the application. The commands that are available from the DEBUG menu or the Debug toolbar are summarized in the table in this figure. You can also use shortcut keys to start these commands.

To execute the statements of an application one at a time, you use the Step Into command. Each time you use this command, the application executes the next statement, then returns to break mode so you can check the values of properties and variables and perform other debugging functions. The Step Over command is similar to the Step Into command, but it executes the statements in called methods without interruption (they are "stepped over").

The Step Out command executes the remaining statements in a method without interruption. When the method finishes, the application enters break mode before the next statement in the calling method is executed.

If your application gets caught in a processing loop so it keeps executing indefinitely without generating a page, you can force it into break mode by choosing the DEBUG→Break All command. This command lets you enter break mode any time during the execution of an application.

The Shopping Cart application in break mode

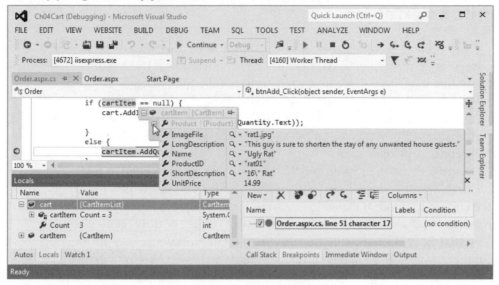

Commands in the DEBUG menu and toolbar

Command	Keyboard	Function
Start/Continue	F5	Start or continue execution of the application.
Break All	Ctrl+Alt+Break	Stop execution and enter break mode.
Stop Debugging	Shift+F5	Stop debugging and end execution of the application.
Restart	Ctrl+Shift+F5	Restart the entire application.
Step Into	F11	Execute one statement at a time.
Step Over	F10	Execute one statement at a time except for called methods.
Step Out	Shift+F11	Execute the remaining lines in the current method.

Description

- When you enter break mode, the debugger highlights the next statement to be executed. Then, you can use the debugging windows and the buttons in the DEBUG menu and toolbar to control the execution of the program and determine the cause of an exception.

- To display the value of a variable or property in a *data tip,* position the mouse pointer over the variable or property in the Code Editor window.

- To display the members of an array, structure, or object in a data tip, position the mouse pointer over it to display its data tip, and then point to the plus sign in the data tip.

- You can use the Step Into, Step Over, and Step Out commands to execute one or more statements and return to break mode.

- To stop an application that's caught in a loop, switch to the Visual Studio window and use the DEBUG→Break All command.

Figure 5-7   How to work in break mode

How to use the debugging windows to monitor variables

If you need to see the values of several application variables or properties, you can do that using the Autos, Locals, or Watch windows. By default, these windows are displayed in the lower left corner of the IDE when an application enters break mode. If they're not displayed, you can display them by selecting the appropriate command from the DEBUG→Windows menu. Note, however, that the Express Edition of Visual Studio provides only one Watch window, but the full editions provide four.

The contents of the Locals and Watch windows are illustrated in figure 5-8. The Locals window displays information about the variables within the scope of the current method. If the code in a form is currently executing, this window also includes information about the form and all of the controls on the form. The Autos window is similar to the Locals window, but it only displays information about the variables used in the current statement and the previous statement.

Unlike the Autos and Locals windows, the Watch windows let you choose the values that are displayed. For example, the Watch window in this figure displays the SelectedValue property of the ddlProducts control. You can also add properties of the page or of business classes to the Watch window, as well as the values of expressions. In fact, an expression doesn't have to exist in the application for you to add it to a Watch window.

To add an item to a Watch window, you can type it directly into the Name column. Alternatively, if the item appears in the Code Editor window, you can highlight it in that window and then drag it to a Watch window. You can also highlight the item in the Code Editor or a data tip and then right-click on it and select the Add Watch command to add it to the Watch window that's currently displayed.

The Immediate window is useful for displaying the values of variables or properties that don't appear in the Code Editor window. To display a value, you type a question mark followed by the name of the variable or property. For instance, the first query in the Immediate window in this figure displays a CartItem's properties. In the second query, you can see that IntelliSense is available to help you enter expressions into this window.

The commands that you enter into the Immediate window remain there until you exit from Visual Studio or explicitly delete them using the Clear All command in the shortcut menu for the window. That way, you can edit and reuse the same commands from one execution of an application to another without having to reenter them.

To execute a command that you've already entered in the Immediate window, scroll through the commands in the window to find the one you want. As you scroll, the commands are displayed at the bottom of the window. Then, you can select one and press Enter to execute it.

The Locals window and a Watch window

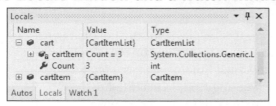 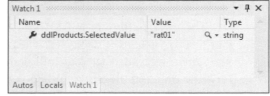

The Immediate window

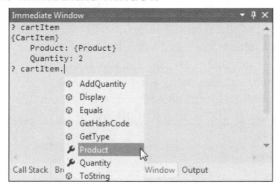

Description

- The Locals window displays information about the variables within the scope of the current method.

- The Watch windows let you view the values of variables and expressions that you specify, called *watch expressions*. You can display up to four Watch windows in the full edition of Visual Studio but only one in the Express edition.

- To add a watch expression, type a variable name or expression into the Name column, or highlight a variable or expression in the Code Editor window and drag it to the Watch window. You can also right-click on a variable, highlighted expression, or data tip in the Code Editor window and choose Add Watch.

- To delete a row from a Watch window, right-click the row and choose Delete Watch. To delete all the rows in a Watch window, right-click the window and choose Select All to select the rows, then right-click and choose Delete Watch.

- You can use the Immediate window to display specific values from a program during execution. To display a value in the Immediate window, enter a question mark followed by the expression whose value you want to display. Then, press the Enter key.

- To remove all commands and output from the Immediate window, right-click the window and choose the Clear All command from the shortcut menu. To execute an existing command, scroll to find it, select it, and press Enter.

- To display any of these windows, click on its tab if it's visible or select the appropriate command from the DEBUG→Windows menu.

Figure 5-8   How to use the debugging windows to monitor variables

How to use the trace feature

The *trace feature* is an ASP.NET feature that displays information that you can't get by using the debugger. The trace feature is most useful when trouble shooting a web site that you can't debug in Visual Studio, such as a production web site on a remote server. When you're working from Visual Studio, though, you shouldn't need the trace feature because the debugger works so well.

How to enable the trace feature

To use the trace feature, you must first enable tracing. To do that, you add a Trace attribute to the Page directive of the page that you want to trace, as shown in the first code example in figure 5-9. Or, to enable tracing for every page in the web site, you add an element to the web.config file, as shown in the second code example in this figure. Then, trace information will be added to the end of each page's output each time the page is requested.

How to interpret trace output

In figure 5-9, you can see the start of the output for the Cart page after the user added an item to the shopping cart. After the request details, the trace information provides a list of trace messages that are generated as the application executes. Here, ASP.NET automatically adds Begin and End messages when major page events such as PreInit, Init, and InitComplete occur. If you scroll down to see all of these trace messages, you can see the variety of events that are raised during the life cycle of a page.

After the trace messages, you'll find information about the controls used by the page, the items in the session state object, the cookies that were included with the HTTP request, the HTTP request headers, and the server variables. In this figure, for example, you can see the session state and cookies data for the Cart page of the Shopping Cart application. In this case, an item named Cart has been added to the session state object. And a cookie named ASP.NET_SessionId is used to keep track of the user's session ID so the user's session state object can be retrieved.

The beginning of the trace output for the Cart page

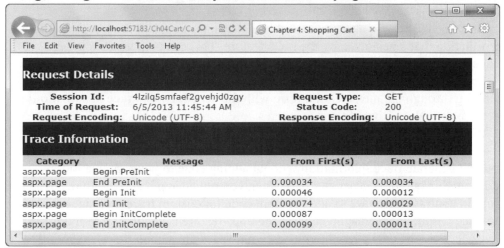

The session and cookies information for the Cart page

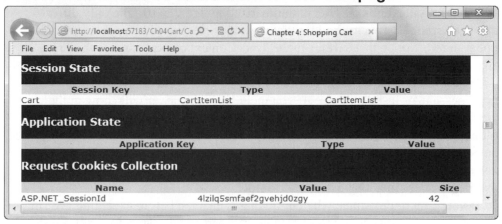

A Page directive that enables tracing for the Cart page

```
<%@ Page Language="C#" AutoEventWireup="true" CodeFile="Cart.aspx.cs"
Inherits="Cart" Trace="true" %>
```

A web.config setting that enables tracing for the entire web site

```
<system.web>
    <trace enabled="true" pageOutput="true" />
</system.web>
```

Description

- The ASP.NET *trace feature* traces the execution of a page and displays trace information in tables at the bottom of that page.

- To activate the trace feature for a page, you add a Trace attribute set to True to its Page directive. To activate the trace feature for the web site, you add a trace element to the web.config file as shown above.

Figure 5-9   How to enable the trace feature and interpret trace output

How to create custom trace messages

In some cases, you may want to add your own messages to the trace information that's generated by the trace feature. This can help you track the sequence in which the methods of a form are executed or the changes in the data as the methods are executed. Although you can also do this type of tracking by stepping through the methods of a form with the debugger, the trace information gives you a static listing of your messages.

Note, however, that you can also create this type of listing using tracepoints as described earlier in this chapter. The advantage to using tracepoints is that you can generate trace information without adding code to your application. In addition, this output is generated only when you run an application with debugging. In contrast, you have to add program code for custom trace messages, and the trace output is generated whenever the trace feature is enabled. If you don't have access to the debugger, though, trace messages are a good troubleshooting option.

To add messages to the trace information, you use the Write or Warn method of the TraceContext object. This is summarized in figure 5-10. The only difference between these two methods is that messages created with the Warn method appear in red. Notice that to refer to the TraceContext object, you use the Trace property of the page.

When you code a Write or Warn method, you can include both a category and a message or just a message. If you include a category, it will show in the category column in the trace output. If you include just a message, the category column is left blank, as shown in this figure. In most cases, you'll include a category because it makes it easy to see the sequence in which the methods were executed. However, leaving the category blank can make it easier to see your custom messages in a long list of trace output.

If you want to determine whether tracing is enabled before executing a Write or Warn method, you can use the IsEnabled property of the TraceContext object as shown in the example in this figure. Normally, though, you won't check the IsEnabled property because trace statements are executed only if tracing is enabled.

Common members of the TraceContext class

Property	Description
IsEnabled	True if tracing is enabled for the page.

Method	Description
Write(message)	Writes a message to the trace output.
Write(category, message)	Writes a message to the trace output with the specified category.
Warn(message)	Writes a message in red type to the trace output.
Warn(category, message)	Writes a message in red type to the trace output with the specified category.

Code that writes a custom trace message

```
if (Trace.IsEnabled)
{
    Trace.Write("Binding products drop-down list.");
}
```

A portion of a trace that includes a custom message

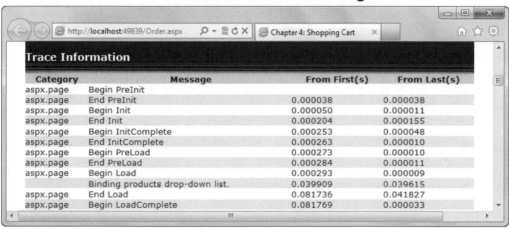

Description

- You can use the TraceContext object to write your own messages to the trace output. The TraceContext object is available through the Trace property of a page.
- Use the Write method to write a basic text message. Use the Warn method to write a message in red type.
- Trace messages are written only if tracing is enabled for the page. To determine whether tracing is enabled, you use the IsEnabled property of the TraceContext object.
- If you are using the Write method, or for some other reason you can't see the red type, trace messages without a category can be easier to find in a long list of trace information.

Figure 5-10   How to create custom trace messages

Perspective

As you can now appreciate, Visual Studio provides a powerful set of tools for debugging ASP.NET applications. For simple applications, you can usually get the debugging done just by using breakpoints, data tips, and the Autos or Locals window. You may also need to step through critical portions of code from time to time.

For complex applications, though, you may discover the need for some of the other features that are presented in this chapter. With tools like these, a difficult debugging job becomes manageable.

Terms

testing	breakpoint
debugging	break mode
browser incompatibilities	tracepoint
concurrency error	data tip
exception	watch expression
debugger	trace feature

Summary

- When you *test* an application, you try to find all of its errors. When you *debug* an application, you find the causes of the errors and fix them.

- To test for *browser incompatibilities*, you need to run your web site in all of the common browsers.

- To test database applications for *concurrency errors*, you need to run your web site in more than one application at the same time and access the same rows in the database.

- Visual Studio's *debugger* provides many features including the ability to set a *breakpoint*, step through the statements in an application when it is in *break mode*, and view the changes in the data after each statement is executed.

- *Tracepoints* are like breakpoints but they also let you perform actions like printing messages in the Output window.

- *Data tips* provide an easy way to view the data when an application is in break mode. But you can also use the Locals, Watch, and Immediate windows to do that.

- The *trace feature* is useful when you have to test an application and Visual Studio isn't available. This happens when the web site has already been deployed on a remote server.

Exercise 5-1   Use the Visual Studio debugger

In this exercise, you'll use the debugger to step through the Shopping Cart application that you studied in chapter 4. However, you'll work with another version of it so you can experiment without changing the original version.

Use breakpoints, step through statements, and view data tips

1. Open the Ex05Cart web site in the aspnet45_cs directory. Then, change this web site so it uses IIS Express, and set the starting page to the Order page.

2. Display the code for the Order page, and set a breakpoint on the statement in the Load event handler that calls the GetSelectedProduct method.

3. Run the application in the default browser. When the application enters break mode, point to the IsPostBack property to see that its value in the data tip is null. Then, point to the data tip and click the pin icon so the data tip remains open.

4. Press the F11 key to execute the next statement. Notice that this statement is in the GetSelectedProduct method. Press the F11 key two more times to see that only one statement is executed each time.

5. Click the Step Out button in the Debug toolbar to skip over the remaining statements in the GetSelectedProduct method. This should return you to the Page_Load method.

6. Click the Continue button in the Debug toolbar. This should execute the remaining statements in the Page_Load method and display the Order page.

7. Select another product from the combo box. This should cause the application to enter break mode again and stop on the statement that calls the GetSelectedProduct method. Notice that the data tip for the IsPostBack property is still displayed, but now its value is True.

8. Press the F10 key to execute the Step Over command. This should step over all statements in the GetSelectedProduct method and enter break mode before the next statement in the Page_Load method is executed. This should also display the data tip for the selectedProduct variable.

9. Point to the plus sign for the selectedProduct data tip to see the values of its members. Next, point to the Text property of the variables that follow to display their values. Then, step through the statements that assign the product properties to the Text property of the labels and note how these values change.

Use the Locals window, a Watch window, and the Immediate window

10. Click on the Locals window tab and note the values that are displayed. Click the plus sign next to the form object (this) to expand it and review the information that's available. When you're done, click the minus sign to collapse the information for this object.

11. Remove the breakpoint from the Page_Load method. Then, set another breakpoint on the statement in the GetSelectedProduct method that sets the value of the selected product's name, continue execution of the application, and select another product. When the application enters break mode again,

click on the Locals window tab and note the variables that are displayed. They should include all of the variables that are in scope.

12. Display a Watch window. Add the Name column of the DataViewRow object to this window by selecting it and then dragging it from the Code Editor window. In the Watch window, it should look something like this:

```
row["Name"].ToString()
```

Then, enter an expression into the Watch window that displays the Count property of the DataView object. It should look something like this:

```
productsTable.Count
```

13. Enter the same expression into the Immediate window, preceded by a question mark. Press the Enter key to see the value that's displayed. It should be 1.

14. Click the Stop Debugging button in the Debug toolbar to end the application. Note that the breakpoint remains in the Code Editor even after you have stopped debugging.

Exercise 5-2   Use the trace feature

In this exercise, you'll use the trace feature of ASP.NET to display trace output on the Order page of the Shopping Cart application that you created in the exercises for chapter 4.

1. If it's not already open, open the Ex05Cart web site.

2. Display the Order page in the Web Forms Designer and switch to Source view. Then, enable tracing for the page by adding a Trace attribute to the Page directive as shown in figure 5-9.

3. Run the application and notice that the trace output is displayed below the controls on the Order page. View the trace information. In particular, review the session state information.

4. Add a product to the cart and go to the Cart page. Notice that the trace output isn't displayed on that page. Click on Continue Shopping to go back to the Order page. View the session state information again and notice there is now a Cart object in the session state data. When you're done viewing the trace information, end the application.

Use custom trace messages

5. Add two custom trace messages to the GetSelectedProduct method as shown in figure 5-10. Put the first message at the top of this method. To do that, use the Trace.Warn method with the method name as the category and have the message indicate that the method is starting. Put the second message at the bottom of the GetSelectedProduct method, right before the return statement. Use the Trace.Write method, but don't include a category, and have the message indicate that a new Product object has been created.

6. Run the application to see what messages are displayed. Then, click the Add to Cart button and see what messages are displayed.

7. End the application, remove the trace messages from the code, and remove the Trace attribute from the Page directive. Then, close and save the solution.

Section 2

ASP.NET essentials

The six chapters in this section expand upon the essentials that you learned in section 1. To start, chapter 6 shows you how to work with the server controls that can be used for developing web pages. Then, chapter 7 shows you how to work with the validation controls, and chapter 8 presents the several ways that you can manage the state of an application or form.

The next three chapters present features of ASP.NET that make it easier to develop professional web sites. Chapter 9 shows you how to use master pages to create pages with common elements, and chapter 10 shows you how to use themes to customize the formatting that's applied to the pages of a web application. Then, chapter 11 shows you how to use ASP.NET routing to provide friendly URLs that improve search engine optimization and how to use the site navigation controls to make it easy for users to navigate through your site.

To a large extent, each of the chapters in this section is an independent unit. As a result, you don't have to read these chapters in sequence. If, for example, you want to know more about state management after you finish section 1, you can go directly to chapter 8. Eventually, though, you're going to want to read all six chapters. So unless you have a compelling reason to skip around, you may as well read the chapters in sequence.

6

How to use the standard server controls

In section 1, you learned the basic skills for working with some of the common server controls: labels, text boxes, buttons, and drop-down lists. Now, you'll learn more about working with those controls as well as how to use the rest of the standard server controls.

An introduction
to the standard server controls

The standard server controls are the ones in the Standard group of the Toolbox. These are the ones that get data from and present data in a web form.

The server controls you'll use the most

The two tables in figure 6-1 summarize the standard *server controls* that you'll use the most. If you've developed Windows applications or HTML pages, you should already be familiar with the operation of most of these controls. For instance, labels, text boxes, check boxes, radio buttons, drop-down lists, and buttons work the same way in Web Forms that they work in Windows applications and HTML pages.

In fact, the ASP.NET server controls are rendered as HTML elements. This is summarized by the second column in the tables in this figure, which present the HTML elements that ASP.NET generates for each type of control. For instance, a Label control is rendered as a span element, and a TextBox control is rendered as an input element. Similarly, some controls get rendered as two or more HTML elements. For instance, an ImageMap control gets rendered as an img element plus a related map element, and a DropDownList control gets rendered as a select element plus one option element for each item in the list.

What isn't shown in this table is that the type attribute of an HTML input element determines how the element looks and works. For instance, a typical text box is rendered as an input element with its type attribute set to "text", a check box is rendered as an input element with its type attribute set to "checkbox", and a file upload control is rendered as an input element with its type attribute set to "file".

For the most part, you don't need to know what HTML elements the server controls are rendered to. But if you use CSS to format those controls, you do need to know what elements are generated so you can code the selectors for the rule sets correctly. If necessary, you can view the source code when a page is rendered in a browser, but this table gives you a general idea of what you can expect.

This figure also answers the question: When should you use HTML elements instead of server controls, and vice versa? In brief, you should use HTML elements whenever the contents aren't going to change. If, for example, a label that identifies a text box isn't going to change, you should use the HTML label element instead of the Label control. In contrast, if the label is going to display text that is changed by the code-behind file based on user actions, the Label control is the right choice.

The other time to use server controls is when you don't know how to code the HTML that you need. Then, you can use the Properties window to set the properties for the corresponding server control and get the result that you want without using HTML. This makes sense when you just want to prototype an application and don't want to take the time to learn how to code the HTML. In the long run, though, you should learn how to use HTML instead of server controls whenever the data in the elements isn't going to change.

Common server controls

Name	HTML	Prefix	Description
Label	**span**	**lbl**	A label that displays descriptive information.
TextBox	**input**	**txt**	A text box that lets the user enter or modify a text value.
CheckBox	**input/label**	**chk**	A check box that can be turned on or off.
RadioButton	**input/label**	**rdo**	A radio button that can be turned on or off, but only one button in a group can be on.
Button	**input**	**btn**	A button that submits a page for processing.
LinkButton	**<a>**	**lbtn**	A link button that submits a page for processing.
ImageButton	**input**	**ibtn**	An image button that submits a page for processing.
Image	**img**	**img**	A control that displays an image.
ImageMap	**img/map**	**imap**	A control that displays an image with one or more clickable areas that submit the page for processing.
HyperLink	**<a>**	**hlnk**	A link that goes to another page or position on a page.
FileUpload	**input**	**upl**	A file upload control that consists of a text box and a Browse button that lets the user upload one or more files.

List server controls

Name	HTML	Prefix	Description
DropDownList	**select/option**	**ddl**	A drop-down list that lets the user choose one item.
ListBox	**select/option**	**lst**	A list box that lets the user choose one or more items.
CheckBoxList	**input/label**	**cbl**	A list of check boxes that can be turned on or off.
RadioButtonList	**input/label**	**rbl**	A list of radio buttons, but only one can be turned on or off.
BulletedList	**ul or ol/li**	**blst**	A bulleted list or numbered list.

When to use HTML elements instead of server controls

- When the contents of the controls aren't going to change, you should use HTML elements instead of server controls because server controls have some overhead.

When to use server controls instead of HTML

- When the contents of the controls are going to change, you should use server controls so it's easy to change the controls by using C# in the code-behind file.

- If you don't know how to code the HTML for the elements you want to use, server controls can help you get around that. Just add the controls to a form, use the Properties window to set their attributes, and let ASP.NET generate the HTML.

Description

- In the tables above, the HTML column shows the HTML elements that are rendered for each *server control*. The Prefix column shows prefixes that are commonly used in the IDs for these controls.

Figure 6-1   The standard server controls that you'll use the most

How to use C# to work with the data in server controls

Like other objects, server controls have events that are fired when certain actions are performed on them. The table at the top of figure 6-2 summarizes some of these events for the common controls. When you click on a button control, for example, the Click event is fired. And when you change the text in a text box, the TextChanged event is fired.

If your application needs to respond to an event, you code a method called an *event handler*. When you generate an event handler from Visual Studio, as explained in chapter 2, an event attribute that names the event handler is added to the aspx code for the control. Then, you enter the C# code for the event handler in the code-behind file. This is illustrated by the first example in this figure. Here, the OnClick attribute of a button named btnCancel indicates that an event handler named btnCancel_Click will be executed when the Click event of the control is raised.

Often, though, you'll use the Load event handler to load data into the server controls of a form. This is illustrated by the second example in this figure. Here, data from a database is used to change the Text properties of two Label controls and the ImageUrl property of an Image control. This example is taken from the Cart application that you studied in chapter 4, and it shows how easy it is to change the data in server controls.

The third example in this figure presents a method that gets the data from server controls and stores it in a Customer object that is then saved in the Session object. Here, the Text property is used to get the data from two text boxes, and the SelectedValue property is used to get the data from a DropDownList control and a RadioButtonList control. You'll learn more about working with the list controls as you go through this chapter.

You can also use one event handler to handle events from two or more controls. To do that, you name the same event handler in the event attribute of each control. For instance, you can use the same event handler for the Click event of two different buttons. You'll see an example of an event handler like this later in this chapter.

Common control events

Event	Attribute	Controls
Click	OnClick	Button, image button, link button, image map
Command	OnCommand	Button, image button, link button
TextChanged	OnTextChanged	Text box
CheckedChanged	OnCheckedChanged	Check box, radio button
SelectedIndexChanged	OnSelectedIndexChanged	Drop-down list, list box, radio button list, check box list

A Click event hander

The aspx for a button control

```
<asp:Button id="btnCancel" runat="server" Text="Cancel Order"
    OnClick="btnCancel_Click" />
```

The event handler for the Click event of the control

```
protected void btnCancel_Click(object sender, EventArgs e)
{
    Session.Remove("Cart");
    Response.Redirect("Order.aspx");
}
```

A Load event handler that changes the data in server controls

```
protected void Page_Load(object sender, EventArgs e) {
    if (!IsPostBack) ddlProducts.DataBind();
    selectedProduct = this.GetSelectedProduct();
    lblName.Text = selectedProduct.Name;
    lblShortDescription.Text = selectedProduct.ShortDescription;
    imgProduct.ImageUrl = "Images/Products/" + selectedProduct.ImageFile;
}
```

A method that gets data from controls and puts them into a Customer object

```
private void GetCustomerData()
{
    if (customer == null)
        customer = new Customer();
    customer.EmailAddress = txtEmail.Text;
    customer.FirstName = txtFirstName.Text;
    customer.State = ddlState.SelectedValue;
    customer.ContactVia = rblContact.SelectedValue;
    Session["Customer"] = customer;
}
```

Description

- You can code *event handlers* that are called when a button is clicked, a value in a text box is changed, a check box or radio button is checked or unchecked, or the selection in a list is changed. Often, though, you'll process the data in the Load event handler for the page.

Figure 6-2   How to use C# to work with the data in server controls

How to set the focus, default button, tab order, and access keys for a form

Before you learn how to use specific server controls, figure 6-3 shows you how to do some housekeeping for the controls on a form. First, it shows how to set the control that receives the *focus* when the form is rendered in the browser. To do that, you can use the DefaultFocus attribute of the form. In the aspx example in this figure, this attribute is set to the txtName control, which is the first text box on the form, so the user can start entering data in that text box.

Second, this figure shows how to set the *default button* for a form. That's the button that's activated by default when you press the Enter key. To identify that button, you set the DefaultButton attribute of the form. In the aspx example in this figure, this attribute is set to the btnSubmit button. Because of that, the form is posted back to the server when the Enter key is pressed, and the event handler for the Click event of that button is executed.

Third, this figure shows how to set the *tab order* for the controls on a form. That's the order in which the focus is moved from one control to another when the user presses the Tab key. By default, this is the sequence of the controls in the HTML, not including labels, and most browsers include links in the tab order. That means that if you set the focus to the first control on the form, the tab order is likely to work the way you want it to. Otherwise, you can use the TabIndex attribute to set the tab order for specific controls, but you usually won't need to do that.

Last, this figure shows how to set the *access keys* for the controls on a form. These let the user select controls by using keyboard shortcuts. If, for example, you designate F as the access key for an input field that accepts a customer's first name, the user can move the focus directly to this field by pressing Alt+F in the Internet Explorer, Chrome, or Safari browsers.

To create an access key, you add the AccessKey attribute to the control you want to create the keyboard shortcut for. Note, however, that the access keys that you define can conflict with the access keys that are defined for a browser. Because of that, you'll want to be sure to test them with all the modern browsers.

When you use access keys with text boxes that are identified by label elements or Label controls, you can assign the access key to the label and then underline the appropriate letter of the label. In this case, you should also code the for attribute for a label element or the AssociatedControlID attribute for a Label control to specify the control that should receive the focus when the user presses the access key.

You can also specify an access key for a button control as illustrated by the aspx code in this figure. However, you can't underline the access key in a Button control. That's because buttons are rendered by an input element that has "submit" as its type attribute, and that type of element doesn't provide a way to format the text that's displayed by the button.

The form attributes for setting the focus and default button

Attribute	Description
DefaultFocus	Sets the focus to the control that's identified.
DefaultButton	Sets the default button to the button that's identified.

The control attributes for setting the tab order and access keys

Attribute	HTML	Description
AssociatedControlID	for	Associates a label with a control.
TabIndex	tabindex	Sets the tab order for a control with a value of 0 or more. To take a control out of the tab order, use a negative value, like -1.
AccessKey	accesskey	Sets a keyboard key that can be pressed in combination with a control key to move the focus to the control.

The aspx code for a form

```
<form id="form1" runat="server" DefaultFocus="txtName"
      DefaultButton="btnSubmit">
    <p>Please enter your contact information:</p>
    <label for="txtName"><u>N</u>ame:</label>
    <asp:TextBox ID="txtName" runat="server" AccessKey="N"></asp:TextBox>
    <label><u>E</u>mail:</label>
    <asp:TextBox ID="txtEmail" runat="server" AccessKey="E"></asp:TextBox>
    <asp:Button ID="btnSubmit" runat="server" AccessKey="S" Text="Submit"
/>
</form>
```

Description

- To set the control that receives the *focus* when a form is first displayed, you can use the DefaultFocus attribute of the form. You can also use the focus method of C# or JavaScript to set the focus on a control.

- To set the *default button* that causes a form to be submitted when the user presses the Enter key, you can use the DefaultButton attribute of the form.

- The *tab order* for a form is the sequence in which the controls receive the focus when the Tab key is pressed. By default, the tab order is the order of the controls in the HTML, not including labels, and most browsers include links in the default tab order.

- *Access keys* are shortcut keys that the user can press to move the focus to specific controls on a form. If you assign an access key to a label, the focus is moved to the control that's associated with the label since labels can't receive the focus.

- To show the user what the access key for a text box is, you can underline the letter for the key in the label that identifies the text box.

- To use an access key, you press a control key plus the access key. For IE, Chrome, and Safari, use the Alt key. For Firefox, use Alt+Shift. And for Opera, use Alt+Esc to get a list of available access keys.

Figure 6-3   How to set the focus, default button, tab order, and access keys for a form

How to use the common server controls

The topics that follow show you how to use some of the common server controls. For the most part, it's just a matter of dragging a control onto a form and using the Properties window to set the Appearance and Behavior properties (or attributes) that make the control work the way you want it to.

How to use labels and text boxes

Figure 6-4 presents the attributes that you need for working with *labels* and *text boxes*. For both of these controls, the Text attribute specifies the text that's stored in the control.

For a label, the AssociatedControlID attribute specifies the control that the label identifies. Although you don't need to set this attribute for all label controls, you do need to use it when you provide an access key for a label, as shown in the last figure. Note that this attribute is converted to a for attribute in the HTML for the label.

For a text box, the TextMode attribute determines whether the box can accept and display one or more lines of text (SingleLine or MultiLine). Then, for a multiline text box, you can use the Rows attribute to specify the number of lines that are shown in the text box and the Wrap attribute to specify whether the lines are automatically wrapped when they exceed the width of the box.

For both single and multiline text boxes, you can use the MaxLength attribute to specify the maximum number of characters that the user can enter into the box. You can also use the Columns attribute to specify the width of the box in characters. Although you can also use CSS to set the appearance of a text box, including its width, please note that ASP.NET generates an HTML textarea element for a multiline text box, not an input element.

For a SingleLine control (the default), the TextMode attribute can be used to specify the HTML type attribute for the input element that's generated for the control. If, for example, you set the TextMode attribute to Password, the characters that the user enters are masked so they can't be read.

Beyond that, the TextMode attribute can be used to specify the HTML5 type attributes that are listed in this figure. For instance, the TextMode attribute can be set to "email" if the text box is supposed to get an email address, and it can be set to tel if the text box is supposed to get a telephone number. For semantic reasons, it's good to set these HTML5 attributes because they indicate what type of data each control is for.

At present, though, the browser support for the HTML5 type attributes varies from one browser to another. At this writing, for example, Firefox, Chrome, and Opera support the email type by providing automatic data validation for the entry in the text box, but Internet Explorer and Safari treat an email text box just like any other text box. Similarly, Opera fully supports the datetime type by offering a calendar widget when the text box receives the focus, but the other browsers treat a datetime text box just like any other text box.

In contrast, the browsers for mobile devices do a better job of supporting the HTML5 type attributes. For instance, the iPhone and iPad support the email and

Common label attributes

Attribute	HTML	Description
AssociatedControlID	for	Associates a label with a control. Sometimes, this attribute is required, like when working with check boxes and radio buttons.
Text		The text content of the label.

Common text box attributes

Attribute	Description
TextMode	The type of text box. SingleLine (the default) creates a standard text box, MultiLine creates a text box that has more than one line of text, and Password causes the characters that are entered to be masked. This attribute can also be used to generate the HTML5 type attribute for the input element that is rendered for a text box.
Text	The text content of the text box.
MaxLength	The maximum number of characters that can be entered into the text box.
Wrap	Determines whether or not text wraps automatically when it reaches the end of a line in a multiline text box. The default is True.
ReadOnly	Determines whether the user can change the text in the text box. The default value is False, which means that the text can be changed.
Columns	The width of the text box in characters. The actual width is based on the font that's used for the entry.
Rows	The height of a multiline text box in lines. The default value is 0, which sets the height to a single line.

TextMode values for the HTML5 type attributes for input elements

| email | url | tel | number | range |
| datetime | time | search | color | |

The aspx for a label and a multiline text box

```
<label for="txtMessage">Please enter any special instructions</label>
<asp:TextBox ID="txtMessage" runat="server" Rows="5" TextMode="MultiLine">
</asp:TextBox>
```

The aspx for a text box that gets an email address

```
<asp:TextBox ID="txtEmail" runat="server" TextMode="Email"></asp:TextBox>
```

Description

- The HTML5 TextMode values get rendered as type attributes for input elements. For semantic reasons, it's good to use these attributes because they indicate what type of data each control is for.

- At present, the HTML5 type values are supported at varied levels by desktop and laptop browsers, but mobile devices provide better support. For instance, most mobile devices adjust the keyboard for the email, url, and tel types to make data entry easier.

Figure 6-4   How to work use labels and text boxes

tel types by displaying a keyboard that is optimized for email or phone entries. For that reason, we recommend that you use the TextMode attribute to set the HTML5 type attributes for TextBox controls. This can only help because the HTML5 type attributes are ignored if they aren't supported.

How to use check boxes and radio buttons

Figure 6-5 shows how to use the controls for *check boxes* or *radio buttons*. The main difference between these two types of controls is that only one radio button in a group can be selected, but check boxes are independent so more than one can be checked.

To create a group of radio buttons, you specify the same name for the GroupName attribute of each button in the group. If you want to create two or more groups of radio buttons on a single form, you use a different group name for each group. Note, however, that if you don't specify a group name for a radio button, that button won't be a part of any group. Instead, it will be processed independently of any other radio buttons on the form.

To specify whether a radio button or check box should be checked when a form is rendered in a browser, you use the Checked attribute. But since only one radio button in a group can be selected, you should only set the Checked attribute to True for one button. If you set this property to True for more than one button in a group, the last one will be selected.

If you want to use C# to get the value of a check box (whether it's checked or unchecked) whenever the user changes it, you can use the code in the check box example in this figure. This event handler is executed whenever the value of the check box changes. Then, the one statement in this handler assigns the value of the checked property of the check box to the NewProductInfo property of a customer object. That value will either be true or false, depending on whether or not the box is checked.

If you want to use C# to get the value of a radio button whenever the user selects it, you can use the code in the first radio button example in this figure. Here, the event handler for the CheckedChanged event of the rdoTwitter button is executed. Since this event only occurs when the user selects the button, the one statement in this handler assigns a value of "Twitter" to the ContactBy property of a customer object.

The second radio button example shows how you can use if statements to find out which radio button in a group has been selected. Here, the first if statement tests whether the button with an id of "rdoTwitter" is selected. In this statement, the condition is just the checked property of the control, which tests whether that property is true. If it is. the code sets the ContactBy property of a customer object to "Twitter". Then, the second statement tests whether the second button is checked, and it sets the ContactBy property to Facebook if it is. Since only one of these buttons can be checked, only one of the conditions in these if statements can be true.

If you use CSS to format check boxes and radio buttons, remember that each one is rendered as in input element followed by a label element that contains

Common check box and radio button attributes

Attribute	Description
Text	The text that's displayed next to the check box or radio button.
Checked	Indicates whether the check box or radio button is selected. The default is False.
GroupName	The name of the group that the radio button belongs to (not used for check boxes).

Three check boxes and two radio buttons in a browser

The aspx code for the three check boxes

```
<asp:CheckBox ID="chkNewProducts" runat="server" Text="New products" />
<asp:CheckBox ID="chkRevisions" runat="server" Text="New Revisions" />
<asp:CheckBox ID="chkSpecial" runat="server" Text="Special offers" />
```

C# code that gets the value of the first check box whenever it changes

```
protected void chkNew_CheckedChanged(object sender, EventArgs e)
{
    customer.NewProductInfo = chkNewProducts.checked;
}
```

The aspx code for the two radio buttons

```
<asp:RadioButton ID="rdoTwitter" runat="server"
    Checked="True" GroupName="ContactBy" Text="Twitter" />
<asp:RadioButton ID="rdoFacebook" runat="server"
    GroupName="ContactBy" Text="Facebook" />
```

C# code that gets the value of a radio button when it is turned on

```
protected void rdoTwitter_CheckedChanged(object sender, EventArgs e)
{
    customer.ContactBy = "Twitter";
}
```

Two if statements that set a value for the checked radio button

```
if (rdoTwitter.checked) { customer.ContactBy = "Twitter"; }
if (rdoFacebook.checked) { customer.ContactBy = "Facebook"; }
```

Description

- A *check box* displays a single option that the user can either check or uncheck.
- *Radio buttons* present a group of options from which the user can select just one.
- For a check box, the CheckedChanged event is raised whenever its checked property is changed. For a radio button, this event is raised only when its checked property is changed to checked.
- To determine whether a check box or radio button is selected, test its checked property.

Figure 6-5   How to use check boxes and radio buttons

the text. Since this is the reverse of how labels and input elements are normally sequenced, this can make your CSS selectors more complicated. As you will see, however, check box lists and radio button lists can simplify the CSS.

How to use image and hyperlink controls

Figure 6-6 shows how to use an *image control*. You've seen this control used to display a product image in the Shopping Cart application of chapter 4. To do that, you just set the ImageURL control to the URL of the image that you want displayed.

For user accessibility, though, it's also good to set the AlternateText attribute of an image control. That way, an assistive device for a visually-impaired user can read a description of the control.

If you need to set the width or height of an image, you can set the Width or Height attribute. Otherwise, the image will be displayed at its full size, unless the width or height is specified by CSS. In general, though, the images that you use should be the size that you want so you shouldn't have to set their widths or heights. To convert the images to the right size, you can use an image editor.

This figure also shows how to use a *hyperlink control*. This control navigates to the web page specified in the NavigateUrl attribute when the user clicks the control. To display text for a hyperlink control, you set the Text attribute or code the text as content between the start and end tags. Either way, the text is underlined by default, although you can use CSS to change that.

The other alternative is to display an image for a hyperlink. To do that, you set the ImageUrl attribute to the URL of the image you want to display. Then, the control navigates to the web page that's specified when the user clicks on the image.

Remember, though, that you shouldn't use these controls unless the images or links are going to be changed by C# code based on the actions of the user. Otherwise, you should use an HTML img element to display an image and an <a> element for a link.

Common image attributes

Attribute	Description
ImageUrl	The absolute or relative URL of the image.
AlternateText	The text that's used in place of the image if the browser can't display the image.
Width	The width of the image.
Height	The height of the image.

The aspx for an image control

```
<asp:Image ID="imgProduct" runat="server" />
```

C# code that sets the URL and alternate text of an image control

```
imgProduct.ImageUrl = "Images/Products/" + selectedProduct.ImageFile;
imgProduct.AlternateText = selectedProduct.AlternateText;
```

The Common hyperlink attributes

Attribute	Description
NavigateUrl	The absolute or relative URL of the page that's displayed when the control is clicked.
Text	The text that's displayed for the control.
ImageUrl	The absolute or relative URL of the image that's displayed for the control.

A hyperlink in a browser

Go to our web site

The aspx for the hyperlink control

```
<asp:HyperLink ID="link1" runat="server"
    NavigateUrl="http://www.murach.com">Go to our web site
</asp:HyperLink>
```

Description

- An *image control* displays a graphic image, typically in GIF (Graphic Interchange Format), JPEG (Joint Photographic Experts Group), or PNG (Portable Network Graphics) format.

- If you don't specify the Height or Width attributes of an image control, the image will be displayed at full size unless the size is specified by CSS.

- When a *hyperlink control* is clicked, it navigates to another web page or another location on the same page control. The attributes let you display either text or an image for the link.

Figure 6-6   How to use image and hyperlink controls

How to use the file upload control

Figure 6-7 shows how to use a *file upload control*. This control lets a user upload one or more files to a web site. As this figure shows, this control is rendered as a text box that lets the user enter the path of each file to be uploaded, plus a Browse button that displays a dialog box that lets the user locate and select a file so the path is automatically put into the text box.

To upload the selected file or files, you must also provide a separate control that does a postback, like the Upload button in this figure. When the user clicks this button, the page is posted and the paths for the files that have been selected are sent to the server along with the HTTP request.

The first example in this figure shows the aspx code that declares a file upload control and an Upload button. Note here that the file upload control doesn't include an attribute that specifies where the file should be saved on the server. That's because the file upload control doesn't automatically save the uploaded file. Instead, you must write code that calls the SaveAs method of this control. The second example in this figure shows how to write this code.

Before you call the SaveAs method, you should test the HasFile property to make sure the user has selected a file. If the user has selected a valid file and it was successfully uploaded to the server, the HasFile property will be True. Then, you can use the FileName property to get the name of the selected file, and you can combine the file name with the path where you want the file saved. In this figure, the file is stored in the C:\Uploads directory.

To illustrate the use of the PostedFile.ContentLength property, the event handler in this figure uses this property to get the size of the uploaded file. Then, it displays this size in the message for the successful upload.

If you use the AllowMultiple attribute with the file upload control, the user can select more than one file for uploading. This ASP.NET attribute gets rendered as the HTML5 multiple attribute, so some browsers don't support it. For instance, IE 9 doesn't support it, but IE 10 does. For this reason, you may want to put off using the AllowMultiple attribute until it has broader support. For more information about using it and for examples that use it, you can search the Internet.

An attribute of the file upload control

Attribute	Description
`AllowMultiple`	If True, the user can upload more than one file.

Properties and methods of the FileUpload class

Property	Description
`HasFile`	If True, the user has selected a file to upload.
`FileName`	The name of the file to be uploaded.
`PostedFile`	The HttpPostedFile object that represents the file that was posted. You can use this object's ContentLength property to determine the size of the posted file.

Method	Description
`SaveAs(string)`	Saves the posted file to the specified path.

A file upload control in a browser

The aspx code for the file upload control

```
File upload:<br />
<asp:FileUpload ID="FileUpload1" runat="server" /><br /><br />
<asp:Button ID="btnUpload" runat="server" Text="Upload"
    OnClick="btnUpload_Click" /><br /><br />
```

The Click event handler for the Upload button

```
protected void btnUpload_Click(object sender, EventArgs e
{
    if (FileUpload1.HasFile)
    {
        string path = "C:\\Uploads\\" + FileUpload1.FileName;
        FileUpload1.SaveAs(path);
        lblMessage.Text = "File uploaded to " + path + "\n" +
            "File size is " + FileUpload1.PostedFile.ContentLength;
    }
}
```

Description

- The *file upload control* displays a text box and a Browse button that lets the user browse the client computer's file system to locate a file to be uploaded.

- Because the file upload control doesn't provide a button to upload the file, you must provide a button or other control to post the page. Then, in the button's Click event handler, you must call the SaveAs method of the file upload control to save the file.

Figure 6-7   How to use the file upload control

How to use the button controls

Most web forms have at least one button control that the user can click to submit the form to the server for processing. That button is commonly called a *submit button*. In the topics that follow, you'll learn how to use all three of the ASP.NET button controls: buttons, link buttons, and image buttons.

How to use buttons, link buttons, and image buttons

Figure 6-8 presents the three types of button controls. These controls differ only in how they appear to the user. This is illustrated by the three buttons shown in this figure. As you can see, a *button* displays text within a rectangular area. A *link button* displays text that looks like a hyperlink. And an *image button* displays an image.

This figure also presents the aspx for the three buttons that are illustrated. For the button and link button, the Text attribute provides the text that's displayed for the control. For the image button, the ImageUrl attribute provides the URL address of the image that's displayed on the button. To make an image button accessible to the visually impaired, you should also code its AlternateText attribute.

When a user clicks one of the button controls, ASP.NET raises two events: Click and Command. Then, you can provide event handlers for one or both of these events. In this figure, for example, you can see an event handler for the Click event of the Add to Cart button.

Note that the event handler for the Click event receives two arguments. The sender argument represents the control that was clicked. Because this argument has a type of object, you need to cast it to a button control if you want to access the properties and methods of the control. You might want to do that, for example, if you code a method that handles the processing for more than one button. Then, you can use the ID property of the control to determine which button was clicked.

The second argument that's passed to the event handler of a Click event is the e argument, which contains information about the event. You're most likely to use that argument with an image button control to determine where the user clicked on the image. To do that, you can use the X and Y properties of the e argument, which return the X and Y coordinates for where on the image the user clicked.

Of course, the Click and Command event handlers are executed only if the page posts back to itself. In contrast, if a value is specified for the PostBackUrl attribute, the page at the specified URL is executed and displayed. This is the cross-page posting feature you learned about in chapter 4.

Common attributes for Button, LinkButton, and ImageButton controls

Attribute	Description
Text	(Button and LinkButton only) The text displayed by the button. For a LinkButton control, the text can be coded as content between the start and end tags or as the value of the Text attribute.
ImageUrl	(ImageButton only) The image displayed for the button.
AlternateText	(ImageButton only) The text displayed if the browser can't display the image.
CausesValidation	If True (the default), page validation occurs when the button is clicked.
CommandName	An object that's passed to the Command event when a user clicks the button.
CommandArgument	An object that's passed to the Command event when a user clicks the button.
PostBackUrl	The URL of the page that is requested when the user clicks the button.

Button, LinkButton, and ImageButton controls

The aspx for the three buttons

```
<asp:Button ID="btnAdd" runat="server" Text="Add to Cart"
    OnClick="btnAdd_Click" />
<asp:LinkButton ID="lbtnCheckOut" runat="server"
    PostBackUrl="~/CheckOut1.aspx">Check Out</asp:LinkButton>
<asp:ImageButton ID="ibtnCart" runat="server" AlternateText="Cart"
    ImageUrl="~/Images/cart.gif" PostBackUrl="~/Cart.aspx" />
```

An event handler for the Click event of a button control

```
protected void btnAdd_Click(object sender, EventArgs e)
{
    this.AddInvoice();
    Response.Redirect("~/Confirmation.aspx");
}
```

Description

- The *button*, *link button*, and *image button* controls are *submit buttons*.
- If the PostBackUrl attribute isn't coded for one of these buttons, the page is posted back to the server when the button is clicked, and the Click and Command events are raised. You can code event handlers for either or both of these events.
- If the PostBackUrl attribute is coded for one of these buttons, the page specified in the PostBackUrl attribute is loaded and executed.
- Two arguments are passed to the Click event handler: sender and e. Sender is the control that the user clicked, and e contains information about the events. For instance, the X and Y properties return the X and Y coordinates for where on the image the user clicked.

Figure 6-8   How to use buttons, link buttons, and image buttons

How to use the Command event

Figure 6-9 shows how you can use the Command event to process a group of button controls with a single event handler. Like the Click event, this event receives both a sender argument and an e argument. In this case, though, the e argument represents a CommandEventArgs object.

The two properties of the CommandEventArgs class are shown in this figure. You can use these properties to get the CommandName and CommandArgument properties of a control. When you create a button control, you can set the CommandName and CommandArgument properties to any string value. Then, you can test them in the Command event handler to determine how the application should respond when the user clicks the button.

The example in this figure illustrates how this works. The first part of the example shows the aspx code for four button controls. Note here that a different CommandName value is assigned to each button. Note too that the same event handler is named in the OnCommand attributes. That way, the same event handler will handle the Command event of all four controls. Although you can also assign CommandArgument values to each control, that isn't needed for this example.

The second part of this example shows an event handler that processes the Command event of all four controls. To do that, it uses a switch statement that tests the value of the CommandName property of the e argument, and calls a different method for each value. Since this value indicates which button was clicked, the effect is to call the right method for the button that was clicked.

Properties of the CommandEventArgs class

Property	Description
CommandName	The value in the CommandName property for the control that generated the Command event.
CommandArgument	The value in the CommandArgument property for the control that generated the Command event.

Four buttons in a browser

The aspx for the four buttons with CommandName attributes

```
<asp:Button ID="btnFirst" runat="server" Text="<<"
    CommandName="First" OnCommand="NavigationButtons_Command" />
<asp:Button ID="btnPrevious" runat="server" Text="<"
    CommandName="Previous" OnCommand="NavigationButtons_Command" />
<asp:Button ID="btnNext" runat="server" Text=">"
    CommandName="Next" OnCommand="NavigationButtons_Command" />
<asp:Button ID="btnLast" runat="server" Text=">>"
    CommandName="Last" OnCommand="NavigationButtons_Command" />
```

An event handler for the Command events of the buttons

```
protected void NavigationButtons_Command(object sender, CommandEventArgs e)
{
    switch (e.CommandName)
    {
        case "First":
            this.GoToFirstRow();
            break;
        case "Previous":
            this.GoToPreviousRow();
            break;
        case "Next":
            this.GoToNextRow();
            break;
        case "Last":
            this.GoToLastRow();
            break;
    }
}
```

Description

- The Command event is raised whenever a user clicks a button control. It can be used instead of the Click event when you want to use one event handler for a group of buttons.

- The e argument that's passed to a Command event handler is a CommandEventArgs object. It has properties for the CommandName and CommandArgument properties of the control that was clicked.

- When a button is clicked, the Click event is raised before the Command event.

Figure 6-9   How to use the Command event

How to use the list controls

If you look back to figure 6-1, you can see that ASP.NET provides five different list controls. The topics that follow will show you how to use them.

How to create drop-down lists and list boxes

Figure 6-10 presents the attributes for creating *drop-down lists* and *list boxes* as well as the items that they contain. To illustrate, the aspx code in this figure creates a list box with four list items that lets the user select more than one item. Also, the first item in the list is selected when the list is rendered in a browser.

Note here that the Value attribute for a form only has to be coded when the value is different from the content for the list item. That's true for the third item in the list because it's content is "Text Message" and its value is "Text". In contrast, the values for the other three controls are the same as their content so the Value attributes aren't required.

After you add any list control to a form, you can use the Collection Editor to add the items for the control. In fact, the items in the aspx code were generated from the items in the Collection Editor in this figure. The easiest way to start the Collection Editor for a list control is to click on the control's smart tag and select Edit Items.

When you first display the ListItem Collection Editor, the list is empty. Then, you can click the Add button below the Members list to add an item to the list. When you do, the item appears in the Members list and its properties appear in the Properties list. The first property lets you disable a list item so it doesn't appear in the list. The other three properties correspond to those in the second table in this figure. When you set the Text property for an item, the Value property defaults to the same value, but you can change that if that isn't what you want.

Common attributes of list box controls

Property	Description
Rows	Specifies the number of items that are displayed in a list box at one time. If all of the items can't be displayed, a scroll bar is added to the list box.
SelectionMode	Indicates whether a list box allows one (Single) or more (Multiple) selections.

Common attributes of list items

Property	Description
Text	The text that's displayed for the list item.
Value	A string value associated with the list item.
Selected	Indicates whether the item is selected.

The aspx for a list box

```
<asp:ListBox ID="lstContactVia" runat="server" SelectionMode="Multiple">
    <asp:ListItem Selected="True">Twitter</asp:ListItem>
    <asp:ListItem>Facebook</asp:ListItem>
    <asp:ListItem Value="Text">Text Message</asp:ListItem>
    <asp:ListItem>Email</asp:ListItem>
</asp:ListBox>
```

The Collection Editor for creating and editing lists

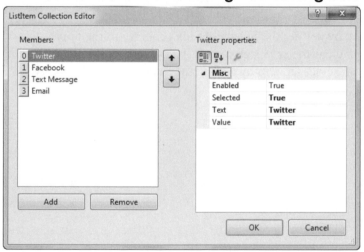

Description

- A *drop-down list* lets the user select one item in the last. A *list box* lets the user select one or more items in the list.
- To use the Collection Editor to add or edit the items in any list control, select Edit Items from the smart tag menu for the control. Or, select the control and then click the ellipsis button that appears when you select the Items property in the Properties window.

Figure 6-10   How to create drop-down lists and list boxes

How to use the properties
for working with list controls

Figure 6-11 presents some common properties for working with list controls. As you just saw, these controls contain ListItem objects that define the items in the list. Then, you can use the properties in the first table in this figure to get the selected ListItem object, the index of the selected object, or the value of the selected object.

This is illustrated by the examples in this figure. All three are for drop-down lists, but they work the same for any type of list control. Here, the first example gets the value of the selected item in the list. And the second example gets the text for the selected item in the list.

The third example gets the value of the selected item right after it is changed because it is coded in the event handler for a list control's SelectedIndexChanged event. This event occurs any time the item that's selected changes between posts to the server. If you want the page to post immediately when the user selects an item, you should set the AutoPostBack property of the control to True.

By default, the SelectedIndex property of a drop-down list is set to zero, which means that the first item is selected. In contrast, the SelectedIndex property of a list box is set to -1 by default, which means that none of the items in the list are selected. Then, you can check if the user has selected an item in a list box by using code like this:

```
if (lstContactVia.SelectedIndex > -1) { ... }
```

You can also select an item by setting the SelectedIndex property to the appropriate index value. You can clear the selection from a list box by setting this property to -1. And you can select an item by setting the SelectedValue property to the appropriate value.

Common properties of list controls

Property	Description
SelectedItem	The ListItem object for the selected item, or the ListItem object for the item with the lowest index if more than one item is selected in a list box.
SelectedIndex	The index of the selected item, or the index of the first selected item if more than one item is selected in a list box. If no item is selected in a list box, the value of this property is -1.
SelectedValue	The value of the selected item, or the value of the first selected item if more than one item is selected in a list box. If no item is selected in a list box, the value of this property is an empty string ("").

A common event of all list controls

Event	Description
SelectedIndexChanged	This event is raised when the user selects a different item in a list.

The aspx code for a drop-down list

```
<asp:DropDownList ID="ddlDay" runat="server">
    <asp:ListItem Value="1">Sunday</asp:ListItem>
    <asp:ListItem Value="2">Monday</asp:ListItem>
    <asp:ListItem Value="3">Tuesday</asp:ListItem>
    <asp:ListItem Value="4">Wednesday</asp:ListItem>
    <asp:ListItem Value="5">Thursday</asp:ListItem>
    <asp:ListItem Value="6">Friday</asp:ListItem>
    <asp:ListItem Value="7">Saturday</asp:ListItem>
</asp:DropDownList>
```

C# code that gets the value of the selected item in the drop-down list

```
int dayNumber = Convert.ToInt32(ddlDay.SelectedValue);
```

C# code that gets the text for the selected item in the drop-down list

```
string dayName = ddlDay.SelectedItem.Text;
```

C# code that uses the SelectedIndexChanged event of the drop-down list

```
protected void ddlDay_SelectedIndexChanged(object sender, EventArgs e)
{
    int dayNumber = Convert.ToInt32(ddlDay.SelectedValue);
}
```

Description

- The properties of a list control let you get the selected ListItem object, the index of the selected object, or the value of the selected object.

Figure 6-11   How to use the properties for working with list controls

How to use the members for list item collections

Figure 6-12 presents some common members for working with a collection of list item objects. To get the item at a specific index, for example, you can use the indexer. And to get a count of the number of items in the collection, you can use the Count property.

The method in this summary that you're most likely to use is the Add method. It adds an item to the end of a collection. The examples in this figure show two different ways you can use this method.

The first example shows the for loop that was used in the Future Value application of chapter 2 to load the values from 50 to 500 into a drop-down list. Here, the Add method is used to add an item with the specified string value. When you code the Add method this way, the value you specify is assigned to both the Text and Value properties of the item.

However, if you want to assign different values to the Text and Value properties of an item, you use the technique in the second example. Here, a new list item object is created with two string values. The first string is stored in the Text property, and the second string is stored in the Value property. Then, the Add method is used to add the new item to the list item collection of the drop-down list.

Notice in both of these examples that the Items property is used to refer to the collection of list item objects for the control. You can also use the SelectedIndex property of a control to refer to an item at a specific index. For example, you could use a statement like this to remove the selected item from a drop-down list:

```
ddlDay.Items.RemoveAt(ddlDay.SelectedIndex);
```

Common property of a list control

Property	Description
Items	The collection of ListItem objects that represents the items in the control. This property returns a ListItemCollection object.

Common members of a ListItemCollection object

Property	Description
Count	The number of items in the collection.

Indexer	Description
[integer]	A ListItem object that represents the item at the specified index.

Method	Description
Add(string)	Adds a new item to the end of the collection, and assigns the string value to both the Text and Value properties of the item.
Add(ListItem)	Adds the specified list item to the end of the collection.
Insert(integer, string)	Inserts an item at the specified index location in the collection, and assigns the specified string value to the Text property of the item.
Insert(integer, ListItem)	Inserts the specified list item at the specified index in the collection.
Remove(string)	Removes the item whose Value property equals the specified string.
Remove(ListItem)	Removes the specified list item from the collection.
RemoveAt(integer)	Removes the item at the specified index from the collection.
Clear()	Removes all the items from the collection.

C# code that loads items into a drop-down list using strings

```
for (int i = 50; i <= 500; i += 50)
{
    ddlMonthlyInvestment.Items.Add(i.ToString());
}
```

C# code that loads items into a drop-down list using ListItem objects

```
ddlDay.Items.Add(New ListItem("Sunday", "1"));
ddlDay.Items.Add(New ListItem("Monday", "2"));
ddlDay.Items.Add(New ListItem("Tuesday", "3"));
```

Description

- The ListItemCollection object is a collection of ListItem objects. Each ListItem object represents one item in the list.
- Items in a ListItemCollection object are numbered from 0.
- When you load items into a list box using strings, both the Text and Value properties of the list item are set to the string value you specify.
- To set the Text and Value properties of a list item to different values, you must create a list item object and then add that item to the collection.

Figure 6-12   How to use the members for list item collections

How to use check box lists and radio button lists

Earlier in this chapter, you learned how to use radio buttons and check boxes. But ASP.NET also provides *check box lists* and *radio button lists* that you can use to create lists of check boxes and radio buttons. As figure 6-13 shows, these controls work like the other list controls.

In the aspx code for the check box list and radio button list in this figure, you can see the ListItem objects. You can use the Collection Editor to add these objects after you add a check box list or radio button list to a form. Like check boxes and radio buttons, more than one item can be checked in a check box list, but only one item can be selected in a radio button list. You can also use the SelectedValue property to get or set the value of the selected item in a radio button list, but note in the first example that this code is simpler for a radio button list than it is when you're using radio buttons in a group.

Like a list box, you can select more than one item in a check box list. Because of that, you'll usually determine whether an item in the list is selected by using the Selected property of the item. This is illustrated in the second example in this figure. Here, the Items property of a check box list is used to get the item at index 0. Then, the Selected property of that item is used to determine if the item is selected. Notice here that you can't refer to individual check boxes by name when you use a check box list.

To set the layout of the items in a radio button or check box list, you use the attributes shown in this figure. The RepeatLayout attribute determines how ASP.NET aligns the buttons or check boxes in a list. In most cases, you'll use a table, which is the default. Then, ASP.NET generates the input and label elements for the boxes or buttons within the rows and columns of the table, which should limit the need for CSS formatting.

Similarly, the RepeatDirection attribute determines whether the controls are listed horizontally or vertically. And the RepeatColumns attribute specifies the number of columns in the radio button or check box list. If you experiment with these, you should get the boxes and buttons aligned the way you want them. And this can be much easier than using CSS to align check boxes and radio buttons that aren't in lists.

How to use bulleted lists

The BulletedList control lets you create a *bulleted* or *numbered list*. It works like the other list controls, but it has different attributes. For instance, the BulletStyle attribute determines whether the list will be bulleted or numbered, and the BulletImageUrl, FirstBulletNumber, and DisplayMode attributes provide other formatting details. If you experiment with these attributes, you should be able to get the results that you want. Unless the items in the lists are going to change, though, you should use HTML instead of the server control.

Attributes for formatting radio button and check box lists

Attribute	Description
RepeatLayout	Specifies whether ASP.NET should use a table (Table), an unordered list (UnorderedList), an ordered list (OrderedList), or normal HTML flow (Flow) to format the list when it renders the control. The default is Table.
RepeatDirection	Specifies the direction in which the controls should be repeated. The available values are Horizontal and Vertical. The default is Vertical.
RepeatColumns	Specifies the number of columns for the controls. The default is 0.

A check box list and a radio button list in a browser

Please let me know about:
☑ New products   ☐ Special offers   ☐ New editions
Please contact me via:
◉ Twitter
○ Facebook

The aspx code for the check box list

```
Please let me know about:
<asp:CheckBoxList ID="cblAboutList"  runat="server"
    RepeatDirection="Horizontal">
    <asp:ListItem Value="New" Selected="True">New products</asp:ListItem>
    <asp:ListItem Value="Special">Special offers</asp:ListItem>
    <asp:ListItem Value="Revisions">New editions</asp:ListItem>
</asp:CheckBoxList>
```

A statement that checks if the first item in a check box list is selected

```
if (cblAboutList.Items[0].Selected) ...
```

The aspx code for the radio button list

```
Please contact me via:
<asp:RadioButtonList ID="rblContactVia" runat="server" >
    <asp:ListItem Selected="True">Twitter</asp:ListItem>
    <asp:ListItem>Facebook</asp:ListItem>
</asp:RadioButtonList>
```

A statement that gets the value of the selected item in a radio button list

```
customer.ContactVia = rblContactVia.SelectedValue;
```

Description

- A *radio button list* presents a list of mutually exclusive options.
- A *check box list* presents a list of independent options.
- These controls contain a collection of ListItem objects that you refer to through the Items property of the control. These controls also have SelectedItem, SelectedIndex, and SelectedValue properties.

Figure 6-13   How to use check box lists and radio button lists

A CheckOut page
that uses server controls

Now, to show you how the server controls can be used in a web page, this chapter ends by presenting a first CheckOut page of the Shopping Cart application.

The user interface and link elements

Figure 6-14 shows the user interface for the first CheckOut page of the application. It starts with text boxes and a drop-down list that are identified by HTML label elements. Then, after the last text box, this form uses a check box list and a radio button list. They are followed by two Button controls and a LinkButton control.

Most of the formatting for this page is done by the CSS in the two files that are referred to in the link elements of the head section of the HTML. The first is the Main.css file that does the basic formatting for all of the pages in the web site. The second provides any other formatting that's needed by the CheckOut page.

Some of the layout for the check box and radio button lists is done by the tables that ASP.NET has generated for these controls. Specifically, the input and label elements that are generated for the check boxes and radio buttons are stored in the cells of tables. Although the CSS in the Checkout.css file has made some minor adjustments to this formatting, the primary layout comes from the attributes of these controls.

In this figure, you can see a message that's displayed for the state code text box because the user didn't select a value from the list. In fact, all of the text boxes and the drop-down list have required field validators. They aren't shown in the aspx code in the next figure, though, because the focus of this chapter is server controls.

A CheckOut page that uses standard server controls

The head section in the HTML for the page

```
<head runat="server">
    <title>Chapter 6: Shopping Cart</title>
    <link href="Styles/Main.css" rel="stylesheet" />
    <link href="Styles/CheckOut.css" rel="stylesheet" />
</head>
```

Description

- This is the first CheckOut page for the Shopping Cart application.
- HTML label elements are used to identify all of the server controls on this page. The last two controls before the buttons are a check box list and a radio button list.
- Most of the page layout is done by the two CSS files that are identified in the head section of the HTML. However, most of the formatting for the check box and radio button lists is done by the way their attributes have been set.
- All of the text boxes and the drop-down list have required field validators, but they aren't shown in the aspx code in the next figure.

Figure 6-14   A CheckOut page that uses standard server controls

The aspx code

Figure 6-15 presents the aspx code for the CheckOut page. Here, you can see the use of the label elements and the server controls. For brevity, though, the required field validators for the text boxes and drop-down list aren't shown.

To start, notice how the attributes for the form element are set. Because the DefaultFocus attribute is set to the first text box on the form, the user will be able to use the Tab key to move from the first text box to those that follow. Because the DefaultButton attribute is set to the Check Out button, the user will be able to press the Enter key to submit the form to the server.

Then, notice that the TextMode attribute of the first text box is set to Email. It becomes the HTML5 type attribute of the input element that is rendered for the text box. Similarly, the TextMode attribute of the phone number text box is set to Tel, although that control isn't included in this aspx code. Both of these attributes indicate what type of data is expected, and the browsers for some mobile devices will display keyboards that are appropriate for those entries.

Of special note is the way the drop-down list uses a SQL data source to add list items for each state to the list. The text that's displayed for each item is the state name, and the value for each item is the state code. The ListItem object that is coded within the drop-down list sets the Text and Value fields for the first item in the list to empty strings. Then, if the user doesn't select an item from the list, a required field validator will be activated so the form won't be submitted to the server.

This code also shows how some of the attributes for server controls are used. For instance, the MaxLength attribute of the text box for the zip code limits the number of characters that can be entered to 5. The RepeatColumns attribute of the check box list is set to 2, and you can see how that is rendered in the previous figure. Similarly, the RepeatDirection attribute of the radio button list is set to Horizontal, and you can see how that is rendered in the previous figure.

The aspx code for the form on the CheckOut page

```
<form id="form1" runat="server" DefaultFocus="txtEmail1"
    DefaultButton="btnCheckOut">
    <h2>Contact information</h2>
    <label>Email: </label>
    <asp:TextBox ID="txtEmail1" runat="server" CssClass="entry"
        TextMode="Email" ></asp:TextBox><br />
    <label>Email Re-entry: </label>
    <asp:TextBox ID="txtEmail2" runat="server" CssClass="entry" >
    </asp:TextBox><br />
    <%-- labels and text boxes for first name, last name, and phone --%>

    <h2>Billing address</h2>
    <%-- labels and text boxes for address and city --%>
    <label>State: </label>
    <asp:DropDownList ID="ddlState" runat="server" CssClass="entry"
        AppendDataBoundItems="True" DataSourceID="SqlDataSource1"
        DataTextField="StateName" DataValueField="StateCode">
        <asp:ListItem Text="" Value="" Selected="True"></asp:ListItem>
    </asp:DropDownList><br />
    <asp:SqlDataSource ID="SqlDataSource1" runat="server"
        ConnectionString="<%$ ConnectionStrings:HalloweenConnection %>"
        SelectCommand="SELECT [StateCode], [StateName] FROM [States]
            ORDER BY [StateCode]"></asp:SqlDataSource>
    <label>Zip code: </label>
    <asp:TextBox ID="txtZip" runat="server" CssClass="entry"
        MaxLength="5"></asp:TextBox>

    <h2>Optional data</h2>
    <div id="optionalData">
        Please let me know about:
        <asp:CheckBoxList ID="cblAboutList"  runat="server"
            RepeatColumns="2">
            <asp:ListItem Value="New">New products</asp:ListItem>
            <asp:ListItem Value="Special">Special offers</asp:ListItem>
            <asp:ListItem Value="Revisions">New editions</asp:ListItem>
            <asp:ListItem Value="Local">Local events</asp:ListItem>
        </asp:CheckBoxList>
        Please contact me via:
        <asp:RadioButtonList ID="rblContactVia" runat="server"
            RepeatDirection="Horizontal">
            <asp:ListItem Selected="True">Twitter</asp:ListItem>
            <asp:ListItem>Facebook</asp:ListItem>
            <asp:ListItem Value="Text">Text Message</asp:ListItem>
            <asp:ListItem>Email</asp:ListItem>
        </asp:RadioButtonList>
    </div>

    <asp:Button ID="btnCheckOut" runat="server" Text="Check Out"
        OnClick="btnCheckOut_Click" CssClass="button" />
    <asp:Button ID="btnCancel" runat="server" Text="Cancel Order"
        CausesValidation="False" OnClick="btnCancel_Click" CssClass="button" />
    <asp:LinkButton ID="lbtnContinueShopping" runat="server"
        PostBackUrl="~/Order.aspx" CausesValidation="False">Continue
        Shopping</asp:LinkButton>
</form>
```

Figure 6-15   The aspx code for the CheckOut page

The code-behind file for the CheckOut page

Figure 6-16 presents the code-behind file for the CheckOut page. The first thing to notice about this code is that it contains a private Customer object. This will store customer information retrieved from Session state or from the page, and it is used by most of the methods in the file.

As you've seen before, the Page_Load event handler method first tests to see whether the page is a postback. If it isn't, that means it's being requested for the first time. In that case, this method gets the Customer object from the Session object if there is one, and it calls the LoadCustomerData method to load the data from the Customer object into the controls of the CheckOut page. Once the data is loaded in to the page's controls, it will be preserved between postbacks in ViewState. That's why you only have to retrieve the customer information from Session the first time the page loads.

In the LoadCustomerData method, you can see how the data from the customer object is loaded into the controls. But note that this is only done if the customer object isn't null. If the object isn't null, it means that the user had entered the data for the first CheckOut page, gone back to the Cart page, and returned to the CheckOut page.

If the user clicks the Check Out button, the btnCheckOut_Click event handler is executed. It first checks to see if the data in the controls is valid. If it is, this method calls the GetCustomerData method to get the data from the controls on the form and save the data in the properties of the customer object. After that, it uses the Response.Redirect method to go to the second CheckOut page.

In the GetCustomerData method, you can see how the statements get the data from the controls and save them in the properties of the customer object. When all of the data has been stored in the customer object, the object is added to the Session object.

On the other hand, if the user clicks the Cancel Order button, the btnCancel_Click event handler is executed. This method removes the Cart and Customer objects from the Session object, and redirects to the Order page.

The code-behind file for capturing the data

```csharp
public partial class CheckOut : System.Web.UI.Page
{
    private Customer customer;
    protected void Page_Load(object sender, EventArgs e)
    {
        if (!IsPostBack)
        {
            customer = (Customer)Session["Customer"];
            this.LoadCustomerData();
        }
    }

    protected void btnCheckOut_Click(object sender, EventArgs e)
    {
        if (Page.IsValid)
        {
            this.GetCustomerData();
            Response.Redirect("~/CheckOut2.aspx");
        }
    }
    protected void btnCancel_Click(object sender, EventArgs e)
    {
        Session.Remove("Cart");
        Session.Remove("Customer");
        Response.Redirect("~/Order.aspx");
    }
    private void LoadCustomerData()
    {
        if (customer != null)
        {
            txtFirstName.Text = customer.FirstName;
            // load data into other text boxes from customer object
            ddlState.SelectedValue = customer.State;
            rblContactVia.SelectedValue = customer.ContactVia;
            cblAboutList.Items[0].Selected = customer.NewProductsInfo;
            cblAboutList.Items[1].Selected = customer.SpecialPromosInfo;
            cblAboutList.Items[2].Selected = customer.NewRevisionsInfo;
            cblAboutList.Items[3].Selected = customer.LocalEventsInfo;
        }
    }
    private void GetCustomerData()
    {
        if (customer == null)
            customer = new Customer();
        customer.FirstName = txtFirstName.Text;
        // get data from the other text boxes and load into customer object
        customer.State = ddlState.SelectedValue;
        customer.ContactVia = rblContactVia.SelectedValue;
        customer.NewProductsInfo = cblAboutList.Items[0].Selected;
        customer.SpecialPromosInfo = cblAboutList.Items[1].Selected;
        customer.NewRevisionsInfo = cblAboutList.Items[2].Selected;
        customer.LocalEventsInfo = cblAboutList.Items[3].Selected;
        Session["Customer"] = customer;
    }
}
```

Figure 6-16   The code-behind file for the CheckOut page

An introduction to the other standard server controls

Now that you've learned how to use the common server controls, you may be wondering what the other controls do and whether you need to learn how to use them. So here's a quick introduction to them.

When and how to use the other standard server controls

The table at the top of figure 6-17 summarizes the other standard server controls that you may be interested in. In particular, the Wizard and MultiView controls let you set up several steps or views that get user entries in a single web form. For instance, you can set up all of the steps of a CheckOut procedure with one Wizard control, as shown in the next figure. One benefit of doing that is you can get the data from all of the steps or views in a single code-behind file.

Of course, you can get the same result by using one web form for each step. You can also get the same result by using one HTML div element for each step and then using jQuery to move from one step to the next. With that approach, all of the data is collected by a single web form, just as it is with a Wizard control.

Similarly, the ASP.NET Calendar control is a useful control. But the jQuery UI DatePicker widget works even better.

The message here is that if you're a professional ASP.NET developer, you should also know how to use jQuery, how to use the jQuery UI (User Interface) *widgets*, and what jQuery *plugins* are available. Then, you can decide whether you want to use an ASP.NET control like the Wizard or use a jQuery approach to get the same result.

If you decide that you want to use one of the other standard server controls, you can search the Internet to get the information and examples that you need for using it. In fact, controls like the Wizard and MultiView controls can work well for quickly prototyping an application. Then, when the prototype is working the way you want it to, you can decide whether you want to keep the application that way or convert it to another approach.

Other standard server controls that you may want to use

Name	Description
Calendar	Displays a calendar that lets the user select a date.
AdRotator	Provides a convenient way to display advertisements on your web pages.
Wizard	Lets you build the steps of a procedure in a single web form.
MultiView	Acts as a container for View controls, and lets you provide two or more views in a single web form.
View	Acts as a container for other controls and HTML.
Panel	Acts as a container for other controls and HTML that can be displayed or hidden as a group.

jQuery UI widgets that you should be aware of

Control	Description
DatePicker	A calendar that can be toggled from a text box or dislayed inline.
Accordion	Collapsible content panels that can be displayed by clicking on a panel's header.
Tabs	A set of tabs that reveals one tab's contents at a time when its tab is clicked.
Dialog	A modal dialog box that is resizable and draggable.

Some common types of jQuery plugins that you should be aware of

Control	Description
Lightbox	Can be used to open a larger version of a thumbnail image, and then lets the user use the next and previous buttons to step through the set of images.
Carousel	Displays one or more images and lets the user use the next and previous buttons to step through the set of images.
Slideshow	Automatically presents one image at a time from a set of images.

Description

* The ASP.NET Calendar control displays a calendar that lets the user select a date, but the jQuery UI control works even better.
* The Wizard and MultiView controls let you provide several different steps or views in a single form, but you can get the same result by using HTML div elements that are manipulated by jQuery.
* The Wizard or MultiView control can be used to quickly prototype the steps or views of an application. Then, if necessary, the steps or views can be redone using jQuery.
* If you're an ASP.NET developer, you should know how to use jQuery, the jQuery UI *widgets*, and jQuery *plugins*. Then, you can decide whether you want to use an ASP.NET control or jQuery to get the results that you want.
* To learn more about using the other ASP.NET controls, you can search the Internet for information and examples, which are plentiful.

Figure 6-17   When and how to use the other standard server controls

How to use the Wizard control

To give you a better idea of how the Wizard control works and how you can use it, figure 6-18 presents an example of this control in use. Here, you can see three steps of a CheckOut procedure. Remember that all of the data collected in these steps is in a single web form, so you can capture all of the data in a single code-behind file.

After you add a Wizard control to a form, you can use the Wizard Collection Editor to add the steps that you want to the Wizard. These are added as WizardStep controls, as shown in the aspx code in this figure. When you're through with the Collection Editor, ASP.NET adds the sidebar links and buttons to the steps that let the user move from one step to another.

At that point, you can add the HTML and controls for each step. You can also use the templates and styles that ASP.NET provides for the controls that are generated by the Wizard. This shows how useful the Wizard Control can be for prototyping. Then, you can decide whether the result is the way you want it, or whether you want to convert it to another approach.

Three steps of a Wizard control

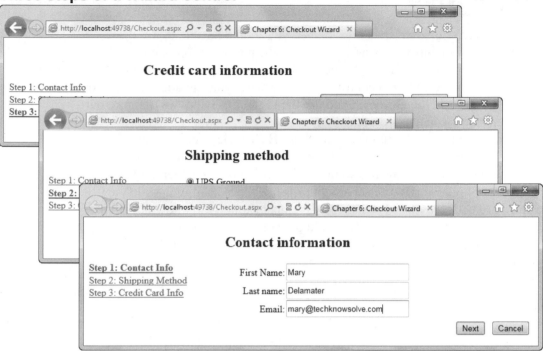

The starting aspx for a Wizard control

```
<asp:Wizard ID="Wizard1" runat="server" ActiveStepIndex="0">
    <WizardSteps>
        <asp:WizardStep runat="server" Title="Step 1">
            <h2>Contact information</h2>
            ...
        </asp:WizardStep>
        <asp:WizardStep runat="server" Title="Step 2">
            <h2>Shipping method</h2>
            ...
        </asp:WizardStep>
        <asp:WizardStep runat="server" Title="Step 3">
            <h2>Credit card information</h2>
            ...
        </asp:WizardStep>
    </WizardSteps>
</asp:Wizard>
```

Description

- To add or remove the steps for a Wizard, you can use the WizardStep Collection Editor. Then, after you set up the steps, you can add the controls and HTML for each of the steps.

- The sidebar that provides the links for the steps and the Next, Previous, and Finish buttons are generated by ASP.NET.

- Because all of the steps are on one web page, you can get the data from the controls for all of the steps in a single code-behind file.

Figure 6-18   How to use the Wizard control

Perspective

Now that you've finished this chapter, you should be able to use the common server controls whenever you need them in your applications. If necessary, you can refer to the figures in this chapter to see what attributes you need to set for the common controls. But otherwise, you can add a control to a form, select it in the Designer, and use the Properties windows to figure out what attributes you need to set.

Remember, though, that you should use HTML elements instead of server controls whenever the data in the elements isn't going to change while the application runs. You may also want to use JavaScript and jQuery, jQuery UI, or jQuery plugins instead of server controls like the Wizard and MultiView controls. That's why every ASP.NET developer should also know how to use HTML, CSS, JavaScript, and jQuery, and that's why you should also have *Murach's HTML5 and CSS3* and *Murach's JavaScript and jQuery* in your professional library.

Terms

server control	file upload control
event handler	submit button
focus	button
default button	link button
tab order	image button
access key	drop-down list
label	list box
text box	check box list
check box	radio button list
radio button	bulleted list
image control	numbered list
hyperlink	

Summary

- The *server controls* in the Standards group of the Visual Studio Toolbox are the ones that you use to get data entries from users and to display data for users. These controls are rendered into HTML elements when a form is displayed in a browser.

- You can code event handlers for the Click and Command events of *buttons*, the TextChanged event of a *text box*, the CheckChanged event of *check boxes* and *radio buttons*, and the SelectedIndexChanged event of list controls like *drop-down lists* and *list boxes*.

- To make it easier for users to work with the controls of a form, you should set the starting *focus* and the *default button* for each form. You should also make sure the *tab order* provides for easy movement through the controls of the form, and you may also want to provide *access keys* for some of the controls.

- In general, you should use HTML elements instead of server controls when the data in the controls isn't going to change. However, you may also want to use server controls when you don't know how to code the HTML elements, even though the data in the controls isn't going to change.

- One of the benefits of using server controls is that they provide properties that make it easy to change their data with C# code. The Properties window in the Designer also makes it easy to set the attributes of the controls.

- With ASP.NET, a list control is treated as a ListItemCollection object that contains ListItem objects. The ListItem Collection Editor makes it easy to create the list items for a list control, and the members of the collection object provide the property, indexer, and methods that let you use C# for working with the items.

- Although ASP.NET provides advanced server controls like the Calendar, Wizard, and MultiView controls, you should be aware that you can get the same or better results by using jQuery, jQuery UI *widgets*, and jQuery *plugins*. Then, you need to decide which approach to use for your web site.

Exercise 6-1   Modify the Check Out page

In this exercise, you'll modify the Check Out page of the Shopping Cart application that's presented in this chapter.

Open, review, and run the Shopping Cart application

1. Open the Ex06Cart web site that's in the aspnet45_cs directory, and review the Order and Cart pages to see that they're like the ones in chapter 4.

2. Test the application to see how it works. Without entering any data on the Check Out page, click the Check Out button to see that all of the text boxes and the drop-down list have required field validators.

3. Enter valid data for all of the fields and click on the Check Out button to go to the CheckOut2 page and note that this displays a page that lists the entries that you made. Then, close the browser and switch to Visual Studio.

4. Review the code in the Customer.cs file in the App_Code folder to see the properties of the Customer object. Then, review the code-behind file for the CheckOut page to see how the user entries are stored in the Customer object and how the Customer object is stored in the Session object. Note that the ContactVia values are stored in a way that differs from figure 6-16.

5. Review the code-behind file for the CheckOut2 page to see how the Customer object is retrieved from the Session object and the properties in the Customer object are displayed on the web page.

Change the radio button list to a list box

6.   In the aspx code for the CheckOut page, comment out the code for the radio button list. Then, add a ListBox control above the commented out code that looks like this:

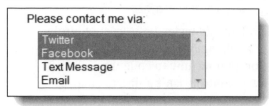

7.   Use the Collection Editor as shown in figure 6-10 to add the items to the list box. Also, set the SelectionMode attribute of the control to Multiple so the user can select more than one item. For formatting, you need to add one br element after the inline text and two after the list box.

8.   Try to run the page, but note the errors that are displayed when you do that. To fix that, comment out the lines in the code-behind file that the messages refer to. Then, test the page to see how the list box looks in the browser. To select one or more items in Internet Explorer, hold down the Ctrl or Shift key as you click on items.

9.   Modify the GetCustomerData method in the code-behind file for the CheckOut page so it sets the ContactVia values in the customer object to the values that the user has selected in the list box. Then, test the application to make sure that the user entries and selections are correctly displayed on the CheckOut2 page.

10.   Modify the LoadCustomerData method in the code-behind file for the CheckOut page so it sets the values in the list box to the ones in the customer object when the page request isn't a postback. Then, test this method by entering valid data in the Check Out form, clicking the Check Out button to save the values in the Session object, and then clicking in sequence: the Back button, the Continue Shopping link, the Go to Cart button, and the Check Out button. If your code works, all of the data should be displayed in the form except for the second email address entry.

7

How to use the validation controls

In chapter 2, you learned the basic skills for using two of the validation controls: the required field validator and the range validator. Now, you'll learn more about using those controls as well as how to use the other validation controls. As you'll see, you can use the validation controls to perform most of the data validation required by web forms.

Introduction to the validation controls

ASP.NET provides six *validation controls* that you can use to validate the data on a web form. You'll learn the basic skills for using these controls in the topics that follow.

How ASP.NET processes the validation controls

Figure 7-1 summarizes the *validation controls* that are available with ASP. NET. As you learned in chapter 2, the first five controls are called *validators*. These are the controls that you use to check that the user has entered valid data into the input controls on a web form. In contrast, you use the validation summary control to display a summary of all the errors on a page.

To refresh your memory about how the validation controls work, this figure summarizes the key points. To start, you should realize that the validation tests are typically done on the client before the page is posted to the server. That way, a round trip to the server isn't required if any invalid data is detected.

In most cases, client-side validation is done when the focus leaves an input control that has validators associated with it. That can happen when the user presses the Tab key to move to the next control or clicks another control to move the focus to that control.

However, the required field validator works a bit differently. When you use this validator, the validation isn't done until the user clicks a button whose CausesValidation property is set to True. The exception is if the user enters a value into an input control and then tries to clear the value. In that case, an error will be detected when the focus leaves the control.

To perform client-side validation, a browser must support JavaScript and JavaScript must be enabled. Because that's the norm, validation is usually done on the client. In case JavaScript isn't enabled in the browser, though, validation is always done on the server when a page is submitted. ASP.NET does this validation after it initializes the page.

When ASP.NET performs the validation tests on the server, it sets the IsValid property of each validator to True or False. In addition, it sets the IsValid property of the page to True or False based on whether the IsValid property of all the input data is true. The IsValid property for the page is usually tested to make sure it's true before the data that has been submitted is processed. In the example in this figure, you can see how this property is tested in the event handler for the Click event for an Add button.

If you want to bypass client-side validation and just perform the validation on the server, you can set the EnableClientScript property of the validation controls to False. Then, the JavaScript for client-side validation isn't generated, and the validation is only done on the server.

The validation controls provided by ASP.NET

Name	Description
RequiredFieldValidator	Checks that an entry has been made.
CompareValidator	Checks an entry against a constant value or the value of another control. Can also be used to check for a specific data type.
RangeValidator	Checks that an entry is within a specified range.
RegularExpressionValidator	Checks that an entry matches a pattern that's defined by a regular expression.
CustomValidator	Checks an entry on the server using C# validation code.
ValidationSummary	Displays a summary of error messages from the other validation controls.

Typical code for processing a page that contains validation controls

```
protected void btnAdd_Click(object sender, EventArgs e)
{
    if (Page.IsValid)
    {
        // code for processing the valid data
    }
}
```

Description

- If a browser has JavaScript enabled, the *validation controls* do their validation on the client. That way, the validation is done and error messages are displayed without the page being posted to the server.

- Validation is always done on the server too, right after the page is initialized, so the validation is done whether or not the browser supports JavaScript.

- Validation is always done when you click a button whose CausesValidation property is set to True. To create a button that doesn't cause validation, you can set this property to False.

- Validation is also done on the client when the focus leaves an input control. The exception is a required field validator, which does its validation only when you click a button whose CausesValidation property is set to True or when you enter a value into a control and then clear and leave the control.

- If a validation control finds invalid data, the IsValid property of that control is set to False and the IsValid property of the page is set to False. These properties can be tested in your C# code.

- If you want to perform validation only on the server, you can set the EnableClientScript properties of the validation controls to False. Then, the JavaScript for validation on the client isn't generated.

Figure 7-1   How ASP.NET processes the validation controls

How to set the attributes of the validators

Figure 7-2 summarizes the common attributes for the validators. These are the ones you can use with any validator. The most important property is the ControlToValidate property, which associates the validator with an input control on the page.

The Display property determines how the error message for a validator is displayed. In most cases, Dynamic works the best because space is only generated for the message when it is displayed. In some cases, though, the other options can be useful.

You use the ErrorMessage and Text properties to specify messages that are displayed when the validator detects an error. You can set one or both of these properties depending on whether you use a validation summary control. If you want the same message in both the validator and the validation summary control, just set the ErrorMessage property. But if you want different messages, set the ErrorMessage property to the message you want in the validation summary control and the Text property to the message you want in the validator.

If the Enabled property of a validator is set to True, the validation test for the validator is performed. But if you want to skip the validation that's done by a validator, you can set this property to False. In contrast, the EnableClientScript property determines whether the client-side JavaScript for the validation is generated. If this property is set to False, the validation is only done on the server.

Besides the attributes in the table in this figure, you will use other attributes for specific controls. You will find most of these in the Behavior category of the Properties window when the validator is selected in the Designer. For instance, you can use the drop-down list for the Operator attribute when you're setting the attributes for a compare validator. You'll learn more about these attributes as you read about specific validators.

Common validator attributes and properties

Property	Description
ControlToValidate	The ID of the control to be validated.
Display	Determines how the error message is to be displayed. Static is the default and allocates space for the message in the page layout. Dynamic allocates space only when an error occurs. None displays errors only in a validation summary control.
Text	The message that's displayed in the validator.
ErrorMessage	The message that's displayed in the validation summary control when the validation fails. This message is also displayed in the validator if the Text property hasn't been set.
Enabled	Indicates whether the validation control is enabled.
EnableClientScript	Indicates whether the validation will be done on the client.
SetFocusOnError	Indicates whether the focus will be moved to the control if it's invalid.
ValidationGroup	Indicates which group the validation control is part of.

The Behavior category in the Properties window for a Compare validator

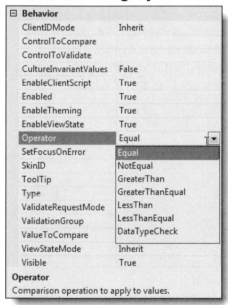

Description

- The Appearance category in the Properties window provides the Display, ErrorMessage, and Text properties.

- The Behavior category provides the attributes that you need for getting the control to work right.

Figure 7-2   How to set the attributes of the validators

How to provide for unobtrusive validation

In chapter 2, you were introduced to *unobtrusive validation*. When it is used, the validation on the client uses jQuery, which is a JavaScript library. The benefit of using jQuery is that it reduces the amount of JavaScript that has to be generated and takes advantage of jQuery features like cross-browser compatibility.

Even though unobtrusive validation is on by default when you start a new web site, it has been turned off in all of the applications that you've studied so far. But now, figure 7-3 shows the easiest way to implement unobtrusive validation. That is, by installing the *NuGet package* for it.

After you use the procedure in this figure to install the NuGet package for jQuery validation, you'll see that several folders and files have been added to the Solution Explorer. First, a dll file has been added to the Bin folder that contains the AspNet.ScriptManager.jQuery assembly that will automatically register the jQuery library with the ScriptManager as "jquery". This registration is what tells ASP.NET where to find the jQuery files.

Second, a Scripts folder has been added that contains three JavaScript files and a map file for jQuery. Third, a packages.config file has been added. This file is used by the NuGet infrastructure to track the versions of installed packages.

Now that you know the easiest way to implement unobtrusive validation, we recommend that you do that for all of your production applications. For most of the applications in this book, however, unobtrusive validation is turned off so the number of folders and files in the Solution Explorer are kept to a minimum.

The Manage NuGet Packages dialog box

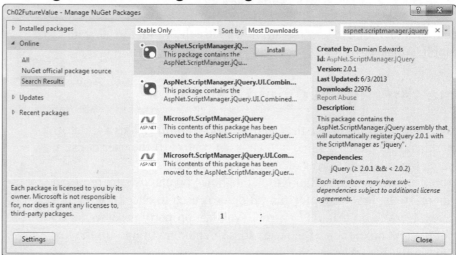

How to install the NuGet package for jQuery validation

- Right-click on the project and select Manage NuGet Packages.

- In the left panel of the dialog box that appears, select Online→NuGet Official Package Source. Next, use the box in the upper right to search for AspNet. ScriptManager.jQuery. Then, click on the Install button.

The Solution Explorer after the NuGet package is installed

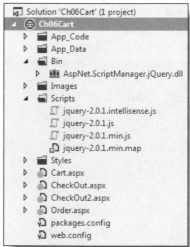

Description

- *Unobtrusive validation* is on by default when you start a new web site from the Empty Web Site Template.

- The easiest way to provide unobtrusive validation is to install the *NuGet package* for it. That adds a Scripts folder that contains the jQuery files to the project as well as the files that reference the jQuery files and manage the validation.

Figure 7-3   How to provide for unobtrusive validation

How to use the validators

In the topics that follow, you'll learn how to use the validators as you develop applications.

How to use the required field validator

Figure 7-4 shows how to use the *required field validator*. This validator checks that the user entered a value into an input control. If the user doesn't enter a value, the validator's error message is displayed.

The three examples in this figure illustrate how you can use the required field validator. In the first example, this validator is used to check for a required entry in a text box. To do that, its ControlToValidate property is set to the ID property of the text box. Then, if the user doesn't enter anything into the text box, the text in the ErrorMessage property is displayed.

The second and third examples show how you can use the InitialValue property of the required field validator to check that the user changed the initial value of a control. For this to work right, this property must be set to the initial value of the field that's being validated.

In the second example, this technique is used with a text box. Here, the initial value of the text box indicates the format for a date entry. If the user doesn't change this value, the validation test will fail. This doesn't work as well as you might want it to, though, because the users have to delete the initial value in the field before they can enter the new value, which isn't as easy as entering a value into an empty text box.

The third example uses the InitialValue property with a list box. Here, the InitialValue property is set to None, which is the value of the first item in the list. That way, if the user doesn't select another item, the validation test will fail. You can also use this technique with a drop-down list or a radio button list.

A property of the required field validator

Property	Description
InitialValue	The initial value of the control that's validated. If this value isn't changed, the validation fails. The default is an empty string.

A validator that checks for a required entry

```
<asp:TextBox ID="txtName" runat="server"></asp:TextBox> 
<asp:RequiredFieldValidator ID="RequiredFieldValidator1" runat="server"
    ControlToValidate="txtName"
    ErrorMessage="You must enter a name." >
</asp:RequiredFieldValidator>
```

A validator that checks that an initial value is changed

```
<asp:TextBox ID="txtBirthDate" runat="server">mm/dd/yyyy</asp:TextBox> 
<asp:RequiredFieldValidator ID="RequiredFieldValidator2" runat="server"
    ControlToValidate="txtBirthDate"
    InitialValue="mm/dd/yyyy"
    ErrorMessage="You must enter a birthdate.">
</asp:RequiredFieldValidator>
```

A required field validator that forces an option to be chosen from a list box

```
<asp:ListBox ID="lstCardType" runat="server">
    <asp:ListItem Selected="True" Value="None">Select a credit card
    </asp:ListItem>
    <asp:ListItem Value="Visa">Visa</asp:ListItem>
    <asp:ListItem Value="MC">MasterCard</asp:ListItem>
    <asp:ListItem Value="AmEx">American Express</asp:ListItem>
</asp:ListBox> 
<asp:RequiredFieldValidator ID="RequiredFieldValidator3" runat="server"
    ControlToValidate="lstCardType"
    InitialValue="None"
    ErrorMessage="You must select a credit card type.">
</asp:RequiredFieldValidator>
```

Description

- The *required field validator* checks that the user entered data into an input control. It's typically used with text box controls, but can also be used with list controls.

- If you set the InititalValue attribute of a required field validator, you should set the starting value for the field that's being validated to the same value. This technique can be used to show the format that should be used for an entry.

Figure 7-4   How to use the required field validator

How to use the compare validator

Figure 7-5 shows how you use the *compare validator*. This validator lets you compare the value entered into an input control with a constant value or the value of another control. You can also use the compare validator to make sure that the value is a particular data type.

To define a compare validator, you use the four properties shown in this figure. To compare the input data with a constant value, you specify the value in the ValueToCompare property. Then, you set the Operator property to indicate the type of comparison you want to perform, and you set the Type property to the type of data you're comparing.

The first example illustrates how this works. Here, the value entered into a text box is tested to be sure that it's an integer that's greater than zero. Then, if the user enters a value that isn't an integer, or if the user enters an integer that isn't greater than zero, the error message will be displayed.

To test for just a data type, you set the Type property to the type of data you're testing for, and you set the Operator property to DataTypeCheck. This is illustrated by the second example. Here, the value entered into a text box is tested to be sure that it's an integer.

The third example shows how to compare the value of an input control with the value of another control. To do that, you set the Operator and Type properties just as you do when you compare an input value with a constant. Instead of setting the ValueToCompare property, however, you set the ControlToCompare property to the ID of the control whose value you want to compare. This example tests that a date that's entered into one text box is after the date entered into another text box.

When you work with compare validators, you should know that if the user doesn't enter a value into a control, the control will pass the test of its compare validator. Because of that, you must use a required field validator along with the compare validator if you want to be sure that the user enters a value into a control.

You should also realize that if you compare the value of a control against the value of another control, the validation test will pass if the user doesn't enter a value into the other control or the value of the other control can't be converted to the correct type. To avoid that problem, you'll want to be sure that the other control is also validated properly.

Properties of the compare validator

Property	Description
`ValueToCompare`	The value that the control specified in the ControlToValidate property should be compared to.
`Operator`	The type of comparison to perform (Equal, NotEqual, GreaterThan, GreaterThanEqual, LessThan, LessThanEqual, or DataTypeCheck).
`Type`	The data type for the comparison (String, Integer, Double, Date, or Currency).
`ControlToCompare`	The ID of the control that the value of the control specified in the ControlToValidate property should be compared to.

A compare validator that checks for a value greater than zero

```
<asp:TextBox ID="txtQuantity" runat="server"></asp:TextBox> 
<asp:CompareValidator ID="CompareValidator1" runat="server"
    ControlToValidate="txtQuantity"
    Type="Integer"
    Operator="GreaterThan"
    ValueToCompare="0"
    ErrorMessage="Quantity must be greater than zero.">
</asp:CompareValidator>
```

A compare validator that checks for an integer value

```
<asp:TextBox id="txtQuantity" runat="server"></asp:TextBox> 
<asp:CompareValidator ID="CompareValidator2" runat="server"
    ControlToValidate="txtQuantity"
    Operator="DataTypeCheck"
    Type="Integer"
    ErrorMessage="Quantity must be an integer.">
</asp:CompareValidator>
```

A compare validator that compares the values of two text boxes

```
<asp:TextBox ID="txtStartDate" runat="server"></asp:TextBox><br /><br />
<asp:TextBox ID="txtEndDate" runat="server"></asp:TextBox> 
<asp:CompareValidator
    ID="CompareValidator3" runat="server"
    ControlToValidate="txtEndDate"
    Operator="GreaterThan"
    Type="Date"
    ControlToCompare="txtStartDate"
    ErrorMessage="End Date must be greater than Start Date.">
</asp:CompareValidator>
```

Description

- The *compare validator* compares the value entered into a control with a constant value or with the value entered into another control.

- You can also use the compare validator to check that the user entered a specific data type.

Figure 7-5   How to use the compare validator

How to use the range validator

The *range validator*, shown in figure 7-6, validates user input by making sure that it falls within a given range of values. To specify the valid range, you set the MinimumValue and MaximumValue properties. You must also set the Type property to the type of data you're checking. For instance, the first example in this figure checks that the user enters an integer between 1 and 14 into a text box.

The second example in this figure shows how you can set the range for a range validator at runtime. Here, you can see that the MinimumValue and MaximumValue properties aren't set when the range validator is declared. Instead, they're set when the page is loaded for the first time. In this case, the MinimumValue property is set to the current date, and the MaximumValue property is set to 30 days after the current date.

Like the compare validator, you should realize that the range validator will pass its validation test if the user doesn't enter anything into the associated control. Because of that, you'll need to use a required field validator along with the range validator if the user must enter a value.

Properties of the range validator

Property	Description
MinimumValue	The minimum value allowed for the control.
MaximumValue	The maximum value allowed for the control.
Type	The data type for the comparison (String, Integer, Double, Date, or Currency).

A range validator that checks for a numeric range

```
<asp:TextBox ID="txtDays" runat="server"></asp:TextBox> 
<asp:RangeValidator ID="RangeValidator1" runat="server"
    ControlToValidate="txtDays"
    Type="Integer"
    MinimumValue="1"
    MaximumValue="14"
    ErrorMessage="Days must be between 1 and 14.">
</asp:RangeValidator>
```

How to set a range at runtime

A range validator that checks a date range that's set at runtime

```
<asp:TextBox ID="txtArrival" runat="server">01/01/12</asp:TextBox> 
<asp:RangeValidator ID="valArrival" runat="server"
    ControlToValidate="txtArrival"
    Type="Date"
    ErrorMessage="You must arrive within 30 days.">
</asp:RangeValidator>
```

Code that sets the minimum and maximum values when the page is loaded

```
protected void Page_Load(object sender, EventArgs e)
{
    if (!IsPostBack)
    {
        valArrival.MinimumValue
            = DateTime.Today.ToShortDateString();
        valArrival.MaximumValue
            = DateTime.Today.AddDays(30).ToShortDateString();
    }
}
```

Description

- The *range validator* checks that the user enters a value that falls within the range specified by the MinimumValue and MaximumValue properties. These properties can be set when the range validator is created or when the page is loaded.

- If the user enters a value that can't be converted to the correct data type, the validation fails.

- If the user doesn't enter a value in the input control, the range validator passes its validation test. As a result, you should also provide a required field validator if a value is required.

Figure 7-6   How to use the range validator

How to use the regular expression validator

A *regular expression* is a string made up of special pattern-matching symbols. You can use regular expressions with the *regular expression validator* to make sure that a user's entry matches a specific pattern, like one for a zip code, phone number, or email address. Figure 7-7 shows how to use the regular expression validator.

As you can see, the ValidationExpression property specifies the regular expression the input data must match. For instance, the code for the first regular expression validator in this figure specifies that the input data must contain five decimal digits (\d{5}). And the regular expression for the second validator specifies that the input data must be in the format of a U.S. phone number.

If you access the Regular Expression Editor that's shown in this figure, you can select one of the expressions provided by Visual Studio. These expressions define common patterns for phone numbers and postal codes in the United States and some other countries, as well as social security numbers, email addresses, and URLs.

You can also create a custom expression that's based on a standard expression by selecting an expression in the Regular Expression Editor so its pattern appears in the text box at the bottom of the dialog box. Then, you can modify the expression and click on the OK button to insert it into the aspx code for the validator. In the next figure, you'll learn more about creating a regular expression.

A property of the regular expression validator

Property	Description
`ValidationExpression`	A string that specifies a regular expression. The regular expression defines a pattern that the input data must match to be valid.

The Regular Expression Editor dialog box

A regular expression validator that validates five-digit numbers

```
<asp:TextBox ID="txtZipCode" runat="server"></asp:TextBox> 
<asp:RegularExpressionValidator ID="RegularExpressionValidator1"
    runat="server" ControlToValidate="txtZipCode"
    ValidationExpression="\d{5}"
    ErrorMessage="Must be a five-digit U.S. zip code.">
</asp:RegularExpressionValidator>
```

A regular expression validator that validates U.S. phone numbers

```
<asp:TextBox ID="txtPhone" runat="server"></asp:TextBox> 
<asp:RegularExpressionValidator ID="RegularExpressionValidator2"
    runat="server" ControlToValidate="txtPhone"
    ValidationExpression="((\(\d{3}\) ?)|(\d{3}-))?\d{3}-\d{4}"
    ErrorMessage="Must be a valid U.S. phone number.">
</asp:RegularExpressionValidator>
```

Description

- The *regular expression validator* matches the user's entry with the pattern specified by the *regular expression* that's identified by the ValidationExpression property. If the entry doesn't match the pattern, the validation fails.

- ASP.NET provides some common regular expressions that you can access from the Regular Expression Editor. To display its dialog box, select the validation control, select the ValidationExpression property in the Properties window, and click its ellipsis button.

- You can also use the Regular Expression Editor to create a custom expression that's based on a standard expression. To do that, select the standard expression and then edit it in the Validation Expression text box.

Figure 7-7   How to use the regular expression validator

How to create regular expressions

Figure 7-8 presents the basic elements of regular expressions. Although the .NET Framework provides many other elements that you can use in regular expressions, you can create expressions of considerable complexity using just the ones shown here. In fact, all of the standard expressions provided by ASP. NET use only these elements.

To start, you can specify any ordinary character, such as a letter or a decimal digit. If a character must be an A, for example, you just include that character in the expression. To include a character other than an ordinary character, you must precede it with a backslash. For example, \(specifies that the character must be a left parenthesis, \] specifies that the character must be a right bracket, and \\ specifies that the character must be a backslash. A backslash that's used in this way is called an *escape character*.

You can also specify a *character class*, which consists of a set of characters. For example, \d indicates that the character must be a decimal digit, \w indicates that the character must be a *word character*, and \s indicates that the character must be a *whitespace character*. The uppercase versions of these elements—\D, \W, and \S—match any character that is not a decimal digit, word character, or whitespace character.

To create a list of possible characters, you enclose them in brackets. For example, [abc] specifies that the character must be the letter a, b, or c, and [a-z] specifies that the character must be a lowercase letter. One common construct is [a-zA-Z], which specifies that the character must be a lowercase or uppercase letter.

You can also use *quantifiers* to indicate how many of the preceding element the input data must contain. To specify an exact number, you just code it in brackets. For example, \d{5} specifies that the input data must be a five-digit number. You can also specify a minimum number and a maximum number of characters. For example, \w{6,20} specifies that the input data must contain from six to twenty word characters. You can also omit the maximum number to require just a minimum number of characters. For example, \w{6,} specifies that the input data must contain at least 6 word characters. You can also use the *, ?, and + quantifiers to specify zero or more, zero or one, or one or more characters.

If the input data can match one or more patterns, you can use the vertical bar to separate elements. For example, \w+|\s{1} means that the input data must contain one or more word characters or a single whitespace character.

To create groups of elements, you use parentheses. Then, you can apply quantifiers to the entire group or you can separate groups with a vertical bar. For example, (AB)|(SB) specifies that the input characters must be either AB or SB. And (\d{3}-)? specifies that the input characters must contain zero or one occurrence of a three-digit number followed by a hyphen.

This of course is just an introduction to regular expressions. For more information, try searching the Internet. The information is plentiful, and you can probably find an example of an expression that does just what you're looking for.

Common regular expression elements

Element	Description
Ordinary character	Matches any character other than ., $, ^, [, {, (, |,), *, +, ?, or \.
\	Matches the character that follows.
\d	Matches any decimal digit (0-9).
\D	Matches any character other than a decimal digit.
\w	Matches any word character (a-z, A-Z, and 0-9).
\W	Matches any character other than a word character.
\s	Matches any white space character (space, tab, new line, etc.).
\S	Matches any character other than a whitespace character.
[abcd]	Matches any character included between the brackets.
[^abcd]	Matches any character that is not included between the brackets.
[a-z]	Matches any characters in the indicated range.
{n}	Matches exactly *n* occurrences of the preceding element or group.
{n,}	Matches at least *n* occurrences of the preceding element or group.
{n,m}	Matches at least *n* but no more than *m* occurrences of the preceding element.
*	Matches zero or more occurrences of the preceding element.
?	Matches zero or one occurrence of the preceding element.
+	Matches one or more occurrences of the preceding element.
|	Matches any of the elements separated by the vertical bar.
( )	Groups the elements that appear between the parentheses.

Examples of regular expressions

Expression	Example	Description
\d{3}	289	A three digit number.
\w{8,20}	Frankenstein	At least eight but no more than twenty word characters.
\d{2}-\d{4}	10-3944	A two-digit number followed by a hyphen and a four-digit number.
\w{1,8}.\w{1,3}	freddy.jpg	Up to eight letters or numbers, followed by a period and up to three letters or numbers.
(AB)|(SB)-\d{1,5}	SB-3276	The letters AB or SB, followed by a hyphen and a one- to five-digit number.
\d{5}(-\d{4})?	93711-2765	A five-digit number, optionally followed by a hyphen and a four-digit number.
\w*\d\w*	arm01	A text entry that contains at least one numeral.
[xyz]\d{3}	x023	The letter x, y, or z, followed by a three-digit number.

Description

- For more information and for specific types of expressions, you can search the Internet.

Figure 7-8   How to create regular expressions

How to use a custom validator

If none of the other validators provide the data validation that your program requires, you can use a *custom validator*. Then, you can code your own validation routine that's executed when the page is submitted to the server. This technique is frequently used to validate input data that requires a database lookup.

Figure 7-9 shows how you use a custom validator. In this example, a custom validator is used to check that a value entered by the user is a valid product code in a table of products. To do that, the code includes an event handler for the ServerValidate event of the custom validator. This event occurs whenever validation is performed on the server.

When the ServerValidate event occurs, the event handler receives an argument named args that you can use to validate the data the user entered. The Value property of this argument contains the user's entry. Then, the event handler can perform the tests that are necessary to determine if this value is valid. If it is valid, the event handler assigns a True value to the IsValid property of the args argument so the validator passes its test. If it isn't valid, the event handler assigns a False value to the IsValid property of this argument so the validator doesn't pass its test. This causes the error message specified by the validator to be displayed in the browser.

In this figure, for example, the event handler calls the CheckProductCode method of the HalloweenDB class. Although you haven't seen this class or method before, all you need to know is that it checks the product code by looking it up in a database. If the product code exists, this method returns a value of True. Otherwise, it returns a value of False. In either case, the returned value is assigned to the IsValid property of the args argument.

Properties of the ServerValidateEventArgs class

Property	Description
Value	The text string to be validated.
IsValid	A Boolean property that you set to True if the value passes the validation test or to False if it fails.

The aspx code for a text box and a custom validator

```
<asp:TextBox ID="txtProductCode" runat="server"></asp:TextBox> 
<asp:CustomValidator id="valProductCode" runat="server"
    ControlToValidate="txtProductCode"
    ErrorMessage="Product code must be in database."
    OnServerValidate="valProductCode_ServerValidate">
</asp:CustomValidator>
```

C# code for the custom validator

```
protected void valProductCode_ServerValidate(object source,
    ServerValidateEventArgs args)
{
    args.IsValid = HalloweenDB.CheckProductCode(args.Value);
}
```

Description

- You can use a *custom validator* to validate input data using the validation tests you specify.

- For a customer validator, you code the validation tests within an event handler for the ServerValidate event of the custom validator. This event is raised whenever validation is performed on the server. Because of that, the form must be submitted before the validation can be done.

- To start the event handler for the ServerValidate event in the code-behind file for a form, you can double-click on the custom validator control in the Designer. Then, you can use the properties of the args argument that's passed to this event handler to test the input data (args.value) and indicate whether the data passed the validation test (args.IsValid).

- If you set the IsValid property of the args argument to False, the error message you specified for the custom validator is displayed in the browser.

- If the user doesn't enter a value into the associated input control, the custom validator doesn't perform its validation test. As a result, you should also provide a required field validator if a value is required.

Figure 7-9   How to use a custom validator

Validation techniques

Now that you're familiar with the validators, you're ready to learn how to use the validation summary control and validation groups.

How to use the validation summary control

The *validation summary control* lets you summarize all the errors on a page. The summary can be a simple message like "There were errors on the page," or a more elaborate message that includes information about each error. The summary can be displayed directly on the page or in a separate message box.

Figure 7-10 shows how to use the validation summary control. The only tricky part of using this control is knowing how to code the Text and ErrorMessage properties of a validator. To display the same message in both the validator and the validation summary control, for example, you set the ErrorMessage property to that message.

To display different messages, you set the ErrorMessage property to the message you want in the summary control and the Text property to the message you want in the validator. This is illustrated in the example in this figure. Here, the message for each field in the validation control specifies the name of the field, and the message in the validator describes the error. Note that in this case, the message in the validator is coded as content of the control rather than in the Text property.

If you don't want to display individual error messages in the summary control, just set the HeaderText property of the control to the generic message you want to display. Then, leave the ErrorMessage property of each validator blank. Otherwise, you can set the HeaderText property to a value like the one in this figure, or you can leave it at its default value so no heading is displayed. Last, if you want to display an error message in the validation summary control but not in a validator, you can set the Display property of the validator to None.

By default, the error messages displayed by a validation summary control are formatted as a bulleted list as shown in this figure. However, you can display the errors in a list or paragraph by setting the DisplayMode property. You can also display the error messages in a message box rather than on the web page by setting the ShowMessageBox property to True and the ShowSummary property to False.

To format a validation summary control, you can use its Appearance properties as shown in this example. Here, the BorderColor, BorderStyle, and BorderWidth properties put a border around the summary control. This is easier than using CSS, because it's hard to tell what HTML elements are generated for a summary control. That's because the elements are generated by JavaScript or jQuery when errors are detected on the client, which means that you can't find out what the elements are by viewing them in the source code for a page.

If you use a bulleted list for a summary control, though, you do know that the error messages will be in li items within an ul item, so you can apply CSS to those elements. In this figure, for example, CSS has been used to add spacing before and after the error messages (li elements).

Properties of the validation summary control

Property	Description
DisplayMode	Specifies how the error messages from the validators are displayed. The options are BulletList (the default), List, and SingleParagraph.
HeaderText	The text that's displayed before the list of error messages.
ShowSummary	A Boolean value that determines whether the validation summary is displayed on the web page. The default is True.
ShowMessageBox	A Boolean value that determines whether the validation summary is displayed in a message box. The default is False.

The aspx code for a validation summary control and two validators

```
<asp:ValidationSummary ID="ValidationSummary1" runat="server"
    HeaderText="Please correct these entries" BorderColor="Black"
    BorderStyle="Solid" BorderWidth="1px" />
<h2>Contact information</h2>
<label>Email address: </label>
<asp:TextBox ID="txtEmail1" runat="server" CssClass="entry"></asp:TextBox>
    <asp:RequiredFieldValidator ID="rfvEmail1" runat="server"
        CssClass="validator" Display="Dynamic" ControlToValidate="txtEmail1"
        ErrorMessage="First email address">Email is required
    </asp:RequiredFieldValidator><br />
<label>Email Re-entry: </label>
<asp:TextBox ID="txtEmail2" runat="server" CssClass="entry"></asp:TextBox>
    <asp:CompareValidator ID="cvEmail2" runat="server"
        ErrorMessage="Second email address" ControlToCompare="txtEmail1"
        ControlToValidate="txtEmail2" CssClass="validator">
        Must match first entry</asp:CompareValidator><br />
```

How the error messages appear on the web page

Description

- The *validation summary control* displays a summary of the error messages that are generated by the page's validators. These messages can be displayed on the form or in a message box.

- The error messages in a summary control come from the ErrorMessage properties of the page's validators. If you want to display a different message in a validator, set the Text property of the validator or code the text as the content of the control.

- If you want to display a message in the validation summary control but not in the validator, you can set the validator's display property to None.

Figure 7-10   How to use the validation summary control

How to use validation groups

The *validation group* feature of ASP.NET lets you group validation controls and specify which group should be validated when a page is posted. Figure 7-11 shows how to use these groups.

To illustrate, the web page in this figure provides for a billing address and a shipping address, with a check box to indicate whether the shipping address is the same as the billing address. Then, if the check box is checked, the shipping address isn't required. As a result, the validators for the shipping fields shouldn't be executed. To implement this type of validation, you can use two validation groups: one for the billing fields, the other for the shipping fields.

The first example in this figure shows just one of the shipping address text boxes and a validator that's assigned to a validation group named ShipTo. For the purpose of this example, though, you can assume that the other shipping fields also have validators assigned to the ShipTo group.

The second example shows a button that submits the page. Here, the button specifies ShipTo as its validation group. Because of that, only the shipping fields will be validated when the user posts the form. For this to work, the CausesValidation property of the button must be set to True, but that's the default for a button.

The third example shows how you can invoke the ShipTo validators in your C# code if the check box is left unchecked. Here, the Validate method of the Page class is executed with the name of the validation group as its argument. That causes the Validate method of each validator in the ShipTo group to be executed. As a result, the shipping fields will be validated on the server, but only if the check box isn't checked.

Note that any validation controls that don't have a ValidationGroup attribute are considered part of the *default group*. The validators in this group are executed only when the page is posted with a button or other control that causes validation but doesn't specify a validation group, or when the Page.Validate method is called without specifying a validation group.

This means that you need two buttons or controls to start the validation for the two groups: one for the default group and one for validation group. Or, you need to use one control to validate the default group on the client, and then you need to validate the validation group only on the server. Since neither alternative is efficient, the use of validation groups has limited application. In fact, you'll see another way to get around this problem in the CheckOut page that's presented next.

The property for working with validation groups

Property	Description
`ValidationGroup`	For an entry control, this property specifies the validation group that the control belongs to. For a control that causes validation, this property specifies the validation group that should be validated.

Part of a web form that accepts billing and shipping addresses

Billing address

Address: `123 Wistful Vista`

City: `Portland`

State: `Oregon`

Zip code: `99999`

Shipping address

☑ Same as billing address

Address: `123 Wistful Vista`

City: `Portland`

State: `Oregon`

Zip code: `9999`

A text box with a validator that specifies a validation group

The aspx code

```
<asp:TextBox ID="txtShipToAddress" runat="server" />
<asp:RequiredFieldValidator ID="RequiredFieldValidator1" runat="server"
    ControlToValidate="txtShipToAddress"
    ErrorMessage="You must enter a shipping address."
    ValidationGroup="ShipTo"></asp:RequiredFieldValidator>
```

A button that starts the validation of the group

```
<asp:Button ID="btnContinue" runat="server" Text="Continue"
    ValidationGroup="ShipTo" OnClick="btnContinue_Click" />
```

C# code that conditionally validates the group

```
if (!chkShipToSameAsBillTo.Checked)
    Page.Validate("ShipTo");
```

Description

- A *validation group* is a group of validators that are run when a page is posted.

- To group validators, set the ValidationGroup attribute for each validator. To run the validators for the group, set this attribute for a control that causes validation.

- You can also use C# code to do the validation for a group by using the Page. Validate method with the name of the validation group as the argument.

- Any validators that don't specify the ValidationGroup attribute are part of the *default group*. This group is executed when started by a button or control that doesn't specify a validation group or when the Page.Validate method is used without an argument.

Figure 7-11   How to use validation groups

A CheckOut page
that uses validation controls

Now, to show you how the validation controls work in a complete application, this chapter ends by presenting a CheckOut page that uses most of the validation controls.

The user interface

Figure 7-12 presents the user interface for the CheckOut page. At the top of this page, you can see a validation summary control that lists the fields that need to be corrected. Then, to the right of those fields, you can see the error messages that describe what's wrong.

In the shipping-address portion of the page, you can see the check box that determines whether the shipping address is the same as the billing address. If the user checks this box, the page is posted to the server, the four shipping-address fields and their validators are disabled, and the page is returned to the browser. If the user unchecks this box, this process is reversed. Either way, when the user clicks the Check Out button, the appropriate validators are executed. In this figure, the shipping fields and their validators aren't enabled so only the other validators are executed when the user clicks the Check Out button.

The Check Out page with validation

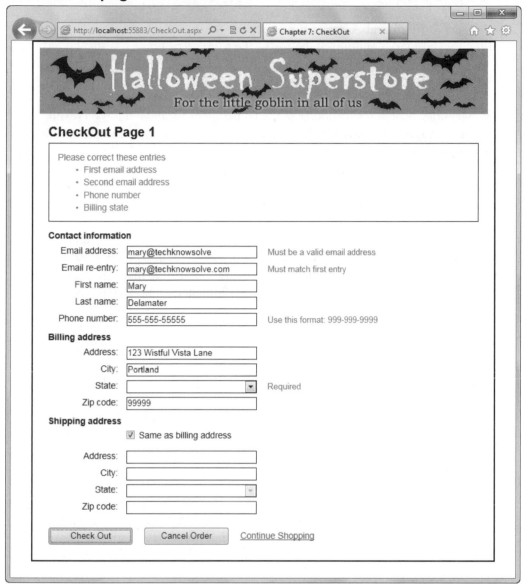

Description

- This web form has a validation control at the top of the form that doesn't show unless the validators detect errors.
- This form uses required field validators, one compare validator, and regular expression validators.
- When the user clicks on the check box that indicates whether the shipping address is the same as the billing address, the page is posted to the server and the text boxes and validators for the shipping fields are either enabled or disabled.

Figure 7-12   The CheckOut page for the Shopping Cart application

The aspx code

Figure 7-13 presents some of the aspx code for the CheckOut page. Here, the validation summary control is at the top of the form so its content is displayed prominently on the page. This is followed by the labels, controls, and validators for the user entries.

As you can see, the validators for all of the fields have one message in the ErrorMessage attribute and another in the text content for the field. As a result, the first message is displayed in the validation summary control, and the second message is displayed in the validator.

If you look down the page to the first required field validator for the shipping-address portion of the page, you can see another way to provide the message that's displayed in the validator. Here, the Text attribute for the validator is used to store the message.

The first block of code in this figure also illustrates the use of a regular expression validator and a compare validator. In the regular expression validator for the first email address entry, the regular expression is one that is provided by the Regular Express Editor. So even though it's long and complicated, you can trust it to do its job.

In the compare validator, the email address entry in the related text box is compared with the address in the preceding text box. Because the Operator attribute isn't specified, an equal comparison is assumed. As a result, the error messages are displayed if the entries in the first two text boxes aren't equal.

In the aspx code for the shipping-address portion of the page, you can see the code for the check box that determines whether the shipping address is different from the billing address. This control is coded within a div element so CSS can be used to format the input and label elements that are generated for the check box as shown in the previous figure. Without the div element and the CSS, the label would be floated ahead of the check box, and the result would be a mess.

To make this form work right, the AutoPostBack attribute of the check box is set to true. Also, by default, its CausesValidation property is set to False. As a result, the page is posted back to the server when this button is checked or unchecked.

The start of the aspx code for the CheckOut page

```
<h1>CheckOut Page 1</h1>
<form id="form1" runat="server" defaultfocus="txtEmail1"
      defaultbutton="btnCheckOut">
    <asp:ValidationSummary ID="ValidationSummary1" runat="server"
       HeaderText="Please correct these entries" BorderColor="Black"
       BorderStyle="Solid" BorderWidth="1px" />
    <h2>Contact information</h2>
    <label>Email address: </label>
    <asp:TextBox ID="txtEmail1" runat="server" CssClass="entry">
    </asp:TextBox>
        <asp:RequiredFieldValidator ID="rfvEmail1" runat="server"
           CssClass="validator" ErrorMessage="First email address"
           Display="Dynamic" ControlToValidate="txtEmail1"  >Required
        </asp:RequiredFieldValidator>
        <asp:RegularExpressionValidator ID="revtxtEmail1" runat="server"
           ErrorMessage="First email address" CssClass="validator"
           Display="Dynamic" ValidationExpression=
               "\w+([-+.']\w+)*@\w+([-.]\w+)*\.\w+([-.]\w+)*"
           ControlToValidate="txtEmail1">Must be a valid email address
        </asp:RegularExpressionValidator><br />
    <label>Email re-entry: </label>
    <asp:TextBox ID="txtEmail2" runat="server" CssClass="entry">
    </asp:TextBox>
        <asp:RequiredFieldValidator ID="rfvEmail2" runat="server"
           ErrorMessage="Second email address" CssClass="validator"
           Display="Dynamic" ControlToValidate="txtEmail2">Required
        </asp:RequiredFieldValidator>
        <asp:CompareValidator ID="cvEmail2" runat="server"
           ErrorMessage="Second email address"
           ControlToCompare="txtEmail1" ControlToValidate="txtEmail2"
           CssClass="validator" Display="Dynamic">Must match first entry
        </asp:CompareValidator><br />
```

The start of the aspx code for the shipping-address portion of the page

```
<h2>Shipping address</h2>
<div id="sameAsBilling">
    <asp:CheckBox ID="chkSameAsBilling" runat="server"
       Text="Same as billing address" AutoPostBack="True"
       OnCheckedChanged="chkSameAsBilling_CheckedChanged"/><br /><br />
</div>
<label>Address: </label>
<asp:TextBox ID="txtShipAddress" runat="server" CssClass="entry">
</asp:TextBox>
    <asp:RequiredFieldValidator ID="rfvShipAddress" runat="server"
       ErrorMessage="Shipping address" CssClass="validator"
       Display="Dynamic" ControlToValidate="txtShipAddress"
       Text="Required"></asp:RequiredFieldValidator><br />
<label>City: </label>
<asp:TextBox ID="txtShipCity" runat="server" CssClass="entry" >
</asp:TextBox>
    <asp:RequiredFieldValidator ID="rfvShipCity" runat="server"
       ErrorMessage="Shipping city" CssClass="validator"
       Display="Dynamic" ControlToValidate="txtShipCity"
       Text="Required"></asp:RequiredFieldValidator><br />
```

Figure 7-13   Some of the aspx code for the CheckOut page

The C# code

Figure 7-14 shows some of the C# code in the code-behind file for the page. This is like the code you reviewed in the previous chapter with two exceptions.

First, the GetCustomerData method not only gets the data for the contact information and the billing address, but also the data for the shipping address. This is done by the shaded lines in the GetCustomerData method that add the shipping fields to the customer object.

Second, the last event handler in this figure is executed when the CheckedChanged event of the check box occurs. This event occurs when the user checks or unchecks the box. To cause a postback when the check box is changed, its AutoPostBack property has been set to True. Also, the CausesValidation property of a check box is set to False by default, so checking the box won't cause validation.

Within this event handler, you can see an if statement that tests whether the check box is *not* checked. If it isn't, the code that follows sets the Enabled properties of both the text boxes and the validators for the shipping-address fields to true. If the box is checked, though, this code sets the Enabled properties for the text boxes and validators to false. This means that the user can only enter data in these fields when the box isn't checked.

You could take this code one step further and set the values in the shipping fields to empty strings when the box is checked. That would remove any data that might be in those fields. You could also modify the code in the GetCustomerData method so it uses an if statement to put the billing entries into the shipping properties of the customer object if the check box is checked. That way, the same data would be in the billing fields and the shipping fields. As it is, the shipping fields will be null when the check box is checked.

You could also use JavaScript and jQuery to handle the check box event on the client instead of the server, including enabling or disabling fields. Then, a round trip wouldn't be required each time the user changes the check box, and you wouldn't need the CheckedChanged event handler in the code-behind file. Since this is a better way to handle the check box changes, this is one more reason for learning how to use JavaScript and jQuery.

Some of the C# code in the code-behind file for the Check Out page

```
public partial class CheckOut : System.Web.UI.Page
{
    private Customer customer;
    protected void Page_Load(object sender, EventArgs e)
    {
        if (!IsPostBack)
        {
            customer = (Customer)Session["Customer"];
            this.LoadCustomerData();
        }
    }
    protected void btnCheckOut_Click(object sender, EventArgs e)
    {
        if (Page.IsValid)
        {
            this.GetCustomerData();
            Response.Redirect("~/CheckOut2.aspx");
        }
    }
    private void GetCustomerData()
    {
        if (customer == null)
            customer = new Customer();
        // statements that get the data from the billing fields
        customer.ShippingAddress = txtShipAddress.Text;
        customer.ShippingCity = txtShipCity.Text;
        customer.ShippingState = ddlShipState.SelectedValue;
        customer.ShippingZip = txtShipZip.Text;
        Session["Customer"] = customer;
    }
}
protected void chkSameAsBilling_CheckedChanged(object sender, EventArgs e)
{
    if (!chkSameAsBilling.Checked) {
        rfvShipAddress.Enabled = true;
        rfvShipCity.Enabled = true;
        rfvShipState.Enabled = true;
        rfvShipZip.Enabled = true;
        txtShipAddress.Enabled = true;
        txtShipCity.Enabled = true;
        ddlShipState.Enabled = true;
        txtShipZip.Enabled = true;
    }
    else {
        rfvShipAddress.Enabled = false;
        rfvShipCity.Enabled = false;
        rfvShipState.Enabled = false;
        rfvShipZip.Enabled = false;
        txtShipAddress.Enabled = false;
        txtShipCity.Enabled = false;
        ddlShipState.Enabled = false;
        txtShipZip.Enabled = false;
    }
}
```

Figure 7-14   Some of the C# code for the Check Out page

Perspective

Now that you've completed this chapter, you should be able to create web forms that provide most or all of the data validation that your applications require. Keep in mind, though, that after you add validators to a form, you need to test them thoroughly to be sure that they detect all invalid entries. Although that can be time-consuming, it's an essential part of developing professional web applications.

Terms

validation control	regular expression validator
validator	regular expression
unobtrusive validation	custom validator
NuGet package	validation summary control
required field validator	validation group
compare validator	default group
range validator	

Summary

- ASP.NET provides six *validation controls*, including five *validators* and one validation summary control.

- If a browser has JavaScript enabled as most browsers do, the validation that's specified by the validators is done on the client, but it is always done on the server too. In the code-behind file for a page, the IsValid property of the page can be tested to see whether the data in all of the controls is valid.

- When *unobtrusive validation* is on, jQuery is used for the validation that's done on the client. Since jQuery is a JavaScript library, this means that ASP.NET generates less JavaScript code for the page. To implement unobtrusive validation, you can install the *NuGet package* for it.

- The *required field validator* lets you check to see if an entry has been made. The *compare validator* lets you compare an entry to another entry or a constant. And the *range validator* lets you check whether an entry falls within a specified range.

- The *regular expression validator* lets you check an entry to see whether it conforms to a pattern that's defined by a *regular expression*. Visual Studio's Regular Expression Editor lets you select regular expressions for common entries like email addresses and phone numbers.

- A *custom validator* lets you provide your own validation code in the code-behind file for the page.

- A *validation summary control* lets you display error messages for the entries in a separate portion of the page as well as in the validators.

- *Validation groups* let you validate one group of controls at a time.

Exercise 7-1   Modify the CheckOut page

In this exercise, you'll modify the Check Out page that's presented in this chapter.

Open, review, and run the CheckOut page

1. Open the Ex07Cart web site that's in the aspnet45_cs directory, and review the CheckOut page and its code-behind file. Refer back to these files as you test the application to see how the aspx and C# code works.

2. Test the application to see how it works. Without entering any data on the CheckOut page, click the Check Out button to see how the error messages are displayed in the validation summary control as well as in the validators.

3. Click on the check box to check it and note that the validation messages disappear. Next, click on the Check Out button again, and note that no error messages are displayed for the shipping fields. Then, click in one of the shipping text boxes and note that it is disabled.

4. Click on the check box again to uncheck it, and click on the Check Out button again. Then, note that error messages are displayed for all of the fields.

5. Test the validators for each field by entering both valid and invalid entries and clicking on the Check Out button. In the first text box, for example, enter an invalid email address to see how the regular expression validator works. And in the second text box, enter a value that's different from the one in the first text box.

6. Eventually, enter valid data for all fields, and click the Check Out button. Then, in the Check Out 2 page, note the data that has been retrieved from the customer object.

Implement unobtrusive validation for the web site

7. Open the web.config file and note that unobtrusive validation has been turned off for the web site. Now, delete the elements that turn it off, and test the application again. Note that the application won't run because it needs a ScriptResourceMapping for jQuery.

8. Install the NuGet package for unobtrusive validation as shown in figure 7-3, and note the folders and files that have been added to the Solution Explorer. Then, test the application again. This time, the validation should work.

Add validators to the web form

9. Add an initial value of 999-999-9999 to the phone number field to show the format for the phone number entry. Next, add an InitialValue attribute to the required field validator for this text box that has the same initial value. Then, test this change to see how it works.

10. Add a regular expression validator for the billing zip code field so it will accept an entry in either of these formats: 99999 or 99999-9999. The validator message should be: "Use this format: 99999 or 99999-9999". Then, test to make sure that both formats are accepted as valid and that the right messages are displayed in the validation summary control and the validator.

11. Add a "Date of birth" field after the Phone number field. Don't add a required field validator for this field because it will be optional, but add a regular expression validator for the field that tests to make sure the data is in this format: mm/dd/yyyy. Also, set the initial value for the text field to "mm/dd/yyyy", and be sure to provide appropriate messages for both the validation summary control and the validator. For the regular expression, you can use this code:

    ```
    [01]?\d\/[0-3]\d\/\d{4}
    ```

Modify the Customer class and two code-behind files

12. Open the Customer.cs file in the App_Code folder, and add a birthdate property to the Customer class. To keep this simple, the property should be a string (not a DateTime value).

13. Open the code-behind file for the CheckOut page, and modify the code so the birthdate entry is added to the customer object.

14. Open the code-behind file for the CheckOut2 page, and modify the code so the birthdate entry is displayed when a valid form has been posted back to the CheckOut page and the CheckOut2 page is displayed.

15. When you're through testing and experimenting, close the application.

8

How to work with state, cookies, and URL encoding

In chapters 2 and 4, you were introduced to the way that view state and session state are used. Now you'll learn more about using these states, and you'll also learn how to use, and not use, application state and caching. Beyond that, you'll learn how to use cookies and URL encoding to pass data between the server and the client. Because HTTP is a stateless protocol, these are essential skills for every web developer.

How to use view state

For the most part, *view state* is automatic. Because of that, you don't have to set any properties or write any code to use it. Nevertheless, you should understand how view state works and how to use it to your advantage. In some cases, you may even want to add your own data to view state.

How to work with view state

As the summary in figure 8-1 says, view state works by saving data in the HTML stream that's sent to the browser when a page is requested. This data is saved as a hidden input field named _VIEWSTATE. Because the field is hidden, it isn't displayed in the browser. And because the field is an input field, it's automatically sent back to the server when the user posts the page.

View state is used to retain the values of the form and control properties that you set in code. In the Future Value application of chapter 2, for example, the values in the drop-down list were set by code. As a result, those values don't need to be reset by code each time the page is posted back to the server. Instead, they're automatically reset by view state.

The EnableViewState property of a page and its controls determines if view state is enabled, which it is by default. Although this is usually what you want, you may occasionally want to disable view state. One reason for doing that is to get a control to work the way you want it to. Another reason is to improve performance when view state gets so large that it degrades performance. In practice, though, you probably won't turn off view state until you discover that it's creating either a programming or performance problem.

If, for example, you change the value of a control property in code, but you want the initial value of that property restored each time the page is loaded, you can turn off view state to get the page to work right. Or, if a page is never posted back to itself, you can turn off view state to improve performance. To disable view state for a control, page, or entire application, you can use the techniques in this figure.

To disable view state for all but a few controls on a page, you can use the technique under the fourth heading in this figure, but this is tricky. First, you need to set the EnableViewState property of the page and controls that you want to use view state for to True. That's because you can't enable view state for any controls if view state is turned off for the page. Then, you set the ViewStateMode property of the Page directive to disabled so view state is disabled for all controls. Last, you set the ViewStateMode property for each of the controls that you want view state enabled for to True.

To determine the size of view state, you can enable the ASP.NET trace feature as described in chapter 5. Then, you can scroll to the Control Tree section of the trace output to see which controls are using view state and how many bytes they're using. That way, you can tell whether it's worth the effort to turn view state off.

View state concepts

- *View state* is an ASP.NET feature that provides for retaining the values of page and control properties that change from one execution of a page to another.

- Before ASP.NET sends a page back to the client, it determines what changes the program has made to the properties of the page and its controls. These changes are encoded in a string that's assigned to the value of a hidden input field named _VIEWSTATE.

- When the page is posted back to the server, the _VIEWSTATE field is sent back to the server along with the HTTP request. Then, ASP.NET retrieves the property values from the _VIEWSTATE field and uses them to restore the page and control properties.

- ASP.NET also uses view state to save the values of the page properties it uses, such as IsPostBack.

- View state is *not* used to restore data entered by a user into a text box or any other input control unless the control responds to change events.

- If view state is enabled for a data-bound control, the control will not be bound again when the page is reposted. Instead, the control's values will be restored from view state.

Two cases when you may want to disable view state

- When restoring the control properties for a page affects the way you want the form to work, you may want to disable view state for one or more controls.

- When the size of the view state field gets so large that it affects performance, you may want to disable view state for one or more controls or for an entire page.

How to disable view state

- To disable view state for a control, set the control's EnableViewState property to False.

- To disable view state for an entire page, set the EnableViewState property of the Page directive to False. That disables view state for all the controls on the page.

- To disable view state for the entire application, set the enableViewState attribute of the pages element in the system.web element of the web.config file to False.

How to enable view state for selected controls

- Set the EnableViewState property of the page and the controls whose view state you want to enable to True.

- Set the ViewStateMode property of the Page directive to Disabled.

- Set the ViewStateMode property of the selected controls to Enabled.

How to determine the size of view state for a page

- Enable the page's trace feature by setting the Trace attribute of the Page directive to True as described in chapter 5. Then, scroll down to the Control Tree section of the trace output to see the number of bytes of view state used by the page and its controls.

Figure 8-1   How to work with view state

How to use view state for your own data

Although view state is designed to automatically save page and control property values across round trips to the browser, you can also add your own data to view state. To do that, you store the data in a *view state object* that's created from the StateBag class as shown in figure 8-2.

Like the session state object, the view state object contains a collection of key/value pairs that represent the items saved in view state. To access this object, you use the ViewState property of the page. Then, you can use the methods listed in this figure to work with the view state object.

To illustrate, the first two examples in this figure show how you can add or update a view state item named TimeStamp. The third example shows how to retrieve that item. And the last example shows how to remove it. Notice in the third example that because a view state item is stored as an object type, the code must cast the object to the DateTime data type.

Keep in mind that you usually use session state, not view state, to save data across round trips to the browser. Occasionally, though, it does make sense to use view state for passing small amounts of data, especially when you want to associate the data with a specific page. In chapter 20, you'll see an example of that.

Common members of the StateBag class

Indexer	Description
`[name]`	The value of the view state item with the specified name. If you set the value of an item that doesn't exist, that item is created.

Property	Description
`Count`	The number of items in the view state collection.
`Keys`	A collection of keys for all of the items in the view state collection.
`Values`	A collection of values for all of the items in the view state collection.

Method	Description
`Add(name, value)`	Adds an item to the view state collection. If the item already exists, its value is updated.
`Clear()`	Removes all items from the view state collection.
`Remove(name)`	Removes the item with the specified name from the view state collection.

A statement that adds or updates a view state item

```
ViewState.Add("TimeStamp", DateTime.Now);
```

Another way to add or update a view state item

```
ViewState["TimeStamp"] = DateTime.Now;
```

A statement that retrieves the value of a view state item

```
DateTime timeStamp = (DateTime) ViewState["TimeStamp"];
```

A statement that removes an item from view state

```
ViewState.Remove("TimeStamp");
```

Description

- View state is implemented with a *view state object* that's defined by the StateBag class. This class defines a collection of view state items.

- Although the form and control properties are automatically saved in view state, you can also save other data in view state.

- To access the view state object for a page, you use the ViewState property of the page.

Figure 8-2   How to use view state for your own data

How to use session state

In chapter 4, you learned some basic skills for using session state to save data across round trips to the browser. The topics that follow review and expand on that information.

How to work with session state

As you have learned, ASP.NET uses *session state* to track the state of each user of an application. To do that, it creates a *session state object* that contains a unique *session ID* for each user's session. This ID is passed back to the browser as part of a response and returned to the server with the next request. ASP.NET can then use the session ID to get the session state object that's associated with the request.

To manage a user session, you can store data in the session state object as shown in figure 8-3. Since you've already seen how session state is used in the Shopping Cart application, you shouldn't have any trouble understanding these examples. The first one adds or updates a session state item named EMail. The second one retrieves the value of the EMail item and stores it in a string variable. And the third one removes the EMail item from session state.

All three of these examples assume that session state is being accessed from the code-behind file of a web page. In that case, you refer to the session state object by using the Session property of the page. To access session state from outside of a web page, however, you use the Session property of the HttpContext object for the current request as illustrated in the fourth example.

Common members of the HttpSessionState class

Indexer	Description
`[name]`	The value of the session state item with the specified name. If you set the value of an item that doesn't exist, that item is created.

Property	Description
`SessionID`	The unique ID of the session.
`Count`	The number of items in the session state collection.

Method	Description
`Add(name, value)`	Adds an item to the session state collection. If the item already exists, its value is updated.
`Clear()`	Removes all items from the session state collection.
`Remove(name)`	Removes the item with the specified name from the session state collection.

A statement that adds or updates a session state item

```
Session["EMail"] = email;
```

A statement that retrieves the value of a session state item

```
string email = Session["EMail"].ToString();
```

A statement that removes an item from session state

```
Session.Remove("EMail");
```

A statement that retrieves a session state item from a non-page class

```
string email = HttpContext.Current.Session["EMail"].ToString();
```

Description

- ASP.NET uses *session state* to track the state of each user of an application. To do that, it creates a *session state object* that contains a *session ID*. This ID is passed to the browser and then back to the server with the next request so the server can identify the session state object associated with that request.

- Because session state sends only the session ID to the browser, it doesn't slow response time. By default, though, session state objects are maintained in server memory so they can slow performance on the server side.

- To work with the data in session state, you use the HttpSessionState class, which defines a collection of session state items.

- To access the session state object from the code-behind file for a web form, use the Session property of the page.

- To access the session state object from a class other than a code-behind file, use the Current property of the HttpContext class to get the HttpContext object for the current request. Then, use the Session property to get the session state object.

Figure 8-3   How to work with session state

When to save and retrieve session state items

Most ASP.NET developers use session state in a consistent way. First, an application retrieves data from session state and stores it in variables. Then, the application uses these variables when it processes the user events. Finally, the application saves the updated variables back to session state so they can be retrieved the next time the page is posted back to the server.

If an item in session state is used within a single method in an application, you can retrieve, process, and save that item within that method. However, it's more common for an application to use a session state item in two or more methods. Because of that, it makes sense to retrieve the item when the application first starts and save it just before it ends. To do that, you can use the Load and PreRender events of the page, as shown in figure 8-4.

The first two examples in this figure are taken from the Shopping Cart application of chapter 4 so you shouldn't have any trouble understanding them. The first example uses the GetCart method of the CartItemList class to get a CartItemList object from the session state object, and it stores it in a variable named cart. The second example updates the cart by removing an item from it if an item in the cart is selected.

The third example shows how to use an event handler for the PreRender event to update an item named "Count" with the value of a variable named sessionCount. Note, however, that this event handler is only needed because sessionCount is a value-based variable, which means that the value is actually stored in the variable.

In contrast, if you update a reference-type variable such as a string or other object variable, the session state item is updated automatically when you update the object. That's because the variable contains a pointer to the object, not the data itself. Then, since the session state item also contains a pointer to that object, you don't have to update the session state item explicitly. That's the way the CartItemList object in the session state object is handled in the first two examples in this figure.

The event handlers that can be used to get and save session state data

Event	Handler name	Description
Load	Page_Load	This event occurs when a page is requested from the server, after all controls have been initialized and view state has been restored. You can use the handler for this event to test whether the session state object already exists, to get data from it if it does, and to create one if it doesn't.
PreRender	Page_PreRender	This event occurs after all the control events for the page have been processed but before the HTML that will be sent back to the browser is generated. You can use it to update value-type variables in the object, but you don't need to do that for reference-type variables.

A Load event handler that gets the session state object named cart

```
private CartItemList cart;
protected void Page_Load(object sender, EventArgs e)
{
    //retrieve cart object from session state on every post back
    cart = CartItemList.GetCart();
    ...
    ...
}
```

A Click event handler that updates the cart object

```
protected void btnRemove_Click(object sender, EventArgs e)
{
    //if cart contains items and user has selected an item...
    if (cart.Count > 0) {
        if (lstCart.SelectedIndex > -1) {
            //remove selected item from cart and re-display cart
            cart.RemoveAt(lstCart.SelectedIndex);
            this.DisplayCart(); }
        else { //if no item is selected, notify user
            lblMessage.Text = "Please select an item to remove."; }
    }
}
```

A PreRender event handler that updates a value in the cart object

```
protected void Page_PreRender(object sender, EventArgs e)
{
    cart["Count"] = sessionCount;
}
```

Description

- You only need to update a session state item explicitly if it's stored in a value-type variable. If it's stored in a reference-type variable, the session state item is updated when the variable is updated because the variable is a pointer to the object that's updated.

Figure 8-4   When to save and retrieve session state items

Options for storing session state data and tracking session IDs

By default, ASP.NET stores session state data in server memory and tracks user sessions using cookies. However, as figure 8-5 shows, ASP.NET actually provides four options for storing session state data and two options for tracking session IDs. Although you typically use the default options, you should be familiar with the other options in case you ever need them.

The default for storing session state data is *in-process mode*. With this mode, session state data is stored in server memory within the same process that your ASP.NET application runs. This is the most efficient way to store session state data, but it only works for applications that are hosted on a single web server.

If your application has so many users that a single web server can't carry the load, you can deploy the application on two or more servers. When you do that, you need to store session state data in a location that can be accessed by all of the servers. To do that, you can use either the *State Server mode* or the *SQL Server mode* that are described in the first table in this figure.

The last option for storing session state data is *custom mode*. With this mode, you create your own *session state store provider* that saves and retrieves session state data. You might use this option, for example, if you want to save session state data in an Oracle database instead of Microsoft SQL Server.

Fortunately, the programming requirements for all four session state modes are identical. So you can change an application from one mode to another without changing any of the application's code, with one caveat. If you haven't made your custom objects *serializable* when working in in-process mode, you'll need to do so when you move to state server or SQL server mode.

By default, ASP.NET maintains session state by sending the session ID for a user session to the browser as a *cookie*. Then, the cookie is returned to the server with the next request so the server can associate the browser with the session. This is called *cookie-based session tracking*, and this is the most reliable and secure way to track sessions.

If a browser doesn't support cookies, however, session state won't work unless you switch to *cookieless session tracking*. Cookieless session tracking works by adding the session ID to the URL that's used to request the ASP.NET page. Unfortunately, because the URL is visible to the user and isn't encrypted, the use of cookieless session tracking creates a security risk.

Ideally, then, you should use cookie-based session tracking when cookies are supported and cookieless session tracking when they're not. As you can see in the third table and the coding example, ASP.NET lets you do that by modifying the system.web element in the web.config file. In this example, the mode attribute indicates that in-process mode should be used. The cookieless attribute indicates that cookies should be used if they're supported, and URLs should be used if they're not. And the timeout attribute increases the time that the session will be maintained without activity to 30 minutes.

If you use a mode other than in-process mode, you're probably going to be in a large shop. In that case, you should be able to get help from the server manager when it's time to set the attributes in the web.config file.

Four modes for storing session state data

Mode	Description
In-process	Stores the data in IIS server memory in the same process as the application. This is the default, but it's only suitable when a single server is used for the application.
State Server	Stores the data in server memory under the control of the *ASP.NET state service*. This service can be accessed by other IIS servers, so it can be used when an application is hosted on a web farm.
SQL Server	Stores the data in a SQL Server database. This mode is used for applications that require more than one IIS server. This mode is slower than In-process mode and State Server mode, but it's the most reliable.
Custom	Lets you write your own *session state store provider* class for session state data.

Two options for tracking session IDs

Option	Description
Cookie-based	Uses cookies.
Cookieless	The session ID is encoded as part of the URL.

Attributes of the session state element in the web.config file

Attribute	Values
Mode	Off, InProc (the default), StateServer, SQLServer, or Custom.
Cookieless	UseCookies (the default). AutoDetect uses cookies if they're supported and a query string if they're not. UseUri uses a query string.
Timeout	The minutes (20 is the default) that a session should be maintained without any user activity.
StateConnectionString	The server name or IP address and port number (always 42424) of the server that runs the ASP.NET state service.
SqlConnectionString	A connection string for the instance of SQL Server that contains the database that's used to store the session state data.
AllowCustomSqlDatabase	A Boolean value that determines if the SqlConnectionString can specify the name of the database used to store state information.

A sessionState element in the web.config file that uses in-process mode

```
<system.web>
    <sessionState mode="InProc" cookieless="AutoDetect" timeout="30" />
</system.web>
```

Description

- The programming requirements for all four session state modes are the same, but the State Server and SQL Server modes require objects in session state to be *serializable*. To make an item serializable, add a Serializable attribute to its class declaration.

Figure 8-5   Options for storing session state data and tracking session IDs

How to use application state and caching

In contrast to session state, which stores data for a single user session, application state and caching let you store data that is shared by all users of an application. In the topics that follow, you'll learn how to use application state and caching.

How application state and caching work

Figure 8-6 presents the concepts you need for working with *application state* and *caching*. To start, an *application* is made up of all the pages, code, and other files that are located under a single directory in an IIS web server.

The first time a user requests a page that resides in an application's directory, ASP.NET initializes the application. During that process, ASP.NET creates an *application object* from the HttpApplication class, an *application state object* from the HttpApplicationState class, and a *cache object* from the Cache class. You can use the application state object or the cache object to store data in server memory that can be accessed by any page that's part of the application.

These objects exist until the application ends, which normally doesn't happen until IIS shuts down. However, the application is also restarted each time you rebuild the application or edit the application's web.config file.

So which application-level storage should you use? Generally, you'll want to use the cache object, because it's more flexible. This is because you can set expiration dates for items stored in the cache, and because the server is allowed to *scavenge* the cache when memory is running low. Because of this, you can store just about anything you want in the cache without worrying about negatively affecting the server, as long as you remember that the items may not be there when you come back for them. So, always check for null values in your code before trying to use something you've retrieved from cache.

Caching is typically used to store application-specific data that changes infrequently. For example, you might use the cache to store discount terms and tax rates for an ordering system, or a list of the 50 states. Although you could retrieve this type of information from a database each time it's needed, it can be retrieved more quickly from cache. As a result, using cached data can improve your application's performance.

In contrast, items stored in application state stay in memory until they are specifically removed or until the application ends. This can have a negative effect on a server's performance if a lot of data is stored. For this reason, it's best to use application state for small items of data, such as keeping track of the users that are logged on to an application that provides a chat room or a forum.

Application concepts

- An ASP.NET *application* is the collection of pages, code, and other files within a single directory on a web server. In most cases, an ASP.NET application corresponds to a single Visual Studio web project.

- An application begins when the first user requests a page that's a part of the application. Then, ASP.NET initializes the application before it processes the request for the page.

- As part of its initialization, ASP.NET creates an *application object* from the HttpApplication class, an *application state object* from the HttpApplicationState class, and a *cache object* from the Cache class. These objects exist for the duration of the application, and items stored in application state or cache are available to all users of the application.

- Once an application has started, it doesn't normally end until the web server is shut down. However, if you rebuild the application or edit the web.config file, the application will be restarted the next time a user requests a page that's part of the application.

Cache concepts

- Items stored in the cache object don't necessarily stay in server memory until the application ends. They can be set with an expiration date, and they can be *scavenged* by the server to recover memory when memory is low.

- Because of the way caching works, you can store larger amounts of data in the cache. However, you'll always need to check whether the data is still there before using it.

- The cache object is typically used to store data that changes infrequently, such as a list of states or countries. Storing data like this in cache improves performance by reducing the number of times you need to retrieve it from the database or other data store.

- Caching in ASP.NET can be done declaratively with output caching, and cache items can be removed automatically via dependencies, but that's beyond the scope of this book. Cashing can also be used by data source server controls.

Application state concepts

- Items stored in the application state object stay in server memory until they are specifically removed, or until the application ends. Because this can stress the server, application state should be used sparingly.

- Application state is most appropriate for storing small items of data that change as an application executes, such as how many users have requested the application.

- To make sure the application object is not accessed by more than one user at a time, it should be locked while updating and unlocked when the update is completed.

Figure 8-6   How application state and caching work

How to work with application state and cache data

Figure 8-7 presents the details for working with application state and cache data. The first table in this figure shows the members that are common to both classes, while the second and third tables show some methods specific to the Cache and HttpApplicationState classes.

As you can see from the examples below the tables, the techniques you use to add items to and retrieve items from application state and cache are similar to the techniques you use to work with items in session state. The main difference is that you use the Application or Cache property of the page to access the objects from a code-behind file, and you use the Application or Cache property of the HttpContext object for the current request to access the objects from a class other than a code-behind file.

However, if you want to set an expiration for an item you're adding to the cache, you'll need to use the Insert method of the Cache object. The Insert method is an overloaded method, but the one you'll most commonly use to set an expiration is shown in the second table in this figure. There are five parameters for this method.

The first and second parameters are the name and value of the object to be stored, just like with the Add method. The third parameter is a CacheDependency object. While not illustrated here, cache dependencies allow you to automatically remove an item from the cache when something it is associated with changes. For example, if your cached item is associated with an item in a database, the cached item can be removed when the item in the database changes. Most of the time, though, you'll enter a value of null for this parameter.

The fourth and fifth parameters determine the expiration time for the cached item. The fourth parameter sets an absolute expiration, such as 20 minutes from now, while the fifth parameter sets a sliding expiration, such as 20 minutes from the last time the item was accessed. If you try to set a value for both of these parameters, you'll get an error. Rather, you must set only one, and then use the System.Web.Caching.Cache enumeration to set a value of NoAbsoluteExpiration or NoSlidingExpiration for the other, as shown in the last example in this figure.

Common members of the HttpApplicationState and Cache classes

Indexer	Description
[name]	The value of the item with the specified name. If you set the value of an item that doesn't exist, that item is created.

Property	Description
Count	The number of items in the collection.

Method	Description
Add(name, value)	Adds an item to the collection.
Remove(name)	Removes the item with the specified name from the collection.

The Insert method of the Cache class

Method	Description
Insert(name, value, dependency, absolute, sliding)	Adds an item to the cache collection with a CacheDependency object (which can be null) and either an absolute expiration (like 20 minutes from now) or a sliding expiration (like 20 minutes from last usage). Use the System.Web.Caching.Cache enumeration for the expiration.

Common methods of the HttpApplicationState class

Method	Description
Clear()	Removes all items from the application state collection.
Lock()	Locks the application state collection so only the current user can access it.
Unlock()	Unlocks the application state collection so other users can access it.

Two statements that add items to application state and cache

```
Application.Add("ClickCount", 0);
Cache.Add("states", states);
```

Two statements that retrieve an item from application state and cache

```
int applicationCount = Convert.ToInt32(Application["ClickCount"]);
List<string> states = (List<string>)Cache["states"];
```

Two statements that retrieve an item from a non-page class

```
int applicationCount =
    Convert.ToInt32(HttpContext.Current.Application["ClickCount"]);
List<string> states = (List<string>)HttpContext.Current.Cache["states"];
```

A statement that adds an item to cache with an absolute expiration time

```
Cache.Insert("states", states, null, DateTime.Now.AddMinutes(20),
    System.Web.Caching.Cache.NoSlidingExpiration);
```

Figure 8-7   How to work with application state and cache data

How to work with application events

Besides providing storage, the application object also raises several events that you can use to run code at various points in the life of an application, such as when it starts, when it ends, or when an error occurs. One of the uses of these events is to initialize the values of application state items, as shown in figure 8-8. To work with these events, you first add a Global.asax file to the project as described in this figure.

By default, this file contains method declarations for five event handlers as shown in the example in this figure. Then, you can add code to any of these event handlers. This figure summarizes the four events you're most likely to use.

The example in this figure shows how you can initialize and update a session state item named HitCount that keeps track of the number of times a new session is started for an application. In this example, the Application_Start event handler retrieves the current hit count number from a database and adds an application state item named HitCount to the application state object. Similarly, the Application_End event handler saves the HitCount item to the database so it will be accurate when it's retrieved the next time the application starts. Although the HalloweenDB class that includes the methods that are used to retrieve and update the count isn't shown here, all you need to know is that the GetHitCount method retrieves the current hit count from the database as an integer value, and the UpdateHitCount method saves the integer value to the database.

The updating of the HitCount item takes place in the Session_Start event handler, which is raised whenever a new user session begins. Note that the code that updates the HitCount item uses the Lock and Unlock methods of the Application object.

When you're working with application state data, you'll want to lock the application state collection when you modify any of its data. To minimize the length of time the application state object is locked, you should do as little processing as possible between the Lock and Unlock methods.

If you don't lock the application state collection while the count is updated, two or more users could access the count at the same time. To illustrate why that's a problem, let's assume that three users access the count item at the same time when its value is 11. Then, when each of those users increment the count it becomes 12, and that's the value that each user stores in the application state collection. In this case, though, the correct count should be 14.

Four common application events

Event	Description
Application_Start	This event is raised when the first page of an application is requested by any user. It is often used to initialize the values of application state items.
Application_End	This event is raised when an application is about to terminate. It can be used to write the values of application state items to a database or file.
Session_Start	This event is raised when a user session begins. It can be used to initialize session state items, update application state items, or authorize user access.
Session_End	This event is raised when a user session is about to terminate. It can be used to free resources held by the user or to log the user off the application. It is raised only when in-process mode is used.

A Global.asax file that creates an object in application state

```
<%@ Application Language="C#" %>
<script runat="server">
    void Application_Start(object sender, EventArgs e)
    {
        // Code that runs on application startup
        Application.Add("HitCount", HalloweenDB.GetHitCount());
    }
    void Application_End(object sender, EventArgs e)
    {
        //  Code that runs on application shutdown
        HalloweenDB.UpdateHitCount(Application["HitCount"]);
    }
    void Application_Error(object sender, EventArgs e)
    {
        // Code that runs when an unhandled error occurs
    }
    void Session_Start(object sender, EventArgs e)
    {
        // Code that runs when a new session is started
        Application.Lock();
            int hitCount = Convert.ToInt32(Application["HitCount"]) + 1;
            Application["HitCount"] = hitCount;
        Application.UnLock();
    }
    void Session_End(object sender, EventArgs e)
    {
        // Code that runs when a session ends.
    }
</script>
```

Description

- To create a Global.asax file, right-click the application and select Add→Add New Item. Or, select the WEBSITE→Add New Item command. Then, choose the Global Application Class template.

- The Global.asax file provides event handlers for application events. The event handlers are coded within a Script element that defines a code declaration block.

Figure 8-8   How to work with application events

How to use cookies and URL encoding

Earlier in this chapter, you learned that view state data is stored in a hidden field on a page that's sent to and from the browser. That's one way to maintain data between round trips. Two others are using cookies and URL encoding.

How to create cookies

A *cookie* is a name/value pair that is stored on the client's computer. For instance, the name of the first cookie in figure 8-9 is ASP.NET_SessionId, and its value is

```
jsswpu5530hcyx2w3jfa5u55
```

This is a typical session ID for a cookie that's generated by ASP.NET to keep track of a session. The other cookie examples are typical of cookies that you create yourself.

To create a cookie, you instantiate an object from the HttpCookie class. Then, you include it in the HTTP response that the server sends back to the browser, and the user's browser stores the cookie either in its own memory or in a text file on the client machine's disk.

A cookie that's stored in the browser's memory is called a *session cookie* because it exists only for that session. When the browser session ends, the contents of any session cookies are lost. Session cookies are what ASP.NET uses to track session ID's. In contrast, *persistent cookies* are written to disk, so they are maintained after the browser session ends. Whether session or persistent, though, once a cookie is sent to a browser, it's automatically returned to the server with each HTTP request.

Besides using cookies for session IDs, you can use cookies to save information that identifies each user so the users don't have to enter that information each time they visit your web site. You can also use cookies to store information that lets you personalize the web pages that are displayed for a user.

When you use cookies to store this type of information, you should keep in mind that some users may have disabled cookies on their browsers. In that case, you won't be able to save cookies on the user's computer. Unfortunately, ASP.NET doesn't provide a way for you to determine whether a user has disabled cookies. As a result, if you use cookies in an application, you may need to notify the user that cookies must be enabled to use it.

This figure also presents some properties of the HttpCookie class. Then, the first example shows how to create a session cookie. Here, both the cookie's name and value are specified in the constructor. Because the Expires property isn't set, it's given a default value of 12:00 a.m. on January 1, 0001. Because this value has already passed, the cookie is deleted when the session ends.

If you don't set the value of a cookie when you create it, you can use the Value property to set it later on. In addition, you can use the Expires property to set the expiration date for a persistent cookie. This is illustrated by the second example in this figure.

Examples of cookies

```
ASP.NET_SessionId=jsswpu5530hcyx2w3jfa5u55
EMail=mary@techknowsolve.com
user_ID=4993
```

Two ways to create a cookie

```
New HttpCookie(name)
New HttpCookie(name, value)
```

Common properties of the HttpCookie class

Property	Description
Expires	A DateTime value that indicates when the cookie should expire.
Name	The cookie's name.
Secure	A Boolean value that indicates whether the cookie should be sent only when a secure connection is used. See chapter 18 for information on secure connections.
Value	The string value assigned to the cookie.

Code that creates a session cookie

```
HttpCookie nameCookie = new HttpCookie("UserName", userName);
```

Code that creates a persistent cookie

```
HttpCookie nameCookie = new HttpCookie("UserName");
nameCookie.Value = userName;
nameCookie.Expires = DateTime.Now.AddYears(1);
```

Description

- A *cookie* is a name/value pair that's stored in the user's browser or on the user's disk.

- A web application sends a cookie to a browser via an HTTP response. Then, each time the browser sends an HTTP request to the server, it attaches any cookies that are associated with that server.

- By default, ASP.NET uses a cookie to store the session ID for a session, but you can also create and send your own cookies to a user's browser.

- A *session cookie* is kept in the browser's memory and exists only for the duration of the browser session. A *persistent cookie* is kept on the user's disk and is retained until the cookie's expiration date.

- To create a cookie, you specify its name or its name and value. To create a persistent cookie, you must also set the Expires property to the time you want the cookie to expire.

Figure 8-9   How to create cookies

How to work with cookies

After you create a cookie, you work with it using the members of the HttpCookieCollection class shown in figure 8-10. This class defines a collection of HttpCookie objects. To refer to a cookie in a cookies collection, for example, you use the indexer of the collection. And to add a cookie to the collection, you use the Add method of the collection.

The key to working with cookies is realizing that you must deal with two instances of the HttpCookieCollection class. The first one contains the collection of cookies that have been sent to the server from the client. You access this collection using the Cookies property of the HttpRequest object. The second one contains the collection of cookies that will be sent back to the browser. You access this collection using the Cookies property of the HttpResponse object.

To send a new cookie to the client, you create the cookie and then add it to the collection of cookies in the HttpResponse object. This is illustrated in the first example in this figure. Here, a cookie named UserName is created and added to the HttpResponse object.

The second example shows you how to retrieve the value of a cookie that's sent from the browser. Here, the Request property of the page is used to refer to the HttpRequest object. Then, the indexer of the Cookies collection of the request object is used to get the cookie, and the Value property of the cookie is used to get the cookie's value.

The last example in this figure shows how to delete a persistent cookie. To do that, you create a cookie with the same name as the cookie you want to delete, and you set its Expires property to a time in the past. In this example, the date is set to one second before the current time. Then, you add the cookie to the HttpResponse object so it's sent back to the browser. When the browser receives the cookie, it replaces the existing cookie with the new cookie. When the client's system detects that the cookie has expired, it deletes it.

Common members of the HttpCookieCollection class

Indexer	Description
[name]	The cookie with the specified name.
Property	**Description**
Count	The number of cookies in the collection.
Method	**Description**
Add(cookie)	Adds a cookie to the collection.
Clear()	Removes all cookies from the collection.
Remove(name)	Removes the cookie with the specified name from the collection.

A method that creates a new cookie and adds it to the HttpResponse object

```
private void AddCookie()
{
    HttpCookie nameCookie = new HttpCookie("UserName", txtUserName.Text);
    nameCookie.Expires = DateTime.Now.AddYears(1);
    Response.Cookies.Add(nameCookie);
}
```

A method that retrieves the value of a cookie from the HttpRequest object

```
protected void Page_Load(object sender, EventArgs e)
{
    if (!IsPostBack)
        if (!(Request.Cookies["UserName"] == null))
            lblUserName.Text = "Welcome back, "
                                + Request.Cookies["UserName"].Value + ".";
}
```

A method that deletes a persistent cookie

```
private void DeleteCookie()
{
    HttpCookie nameCookie = new HttpCookie("UserName");
    nameCookie.Expires = DateTime.Now.AddSeconds(-1);
    Response.Cookies.Add(nameCookie);
}
```

Description

- Cookies are managed in collections defined by the HttpCookieCollection class.

- To access the cookies collection for a request or response, use the Cookies property of the HttpRequest or HttpResponse object. To refer to these objects, use the Request and Response properties of the page.

- To delete a persistent cookie, create a cookie with the same name as the cookie you want to delete and set its Expires property to a time that has already passed. Then, when the client's system detects that the cookie has expired, it deletes it.

Figure 8-10   How to work with cookies

How to enable or disable cookies

If an application relies on the use of cookies, you'll want to be sure that cookies are enabled in your browser as you test the application. Conversely, to test an application that's intended to work even if cookies have been disabled, you'll need to disable cookies in your browser. To do that, you can use the techniques presented in figure 8-11.

If you're using Internet Explorer, you use a slider control to determine what cookies are allowed. The default setting is Medium, which enables both session and persistent cookies. To disable both types of cookies, you can select a privacy setting that blocks all cookies. Alternatively, you can use the dialog box that's displayed when you click the Advanced button to override the default settings so your browser accepts session cookies but disables persistent cookies.

This figure also describes how to enable or disable cookies if you're using Google Chrome or Mozilla Firefox. Although these techniques differ from browser to browser and they may change in later browser versions, you should be able to figure out what you need to do for any browser that you use.

An Internet Explorer dialog box with disabled cookies

How to enable or disable cookies for Internet Explorer

1. Select the Tools→Internet Options command.
2. Select the Privacy tab, then use the slider control to set the security level to accept or block cookies.
3. To enable or disable persistent cookies and session cookies separately, click the Advanced button and select from the advanced privacy settings.

How to enable or disable cookies for Google Chrome

1. Click the menu icon to the right of the address bar, and then select Settings.
2. Scroll to the bottom of the page and click on the Show Advanced Settings link.
3. Select Privacy and then Content Settings, then select the Block Sites From Setting Any Data button.

How to enable or disable cookies for Mozilla Firefox

1. Select the Tools→Options command from the menu bar.
2. Click the Privacy icon, then select the Use Custom Settings for History option from the Firefox Will drop-down list.
3. Check or uncheck the Accept Cookies From Sites option, and select an item from the Keep Until drop-down list.

Figure 8-11   How to enable or disable cookies

How to use URL encoding

URL encoding provides another way to maintain state by storing information in a page on the client. This information is stored in a *query string* that's added to the end of the URL, as shown in figure 8-12. Since using query strings is a common technique, you've probably seen them used on search sites like Google and shopping sites like Ebay and Amazon.

At the top of this figure, you can see two URLs that include query strings. The first one includes a single attribute named cat (for category), and the second one includes two attributes named cat and prod. As you can see, you add a query string by coding a question mark after the URL. Then, you code the name of the first attribute, an equal sign, and the value you want to assign to the attribute. To include another attribute, you code an ampersand (&), followed by the name and value of the attribute.

In most cases, you'll use query strings within hyperlinks or anchor (<a>) elements to pass information from one page of an application to another. The second example in this figure shows how to use query strings with hyperlinks. Here, the NavigateUrl attribute of the hyperlink indicates that it will link to a page named Product.aspx. In addition, the URL includes a query string that contains a category and a product value. The Product page can then use these values to display information for the specified product.

You use query strings with anchor elements in the much the same way. This is illustrated in the third example in this figure. Here, the href attribute specifies the URL with the query string.

To retrieve the values included in a query string, you use the QueryString property of the Request object as illustrated in the fourth example. The two statements in this example retrieve the two values passed by the query string in the second and third examples.

The fifth example shows that you can also use query strings in the URLs that you code for Redirect, RedirectPermanent, or Transfer methods. Here, the URL contains a query string with a single attribute that contains a category ID. You should also realize that you can code query strings in the PostBackUrl attribute of a button control, although you're not likely to do that.

The last example shows a relatively new way to store information in a URL. This type of URL is often called an *SEO-friendly URL,* or just a *friendly URL*, because search engines won't archive the query strings in normal URLs. With friendly URLs, though, the search engines will archive the entire URLs. They are also called friendly URLs because they're easier for users to read and remember.

Although SEO-friendly URL's require some additional coding, ASP.NET has a routing framework that makes them easy to work with. You'll learn more about this in chapter 11.

Two URLs with query strings

```
~/Order.aspx?cat=costumes
~/Order.aspx?cat=props&prod=rat01
```

A hyperlink with a URL that includes a query string

```
<asp:HyperLink ID="HyperLink1" runat="server"
    NavigateUrl="~/Product.aspx?cat=fx&amp;prod=fog01">Fog machine
</asp:HyperLink>
```

An anchor element with a URL that includes a query string

```
<a href="product.aspx?cat=fx&prod=fog01">Fog machine</a>
```

Statements that retrieve the values of the query string attributes

```
string categoryID = Request.QueryString["cat"];
string productID = Request.QueryString["prod"];
```

Code that uses a URL with a query string in a Redirect method

```
Response.Redirect("~/Order.aspx?cat=" + categoryID);
```

A SEO-friendly URL

```
~/Order.aspx/props/rat01
```

Description

- When you use *URL encoding*, a *query string* that consists of attribute/value pairs is added to the end of a URL. Query strings are frequently used in hyperlinks and anchor <a> elements to pass information from one page of an application to another or to display different information on the same page.

- Query strings can also be used in the URLs that are specified for Response. Redirect, Response.RedirectPermanent, or Server.Transfer calls, and they can be used in the PostBackUrl property of a button control.

- When you use a hyperlink, an anchor element, or a Redirect or Transfer method that specifies a URL for the current page, the page is processed as if it's being requested for the first time.

- To code a query string, follow the URL with a question mark, the name of the attribute, an equal sign, and a value. To code two or more attributes, separate them with ampersands (&) and don't include any spaces in the query string.

- To retrieve the value of a query string attribute, use the QueryString property of the HttpRequest object and specify the attribute name. To refer to the HttpRequest object, use the Request property of the page.

- Different browsers impose different limits on the number of characters in the query string of a URL. Most browsers provide for a URL with at least 2000 characters, however.

- A recent development with URL encoding is *SEO-friendly URLs* that can improve search engine optimization. You'll learn more about them in chapter 11.

Figure 8-12   How to use URL encoding

An application that uses cookies, application state, and caching

To show you how cookies, application state, and caching can be used in an application, this chapter ends by showing two pages of the Shopping Cart application with a couple of added features.

The Order and CheckOut pages

Figure 8-13 shows the Order and first CheckOut page for the Shopping Cart application that you studied in section 1. But now, the Order page includes a Welcome message with the user's first name. This name is stored in a cookie when the user completes the first CheckOut page that's shown in this figure. After that, the name is retrieved from the cookie whenever the Order page is requested.

In addition, the footer of the Order page now contains two lines of data. The first one shows the last date and time that this item was updated in the cache. This value is kept in the cache object for the application. The second line shows the number of times that this page has been accessed during the life of this application. This value is kept in the application state object.

This figure also shows the aspx code for the new items on the Order page. Here, you can see that all the of the items are displayed in label controls. Although this chapter, doesn't show the aspx code for the CheckOut page, the IDs for its three controls are txtFirstName, txtLastName, and btnContinue.

An Order page that uses a cookie and application state

The first CheckOut page

The aspx code for the welcome message and the footer on the Order page

```
<section>
    <asp:Label ID="lblWelcome" runat="server"></asp:Label>
    <form id="form1" runat="server">
        ...
        ...
    </form>
</section>
<footer>
    Last Updated: <asp:Label ID="lblUpdateTime" runat="server">
        </asp:Label><br />
    Number of Page Hits: <asp:Label ID="lblPageHits" runat="server">
        </asp:Label>
</footer>
```

Figure 8-13   An application that uses cookies, application state, and caching

The critical C# code for the Order and CheckOut pages

Figure 8-14 presents the critical C# code in the code-behind files for the Order and CheckOut forms. Look first at the code for the CheckOut page. There, the Click event handler for the Continue button starts by setting a DateTime object named "expiry" to 5 minutes after the current time. Then, the next two statements call the SetResponseCookie method to add FirstName and LastName cookies to the HTTP response for this application. Note, however, that both of these cookies will last for only five minutes. The last statement in this event handler redirects to the Order page.

Now, look at the code for the Load event handler for the Order page. After the SQL data source is bound to the drop-down list, the item named "HitCount" is retrieved from the application state object and stored in an integer variable named hitCount. Then, this variable is increased by one, and the HitCount item in application state is set to the value of this variable. Last, the value of the hitCount variable is converted to a string and stored in the label in the footer of the page.

The next block of code in the Load event handler for the Order page gets the FirstName cookie from the request object. If it isn't null, the value of this cookie is concatenated in the string for the Welcome message, and the message is put into the label at the start of the section element. That displays the message below the header on the Order page.

The third block of code uses caching to get the value of the LastUpdateTime item from the cache object. If the item is null, it sets the object named "lastUpdateTime" to the current date and time. Then, it uses the Insert method of the Cache object to add that item to the cache with a time before expiration of 10 minutes. Note that a using statement for the System.Web.Caching namespace is included at the beginning of this file, so it isn't necessary to qualify the Cache enumeration that's used by the last parameter of this method. Last, this block of code puts the value of the item in the label control in the footer of the page.

The critical code in the code-behind for the Order page

```csharp
protected void Page_Load(object sender, EventArgs e)
{
    //bind drop-down list and update page hit count on first load
    if (!IsPostBack)
    {
        ddlProducts.DataBind();
        Application.Lock();
            int hitCount = Convert.ToInt32(Application["HitCount"]);
            hitCount++;
            Application["HitCount"] = hitCount;
        Application.UnLock();
        lblPageHits.Text = hitCount.ToString();
    }
    //get and show product data on every load
    ...

    //get firstname from cookie and set welcome message if it exists
    HttpCookie cookie = Request.Cookies["FirstName"];
    if (cookie != null)
        lblWelcome.Text = "Welcome back, " + cookie.Value + "!";

    //get last update from cache, then display it
    //or set last update in cache to now plus 10, then display
    object lastUpdateTime = Cache.Get("LastUpdateTime");
    if (lastUpdateTime == null)
    {
        lastUpdateTime = DateTime.Now;
        Cache.Insert("LastUpdateTime", lastUpdateTime, null,
            DateTime.Now.AddMinutes(10), Cache.NoSlidingExpiration);
    }
    lblUpdateTime.Text = lastUpdateTime.ToString();
    ...
```

The critical code in the code-behind file for the first CheckOut page

```csharp
public partial class CheckOut : System.Web.UI.Page
{
    protected void btnContinue_Click(object sender, EventArgs e)
    {
        if (Page.IsValid)
        {
            DateTime expiry = DateTime.Now.AddMinutes(5);
            this.SetResponseCookie("FirstName", txtFirstName.Text, expiry);
            this.SetResponseCookie("LastName", txtLastName.Text, expiry);
        }
        Response.Redirect("~/Order.aspx");
    }
    private void SetResponseCookie(string name, string value,
                                   DateTime expiry)
    {
        HttpCookie cookie = new HttpCookie(name, value);
        cookie.Expires = expiry;
        Response.Cookies.Add(cookie);
    }
}
```

Figure 8-14   The critical C# code for the Order and CheckOut pages

Perspective

If this chapter has succeeded, you should now be able to use view state, session state, application state, caching, cookies, and URL encoding whenever they're appropriate for your applications. As you work with these techniques, you'll often find that you need two or more of them in a single application. Most web applications, for example, use both view state and session state. And many applications also use caching, cookies, and URL encoding.

Terms

view state	application state
view state object	application state object
session state	caching
session state object	cache object
session ID	scavenging the cache
in-process mode	cookie
session state store provider	session cookie
cookie-based session tracking	persistent cookie
cookieless session tracking	URL encoding
serializable	query string
application	SEO-friendly URL
application object	friendly URL

Summary

- *View state* is implemented by a *view state object* that retains the values of page and control properties that change from one execution of a page to another. These values are encoded in a string that's assigned to a hidden input field that's passed to and from the browser.

- Two reasons for disabling view state for a page or control are (1) because view state restores data that you don't want restored, and (2) because view state storage is so large that it affects the performance of the page.

- ASP.NET uses *session state* to track each user's session. To do that, it creates a *session state object* that contains a *session ID*, and it passes this ID to and from the browser. The server uses this ID to get the session state object for the user.

- To work with the items in a view state object or a session state object, you can use the indexer, properties, and methods of their classes: the StateBag class for view state and the HttpSessionState class for session state.

- To get data from a session state object, you often use the Load event handler for a page. To get or update the data in the object, you can use any event handler. And to update value-based data, you can use the PreRender event handler, although you don't need to do that for reference-based data.

- Although *cookies* are normally used to pass the session ID for a session state object to and from the browser, you can also set up *cookieless session tracking*. Then, the session ID is coded in the URL for the page. A third option uses a cookie if cookies are supported by a browser or the URL if they aren't.

- When an *application* starts, ASP.NET creates an *application object*, an *application state object*, and a *cache object*. These objects exist as long as the application is running on IIS, and items stored in the application state object and cache object are available to all users of the application.

- The application state object is best used for small items of data, but the cache object can be used for larger items since they don't have to stay in server memory until the application ends. Instead, cache items can have expiration dates, and they can be *scavenged* by the server if memory is needed.

- You can create a Global.asax file for an application that lets you create event handlers for application and session events like the start or end of an application or session.

- A *cookie* is a name/value pair that's stored in the user's browser or on the user's disk. A web application can send a cookie to a browser in an HTTP response. Then, the browser returns the cookie in its HTTP request.

- A *session cookie* exists only for the duration of a browser session. A *persistent cookie* is kept on the user's disk and is retained until the cookie expires.

- *URL encoding* lets you pass data from one page of an application to another by attaching name/value pairs in a *query string* at the end of the URL.

Exercise 8-1   Modify the Shopping Cart application

In this exercise, you'll modify and enhance the Shopping Cart application that's in figures 8-13 and 8-14. Although the way this application works isn't entirely realistic, this exercise will give you a chance to use cookies, session state, and caching.

Open, review, and run the Shopping Cart application

1. Open the Ex08Cart web site that's in the aspnet45_cs directory, and review the code-behind files for the Order and CheckOut pages to see that they're like the ones in figure 8-14.

2. Test the application to see how it works. To go to the CheckOut page, go first to the Cart page, then click its CheckOut button. On the CheckOut page, enter a first name and last name and click on the Continue button. Note that this displays the Order page with a Welcome message displayed.

3. Go back to the CheckOut page, and note that the first name and last name fields are empty. Then, enter a different first name and last name and click on the Continue button to see that the Welcome message has been changed. Now, stop the application and return to Visual Studio.

4. Enable the trace feature for the Order page as shown at the bottom of figure 8-1. Next, run the application and scroll down to see the number of bytes used for view state. Then, turn the trace feature off.

Use cookies or session state to restore the data in the CheckOut page

5. Modify the code-behind file for the CheckOut page so the first and last name fields are restored when the user returns to this page by getting the data from the cookies that are created. Then, test this change. Remember, though, that the cookies have just a five minute life, so you may have to enter the first and last name fields again when you test this change.

6. Test this change again. This time, make sure that the Welcome message is correct if you change the entry in the first name field after it has been restored from the cookie. In other words, if you change the field from Mary to Mike, the Welcome message should reflect that.

7. Comment out the code for using cookies to restore the entries on the CheckOut page. Then, write new code that uses session state to store the first and last name entries after the user enters them, and to restore those entries when the user returns to this page. This should also let the user change the values in the restored entries and have the changes be reflected in the Welcome message. Now, test this change.

Use caching to keep track of the hit count

8. In the code-behind file for the Order page, comment out the code that uses application state to keep track of the hit count. Then, write new code that uses caching to do that with a 5-minute life for the item, and test that change.

9. When you're through testing and experimenting, close the application.

9

How to use master pages

As you develop the pages of a web site, you'll find that many pages require some of the same elements like headers, navigation bars, and footers. For example, both the Order and Cart pages of the Shopping Cart application have the same header. The easiest way to create pages with common elements like that is to use master pages, and that's what you'll learn how to do in this chapter. In fact, we recommend that you use master pages for every site you develop.

How to create master pages

A *master page* is a page that provides the common elements for the other pages of a web site. For instance, master pages make it easy to include headers, navigation menus, and footers that are used by the other pages. In the topics that follow, you'll learn how to create master pages in your ASP.NET applications.

An introduction to master pages

Figure 9-1 shows the basics of how master pages work. As you can see, the page that's actually sent to the browser is created by combining elements from a master page and a *content page*. The content page provides the content that's unique to each page in the application, while the master page provides the elements that are common to all pages.

In this example, the master page (Site.master) provides a header at the top of each page and a navigation menu at the side of each page. The master page also includes a *content placeholder* that indicates where the content for each content page should be displayed. In this example, the content page is the Order.aspx page, and its content is displayed in the content placeholder in the master page.

Notice that the name of the content page is Order.aspx, the same as the Order page that you saw in chapter 4. In other words, when you use master pages, the individual pages of your web application become the content pages.

The Shopping Cart application with a master page

Master page (Site.master) and Content page (Order.aspx)

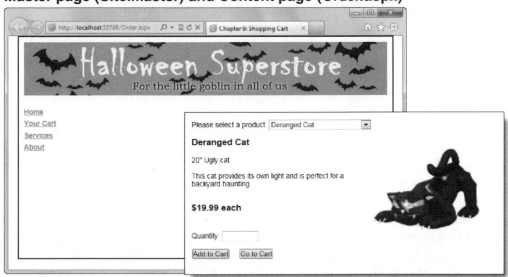

Rendered page

Description

- A *master page* provides a framework in which the content of the pages of the web site can be presented. As a result, master pages make it easy to create pages with a consistent look.

- The pages that provide the content that's displayed in a master page are called *content pages*. The content of each content page is displayed in one or more of the master page's *content placeholders*.

Figure 9-1   An application that uses a master page

How to create a master page

Figure 9-2 shows how to create a master page, and it also shows the starting aspx code for a master page. This code includes two ContentPlaceHolder controls: one in the head element and one in the form element. The one in the head element can contain any element that would normally be coded within the head element, such as links to external style sheets or JavaScript files. The one in the form element marks the location where the content from the content page will displayed.

To develop the content of the master page, you add elements outside of the ContentPlaceHolder controls. This is illustrated by the Visual Studio example at the top of this figure. Here, you can see that an image has been added to a header element at the top of the page, and four links have been added to a nav element that is displayed on the side of the page. Like any page, you can add HTML elements and server controls to a master page. You can also structure the page with HTML5 semantic elements and format the page with CSS.

Although a master page starts with only two content placeholders, you can create other placeholders if you need to. You might want to do that, for example, to create a page layout that has custom content in several areas. To create another content placeholder, you simply drag the ContentPlaceHolder control from the Standard group of the Toolbox onto the master page and give it a unique ID.

Because an application can have more than one master page, you can use one master page for one set of pages within a site and another master page for another set of pages. That way, you can give each set of pages a distinctive page layout. For example, you can use one master page for all of the shopping pages of a web site, and another master page for the checkout pages. Then, each content page specifies which master page to use.

If you look at the starting code for a master page, you can see that it starts with a Master directive with attributes that are similar to those in the Page directive for a content page. Although it isn't included in the starting Master directive, another important attribute is the ClientIDMode attribute. You'll learn about this attribute next.

A master page in Design view with header, aside, and nav elements

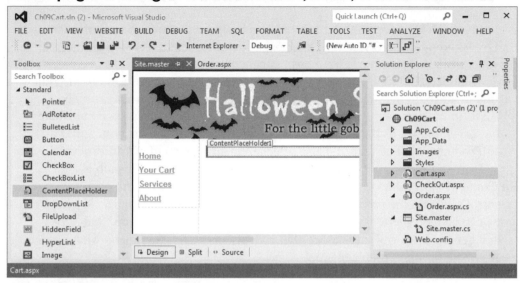

The starting code for a master page

```
<%@ Master Language="C#" AutoEventWireup="true"
CodeFile="MasterPage.master.cs" Inherits="MasterPage" %>

<!DOCTYPE html>
<html xmlns="http://www.w3.org/1999/xhtml">
<head runat="server">
    <title></title>
    <asp:ContentPlaceHolder id="head" runat="server">
    </asp:ContentPlaceHolder>
</head>
<body>
    <form id="form1" runat="server">
    <div>
        <asp:ContentPlaceHolder id="ContentPlaceHolder1" runat="server">
        </asp:ContentPlaceHolder>
    </div>
    </form>
</body>
</html>
```

How to add a master page to a project

- Right-click on the project in the Solution Explorer, then select Add→Master Page, enter a name for the page in the resulting dialog box, and click OK.

Description

- A new master page starts with two content placeholders, but you can add more.
- Any elements you add to the master page will appear on every content page that uses the master page, and any elements that you add inside a content placeholder can be displayed or overridden by a content page.

Figure 9-2   How to create a master page

How to work with the ClientIDMode property

Figure 9-3 shows the Order page after it has been updated to use a master page. Although the CSS for the Order page hasn't changed, something has gone wrong with the formatting. What has happened?

To understand this, you need to know how ASP.NET creates a *client id*. That is the id attribute that ASP.NET assigns to an HTML element when it renders HTML to the browser. As you have seen, ASP.NET usually uses the ID attribute of a server control as the client id. For example, a drop-down list with an ID of "ddlProducts" will be rendered as a select element with an id of "ddlProducts".

However, if a server control is placed inside a parent control, such as a ContentPlaceHolder control, ASP.NET uses a combination of the parent control's ID and the server control's ID to create the client id. You can see how this can be a problem if your CSS expects the id to be "ddlProducts" but ASP.NET generates "formPlaceHolder_ddlProducts" as the id. And that's what has caused the problem in this figure.

The good news is that you can control how a client id is created by using the ClientIDMode attribute of a page or a control. The table in this figure shows the available values for this property, and the code examples show the client ids that are created for a control with an id of "ddlProducts" when using each of the modes.

The default value of the ClientIDMode for a page is Predictable. Then, since the default value for all controls is Inherit, their mode will also be Predictable. This mode is called Predictable because you can predict the client id that ASP.NET is going to produce based on the IDs of the parent control and the server control. For instance, a control with ddlProducts as its ID in a placeholder with formPlaceHolder as its ID will end up with a client id of formPlaceHolder_ddlProducts.

If you are starting a web site from scratch, you'll probably want to leave these settings alone and use the generated client ids when you write the CSS and JavaScript code for the pages. But if you're converting existing pages so they use a master page and you've already written the CSS for them, you may want to change the page's ClientIDMode attribute to Static. Or, if you're converting an older application with CSS that's expecting the ASP.NET-generated client ids, you may want to change the ClientIDMode to AutoID. If you don't want to change the ClientIDMode for the entire page, you can change it for the content placeholders or for the controls that you add to the content pages.

A page with a ClientIDMode of Predictable that has messed up the CSS

Values of the ClientIDMode property

Value	Description
Predictable	The client id is the name of the parent container added to the name of the server control. This is a page's default value. (For a data-bound parent control that generates multiple rows, the value of the control's ClientIDRowSuffix property is added to the end of the child control's id. If this property is blank a sequential number is added.)
Static	The client id is the same as the server control ID. This can cause id conflicts, such as when there are several instances of the same user control on a page.
AutoID	The client id is based on the conventions of ASP.NET versions prior to 4.0.
Inherit	The control inherits the parent's ClientIDMode. This is the default value for a control.

The select elements generated for a drop-down list with ddlProducts as its ID when it's in a placeholder with formPlaceHolder as its ID

When ClientIDMode is Predictable

```
<select name="ctl00$formPlaceHolder$ddlProducts"
    id="formPlaceHolder_ddlProducts">...</select>
```

When ClientIDMode is Static

```
<select name="ctl00$formPlaceHolder$ddlProducts"
    id="ddlProducts">...</select>
```

When ClientIDMode is AutoID

```
<select name="ctl00$formPlaceHolder$ddlProducts"
    id="ctl00_formPlaceHolder_ddlProducts">...</select>
```

Description

- A *client id* is the value of the HTML id attribute that will be generated for a control.

- The ClientIDMode attribute of a page or an individual control determines how the client id for a control will be generated. This affects the ID selectors you use in the CSS for a page.

Figure 9-3   How to use the ClientIDMode property

How to create and develop content pages

Once you create a master page, you can create and develop the content pages for the master page. The topics that follow show how.

How to create a content page

Figure 9-4 shows how to create a content page. To create the Default.aspx content page, you can use the first procedure. For most pages, though, you'll use the same procedure to create a content page that you use to create a regular page, but you'll also check the Select Master Page check box. Then, you can choose the master page you want to use for the content page from the Select a Master Page dialog box that's displayed.

The Visual Studio example in this figure shows the code that's generated when you create a new content page named Order. Although the Page directive includes the same information as a regular ASP.NET page, it also includes a MasterPageFile attribute that specifies the master page that you selected.

Unlike normal ASP.NET pages, though, content pages don't include a DOCTYPE directive or any structural HTML elements such as html, head, body, or form elements. That's because those elements are provided by the master page. Instead, the content page includes one ASP.NET Content element for each content placeholder in the master page. In this case, because the master page contains two placeholders, the content page contains two Content elements.

As you can see, the ContentPlaceHolderID attributes of these elements identify which placeholders they're associated with. Then, you place the content for the page between the start and end tags of the Content elements.

This figure also includes a procedure for converting a regular page to a content page. You'll need to follow this procedure if you start a web site without using master pages, and later decide to use master pages. Unfortunately, though, Visual Studio doesn't provide a way to automatically do this. As a result, you'll have to manually edit each of the pages to add the MasterPageFile attribute to the Page directive, remove the DOCTYPE directive and structural HTML elements (html, head, body, and form), and add one or more Content elements.

Because this conversion procedure is error prone, it pays to use master pages for all but the simplest of applications, even if each master page contains only the content placeholders. Then, when you're ready to provide a consistent look to the pages within the application, you can enhance the master pages.

For the record, you can also use two other methods for specifying which master page is used for a content page. First, you can add a masterPageFile attribute to the pages element in the web.config file that specifies the master page that will apply to all content pages that don't specify a master file. Second, you can specify the master page at runtime by setting the MasterPageFile attribute of the page in the Page_PreInit method. Note, however, that the Web Forms Designer doesn't support either of these techniques so you won't be able to view or edit the content pages in Design view.

The starting code for a new content page

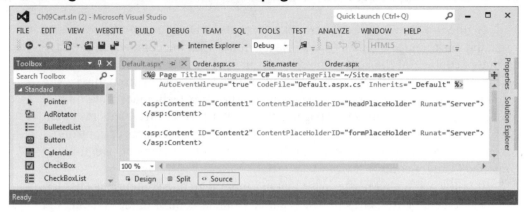

How to create a new content page

- To create the Default.aspx content page for a master page, right-click on the master page in the Solution Explorer, then choose Add Content Page.

- To create other content pages, right-click on the master page in the Solution Explorer, and select Add→Add New Item. Then, select the Web Form template, enter the name for the form, check Select Master Page, and click Add. When the Select a Master Page dialog box appears, select the master page that you want to use, and click OK.

How to convert a regular ASP.NET page to a content page

- Add a MasterPageFile attribute to the Page directive and set its value to the URL of the master page.

- Add a Content control within the form element and move the original contents of the page inside it.

- If the head element contains other elements used by the page, add a Content control within the head element and move the original contents of the head element inside it.

- Delete everything that's outside the Content elements except the Page directive.

Description

- The Page directive in the aspx code for a content page includes a MasterPageFile attribute that specifies the name of the master page.

- The aspx code for a content page includes Content controls that correspond to the placeholders of the master page. Then, you enter the content for the page within these Content controls.

- Although you can also specify the master page for a content page in the web.config file or in the Page_PreInit method, the Web Forms Designer doesn't support either of these techniques. As a result, you won't be able to view the content page in Design view.

Figure 9-4   How to create a content page

How to add content to a page

Figure 9-5 shows how a content page appears in Design view. As you can see, the master page elements are displayed along with the contents of the Content control for the content placeholder in the form element of the master page. However, you can't edit any of the master page elements from this view.

To add content to a content page, you use the same techniques that you use for adding content to any other page. You can enter text, HTML elements, and ASP controls directly into Source view, or you can drag elements or controls from the Toolbox to the content area. Just be sure that the elements are going into the Content control.

If you work with a master page that has more than one content placeholder in the body element, there will be a separate Content control in the content page for each placeholder. For instance, a master page might have one placeholder in its header element, one in its section element, and another in its footer element. Then, when you add content to a content page, you need to make sure you're adding the right content to the right Content control.

The Order page in Design view

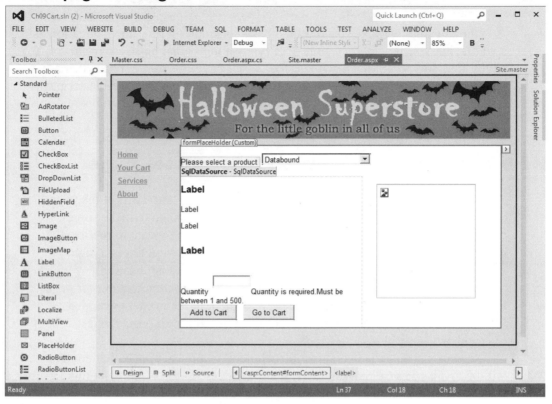

Description

- When you display a content page in Design view, the elements from the master page are displayed so you can see how they will affect the appearance of the page.
- To add content to a content page, you add text, HTML elements, or web controls just as you would for any other page. Just be sure that what you add is within the right Content control.

Figure 9-5   How to add content to a page

How to customize content pages

In many applications, you'll want a basic look and feel for the application as a whole, but you'll want to be able to customize individual pages or groups of pages. One way to do that is with nested master pages, or master pages that are also content pages for other master pages. The problem with nested master pages is that they can quickly become confusing and hard to maintain. For this reason, this topic will present two other ways to customize individual pages.

How to add default content to a master page

Default content is a good way to handle scenarios where most of the pages of an application will be the same, but a few pages will need to make some changes to the master page content. For example, you may want to remove the navigation menu from the checkout pages. Or, you may want to put a login button in the header of some but not all of the pages in an application.

Figure 9-6 shows how to add two types of default content to a master page. First, if you add a title element to the head element in the master page, that title will be displayed in the browser's title bar or tab for all pages, unless it's overridden.

Second, if you add content in a placeholder on a master page, that content will be displayed in all pages, unless it's overridden. In the example in this figure, the default content in the placeholder is a Label control that will be used to display the number of days until Halloween.

How to override and accept the default content from a content page

Figure 9-6 also shows how to override and accept two types of default content on the master page. First, you can override the title on the master page by coding the Title attribute of the Page directive for a content page. If you don't override it, you accept the title element in the master page.

Second, you can accept the default content in a placeholder by clicking on its smart tag and choosing the Default to Master's Content command. That removes the related Content control from the content page. In contrast, if you don't accept the default content, the default content is automatically overridden by whatever you add to the related Content control or by nothing if you don't add anything to it.

If you change your mind after you accept the default content from the master page, you can click the smart tag for the default content and select Create Custom Content from the smart tag menu, as shown in this figure. That restores the Content control so you can add whatever content you want to it.

A master page's default content in the footer of a content page

How set the default title in a master page and override it in a content page

To set the default title in a master page, enter the content for the title element

```
<title>Chapter 9: Shopping Cart</title>
```

To override the default title in a content page, use the Title attribute of the Page directive

```
<%@ Page Title="Your Shopping Cart" Language="C#" ... %>
```

How to set default content in a master page

Just add content to a placeholder control

```
<asp:ContentPlaceHolder id="footerPlaceHolder" runat="server">
    <asp:Label ID="lblDaysUntilHalloween" runat="server"></asp:Label>
</asp:ContentPlaceHolder>
```

How to accept the master page's default content in a content page

- Click the smart tag of the Content control and choose Default to Master's Content.

How to override a master page's default content in a content page

- Add content to the Content control for the related placeholder. But if you've already accepted the default content for that control, click the smart tag of the Content control and choose Create Custom Content.

Description

- You will often want to provide *default content* in a master page that can be over-ridden by a content page. To do that, you just add content to a placeholder in a master page.

Figure 9-6   How to add default content to a master page and how to override it

How to expose a public property in a master page

Another way to provide content on a master page that can be overridden by a content page is to use *public properties*. For instance, you can use a public property for an h1 element that will be displayed at the top of every page. Then, the content pages can override the value in this h1 element. This helps to insure that there will be an h1 heading at the top of every page, which is one of the principles of search engine optimization.

To *expose* a public property in a master page, you can use the technique in figure 9-7. The example in this figure only provides a way to set the text of the h1 element, but you can also provide a get accessor for getting the value of an exposed property. In this example, the content pages only need to set the heading's text, so the property on the master page is a write-only property.

When you use public properties, you can expose properties of the master page itself, such as its width. You can expose entire server controls, such as a message label. And you can expose individual properties of a server control, such as the Text property of a message label. In general, you should expose only what you're going to work with. So, if all you need to do is change a label's text, you should expose only the Text property, not the entire label control.

How to access a public property from a content page

The easiest way to access a master page's public properties from a content page is by adding a MasterType directive to the content page as shown in figure figure 9-7. Then, you use the TypeName or VirtualPath attribute to specify the type of object that's returned by the content page's Master property. In this example, the master page is Site.master, so its type is Site. As a result, you either add Site in the TypeName attribute, or you add the path to the master page in the VirtualPath attribute. Either option will work, but Visual Studio provides Intellisense for the VirtualPath attribute.

After you add the MasterType directive, you can work with the content page's Master property to access any public property on the master page, as shown in this figure. Here, the PageH1Text property is being updated to the heading that will be displayed at the top of the page, "Your Shopping Cart".

You should also know that you can work with the content page's Master property even if you don't add a MasterType directive. In that case, though, the Master property will return an object of type Master, and you'll need to cast it to the specific type you want to work with, like this:

```
MasterPage mp = (Site) this.Master;
```

To avoid this awkward bit of casting, you'll usually want to use the MasterType directive.

Attributes of the MasterType directive

Attribute	Description
TypeName	Specifies the type name for the master page. For instance, for a master page named Site.master, the TypeName is Site.
VirtualPath	Specifies the path to the master page file that generates the type. When you use this attribute, Intellisense helps you pick the master page.

How to expose a property in a master page

The aspx code for the element in the master page

```
<form id="form" runat="server">
    <h1><asp:Label ID="lblH1" runat="server"></asp:Label></h1>
    <asp:ContentPlaceHolder id="formPlaceHolder" runat="server">
    </asp:ContentPlaceHolder>
</form>
```

The C# in the code-behind file that exposes the property

```
public string PageH1Text {
    set { lblH1.Text = value; }
}
```

How to access a public property from a content page

The MasterType directive for a content page

```
<%@ MasterType VirtualPath="~/Site.master" %>
```

The C# code in the code-behind file that accesses the public property

```
this.Master.PageH1Text = "Your Shopping Cart";
```

Description

- You can create *public properties* in a master page that expose elements of the master page to the content pages. A public property can have both get and set accessors, just a get accessor, and or just a set accessor.

- You can use public properties to *expose* properties of the master page itself, such as the width; server controls on the master page, such as a text box; or individual properties of a server control, such as the Text property of a label.

- To access a master page's public properties, a content page must have a MasterType directive with either a TypeName or VirtualPath attribute.

Figure 9-7   How to expose and access properties in a master page

The Shopping Cart application

To give you a better idea of how master pages work, this chapter ends by presenting two pages of the shopping cart application that use the same master page.

Two pages of the Shopping Cart application

Figure 9-8 presents the Order page and Cart page of the Shopping Cart application. Here, the header, sidebar with four links, and the footer are part of the master page.

The master page also has two types of default content. First, it provides a default but empty h1 element at the top of the content for each page. Because the master page exposes the Text property for this element, it can be changed by the content pages. In this example, the Cart page has done that, but the Order page hasn't.

Second, the master page provides content for its footer. This is a label that shows the number of days left until Halloween. Note that this label is displayed in the Order page, but overridden in the Cart page by nothing.

The Order page

The Cart page

Figure 9-8   Two Shopping Cart pages that use a master page

The aspx code for the master page

Figure 9-9 presents the complete aspx code for the master page of the Shopping Cart application. To start, you should notice that the content for the title element in the document head is "Chapter 9: Shopping Cart". As a result, this title will be displayed in the browser's title bar or tab for all pages, unless it's overridden.

You should also notice that the head element contains a link element that links the external style sheet named Master.css in the Styles directory to the page. In addition, the document head contains the content placeholder that's added by default. This placeholder can be used by the content pages to add other elements to the document head.

Next, notice that the page uses HTML5 semantic elements to structure the content of the master page. The header element contains the image that's displayed at the top of the page. The aside element creates the sidebar on the left side of the page. The nav element within the aside element contains the hyperlinks that create the navigation menu in the sidebar. The section element contains the content placeholder for the form. And the footer element contains the content placeholder for the footer, along with the default content for the placeholder.

These elements are used by the external style sheet to format the master page so it appears as in the previous figure. Because the external style sheet contains references to the IDs of individual controls, the master page's ClientIDMode is set to Static in the Master directive so the IDs will be rendered the way the style sheet expects. However, you could also set the ClientIDMode of the ContentPlaceHolders instead of setting the mode in the Master directive.

The aspx code for the master page

```
<%@ Master Language="C#" AutoEventWireup="true" CodeFile="Site.master.cs"
    Inherits="Site" ClientIDMode="Static" %>

<!DOCTYPE html>
<html xmlns="http://www.w3.org/1999/xhtml">
<head id="Head1" runat="server">
    <title>Chapter 9: Shopping Cart</title>
    <link href="Styles/Master.css" rel="stylesheet" />
    <asp:ContentPlaceHolder id="headPlaceHolder" runat="server">
    </asp:ContentPlaceHolder>
</head>
<body>
    <header>
        <img src="Images/banner.jpg" alt="Halloween Store banner" /><br />
    </header>
    <aside>
        <nav>
            <ul>
                <li><asp:HyperLink NavigateUrl="~/Order.aspx"
                    runat="server">Home</asp:HyperLink></li>
                <li><asp:HyperLink NavigateUrl="~/Cart.aspx" runat="server">
                    Your Cart</asp:HyperLink></li>
                <li><asp:HyperLink NavigateUrl="~/Service.aspx"
                    runat="server">Services</asp:HyperLink></li>
                <li><asp:HyperLink NavigateUrl="~/About.aspx"
                    runat="server">About</asp:HyperLink></li>
            </ul>
        </nav>
    </aside>
    <section>
        <form id="form" runat="server">
            <%--a label within an h1 element that will be exposed--%>
            <h1><asp:Label ID="lblH1" runat="server"></asp:Label></h1>

            <asp:ContentPlaceHolder id="formPlaceHolder" runat="server">
            </asp:ContentPlaceHolder>
        </form>
    </section>
    <footer>
        <asp:ContentPlaceHolder id="footerPlaceHolder" runat="server">
            <%--the default content that can be overridden--%>
            <asp:Label ID="lblDaysUntilHalloween" runat="server">
            </asp:Label>
        </asp:ContentPlaceHolder>
    </footer>
</body>
</html>
```

Description

- When you use Hyperlink server controls for navigation in a master page, you can use the tilde operator in the NavigateURL property to resolve each file path. That's usually easier than using <a> elements for the links.

- The Label control in the footer of this master page is the footer's default content.

Figure 9-9   The aspx code for the master page

The code-behind file for the master page

Master pages have events just like regular ASP.NET pages. So it's important to realize that most of these events are raised *after* the corresponding events for the content page are raised. For example, the Page Load event for the master page will be processed after the Page Load event for the content page.

Likewise, any control events for the content page are processed before any control events for the master page. Note, however, that the Load events for both the content page and the master page are processed before any of the control events are processed.

Content pages also have a Page Load Completed event that is raised after the Page Load events for the content and master page have fired. This can be a good place to put content page code that needs to run after some code in the master page's Page Load event.

With that in mind, figure 9-10 presents the code-behind file for the master page of the Shopping Cart application. This file includes a Page_Load method that's executed when the master page loads. As you can see, this method calls a method named DaysUntilHalloween that calculates and returns the number of days remaining until October 31. Then, an appropriate message is assigned to the Text property of the lblDaysUntilHalloween label. Remember, though, that this label is default content that can be overridden by a content page. Because of this, the code must first check to make sure the label is there before trying to set its content.

This code-behind file also includes a write-only public property that allows content pages to change the text in the master page's h1 element. If the content page doesn't add any text to this property, the page won't have a page heading. That's because the aspx page hasn't specified any content for this h1 heading.

The code-behind file for the master page

```
using System;
using System.Collections.Generic;
using System.Linq;
using System.Web;
using System.Web.UI;
using System.Web.UI.WebControls;

public partial class Site : System.Web.UI.MasterPage
{
    public string PageH1Text {
        set { lblH1.Text = value; }
    }
    protected void Page_Load(object sender, EventArgs e) {
        if (lblDaysUntilHalloween != null) {
            int daysUntil = DaysUntilHalloween();
            switch (daysUntil) {
                case 0:
                    lblDaysUntilHalloween.Text = "Happy Halloween!";
                    break;
                case 1:
                    lblDaysUntilHalloween.Text = "Tomorrow is Halloween!";
                    break;
                default:
                    lblDaysUntilHalloween.Text = string.Format(
                        "There are only {0} days left until Halloween!",
                         daysUntil);
                    break;
            }
        }
    }
    private int DaysUntilHalloween() {
        DateTime halloween = new DateTime(DateTime.Today.Year, 10, 31);
        if (DateTime.Today > halloween)
            halloween = halloween.AddYears(1);
        TimeSpan ts = halloween - DateTime.Today;
        return ts.Days;
    }
}
```

Description

- Most events for the content page are raised before the corresponding events for the master page. Similarly, events for a content page's controls are raised before events for the master page's controls.

- Content pages also have a Page Load Completed event that is raised after the Page Load events for the content and master page have fired.

- This master page exposes a public property that lets the content pages set the text of the label inside the h1 element.

- The Load event of this master page is used to display the number of days until Halloween in the label in the footer. However, because the label is default content that can be overridden, the code first checks to make sure the label is there.

Figure 9-10   The code-behind file for the master page

The aspx code for the Order page

Figure 9-11 presents the aspx code for the Order page of the Shopping Cart application. As you can see, this code includes two Content controls. The first one includes a link element that identifies the external style sheet that will used to format this page. When the Order page is displayed, the styles in this style sheet will be combined with the styles in the external style sheet for the master page, but the styles in the page style sheet will override the same styles in the master style sheet.

The second Content control contains the main content for the page. This is the same content that would normally be included in the form element of a page. Because of that, you shouldn't have any trouble understanding it.

When you create a content page, ASP.NET generates one Content control for each placeholder in the master page. Note here, though, that the third Content control is missing. That's because the default content for the footer has been accepted, which removed the Content control from the form. If the default content had been overridden, the Content control would still be there.

The Order page also leaves the Title attribute in the Page directive empty, which is how it is by default when the content page is created. Because it's empty, the Order page will display the master page's title in the browser.

The aspx code for the Order content page

```
<%@ Page Title="" Language="C#" MasterPageFile="~/Site.master"
    AutoEventWireup="true" CodeFile="Order.aspx.cs" Inherits="Order" %>

<asp:Content ID="headContent" ContentPlaceHolderID="headPlaceHolder"
        Runat="Server">
    <link href="Styles/Order.css" rel="stylesheet" />
</asp:Content>

<asp:Content ID="formContent" ContentPlaceHolderID="formPlaceHolder"
        Runat="Server">
    <label>Please select a product </label>
    <asp:DropDownList ID="ddlProducts" runat="server" AutoPostBack="True"
        DataSourceID="SqlDataSource" DataTextField="Name"
        DataValueField="ProductID">
    </asp:DropDownList>
    <asp:SqlDataSource ID="SqlDataSource" runat="server"
        ConnectionString='<%$ ConnectionStrings:HalloweenDatabase %>'
        SelectCommand="SELECT [ProductID], [Name], [ShortDescription],
        [LongDescription], [ImageFile], [UnitPrice] FROM [Products] ORDER BY
        [Name]"></asp:SqlDataSource>
    <div id="productData">
        <asp:Label ID="lblName" runat="server" Text="Label"></asp:Label>
        <asp:Label ID="lblShortDescription" runat="server"
            Text="Label"></asp:Label>
        <asp:Label ID="lblLongDescription" runat="server"
            Text="Label"></asp:Label>
        <asp:Label ID="lblUnitPrice" runat="server"
            Text="Label"></asp:Label>
        <label id="lblQuantity">Quantity </label>
        <asp:TextBox ID="txtQuantity" runat="server"></asp:TextBox>
        <asp:RequiredFieldValidator>....</asp:RequiredFieldValidator>
        <asp:RangeValidator>....</asp:RangeValidator>
        <br />
        <asp:Button ID="btnAdd" runat="server" OnClick="btnAdd_Click"
            Text="Add to Cart" CssClass="button" />
        <asp:Button ID="btnCart" runat="server" CausesValidation="False"
            PostBackUrl="~/Cart.aspx" Text="Go to Cart" CssClass="button" />
    </div>
    <asp:Image ID="imgProduct" runat="server" />
</asp:Content>
```

Description

- The Order.aspx page contains a Content control for the form that contains all of the HTML and server controls for the form.

- Since the Order page has its own CSS file, it uses the Content control for the head element to add a link to the CSS file.

- Since the Order page leaves the Title attribute of the Page directive blank, the Order page will use the title value of the master page.

- The Order page's C# code, not shown here, doesn't set the master PageH1Text public property.

Figure 9-11   The aspx code for the Order page

The aspx code for the Cart page

Figure 9-12 presents the aspx code for the Cart page of the Shopping Cart application. Unlike the Order page, this page includes all three Content controls because it has overridden the default content for the footer. But note that the Content control for the footer doesn't contain any elements. This means that it replaces the default content with nothing.

Unlike the Order page, this page does add content to the Title attribute of the Page directive. This means that the content of the Title attribute, rather than the master page's title content, will be displayed in the browser for this page.

The Load event handler in the code-behind file for the Cart page

Figure 9-12 also presents the Page_Load method of the code-behind file for the Cart page. Here, the Cart page adds a value to the PageH1Text property of the master page. This means that the Cart page will have a page heading of "Your Shopping Cart".

The aspx code for the Cart content page

```
<%@ Page Title="Your Shopping Cart" Language="C#"
    MasterPageFile="~/Site.master" AutoEventWireup="true"
    CodeFile="Cart.aspx.cs" Inherits="Cart" %>
<%@ MasterType VirtualPath="~/Site.master" %>

<asp:Content ID="headContent" ContentPlaceHolderID="headPlaceHolder"
        Runat="Server">
    <link href="Styles/Cart.css" rel="stylesheet" />
</asp:Content>

<asp:Content ID="formContent" ContentPlaceHolderID="formPlaceHolder"
        Runat="Server">
    <asp:ListBox ID="lstCart" runat="server"></asp:ListBox>
    <div id="cartbuttons">
        <asp:Button ID="btnRemove" runat="server" CssClass="button"
            Text="Remove Item" OnClick="btnRemove_Click" /><br />
        <asp:Button ID="btnEmpty" runat="server" CssClass="button"
            Text="Empty Cart" OnClick="btnEmpty_Click" />
    </div>
    <div id="shopbuttons">
        <asp:Button ID="btnContinue" runat="server" CssClass="button"
            PostBackUrl="~/Order.aspx" Text="Continue Shopping" />
        <asp:Button ID="btnCheckOut" runat="server" CssClass="button"
            Text="Check Out" OnClick="btnCheckOut_Click" />
    </div>
    <p id="message">
        <asp:Label ID="lblMessage" runat="server"
            EnableViewState="False"></asp:Label>
    </p>
</asp:Content>

<asp:Content ID="footerContent"
    runat="server" contentplaceholderid="footerPlaceHolder">
</asp:Content>
```

The load event for the Cart content page

```
protected void Page_Load(object sender, EventArgs e) {
    cart = CartItemList.GetCart();
    if (!IsPostBack) {
        this.DisplayCart();
        this.Master.PageH1Text = "Your Shopping Cart";
    }
}
```

Description

- The Cart page adds a value to the Title attribute of the Page directive. As a result, that value, rather than the master page's title value, will be shown in the browser.

- The Cart page has overridden the master page's default footer content, but it hasn't replaced it with anything. As a result, the footer won't be displayed.

- The Cart page's C# code sets a value for the master page's PageH1Text public property, so an h1 element will be displayed at the top of the form.

Figure 9-12   The aspx code and Load event handler for the Cart page

Perspective

Because master pages are so valuable, we recommend that you use them for all but the simplest applications, even if you start out with nothing in your master pages but placeholders. Then, when you're ready to provide a professional look to your pages, you can enhance the master pages, which will also enhance all of your content pages.

The alternative is to convert regular content pages so they use the master pages that you develop later on. But that's a time-consuming and error-prone procedure. How much better it is to think ahead.

Terms

master page
content page
content placeholder
default content
client id
public property
expose a property

Summary

- *Master pages* let you provide a consistent look and feel to all of the pages in a web site. A master page provides the elements that are the same for all of the pages. The *content pages* provide the elements that vary from page to page.

- Master pages work by providing *content placeholders* that receive the contents of the pages of the web site. Master pages can also provide *default content* within these placeholders that can be overridden by the content pages when necessary.

- The ClientIDMode attribute of a master page or a control determines how the *client ids* for the controls are generated by ASP.NET. The setting for this attribute is important when the IDs are used by the selectors in the CSS for a page.

- You can code *public properties* in the code-behind file for a master page that *expose* properties in the master page to the content pages. Then, the content pages can access the public properties and change them.

Exercise 9-1   Work with master pages

In this exercise, you'll modify the Shopping Cart application that's presented in this chapter. That will give you a better feel for how master pages work and show you how easy it is to work with them.

Open, run, and review the Shopping Cart application

1. Open the Ex09Cart web site that's in the aspnet45_cs directory. Then, test the application to see how it works and note that the last two links in the navigation list don't work.

2. Review the aspx, code-behind, and CSS files for both the master and content pages to see how everything works.

3. Restore the default content for the footer of the Cart page by using the technique in figure 9-6.

Modify the Order page

4. In the aspx file for the Order page, add content to the Title attribute in the Page directive so "Your Shopping Page" will be displayed in the browser's title bar or tab.

5. In the aspx file for the Order page, override the default content in the footer and replace it with "Your Shopping Page" by using the technique in figure 9-6.

6. In the code-behind file for the Order page, use the exposed property in the master page to set the h1 heading for the Order page to "Your Shopping Page", as shown in figure 9-7. Now, test this page to make sure everything is working.

Create a Checkout page

7. Create a new content page named Checkout.aspx that uses the Site.master master page. Note that it has three Content controls.

8. Keep the default content for the footer by using the technique in figure 9-6.

9. In the Content control for the form, add an h1 element that displays "Checkout Page 1" (don't use the exposed property in the master page to set this heading). Also, change the content for the title element for the page to "Checkout Page 1", but keep the default content for the footer. Now, test this page to make sure everything is working right.

Create a second master page

10. Create a second master page named Checkout.master. The content for this page should be the same as the Site.master content, but without the aside and nav elements and without the h1 element in the section element. Also, the footer should display "Checkout Page" without any default content.

11. Switch the Checkout page to the new master page. Then, run it to see how it works.

12. When you're through experimenting, close the application.

10

How to use themes

When you develop a web site, you want to apply consistent formatting to all of its pages so the entire site has a cohesive look and feel. It's also a best practice to separate the formatting of the web pages from the structure and content of the web pages by using CSS for all page layout and formatting. That way, web designers can focus on making the site look good, and programmers can focus on making the site work the way it should.

To make this work even better, ASP.NET provides a feature known as *themes*. This feature works with CSS to let you create more than one theme for a web site, and then switch between themes. You can even use this feature to let the users choose the themes that they prefer.

An introduction to themes

As you learned in chapter 3, it's a best practice to use HTML for the content and structure of a web site and an external CSS style sheet for the layout and formatting. Although this works well for HTML elements, it can be tricky to get this to work right with ASP.NET server controls, especially the data controls that you'll learn about in section 3. The solution is to use *themes*, which let you specify the formatting for both HTML elements and server controls.

A page with two different themes applied

Figure 10-1 shows the Order page for the Halloween Store application after two different themes have been applied to it. So even though the page works the same with both themes, the two versions look quite different.

For both versions, CSS is used for the basic layout and formatting, just as it has been in the previous chapters. Since the Order page uses a master page, the CSS file for the master page provides some of the formatting, and the CSS file for the Order page provides the rest of it.

Then, the themes provide additional formatting. For instance, the Bats theme uses one image file for the header, and the Spiders theme uses another. The Bats theme also has orange links, an orange border around the buttons, and a small black border around the drop-down list and text box, while the Spiders theme formats these elements another way. The Spiders theme also has a vertical rule between the sidebar and the section, a bottom border below the header, and everything is in black.

As you will see, themes are relatively easy to create. Better yet, you can switch from one theme to another just by changing one setting in the web.config file.

The Order page with the Bats theme applied to it

The Order page with the Spiders theme applied to it

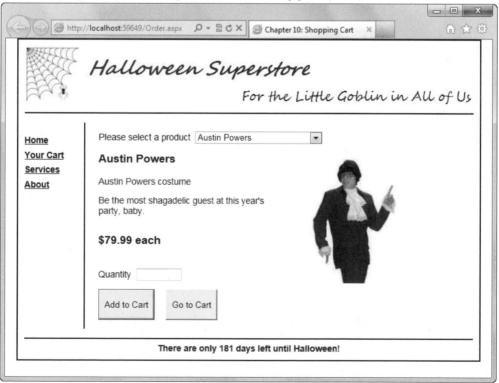

Figure 10-1   A page with two different themes applied

How themes work

Figure 10-2 gives an overview of how themes work. To start, it shows the Solution Explorer for an application that uses themes. Here, the App_Themes folder contains one subfolder for each theme: the Bats theme and the Spiders theme.

The Bats folder shows the three types of files a theme can include. First, a theme folder can include a CSS file for formatting the theme. This file typically has the same name as the theme folder, although that's not required.

Second, a theme folder can contain one or more files for the *skins* that define the appearance of the ASP.NET server controls. A skin file has an extension of skin, and the skins for a theme can be stored in one or more skin files. Typically, though, if a theme has only one skin file, it is given the same name as the theme folder, although that's not required.

Third, a theme folder can contain the files for any images or other resources that are used by the CSS and skins in the theme. For example, the banner.jpg file in the Bats theme folder and the banner.jpg file in the Spiders folder are the images files that are used for the header in each theme. In this case, these image files are stored in the Images subfolders, but these files can be stored in the theme folder or any subfolder of the theme folder.

Note also that this application has a Styles folder that contains the CSS files for the master page, Order page, and Cart page. These files work the same as in the previous chapter to provide the basic formatting for the pages.

The directory structure for a theme

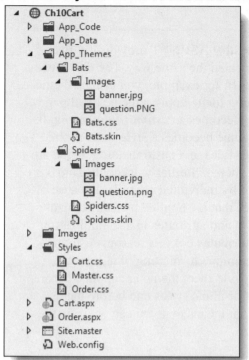

The folders and files for a theme

- One or more CSS files
- One or more skin files
- An Image folder that contains the image files that the theme requires

Description

- The App_Themes folder contains subfolders that define the *themes* for the application.
- The skin files within a theme folder define the *skins* that control the appearance of the ASP.NET server controls.
- The CSS files in a theme folder are automatically applied to all pages that use that theme.
- The CSS files in the Styles folder need to be linked to the pages that use them by a link element in the head element of the HTML for those pages.
- In general, you use the style sheets in the Styles folder to do the basic formatting for master and content pages.

Figure 10-2   The folders and files that make up a theme

The difference between customization and style sheet themes

When you use themes, you should realize that ASP.NET provides for two different types of themes, although they're created the same way. The difference between these themes is how they're applied. If, for example, you use the theme attribute of the pages element in the web.config file to apply a theme to all pages, as shown at the top of figure 10-3, the theme becomes a *customization theme*. If you use the styleSheetTheme attribute, the theme becomes a *style sheet theme*.

As the summary in this figure shows, the styles of a customization theme are applied after any styles specified outside the theme. Similarly, its control attributes are applied after the attributes specified by individual controls. Because of that, you can't override the styles or attributes that are applied by a customization theme. To say that another way, the styles and attributes in a customization theme always override the other styles and attributes For this reason, customization themes are commonly used to apply the unique formatting of a theme.

In contrast, the styles and attributes in a style sheet theme are applied before the styles specified by any external, internal, or inline styles and before the attributes specified by individual controls. That means that you can override the styles that are applied by a style sheet theme.

How to apply a customization theme to all pages of an application

```
<system.web>
    <pages theme="Spiders"></pages>
</system.web>
```

How to apply a style sheet theme to all pages of an application

```
<system.web>
    <pages styleSheetTheme="Bats"></pages>
</system.web>
```

The order in which styles and control attributes are applied

1. Style sheet theme styles and control attributes
2. External, internal, and inline styles and control attributes
3. Customization theme styles and control attributes

Description

-   ASP.NET provides for both *customization themes* and *style sheet themes*. The difference between the two is in how they are applied, not in how they're created.

-   When you use a customization theme, it overrides the external, internal, and inline styles that have been applied. When you use a style sheet theme, the reverse is true.

-   As you will see, you can apply a theme to all the pages of an application or to selected pages.

Figure 10-3   The difference between customization and style sheet themes

How to work with themes and skins

In the topics that follow, you'll learn the basic skills for creating and using themes and skins.

How to create and use themes and skins

Figure 10-4 provides the basic skills for creating themes and skins and for applying skins. After you create the folder for a theme by using the first procedure in this figure, you can add a skin file to it by using the second procedure.

Then, you can add skins to the file by entering the opening tag for the type of control that you want to provide a skin for, entering a RunAt attribute, and entering the closing tag. After that, you can enter whatever attributes you want to use for each skin, including formatting attributes. However, because there's no IntelliSense support in a skin file, it can be faster to add the controls you want to an aspx file first, including any formatting properties, cut and paste them into the skin file, and then remove all but the formatting and Runat attributes from the skins.

You should know, however, that it's a best practice to keep most of the styling information in external style sheets. To do that, you just set the CssClass attribute in the skin, as shown by the first two examples in this figure. Then, you use the CSS style sheet for the theme to format the controls with those classes. That way, you keep all of the styling for the theme in one place.

Of course, you can't always do that. If, for example, a skin for an ImageButton needs to set the ImageUrl attribute, there's no easy way to do that with CSS. In that case, you might need to set some formatting attributes in the skin file, as shown by the third skin in this figure. The trouble is that styles set this way will be converted to inline styles when ASP.NET renders the HTML.

Notice that the first skin in this figure doesn't include a SkinID attribute. As a result, it is a *default skin* that is applied to any control of that type that doesn't include a SkinID attribute. In contrast, the second skin is a *named skin* because it has a SkinID attribute that uniquely identifies the skin. To apply a named skin to a control, you specify its ID in the SkinID attribute for the control. The last two examples in this figure show how this default skin and named skin are applied to two button controls.

How to create a themes folder and the App_Themes folder

- Right-click on the project in the Solution Explorer, select Add→Add ASP.NET Folder→Theme. Then, enter a name for the new folder. If necessary, this will also create the App_Themes folder.

How to add a skin file to a theme folder

- Right-click on the folder for the theme in the Solution Explorer, and select Add New Item. Then, select the Skin File template and enter the name for the file.

How to create a skin

- Enter the aspx code for the type of control that you want to provide a skin for. Then, add whatever attributes you want the control to have, including any formatting attributes.

Two skins for buttons that use styles with class selectors for formatting

A default skin

```
<asp:Button runat="server" CssClass="button" />
```

A named skin

```
<asp:Button SkinID="fancyButton" runat="server" CssClass="fancyButton" />
```

A named skin for an ImageButton control that uses a formatting attribute

```
<asp:ImageButton SkinId="questionMark" runat="server"
    ImageUrl="~/Images/question.PNG" />
```

Two ways to apply skins

A control that uses a default skin (no SkinID attribute)

```
<asp:Button ID="btnAdd" runat="server" OnClick="btnAdd_Click"
    Text="Add to Cart" />
```

A control that specifies a named skin in the SkinID attribute

```
<asp:Button ID="btnCopyToClipboard" SkinID="fancyButton" runat="server"
    OnClick="btnCopyToClipboard_Click" Text="Copy To Clipboard" />
```

Description

- To create a *default skin*, don't specify the SkinID attribute for the skin. Then, the skin will automatically be applied to any control of that type whose SkinID property isn't set.

- To create a *named skin*, you specify the SkinID attribute for the skin. Then, you can use the SkinID attribute of a control to apply the skin to the control.

- All the skins for a theme can be stored in a single file, or they can be grouped in separate files like all button skins in one file and all text box skins in another file.

- If you use ASP.NET attributes to format a skin, you can be sure that they will override any styles that are applied to the control. However, it's better to use styles to format the skins, as shown in the next figure.

Figure 10-4   How to create and use themes and skins

The skin and CSS files for the Bats theme

To give you a better idea of how the skin and CSS files for a theme work, figure 10-5 presents the skin and CSS file for the Bats theme. In this case, all of the skins for the theme are coded in a single skin file. However, the skins would work the same way if they were grouped into two or more skin files.

When you use themes, you typically define one skin for each type of control that you use in your application. Otherwise, a control that doesn't have a skin might not look like the rest of the controls. In this figure, for example, you can see the skins for the TextBox, Button, DropDownList, and Validator controls used by the application.

Note here that formatting attributes aren't used for any of these skins. Instead, a CssClass attribute is coded for each skin. Note too that the same class names can be used for more than one skin. For instance, "entry" is the class name for drop-down lists and text boxes, and "validator" is the class name for all of the validators used by the application.

The CSS file that follows shows how these skins are formatted by the rule sets for the button, entry, and validator classes. Here, for example, the buttons are formatted with an orange border and a white background. The controls in the entry class are formatted with a black border. And the validators are formatted with orange type.

The styles for the skins are followed by a rule set for the div element in the header of the master page, which has banner as its ID. This rule set uses the background property to change the background for the header to the image that's stored in the banner.jpg file. Since this banner changes for each theme, the Spiders theme uses the same rule set to change the background to its banner.jpg file.

The last rule set in the CSS file is for the label that contains the message in the footer. This just sets the font weight to bold, but it could also change the color of the message or otherwise format the message.

If you apply the Bats theme as a customization theme, it will of course override the styles in the CSS files in the Styles folder. That's how easy it is to customize the look of an application when you use themes. However, this also shows how important a thorough knowledge of HTML and CSS is for web development. So, if you have any trouble understanding this CSS code, by all means get a copy of our *HTML5 and CSS3*.

The skin file for the Bats theme (Bats.skin)

```
<%-- Named skins --%>
<asp:ImageButton SkinId="questionMark" runat="server" ImageUrl="Images/
question.PNG" />

<%-- Default skins --%>
<asp:Button runat="server" CssClass="button" />
<asp:TextBox runat="server" CssClass="entry">
</asp:TextBox>
<asp:DropDownList runat="server" CssClass="entry">
</asp:DropDownList>

<asp:RequiredFieldValidator runat="server"
    CssClass="validator"></asp:RequiredFieldValidator>
<asp:RangeValidator runat="server"
    CssClass="validator"></asp:RangeValidator>
<asp:CustomValidator runat="server"
    CssClass="validator"></asp:CustomValidator>
<asp:RegularExpressionValidator runat="server"
    CssClass="validator"></asp:RegularExpressionValidator>
<asp:ValidationSummary runat="server"
    CssClass="validator"></asp:ValidationSummary>
```

The CSS file for the Bats theme (Bats.css)

```
/* the styles for the skins */
.button {
    background-color: white;
    font-weight: bold;
    border: 2px solid #FF6600;
    padding: .5em;
}
.entry {
    border: 1px solid black;
}
.validator {
    color: #FF6600;
    font-weight: bold;
}
/* the style that puts the banner in the header */
#banner {
    width: 100%;
    height: 102px;
    background: white url('Images/banner.jpg') no-repeat;
}
/* the style that boldfaces the label in the footer */
#lblDaysUntilHalloween {
    font-weight: bold;
}
```

Description

- Styles are used to apply all of the formatting for the three skins.
- Styles are also used to change the image in the header for each theme and to format the label in the footer.

Figure 10-5   The skin and CSS files for the Bats theme

How to apply themes and skins

When you use a theme, you can apply the theme to an entire application or to selected pages. You can also apply a skin to individual controls. The techniques for doing that are summarized in figure 10-6.

Usually you'll apply a customization or style sheet theme to the entire application. To do that, you work with the theme or styleSheetTheme attribute of the pages element in the web.config file.

However, you can also apply a theme to a single page at design time or runtime. To apply a theme at design time, you use the Theme or StyleSheetTheme attribute of the Page directive. To apply a customization theme at runtime, you use the Theme property of the Page object. To apply a style sheet theme at runtime, you override the page's style sheet theme.

Note that the code that applies the customization theme at runtime must be executed before the HTML elements or ASP.NET controls are added to the page. Because these are added during the Init event, the theme is typically applied in the PreInit event handler for the page.

By contrast, the code for the changing the style sheet theme for a page at runtime doesn't use the PreInit event of the page. Instead, you override the page's StyleSheetTheme property to get and set the name of the theme. Then, when a page loads, it automatically calls the StyleSheetTheme property to set the style sheet theme.

In the example in this figure, the code that applies the theme at runtime uses a string for a theme that has been stored in the Session object. This is how you can change the theme for an application after the user has selected a theme and you've stored the name of the theme in the session object. Of course, if you want to store the selected theme for future sessions, you need to save it to a persistent data store like a database or a text file.

Earlier, you learned how to use the SkinID attribute to apply a named skin to a server control at design time. Now, this figure ends by reviewing how to do that and also showing how to use the SkinID property of a server control to apply a named skin at runtime. To do that, you can use the PreInit event of the page to make sure that this skin is applied before the control is added to the page. This works the same as it does for applying a customization theme to a page.

How to apply a customization theme

To all pages of an application

```
<system.web>
    <pages theme="Bats"></pages>
</system.web>
```

To a single page at design time

```
<%@ Page Language="C#" Theme="Bats" %>
```

To a single page at run time

```
protected void Page_PreInit(object sender, EventArgs e) {
    Page.Theme = Session["MyTheme"].ToString();
}
```

How to apply a style sheet theme

To all pages of an application

```
<system.web>
    <pages styleSheetTheme="Bats"></pages>
</system.web>
```

To a single page at design time

```
<%@ Page Language="C#" StylesheetTheme="Bats" %>
```

To a single page at run time

```
public override string StyleSheetTheme {
    get { return Session["MyTheme"].ToString(); }
    set { Session["MyTheme"] = value; }
}
```

How to apply a skin to a control

At design time

```
<asp:Label ID="lblMessage" runat="server" SkinID="Head1"></asp:Label>
```

At runtime

```
protected void Page_PreInit(object sender, EventArgs e) {
    lblName.SkinID = Session["MySkinID"].ToString();
}
```

Description

- To apply a theme to all the pages of an application, you can edit the web.config file.

- To apply a theme to a single page at design time, you can use the Theme or StyleSheetTheme attribute of the Page directive.

- To apply a theme to a single page at runtime, you can use the Theme property or override the StyleSheetTheme property of the page.

- To apply a skin to a control, you can use the SkinID attribute or property of the control.

- You add runtime code for customization themes and skins to the event handler for the PreInit event of the page so the code is executed before the HTML elements and ASP.NET controls are added to the page.

Figure 10-6   How to apply themes and skins

How to remove themes

Figure 10-7 shows how to remove a theme from an application, page, or control after you've applied it. Although it isn't shown in this chapter, a web site administrator can set a global theme that applies to all web applications running on the server. In that case, you may want to remove the global theme from all pages of your application. To do that, you can open the web.config file for your application and set the theme or styleSheetTheme attribute of the pages element to an empty string.

Next, this figure shows how to remove a theme from a single page. You may need to do that if you want to apply formatting to that page that's different from the formatting of the theme. Here again, this can be done at design time or runtime by using techniques like those for applying a theme.

This figure also shows how to remove (or disable) a theme that's applied to a control. By default, the EnableTheming property is set to True for all controls so the theme for the application or page is applied to all controls. In most cases, that's what you want. However, since an attribute that's set in a skin in a customization theme overrides the same attribute that's set at the control level, you may want to remove the theme from the control so the formatting that's specified by the control is applied instead.

To remove the theme from a control, you can set the EnableTheming attribute for the control to False. Then, you can use standard ASP.NET formatting techniques to format the control. For instance, the example in this figure sets the CssClass attribute to a different class so the formatting for that class will be applied to it.

If you need to set the EnableTheming property at runtime, you can use the PreInit event of the page to make sure that this skin is removed before the HTML elements and controls are added to the page. This works the same as it does for applying a theme to a page.

Of course, you can also override a class rule set in a CSS file by applying a id rule set. That's because an id selector is more specific than a class selector. If you do it that way, you don't need to make any other design time or runtime changes.

Although you can also remove a style sheet theme from a control by setting the control's EnableTheming property to False, you're not likely to do that. That's because any attributes you specify for individual controls are applied after the styles specified by the style sheet theme. So if you need to override an attribute that's set by a theme, you can simply include that attribute on the control. That's the main advantage of using style sheet themes.

How to remove a customization theme

From all pages of an application

```
<system.web>
    <pages theme=""></pages>
</system.web>
```

From a single page at design time

```
<%@ Page Language="C#" Theme="" %>
```

From a single page at run time

```
protected void Page_PreInit(object sender, EventArgs e) {
    Page.Theme = "";
}
```

From a control at design time

```
<asp:Button ID="btnAdd" runat="server"
    EnableTheming="False" CssClass="otherbutton"></asp:Button>
```

From a control at runtime

```
protected void Page_PreInit(object sender, EventArgs e) {
    btnAdd.EnableTheming = false;
    btnAdd.CssClass = "otherbutton";
}
```

How to remove a style sheet theme

From all pages of an application

```
<system.web>
    <pages styleSheetTheme=""></pages>
</system.web>
```

From a single page at design time

```
<%@ Page Language="C#" StylesheetTheme="" %>
```

From a single page at run time

```
public override string StyleSheetTheme {
    get { return ""; }
    set { }
}
```

Description

- To remove a theme from an application or single page, you use techniques like those for applying a theme.
- To remove a theme from a control, you can set its EnableTheming property to false. However, you usually won't need to do that for a style sheet theme since you can override it by setting attributes on the control.
- As before, you use the PreInit event of the page if you want the code to be executed before the HTML elements and ASP.NET controls are added to the page.

Figure 10-7   How to remove themes

Perspective

In this chapter, you learned how themes work and how they can be used to separate the formatting of an application from the code of an application. In particular, you learned how you can use skins to control the formatting of controls. Now, if you combine that knowledge with the information that was presented in chapter 3 on cascading style sheets, you should be able to work with a web designer to create a suitable theme for your application.

Terms

theme	style sheet theme
skin	default skin
customization theme	named skin

Summary

- A *theme* consists of the CSS files, skins, images, and other resources that the theme requires. If an application has two or more themes, the theme can be changed just by changing one setting in the web.config file.

- *Customization themes* and *style sheet themes* are developed the same way, but they are applied differently. In particular, a customization theme over-rides the external, internal, and inline styles for a page, but the reverse is true for a style sheet theme.

- A *skin* defines the appearance of a server control. A *default skin* for a control type applies to all controls of that type. A *named skin* applies only to the controls of that type that have their SkinID attributes set to the name of the skin.

- Although you can format skins by coding formatting attributes for them, it's better to use CSS and class selectors to format the skins.

- You can apply a theme to all pages of an application and to individual pages, which also applies the theme to the controls on the pages. To remove a theme from a control on a page, you can set its EnableTheme property to false, either at design time or runtime.

Exercise 10-1   Work with themes

In this exercise, you'll modify the Shopping Cart application that's presented in this chapter. That will give you a better feel for how themes work and show you how easy it is to work with them.

Open, run, and review the Shopping Cart application

1. Open the Ex10Cart web site that's in the aspnet45_cs directory. Then, test the application to see how it works and note that the Spiders theme has been applied to all of the pages.

2. Stop the application, and review the files in the themes folders to see how they work.

3. Switch the theme for all of the pages to the Bats theme. Then, test the application to see how this theme looks.

Create a skin for the links in the sidebar

4. Create a new skin file for the Bats theme named Links.skin. Then, add one default skin to it for HyperLink controls. This skin should have its CssClass attribute set to "link".

5. Add this rule set for the "link" class to the CSS file for the Bats theme:

```
.link {
    border: 2px solid black;
    padding: .25em .5em;
    text-decoration: none;
    display: block;
}
```

Now, test this change to see how the links in the sidebar have changed. This also shows that skins work the same whether they're stored in one file or more than one file.

Add a vertical rule between the sidebar and the section

6. Add this rule set to the CSS file for the Bats theme:

```
section {
    border-left: 2px solid #FF6600;
}
```

Now, test this change to see the vertical rule between the sidebar and the section.

7. Experiment on your own to see how easy it is to work with themes. When you're through experimenting, close the solution.

11

How to use site navigation and ASP.NET routing

The ASP.NET site navigation controls make it easy for you to provide the features that let your users navigate to the pages in your web site. The ASP. NET routing feature lets you provide friendly URLs for your pages that improve search engine optimization. This chapter shows you how to get the most from both of these features, and it shows you how to use these features separately or together.

How to use the navigation controls

ASP.NET's *site navigation* features are designed to simplify the task of creating menus and other navigation features that let users find their way around your web site. To implement these features, ASP.NET provides a site map data source control and three navigation controls.

An introduction to the navigation controls

Figure 11-1 shows a page from the Shopping Cart application that you've been working with. It illustrates the three navigation controls that ASP.NET provides in the Navigation group of the Toolbox.

The Menu control creates menus that expand when you hover the mouse over a menu item that contains subitems. If, for example, you hover the mouse over the Support item in the menu in this figure, a submenu with these items is displayed: Customer Service, Product Support, and Site Map.

The SiteMapPath control displays a list of links that lead from the web site's home page to the current page. This makes it easy for the user to return to the home page or to a parent of the current page. These links are sometimes called *bread crumbs* because they let the user find his or her way back to the home page.

The TreeView control displays the pages of a web site in a tree structure that's similar to a directory tree displayed by Windows Explorer. The user can expand or collapse a node by clicking the icon that appears next to each node that has children. If, for example, the user clicks on the icon before the Categories item in this figure, the children will be hidden.

The TreeView and the Menu controls are used with a SiteMapDataSource control that binds the controls to a file named web.sitemap. This file contains the XML that defines the structure of the pages that make up the web site.

In many cases, you'll use a Menu or SiteMapPath control in a master page. That way, these controls will be available on any page that uses the master page. You may also want to offer a separate Site Map page that includes a TreeView control so the user can locate any page within the web site.

A page with three site navigation controls

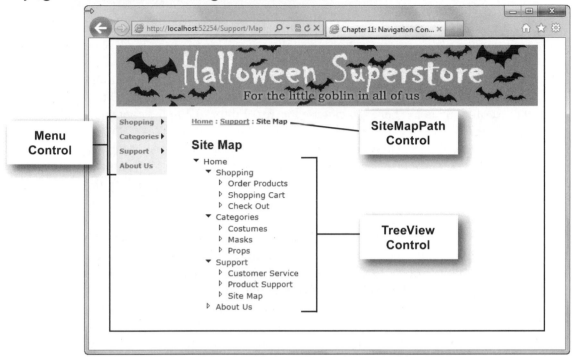

ASP.NET navigation controls

Control	Description
TreeView	Provides a hierarchical view of the site's structure. The user can click the icon next to a node to expand or collapse the node. Must be bound to a SiteMapDataSource control.
Menu	Creates a horizontal or vertical menu. Must be bound to a SiteMapDataSource control.
SiteMapPath	Displays a list of links from the application's root page (the home page) to the current page. Doesn't need to be bound to a SiteMapDataSource control.
SiteMapDataSource	Connects a navigation control to the site hierarchy specified by the web. sitemap file. Located in the Data group of the Toolbox.

Description

- ASP.NET provides TreeView, Menu, and SiteMapPath controls in the Navigation group of the Toolbox. It also provides a SiteMapDataSource control in the Data group of the Toolbox.

- The navigation structure of a web site is defined by an XML file named web. sitemap that's located in the application's root folder. You must create this file before you can work with any of the navigation controls.

Figure 11-1   An introduction to the site navigation controls

How to create a web.sitemap file

Before you can use one of the site navigation controls, you must create a web.sitemap file in the application's root directory. This file uses XML to define the hierarchical structure of the pages that make up the application.

As figure 11-2 shows, you can add a web.sitemap file to an application by choosing the WEBSITE→Add New Item command and selecting Site Map from the list of templates. Then, you can use the Text Editor to edit the contents of this file.

The web.sitemap file contains two types of XML elements: siteMap and siteMapNode. The siteMap element is the root element for the XML file and should occur only once in the file. You usually don't need to modify this element.

In contrast, you need to create a siteMapNode element for each page in the web site that you want to include in the navigation controls. In the siteMapNode element, you specify the URL of the page (relative to the application's root folder); the page title that's displayed as the link in a menu, map path, or tree; and a description of the page that works as a tool tip.

To indicate the hierarchy of the pages in the site map, you nest the siteMap-Node elements. The file should contain just one top-level siteMapNode element that represents the site's home page. Then, additional elements can be nested between the start and end tags for that siteMapNode. Within each siteMapNode element, the URL must be unique. That means each page in the web site can appear only once in the site map.

Note, however, that you don't have to include all of the pages in the web site in the sitemap file. Instead, you should only include those pages that you want to make available via the site's navigation controls. If, for example, the site uses a two-page checkout process, you may not want to include the second checkout page in the sitemap file. That way, the user will be able to access the first check-out page from a menu or tree view control, but not the second checkout page.

To show how a sitemap file works, this figure presents the start of the web.sitemap file that's used by the controls in figure 11-1. If you compare the siteMapNode elements in this file with the items listed in the TreeView control, you can see how the nesting of the siteMapNode elements specifies the site's hierarchical structure.

Attributes of the siteMapNode element

Attribute	Description
Url	The URL for the page, which must be a unique value for each element.
Title	The text that will appear in the menu for the page.
Description	The tool tip for the page.

How to create a web.sitemap file

- Choose the WEBSITE→Add New Item command, select Site Map from the list of available templates, and click Add.

The web.sitemap file created from the Site Map template

```
<?xml version="1.0" encoding="utf-8" ?>
<siteMap xmlns="http://schemas.microsoft.com/AspNet/SiteMap-File-1.0" >
    <siteMapNode url="" title=""  description="">
        <siteMapNode url="" title=""  description="" />
        <siteMapNode url="" title=""  description="" />
    </siteMapNode>
</siteMap>
```

The start of the web.sitemap file used for the controls in figure 11-1

```
<?xml version="1.0" encoding="utf-8" ?>
<siteMap xmlns="http://schemas.microsoft.com/AspNet/SiteMap-File-1.0" >
    <siteMapNode url="~/Default.aspx" title="Home"
        description="Home page.">
        <siteMapNode url="~/Shopping.aspx" title="Shopping"
            description="Shop for your favorite products.">
            <siteMapNode url="~/Order.aspx" title="Order Products"
                description="Order a product.">
            </siteMapNode>
            <siteMapNode url="~/Cart.aspx" title="Shopping Cart"
                description="View your shopping cart.">
            </siteMapNode>
            <siteMapNode url="~/Checkout1.aspx" title="Check Out"
                description="Complete your purchase.">
            </siteMapNode>
        </siteMapNode>
        <siteMapNode url="~/Categories.aspx" title="Categories"
            description="View our products by category">
            <siteMapNode url="~/Costumes.aspx" title="Costumes"
            ...
        ...
    </siteMapNode>
</siteMap>
```

Description

- The web.sitemap file contains the XML that describes the navigation hierarchy of an ASP.NET application.

- To create a site map, you nest siteMapNode elements within other siteMapNode elements. However, you don't have to include all the pages of a web site in the site map.

Figure 11-2   How to create a web.sitemap file

How to create a SiteMapDataSource control

Figure 11-3 shows how to create a SiteMapDataSource control. One way is to drag this control from the Data group of the Toolbox to a page. The other way is to click the smart tag for a TreeView or Menu control, and choose New Data Source from the menu that appears. This brings up the Data Source Configuration Wizard dialog box shown in this figure. Then, you can select Site Map and click OK to create a *site map data source*.

To customize the behavior of the site map data source, you can use the attributes listed in this figure. For example, the ShowStartingNode attribute determines whether the highest-level siteMapNode element in the web.sitemap file will be included in the menu or tree. Usually, you'll leave this attribute set to its default of True for TreeView controls, and you'll set it to False for Menu controls.

The StartFromCurrentNode and StartingNodeUrl attributes let you bind a TreeView or Menu control to just a portion of the site map. If you specify True for the StartFromCurrentNode attribute, the menu or tree will start from the current page. As a result, only child pages of the current page will appear in the tree or menu. The StartingNodeUrl attribute lets you select any node in the site map as the starting node for the menu or tree.

The Data Source Configuration Wizard dialog box

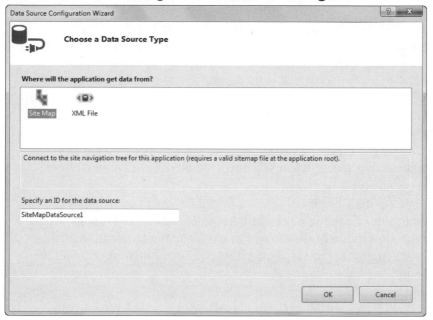

Two ways to create a SiteMapDataSource control

- Drag the control from the Data group of the Toolbox to a page.
- Click the smart tag of a TreeView or Menu control, then select New Data Source in the Choose Data Source drop-down list.

Common attributes of the SiteMapDataSource control

Attribute	Description
StartingNodeUrl	The URL of the node the SiteMapDataSource control should use as its starting node.
ShowStartingNode	Set to False to omit the starting node. The default is True.
StartFromCurrentNode	Set to True to start the navigation from the current node. The default is False, which starts the navigation from the root node specified in the web.sitemap file.

A default SiteMapDataSource control

```
<asp:SiteMapDataSource ID="SiteMapDataSource1" runat="server" />
```

A SiteMapDataSource control that specifies a starting level

```
<asp:SiteMapDataSource ID="SiteMapDataSource1" runat="server"
    StartingNodeUrl="Categories.aspx" />
```

Description

- You use a SiteMapDataSource control to bind a TreeView or Menu control to the navigation structure defined by the web.sitemap file.

Figure 11-3   How to create a SiteMapDataSource control

How to use the Menu control

Figure 11-4 shows how to use the Menu control, which lets you create menus that are arranged either vertically or horizontally. *Vertical menus* are usually used in a sidebar alongside the content placeholder in a master page. *Horizontal menus* typically appear below the header and above the sidebar and content placeholder.

Each item in a menu can contain a submenu. For example, the Support submenu in this figure doesn't appear until you hover the mouse over the Support item. The part of the menu that is always displayed is called the *static menu*. The submenus that appear when you hover the mouse over a menu item are called *dynamic menus*.

The Menu control must be bound to a site map data source by using the DataSourceID attribute. Then, the other attributes in the table in this figure let you customize the appearance of the menu. For example, the Orientation attribute determines whether the menu is arranged vertically or horizontally. And the MaximumDynamicDisplay attribute determines how many layers of dynamic submenus should be displayed.

The IncludeStyleBlock attribute determines whether a style element with the CSS that's used to format the menu is generated. If you set the value of this attribute to False, you can customize the appearance of the menu by coding your own CSS. The easiest way to do that is to display the page in a browser with the value of this attribute set to True. Then, you can display the HTML for the page, copy the generated CSS, paste it into an external style sheet, and modify it any way you like.

As you set the properties for a Menu control, you'll see that it includes many style properties that aren't listed in this figure. You can set these properties to control the formatting that's used to display the menu.

Alternatively, you can apply a predefined scheme to a Menu control by selecting Auto Format from its smart tag menu. When you select a scheme, Visual Studio generates the attributes and style elements that apply the formatting that you selected. Then, you can customize these attributes and elements any way you like.

Later, if you want to separate the formatting from the control, you can move the styling to skin and CSS files. To do that, you can use the skills that you learned in the last chapter.

Common attributes of the Menu control

Attribute	Description
`DataSourceID`	The ID of the SiteMapDataSource control the menu is bound to.
`IncludeStyleBlock`	If True (the default), the CSS that formats the menu is included in a style element in the rendered HTML. If False, no style element is generated.
`ItemWrap`	If True, words in the menu items will be word-wrapped if necessary. The default is False.
`MaximumDynamicDisplay`	The number of levels of dynamic submenus to display. The default is 3.
`Orientation`	Horizontal or Vertical. The default is Vertical.
`StaticDisplayLevels`	The number of levels that should always be displayed. The default is 1.
`StaticEnableDefaultPopOutImage`	If True (the default), an arrow graphic is displayed next to any menu item that has a submenu.

A menu with vertical orientation

A menu with horizontal orientation

The aspx code for the menu with horizontal orientation

```
<asp:Menu ID="Menu1" Orientation="Horizontal" runat="server"
    DataSourceID="SiteMapDataSource1">
</asp:Menu>
```

Description

- The Menu control displays site navigation data in a menu. Submenus automatically appear when the user hovers the mouse over a menu item that has a submenu.

- To display an application's navigation structure, the Menu control must be bound to a SiteMapDataSource control.

- The Menu control has many formatting attributes that aren't listed in this figure. To apply a predefined scheme of formatting attributes, click the smart tag of the Menu control and choose Auto Format. Then, select a scheme.

Figure 11-4   How to use the Menu control

How to use the TreeView control

Figure 11-5 shows how to use the TreeView control, which must be bound to a site map data source. The table in this figure lists the attributes you're most likely to use with this control. In particular, the DataSourceID attribute specifies the ID of the data source that provides the site map data.

The other attributes let you customize the appearance and behavior of the TreeView control. For example, you can use the ExpandDepth attribute to set the number of levels that are expanded when the TreeView is first displayed. You can also use the ShowLines attribute to include lines that graphically show the tree's hierarchical structure.

The best way to learn how these attributes affect the TreeView control is to experiment with them. Like the Menu control, you can also use the Auto Format command to apply a predefined scheme and then move the styling to skin and CSS files.

How to use the SiteMapPath control

Figure 11-5 also shows how to use the SiteMapPath control. Unlike the TreeView and Menu controls, the SiteMapPath control doesn't need to be bound to a data source. Instead, it gets the site navigation information directly from the web.sitemap file.

The attributes listed in this figure let you customize the appearance of the SiteMapPath control. In particular, you can indicate how many parent nodes to list, which direction the nodes are listed in, what text to use to separate the nodes, and whether the current page should be formatted as a link or just plain text.

Although this figure doesn't show it, the SiteMapPath control also provides other attributes that let you customize the appearance of the site map path. Like the Menu and TreeView controls, you can also use the Auto Format command to apply a predefined scheme and then move the styling information to skin and CSS files.

Common attributes of the TreeView control

Attribute	Description
DataSourceID	The ID of the SiteMapDataSource control the tree is bound to.
ExpandDepth	The number of levels to be expanded when the tree is initially displayed. The default is FullyExpand.
MaxDepthDataBind	The maximum depth of the tree. The default is -1, which means no limit.
NodeIndent	The number of pixels to indent each level. The default is 20.
NodeWrap	If True, wraps the text of each node. The default is False.
ShowExpandCollapse	If False, hides the Expand/Collapse icons. The default is True.
ShowLines	If True, includes lines that show the structure. The default is False.

The aspx code for the TreeView control in figure 11-1

```
<asp:TreeView ID="TreeView1" runat="server"
    DataSourceID="SiteMapDataSource1" ImageSet="Arrows">
</asp:TreeView>
```

Common attributes of the SiteMapPath control

Attribute	Description
ParentLevelsDisplayed	The maximum number of parent nodes to display. The default is -1, which displays all parent nodes.
PathDirection	Indicates the order in which nodes should be listed. Allowable values are RootToCurrent (the default) and CurrentToRoot.
PathSeparator	The string displayed between each node of the path. The default is >.
RenderCurrentNodeAsLink	If True, the node that represents the current page will be rendered as a link. The default is False.

The aspx code for the SiteMapPath control in figure 11-1

```
<asp:SiteMapPath ID="SiteMapPath1" runat="server" PathSeparator=" : ">
</asp:SiteMapPath>
```

Description

- The TreeView control must be bound to a SiteMapDataSource control.
- The SiteMapPath control automatically uses the web.sitemap file, so it doesn't need to be bound to a site map data source.

Figure 11-5   How to use the TreeView and SiteMapPath controls

The aspx code for the master page of the Shopping Cart application

To show you how the navigation controls work together, figure 11-6 presents the aspx code for the form element of a master page that includes both a menu and a site map path. This is from the master page for the web site in figure 11-1. Notice that the menu uses the SiteMapDataSource control on the page, but the site map doesn't.

This master page is a little bit different than one you were introduced to in chapter 9. In that master page, the section element contained the form element, but in this one the section and aside elements are both inside the form element. This is necessary because the site navigation controls don't work unless they're in a form element. Otherwise, the structure and CSS of this master page are the same.

Note here that both the Menu and SiteMapPath controls include several style elements that specify the appearance of the controls. These elements were generated by selecting the Auto Format command in the smart tag menu for the controls and then choosing the Professional scheme. Usually, you will want to move formatting like this to skin and CSS files after you get the controls the way you want them.

The aspx code for the form element of the master page

```
<form id="form1" runat="server">
<aside>
  <nav>
    <asp:Menu ID="Menu1" runat="server" DataSourceID="SiteMapDataSource1"
          DynamicHorizontalOffset="2" StaticSubMenuIndent="10px"
          BackColor="#F7F6F3" Font-Names="Verdana" Font-Size="0.8em"
          ForeColor="#7C6F57">
        <StaticSelectedStyle BackColor="#5D7B9D" />
        <StaticMenuItemStyle HorizontalPadding="5px"
            VerticalPadding="2px" />
        <StaticHoverStyle BackColor="#7C6F57" Font-Bold="True"
            ForeColor="White" />
        <DynamicHoverStyle BackColor="#7C6F57" Font-Bold="True"
            ForeColor="White" />
        <DynamicMenuStyle BackColor="#F7F6F3" />
        <DynamicSelectedStyle BackColor="#5D7B9D" />
        <StaticHoverStyle BackColor="#7C6F57" Font-Bold="True"
            ForeColor="White"></StaticHoverStyle>
        <StaticSelectedStyle BackColor="#5D7B9D"></StaticSelectedStyle>
        <DynamicMenuItemStyle HorizontalPadding="5px"
            VerticalPadding="2px"/>
    </asp:Menu>

    <asp:SiteMapDataSource ID="SiteMapDataSource1" runat="server"
        ShowStartingNode="False" />
  </nav>
</aside>
<section>
    <asp:SiteMapPath ID="SiteMapPath1" runat="server" Font-Names="Verdana"
          Font-Size="0.8em" PathSeparator=" : " >
        <CurrentNodeStyle ForeColor="#333333"></CurrentNodeStyle>
        <NodeStyle Font-Bold="True" ForeColor="#7C6F57"></NodeStyle>
        <PathSeparatorStyle Font-Bold="True" ForeColor="#5D7B9D">
        </PathSeparatorStyle>
        <RootNodeStyle Font-Bold="True" ForeColor="#5D7B9D"></RootNodeStyle>
    </asp:SiteMapPath>

    <asp:ContentPlaceHolder id="formPlaceholder" runat="server">
    </asp:ContentPlaceHolder>
</section>
</form>
```

Description

- The navigation controls must be placed inside a form element.

- The styling for the Menu and SiteMapPath controls was generated by the Professional scheme that's available with the AutoFormat feature.

- It's a good practice to move the styling generated by the AutoFormat feature into skin and CSS files.

Figure 11-6   The aspx code for the master page of the Shopping Cart application

How to use ASP.NET routing

ASP.NET routing is a feature that lets you use friendly URLs for the pages of a web site. This feature provides several benefits, and it can be used with or without the site navigation controls.

An introduction to ASP.NET routing and friendly URLs

As you learned in chapter 1, a URL consists of several parts, including protocol, domain, path, and file name. Also, as you learned in chapter 8, one way to pass data between the pages of a web site is to use URL encoding with *query strings* that are coded at the end of the URLs. This is illustrated by the first example in figure 11-7.

In contrast, when you use ASP.NET routing, the data that's passed between pages becomes part of a *friendly URL*. This is illustrated by the second example in this figure. Here, the parameter is cat01, which identifies a product that has that ID in the database for the web site.

One of the main benefits of friendly URLs is improved *search engine optimization*, or *SEO*. That's why friendly URLs are sometimes referred to as *SEO-friendly URLs*. The improvement in SEO happens because all of the pages with friendly URLs get archived by the search engines. In contrast, most search engines don't archive the query string in a traditional URL.

In this figure, for example, the traditional URL with a query string is this:

```
http://halloweenstore.com/Order.aspx?ProductID=cat01
```

However, most search engines will only archive this portion of it:

```
http://halloweenstore.com/Order.aspx
```

In contrast, all of the friendly URLs will be archived.

Friendly URLs also benefit users because they're easier to read and remember. For instance, you can probably imagine a customer typing the second URL in this figure into the address bar of a browser, but it's not so easy to imagine him typing in the first one.

A third benefit of friendly URLs is that they let web developers organize their physical files without worrying about the navigation structure of the web site. In contrast, when you use traditional URLs, the physical files must mirror the navigation structure. If, for example, you want the Costumes page to be in a submenu for the Categories page, you have to place the Categories.aspx file in the root directory, and the Costumes.aspx file in the Categories directory.

The two pages and the table in this figure show how friendly URLs work. In the table, you can see that the friendly URLs have no relation to the directory structure of the site. For instance, there isn't a Categories directory that contains a Costumes page. Instead, the Categories.aspx and Costumes.aspx files are both in the root directory. Similarly, there isn't a directory named Shopping that contains an Order page. Instead, the Order.aspx file is in the root directory. Last, there isn't a directory for cat01 or hippie01. Instead, those are the product IDs that have been added to the ends of the URLs.

Friendly URLs in the Shopping Cart application

A URL with a query string parameter

```
http://halloweenstore.com/Order.aspx?ProductID=cat01
```

A friendly URL with the same parameter

```
http://halloweenstore.com/Shopping/Order/cat01
```

Benefits of friendly URLs

- They improve search engine optimization because *friendly URLs* with parameters are archived by search engines.

- They are easier for users to read and remember.

- They let developers use URLs that don't depend on the directory structure of the site.

Friendly URLs in the Shopping Cart application and their actual file paths

Friendly URL	Actual file path
/Categories/	/Categories.aspx
/Categories/Costumes	/Costumes.aspx
/Shopping/Order/cat01	/Order.aspx
/Shopping/Order/hippie01	/Order.aspx

Figure 11-7   An introduction to ASP.NET routing and friendly URLs

How to create a route collection

The ASP.NET routing framework is what makes friendly URLs possible in an ASP.NET application. The routing framework was originally developed for ASP.NET MVC, but starting with ASP.NET 3.5, it became available to Web Forms projects as well.

To use the routing framework, you must first map your application's routes. A *route* is a URL pattern that identifies a page, and a route can be either static or dynamic. The difference is that a *static route* will always be the same, like Shopping/Cart, but a *dynamic route* will contain at least one placeholder that represents a URL parameter, like Shopping/Order/cat01.

To map the routes for an application, you use the Routes property of the RouteTable class. This property is a RouteCollection object that stores all of the routes for an application. To add a route to this collection, you use the MapPageRoute method of the Routes property (the RouteCollection object).

The common parameters for this method are summarized in the table in figure 11-8. The first three are required for static routes, but all five can be used for dynamic routes. To provide a default value for the fifth parameter, you need to create a RouteValueDictionary object and assign a value to it.

This figure illustrates a standard procedure for creating the route collection for an application. Here, you can see that the code for mapping the routes starts in the Application_Start event handler in the global.asax file. For this to work, however, you must import the System.Web.Routing namespace.

The typical code in the event handler is just a call to a method named RegisterRoutes with the Routes property of the RouteTable class passed to the method as a parameter. Then, in the RegisterRoutes method, the MapPageRoute method of the Routes property is used to map the routes. In this example, the RegisterRoutes method is coded in the global.asax file, but it could also be in a separate class.

Note, however, that the RegisterRoutes method should start by executing the Ignore method of the Routes property. This tells the routing framework to ignore any of the .axd resource files that are used by ASP.NET. That way, ASP.NET routing won't interfere with other ASP.NET functions. This line of code appears by default in ASP.NET MVC projects, and it must come before any mapping code.

In the next statement of the RegisterRoutes method, you can see how a static route is coded. It consists of the name of the route, the friendly URL for the route, and the URL for the physical file that the route maps to. In this case, Shopping/Cart is the friendly URL, and it will call the Cart.aspx file in the root directory of the application.

In contrast, the last statement in this method is for a dynamic route. Here, the friendly URL includes a parameter called productID that's coded within braces, and it maps to the Order.aspx file in the root directory. Then, the fifth parameter provides a default value of an empty string for this parameter. To do that, it creates a new RouteValueDictionary object with productID as its key and an empty string as its value. As a result, an empty string is the default value for the parameter when the route is called and a value isn't passed to it.

Common parameters of the MapPageRoute method of the Routes property

Parameter	Description
routeName	The name of the route.
routeURL	The friendly URL for the route. For dynamic routes, the pattern should contain placeholders within braces for any parameters.
physicalFile	The physical file that the route maps to.
checkPhysicalUrlAccess	A Boolean value that indicates whether ASP.NET should validate that the user has the authority to access the physical URL. (The route URL is always checked.) The default value is True.
defaults	A RouteValueDictionary object that contains default values for the route parameters.

Creating a route collection in a global.asax file

```
<%@ Import Namespace="System.Web.Routing" %>
...
    void Application_Start(object sender, EventArgs e)
    {
        // Code that runs on application startup
        RegisterRoutes(RouteTable.Routes);
    }

    public static void RegisterRoutes(RouteCollection routes)
    {
        //ignore WebResource.axd file
        routes.Ignore("{resource}.axd/{*pathInfo}");

        //map static pages
        routes.MapPageRoute("Cart", "Shopping/Cart", "~/Cart.aspx");

        //map dynamic pages
        routes.MapPageRoute("Order", "Shopping/Order/{productID}",
            "~/Order.aspx", false,
            new RouteValueDictionary { { "productID", "" } });
    }
```

Description

- A *route* is the URL pattern used in a friendly URL.
- The RouteTable class has a static property named Routes, which is a RouteCollection object that contains all of the routes for an application. The routes are added to the *route collection* when the application starts.
- A standard procedure for creating a route collection is to call a RegisterRoutes method from the Application_Start event handler in the global.asax file and pass the Routes property to it. Then, in the RegisterRoutes method, the MapPageRoute method of the Routes property is used to add the routes to the collection.
- The RegisterRoutes method must start by using the Ignore method of the Routes property to tell the routing framework to ignore any of the .axd resource files that are used by ASP.NET. That way, ASP.NET routing won't interfere with other ASP.NET functions.

Figure 11-8   How to create a route collection

How to work with route parameters

In chapter 8, you learned how to retrieve parameters from a traditional URL query string by using the QueryString collection of the page's Request property. Similarly, you can retrieve the parameters from a friendly URL by using the Values collection of the page's RouteData property, as shown in the first example in figure 11-9.

You can also retrieve URL parameters from outside of a web page. To do that, you use the current request's RequestContext property to get the RouteData property, and then use the Values collection of that property, as shown in the second example in this figure.

Like the other collections, the Values collection of the RouteData property stores items as objects. This means that when you retrieve them, you must cast them to their specific data types. Once you've retrieved and cast a parameter from the Values collection, you can work with it in code like any other variable.

Besides retrieving route parameters in code, you can use them with data source controls. For instance, the third example in this figure shows a SqlDataSource control that uses a route parameter as a select parameter. Here, the RouteKey attribute is the name given to the placeholder in the global.asax file. The Name attribute is the name of the field in the Select statement. And the Type attribute is the data type of the value. All three of these attributes are required, and you can also set an optional DefaultValue attribute. (Although using route parameters with data source controls can be useful in some applications, they aren't illustrated in this chapter).

How to work with file paths

When you use ASP.NET routing for a page, it can sometimes have unexpected effects on the file paths that ASP.NET renders for static resources such as images, CSS files, and JavaScript files. Figure 11-9 shows three ways to deal with the file paths for static resources so they won't cause problems.

All three techniques make the file paths relative to the root directory of the site, rather than to the current file. First, you can start the file path with a forward slash ("/"). Second, for a server control, you can use the tilde operator in the file path. Remember that this operator causes the URL to be based on the root directory of the site.

Third, for an HTML element, you can make the path relative to the root directory by using the ResolveUrl method of the page class along with the tilde operator. This resolves any conflicts that might occur when the page is rendered. But note again that this is only a problem for pages that are accessed with friendly URLs.

This figure also shows one other way to get around this problem, but it only works with images. Rather than using image elements in your HTML, you can use CSS to treat the images as background images for other HTML elements.

How to retrieve a route parameter

In a code-behind file

```
string catID = RouteData.Values["catID"].ToString();
```

In a non-page class

```
string catID =
HttpContext.Current.Request.RequestContext.RouteData.Values["catID"].ToString();
```

How to use a route parameter as the parameter for a SQL data source

```
<asp:SqlDataSource ID="SqlDataSource1" runat="server"
    ConnectionString='<%$ ConnectionStrings:HalloweenDatabase %>'
    SelectCommand="SELECT [ProductID], [Name], [LongDescription],
        [CategoryID], [UnitPrice], [ImageFile] FROM [Products] WHERE
        ([ProductID] = @ProductID)">
    <SelectParameters>
        <asp:RouteParameter RouteKey="productID" Name="ProductID"
            DefaultValue="pow01" Type="String">
        </asp:RouteParameter>
    </SelectParameters>
</asp:SqlDataSource>
```

Three ways to make a file path relative to the root directory

Start the path with a forward slash

```
<link href="/Styles/Order.css" rel="stylesheet" />
```

Use the tilde operator with server controls.

```
<asp:Image ID="Image1" runat="server" ImageUrl="~/Images/banner.jpg"
    AlternateText="Halloween Store" />
```

Use the tilde operator and the ResolveURL method with HTML elements

```
<img src='<%=ResolveUrl("~/Images/banner.jpg")%>' alt="Halloween Store" />
```

Another way to handle the file path for an image

- Use CSS to treat the image as the background image for another HTML element.

Description

- If a page is running in response to a request made through ASP.NET routing, the page's RouteData property provides access to the parameter values that were in the URL.

- To use a route parameter as the select parameter for a SQL data source, you code a RouteParameter element within the SelectParameters element of the data source, as shown above.

- When you use routing, it can have unexpected effects on the file paths that ASP.NET renders for static resources such as images, CSS files, and JavaScript files. To correct this, you should make the paths to these resources relative to the root directory.

- One way to make sure that the URL for a static resource will be rendered correctly is to combine the use of the tilde operator with the ResolveURL method of the page class.

Figure 11-9   How to work with route parameters and file paths

The C# code for the Order page with a dynamic route

If you look back to the Order page in figure 11-7, you can see that the last portion of its friendly URL is the parameter that contains the product ID for the product that's displayed. Then, if you look at the code in figure 11-8, you can see that a dynamic route has been created for this page with an empty string as the default value for the ProductID parameter. This means that the code-behind file for the Order page has to do something with the parameter that it receives.

Figure 11-10 starts by showing one version of a Load event handler for the Order page. This handler checks the IsPostBack property, and binds the drop-down list to its SQL data source if this is the initial load of the page. This is the same as the code in previous versions of the Order page.

But next, this handler uses the Values collection of the page's RouteData property to get the value of a URL parameter named "productID". If it finds one, it sets the selected value of the drop-down list to that value. The selected value is then used by the ShowSelectedProduct method to get and display the product data.

From a coding standpoint, nothing is wrong with this code. It displays the right product data when another page sends a URL parameter or when its own drop-down list posts back to the page. The problem is the URL that is displayed when a user selects a new product in the drop-down list. For example, figure 11-7 shows the page that is rendered when the id for the Deranged Cat product has been sent to the Orders page: /Shopping/Order/cat01. But if the user then selects "Hippie" from the drop-down list, the Hippie data will be displayed but the URL will still be /Shopping/Order/cat01.

The second example in this figure fixes this problem by improving the Load event handler, adding an event handler for the SelectedIndexChanged event of the drop-down list, and adding an AddProductIdToUrlAndRedirect method. Here's how it works.

When the drop-down selection changes, the Load event is called, but the Load event code doesn't run because it is a postback. As a result, the execution continues with the event handler for the SelectedIndexChanged event. Then, this hander calls the AddProductIdToUrlAndRedirect helper method, which builds a friendly URL based on the selected value of the drop-down list, and then passes the new URL to the Redirect method of the Response object.

This causes the page to be reloaded with the new URL, and since it isn't a postback, all the code in the Load event handler runs. Then, since the new URL contains a parameter for the selected product, the code retrieves it and uses it to set the selected value and display product information.

The revised Load event handler calls the same helper method when no productID can be found in the URL, which will happen when the user first navigates to the Order page. In that case, the selected value of the drop-down list will be the first product in the list, so that's what will display on the page and in the URL after the page reloads.

This correction uses a design pattern called the *Post-Redirect-Get (PRG) pattern*. It is commonly used in ASP.NET MVC applications and also to correct backbutton problems, as you'll see later in the book.

A Load event handler for the Order page that has a problem

```
protected void Page_Load(object sender, EventArgs e) {
    if (!IsPostBack)
    {
        // bind drop-down list to product data from database
        ddlProducts.DataBind();

        // get the 'productID' parameter from the page's RouteData object
        string routeProductID = RouteData.Values["productID"].ToString();

        // if there is a parameter, use it to set drop-down value
        if (routeProductID != "")
                this.ddlProducts.SelectedValue = routeProductID;
    }
    //Display information about the selected product in the form
    ShowSelectedProduct();
}
```

Improved C# code for the Order page

```
protected void Page_Load(object sender, EventArgs e)
{
    if (!IsPostBack) //initial page load
    {
        // bind drop-down list to product data from database
        ddlProducts.DataBind();

        // get the 'productID' parameter from the page's RouteData object
        string routeProductID = RouteData.Values["productID"].ToString();

        // if no parameter, add product ID to the URL and re-load page
        if (routeProductID == "")
            AddProductIdToUrlAndRedirect();
        else //URL has product ID so use it to set drop-down value
            this.ddlProducts.SelectedValue = routeProductID;
    }
    else
    {
        //postback - always add productID to URL and re-load page
        AddProductIdToUrlAndRedirect();
    }
    //Display information about the selected product in the form
    ShowSelectedProduct();
}
protected void ddlProducts_SelectedIndexChanged(object sender, EventArgs e)
{
    AddProductIdToUrlAndRedirect();
}
private void AddProductIdToUrlAndRedirect() {
    //add selected product to the friendly URL and re-load page
    Response.Redirect("~/Shopping/Order/" + ddlProducts.SelectedValue);
}
```

Figure 11-10   The C# code for the Order page with friendly URLs

How to use the navigation controls with ASP.NET routing

In this chapter, you first learned how to use the navigation controls without ASP.NET routing. Then, you learned how to use ASP.NET routing, especially for an Order page that receives parameters in friendly URLs. Now, you'll learn how to use the navigation controls with ASP.NET routing.

But first, it's important to note we had to change the database that's used for the other applications in this book so it would work right with ASP.NET routing. That's because the ProductID column in the Products table in the Halloween database for the other applications is defined as char(10), which means an ID that is less than 10 characters will have spaces added to it. The trouble is that an ID of cat01 becomes cat01 followed by five spaces, and those extra spaces will cause the routing to fail.

The best solution to a problem like this is to change the database so it works properly with ASP.NET routing. In this case, the ProductID column should have been defined as varchar(10) in the first place, which trims the extra spaces from the ID if it's less than 10 characters. Keep in mind, though, that this is the only application that uses this version of the database.

The global.asax file for the Shopping Cart application with friendly URLs

Back in figure 11-7, you can see two pages of a Shopping Cart application that uses friendly URLs for all of the pages. That includes the pages that are accessed by the Menu and SiteMapPath controls that are in the master page of the application. Note, however, that the SiteMapPath control isn't displayed on the Order page because that control doesn't work with dynamic routes unless you create a special provider for it.

Figure 11-11 shows the global.asax file for this application. Here, you can see the code for adding all of the routes to the route collection in the event handler for the Application_Start method. You can also see the code for importing the System.Web.Routing namespace at the top of the file. Without that code, you will get syntax errors when you try to code the routes.

The first statement in the RegisterRoutes method uses the Ignore method of the static Routes property to tell the routing framework to ignore any of ASP.NET's .axd resource files. This is followed by the calls to the MapPageRoute method that map the site's static routes. The last statement in this method adds the dynamic route for the Order page to the route collection.

Note that if you create a dynamic route and a user types in a URL with no value for the parameter, the user will get a "404 File Not Found" error. That's why it's a best practice to send in a RouteValueDictionary object with default values for the parameter. So that's what the route for the Order page does.

The global.asax file for the Shopping Cart application with friendly URLs

```
<%@ Application Language="C#" %>
<%@ Import Namespace="System.Web.Routing" %>

<script runat="server">

    void Application_Start(object sender, EventArgs e){
        // Code that runs on application startup
        RegisterRoutes(RouteTable.Routes);
    }

    public static void RegisterRoutes(RouteCollection routes) {
        routes.Ignore("{resource}.axd/{*pathInfo}");

        //map static pages
        routes.MapPageRoute("Home", "Home", "~/Default.aspx");

        routes.MapPageRoute("Shopping", "Shopping", "~/Shopping.aspx");
        routes.MapPageRoute("Cart", "Shopping/Cart", "~/Cart.aspx");
        routes.MapPageRoute("Checkout", "Shopping/Checkout",
            "~/Checkout.aspx");

        routes.MapPageRoute("Categories", "Categories",
            "~/Categories.aspx");
        routes.MapPageRoute("Costumes", "Categories/Costumes",
            "~/Costumes.aspx");
        routes.MapPageRoute("Masks", "Categories/Masks", "~/Masks.aspx");
        routes.MapPageRoute("Props", "Categories/Props", "~/Props.aspx");

        routes.MapPageRoute("Support", "Support", "~/Support.aspx");
        routes.MapPageRoute("Service", "Support/Service",
            "~/CustomerService.aspx");
        routes.MapPageRoute("Product", "Support/Product",
            "~/ProductSupport.aspx");
        routes.MapPageRoute("Map", "Support/Map", "~/Map.aspx");

        routes.MapPageRoute("About", "About", "~/About.aspx");

        //map dynamic pages
        routes.MapPageRoute("Order", "Shopping/Order/{productID}",
            "~/Order.aspx", false,
            new RouteValueDictionary { { "productID", "" } });
    }
    ...
</script>
```

Description

- To use ASP.NET routing, you must import the System.Web.Routing namespace.
- To provide a default value for a route parameter, you create a new RouteValueDictionary object for the parameter and give it a starting value.

Figure 11-11   The global.asax file for the Shopping Cart application with friendly URLs

The web.sitemap file with traditional URLs

Figure 11-12 starts by showing the complete web.sitemap file for the Shopping Cart application *when traditional URLs are used*. This file is presented in this figure so you can easily see the difference between a web.sitemap file with traditional URLs and one with friendly URLs. To save space, though, the Description attributes have been removed and the inner nodes use self-closing tags, which is different than the way the web.sitemap file looks in figure 11-2.

This site navigation structure corresponds to the structure shown in the TreeView control in figure 11-1. Here, the url attributes contain the paths of the physical aspx files. To do that, these attributes use the tilde operator, so the paths are relative to the root directory.

The web.sitemap file with friendly URLs

By contrast, the second version of the web.sitemap file in figure 11-12 uses ASP.NET routing and friendly URLs. As a result, the url attribute for each page contains the friendly URL of the route that was registered for the page in the global.asax file in the last figure. Here again, the tilde operator is used so the paths are relative to the root directory.

Note here that the url attribute for the Order page is coded just like the attributes for the other pages, even though the Order page has a dynamic route with a URL parameter named productID and the code-behind file for the Order page has code that uses that parameter. Similarly, as long as the url attributes for the other pages contain the friendly URLs for those pages, the Menu and TreeView controls that use the web.sitemap file will work correctly.

But note again that the SiteMapPath control doesn't work with dynamic routes unless you develop a custom provider for it. Because that can be more trouble than it's worth, you may well decide to remove the SiteMapPath controls from pages that are accessed by dynamic routes.

Incidentally, you can mix traditional and friendly URLs in the web.sitemap file for an application. For instance, you could use traditional URLs for all of the static routes in the Shopping Cart application and friendly URLs for just the Order page. That would give you the benefit of friendly URLs for the Order page without all of the trouble of setting up the routes for the other pages. But the SiteMapPath control still wouldn't work on the Order page.

The web.sitemap file with traditional URLs

```
<siteMap xmlns="http://schemas.microsoft.com/AspNet/SiteMap-File-1.0" >

  <siteMapNode url="~/Default.aspx" title="Home">

    <siteMapNode url="~/Shopping.aspx" title="Shopping">
      <siteMapNode url="~/Order.aspx" title="Order Products" />
      <siteMapNode url="~/Cart.aspx" title="Shopping Cart" />
      <siteMapNode url="~/Checkout.aspx" title="Check Out" />
    </siteMapNode>

    <siteMapNode url="~/Categories.aspx" title="Categories">
      <siteMapNode url="~/Costumes.aspx" title="Costumes" />
      <siteMapNode url="~/Masks.aspx" title="Masks" />
      <siteMapNode url="~/Props.aspx" title="Props" />
    </siteMapNode>

    <siteMapNode url="~/Support.aspx" title="Support">
      <siteMapNode url="~/CustomerService.aspx" title="Customer Service" />
      <siteMapNode url="~/ProductSupport.aspx" title="Product Support" />
      <siteMapNode url="~/Map.aspx" title="Site Map" />
    </siteMapNode>

    <siteMapNode url="~/About.aspx" title="About Us"></siteMapNode>

  </siteMapNode>
</siteMap>
```

The web.sitemap file with ASP.NET routing

```
<siteMap xmlns="http://schemas.microsoft.com/AspNet/SiteMap-File-1.0" >

  <siteMapNode url="~/Home" title="Home">

    <siteMapNode url="~/Shopping" title="Shopping">
      <siteMapNode url="~/Shopping/Order" title="Order Products" />
      <siteMapNode url="~/Shopping/Cart" title="Shopping Cart" />
      <siteMapNode url="~/Shopping/Checkout" title="Check Out" />
    </siteMapNode>

    <siteMapNode url="~/Categories" title="Categories">
      <siteMapNode url="~/Categories/Costumes" title="Costumes" />
      <siteMapNode url="~/Categories/Masks" title="Masks" />
      <siteMapNode url="~/Categories/Props" title="Props" />
    </siteMapNode>

    <siteMapNode url="~/Support" title="Support">
      <siteMapNode url="~/Support/Service" title="Customer Service" />
      <siteMapNode url="~/Support/Product" title="Product Support" />
      <siteMapNode url="~/Support/Map" title="Site Map" />
    </siteMapNode>

    <siteMapNode url="~/About" title="About Us"></siteMapNode>

  </siteMapNode>
</siteMap>
```

Figure 11-12   Web.sitemap files with traditional and friendly URLs

Perspective

If you experiment with the navigation controls and ASP.NET routing, you'll quickly see how useful they can be. You'll also discover that the TreeView, Menu, and SiteMapPath controls include many attributes that weren't presented in this chapter. However, most of these attributes are designed to let you alter the appearance of the navigation controls, not their behaviors. So, once you master the basics of using these controls, you shouldn't have any trouble learning how to tweak their appearance by using the other attributes.

Terms

site navigation	friendly URL
bread crumbs	SEO (search engine optimization)
site map data source	SEO-friendly URL
vertical menu	route
horizontal menu	route collection
static menu	static route
dynamic menu	dynamic route
ASP.NET routing	PRG (Post-Redirect-Get) pattern
query string	

Summary

- ASP.NET's *site navigation* features simplify the task of providing the navigation for a web site by providing a site map data source control and three navigation controls.

- The Menu control creates a *static menu* plus *dynamic menus* that expand when you hover the mouse over an item that contains submenu items. The TreeView control displays the web site's pages in a tree structure. And the SiteMapPath control displays a list of links, or *bread crumbs*, that lead from the site's home page to the current page.

- The web.sitemap file uses XML tags to define the hierarchical structure of the application's pages. It is required for using the site navigation controls.

- The Menu control and the TreeView control use SiteMapDataSource controls that are bound to the web.sitemap file. The SiteMapPath control binds directly to the web.sitemap file, so it doesn't need a *site map data source*.

- *ASP.NET routing* lets you create *friendly URLs* for your site. Routing can be used in conjunction with the site navigation controls, but it doesn't have to be.

- To work with ASP.NET routing you must define your site's routes at application startup. A *route* is a URL pattern and can be *static* or *dynamic*.

- You map your site's routes to its physical files by using the MapPageRoute method of the static Routes property of the RouteTable class.

- You retrieve parameters from a friendly URL by using the page's RouteData collection. You can also use URL parameters with data source controls.

- ASP.NET routing can cause problems with the paths of static resources. You can correct for this by making the file paths relative to the root directory.

- ASP.NET routing can also cause a page's URL to be out of sync with the data it is displaying. You can correct for this by using the *PRG (Post-Redirect-Get) pattern.*

Exercise 11-1   Modify the Navigation application

In this application, you'll review, fix, and enhance the Navigation application that's presented in this chapter. It uses ASP.NET routing and friendly URLs in combination with the three navigation controls.

Before you start, keep in mind that the local database for just this one application has been changed so the ProductID column in the Products table is defined as varchar(10), not char(10). This means that if you try to run this application with the database that's used for any of the other applications, it won't work.

Open, run, and review the Shopping Cart application
1. Open the Ex11CartNavigation web site that's in the aspnet45_cs directory. Then, review any of the files that you're interested in, like the Global.asax, Web.sitemap, or Site.master files.

2. Start the application and test the Order page of the site to see that friendly URLs are used for the pages, whether you select a product on the Default.aspx page (the Home page) or select a product from the drop-down list on the Order page.

3. Use the menus and site map path to go to the other pages of the site, and note that the formatting of the Cart page is messed up. Then, go to the Order page and click on the Go to Cart button to find that the formatting of the Cart page is improved, but it no longer has the site map path on it and the URL in the address bar in the browser is a traditional URL, not a friendly URL.

Fix the Cart page
4. To fix the Cart page, you need to change the PostBackUrl attribute of the Go to Cart button on the Order page so it uses the friendly URL for the page. Do that, and test the application again.

5. That fixed the URL for the page, but the formatting is still messed up. To fix that, use the ResolveUrl method to resolve the URL that identifies the CSS style sheet for the Cart page. Now, test that change.

6. On the Cart page, click the Continue Shopping button, and note that you need to fix the PostBackUrl attribute for that button too. Now, test that change.

Enhance the Menu control

7. Use the smart tag menu for the Menu control on the master page to access the AutoFormat dialog box and remove the formatting that has been applied to the menus. Then, test that change and note that the formatting is now being done by the CSS file for the master page.

8. Use the AutoFormat feature to change the formatting for the menus to the Colorful scheme, and test that change.

9. Add two submenu items to the About Us item in the Menu control. The first one should be Our Mission and go to the page named Mission.aspx that's in the root directory. The second one should be Our History and go to the page named History.aspx that's in the root directory. To do that with traditional URLs, you just need to add these items to the web.sitemap file. Now, make and test those changes.

10. To use the new menu items with friendly URLs, you need to add the routes to the global.asax file and then change the web.sitemap file so it uses the friendly URLs. For the Mission.aspx file, use About/Mission as the friendly URL. For the History.aspx file, use About/History as the friendly URL. Now, make and test those changes.

Experiment on your own

11. If you're interested, continue to experiment with the formatting or behavior of any of the navigation controls. When you're through, close the application.

Section 3

ASP.NET database programming

Since most ASP.NET applications store their data in databases, this section is devoted to the essentials of database programming. To start, chapter 12 introduces you to the concepts and terms you need to know for developing database applications.

Then, chapter 13 shows you how to use SQL data sources and the DataList control to get data from a database. Chapter 14 shows you how to use the GridView control to create more complex applications. Chapter 15 shows you how to use the DetailsView and FormView controls. And chapter 16 shows you how to use the ListView and DataPager controls. By using SQL data sources and the data controls, you'll be able to develop powerful applications with a minimum of code.

Finally, chapter 17 shows you how to use object data sources to develop 3-layer database applications. If you already know how to use ADO.NET directly, you should be able to use object data sources when you complete this chapter. Otherwise, you will at least understand the concepts and recognize the need for learning ADO.NET.

12

An introduction to database programming

This chapter introduces you to the basic concepts and terms that apply to database applications. In particular, it explains what a relational database is and describes how you work with it using SQL. It also introduces the basic ADO.NET components that are used to access and update the data in relational databases.

An introduction to relational databases

In 1970, Dr. E. F. Codd developed a model for what was then a new and revolutionary type of database called a *relational database.* This type of database eliminated some of the problems that were associated with standard files and other database designs. By using the relational model, you can reduce data redundancy, which saves disk storage and leads to efficient data retrieval. You can also view and manipulate data in a way that is both intuitive and efficient. Today, relational databases are the de facto standard for database applications.

How a table is organized

The model for a relational database states that data is stored in one or more *tables.* It also states that each table can be viewed as a two-dimensional matrix consisting of *rows* and *columns.* This is illustrated by the relational table in figure 12-1. Each row in this table contains information about a single product.

In practice, the rows and columns of a relational database table are sometimes referred to by the more traditional terms, *records* and *fields.* In fact, some software packages use one set of terms, some use the other, and some use a combination. In this book, I've used the terms *rows* and *columns* for consistency.

If a table contains one or more columns that uniquely identify each row in the table, you can define these columns as the *primary key* of the table. For instance, the primary key of the Products table in this figure is the ProductID column. Here, the primary key consists of a single column. However, a primary key can also consist of two or more columns, in which case it's called a *composite primary key.*

In addition to primary keys, some database management systems let you define additional keys that uniquely identify each row in a table. If, for example, the Name column in the Products table contains a unique name for each product, it can be defined as a *non-primary key.* In SQL Server, this is called a *unique key,* and it's implemented by defining a *unique key constraint* (also known simply as a *unique constraint*). The only difference between a unique key and a primary key is that a unique key can contain a null value and a primary key can't.

Indexes provide an efficient way to access the rows in a table based on the values in one or more columns. Because applications typically access the rows in a table by referring to their key values, an index is automatically created for each key you define. However, you can define indexes for other columns as well. If, for example, you frequently need to sort the rows in the Products table by the CategoryID column, you can set up an index for that column. Like a key, an index can include one or more columns.

The Products table in a Halloween database

Primary key | Columns | Rows

ProductID	Name	ShortDescripti...	LongDescription	CategoryID	ImageFile	UnitPrice	OnHand
arm01	Freddie Arm	Life-size Freddy...	This arm will gi...	props	arm1.jpg	20.9500	200
bats01	Flying Bats	Bats flying in fr...	Bats flying in fr...	props	cool1.jpg	69.9900	25
bl01	Black Light	Black light with...	Create that cree...	fx	blacklight1.jpg	19.9900	200
cat01	Deranged Cat	20" Ugly cat	This cat provid...	props	cat1.jpg	19.9900	45
fog01	Fog Machine	600W Fog mac...	The perfect fog...	fx	fog1.jpg	34.9900	100
fogj01	Fog Juice (1qt)	1 qt Bottle of fo...	Fill up your fog ...	fx	fogjuice1.jpg	9.9900	500
frankc01	Frankenstein	Frankenstein co...	Have all your fri...	costumes	frank1.jpg	39.9900	100
fred01	Freddie	Freddie Krueger...	The ultimate in ...	masks	freddy1.jpg	29.9900	50
head01	Michael Head	Mini Michael M...	For classic horr...	props	head1.jpg	29.9900	100
head02	Saw Head	Jigsaw head sca...	Perfect for getti...	props	head2.jpg	29.9900	100
hippie01	Hippie	Women's hippi...	Share the peace...	costumes	hippie1.jpg	79.9900	40
jar01	JarJar	Jar Jar Binks	Meesa happy t...	costumes	jarjar1.jpg	59.9900	25
martian01	Martian	Martian costume	Now includes a...	costumes	martian1.jpg	69.9900	100
mum01	Mummy	Mummy mask	All wrapped up ...	masks	mummy1.jpg	39.9900	30
pow01	Austin Powers	Austin Powers ...	Be the most sh...	costumes	powers1.jpg	79.9900	25
rat01	Ugly Rat	16" Rat	This guy is sure...	props	rat1.jpg	14.9900	75
rat02	Uglier Rat	20" Rat	Yuch! This one ...	props	rat2.jpg	19.9900	50
skel01	Life-size Skeleton	Life-size plastic ...	This blown plas...	props	skel1.jpg	14.9500	10
skullfog01	Skull Fogger	2,800 cubic foo...	This fogger put...	fx	skullfog1.jpg	39.9500	50
str01	Mini-strobe	Black mini stro...	Perfect for crea...	fx	strobe1.jpg	13.9900	200
super01	Superman	Superman cost...	Look, up in the ...	costumes	superman1.jpg	39.9900	100
tlm01	T&L Machine	Thunder & Lig...	Flash! Boom! Cr...	fx	tlm1.jpg	99.9900	10
vader01	Darth Vader Ma...	The legendary ...	OB1 has taught...	masks	vader1.jpg	19.9900	100

Concepts

- A *relational database* uses *tables* to store and manipulate data. Each table consists of one or more *records*, or *rows*, that contain the data for a single entry. Each row contains one or more *fields*, or *columns*, with each column representing a single item of data.

- Most tables contain a *primary key* that uniquely identifies each row in the table. The primary key often consists of a single column, but it can also consist of two or more columns. If a primary key uses two or more columns, it's called a *composite primary key*.

- In addition to primary keys, some database management systems let you define one or more *non-primary keys*. In SQL Server, these keys are called *unique keys*, and they're implemented using *unique key constraints*. Like a primary key, a non-primary key uniquely identifies each row in the table.

- A table can also be defined with one or more *indexes*. An index provides an efficient way to access data from a table based on the values in specific columns. An index is automatically created for a table's primary and non-primary keys.

Figure 12-1   How a table is organized

How the tables in a database are related

The tables in a relational database can be related to other tables by values in specific columns. The two tables shown in figure 12-2 illustrate this concept. Here, each row in the Categories table is related to one or more rows in the Products table. This is called a *one-to-many relationship*.

Typically, relationships exist between the primary key in one table and the *foreign key* in another table. The foreign key is simply one or more columns in a table that refer to a primary key in another table. In SQL Server, relationships can also exist between a unique key in one table and a foreign key in another table.

Although one-to-many relationships are the most common, two tables can also have a one-to-one or many-to-many relationship. If a table has a *one-to-one relationship* with another table, the data in the two tables could be stored in a single table. Because of that, one-to-one relationships are used infrequently.

In contrast, a *many-to-many relationship* is usually implemented by using an intermediate table, called a *linking table*, that has a one-to-many relationship with the two tables in the many-to-many relationship. In other words, a many-to-many relationship can usually be broken down into two one-to-many relationships.

The relationship between the Categories and Products tables

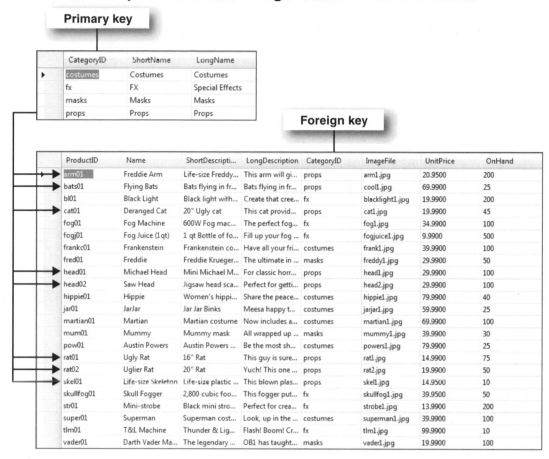

Concepts

- The tables in a relational database are related to each other through their key columns. For example, the CategoryID column is used to relate the Categories and Products tables above. The CategoryID column in the Products table is called a *foreign key* because it identifies a related row in the Categories table.

- Usually, a foreign key corresponds to the primary key in the related table. In SQL Server, however, a foreign key can also correspond to a unique key in the related table.

- When two tables are related via a foreign key, the table with the foreign key is referred to as the *foreign key table* and the table with the primary key is referred to as the *primary key table*.

- The relationships between the tables in a database correspond to the relationships between the entities they represent. The most common type of relationship is a *one-to-many* relationship as illustrated by the Categories and Products tables. A table can also have a *one-to-one relationship* or a *many-to-many relationship* with another table.

Figure 12-2   How the tables in a database are related

How the columns in a table are defined

When you define a column in a table, you assign properties to it as indicated by the design of the Products table in figure 12-3. The two most important properties for a column are Name, which provides an identifying name for the column, and Data Type, which specifies the type of information that can be stored in the column. With SQL Server, you can choose from *system data types* like the ones in this figure, and you can define your own data types that are based on the system data types. As you define each column in a table, you generally try to assign the data type that will minimize the use of disk storage because that will improve the performance of the queries later.

In addition to a data type, you must indicate whether the column can store a *null value*. A null represents a value that's unknown, unavailable, or not applicable. The Products table, for example, allows nulls in its ImageFile column.

You can also assign a *default value* to each column. Then, that value is assigned to the column if another value isn't provided. If a column doesn't allow nulls and doesn't have a default value, you must supply a value for the column when you add a new row to the table. Otherwise, an error will occur.

Each table can also contain a numeric column whose value is generated automatically by the DBMS. In SQL Server, a column like this is called an *identity column*, and you establish it using the Identity, Identity Seed, and Identity Increment properties. Identity columns are often used as the primary key for a table.

A *check constraint* defines the acceptable values for a column. For example, you can define a check constraint for the Products table in this figure to make sure that the UnitPrice column is greater than zero. A check constraint like this can be defined at the column level because it refers only to the column it constrains. If the check constraint for a column needs to refer to other columns in the table, however, it can be defined at the table level.

After you define the constraints for a database, they're managed by the DBMS. If, for example, a user tries to add a row with data that violates a constraint, the DBMS sends an appropriate error code back to the application without adding the row to the database. The application can then respond to the error code.

Another alternative is to validate the data that is going to be added to a database before the program tries to add it. That way, the constraints shouldn't be needed and the program should run more efficiently. In many cases, both data validation and constraints are used. That way, the programs run more efficiently if the data validation routines work, but the constraints are there in case the data validation routines don't work or aren't coded.

The Server Explorer design view window for the Products table

Name	Data Type	Allow Nulls	Default
ProductID	char(10)	☐	
Name	varchar(50)	☐	
ShortDescription	varchar(200)	☐	
LongDescription	varchar(2000)	☐	
CategoryID	varchar(10)	☐	
ImageFile	varchar(30)	☑	
UnitPrice	money	☐	
OnHand	int	☐	
		☐	

▲ **Keys** (1)
    PK_Products (Primary Key, Clustered: ProductID)
Check Constraints (0)
Indexes (0)
Foreign Keys (0)
Triggers (0)

Common SQL Server data types

Type	Description
bit	A value of 1 or 0 that represents a True or False value.
char, varchar, text	Any combination of letters, symbols, and numbers.
date, time, datetime, smalldatetime	Alphanumeric data that represents a date, a time, or both a date and time. Various formats are acceptable.
decimal, numeric	Numeric data that is accurate to the least significant digit. The data can contain an integer and a fractional portion.
float, real	Floating-point values that contain an approximation of a decimal value.
bigint, int, smallint, tinyint	Numeric data that contains only an integer portion.
money, smallmoney	Monetary values that are accurate to four decimal places.

Description

- The *data type* that's assigned to a column determines the type of information that can be stored in the column. Depending on the data type, the column definition can also include its length, precision, and scale.

- Each column definition also indicates whether or not the column can contain *null values*. A null value indicates that the value of the column is not known.

- A column can be defined with a *default value*. Then, that value is used for the column if another value isn't provided when a row is added to the table.

- A column can also be defined as an *identity column*. An identity column is a numeric column whose value is generated automatically when a row is added to the table.

- To restrict the values that a column can hold, you define *check constraints*. Check constraints can be defined at either the column level or the table level.

Note

- When you select a column in design view, its properties are displayed in the Properties window. Then you can use this window to change any of the properties of the column, including those that aren't displayed in design view.

Figure 12-3   How the columns in a table are defined

The design of the Halloween database

Now that you've seen how the basic elements of a relational database work, figure 12-4 shows the design of the Halloween database that's used in the programming examples throughout this book. Although this database may seem complicated, its design is actually much simpler than most databases you'll encounter when you work on actual database applications.

The purpose of the Halloween database is to track orders placed at an online Halloween products store. To do that, the database must track not only invoices, but also products and customers.

The central table for this database is the Invoices table, which contains one row for each order placed by the company's customers. The primary key for this table is the InvoiceNumber column, which is an identity column. As a result, invoice numbers are generated automatically by SQL Server whenever new invoices are created.

The LineItems table contains the line item details for each invoice. The primary key for this table is a combination of the InvoiceNumber and ProductID columns. The InvoiceNumber column relates each line item to an invoice, and the ProductID column relates each line item to a product. As a result, each invoice can have only one line item for a given product.

The Products and Categories tables work together to store information about the products offered by the Halloween store. The Category table has just three columns: CategoryID, ShortName, and LongName. The CategoryID column is a 10-character code that uniquely identifies each category. The ShortName and LongName columns provide two different descriptions of the category that the application can use, depending on how much room is available to display the category information.

The Products table contains one row for each product. Its primary key is the ProductID column. The Name, ShortDescription, and LongDescription columns provide descriptive information about the product. The ImageFile column provides the name of a separate image file that depicts the product, if one exists. This column specifies just the name of each image file, not the complete path. In the applications in this book, the image files are stored in a directory named Images beneath the application's main directory, so the application knows where to find them. If an image isn't available for a product, this column contains a null value.

The Customers table contains a row for each customer who has purchased from the Halloween Store. The primary key for this table is the customer's email address. The other columns in this table contain the customer's name, address, and phone number. The State column relates each customer to a state in the States table. The primary key for the States table is the 2-character StateCode column.

The tables that make up the Halloween database

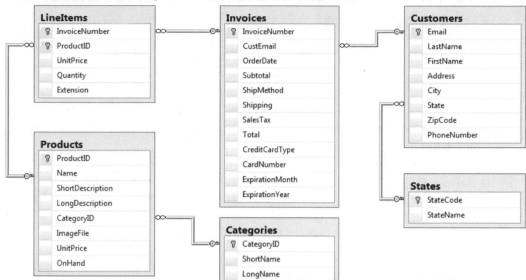

Description

- The Categories table contains a row for each product category. Its primary key is CategoryID, a 10-character code that identifies each category.

- The Products table contains a row for each product. Its primary key is ProductID, a 10-character code that identifies each product. CategoryID is a foreign key that relates each product to a row in the Categories table.

- The States table contains a row for each state. Its primary key is StateCode, a 2-character code that identifies each state.

- The Customers table contains a row for each customer. Its primary key is Email, which identifies each customer by his or her email address. State is a foreign key that relates each customer to a row in the States table.

- The Invoices table contains a row for each invoice. Its primary key is InvoiceNumber, an identity column that's generated automatically when a new invoice is created. CustEmail is a foreign key that relates each invoice to a row in the Customers table.

- The LineItems table contains one row for each line item of each invoice. Its primary key is a combination of InvoiceNumber and ProductID. InvoiceNumber is a foreign key that relates each line item to an invoice, and ProductID is a foreign key that relates each line item to a product.

- The relationships between the tables in this diagram appear as links, where the endpoints indicate the type of relationship. A key indicates the "one" side of a relationship, and the infinity symbol (∞) indicates the "many" side.

Figure 12-4   The design of the Halloween database

How to use SQL to work with the data in a relational database

To access or update the data in a relational database, you use a standard language called *SQL* (*Structured Query Language*). In practice, SQL is either pronounced as the letters S-Q-L or as sequel, and the writing in this section assumes the sequel pronunciation. In the topics that follow, you'll learn about the four *SQL statements* that retrieve and update data: the Select, Insert, Update, and Delete statements.

Although SQL is a standard language, each DBMS is likely to have its own *SQL dialect*, which includes extensions to the standard language. So when you use SQL, you need to make sure that you're using the dialect that's supported by your DBMS. In this chapter and throughout this book, all of the SQL examples are for Microsoft SQL Server's dialect, which is called *Transact-SQL*.

How to query a single table

Figure 12-5 shows how to use a Select statement to query a single table in a database. In the syntax summary at the top of this figure, you can see that the Select clause names the columns to be retrieved and the From clause names the table that contains the columns. You can also code a Where clause that gives criteria for the rows to be selected. And you can code an Order By clause that names one or more columns that the results should be sorted by and indicates whether each column should be sorted in ascending or descending sequence.

If you study the Select statement below the syntax summary, you can see how this works. Here, the Select statement retrieves three columns from the Products table. It selects a row only if the CategoryID column for the row has a value of "props." And it sorts the returned rows by UnitPrice, so the least expensive products are listed first.

This figure also shows the *result table*, or *result set*, that's returned by the Select statement. A result set is a logical table that's created temporarily within the database. When an application requests data from a database, it receives a result set.

Although it's not shown here, you should realize that a result set can include columns that are calculated from other columns in the table. For example, you could create a column for the total value of each product in the Products table by multiplying the OnHand column in that table by the UnitPrice column. This type of column is called a *calculated column*, and it exists only in the results of the query.

Simplified syntax of the Select statement

```
Select column-1 [, column-2]...
From table-1
[Where selection-criteria]
[Order By column-1 [Asc|Desc] [, column-2 [Asc|Desc]]...]
```

A Select statement that retrieves and sorts selected columns and rows from the Products table

```
Select ProductID, Name, UnitPrice
From Products
Where CategoryID = 'props'
Order By UnitPrice
```

The result set defined by the Select statement

	ProductID	Name	UnitPrice
1	skel01	Life-size Skeleton	14.95
2	rat01	Ugly Rat	14.99
3	rat02	Uglier Rat	19.99
4	cat01	Deranged Cat	19.99
5	arm01	Freddie Arm	20.95
6	head01	Michael Head	29.99
7	head02	Saw Head	29.99
8	bats01	Flying Bats	69.99

Concepts

- To access and update the data in a relational database, you use *Structured Query Language*, or *SQL* (pronounced as sequel or the letters S-Q-L).

- The Select statement is a *SQL statement* that gets data from a database and returns it in a *result table*, or *result set*. A result set is a logical set of rows that consists of all of the columns and rows requested by the Select statement.

- A result set can include *calculated columns* that are calculated from other columns in the table.

- To select all of the columns in a table, you can code an asterisk (*) in place of the column names. For example, this statement will select all of the columns from the Products table:

```
Select * From Products
```

However, this technique is typically not used in production applications because it can retrieve more data than is needed or introduce errors if the table changes.

Figure 12-5   How to query a single table

How to join data from two or more tables

Figure 12-6 presents the syntax of the Select statement for retrieving data from two tables. This type of operation is called a *join* because the data from the two tables is joined together into a single result set. For example, the Select statement in this figure joins data from the Categories and Products tables into a single result set.

An *inner join* is the most common type of join. When you use an inner join, rows from the two tables in the join are included in the result set only if their related columns match. These matching columns are specified in the From clause of the Select statement. In the Select statement in this figure, for example, rows from the Categories and Products tables are included only if the value of the CategoryID column in the Categories table matches the value of the CategoryID column in one or more rows in the Products table. If there aren't any products for a particular category, that category won't be included in the result set.

Notice that the Select clause in this statement doesn't indicate which table contains each column. That's because each of the columns exists in only one of the tables. If a column existed in both tables, however, you would need to indicate which table you wanted to retrieve the column from. If you wanted to retrieve the CategoryID column from the Categories table, for example, you would need to code that column like this:

```
Categories.CategoryID
```

Although this figure shows how to join data from two tables, you should know that you can extend this syntax to join data from additional tables. If, for example, you want to include data from the LineItems table in the results shown in this figure, you can code the From clause of the Select statement like this:

```
From Categories
    Inner Join Products
        On Categories.CategoryID = Products.CategoryID
    Inner Join LineItems
        On Products.ProductID = LineItems.ProductID
```

Then, in the column list of the Select statement, you can include any of the columns in the LineItems table.

The syntax of the Select statement for joining two tables

```
Select column-list
From table-1
    [Inner] Join table-2
      On table-1.column-1 {=|<|>|<=|>=|<>} table-2.column-2
[Where selection-criteria]
[Order By column-list]
```

A Select statement that joins data
from the Products and Categories tables

```
Select ShortName, ProductID, Name, UnitPrice
From Categories Inner Join Products
    On Categories.CategoryID = Products.CategoryID
Order By Categories.CategoryID
```

The result set defined by the Select statement

	ShortName	ProductID	Name	UnitPrice
1	Costumes	frankc01	Frankenstein	39.99
2	Costumes	hippie01	Hippie	79.99
3	Costumes	jar01	JarJar	59.99
4	Costumes	martian01	Martian	69.99
5	Costumes	pow01	Austin Powers	79.99
6	Costumes	super01	Superman	39.99
7	FX	tlm01	T&L Machine	99.99
8	FX	fog01	Fog Machine	34.99
9	FX	fogj01	Fog Juice (1qt)	9.99
10	FX	skullfog01	Skull Fogger	39.95
11	FX	str01	Mini-strobe	13.99
12	FX	bl01	Black Light	19.99
13	Masks	fred01	Freddie	29.99
14	Masks	mum01	Mummy	39.99
15	Masks	vader01	Darth Vader ...	19.99
16	Props	rat01	Ugly Rat	14.99
17	Props	rat02	Uglier Rat	19.99
18	Props	skel01	Life-size Skel...	14.95
19	Props	head01	Michael Head	29.99
20	Props	head02	Saw Head	29.99
21	Props	cat01	Deranged Cat	19.99
22	Props	arm01	Freddie Arm	20.95
23	Props	bats01	Flying Bats	69.99

Concepts

- A *join* lets you combine data from two or more tables into a single result set.
- The most common type of join is an *inner join*. This type of join returns rows from both tables only if their related columns match.

Figure 12-6   How to join data from two or more tables

How to add, update, and delete data in a table

Figure 12-7 presents the basic syntax of the SQL Insert, Update, and Delete statements. You use these statements to add new rows to a table, to update the data in existing rows, and to delete existing rows.

To add a single row to a table, you use an Insert statement with the syntax shown in this figure. With this syntax, you specify the name of the table you want to add the row to, the names of the columns you're supplying data for, and the values for those columns. In the example, the Insert statement adds a row to the Categories table and supplies a value for each of the three columns in that table. If a table allows nulls or provides default values for some columns, though, the Insert statement doesn't have to provide values for those columns. In addition, an Insert statement never provides a value for an identity column because that value is generated by the DBMS.

To change the values of one or more columns in one or more rows, you use the Update statement. On this statement, you specify the name of the table you want to update, expressions that indicate the columns you want to change and how you want to change them, and a condition that identifies the rows you want to change. In the example, the Update statement changes the ShortName value for just the one row in the Categories table that has a CategoryID value of "food."

To delete one or more rows from a table, you use the Delete statement. On this statement, you specify the table you want to delete rows from and a condition that indicates the rows you want to delete. In the example, the Delete statement deletes just the one row in the Categories table whose CategoryID column is "food."

How to add a single row

The syntax of the Insert statement for adding a single row

```
Insert [Into] table-name [(column-list)]
    Values (value-list)
```

A statement that adds a single row to a table

```
Insert Into Categories (CategoryID, ShortName, LongName)
    Values ('food', 'Spooky Food', 'The very best in Halloween cuisine')
```

How to update rows

The syntax of the Update statement

```
Update table-name
    Set expression-1 [, expression-2]...
    [Where selection-criteria]
```

A statement that changes the value of the ShortName column for a selected row

```
Update Categories
    Set ShortName = 'Halloween cuisine'
    Where CategoryID = 'food'
```

How to delete rows

The syntax of the Delete statement

```
Delete [From] table-name
    [Where selection-criteria]
```

A statement that deletes a specified category

```
Delete From Categories
    Where CategoryID = 'food'
```

Description

- You use the Insert, Update, and Delete statements to maintain the data in a database table.

- The Insert statement can be used to add one or more rows to a table. Although the syntax shown above is for adding just one row, there is another syntax for adding more than one row.

- The Update and Delete statements can be used for updating or deleting one or more rows in a table using the syntax shown above.

Warning

- If you code an Update statement without a Where clause, all of the rows in the table will be updated. Similarly, if you code a Delete statement without a Where clause, all of the rows in the table will be deleted.

Figure 12-7   How to add, update, and delete data in a table

How to work with other database objects

In addition to the tables you've already learned about, relational databases can contain other database objects like views and stored procedures. In the topics that follow, you'll be introduced to these objects.

How to work with views

A *view* is a predefined query that's stored in a database. To create a view, you use the Create View statement as shown in figure 12-8. This statement causes the Select statement you specify to be stored with the database. In this case, the Create View statement creates a view named CustomersMin that retrieves four columns from the Customers table.

To access a view, you issue a Select statement that refers to the view. This causes a *virtual table*—a temporary table that's created on the server—to be created from the Select statement in the view. Then, the Select statement that referred to the view is executed on this virtual table to create the result set.

Although views can be quite useful, they require some additional overhead. That's because every time an application refers to a view, the view has to be created from scratch. If that's a problem, an alternative is to use stored procedures.

A Create View statement for a view named CustomersMin

```
Create View CustomersMin AS
    Select LastName, FirstName, State, Email
    From Customers
```

A Select statement that uses the CustomersMin view

```
Select * FROM CustomersMin
Where State = 'CA'
Order By LastName, FirstName
```

The virtual table that's created for the Select statement

	LastName	FirstName	State	Email
1	Molunguri	A	AL	A8@webemaxmjKd.com
2	Antosca	Andrew	MI	AAntosca@netYduo.com
3	Antony	Abdul	NC	Abdul70@matminvV.edu
4	Johnson	Ajith	CA	Ajith@xgMaster.edu
5	Rose	Alan	FL	Alan@NsiYYGE.net
6	Browning	Albert	GA	Albert@masterxmlrad.com
7	Litterson	Anthony	PA	ALitterson@mastermaster.c
8	Lee	Andra	NY	Andra91@webtechdotca.edu
9	Latheef	Andrea c.	FL	Andrea c.@sWGrUDweb.com

The result set that's created from the view

	LastName	FirstName	State	Email
1	Armalie	Dennis	CA	DArmalie@ShwildOHrad.com
2	Arutla	Jerry I.	CA	Jerry I.@progwildbioY.com
3	Blake	John	CA	John@netEw.edu
4	Bommana	Ilya	CA	IIBommana@radassoc.net
5	Brown	Srikanth	CA	Srikanth@XyRbduocare.gov
6	Carroll	Sam	CA	Sam91@OSZqlKrNxmlE.gov
7	Condron	Michael	CA	Michael@zmasterftRW.com
8	Curless	Darald	CA	Darald@DDiHYzrmaste.net
9	Diop	John	CA	JoDiop@netcaremaste.edu

Description

- A *view* consists of a Select statement that's stored with the database. Because views are stored as part of the database, they can be managed independently of the applications that use them.

- When you refer to a view, a *virtual table* is created on the server that represents the view. Then, the result set is extracted from this virtual table. For this reason, a view is also called a *viewed table*.

- Views can be used to restrict the data that a user is allowed to access or to present data in a form that's easy for the user to understand. In some databases, users may be allowed to access data only through views.

Figure 12-8   How to work with views

How to work with stored procedures

A *stored procedure* is a set of one or more SQL statements that are stored together in a database. To create a stored procedure, you use the Create Procedure statement as shown in figure 12-9. Here, the stored procedure contains a single Select statement. To use the stored procedure, you send a request for it to be executed.

When the server receives the request, it executes the stored procedure. If the stored procedure contains a Select statement like the one in this figure, the result set is sent back to the calling program. If the stored procedure contains Insert, Update, or Delete statements, the appropriate processing is performed.

Notice that the stored procedure in this figure accepts an *input parameter* named @State from the calling program. The value of this parameter is then substituted for the parameter in the Where clause so only customers in the specified state are included in the result set.

When it's done with its processing, a stored procedure can also pass *output parameters* back to the calling program. In addition, stored procedures can include *control-of-flow language* that determines the processing that's done based on specific conditions.

A Create Procedure statement
for a procedure named spCustomersByState

```
Create Procedure spCustomersByState @State char AS
    Select LastName, FirstName, State, Email
    From Customers
    Where State = @State
    Order By LastName, FirstName
```

The result set that's created when the stored procedure is executed
with the @State variable set to 'CA'

	LastName	FirstName	State	Email
1	Armalie	Dennis	CA	DArmalie@ShwildOHrad.com
2	Arutla	Jerry I.	CA	Jerry I.@progwildbioY.com
3	Blake	John	CA	John@netEw.edu
4	Bommana	Ilya	CA	IIBommana@radassoc.net
5	Brown	Srikanth	CA	Srikanth@XyRbduocare.gov
6	Carroll	Sam	CA	Sam91@OSZqIKrNxmlE.gov
7	Condron	Michael	CA	Michael@zmasterftRW.com
8	Curless	Darald	CA	Darald@DDiHYzrmaste.net
9	Diop	John	CA	JoDiop@netcaremaste.edu

Concepts

- A *stored procedure* consists of one or more SQL statements that have been compiled and stored with the database. A stored procedure can be started by application code on the client.

- Stored procedures can improve database performance because the SQL statements in each procedure are only compiled and optimized the first time they're executed. In contrast, SQL statements that are sent from a client to the server have to be compiled and optimized every time they're executed.

- In addition to Select statements, a stored procedure can contain other SQL statements such as Insert, Update, and Delete statements. It can also contain *control-of-flow language*, which lets you perform conditional processing within the stored procedure.

Figure 12-9   How to work with stored procedures

An introduction to ADO.NET 4.5

ADO.NET 4.5 (*ActiveX Data Objects*) is the primary data access API for the .NET Framework. It provides the classes that are used when you develop database applications. The topics that follow introduce you to the important ADO.NET concepts.

How the basic ADO.NET components work

Figure 12-10 presents the primary ADO.NET objects that are used when you develop database applications. To start, the data that's retrieved from a database is stored in a *dataset* that contains one or more *data tables*. Then, the data in the data tables can be displayed in one or more controls on the page. When the data in a control is updated, the change is reflected in the data table and is passed on to the database.

To manage the flow of data between a dataset and a database, ADO.NET uses a *data adapter*. The data adapter uses *commands* that define the SQL statements to be issued. If a command contains a Select statement, for example, the command connects to the database using a *connection* and passes the Select statement to the database. After the Select statement is executed, the result set it produces is sent back to the data adapter, which stores the results in the data table.

To update the data in a database, the data adapter can use a command that contains an Insert, Update, or Delete statement for a data table. Then, the command uses the connection to connect to the database and perform the requested operation.

When you use a SQL data source to work with the data in a database as shown in chapter 4, the data is stored in a dataset by default. Then, the data source provides the information ADO.NET needs to connect to the database, and it specifies the SQL statements ADO.NET uses to retrieve and update the data. You'll learn more about that in the chapters that follow.

The ADO.NET classes for the data adapters, commands, and connections that work directly with a database are provided by the *.NET data providers*. The .NET Framework currently includes data providers for SQL Server, Oracle, OLE DB, and ODBC, although the Oracle data provider has been deprecated. You can use SQL data source to work with any of these data providers.

Although it's not apparent in this figure, the data in a dataset is independent of the database that the data was retrieved from. In fact, when you use a SQL data source, the connection to the database is automatically closed after each operation. Because of that, the application must work with the copy of the data that's stored in the dataset. The architecture that's used to implement this type of data processing is referred to as a *disconnected data architecture*.

Although a disconnected data architecture is more complicated than a connected architecture, it improves system performance by using fewer system resources for maintaining connections. It also works well with ASP.NET web applications, which are inherently disconnected.

Basic ADO.NET objects

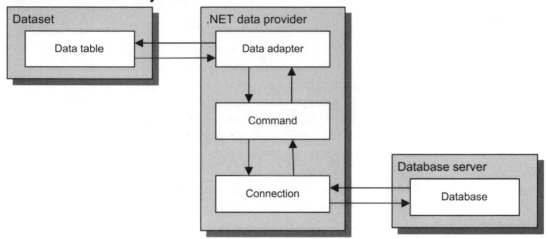

Description

- ADO.NET uses two types of objects to access the data in a database: *datasets*, which can contain one or more *data tables*, and *.NET data provider* objects, which include data adapters, commands, and connections.

- A dataset stores data from the database so it can be accessed by the application. The .NET data provider objects retrieve data from and update data in the database.

- To retrieve data from a database and store it in a data table, a *data adapter* object issues a Select statement that's stored in a *command* object. Next, the command object uses a *connection* object to connect to the database and retrieve the data. Then, the data is passed back to the data adapter, which stores the data in a table within the dataset.

- To update the data in a database based on the data in a data table, the data adapter object issues an Insert, Update, or Delete statement that's stored in a command object. Then, the command object uses a connection to connect to the database and update the data.

- When you use a SQL data source, it specifies the information for connecting to the database and for retrieving and updating data.

- The data provider remains connected to the database only long enough to retrieve or update the specified data. Then, it disconnects from the database and the application works with the data via the dataset object. This is referred to as a *disconnected data architecture*.

- All of the ADO.NET objects are implemented by classes in the System.Data namespace of the .NET Framework. However, the specific classes used to implement the connection, command, and data adapter objects depend on the .NET data provider you use.

Figure 12-10   How the basic ADO.NET components work

Concurrency and the disconnected data architecture

Although the disconnected data architecture has advantages, it also has some disadvantages. One of those is the conflict that can occur when two or more users retrieve and then try to update data in the same row of a table. This is called a *concurrency* problem. This is possible because once a program retrieves data from a database, the connection to that database is dropped. As a result, the database management system can't manage the update process.

To illustrate, consider the situation shown in figure 12-11. Here, two users are using the Products table at the same time. These users could be using the same page of a web site or different pages that have accessed the Products table. Now, suppose that user 1 modifies the unit price in the row for a product and updates the Products table in the database. Suppose too that user 2 modifies the description in the row for the same product, and then tries to update the Products table in the database. What will happen? That will depend on the *concurrency control* that's used by the programs.

When you use ADO.NET, you have two choices for concurrency control. First, you can use *optimistic concurrency*, which checks whether a row has been changed since it was retrieved. If it has, the update or deletion will be refused and a *concurrency exception* will be thrown. Then, the program should handle the error. For example, it could display an error message that tells the user that the row could not be updated and then retrieve the updated row so the user can make the change again.

Second, you can use the *"last in wins"* technique, which works the way its name implies. Since no checking is done with this technique, the row that's updated by the last user overwrites any changes made to the row by a previous user. For the example above, the row updated by user 2 will overwrite changes made by user 1, which means that the description will be right but the unit price will be wrong. Since errors like this corrupt the data in a database, optimistic concurrency is used by most programs.

If you know that concurrency will be a problem, you can use a couple of programming techniques to limit concurrency exceptions. If a program uses a dataset, one technique is to update the database frequently so other users can retrieve the current data. The program should also refresh its dataset frequently so it contains the recent changes made by other users.

Another way to avoid concurrency exceptions is to retrieve and work with just one row at a time. That way, it's less likely that two users will update the same row at the same time. In contrast, if two users retrieve the same table, they will of course retrieve the same rows. Then, if they both update the same row in the table, even though it may not be at the same time, a concurrency exception will occur when they try to update the database.

Two users who are working with copies of the same data

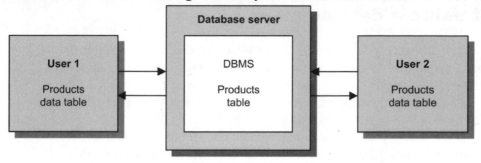

What happens when two users try to update the same row

- When two or more users retrieve the data in the same row of a database table at the same time, it is called *concurrency*. Because ADO.NET uses a disconnected data architecture, the database management system can't prevent this from happening.

- If two users try to update the same row in a database table at the same time, the second user's changes could overwrite the changes made by the first user. Whether or not that happens depends on the *concurrency control* that the programs use.

- With *optimistic concurrency*, the program checks to see whether the database row that's going to be updated or deleted has been changed since it was retrieved. If it has, a *concurrency exception* occurs and the update or deletion is refused. Then, the program should handle the exception.

- If optimistic concurrency isn't in effect, the program doesn't check to see whether a row has been changed before an update or deletion takes place. Instead, the operation proceeds without throwing an exception. This is referred to as "*last in wins*" because the last update overwrites any previous update. And this can lead to errors in the database.

How to avoid concurrency errors

- For many applications, concurrency errors rarely occur. As a result, optimistic concurrency is adequate because the users will rarely have to resubmit an update or deletion that is refused.

- If concurrency is likely to be a problem, a program that uses a dataset can be designed so it updates the database and refreshes the dataset frequently. That way, concurrency errors are less likely to occur.

- Another way to avoid concurrency errors is to design a program so it retrieves and updates just one row at a time. That way, there's less chance that two users will retrieve and update the same row at the same time.

Figure 12-11   Concurrency and the disconnected data architecture

How to work with data without using a data adapter

By default, when you use a SQL data source to work with the data in a database, a data adapter is used to retrieve that data and store it in a dataset as described earlier in this chapter. You should know, however, that you can also work with the data in a database without using a data adapter. Figure 12-12 shows you how.

As you can see, you still use command and connection objects to access the database. Instead of using a data adapter to execute the commands, though, you execute the commands directly. When you do that, you also have to provide code to handle the result of the command. If you issue a command that contains an Insert, Update, or Delete statement, for example, the result is an integer that indicates the number of rows that were affected by the operation. You can use that information to determine if the operation was successful.

If you execute a command that contains a Select statement, the result is a result set that contains the rows you requested. To read through the rows in the result set, you use a *data reader* object. Although a data reader provides an efficient way of reading the rows in a result set, you can't use it to modify those rows. In addition, it only lets you read rows in a forward direction. Once you read the next row, the previous row is unavailable. Because of that, you typically use a data reader to retrieve and work with a single database row at a time or to retrieve rows that won't change.

As you'll see in the next chapter, you can use this technique with a SQL data source instead of using a dataset. That can improve the efficiency of an application. You can also use this technique with object data sources as described in chapter 17. As you'll see in that chapter, though, you have to write all of the data access code yourself when you use object data sources.

ADO.NET components for accessing a database directly

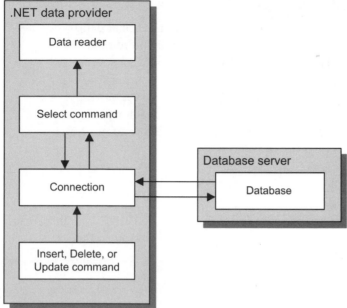

Description

- Instead of using a data adapter to execute commands to retrieve, insert, update, and delete data from a database, you can execute those commands directly.

- To retrieve data from a database, you execute a command object that contains a Select statement. Then, the command object uses a connection to connect to the database and retrieve the data. You can then read the results one row at a time using a *data reader* object.

- To insert, update, or delete data in a database, you execute a command object that contains an Insert, Update, or Delete statement. Then, the command object uses a connection to connect to the database and update the data. You can then check the value that's returned to determine if the operation was successful.

- If you use this technique in an application that maintains the data in a database, you typically work with a single row at a time. Because of that, the chance of a concurrency error is reduced.

- To use this technique with ASP.NET applications, you can use object data sources. See chapter 17 for details.

Figure 12-12   How to work with data without using a data adapter

Perspective

This chapter has introduced you to the basic concepts of relational databases and the basic SQL statements. With that as background, you're ready to learn how to develop ASP.NET database applications with SQL data sources, ASP.NET data controls, and object data sources.

Before you continue, though, you should know that there's a lot more to SQL and SQL Server than what has been presented in this chapter. For a complete treatment of SQL Server, please refer to the latest edition of our SQL Server book.

Terms

relational database	SQL dialect
table	Transact-SQL
record	result table
row	result set
field	calculated column
column	join
primary key	inner join
composite primary key	view
non-primary key	virtual table
unique key	stored procedure
unique key constraint	input parameter
unique constraint	output parameter
index	control-of-flow language
foreign key	ADO.NET
foreign key table	ActiveX Data Objects .NET
primary key table	dataset
one-to-many relationship	data table
one-to-one relationship	.NET data provider
many-to-many relationship	data adapter
linking table	command
data type	connection
system data type	disconnected data architecture
null value	concurrency
default value	concurrency control
identity column	optimistic concurrency
check constraint	concurrency exception
SQL (Structured Query Language)	last in wins
SQL statement	data reader

Summary

- A *relational database* consists of *tables* that store data in *rows* and *columns*. A *primary key* is used to identify each row in a table.

- The tables in a relational database are related by *foreign keys* in one table that have the same values as primary keys in another table. Usually, these tables have a *one-to-many* relationship.

- Each column in a database table is defined with a *data type* that determines what can be stored in that column. In addition, the column definition specifies whether the column allows *null values* or has a *default value*.

- To work with the data in a database, you use *SQL (Structured Query Language)*. To access and update the data in a database, you use these *SQL statements*: Select, Insert, Update, and Delete.

- The Select statement returns data from one or more tables in a *result set*. To return data from two or more tables, you *join* the tables based on the data in related fields. An *inner join* returns a result set that includes data only if the related fields match.

- A *view* consists of a Select statement that's stored with the database. Views can be used to restrict the data that a user is allowed to access.

- A *stored procedure* consists of one or more SQL statements that have been compiled and stored with the database. Stored procedures can improve database performance because they're only compiled and optimized the first time they're executed.

- *ADO.NET (ActiveX Data Objects)* is the primary data access API for the .NET Framework. It provides the classes that are used by the *data provider* when you develop database applications with SQL data sources. The members in these classes can also be used directly by the programmer.

- ADO.NET uses a *disconnected data architecture*, which means that the database is disconnected from the web server as soon as each database operation is completed. This has some advantages, but it can also lead to *concurrency* problems. These occur when two or more users try to update the same row in a database table at the same time.

13

How to use SQL data sources

In this chapter, you'll learn more about using the SqlDataSource control, which lets you access data from a relational database with little or no programming. Along the way, you'll also learn how to use the DataList control, which lets you create a list of the data that's retrieved by a data source.

How to create a SQL data source

In chapter 4, you learned the basics of using the SqlDataSource control to get data from a SQL Server database. Now, in the topics that follow, you'll learn more about how to use this control, which can be referred to as a *SQL data source*.

Just as in chapter 4, all of the applications in this chapter and in the rest of this section use the Microsoft *SQL Server 2012 Express LocalDB* database engine that comes with Visual Studio 2012. Because LocalDB is based on SQL Server 2012, the applications you develop with LocalDB are compatible with applications you develop with SQL Server 2012. The only difference is the connection string you use to connect to the database.

How the SqlDataSource control works

Figure 13-1 illustrates how the SqlDataSource control works and presents its basic attributes. In the example in this figure, the data source is bound to a drop-down list that displays all the categories in the Categories table. You can see the Select statement that retrieves this data in the SelectCommand attribute of the SqlDataSource control.

The ConnectionString attribute of the data source provides the information that's needed to connect to the database that contains the Categories table. In this case, the attribute refers to a connection string that's stored in the application's web.config file. You'll learn more about that later in this chapter.

A SqlDataSource that's bound to a drop-down list

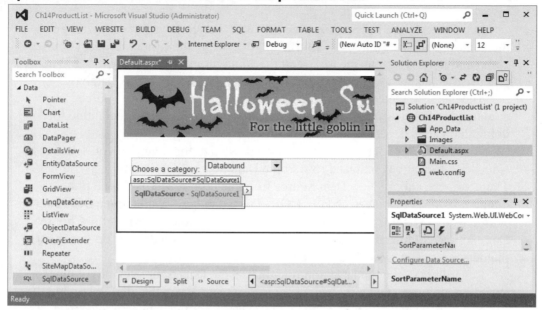

The aspx code for the SqlDataSource control

```
<asp:SqlDataSource ID="SqlDataSource1" runat="server"
    ConnectionString="<%$ ConnectionStrings:HalloweenConnectionString %>"
    SelectCommand="SELECT [CategoryID], [LongName] FROM [Categories]
        ORDER BY [LongName]">
</asp:SqlDataSource>
```

Basic SqlDataSource control attributes

Attribute	Description
ID	The ID for the SqlDataSource control.
Runat	Must specify "server."
ConnectionString	The connection string. In most cases, you should use a <%$ expression to specify the name of a connection string saved in the web.config file (see figure 13-4).
ProviderName	The name of the .NET data provider used to access the database. The default is System.Data.SqlClient.
SelectCommand	The SQL Select statement executed by the data source to retrieve data.

Description

- A SqlDataSource control (or *SQL data source*) provides the information an application needs to connect to a database and retrieve the data needed by the application. It can also be used to insert, update, and delete data.

- A SQL data source can be bound to another control, such as a drop-down list or a DataList control. Then, the data that's retrieved by the data source is displayed in that control.

Figure 13-1   How the SqlDataSource control works

How to choose a data source type

In chapter 4, you learned how to create a SqlDataSource control by dragging the control from the Toolbox to a form and then using the Configure Data Source command in its smart tag menu to start the Configure Data Source wizard. When you use this technique, the data source type is automatically set to Database.

You can also create a SQL data source using the Choose Data Source command in the smart tag menu of a bindable control. The exact technique for doing that varies depending on the control you're binding.

To create a SQL data source for a drop-down list, for example, you select the Choose Data Source command to start the Data Source Configuration Wizard. Then, you can choose New Data Source from the drop-down list in the first dialog box that's displayed and click OK. The technique for creating a SQL data source from a DataList control is similar. The only difference is that the Choose Data Source command in the control's smart tag menu includes a drop-down list that lets you select New Data Source.

Regardless of the bindable control you use, the Data Source Configuration Wizard dialog box shown in figure 13-2 is displayed. From this dialog box, you can select the Database icon and click OK. That drops the data source control onto the form next to the bindable control and brings you to the Configure Data Source dialog box.

How to choose a data connection

The Configure Data Source dialog box, also shown in figure 13-2, lets you choose the data connection you want to use to connect to the database. From this dialog box, you can select a database file that's included in the App_Data folder of the project, or you can select an existing connection (one you've already created for this project or for another project). You can also click the New Connection button to display the Add Connection dialog box that's shown in the next figure.

To be sure you use the right connection, you can click the button with the plus sign on it to display the connection string. In this example, you can see that the connection string will attach the Halloween.mdf file at the specified location to the LocalDB engine. Here, DataDirectory refers to the project's App_Data folder.

Note that when you run an application that uses LocalDB, the database engine is started if it isn't already running, and the database is attached. In addition, the first time you try to connect to the LocalDB engine, an instance of the engine has to be created before it's started. Because of that, the connection may fail with a timeout message. If that happens, you should wait a few seconds while the creation finishes and then run the application again.

The dialog boxes for choosing a data source type and connection

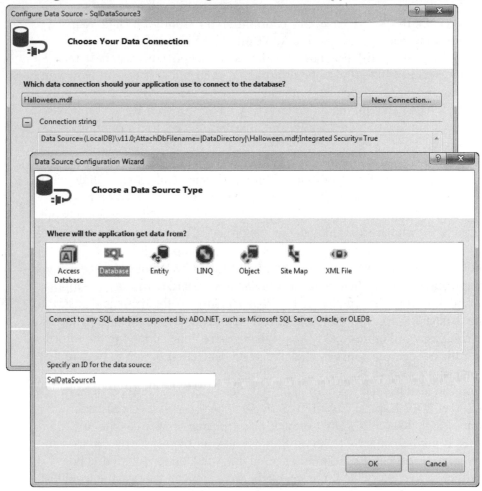

How to choose a data source type

- When you drag a SqlDataSource control onto the form, the data source type is automatically set to Database and the first page of the Configure Data Source wizard shown above is displayed.

- To use the Data Source Configuration Wizard to choose a data source type, use the Choose Data Source command in the smart tag menu of a bindable control, select the Database icon in the dialog box that's displayed, and click OK.

How to choose a connection

- If your project contains a database file or you've previously created a connection for the database you want to use, you can select the file or connection from the drop-down list. To see the connection string for that connection, click the + button below the list.

- To create a new connection, click the New Connection button.

Figure 13-2   How to choose a data source type and connection

How to create a connection

If you click the New Connection button from the Configure Data Source dialog box shown in figure 13-2, the Add Connection dialog box shown in figure 13-3 is displayed. This dialog box helps you identify the database that you want to access and provide the information you need to access it. How you do that, though, varies depending on whether you're using SQL Server Express LocalDB, which can only run on your own PC; a SQL Server Express database server that's running on your own PC; or a database server that's running on a remote server.

If you're using SQL Server Express LocalDB, you can select the Microsoft SQL Server Database File data source from the Change Data Source dialog box. Then, you just identify the database file in the Add Connection dialog box. In this figure, for example, the connection is for the Halloween database file. Note that the file shown here isn't included in the project. That shows that you can use LocalDB to work with a database file that's outside the project.

For the logon information, you should select the Use Windows Authentication option. Then, SQL Server Express LocalDB will use the login name and password that you use to log in to Windows as the name and password for the database server too. As a result, you won't need to provide a separate user name and password in this dialog box. When you're done supplying the information for the connection, you can click the Test Connection button to be sure that the connection works.

You can also use the full edition of SQL Server 2012 Express instead of SQL Server 2012 Express LocalDB. *SQL Server Express* is a scaled-back version of SQL Server 2012 that provides all the same services as the full editions. If you're using SQL Server Express on your own PC, you can use the Microsoft SQL Server data source. Then, in the Add Connection dialog box, you will need to specify the server name. In this case, you can use the localhost keyword to specify that the database server is running on the same PC as the application. This keyword should be followed by a backslash and the name of the database server: SqlExpress. Alternatively, you can select the server name from the drop-down list, which will include your computer name like this: ANNE-PC\SQLEXPRESS. If you will be porting your applications from one computer to another, though, it's best to use localhost.

After you enter the name of the server, you can enter or select the name of the database you want to connect to. You can also enter the required logon information. Just as you do when you use SQL Server Express LocalDB, though, you typically use Windows authentication with SQL Server Express.

If you need to connect to a SQL Server database that's running on a database server that's available through a network, you can use the Microsoft SQL Server data source just like you do for SQL Server Express. This works for SQL Server 2005, 2008, and 2012 databases. Then, you need to get the connection information from the network or database administrator. This information will include the name of the database server, logon information, and the name of the database. Once you establish a connection to the database, you can use that connection for all of the other applications that use that database.

The dialog boxes for defining a connection

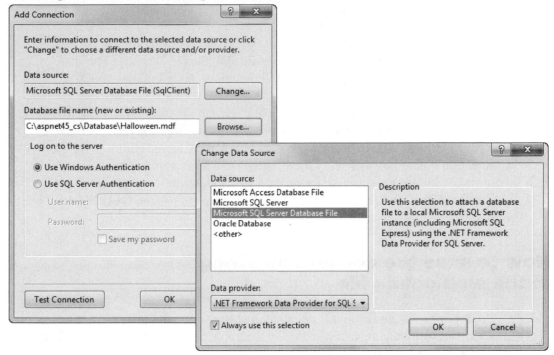

Description

- The first time you create a connection, the Change Data Source dialog box is displayed so you can select the data source and data provider you want to use. If you check the Always Use This Selection option, your selections will be used each time you create a connection. To change these options, click the Change button in the Add Connection dialog box.

- To create a connection for a database file that uses SQL Server Express LocalDB, use the Microsoft SQL Server Database File data source. Then, specify the name and path for the file and enter the information that's required to log on to the server in the Add Connection dialog box.

- To create a connection for a database on a local or remote SQL Server database server, use the Microsoft SQL Server data source. Then, specify the name of the server that contains the database, enter the information that's required to log on to the server, and specify the name of the database you want to connect to in the Add Connection dialog box.

- To be sure that the connection is configured properly, you can click the Test Connection button in the Add Connection dialog box.

Figure 13-3   How to create a connection

The first time you create a connection, Visual Studio automatically displays the Change Data Source dialog box so you can select the data source and data provider you want to use. In most cases, the data provider that's selected by default when you select a data source will be the one you want to use. If you select the Microsoft SQL Server or Microsoft SQL Server Database File data source, for example, the data provider will default to .NET Framework Data Provider for SQL Server.

You can also check the Always Use This Selection option if you want to use the selected data provider by default. Then, if you ever need to create a connection for a different type of database, you can click the Change button in the Add Connection dialog box to display the Change Data Source dialog box again. If you want to create a connection for an Access database, for example, you can select the Microsoft Access Database File data source to use the OLE DB data provider.

How to save the connection string
in the web.config file

Although you can hard-code connection strings into your programs, it's much better to store connection strings in the application's web.config file. That way, if you move the database to another server or make some other change that affects the connection string, you won't have to recompile the application. Instead, you can simply change the connection string in the web.config file.

As figure 13-4 shows, ASP.NET can store connection strings in the web.config file automatically if you check the Yes box in the next step of the Configure Data Source wizard. That way, you don't have to manually edit the web.config file or write code to retrieve the connection string. When you select this check box, the connection string will automatically be saved with the name that you supply.

This figure also shows the entries made in the web.config file when a connection string is saved. Here, the web.config file has a connectionStrings element that contains an add element for each connection string. In the example, the connection string is named HalloweenConnectionString, and the connection string refers to a LocalDB database named Halloween that's stored in the project's App_Data folder.

Last, this figure shows how the aspx code that's generated for a data source can refer to the connection string by name. Here, the shaded portion of the example shows the value of the ConnectionString attribute. As you can see, it begins with the word ConnectionStrings followed by a colon and the name of the connection string you want to use. Note that this code is automatically generated by the Configure Data Source wizard, so you don't have to write it yourself.

The dialog box for saving the connection string in the web.config file

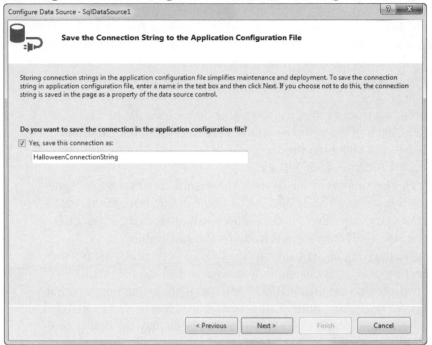

The ConnectionStrings section of the web.config file

```
<connectionStrings>
    <add name="HalloweenConnectionString"
      connectionString="Data Source=(LocalDB)\v11.0;
      AttachDbFilename=|DataDirectory|\Halloween.mdf;
      Integrated Security=True" providerName="System.Data.SqlClient" />
</connectionStrings>
```

Aspx code that refers to a connection string in the web.config file

```
<asp:SqlDataSource ID="SqlDataSource1" runat="server"
    ConnectionString="<%$ ConnectionStrings:HalloweenConnectionString %>"
    SelectCommand="SELECT [CategoryID], [LongName] FROM [Categories]
        ORDER BY [LongName]">
</asp:SqlDataSource>
```

Description

- ASP.NET applications can store connection strings in the web.config file.

- If you save the connection string in the web.config file, the ConnectionString attribute of the data source control will include a special code that retrieves the connection string from the web.config file.

- If you don't save the connection string in the web.config file, the ConnectionString attribute will specify the actual connection string.

- It's best to always save the connection string in the web.config file. Then, if the location of the database changes, you can change the connection string in the web.config file rather than in each data source that uses the connection.

Figure 13-4   How to save the connection string in the web.config file

How to configure the Select statement

Figure 13-5 shows how to configure the Select statement for a data source as you proceed through the steps of the wizard. The easiest way to do that is to choose the columns for the query from a single table or view. You can also specify a custom SQL statement or stored procedure as shown later in this chapter.

To select columns from a table, use the Name drop-down list to select the table. Then, check each of the columns you want to retrieve in the Columns list box. In this figure, I chose the Products table and selected four columns: ProductID, Name, UnitPrice, and OnHand.

As you check the columns in the list box, the wizard creates a Select statement that's shown in the text box at the bottom of the dialog box. In this case, the Select statement indicates that the data source will retrieve the ProductID, Name, UnitPrice, and OnHand columns from the Products table.

The buttons to the right of the Columns list box let you specify additional options for selecting data. If, for example, you want to sort the data that's retrieved, you can click on the ORDER BY button to display a dialog box that lets you select up to three sort columns. If you want to select rows that satisfy certain criteria, you can click on the WHERE button to display the dialog box that's described in the next figure. And if you want to use an advanced feature, you can click on the Advanced button to display the dialog box that's described in figure 13-18.

When you finish specifying the data you want the data source to retrieve, click Next. This takes you to a dialog box that includes a Test Query button. If you click this button, the wizard immediately retrieves the data that you specified. You can then look over this data to make sure the query retrieves the data you expected. If it doesn't, you can click the Back button and adjust the query as needed.

The dialog box for defining the Select statement

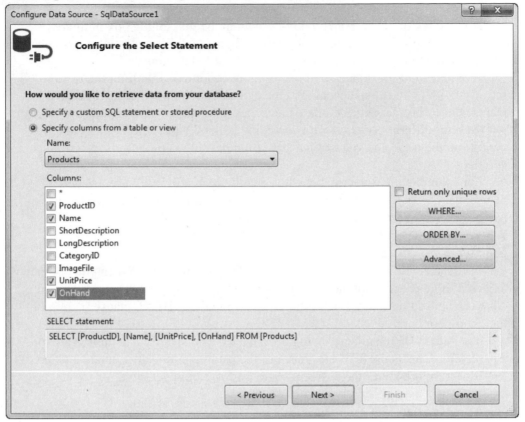

Description

- To configure the Select statement, you choose whether you want to use a custom SQL statement or specify the columns from a table or view in the database.

- If you choose to select the columns from a table or view, you can choose the table or view and columns you want retrieved. You can click the ORDER BY button to specify how the records should be sorted. And you can click the WHERE button to specify the selection criteria as shown in figure 13-6.

- If you choose to use custom SQL statements, the next dialog box lets you enter the SQL statements as shown in figure 13-8 or click the Query Builder button to build the query as shown in figure 13-9.

Figure 13-5   How to configure the Select statement

How to create a Where clause

If you click on the WHERE button shown in the first dialog box in figure 13-5, the Add WHERE Clause dialog box in figure 13-6 is displayed. It lets you create a Where clause and parameters for the Select statement.

A Where clause is made up of one or more conditions that limit the rows retrieved by the Select statement. To create these conditions, the Add WHERE Clause dialog box lets you compare the values in the columns of a database table with several different types of data, including a literal value, the value of another control on the page, the value of a query string passed via the page's URL, or a cookie.

For example, the Select statement shown in figure 13-5 will use a Where clause that compares the CategoryID column in the Products table with the category selected from a drop-down list named ddlCategory. To create this Where clause, select CategoryID in the Column drop-down list, the equals operator in the Operator drop-down list, and Control in the Source drop-down list. Next, select ddlCategory in the Control ID drop-down list. When you do, the SelectedValue property of the control is automatically selected. Then, when you click on the Add button, this condition is shown in the WHERE clause section of the dialog box.

The Add WHERE Clause dialog box also lets you specify a default value for a parameter. This is useful if the source of the parameter doesn't contain a value. You'll learn more about the different sources for a parameter next.

The Add WHERE Clause dialog box

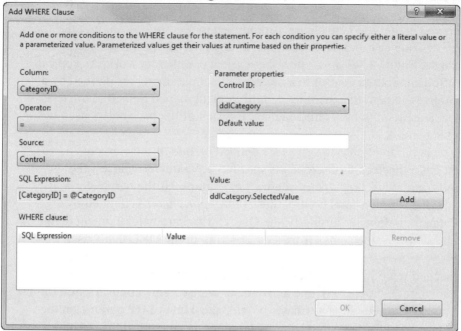

The WHERE clause section after a condition has been added

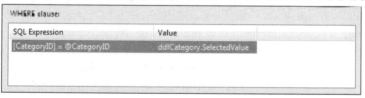

Description

- The Add WHERE Clause dialog box lets you specify a Where clause for the Select statement.

- The Where clause consists of one or more conditions that you construct by using the controls in this dialog box. To create a condition, you select the column you want to compare, the operator you want to use for the comparison, and the source of the data to use for the comparison. Then, you must click Add to add the condition to the list of Where clause conditions.

- The source of the data for the comparison can be a literal value, the value of another control on the form, a cookie, an HTML form field, a profile property, a query string in the URL for the page, a value stored in session state, or a route.

- You can also specify a default value for a parameter. Then, that value is used if the source doesn't contain a value.

Remember

- After you construct a condition, be sure to click the Add button to add the condition to the generated Where clause.

Figure 13-6 How to create a Where clause

How select parameters work

When you create a Where clause as described in the previous figure, the wizard creates one or more *select parameters* that provide the values used by the Where clause. Figure 13-7 shows how these select parameters work. As you can see, each SqlDataSource control that includes select parameters is defined by a SqlDataSource element that includes a child element named SelectParameters. Then, this element contains a child element for each of the parameters used by the Select statement.

The select parameters themselves are defined by one of the elements listed in the first table. Each of these elements specifies a parameter whose value is obtained from a different type of source. For example, if the parameter's value is obtained from a form control, this *control parameter* is defined by a ControlParameter element. Similarly, the QueryStringParameter element defines a parameter whose value comes from a query string in the URL that's used for the page.

The second table in this figure lists the attributes used by the ControlParameter element to define a parameter whose value comes from a form control. As you can see, these attributes provide the name of the parameter, the SQL data type used for the parameter, the ID of the form control that provides the value, the name of the property used to obtain the value, and, optionally, a default value for the parameter.

The code example in this figure shows the aspx code generated for a SqlDataSource control with a Select statement that includes the Where clause shown in the previous figure. Here, the Select statement uses one parameter named CategoryID. This parameter is defined by a ControlParameter element whose Name attribute is set to CategoryID. The SQL data type for this parameter is String, and the parameter's value is obtained from the SelectedValue property of the form control whose ID is ddlCategory.

Please note that the code in this example is generated by the Web Forms Designer when you configure the data source using the Configure Data Source wizard. As a result, you don't have to write this code yourself.

Elements used to define select parameters

Element	Description
SelectParameters	Contains a child element for each parameter used by the data source's Select statement.
Parameter	Defines a parameter with a constant value.
ControlParameter	Defines a parameter that gets its value from a control on the page.
QueryStringParameter	Defines a parameter that gets its value from a query string in the URL used to request the page.
FormParameter	Defines a parameter that gets its value from an HTML form field.
SessionParameter	Defines a parameter that gets its value from an item in session state.
ProfileParameter	Defines a parameter that gets its value from a profile property.
CookieParameter	Defines a parameter that gets its value from a cookie.
RouteParameter	Defines a parameter that gets its value from a route.

Attributes of the ControlParameter element

Attribute	Description
Name	The parameter name.
Type	The SQL data type of the parameter.
ControlID	The ID of the web form control that supplies the value for the parameter.
PropertyName	The name of the property from the web form control that supplies the value for the parameter.
DefaultValue	The value that's used if a value isn't provided by the specified property of the web form control.

The aspx code for a SqlDataSource control that includes a select parameter

```
<asp:SqlDataSource ID="SqlDataSource2" runat="server"
    ConnectionString="<%$ ConnectionStrings:HalloweenConnectionString %>"
    SelectCommand="SELECT [ProductID], [Name], [UnitPrice], [OnHand]
        FROM [Products] WHERE ([CategoryID] = @CategoryID)
        ORDER BY [ProductID]">
    <SelectParameters>
        <asp:ControlParameter Name="CategoryID" Type="String"
            ControlID="ddlCategory" PropertyName="SelectedValue" />
    </SelectParameters>
</asp:SqlDataSource>
```

Description

- The SelectParameters element defines the *select parameters* that are used by the Select statement of a data source. The aspx code that defines these parameters is generated automatically when you use the Add WHERE Clause dialog box to create parameters.

- A *control parameter* is a parameter whose value is obtained from another control on a web form, such as the value selected by a drop-down list. Control parameters are defined by the ControlParameter element.

- Once you understand how to use control parameters, you shouldn't have any trouble learning how to use the other types of parameters on your own.

Figure 13-7   How select parameters work

How to use custom statements and stored procedures

Earlier in this chapter, you learned how to configure the Select statement for a SQL data source by selecting columns from a table. If you need to code a Select statement that's more complex than what you can create using this technique, you can define your own custom statements. To do that, you can enter the statements directly, or you can use the Query Builder. You can also use stored procedures that have been defined within the database.

How to enter custom statements

If you select the first option from the dialog box shown in figure 13-5 and then click the Next button, the dialog box shown in figure 13-8 is displayed. As you can see, this dialog box includes tabs that let you enter Select, Update, Insert, and Delete statements for the data source. In this case, the Select statement is the same as the one that was generated by the wizard as shown earlier in this chapter. Because of that, you might think that you wouldn't need to enter a custom Select statement. Keep in mind, though, that when you create a Select statement by selecting columns from a table, you have no control over the Update, Insert, and Delete statements that are generated. So if you want to use statements other than those that are generated automatically, you can do that by entering custom statements.

How to select stored procedures

If the stored procedures you want to use to select, insert, update, and delete data have already been defined in the database, you can easily use them in a SQL data source. To do that, you select the Stored Procedure option from the appropriate tab of the dialog box shown in figure 13-8. Then, you select the stored procedure you want to use for the operation from the drop-down list that becomes available.

The dialog box for entering a custom Select statement

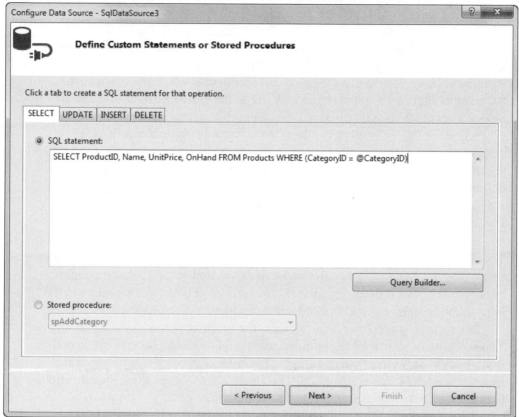

Description

- To use custom statements with a SQL data source, select the SQL Statement option and then enter the statement into the text box. You can enter Select, Update, Insert, and Delete statements by selecting the appropriate tab.

- You can also use the Query Builder to generate custom statements, as shown in the next figure.

- To use stored procedures with a SQL data source, select the Stored Procedure option and then select the stored procedure you want to use from the drop-down list that's displayed.

- When you use custom statements, Visual Studio doesn't generate Update, Insert, and Delete statements from the Select statement you enter. Because of that, you have to enter each of these statements yourself or use the Query Builder to generate them.

Figure 13-8   How to enter custom statements or select stored procedures

How to create a Select statement with the Query Builder

The *Query Builder* makes it easy to generate SQL statements without even knowing the proper syntax for them. Even if you do know the proper syntax, it can be much easier to use the Query Builder than to enter your own custom statements. Figure 13-9 shows you how to use the Query Builder to create a Select statement. You can use similar techniques to create other SQL statements.

When the Query Builder window opens, the Add Table dialog box is displayed. This dialog box, which isn't shown in this figure, lists all of the tables and views in the database that the data source is connected to. You can use this dialog box to add one or more tables to the *diagram pane* of the Query Builder window so you can use them in your query. In this figure, for example, the Products table has been added to the diagram pane.

In the *grid pane*, you can see the columns that will be included in the query. To add columns to this pane, you just check the boxes before the column names in the diagram pane. You can also enter an expression in the Column column of the grid pane to create a calculated column, and you can enter a name in the Alias column to give the calculated column a name.

Once the columns have been added to the grid pane, you can use the Sort Type column to identify any columns that should be used to sort the returned rows and the Sort Order column to give the order of precedence for the sort if more than one column is identified. The Query Builder uses these specifications to build the Order By clause for the Select statement.

You can use the Filter column to establish the criteria to be used to select the rows that will be retrieved by the query. For the query in this figure, a parameter named @CategoryID is specified for the CategoryID column. As a result, only the products whose CategoryID column matches the value of the @CategoryID parameter will be retrieved.

Notice in this figure that the Output column for the CategoryID column in the grid pane isn't selected. That means that this column won't be included in the query output. However, it's included in the grid pane so it can be used to specify the filter criteria.

The Query Builder dialog box

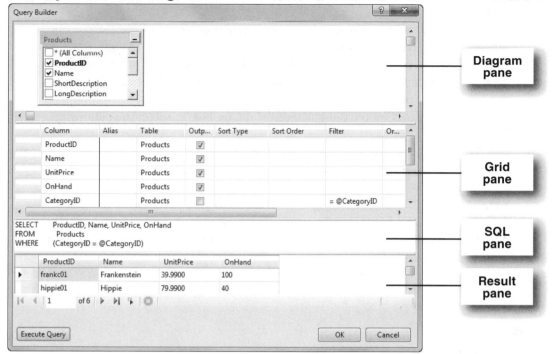

Description

- The *Query Builder* is displayed if you choose to enter a custom SQL statement, and then click the Query Builder button in the dialog box that follows.

- The Query Builder lets you build a Select statement by choosing columns from one or more tables and views and specifying the sort order and filter criteria for each column.

- When you first start the Query Builder, a dialog box is displayed that lets you select the database tables you want to include in the query. Each table you select is displayed in the *diagram pane* at the top of the Query Builder window.

- If you add two related tables to the diagram pane, the Query Builder automatically joins the two tables by including a Join phrase in the From clause.

- To include a column from a table, use the check box that appears next to the column in the diagram pane. This adds the column to the *grid pane*. Then, you can specify any sorting or filtering requirements for the column.

- You can use a parameter in an expression in the Filter column to create a parameterized query. If you use one or more parameters in the query, the Data Source Configuration Wizard lets you specify the source of each parameter value, as described in figure 13-10.

- As you select columns and specify sort and selection criteria, the Query Builder builds the Select statement and displays it in the *SQL pane*.

- To display the results of the query in the *results pane*, click the Execute Query button. If the query includes parameters, you will be asked to enter the value of each parameter.

Figure 13-9   How to create a Select statement with the Query Builder

How to define the parameters

If you specify one or more parameters when you create a Select statement with the Query Builder, the next dialog box lets you define those parameters as shown in figure 13-10. Here, the list box on the left side of the dialog box lists each of the parameters you created in the Query Builder. To define the source for one of these parameters, you select the parameter in this list box. Then, you can use the controls on the right side of the dialog box to select the parameter's source.

In this example, the source of the CategoryID parameter is set to the SelectedValue property of the control named ddlCategory. When I selected the ddlCategory control, the SelectedValue property was selected by default. If you want to use a different property as the source for a parameter, however, you can click the Show Advanced Properties link to display a list of the parameter properties. Then, you can set the PropertyName property to the control property you want to use.

The dialog box for defining parameters

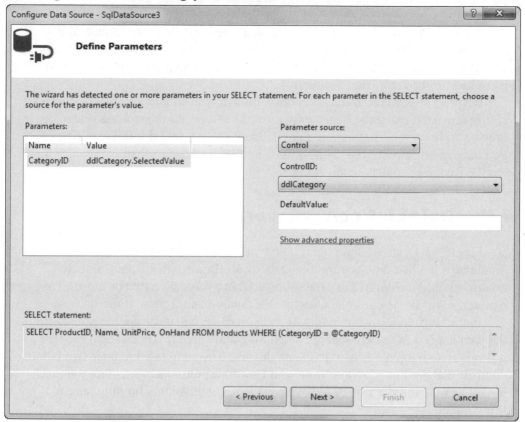

Parameter sources

Source	Description
Control	The parameter's value comes from a control on the page.
QueryString	The parameter's value comes from a query string in the URL used to request the page.
Form	The parameter's value comes from an HTML form field.
Session	The parameter's value comes from an item in session state.
Profile	The parameter's value comes from a profile property.
Cookie	The parameter's value comes from a cookie.
Route	The parameter's value comes from a route.

Description

- If you specify one or more parameters when you create a custom Select statement, the next dialog box lets you define those parameters.

- To define a parameter, you specify the source of the value for each parameter. You can also specify a default value for the parameter.

Figure 13-10   How to define the parameters

How to use the DataList control

A DataList control displays items from a repeating data source such as a data table. In the topics that follow, you'll learn how the DataList control works, you'll learn how to create the templates that define a DataList control, and you'll learn how to format a DataList control.

Before I present the DataList control, though, you should know that you can also create a list using the Repeater control. The Repeater control has one major drawback, however. That is, you can't define it using a visual interface. Instead, you have to enter code directly into the aspx file. Because of that, we won't present the Repeater control in this book.

How the DataList control works

Figure 13-11 shows a simple *data list* that consists of two columns of data. To create a list like this, you use the DataSourceID attribute of the DataList control to bind the control to a data source. Then, you define one or more *templates* within the control that define the content and format of the list.

In the aspx code shown in this figure, you can see that the source of data for the data list is a SQL data source named SqlDataSource2. You can also see that a single Item template is used to create this list. This template includes two label controls that are bound to the Name and UnitPrice columns of the data source. You'll learn about the expressions you use to accomplish this binding later in this chapter.

A simple list displayed by a DataList control

```
Austin Powers $79.99
Frankenstein $39.99
Hippie $79.99
JarJar $59.99
Martian $69.99
Superman $39.99
```

The aspx code for the DataList control

```
<asp:DataList ID="DataList1" runat="server" DataSourceID="SqlDataSource2">
    <ItemTemplate>
        <asp:Label ID="lblName" runat="server"
            Text='<%# Eval("Name") %>'></asp:Label>
        <asp:Label ID="lblUnitPrice" runat="server"
            Text='<%# Eval("UnitPrice", "{0:C}") %>'></asp:Label>
    </ItemTemplate>
</asp:DataList>
```

Basic attributes of the DataList control

Attribute	Description
ID	The ID for the DataList control.
Runat	Must specify "server."
DataSourceID	The ID of the data source to bind the data list to.

Description

- A *data list* displays a list of items from the data source that it's bound to. To bind a data list to a data source, use the Choose Data Source command in the control's smart tag menu.

- To define the information to be displayed in a data list, you create one or more *templates*. Visual Studio provides a designer interface you can use to create the templates as shown in the next figure.

- To display the data from a column in the data source in a data list, you add a control to a template and then bind that control. See figure 13-15 for more information.

- You can use a DataList control for edit operations as well as display operations. However, you're more likely to use the GridView, DetailsView, FormView, and ListView controls for edit operations.

Figure 13-11   How the DataList control works

How to define the templates for a data list

Figure 13-12 shows you how to define the templates for a data list. The table in this figure lists the templates you're most likely to use. Although you can also create templates that let the user select and edit items in the list, you're not likely to use a DataList control for these functions. Instead, you'll use the GridView, DetailsView, FormView, or ListView controls that are described in the next three chapters.

The only template that's required for a data list is the Item template, which defines how each item in the data source is displayed. Depending on the requirements of your application, though, you may need to use one or more of the other templates as well. For example, you'll typically use a Header template to create headings that are displayed in the first row of the data list.

To define the templates for a data list, you work in *template-editing mode*. At the top of this figure, for example, you can see the Item template for a list that includes four columns. This template is displayed by default when you enter template-editing mode. To display a different template, you can use the Display drop-down list in the smart tag menu for the control. You can also display a group of related templates by selecting the group name from this list. For example, you can display both the Header and Footer templates by selecting the Header and Footer Templates item.

If a data list consists of two or more columns, you'll want to place the text and controls in each template within a table. That way, you can set the width of each column in the data list by setting the widths of the columns in the table. In addition, if you add two or more templates to a data list, you can align the columns in the templates by setting the widths of the corresponding table columns to the same values. In this illustration, for example, I set the widths of the corresponding columns in the Item template and the Header template to the same values.

Before I go on, you should realize that you use templates to define the content of a data list and not its appearance. For example, you use the AlternatingItem template to display different content for every other row in a data list, not to shade or highlight every other row. To format a data list, you use styles as shown in the next figure.

The Item template in template-editing mode

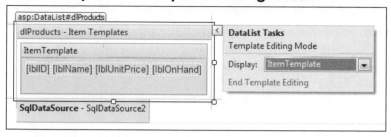

A Header template

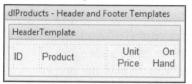

Common template elements for a data list

Element	Description
HeaderTemplate	Displayed before the first item in the data source.
FooterTemplate	Displayed after the last item in the data source.
ItemTemplate	Displayed for each item in the data source.
AlternatingItemTemplate	Displayed for alternating items in the data source.
SeparatorTemplate	Displayed between items.

Description

- The templates you define for a data list specify what content to display and what controls to use to display it. At the least, you must create an Item template that defines the items from the data source that you want to display.

- To create a template, choose Edit Templates from the smart tag menu for the control to display the control in *template-editing mode*. Then, select the template or group of templates you want to edit from the smart tag menu.

- To add text to a template, click in the template and begin typing. To add a control to a template, drag the control from the Toolbox onto the template, then use the Properties window or the control's smart tag menu to set its properties. When you're finished, choose End Template Editing from the smart tag menu.

- To line up the text and controls in two or more templates, place them in tables within the templates and set the column widths to the same values.

- When you set the data source for a DataList control, Visual Studio creates a default Item template. This template includes a text box for each column in the data source preceded by text that identifies the column.

Figure 13-12   How to define the templates for a data list

How to format a data list

To format a data list, you can use one of the techniques presented in figure 13-13. The easiest way is to use the Auto Format dialog box. This dialog box lets you select one of 17 predefined schemes that use different combinations of colors and borders for the items in the data list.

Another way to format a data list is to use the Format page of the Properties dialog box shown in this figure. This dialog box lets you set the colors, fonts, alignment, and other formatting options for the data list and each of its templates. Note that you can use this dialog box to customize an Auto Format scheme or to design your own scheme.

The Auto Format and Properties dialog boxes provide convenient ways to format a data list. However, you can also apply formatting directly from the Properties window. To do that, you use the properties in the Appearance and Style sections of this window, which are available when you display the properties by category. The properties in the Appearance section apply to the data list as a whole, and the properties in the Style section apply to the templates that make up the data list. To set the properties for the Item template, for example, you can expand the ItemStyle group, and to set the properties for the Header template, you can expand the HeaderStyle group.

This figure also presents the five style elements you're most likely to use with a data list. When you use one of the techniques in this figure to format the templates in a data list, the appropriate style elements are generated for you. Of course, you can also format a data list by entering style elements directly into the aspx code. That's not usually necessary, however.

Instead of using the style elements shown here to format a data list, you can use CSS. Because a data list is rendered to nested HTML tables, though, that can be difficult to do. You can also move the style elements to a skin as described in chapter 10. For the purposes of this chapter, though, we'll include the style elements in the aspx code so you can see the styles that are applied.

The Format page of the Properties dialog box

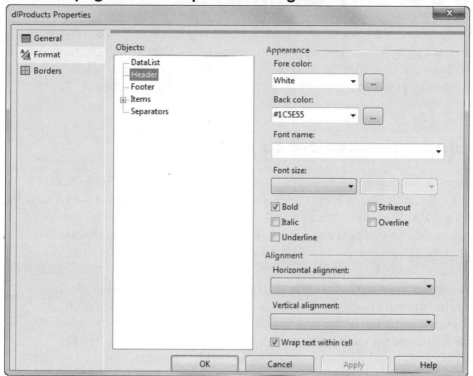

Common style elements for a data list

Element	Description
HeaderStyle	The style used for the header.
FooterStyle	The style used for the footer.
ItemStyle	The style used for each item in the data source.
AlternatingItemStyle	The style used for alternating items in the data source.
SeparatorStyle	The style for the separator.

The asp tag for a Header style

```
<HeaderStyle BackColor="#1C5E55" Font-Bold="True" ForeColor="White" />
```

Description

- You can format a data list by applying a predefined scheme, by using the Properties dialog box, by using the Properties window, or by editing the aspx code.
- To apply a scheme, choose Auto Format from the control's smart tag menu and then select the scheme you want to apply.
- To use the Properties dialog box, choose Property Builder from the control's smart tag menu and then set the properties for the data list and its templates.
- To use the Properties window to format a template, expand the style property for that template and then set its properties.

Figure 13-13   How to format a data list

How to use data binding

Once you've configured a data source control, you can bind it to a web form control to automatically display the data retrieved by the data source on the page. In the following topics, you'll learn how to bind a list control to a data source and how to bind controls defined within the templates of another control like a DataList control.

How to bind a list control to a data source

Figure 13-14 shows how to bind a list control to a data source. To do that, you use the three attributes in the table in this figure. The DataSourceID attribute provides the ID of the data source. The DataTextField attribute provides the name of the data source field that's displayed in the list. And the DataValueField attribute provides the name of the data source field that is returned by the SelectedValue property when the user selects an item from the list.

You can set these attributes manually by using the Properties window or by editing the aspx code. Or, you can use the Data Source Configuration Wizard shown at the top of this figure to set these properties. To do that, display the smart tag menu for the list and select Choose Data Source. Then, use the wizard's controls to set the data source, display field, and value field.

The code example in this figure shows a drop-down list that's bound to a data source named SqlDataSource1. The field named LongName provides the values that are displayed in the drop-down list, and the field named CategoryID supplies the value that's returned by the SelectedValue property when the user selects an item from the list.

The Data Source Configuration Wizard for binding a drop-down list

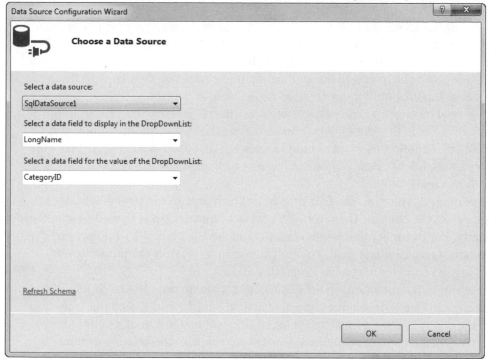

List control attributes for data binding

Attribute	Description
DataSourceID	The ID of the data source to bind the list to.
DataTextField	The name of the data source field that should be displayed in the list.
DataValueField	The name of the data source field whose value should be returned by the SelectedValue property of the list.

The aspx code for a drop-down list that's bound to a SQL data source

```
<asp:DropDownList ID="ddlCategory" runat="server"
    AutoPostBack="True" DataSourceID="SqlDataSource1"
    DataTextField="LongName" DataValueField="CategoryID">
</asp:DropDownList>
```

Description

- You can bind any of the controls that inherit the ListControl class to a data source. That includes the list box control, the drop-down list control, the check box list control, and the radio button list control.

- You can use the Data Source Configuration Wizard to select the data source for a list control, the data field to display in the list, and the data value to return for the selected item.

- You can also use the DataTextFormatString attribute of a list control to specify a format string you want to apply to the text that's displayed in the control.

Figure 13-14   How to bind a list control to a data source

How to bind the controls in a template

Figure 13-15 shows how you can bind the controls in a template to columns of a data source. This technique can be used with any control that uses templates and specifies a data source. That includes the data controls that you'll learn about in the next three chapters. In the application in the next two figures, you'll see how these binding techniques are used for a DataList control.

To bind a control to a column of the data source, you use the DataBindings dialog box. From this dialog box, you can select the Field Binding option and then select the field you want to bind to from the first drop-down list. If you want to format the bound data, you can also select a format from the second drop-down list.

By default, you bind the Text property of a control so the bound data is displayed in the control. However, you may occasionally want to bind to another property. For example, you might want to bind the Enabled or Visible property of a control to a Boolean field. To do that, you simply select the property you want to bind from the Bindable Properties list.

As you make selections in the DataBindings dialog box, Visual Studio generates an Eval method that contains the data binding expression that's used to bind the control. You can see the syntax of the Eval method in this figure along with two examples. If you compare these examples with the binding options in the DataBindings dialog box, you shouldn't have any trouble understanding how this method works.

Although the drop-down lists in the DataBindings dialog box make it easy to create a data binding expression, you can also create your own custom binding expressions. To do that, you just select the Custom Binding option and then enter the binding expression in the Code Expression text box. You might want to do that, for example, if you need to apply a custom format to the data. Or, you might want to code a custom expression that uses the Bind method instead of the Eval method.

Unlike the Eval method, which only provides for displaying bound data, the Bind method provides for both displaying and updating data. This method implements a feature called *two-way binding*. You'll see an application that uses two-way binding in the next chapter.

The DataBindings dialog box for binding a control

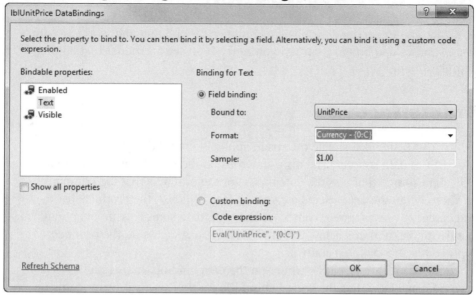

The syntax of the Eval and Bind methods

```
<%# {Eval|Bind}(NameString [, FormatString]) %>
```

Code examples

```
<%# Eval("Name") %>
<%# Eval("UnitPrice", "{0:C}") %>
<%# Bind("UnitPrice", "{0:C}") %>
```

Description

- To bind a control in a template, select the Edit DataBindings command from the smart tag menu for the control to display the DataBindings dialog box. Then, select the property you want to bind to (usually Text), select the Field Binding option, and select the field you want to bind to from the Bound To drop-down list.

- If you want to apply a format to the bound data, select a format from the Format drop-down list.

- As you specify the binding for a control, Visual Studio generates a data binding expression that uses the Eval method. You can see this method in the Code Expression box at the bottom of the DataBindings dialog box.

- You can also create a custom binding expression by selecting the Custom Binding option and then entering the expression in the Code Expression text box.

- The Eval method provides only for displaying data from a data source in a control. In contrast, the Bind method provides for *two-way binding*, which means that it can be used to display as well as update data from a data source.

Note

- If the Field Binding option isn't enabled, you can click the Refresh Schema link to enable it.

Figure 13-15   How to bind the controls in a template

A Product List application

Now that you understand the basic techniques for creating and working with SQL data sources and bound controls, you're ready to see a Product List application that uses them.

The user interface

Figure 13-16 shows a simple one-page application that demonstrates the use of two SQL data sources. The drop-down list at the top of the page is bound to a SQL data source that gets the categories for the products that the company offers. Then, when the user selects a category from this list, the products for the selected category are retrieved from a second SQL data source, which is bound to a DataList control that's below the drop-down list. As a result, the products are displayed in the DataList control.

Since this application relies entirely on the data binding that's established in the Web Forms Designer, the code-behind file for this application contains no C# code. Although this is a simple application, even complicated applications that insert, update, and delete database data can often be written with little or no code.

That's not to say that most ASP.NET database applications are code-free. In the next three chapters, for example, you'll see applications that require database handling code. In particular, these applications require code to detect database errors and concurrency violations and display appropriate error messages. Also, as you'll learn in chapter 17, you can use object data sources to build 3-layer applications that require extensive amounts of database handling code.

The Product List application displayed in a web browser

Description

- The Product List application uses two SqlDataSource controls to get category and product data from a SQL Server database and display it in two bound controls.

- The drop-down list near the top of the form displays the product categories. This control is bound to the first data source control.

- The DataList control, which is bound to the second data source control, displays the data for the products that are in the category that's selected in the drop-down list.

- This application requires no C# code in the code-behind file.

Figure 13-16   The Product List application

The aspx file

Figure 13-17 presents the aspx code for the Product List application. To make it easier for you to follow this code, I've shaded parts of the data source controls and the controls they're bound to. Because this application relies entirely on the data binding declared in this aspx file, it doesn't require any C# code.

The first control is the drop-down list that's bound to the first SqlDataSource control, SqlDataSource1. Here, the AutoPostBack attribute for the drop-down list is set to True so the page is automatically posted back to the server when the user selects a category.

The second control is the first SqlDataSource control, which uses this Select statement to get the required data:

```
SELECT [CategoryID], [LongName] FROM [Categories]
    ORDER BY [LongName]
```

As a result, this data source gets the CategoryID and LongName columns for each row in the Categories table and sorts the result based on the LongName column. Then, these columns are used by the drop-down list that's bound to this data source.

The third control is a DataList control that's bound to the second SqlDataSource control, SqlDataSource2. The Header template for this control provides for a row of headings that are defined within a row of a table. Then, the Item template defines the table rows that display the data in the rows that are retrieved by the data source. As you can see, each column in the table contains a label whose Text attribute is bound to a column in the data source. Also notice that the columns in the Item template use the same style classes as the columns in the Header template. Although you can't see these style classes here, they specify the widths of the columns. Because of that, the columns in the two templates are aligned. In addition, the last two columns in each template are right aligned since they contain numeric data.

The last two elements for the DataList control define the styles for alternating items and for the header. You saw the Header style earlier in this chapter. It indicates that the header text should be displayed in a white, boldface font on a green background. The AlternatingItem style indicates that every other row in the data list should be displayed on a light green background. Since no Item style is included, the other rows will be displayed on a white background.

The fourth control, SqlDataSource2, uses this Select statement:

```
SELECT [ProductID], [Name], [UnitPrice], [OnHand]
    FROM [Products]
    WHERE ([CategoryID] = @CategoryID)
    ORDER BY [ProductID]
```

Here, the Where clause specifies that only those rows whose CategoryID column equals the value of the CategoryID parameter should be retrieved. To make this work, the ControlParameter element specifies that the value of the CategoryID parameter is obtained from the SelectedValue property of the ddlCategory control.

The Default.aspx file

```
<body>
    <header>
        <img src="Images/banner.jpg" alt="Halloween Store" />
    </header>
    <section>
    <form id="form1" runat="server">
        <label>Choose a category: </label>
        <asp:DropDownList ID="ddlCategory" runat="server"
            DataSourceID="SqlDataSource1" DataTextField="LongName"
            DataValueField="CategoryID" AutoPostBack="True">
        </asp:DropDownList><br />
        <asp:SqlDataSource ID="SqlDataSource1" runat="server"
            ConnectionString="<%$ ConnectionStrings:HalloweenConnectionString %>"
            SelectCommand="SELECT [CategoryID], [LongName] FROM [Categories]
                ORDER BY [LongName]">
        </asp:SqlDataSource>
        <asp:DataList ID="dlProducts" runat="server" DataKeyField="ProductID"
            DataSourceID="SqlDataSource2" CellPadding="4">
            <HeaderTemplate>
                <table><tr>
                    <td class="col1">ID</td>
                    <td class="col2">Product</td>
                    <td class="col3">Unit Price</td>
                    <td class="col4">On Hand</td><tr>
                </table>
            </HeaderTemplate>
            <ItemTemplate>
                <table><tr>
                    <td class="col1">
                        <asp:Label ID="lblID" runat="server"
                            Text='<%# Eval("ProductID") %>' /></td>
                    <td class="col2">
                        <asp:Label ID="lblName" runat="server"
                            Text='<%# Eval("Name") %>' /></td>
                    <td class="col3">
                        <asp:Label ID="lblUnitPrice" runat="server"
                            Text='<%# Eval("UnitPrice", "{0:C}") %>' /></td>
                    <td class="col4">
                        <asp:Label ID="lblOnHand" runat="server"
                            Text='<%# Eval("OnHand") %>' /></td></tr>
                </table>
            </ItemTemplate>
            <AlternatingItemStyle BackColor="#E3EAEB" />
            <HeaderStyle BackColor="#1C5E55" Font-Bold="True" ForeColor="White" />
        </asp:DataList>
        <asp:SqlDataSource ID="SqlDataSource2" runat="server"
            ConnectionString="<%$ ConnectionStrings:HalloweenConnectionString %>"
            SelectCommand="SELECT [ProductID], [Name], [UnitPrice], [OnHand]
                FROM [Products] WHERE ([CategoryID] = @CategoryID)
                ORDER BY [ProductID]">
            <SelectParameters>
                <asp:ControlParameter ControlID="ddlCategory" Name="CategoryID"
                    PropertyName="SelectedValue" Type="String" />
            </SelectParameters>
        </asp:SqlDataSource>
    </form>
    </section>
</body>
```

Figure 13-17   The aspx file for the Product List application

How to use the advanced features of a SQL data source

The SqlDataSource control provides several advanced features that you may want to use in your applications. These features are explained in the topics that follow.

How to create a data source that can update the database

Much like ADO.NET data adapters, a SQL data source can include Insert, Update, and Delete statements that let you automatically update the underlying database based on changes made by the user to bound data controls. To automatically generate these statements, you can check the first box in the dialog box shown in figure 13-18, which is displayed when you click on the Advanced button in the dialog box shown in figure 13-5. You can also check the box for optimistic concurrency, which enhances the generated statements so they check whether updated or deleted rows have changed since the data source retrieved the original data.

Note that for this to work, the primary key column of the table you're updating must be included in the Select statement. That's because this column is used to identify a row that's being updated or deleted. So if the Generate option in the Advanced SQL Generation Options dialog box isn't enabled, it's probably because you haven't selected the primary key column.

The code in this figure shows the aspx elements that are generated when you request Insert, Update, and Delete statements without using optimistic concurrency. Here, the InsertCommand, UpdateCommand, and DeleteCommand attributes provide the statements, and the InsertParameters, UpdateParameters, and DeleteParameters child elements define the parameters used by these statements. Because optimistic concurrency isn't used, these statements will update the database whether or not the data has changed since it was originally retrieved, which could lead to corrupt data.

If you check the Use Optimistic Concurrency check box, though, the update and delete commands will include Where clauses that compare the value of each column with the value originally retrieved. Because these values are passed as parameters, the generated aspx code will include additional elements that define these parameters. The SqlDataSource control will also include two additional attributes. The first one indicates that optimistic concurrency should be used, and the second one indicates the format that should be used for the names of the parameters that will hold the original column values. Then, if the value of any column has changed since it was originally retrieved, the update or delete operation will be refused, and your application needs to provide code that handles that situation. You'll see how that works in chapter 14.

The Advanced SQL Generation Options dialog box

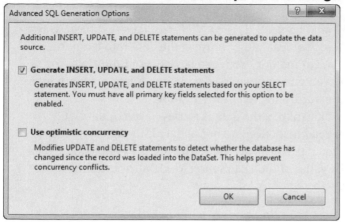

The aspx code for a SqlDataSource control that uses action queries

```
<asp:SqlDataSource ID="SqlDataSource1" runat="server"
    ConnectionString="<%$ ConnectionStrings:HalloweenConnectionString %>"
    SelectCommand="SELECT [CategoryID], [ShortName], [LongName]
                FROM [Categories]"
    InsertCommand="INSERT INTO [Categories] ([CategoryID], [ShortName],
                [LongName]) VALUES (@CategoryID, @ShortName, @LongName)"
    UpdateCommand="UPDATE [Categories] SET [ShortName] = @ShortName,
                [LongName] = @LongName WHERE [CategoryID] = @CategoryID"
    DeleteCommand="DELETE FROM [Categories]
                WHERE [CategoryID] = @CategoryID">
    <DeleteParameters>
        <asp:Parameter Name="CategoryID" Type="String" />
    </DeleteParameters>
    <UpdateParameters>
        <asp:Parameter Name="ShortName" Type="String" />
        <asp:Parameter Name="LongName" Type="String" />
        <asp:Parameter Name="CategoryID" Type="String" />
    </UpdateParameters>
    <InsertParameters>
        <asp:Parameter Name="CategoryID" Type="String" />
        <asp:Parameter Name="ShortName" Type="String" />
        <asp:Parameter Name="LongName" Type="String" />
    </InsertParameters>
</asp:SqlDataSource>
```

Description

- To automatically generate Insert, Update, and Delete statements for a data source, check the first box in the dialog box that you get by clicking on the Advanced button in the first dialog box in figure 13-5. To generate enhanced versions of the Update and Delete statements that use optimistic concurrency, check the second box too.

- The InsertCommand, UpdateCommand, and DeleteCommand attributes in the aspx code define the Insert, Update, and Delete statements used by a data source. If these statements require parameters, the InsertParameters, UpdateParameters, and DeleteParameters elements specify those parameters.

Figure 13-18   How to create a SQL data source that can update the database

How to change the data source mode

As you may remember from chapter 12, ADO.NET provides two basic ways to retrieve data from a database. You can either retrieve the data into a dataset, which retains a copy of the data in memory so it can be accessed multiple times and updated if necessary. Or, you can retrieve the data using a data reader, which lets you retrieve the data in forward-only, read-only fashion.

When you create a SQL data source, the data is retrieved into a dataset by default. If the data will be read just once and not updated, though, you can usually improve the application's performance by retrieving the data using a data reader. To do that, just set the value of the DataSourceMode attribute shown in figure 13-19 to DataReader.

How to use caching

ASP.NET's caching feature lets you save the data retrieved by a data source in cache memory on the server. That way, the next time the data needs to be retrieved, the cached data is used instead of getting it from the database again. Since this reduces database access, it often improves an application's overall performance.

To cache the data that's retrieved by a SQL data source, you use the attributes of the data source that are presented in figure 13-19. To enable caching, you simply set the EnableCaching attribute to True. Then, you can use the CacheDuration attribute to specify how long data should be kept in the cache. If, for example, the cached data rarely changes, you can set a long cache duration value such as 30 minutes or more. If the data changes more frequently, you can set a shorter cache duration value.

But what if the data in the database changes before the duration expires? In that case, the user will view data that is out of date. Sometimes, that's okay so you don't have to worry about it. Otherwise, you can minimize the chance of this happening by setting a shorter duration time.

The DataSourceMode attribute

Attribute	Description
DataSourceMode	DataSet or DataReader. The default is DataSet, but you can specify DataReader if the data source is read-only.

A SqlDataSource control that uses a data reader

```
<asp:SqlDataSource ID="SqlDataSource1" runat="server"
    ConnectionString="<%$ ConnectionStrings:HalloweenConnectionString %>"
    DataSourceMode="DataReader"
    SelectCommand="SELECT [CategoryID], [LongName]
        FROM [Categories]
        ORDER BY [LongName]"
</asp:SqlDataSource>
```

SqlDataSource attributes for caching

Attribute	Description
EnableCaching	A Boolean value that indicates whether caching is enabled for the data source. The default is False.
CacheDuration	The length of time in seconds that the cached data should be saved in cache storage.
CacheExpirationPolicy	If this attribute is set to Absolute, the cache duration timer is started the first time the data is retrieved and is not reset to zero until after the time has expired. If this attribute is set to Sliding, the cache duration timer is reset to zero each time the data is retrieved. The default is Absolute.
CacheKeyDependency	A string that provides a key value associated with the cached data. If you provide a key for the cached data, you can use the key value to programmatically expire the cached data at any time.

A SqlDataSource control that uses caching

```
<asp:SqlDataSource ID="SqlDataSource1" runat="server"
    ConnectionString="<%$ ConnectionStrings:HalloweenConnectionString %>"
    EnableCaching="True" CacheDuration="60"
    SelectCommand="SELECT [CategoryID], [LongName]
        FROM [Categories]
        ORDER BY [LongName]"
</asp:SqlDataSource>
```

Description

- The DataSourceMode attribute lets you specify that data should be retrieved using a data reader rather than being stored in a dataset. For read-only data, a data reader is usually more efficient.

- The data source caching attributes let you specify that data should be stored in cache storage for a specified period of time. For data that changes infrequently, caching can improve performance.

Figure 13-19   How to change the data source mode and use caching

Perspective

In this chapter, you've learned how to use the SqlDataSource control with a DataList control. As you will see, however, the real power of a SQL data source lies in how it can be used with data controls like the GridView, DetailsView, FormView, and ListView controls. Those are the controls that you'll learn how to use in the next three chapters.

When you use SQL data sources as shown in this chapter, the code that's used to manage the user interface is mixed with the code that's used to work with the application's database. One easy way to separate these concerns is to use stored procedures instead of SQL statements with the SqlDataSource control. That way, the SQL statements that access and update the database are in the database itself, separated from the presentation code.

Another way to separate the concerns is to use ObjectDataSource controls instead of SqlDataSource controls, as shown in chapter 17. Then, you create and use data access classes to work with the data, so the code isn't in the aspx file.

Terms

SQL data source	grid pane
SQL Server Express LocalDB	SQL pane
SQL Server Express	results pane
select parameter	data list
control parameter	template
Query Builder	template-editing mode
diagram pane	two-way binding

Summary

- A *SQL data source* provides the information an application needs to connect to a database and retrieve the data needed by the application. A SQL data source can also be used to insert, update, and delete data.

- When you connect a SQL data source to a database, you can select a *SQL Server Express LocalDB* file on your own computer or you can create a connection to a SQL Server database on a database server. Either way, it's best to store the connection string in the web.config file for the application.

- The Configure Data Source wizard helps you generate the Select statement for a SQL data source including the *select* and *control parameters* used in the Where clause. This wizard also lets you enter custom SQL statements with parameters, select stored procedures, and use the *Query Builder* to generate SQL statements.

- The DataList control (or *data list*) displays a list of items from the data source that it's bound to. To define the information that's displayed in the list, you can create one or more *templates* for the list. To format the data in the list, you can use the Properties window or the Properties dialog box.

- You can *bind* a SQL data source to any list control like a drop-down list or list box. You can also bind a SQL data source to the controls that are within a template of a data control like a data list.

- The Configure Data Source wizard lets you automatically generate the Insert, Update, and Delete statements for a SQL data source based on the Select statement for the data source, with or without optimistic concurrency.

- The attributes of a SQL data source let you use a data reader to retrieve the data instead of retrieving the data into a dataset. That is more efficient when the data isn't going to be updated. The attributes also let you specify that the retrieved data should be stored in a *cache*. That can improve performance when the data rarely changes.

Exercise 13-1   Create a DataList application

In this exercise, you'll create an application that lists line items by invoice. To do that, you'll use two SqlDataSource controls and two bound controls. When you're done, the application should look like this:

Create a drop-down list and the data source it's bound to

1. Open the Ex13InvoiceLineItems application in the aspnet45_cs directory. This application contains the starting page and the database, image, and style sheet used by the page.

2. Add a label to the form that contains the text shown above, followed by a non-breaking space and a drop-down list. When the smart tag menu is displayed for the list, select the Choose Data Source command and then select New Data Source from the first drop-down list in the Data Source Configuration Wizard.

3. Configure the data source as shown in figures 13-2 through 13-6, using the Halloween.mdf file in the App_Data folder for the data connection. The data source should include the InvoiceNumber column from the Invoices table for all invoices whose Total column is greater than 300. To create the Where clause for the Select statement, select None from the Source drop-down list.

4. When the Data Source Configuration Wizard is displayed again, accept the defaults so the InvoiceNumber column is displayed in the drop-down list and stored as the value of the drop-down list.

5. Change the name of the drop-down list to ddlInvoice and set its AutoPostBack property to True. Then, in the aspx code, review the Select statement and the select parameter that were generated for the SqlDataSource control.

Create another data source and bind it to a data list

6. Add a second SqlDataSource control to the page. Configure this data source so it uses the connection string that's in the web.config file, so it selects the ProductID, UnitPrice, Quantity, and Extension columns from the LineItems table, and so it selects only the line items for the invoice that's selected from the drop-down list.

7. Add a DataList control to the form, set its data source to the SqlDataSource control you just created, and change its name to dlLineItems. Then, run the application to see how the data is displayed.

Modify the templates for the data list

8. Display the smart tag menu for the DataList control, and select the Edit Templates command to display the Item template. Then, delete the literal text for each column, and add a table at the bottom of the template that consists of one row and four columns and that has a width of 400 pixels.

9. Set the width of each column to 100 pixels, and right-align the second, third, and fourth columns. (To do that, you can create styles that use the width and text-align properties or set the Width and Align properties of the table cells.)

10. Move the labels for the four columns into the four cells of the table, and then delete the space above the table.

11. Select the label for the UnitPrice column, display its smart tag menu, and select Edit DataBindings. Then, use the DataBindings dialog box to apply the Currency format to that column. Do the same for the Extension column.

12. Use the drop-down list in the smart tag menu for the data list to display the header template for the control. Then, add a table like the one you used for the Item template, but enter the values shown in the heading above. When you're done, exit from template-editing mode.

Format the data list

13. Display the smart tag menu for the data list, select the Auto Format command, and highlight one or more of the predefined schemes to see how they look. Then, apply the Simple scheme, and review the aspx code for the DataList control to see the style properties and elements that were generated.

14. Run the application to make sure it's formatted properly. Select a different invoice from the drop-down list to make sure this works. Then, close the browser window.

14

How to use the GridView control

In this chapter, you'll learn how to use the GridView control. This control lets you display the data from a data source in the rows and columns of a table. It includes many advanced features, such as automatic paging and sorting. It lets you update and delete data with minimal C# code. And its appearance is fully customizable.

How to customize the GridView control

The GridView control is one of the most powerful user interface controls available in ASP.NET 4.5. It provides many options that let you customize its appearance and behavior. In the following topics, you'll learn how to define fields, customize the contents and appearance of those fields, enable sorting, and provide for custom paging.

How the GridView control works

As figure 14-1 shows, the GridView control displays data provided by a data source in a row and column format. In fact, the GridView control renders its data as an HTML table with one Tr element for each row in the data source, and one Td element for each column in the data source.

The GridView control at the top of this figure displays the data from the Categories table of the Halloween database. Here, the first three columns of the control display the data from the three columns of the table.

The other two columns of this control display buttons that the user can click to edit or delete a row. In this example, the user has clicked the Edit button for the masks row, which placed that row into edit mode. In this mode, text boxes are displayed in place of the labels for the short and long name columns, the Edit button is replaced by Update and Cancel buttons, and the Delete button is removed.

The table in this figure lists some of the basic attributes of the GridView control, and the aspx code in this figure is the code that creates the GridView control above it. By default, this control contains one column for each of the columns in the data source. These columns are defined by BoundField elements, which are coded within a Columns element. The GridView control in this figure, for example, contains a Columns element with three BoundField elements. Notice that all three BoundField elements contain ItemStyle elements that define the widths of the columns. The Columns element also contains two CommandField elements that define the button columns.

Most of the aspx code for a GridView control is created automatically by Visual Studio when you drag the control from the Toolbox onto the form and when you use the configuration wizard to configure the data source. However, you typically modify this code to customize the appearance and behavior of this control.

A GridView control that provides for updating a table

ID	Short Name	Long Name		
costumes	Costumes	Costumes	Edit	Delete
fx	FX	Special Effects	Edit	Delete
masks	Masks	Masks	Update Cancel	
props	Props	Props	Edit	Delete

The aspx code for the GridView control shown above

```
<asp:GridView ID="GridView1" runat="server" AutoGenerateColumns="False"
            DataSourceID="SqlDataSource1" DataKeyNames="CategoryID">
    <Columns>
        <asp:BoundField DataField="CategoryID" HeaderText="ID"
                        ReadOnly="True" SortExpression="CategoryID">
            <ItemStyle Width="100px" />
        </asp:BoundField>
        <asp:BoundField DataField="ShortName" HeaderText="Short Name"
                        SortExpression="ShortName">
            <ItemStyle Width="150px" />
        </asp:BoundField>
        <asp:BoundField DataField="LongName" HeaderText="Long Name"
                        SortExpression="LongName">
            <ItemStyle Width="200px" />
        </asp:BoundField>
        <asp:CommandField ButtonType="Button" ShowEditButton="True"
                        CausesValidation="False" />
        <asp:CommandField ButtonType="Button" ShowDeleteButton="True"
                        CausesValidation="False" />
    </Columns>
</asp:GridView>
```

Basic attributes of the GridView control

Attribute	Description
DataSourceID	The ID of the data source to bind to.
DataKeyNames	The names of the primary key columns separated by commas.
AutoGenerateColumns	Specifies whether the control's columns should be automatically generated.
SelectedIndex	Specifies the row to be initially selected.

Description

- The GridView control displays data from a data source in a row and column format. The data is rendered as an HTML table.
- To create a GridView control, drag the GridView icon from the Data group of the Toolbox.
- To bind a GridView control to a data source, use the smart tag menu's Choose Data Source command.

Figure 14-1   How the GridView control works

How to define the fields in a GridView control

By default, a GridView control displays one column for each column in the data source. If that's not what you want, you can choose Edit Columns from the control's smart tag menu to display the Fields dialog box shown in figure 14-2. Then, you can use this dialog box to delete fields you don't want to display, change the order of the fields, add additional fields like command buttons, and adjust the properties of the fields.

The Available Fields list box lists all of the available sources for GridView fields, while the Selected Fields list box shows the fields that have already been added to the GridView control. To add an additional field to the GridView control, select the field you want to add in the Available Fields list box and click Add. To change the properties for a field, select the field in the Selected Fields list, and use the Properties list.

The table in this figure lists some of the properties you're most likely to want to change. For example, the HeaderText property determines the text that's displayed for the field's header row, the ItemStyle.Width property sets the width for the field, and the DataFormatString property specifies how you want a field formatted.

Instead of defining each bound field you want to include in a GridView control, you can have the control generate the fields for you automatically. To do that, you select the Auto-generate Fields option in the Fields dialog box. Then, a field will be automatically generated for each column in the data source. Because of that, you'll want to remove any bound fields that were added to the Selected Fields list by default. If you don't, these fields will appear in the GridView control twice.

Note that if you choose to have the bound fields generated automatically, the aspx code for those fields isn't generated until runtime. That means that you can't change the appearance or behavior of these fields at design time. Because of that, you're not likely to use auto-generated fields.

The Fields dialog box

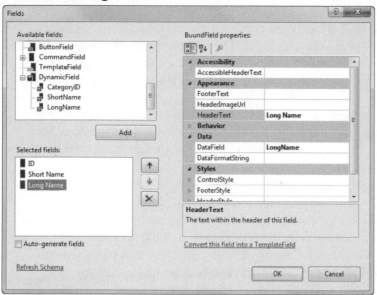

Commonly used field properties

Property	Description
`DataField`	For a bound field, the name of the column in the underlying data source that the field should be bound to.
`DataFormatString`	A format string used to format the data. For example, use {0:c} to format a decimal value as currency.
`ItemStyle.Width`	The width of the field.
`ReadOnly`	True if the field is used for display only.
`NullDisplayText`	The text that's displayed if the data field is null.
`ConvertEmptyStringToNull`	If True (the default), empty strings are treated as nulls when data is updated in the database. Set this property to False if the underlying database field doesn't allow nulls.
`HeaderText`	The text that's displayed in the header row for the field.
`ShowHeader`	True if the header should be displayed for this field.

Description

- By default, the GridView control displays one column for each column in the data source.

- To define the fields that you want to display in the GridView control, display the Fields dialog box by selecting the Edit Columns command in the control's smart tag menu.

- Another way to add a field to a GridView control is to use the Add New Column command in the smart tag menu. You'll see how to use this technique to add command buttons to a DetailsView control in the next chapter.

Figure 14-2   How to define the fields in a GridView control

Elements used to create and format fields

As figure 14-3 shows, the GridView control uses several different types of child elements to create and format its fields. The first element listed here is the Columns element, which defines the collection of columns that are displayed by the control. This element should be placed between the start and end tags for the GridView control.

Between the start and end tags for the Columns element, you can place any combination of the remaining elements listed in the first table in this figure. For example, to create a column that's bound to a column from the data source, you use the BoundField element.

The second table in this figure lists the various types of style elements you can use with a GridView control to set the formatting used for different parts of the control. Some of these elements are used as child elements of the column elements. For example, the ItemStyle element is used in the code example in this figure to set the width for the CategoryID column. The other style elements in this example are used to set the foreground and background colors for different types of rows displayed by the GridView control. Like a DataList control, a GridView control is rendered as an HTML table. Because of that, you typically use these style elements to format a GridView control rather than using CSS. Remember, though, that you can move these style elements to a skin.

Note that you don't have to create these elements yourself. Instead, these elements are created automatically when you use the Fields dialog box as described in the previous figure, when you use the Properties window to specify the styles for an element, or when you apply a scheme to the GridView control using the Auto Format command.

Column field elements

Element	Description
Columns	The columns that are displayed by a GridView control.
asp:BoundField	A field bound to a data source column.
asp:ButtonField	A field that displays a button.
asp:CheckBoxField	A field that displays a check box.
asp:CommandField	A field that contains Select, Edit, Delete, Update, or Cancel buttons.
asp:HyperlinkField	A field that displays a hyperlink.
asp:ImageField	A field that displays an image.
asp:TemplateField	Lets you create a column with custom content.

Style elements

Element	Description
RowStyle	The style used for data rows.
AlternatingRowStyle	The style used for alternating data rows.
SelectedRowStyle	The style used when the row is selected.
EditRowStyle	The style used when the row is being edited.
EmptyDataRowStyle	The style used when the data source is empty.
ItemStyle	The style used for an individual field.
HeaderStyle	The style used for the header row.
FooterStyle	The style used for the footer row.
PagerStyle	The style used for the pager row.

The aspx code for a control that uses field and style elements

```
<asp:GridView ID="GridView1" runat="server" AutoGenerateColumns="False"
            DataKeyNames="CategoryID" DataSourceID="SqlDataSource1">
  <Columns>
    <asp:BoundField DataField="CategoryID" HeaderText="ID" ReadOnly="true">
      <ItemStyle Width="100px" />
    </asp:BoundField>
    .
    .
    .
  </Columns>
  <HeaderStyle BackColor="LightGray" ForeColor="White" Font-Bold="True" />
  <RowStyle BackColor="White" ForeColor="Black" />
  <SelectedRowStyle BackColor="Gray" ForeColor="White" Font-Bold="True" />
  <FooterStyle BackColor="LightGray" ForeColor="Blue" />
  <PagerStyle BackColor="LightGray" ForeColor="Blue"
            HorizontalAlign="Center" />
</asp:GridView>
```

Description

- The GridView control uses several child elements to define the column fields in a row and the styles used to format the data.

Figure 14-3   Elements used to create and format fields

How to enable sorting

The GridView control has a built-in ability to let the user sort the rows based on any or all of the columns displayed by the control. As figure 14-4 shows, all you have to do to enable sorting is set the AllowSorting attribute to True and provide a SortExpression attribute for each column you want to allow sorting for. When sorting is enabled for a column, the user can sort the data by clicking the column header. The first time it's clicked, the data will be sorted in ascending sequence. The second time it's clicked, the data will be sorted in descending sequence. And so on.

Note that a SortExpression attribute is automatically generated for each BoundField column that's included by default or that you create with the Fields dialog box. As a result, instead of adding SortExpression attributes for the columns you want to allow sorting for, you must remove the SortExpression attributes for the columns you don't want to allow sorting for. You can use the Fields dialog box to do that by clearing the SortExpression properties. Or, you can use the HTML Editor to delete the SortExpression attributes.

The code example in this figure allows sorting for three of the five fields displayed by the GridView control. For the first two fields, the SortExpression attribute simply duplicates the name of the data source column the field is bound to. If, for example, the user clicks the header of the ProductID column, the data is sorted on the ProductID field.

In some cases, though, you may want the sort expression to be based on two or more columns. To do that, you just use commas to separate the sort field names. In this example, the sort expression for the CategoryID column is "CategoryID, Name". That way, any rows with the same category ID will be sorted by the Name column. Note that the first time the CategoryID column header is clicked, the rows will be sorted by the Name column in ascending sequence within the CategoryID column in ascending sequence. If the CategoryID column header is clicked again, the category IDs will remain in ascending sequence, but the names will be sorted in descending sequence.

It's important to note that the GridView control doesn't actually do the sorting. Instead, it relies on the underlying data source to sort the data. As a result, sorting will only work if the data source provides for sorting. For a SqlDataSource, this means that you need to use the default DataSet mode.

A GridView control with sorting enabled

ID	Name	Category	Unit Price	On Hand
pow01	Austin Powers	costumes	$79.99	25
frankc01	Frankenstein	costumes	$39.99	100
hippie01	Hippie	costumes	$79.99	40
jar01	JarJar	costumes	$59.99	25
martian01	Martian	costumes	$69.99	100
super01	Superman	costumes	$39.99	100
bl01	Black Light	fx	$19.99	200
fogj01	Fog Juice (1qt)	fx	$9.99	500
fog01	Fog Machine	fx	$34.99	100
str01	Mini-strobe	fx	$13.99	200
skullfog01	Skull Fogger	fx	$39.95	50
tlm01	T&L Machine	fx	$99.99	10

The aspx code for the control shown above

```
<asp:GridView ID="GridView1" runat="server" AllowSorting="True"
    AutoGenerateColumns="False" DataKeyNames="ProductID"
    DataSourceID="SqlDataSource1">
    <Columns>
        <asp:BoundField DataField="ProductID" HeaderText="ID"
            ReadOnly="True" SortExpression="ProductID">
            <HeaderStyle HorizontalAlign="Left" />
            <ItemStyle Width="75px" />
        </asp:BoundField>
        <asp:BoundField DataField="Name" HeaderText="Name"
            SortExpression="Name">
            <HeaderStyle HorizontalAlign="Left" />
            <ItemStyle Width="200px" />
        </asp:BoundField>
        <asp:BoundField DataField="CategoryID" HeaderText="Category"
            SortExpression="CategoryID, Name" />
        <asp:BoundField DataField="UnitPrice" DataFormatString="{0:c}"
            HeaderText="Unit Price">
            <HeaderStyle HorizontalAlign="Right" />
            <ItemStyle Width="85px" HorizontalAlign="Right" />
        </asp:BoundField>
        <asp:BoundField DataField="OnHand" HeaderText="On Hand">
            <HeaderStyle HorizontalAlign="Right" />
            <ItemStyle Width="85px" HorizontalAlign="Right" />
        </asp:BoundField>
    </Columns>
    <HeaderStyle BackColor="#E3EAEB" />
</asp:GridView>
```

Description

- To enable sorting, set the AllowSorting attribute to True. Then, add a SortExpression attribute to each column you want to allow sorting for.

- For sorting to work, the DataSourceMode attribute of the data source must be set to DataSet mode.

Figure 14-4   How to enable sorting

How to enable paging

Paging refers to the ability of the GridView control to display bound data one page at a time, along with paging controls that let the user select which page of data to display next. As figure 14-5 shows, the GridView control lets you enable paging simply by setting the AllowPaging attribute to True.

When you enable paging, an additional row is displayed at the bottom of the GridView control to display the paging controls. If you want, you can provide a PagerStyle element to control how this row is formatted. In the example in this figure, the PagerStyle element specifies a background color for the pager row and centers the pager controls horizontally.

Unlike sorting, the GridView control doesn't delegate the paging function to the underlying data source. Like sorting, however, paging works only for data sources that are in DataSet mode.

A GridView control with paging enabled

ID	Name	Category	Unit Price	On Hand
arm01	Freddie Arm	props	$20.95	200
bats01	Flying Bats	props	$69.99	25
bl01	Black Light	fx	$19.99	200
cat01	Deranged Cat	props	$19.99	45
fog01	Fog Machine	fx	$34.99	100
fogj01	Fog Juice (1qt)	fx	$9.99	500
frankc01	Frankenstein	costumes	$39.99	100
fred01	Freddie	masks	$29.99	50
head01	Michael Head	props	$29.99	100
head02	Saw Head	props	$29.99	100

1 <u>2</u> <u>3</u>

The aspx code for the control shown above

```
<asp:GridView ID="GridView1" runat="server" AllowPaging="True"
    AutoGenerateColumns="False" DataKeyNames="ProductID"
    DataSourceID="SqlDataSource1">
    <Columns>
        <asp:BoundField DataField="ProductID" HeaderText="ID"
            ReadOnly="True">
            <HeaderStyle HorizontalAlign="Left" />
            <ItemStyle Width="75px" />
        </asp:BoundField>
        <asp:BoundField DataField="Name" HeaderText="Name">
            <HeaderStyle HorizontalAlign="Left" />
            <ItemStyle Width="200px" />
        </asp:BoundField>
        <asp:BoundField DataField="CategoryID" HeaderText="Category" />
        <asp:BoundField DataField="UnitPrice" DataFormatString="{0:c}"
            HeaderText="Unit Price">
            <HeaderStyle HorizontalAlign="Right" />
            <ItemStyle Width="85px" HorizontalAlign="Right" />
        </asp:BoundField>
        <asp:BoundField DataField="OnHand" HeaderText="On Hand">
            <HeaderStyle HorizontalAlign="Right" />
            <ItemStyle Width="85px" HorizontalAlign="Right" />
        </asp:BoundField>
    </Columns>
    <HeaderStyle BackColor="#E3EAEB" />
    <PagerStyle BackColor="#E3EAEB" HorizontalAlign="Center" />
</asp:GridView>
```

Description

- To enable *paging*, set the AllowPaging attribute to True. Then, add a PagerStyle element to define the appearance of the pager controls. You can also add a PagerSettings element as described in the next figure to customize the way paging works.

- For paging to work, the DataSourceMode attribute of the data source must be set to DataSet mode.

Figure 14-5   How to enable paging

How to customize paging

Figure 14-6 shows how you can customize the way paging works with a GridView control. To start, the two attributes in the first table let you enable paging and specify the number of data rows that will be displayed on each page. The default setting for the second attribute is 10.

You can also customize the appearance of the pager area by including a PagerSettings element between the start and end tags of a GridView control. Then, you can use the attributes in the second table for the customization. The most important of these attributes is Mode, which determines what buttons are displayed in the pager area. If, for example, you set the mode to NextPrevious, only Next and Previous buttons will be displayed.

If you specify Numeric or NumericFirstLast for the Mode attribute, individual page numbers are displayed in the pager area so the user can go directly to any of the listed pages. You can then use the PageButtonCount attribute to specify how many of these page numbers should be displayed in the pager area. Note that if you specify NumericFirstLast, the first and last buttons are displayed only if the total number of pages exceeds the value you specify for the PageButtonCount attribute and the first or last page isn't displayed.

The remaining attributes in this table let you control the text or image that's displayed for the various buttons. By default, the values for the First, Previous, Next, and Last buttons use less-than and greater-than signs, but the example shows how you can change the text for these buttons.

When you use paging, you should know that, by default, all of the rows from the data source are retrieved each time a different page is displayed. If the data source contains a large number of rows, this can be inefficient. Because of that, ASP.NET 4.5 adds two properties to the GridView control that you can use to read just the rows you need for each page.

The first property, AllowCustomPaging, lets you enable custom paging. Then, when the user clicks a pager control to display another page of data, the application can respond to the PageIndexChanging event. Among other things, the event handler for this event must set the second new property, VirtualItemCount, to the total number of rows in the data source. For more information on how to code this event handler, please see online help.

Attributes of the GridView control that affect paging

Attribute	Description
AllowPaging	Set to True to enable paging.
PageSize	Specifies the number of rows to display on each page. The default is 10.

Attributes of the PagerSettings element

Attribute	Description
Mode	Controls what buttons are displayed in the pager area. You can specify NextPrevious, NextPreviousFirstLast, Numeric, or NumericFirstLast.
FirstPageText	The text to display for the first page button. The default is <<, which displays as <<.
FirstPageImageUrl	The URL of an image file used to display the first page button.
PreviousPageText	The text to display for the previous page button. The default is <, which displays as <.
PreviousPageImageUrl	The URL of an image file used to display the previous page button.
NextPageText	The text to display for the next page button. The default is >, which displays as >.
NextPageImageUrl	The URL of an image file used to display the next page button.
LastPageText	The text to display for the last page button. The default is >>, which displays as >>.
LastPageImageUrl	The URL of an image file used to display the last page button.
PageButtonCount	The number of page buttons to display if the Mode is set to Numeric or NumericFirstLast.
Position	The location of the pager area. You can specify Top, Bottom, or TopAndBottom.
Visible	Set to False to hide the pager controls.

Example

A PagerSettings element

```
<PagerSettings Mode="NextPreviousFirstLast"
          NextPageText="Next" PreviousPageText="Prev"
          FirstPageText="First" LastPageText="Last" />
```

The resulting pager area

First Prev Next Last

Description

- You can use the PageSize attribute of the GridView element to specify the number of rows to display on each page.
- You can also add a PagerSettings element to control the appearance of the pager area.
- By default, each time a different page is displayed, all the rows in the data source are read. To avoid that, you can use the new AllowCustomPaging and VirtualItemCount properties. For more information, see online help.

Figure 14-6   How to customize paging

A list application
that uses a GridView control

Now that you've learned the basics of working with a GridView control, the following topics present the design and code for an application that uses a GridView control to list the rows of a data source. As you'll see, this application provides for sorting and paging and doesn't require a single line of C# code.

The Product List application

Figure 14-7 presents the Product List application. Here, the data from the Products table of the Halloween database is displayed in a GridView control. The data is displayed 8 rows at a time, and numeric page buttons are displayed at the bottom of the GridView control so the user can navigate from page to page. In addition, the user can sort the data by clicking the column headings for the ID, Name, and Category columns.

The Product List application

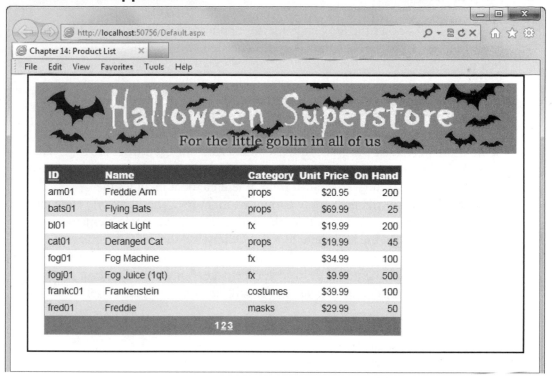

Description

- The Product List application uses a GridView control to display a list of all the products in the Products table. The GridView control is bound to a SqlDataSource control that works in DataSet mode.

- Sorting is enabled for the first three columns. That way, the user can sort the product data by ID, Name, or Category.

- Paging is enabled with 8 products displayed on each page.

- Currency formatting is applied to the Unit Price column.

Figure 14-7   The Product List application

The aspx file

Figure 14-8 shows the aspx code for this application, which is stored in the Default.aspx file. Because no C# code is needed, the code-behind file isn't shown.

Because you've already been introduced to all of the code in the aspx file, you should be able to follow it without much trouble. So I'll just point out a few highlights.

The Columns element contains five BoundField child elements that define the fields displayed by the grid. All five columns are retrieved from the SQL data source. The first three of these BoundField elements include the SortExpression attribute to allow sorting. The fourth BoundField element includes the DataFormatString attribute to apply currency formatting. The ItemStyle elements for the first two fields set the width of the fields, and the ItemStyle elements for the last two fields set the alignment to right. Otherwise, the default formatting is used for the five fields.

A PagerStyle element is used to center the pager buttons in the pager area. Then, a PagerSettings element is used to specify the types of pager controls to display.

Finally, the SqlDataSource control uses this Select statement to retrieve data from the Halloween database:

```
SELECT [ProductID], [Name], [CategoryID],
    [UnitPrice], [OnHand] FROM [Products]
```

Because the DataSourceMode attribute isn't set, the default of DataSet mode is used, which means that sorting and paging can be enabled.

The Default.aspx file

```
<html xmlns="http://www.w3.org/1999/xhtml">
<head id="Head1" runat="server">
    <title>Chapter 14: Product List</title>
    <link href="Main.css" rel="stylesheet" type="text/css" />
</head>
<body>
    <header>
        <img src="Images/banner.jpg" alt="Halloween Store" />
    </header>
    <section>
    <form id="form1" runat="server">
        <asp:GridView ID="grdProducts" runat="server"
            AutoGenerateColumns="False" DataKeyNames="ProductID"
            DataSourceID="SqlDataSource1" AllowPaging="True" PageSize="8"
            AllowSorting="True" CellPadding="4" ForeColor="Black"
            GridLines="None">
            <Columns>
                <asp:BoundField DataField="ProductID" HeaderText="ID"
                    ReadOnly="True" SortExpression="ProductID">
                    <HeaderStyle HorizontalAlign="Left" />
                    <ItemStyle Width="75px" />
                </asp:BoundField>
                <asp:BoundField DataField="Name" HeaderText="Name"
                    SortExpression="Name">
                    <HeaderStyle HorizontalAlign="Left" />
                    <ItemStyle Width="200px" />
                </asp:BoundField>
                <asp:BoundField DataField="CategoryID" HeaderText="Category"
                    SortExpression="CategoryID, Name" />
                <asp:BoundField DataField="UnitPrice"
                    HeaderText="Unit Price" DataFormatString="{0:c}">
                    <ItemStyle HorizontalAlign="Right" />
                </asp:BoundField>
                <asp:BoundField DataField="OnHand" HeaderText="On Hand">
                    <ItemStyle HorizontalAlign="Right" />
                </asp:BoundField>
            </Columns>
            <HeaderStyle BackColor="#1C5E55" Font-Bold="True"
                ForeColor="White" />
            <RowStyle BackColor="White" ForeColor="Black" />
            <AlternatingRowStyle BackColor="#E3EAEB" ForeColor="Black" />
            <PagerStyle BackColor="Gray" ForeColor="White"
                HorizontalAlign="Center" Font-Bold="True" />
            <PagerSettings Mode="NumericFirstLast" />
        </asp:GridView>
        <asp:SqlDataSource ID="SqlDataSource1" runat="server"
          ConnectionString=
              "<%$ ConnectionStrings:HalloweenConnectionString %>"
          SelectCommand="SELECT [ProductID], [Name], [CategoryID],
            [UnitPrice], [OnHand] FROM [Products]">
        </asp:SqlDataSource>
    </form>
    </section>
</body>
</html>
```

Figure 14-8   The aspx file for the Product List application

How to update GridView data

Another impressive feature of the GridView control is its ability to update data in the underlying data source with little additional code. Before you can set that up, though, you must configure the data source with Update, Delete, and Insert statements as described in the last chapter. Once you've done that, you can set up a GridView control so it calls the Update and Delete statements, which you'll learn how to do next. Then, you'll learn how to insert a row into a GridView control.

How to work with command fields

A *command field* is a GridView column that contains one or more command buttons. Figure 14-9 shows five of the command buttons that you can include in each row of a GridView control. Please note, however, that the Update and Cancel buttons are displayed only when a user clicks the Edit button to edit a row. You can't display these buttons in separate command fields.

When the user clicks a Delete button, the GridView control calls the data source control's Delete method, which deletes the selected row from the underlying database. Then, the GridView control redisplays the data without the deleted row.

When the user clicks the Edit button, the GridView control places the selected row in *edit mode*. In this mode, the labels used to display the editable bound fields are replaced by text boxes so the user can enter changes. Also, the row is formatted using the style attributes provided by the EditRowStyle element. Finally, the Edit button itself is replaced by Update and Cancel buttons. Then, if the user clicks the Update button, the GridView control calls the data source control's Update method, which updates the underlying database. But if the user clicks Cancel, any changes made by the user are discarded and the original values are redisplayed.

The Select button lets the user select a row. Then, the selected row is displayed with the settings in the SelectedRowStyle element. Also, the SelectedIndex and SelectedRow properties are updated to reflect the selected row. The Select button is most often used in combination with a FormView or DetailsView control to create pages that show the details for an item selected from the GridView control. You'll learn how this works in chapter 15.

The two tables in this figure show the attributes of a CommandField element. For instance, you can set the ShowEditButton attribute to True to display an Edit button in a command field. And you can use the EditText attribute to set the text that's displayed on that button.

Although a single command field can display more than one button, it's common to create separate command fields for Select, Edit, and Delete buttons. It's also common to set the CausesValidation attribute of the Select and Delete buttons to False since the operations these buttons perform don't require any data validation. On the other hand, you'll usually leave the CausesValidation attribute of the Edit button set to True so validation is performed when the user clicks the Update button. Later in this chapter, you'll learn how to use validation controls with the Edit button by creating template fields.

The Fields dialog box for working with a command field

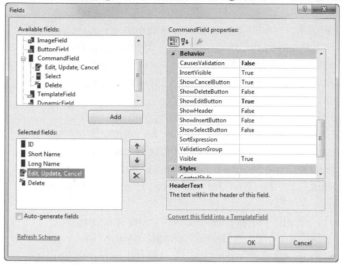

Attributes of the CommandField element

Attribute	Description
ButtonType	Specifies the type of button displayed in the command field. Valid options are Button, Link, or Image.
CausesValidation	Specifies whether validation should be performed if the user clicks the button.
ValidationGroup	Specifies the name of the group to be validated if CausesValidation is True.

Attributes that show buttons and set the text or images they display

Button	Show	Text	Image
Cancel	**ShowCancelButton**	**CancelText**	**CancelImage**
Delete	**ShowDeleteButton**	**DeleteText**	**DeleteImage**
Edit	**ShowEditButton**	**EditText**	**EditImage**
Select	**ShowSelectButton**	**SelectText**	**SelectImage**
Update	n/a	**UpdateText**	**UpdateImage**

Typical code to define command fields

```
<asp:CommandField ButtonType="Button" ShowEditButton="True"
    CausesValidation="False" />
<asp:CommandField ButtonType="Button" ShowDeleteButton="True"
    CausesValidation="False" />
```

Description

- A *command field* adds buttons that let the user edit, delete, or select data.
- The CommandField element also provides for an Insert button, but the GridView control doesn't directly support insert operations.

Figure 14-9   How to work with command fields

How to use events raised by the GridView control

Although the GridView control provides many features automatically, you still must write some code to handle such things as data validation, database exceptions, and concurrency errors. As figure 14-10 shows, most of this code will be in the form of event handlers that respond to one or more of the events raised by the GridView control.

If you look at the list of events in the table in this figure, you'll see that several of them come in pairs, with one event raised before an action is taken and the other after the action completes. For example, when the user clicks the Delete button in a GridView row, two events are raised. The RowDeleting event is raised before the row is deleted, and the RowDeleted event is raised after the row has been deleted.

The most common reason to handle the before-action events is to provide data validation. For example, when the user clicks the Update button, you can handle the RowUpdating event to make sure the user has entered correct data. If not, you can set the e argument's Cancel property to True to cancel the update.

In contrast, the after-action events give you an opportunity to make sure the database operation completed successfully. In most applications, you should test for two conditions. First, you should check for any database exceptions by checking the Exception property of the e argument. If this property refers to a valid object, an exception has occurred and you can notify the user with an appropriate error message.

Second, if optimistic concurrency is used, you should check to see if a concurrency violation has occurred. To do that, you can check the AffectedRows property of the e argument. If this property is zero, which means no rows have been changed, a concurrency error has probably occurred, and you can notify the user with an appropriate error message.

When you use optimistic concurrency, remember that the Where clause in an Update or Delete statement tries to find a row that has the same values as when the row was originally retrieved. If that row can't be found, which means that another user has updated one of the columns or deleted the row, the update or delete operation never takes place so no rows are affected.

When you try to update a row, one of the most common exceptions is caused by an attempt to store a null value in a database column that doesn't allow null values. This occurs when the user doesn't enter a value in one of the columns that's being updated. In this case, you can display an appropriate error message and set the e argument's ExceptionHandled property to True to suppress further processing of the exception. You can also set the KeepInEditMode property to True to leave the GridView control in edit mode. This is illustrated by the event handler that's coded in this figure.

Another event you may use is the RowDataBound event, which occurs when a row is bound to the GridView control. This event is commonly used to format a cell in a row based on the cell's value. If the value of the cell is less than zero, for example, you might assign a different background color to it. To do that, you

Events raised by the GridView control

Event	Raised when ...
`RowCancelingEdit`	The Cancel button of a row in edit mode is clicked.
`RowDataBound`	Data binding completes for a row.
`RowDeleted`	A row has been deleted.
`RowDeleting`	A row is about to be deleted.
`RowEditing`	A row is about to be edited.
`RowUpdated`	A row has been updated.
`RowUpdating`	A row is about to be updated.
`SelectedIndexChanged`	A row has been selected.
`SelectedIndexChanging`	A row is about to be selected.

An event handler for the RowUpdated event

```
protected void GridView1_RowUpdated(object sender,
    GridViewUpdatedEventArgs e)
{
    if (e.Exception != null)
    {
        lblError.Text = "A database error has occurred. " +
            "Message: " + e.Exception.Message;
        e.ExceptionHandled = true;
        e.KeepInEditMode = true;
    }
    else if (e.AffectedRows == 0)
    {
        lblError.Text = "Another user may have updated that category. " +
            "Please try again.";
    }
}
```

Description

- The GridView control raises various events that can be handled when data is updated.

- The RowUpdating and RowDeleting events are often used for data validation. You can cancel the update or delete operation by setting the e argument's Cancel property to True.

- You can handle the RowUpdated and RowDeleted events to ensure that the row was successfully updated or deleted.

- To determine if a SQL exception has occurred, check the Exception property of the e argument. If an exception has occurred, the most likely cause is a null value for a column that doesn't accept nulls. To suppress the exception, you can set the ExceptionHandled property to True. And to keep the control in edit mode, you can set the KeepInEditMode property to True.

- To determine how many rows were updated or deleted, check the AffectedRows property of the e argument. If this property is zero and an exception has *not* been thrown, the most likely cause is a concurrency error.

Figure 14-10   How to use events raised by the GridView control

can use the Row property of the e argument that's passed to the event handler to get the current row. Then, you can use the Cell property with an index to get a cell in the row. Finally, you can set the properties of the cell as appropriate.

How to insert a row in a GridView control

You may have noticed that although the GridView control lets you update and delete rows, it has no provision for inserting new rows. When you use the GridView control in concert with a FormView or DetailsView control, though, you can provide for insert operations with a minimum of code. You'll learn how to do that in chapter 15. Another alternative is to create a page that lets you insert data into a GridView control by using the technique described in figure 14-11.

To provide for insertions, you must first create a set of input controls such as text boxes into which the user can enter data for the row to be inserted. Next, you must provide a button that the user can click to start the insertion. Then, in the event handler for this button, you can set the insert parameter values to the values entered by the user and call the data source's Insert method to add the new row.

This is illustrated by the code in this figure. Here, if the insertion is successful, the contents of the text boxes are cleared. But if an exception is thrown, an error message is displayed. This message indicates that an exception has occurred and uses the Message property of the Exception object to display the message that's stored in the Exception object.

Notice in this example that a parameter is generated for each column in the Categories table. If a table contains an identity column, though, a parameter won't be generated for that column. That makes sense because the value of this column is set by the database when the row is inserted.

Method and properties of the SqlDataSource class for inserting rows

Method	Description
`Insert()`	Executes the Insert command defined for the data source.
Property	**Description**
`InsertCommand`	The Insert command to be executed.
`InsertParameters["name"]`	The parameter with the specified name.

Property of the Parameter class for inserting rows

Property	Description
`DefaultValue`	The default value of a parameter. This value is used if no other value is assigned to the parameter.

Code that uses a SqlDataSource control to insert a row

```
protected void btnAdd_Click(object sender, EventArgs e)
{
    SqlDataSource1.InsertParameters["CategoryID"].DefaultValue
        = txtID.Text;
    SqlDataSource1.InsertParameters["ShortName"].DefaultValue
        = txtShortName.Text;
    SqlDataSource1.InsertParameters["LongName"].DefaultValue
        = txtLongName.Text;
    try
    {
        SqlDataSource1.Insert();
        txtID.Text = "";
        txtShortName.Text = "";
        txtLongName.Text = "";
    }
    catch (Exception ex)
    {
        lblError.Text = "A database error has occurred. " +
            "Message: " + ex.Message;
    }
}
```

Description

- The GridView control doesn't support insert operations, but you can use the GridView's data source to insert rows into the database. When you do, the new row will automatically be shown in the GridView control.

- To provide for inserts, the page should include controls such as text boxes for the user to enter data and a button that the user can click to insert the data.

- To use a SqlDataSource control to insert a database row, first set the DefaultValue property of each insert parameter to the value you want to insert. Then, call the Insert method.

- The Insert method may throw a SqlException if a SQL error occurs. The most likely cause of the exception is a primary key constraint violation.

Figure 14-11   How to insert a row in a GridView control

A maintenance application that uses a GridView control

To give you a better idea of how you can use a GridView control to update, delete, and insert data, the following topics present an application that maintains the Categories table in the Halloween database.

The Category Maintenance application

Figure 14-12 introduces you to the Category Maintenance application. It lets the user update, delete, and insert rows in the Categories table of the Halloween database. Here, a GridView control is used to display the rows in the Categories table along with Edit and Delete buttons. In this figure, the user has clicked the Edit button for the third data row, placing that row in edit mode.

Beneath the GridView control, three text boxes let the user enter data for a new category. Then, if the user clicks the Add New Category button, the data entered in these text boxes is used to add a category row to the database. Although it isn't apparent from this figure, required field validators are used for each text box. Also, there's a label control beneath the GridView control that's used to display error messages when an update, delete, or insert operation fails.

The Category Maintenance application

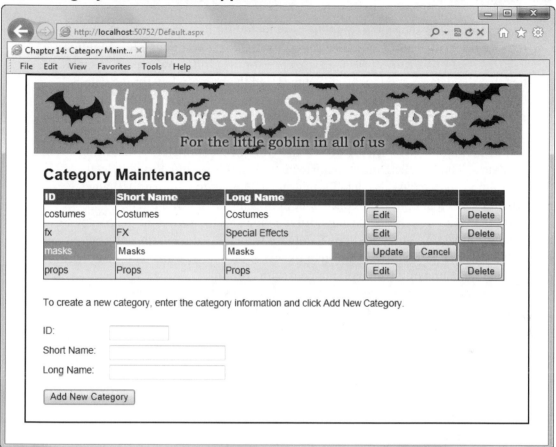

Description

- The Category Maintenance application uses a GridView control to let the user update or delete rows in the Categories table.

- To edit a category, the user clicks the Edit button. This places the GridView control into edit mode. The user can then change the Short Name or Long Name and click Update. Or, the user can click Cancel to leave edit mode.

- To delete a category, the user clicks the Delete button.

- The user can add a category to the table by entering data into the text boxes beneath the GridView control and clicking the Add New Category button.

- If the user attempts to update or add a row with a column that is blank, an error message is displayed.

Figure 14-12   The Category Maintenance application

The aspx file

Figure 14-13 shows the complete aspx listing for this application. Since most of this code has already been introduced, I'll just point out a few highlights.

Part 1 of this figure shows the aspx code for the GridView control. It specifies that the data source is SqlDataSource1 and the primary key for the data is CategoryID. The five columns defined in the Columns element display the three columns from the data source, an Edit button, and a Delete button.

Part 2 of this figure shows the SqlDataSource control. Note that this data source includes the ConflictDetection and OldValuesParameterFormatString attributes. The ConflictDetection attribute indicates how update and delete operations are handled. By default, this attribute is set to CompareAllValues, which means that optimistic concurrency checking will be done. The OldValuesParameterFormatString attribute indicates the format of the parameter names that are used to hold original column values. By default, this attribute is set to original_{0}, which means that the name of each original parameter will include the name of the column prefixed with "original_".

As a result of these two attribute values, these statements are used to retrieve, delete, update, and insert category rows:

```
SELECT [CategoryID], [ShortName], [LongName]
    FROM [Categories]

DELETE FROM [Categories]
    WHERE [CategoryID] = @original_CategoryID
      AND [ShortName] = @original_ShortName
      AND [LongName] = @original_LongName

UPDATE [Categories]
    SET [ShortName] = @ShortName,
        [LongName] = @LongName
    WHERE [CategoryID] = @original_CategoryID
      AND [ShortName] = @original_ShortName
      AND [LongName] = @original_LongName

INSERT INTO [Categories]
    ([CategoryID], [ShortName], [LongName])
    VALUES (@CategoryID, @ShortName, @LongName)
```

Here, the Where clauses implement optimistic concurrency by looking for rows that have the values originally retrieved. Then, the DeleteParameters, UpdateParameters, and InsertParameters elements in the aspx code define the parameters used by these statements.

Finally, part 3 of this figure shows the input controls used to enter the data for a new category. As you can see, each text box is validated by a required field validator that makes sure the user has entered data for the field. This validation is performed when the user clicks the Add New Category button. In addition, the MaxLength attribute is coded for each text box so the user can't enter more characters than are allowed by the associated column in the data source.

The Default.aspx file   Page 1

```
<%@ Page Language="C#" AutoEventWireup="true" CodeFile="Default.aspx.cs"
Inherits="_Default" %>

<!DOCTYPE html>

<html xmlns="http://www.w3.org/1999/xhtml">
<head id="Head1" runat="server">
    <title>Chapter 14: Category Maintenance</title>
    <link href="Main.css" rel="stylesheet" type="text/css" />
</head>
<body>
    <header>
        <img src="Images/banner.jpg" alt="Halloween Store" />
    </header>
    <section>
    <h1>Category Maintenance</h1>
    <form id="form1" runat="server">
        <asp:GridView ID="GridView1" runat="server"
            AutoGenerateColumns="False" DataKeyNames="CategoryID"
            DataSourceID="SqlDataSource1" ForeColor="Black"
            OnRowDeleted="GridView1_RowDeleted"
            OnRowUpdated="GridView1_RowUpdated">
            <Columns>
                <asp:BoundField DataField="CategoryID" HeaderText="ID"
                    ReadOnly="True">
                    <HeaderStyle HorizontalAlign="Left" />
                    <ItemStyle Width="100px" />
                </asp:BoundField>
                <asp:BoundField DataField="ShortName" HeaderText="Short Name"
                    SortExpression="ShortName">
                    <HeaderStyle HorizontalAlign="Left" />
                    <ItemStyle Width="150px" />
                </asp:BoundField>
                <asp:BoundField DataField="LongName" HeaderText="Long Name"
                    SortExpression="LongName">
                    <HeaderStyle HorizontalAlign="Left" />
                    <ItemStyle Width="200px" />
                </asp:BoundField>
                <asp:CommandField ButtonType="Button" CausesValidation="False"
                    ShowEditButton="True" />
                <asp:CommandField ButtonType="Button" CausesValidation="False"
                    ShowDeleteButton="True" />
            </Columns>
            <HeaderStyle BackColor="#1C5E55" Font-Bold="True"
                ForeColor="White" />
            <RowStyle BackColor="White" ForeColor="Black" />
            <AlternatingRowStyle BackColor="#E3EAEB" ForeColor="Black" />
            <EditRowStyle BackColor="#F46D11" ForeColor="White" />
        </asp:GridView>
```

Notes

- The GridView control is bound to the SqlDataSource1 data source.
- The Columns element includes child elements that define five columns. Three are for the bound fields; the other two are for the command buttons.

Figure 14-13   The aspx file for the Category Maintenance application (part 1 of 3)

The Default.aspx file Page 2

```
<asp:SqlDataSource ID="SqlDataSource1" runat="server"
    ConflictDetection="CompareAllValues"
    ConnectionString="<%$ ConnectionStrings:HalloweenConnectionString %>"
    OldValuesParameterFormatString="original_{0}"
    SelectCommand="SELECT [CategoryID], [ShortName], [LongName]
        FROM [Categories]"
    DeleteCommand="DELETE FROM [Categories]
        WHERE [CategoryID] = @original_CategoryID
          AND [ShortName] = @original_ShortName
          AND [LongName] = @original_LongName"
    InsertCommand="INSERT INTO [Categories]
        ([CategoryID], [ShortName], [LongName])
        VALUES (@CategoryID, @ShortName, @LongName)"
    UpdateCommand="UPDATE [Categories]
        SET [ShortName] = @ShortName,
            [LongName] = @LongName
        WHERE [CategoryID] = @original_CategoryID
          AND [ShortName] = @original_ShortName
          AND [LongName] = @original_LongName">
    <DeleteParameters>
        <asp:Parameter Name="original_CategoryID" Type="String" />
        <asp:Parameter Name="original_ShortName" Type="String" />
        <asp:Parameter Name="original_LongName" Type="String" />
    </DeleteParameters>
    <InsertParameters>
        <asp:Parameter Name="CategoryID" Type="String" />
        <asp:Parameter Name="ShortName" Type="String" />
        <asp:Parameter Name="LongName" Type="String" />
    </InsertParameters>
    <UpdateParameters>
        <asp:Parameter Name="ShortName" Type="String" />
        <asp:Parameter Name="LongName" Type="String" />
        <asp:Parameter Name="original_CategoryID" Type="String" />
        <asp:Parameter Name="original_ShortName" Type="String" />
        <asp:Parameter Name="original_LongName" Type="String" />
    </UpdateParameters>
</asp:SqlDataSource>
```

Notes

- The Select statement retrieves all rows in the Categories table.
- The Where clauses in the Delete and Update statements provide for optimistic concurrency.

Figure 14-13   The aspx file for the Category Maintenance application (part 2 of 3)

The Default.aspx file   **Page 3**

```
<p>To create a new category, enter the category information and click
    Add New Category.</p>
<p>
    <asp:Label ID="lblError" runat="server" EnableViewState="False">
    </asp:Label>
</p>
<label>ID:</label>
<asp:TextBox ID="txtID" runat="server" MaxLength="10"
    CssClass="entry">
</asp:TextBox> 
    <asp:RequiredFieldValidator ID="RequiredFieldValidator1"
        runat="server" ControlToValidate="txtID" CssClass="validator"
        ErrorMessage="ID is a required field.">
    </asp:RequiredFieldValidator><br />
<label>Short Name:</label>
<asp:TextBox ID="txtShortName" runat="server" MaxLength="15"
    CssClass="entry">
</asp:TextBox> 
    <asp:RequiredFieldValidator ID="RequiredFieldValidator2"
        runat="server" ControlToValidate="txtShortName"
        CssClass="validator"
        ErrorMessage="Short Name is a required field.">
    </asp:RequiredFieldValidator><br />
<label>Long Name:</label>
<asp:TextBox ID="txtLongName" runat="server" MaxLength="50"
    CssClass="entry">
</asp:TextBox> 
    <asp:RequiredFieldValidator ID="RequiredFieldValidator3"
        runat="server" ControlToValidate="txtLongName"
        CssClass="validator"
        ErrorMessage="Long Name is a required field.">
    </asp:RequiredFieldValidator><br />
<asp:Button ID="btnAdd" runat="server" Text="Add New Category"
    OnClick="btnAdd_Click" />
    </form>
    </section>
</body>
</html>
```

Notes

- The text boxes are used to enter data for a new row.
- The required field validators ensure that the user enters data for each column of a new row.

Figure 14-13   The aspx file for the Category Maintenance application (part 3 of 3)

The code-behind file

Although it would be nice if you could create a robust database application without writing any C# code, you must still write code to insert data into a GridView control and to catch and handle any database or concurrency errors that might occur. Figure 14-14 shows this code for the Category Maintenance application.

As you can see, this code-behind file consists of just three methods. The first, btnAdd_Click, sets the values of the three insert parameters to the values entered by the user. Then, it calls the Insert method of the data source control. If an exception is thrown, an appropriate error message is displayed.

The second method, GridView1_RowUpdated, is called after a row has been updated. This method checks the Exception property of the e argument to determine if an exception has been thrown. If so, an error message is displayed, the ExceptionHandled property is set to True to suppress the exception, and the KeepInEditMode property is set to True to leave the GridView control in edit mode. If an exception hasn't occurred, the e argument's AffectedRows property is checked. If it's zero, it means that a concurrency error has occurred and an appropriate message is displayed.

The third method, GridView1_RowDeleted, is called after a row has been deleted. Like the method that's called after a row is updated, this method checks if an exception has been thrown or if a concurrency error has occurred. The only difference is that this method doesn't set the KeepInEditMode property to True, since the control isn't in edit mode when the Delete button is clicked.

The Default.aspx.cs file

```
public partial class _Default : System.Web.UI.Page
{
    protected void btnAdd_Click(object sender, EventArgs e)
    {
        SqlDataSource1.InsertParameters["CategoryID"].DefaultValue
            = txtID.Text;
        SqlDataSource1.InsertParameters["ShortName"].DefaultValue
            = txtShortName.Text;
        SqlDataSource1.InsertParameters["LongName"].DefaultValue
            = txtLongName.Text;
        try
        {
            SqlDataSource1.Insert();
            txtID.Text = "";
            txtShortName.Text = "";
            txtLongName.Text = "";
        }
        catch (Exception ex)
        {
            lblError.Text = "A database error has occurred.<br /><br />" +
                "Message: " + ex.Message;
        }
    }

    protected void GridView1_RowUpdated(object sender,
        GridViewUpdatedEventArgs e)
    {
        if (e.Exception != null)
        {
            lblError.Text = "A database error has occurred.<br /><br />" +
                "Message: " + e.Exception.Message;
            e.ExceptionHandled = true;
            e.KeepInEditMode = true;
        }
        else if (e.AffectedRows == 0)
        {
            lblError.Text = "Another user may have updated that category." +
                "<br />Please try again.";
        }
    }

    protected void GridView1_RowDeleted(object sender,
        GridViewDeletedEventArgs e)
    {
        if (e.Exception != null)
        {
            lblError.Text = "A database error has occurred.<br /><br />" +
                "Message: " + e.Exception.Message;
            e.ExceptionHandled = true;
        }
        else if (e.AffectedRows == 0)
        {
            lblError.Text = "Another user may have updated that category." +
                "<br />Please try again.";
        }
    }
}
```

Figure 14-14   The code-behind file of the Category Maintenance application

How to work with template fields

Although using bound fields is a convenient way to include bound data in a GridView control, the most flexible way is to use template fields. A *template field* is simply a field that provides one or more templates that are used to render the column. You can include anything you want in these templates, including labels or text boxes, data binding expressions, and validation controls. In fact, including validation controls for editable GridView controls is one of the main reasons for using template fields.

How to create template fields

Figure 14-15 shows how to create template fields. The easiest way to do that is to first create a regular bound field and then convert it to a template field. This changes the BoundField element to a TemplateField element and, more importantly, generates ItemTemplate and EditItemTemplate elements that include labels and text boxes with appropriate binding expressions. In particular, each EditItemTemplate element includes a text box that uses the Bind method to implement two-way binding (please see figure 13-15 for more information about this method).

Once you've converted the bound field to a template, you can edit the template to add any additional elements you want to include, such as validation controls. In the code example in this figure, you can see that I added a RequiredFieldValidator control to the EditItem template for the ShortName column. That way, the user must enter data into the txtGridShortName text box. I also changed the names of the label and the text box that were generated for the Item and EditItem templates from their defaults (Label1 and TextBox1) to lblGridShortName and txtGridShortName.

You can also edit the templates from Design view. To do that, you use the same basic techniques that you use to work with the templates for a DataList control. The main difference is that each bound column in a GridView control has its own templates. In this figure, for example, you can see the EditItem template for the ShortName column.

Although a text box is included in the EditItem template for a column by default, you should know that you can use other types of controls too. For example, you can use a check box to work with a Boolean column, and you can use a Calendar control to work with a date column. You can also use a drop-down list that lets the user select a value from the list. To do that, you must create a separate data source that retrieves the data for the list. Then, you can bind the drop-down list to this data source by setting the DataTextField and DataValueField attributes as shown in the last chapter, and you can bind the drop-down list to a column in the GridView's data source by setting its SelectedValue attribute using the DataBindings dialog box you saw in the last chapter.

How to edit templates

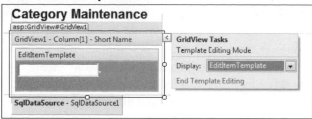

GridView template elements

Element	Description
ItemTemplate	The template used for an individual field.
AlternatingItemTemplate	The template used for alternate rows.
EditItemTemplate	The template used when the row is being edited.
HeaderTemplate	The template used for the header row.
FooterTemplate	The template used for the footer row.

A template field that includes a validation control

```
<asp:TemplateField HeaderText="Short Name">
    <ItemTemplate>
        <asp:Label ID="lblGridShortName" runat="server"
            Text='<%# Bind("ShortName") %>'></asp:Label>
    </ItemTemplate>
    <EditItemTemplate>
        <asp:TextBox ID="txtGridShortName" runat="server"
            width="125px" Text='<%# Bind("ShortName") %>'></asp:TextBox>
        <asp:RequiredFieldValidator
            ID="RequiredFieldValidator5" runat="server"
            ControlToValidate="txtGridShortName"
            ErrorMessage="Short Name is a required field."
            ValidationGroup="Edit">*</asp:RequiredFieldValidator>
    </EditItemTemplate>
    <HeaderStyle HorizontalAlign="Left" />
    <ItemStyle Width="150px" />
</asp:TemplateField>
```

Description

* *Template fields* provide more control over the appearance of the columns in a GridView control than bound fields. A common reason for using template fields is to add validation controls.

* To create a template field, first use the Fields dialog box to create a bound field. Then, click the Convert This Field into a TemplateField link.

* To edit a template, choose Edit Templates from the smart tag menu for the GridView control. Then, select the template you want to edit in the smart tag menu and edit the template by adding text or other controls. You may also want to change the names of the labels and text boxes that were generated when you converted to a template field. When you're finished, choose End Template Editing in the smart tag menu.

Figure 14-15   How to create template fields

The template version
of the Category Maintenance application

Figure 14-16 shows a version of the Category Maintenance application that uses templates instead of bound fields in the GridView control. Then, each EditItem template includes a required field validator. In addition, the page uses a validation summary control to display any error messages that are generated by the required field validators.

The aspx code for the template version

Figure 14-17 shows the aspx code for the template version of the Category Maintenance application. Because this file is similar to the file shown in figure 14-13, this figure shows only the portions that are different. In particular, it shows the code for the GridView control and the ValidationSummary control. Because you've already been introduced to most of this code, I'll just point out a few highlights.

First, the GridView control uses template fields for the ShortName and LongName columns. These templates include required field validators to validate the text box input fields. Here, each validator is assigned to a validation group named Edit. Then, in the CommandField element for the Edit button, the CausesValidation attribute is set to True and the ValidationGroup attribute is set to Edit. As a result, when a row is displayed in edit mode, just the validators that belong to the Edit group will be invoked when the Update button is clicked.

Second, the ErrorMessage attribute of each of the Edit validators provides the error message that's displayed in the ValidationSummary control. For this control, you can see that the ValidationGroup is set to Edit so the right messages will be displayed. In addition, the content of each validator specifies that an asterisk will appear to the right of each field in the GridView control. If you look closely at the screen in the last figure, you can see that these asterisks are displayed in white on the dark row background.

Third, the text boxes in the EditItem templates for the Short Name and Long Name fields include the MaxLength attribute. That way, the user can't enter more characters than are allowed by the data source. This is another advantage of using templates with a GridView control.

Please note that there is one other difference between this version of the application and the previous version that isn't shown in this figure. Because this version uses a validation group for the validators in the GridView control, it must also use a validation group for the validators that are outside of the GridView control. As a result, the three validators for the text boxes as well as the Add New Category button all have a ValidationGroup attribute that assigns them to the New group.

The Category Maintenance application with template fields

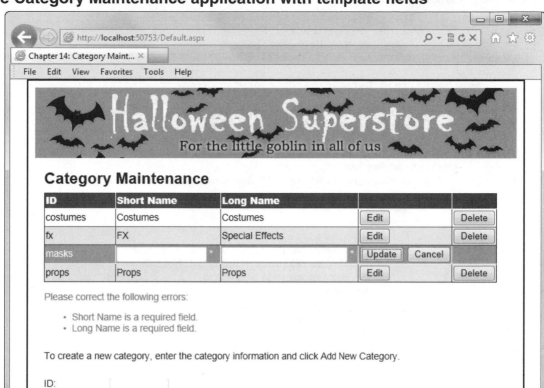

Description

- This version of the Category Maintenance application uses template fields in the GridView control, and the EditItem template for each editable field includes a required field validator.

- A ValidationSummary control is used to display the error messages generated by the required field validators.

- The text boxes in the EditItem templates for the Short Name and Long Name fields include the MaxLength attribute so the user can't enter more characters than are allowed by the data source.

Figure 14-16   The template version of the Category Maintenance application

The Default.aspx file   **Page 1**

```
<asp:GridView ID="GridView1" runat="server"
    AutoGenerateColumns="False" DataKeyNames="CategoryID"
    DataSourceID="SqlDataSource1" ForeColor="Black"
    OnRowDeleted="GridView1_RowDeleted" OnRowUpdated="GridView1_RowUpdated">
    <Columns>
        <asp:BoundField DataField="CategoryID" HeaderText="ID"
            ReadOnly="True" >
        <HeaderStyle HorizontalAlign="Left" />
        <ItemStyle Width="100px" />
        </asp:BoundField>
        <asp:TemplateField HeaderText="Short Name">
            <EditItemTemplate>
                <asp:TextBox ID="txtGridShortName" runat="server"
                    Width="125px" MaxLength="15"
                    Text='<%# Bind("ShortName") %>'>
                </asp:TextBox>
                    <asp:RequiredFieldValidator
                        ID="RequiredFieldValidator4" runat="server"
                        ControlToValidate="txtGridShortName"
                        ErrorMessage="Short Name is a required field."
                        ForeColor="White"
                        ValidationGroup="Edit">*
                    </asp:RequiredFieldValidator>
            </EditItemTemplate>
            <ItemTemplate>
                <asp:Label ID="lblGridShortName" runat="server"
                    Text='<%# Bind("ShortName") %>'>
                </asp:Label>
            </ItemTemplate>
            <HeaderStyle HorizontalAlign="Left" />
            <ItemStyle Width="150px" />
        </asp:TemplateField>
        <asp:TemplateField HeaderText="Long Name">
            <EditItemTemplate>
                <asp:TextBox ID="txtGridLongName" runat="server"
                    Width="180px" MaxLength="50"
                    Text='<%# Bind("LongName") %>'>
                </asp:TextBox>
                    <asp:RequiredFieldValidator
                        ID="RequiredFieldValidator5" runat="server"
                        ControlToValidate="txtGridLongName"
                        ErrorMessage="Long Name is a required field."
                        ForeColor="White"
                        ValidationGroup="Edit">*
                    </asp:RequiredFieldValidator>
            </EditItemTemplate>
            <ItemTemplate>
                <asp:Label ID="lblGridLongName" runat="server"
                    Text='<%# Bind("LongName") %>'>
                </asp:Label>
            </ItemTemplate>
            <HeaderStyle HorizontalAlign="Left" />
            <ItemStyle Width="200px" />
        </asp:TemplateField>
```

Figure 14-17   The aspx code for the template version of the application (part 1 of 2)

The Default.aspx file   Page 2

```
        <asp:CommandField ButtonType="Button" CausesValidation="True"
            ShowEditButton="True" ValidationGroup="Edit" />
        <asp:CommandField ButtonType="Button" CausesValidation="False"
            ShowDeleteButton="True" />
    </Columns>
    <HeaderStyle BackColor="#1C5E55" Font-Bold="True" ForeColor="White" />
    <RowStyle BackColor="White" ForeColor="Black" />
    <AlternatingRowStyle BackColor="#E3EAEB" ForeColor="Black" />
    <EditRowStyle BackColor="#F46D11" ForeColor="White" />
</asp:GridView>
.
.
.
<asp:ValidationSummary ID="ValidationSummary1" runat="server"
    HeaderText="Please correct the following errors:"
    ValidationGroup="Edit" CssClass="error" />
.
.
.
```

Description

- The EditItem templates for the Short Name and Long Name fields include required field validators, which are assigned to a validation group named Edit. This group is also referenced in the code for the Edit button and the ValidationSummary control so only the validators in this group are included.

- The text boxes in the EditItem templates for the Short Name and Long Name fields include the MaxLength attribute so the user can't enter more characters than are allowed by the data source.

- The aspx code that's not shown in this figure is identical to the code in figure 14-13, except that the required field validators for the text boxes for inserting a new category and the Add New Category button specify a validation group named New.

Figure 14-17   The aspx code for the template version of the application (part 2 of 2)

Perspective

The GridView control is ideal for any application that displays a list of items retrieved from a database, and nearly all applications have that need. It's also good for displaying search results and for maintaining tables that consist of just a few columns. In the next chapter, you'll build on your knowledge of the GridView control by learning how to use it with the FormView and DetailsView controls.

Terms

paging	edit mode
command field	template field

Summary

- The GridView control displays data from a data source in a row and column format. The data is rendered as an HTML table.

- By default, the Gridview control displays one column for each column in the data source, but you can change those fields and add other types of fields to the control, like button, command, and hyperlink fields. Then, you can use style elements to format the fields.

- By default, the GridView control lets the users sort the rows based on the data in the columns. However, you do have to enable this feature and remove the sort expressions from those columns for which you don't want to allow sorting.

- To enable *paging* for a GridView control, you just need to set one attribute for the control. Then, you can customize the paging by adding a PagerSettings element to the aspx code for the control.

- *Command fields* are used to add buttons to a GridView control that let the users edit, delete, or select data without requiring any C# code. To insert data, you have to use input controls such as text boxes and a button that users can click to start the insert operation. Then, the event handler for the click event of that button adds the data to the data source that the GridView control is bound to.

- Although the GridView control provides many features automatically, you have to write C# code for handling such things as data validation, database exceptions, and concurrency errors. To do that, you can use the events that are raised by a GridView control, like the RowUpdating and RowUpdated events.

- A *template field* provides one or more templates for rendering a column. These fields can contain standard server controls, binding expressions, and validation controls. One common use of template fields is to provide the validation controls that validate the data in an editable GridView control.

Exercise 14-1	Create a Customer List application

In this exercise, you'll develop a page that displays customers in a GridView control that includes sorting and paging. When you're done, the page should look like this:

Create the GridView control and the SQL data source

1. Open the Ex14CustomerList application in the aspnet45_cs directory. This application contains the starting page and the database, image, and style sheet used by the page.

2. Add a GridView control to the form and change its name to grdCustomers. Then, create a data source for the control that retrieves the LastName, FirstName, State, and City columns from the Customers table sorted by LastName.

3. Use the AutoFormat dialog box to apply the Simple scheme to the control.

4. Use the Fields dialog box to left-align the header for each field and to set the column widths to 175, 150, 75, and 150 respectively.

5. Run the application to see how it looks. Notice that all the customers are displayed on a single page.

Add paging to the GridView control

6. Display the smart tag menu for the GridView control and check the Enable Paging option.

7. Set the Mode property in the PagerSettings group for the GridView control to NextPreviousFirstLast. In addition, set the BackColor property in the PagerStyle group so the background color of the pager area is the same as the background color of the header.

8. Run the application again, and use the paging controls to display different pages.

Add sorting to the GridView control

9. Display the smart tag menu for the GridView control and check the Enable Sorting option.

10. Remove the sort expressions from the FirstName and City fields, and set the sort expression for the State field so it sorts by city within state.

11. Run the application, and click the State heading. The rows should be sorted by city in ascending sequence within state in ascending sequence. Notice that the color of the sorted column changes.

12. Click the State heading again. This time, the rows should be sorted by city in descending sequence within state in ascending sequence, and the column should be displayed in a different color.

13. Close the browser, and delete the four Sorted style elements that were added to the GridView control when you applied the scheme. You can also delete any other style elements that aren't used by this application if you'd like.

14. Run the application one more time, and click the State heading. This time, the formatting shouldn't change. Continue experimenting if you want, and then close the browser.

15

How to use the DetailsView and FormView controls

In this chapter, you'll learn how to use the DetailsView and FormView controls. Although both of these controls are designed to work with the GridView control to display the details of the item selected in that control, they can also be used on their own or in combination with other types of list controls such as drop-down lists or list boxes.

How to use the DetailsView control

The following topics present the basics of working with the DetailsView control. However, much of what you'll learn in these topics applies to the FormView control as well.

An introduction to the DetailsView control

As figure 15-1 shows, the DetailsView control is designed to display the data for a single item of a data source. To use this control effectively, you must provide some way for the user to select which data item to display. The most common way to do that is to use the DetailsView control in combination with another control such as a GridView control or a drop-down list. At the top of this figure, you can see how the DetailsView control works with a drop-down list, and you'll see how it works with a GridView control later in this chapter.

Alternatively, you can enable paging for the DetailsView control. Then, a row of paging controls appears at the bottom of the DetailsView control, and the user can select a data item using those controls. You'll learn how this works in figure 15-3.

As the code example in this figure shows, you use the DataSourceID attribute to specify the data source that a DetailsView control should be bound to. Then, the Fields element contains a set of child elements that define the individual fields to be displayed by the DetailsView control. This is similar to the way the Columns element for a GridView control works.

A DetailsView control can be displayed in one of three modes. In ReadOnly mode, the data for the current data source row is displayed but can't be modified. In Edit mode, the user can modify the data for the current row. And in Insert mode, the user can enter data that will be inserted into the data source as a new row.

A DetailsView control that displays data for a selected product

Choose a product:	Skull Fogger ▼

Product ID:	skullfog01
Name:	Skull Fogger
Short Description:	2,800 cubic foot fogger
Long Description:	This fogger puts out a whopping 2,800 cubic feet of fog per minute. Comes with a 10-foot remote control.
Category ID:	fx
Image File:	skullfog1.jpg
Unit Price:	39.9500
On Hand:	50

The aspx code for the DetailsView control shown above

```
<asp:DetailsView ID="DetailsView1" runat="server" AutoGenerateRows="False"
    DataKeyNames="ProductID" DataSourceID="SqlDataSource2" Width="450px">
    <Fields>
        <asp:BoundField DataField="ProductID" HeaderText="Product ID:"
            ReadOnly="True">
            <HeaderStyle Width="125px" />
            <ItemStyle Width="325px" />
        </asp:BoundField>
        <asp:BoundField DataField="Name" HeaderText="Name:" />
        <asp:BoundField DataField="ShortDescription"
            HeaderText="Short Description:" />
        <asp:BoundField DataField="LongDescription"
            HeaderText="Long Description:" />
        <asp:BoundField DataField="CategoryID" HeaderText="Category ID:" />
        <asp:BoundField DataField="ImageFile" HeaderText="Image File:" />
        <asp:BoundField DataField="UnitPrice" HeaderText="Unit Price:" />
        <asp:BoundField DataField="OnHand" HeaderText="On Hand:" />
    </Fields>
</asp:DetailsView>
```

Three modes of the DetailsView control

Mode	Description
ReadOnly	Used to display an item from the data source.
Edit	Used to edit an item in the data source.
Insert	Used to insert a new item into the data source.

Description

- The DetailsView control displays data for a single row of a data source. It is typically used in combination with a drop-down list or GridView control that is used to select the item to be displayed.

- The DetailsView element includes a Fields element that contains a BoundField element for each field retrieved from the data source.

- You can edit the fields collection by choosing Edit Fields from the smart tag menu of a DetailsView control.

Figure 15-1   An introduction to the DetailsView control

Attributes and child elements for the DetailsView control

The tables in figure 15-2 list the attributes and child elements you can use to declare a DetailsView control. The first table lists the attributes you're most likely to use for this control. You can use the DataKeyNames attribute to list the names of the primary key fields for the data source. And you can set the AutoGenerateRows attribute to True if you want the DetailsView control to automatically generate data fields. Then, you'll want to delete the Fields element that was added when you created the DetailsView control.

By the way, there are many other attributes you can use on the DetailsView element to specify the control's layout and formatting. For example, you can include attributes like Height, Width, BackColor, and ForeColor. To see all of the attributes that are available, you can use the HTML Editor's IntelliSense feature.

The second table in this figure lists the child elements that you can use between the start and end tags of the DetailsView element. Most of these elements provide styles and templates that control the formatting and content for the different parts of the DetailsView control. Like the DataList and GridView controls, the DetailsView control is rendered as a table. So it's best to use the style elements to format the control rather than using CSS. When you use style elements, remember that you can store them in a skin.

The Fields element can contain any of the child elements listed in the third table of this figure. These elements describe the individual fields that are displayed by the DetailsView control. Although this figure doesn't show it, these child elements can themselves include child elements to specify formatting information. For example, you can include HeaderStyle and ItemStyle as child elements of a BoundField element to control the formatting for the header and item sections of a bound field. Here again, you can use the HTML Editor's IntelliSense feature to see what child elements are available and what attributes they support.

Note that when Visual Studio generates a BoundField element for a DetailsView control, it includes a SortExpression attribute just as it does for a GridView control. Because the DetailsView control doesn't support sorting, though, you can delete this attribute if you want to simplify the aspx code.

How to define the fields in a DetailsView control

Just like when you create a GridView control, one BoundField element is created for each column in the data source when you create a DetailsView control. Then, you can work with those fields or create additional fields using the Fields dialog box you saw in figure 14-2 of chapter 14. To display this dialog box, you choose the Edit Fields command from the control's smart tag menu. You can also use the HTML editor to create these fields manually. Or you can use the Add Field dialog box as described later in this chapter.

DetailsView control attributes

Attribute	Description
DataSourceID	The ID of the data source to bind the DetailsView control to.
DataKeyNames	A list of field names that form the primary key for the data source.
AutoGenerateRows	If True, a row is automatically generated for each field in the data source. If False, you must define the rows in the Fields element.
DefaultMode	Sets the initial mode of the DetailsView control. Valid options are Edit, Insert, or ReadOnly.
AllowPaging	Set to True to allow paging.

DetailsView child elements

Element	Description
Fields	The fields that are displayed by a DetailsView control.
RowStyle	The style used for data rows in ReadOnly mode.
AlternatingRowStyle	The style used for alternate rows.
EditRowStyle	The style used for data rows in Edit mode.
InsertRowStyle	The style used for data rows in Insert mode.
CommandRowStyle	The style used for command rows.
EmptyDataRowStyle	The style used for data rows when the data source is empty.
EmptyDataTemplate	The template used when the data source is empty.
HeaderStyle	The style used for the header row.
HeaderTemplate	The template used for the header row.
FooterStyle	The style used for the footer row.
FooterTemplate	The template used for the footer row.
PagerSettings	The settings used to control the pager row.
PagerStyle	The style used for the pager row.
PagerTemplate	The template used for the pager row.

Fields child elements

Element	Description
asp:BoundField	A field bound to a data source column.
asp:ButtonField	A field that displays a button.
asp:CheckBoxField	A field that displays a check box.
asp:CommandField	A field that contains command buttons.
asp:HyperlinkField	A field that displays a hyperlink.
asp:ImageField	A field that displays an image.
asp:TemplateField	A column with custom content.

Figure 15-2   Attributes and child elements for the DetailsView control

How to enable paging

Like the GridView control, the DetailsView control supports paging. As figure 15-3 shows, a row of paging controls is displayed at the bottom of the DetailsView control when you set the AllowPaging attribute to True. Then, you can specify the paging mode by including a PagerSettings element, and you can include PagerStyle and PagerTemplate elements to specify the formatting and content of the pager controls.

Note that if the data source contains more than a few dozen items, paging isn't a practical way to provide for navigation. In most cases, then, a DetailsView control is associated with a list control that is used to select the item to be displayed. You'll learn how to create pages that work this way in the next figure.

A DetailsView control that allows paging

Product ID:	bats01
Name:	Flying Bats
Short Description:	Bats flying in front of moon
Long Description:	Bats flying in front of a full moon make for an eerie spectacle.
Category ID:	props
Image File:	cool1.jpg
Unit Price:	69.9900
On Hand:	25

<<<>>>

The aspx code for the DetailsView control shown above

```
<asp:DetailsView ID="DetailsView1" runat="server" AutoGenerateRows="False"
    DataKeyNames="ProductID" DataSourceID="SqlDataSource1"
    Width="450px" AllowPaging="True">
<PagerSettings Mode="NextPreviousFirstLast" />
<Fields>
    <asp:BoundField DataField="ProductID" HeaderText="ProductID"
        ReadOnly="True">
        <HeaderStyle Width="125px" />
        <ItemStyle Width="325px" />
    </asp:BoundField>
    <asp:BoundField DataField="Name" HeaderText="Name:" />
    <asp:BoundField DataField="ShortDescription"
        HeaderText="Short Description:" />
    <asp:BoundField DataField="LongDescription"
        HeaderText="Long Description:" />
    <asp:BoundField DataField="CategoryID"
        HeaderText="Category ID: " />
    <asp:BoundField DataField="ImageFile" HeaderText="Image File:" />
    <asp:BoundField DataField="UnitPrice" HeaderText="Unit Price:" />
    <asp:BoundField DataField="OnHand" HeaderText="On Hand:" />
</Fields>
</asp:DetailsView>
```

Description

- The DetailsView control supports paging. Then, you can move from one item to the next by using the paging controls. This works much the same as it does for a GridView control, except that data from only one row is displayed at a time.

- For more information about paging, please refer to figure 14-6 in chapter 14.

Figure 15-3   How to enable paging

How to create a Master/Detail page

As figure 15-4 shows, a *Master/Detail page* is a page that displays a list of data items from a data source along with the details for one of the items selected from the list. The list of items can be displayed by any control that allows the user to select an item, including a drop-down list or a GridView control. Then, you can use a DetailsView control to display the details for the selected item. The page shown in figure 15-1 is an example of a Master/Detail page in which the master list is displayed as a drop-down list and a DetailsView control is used to display the details for the selected item.

A Master/Detail page typically uses two data sources. The first retrieves the items to be displayed by the control that contains the list of data items. For efficiency's sake, this data source should retrieve only the data columns necessary to display the list. For example, the data source for the drop-down list in figure 15-1 only needs to retrieve the ProductName and ProductID columns from the Products table in the Halloween database.

The second data source provides the data for the selected item. It usually uses a parameter to specify which row should be retrieved from the database. In the example in this figure, the data source uses a parameter that's bound to the drop-down list. That way, this data source automatically retrieves the data for the product that's selected by the drop-down list.

A Master/Detail page typically contains:

- A control that lets the user choose an item to display, such as a drop-down list or a GridView control.

- A data source that retrieves all of the items to be displayed in the list. The control that contains the list of data items should be bound to this data source.

- A DetailsView control that displays data for the item selected by the user.

- A data source that retrieves the data for the item selected by the user. The DetailsView control should be bound to this data source. To retrieve the selected item, this data source can use a parameter that's bound to the SelectedValue property of the control that contains the list of data items.

A SqlDataSource control with a parameter that's bound to a drop-down list

```
<asp:SqlDataSource ID="SqlDataSource2" runat="server"
    ConnectionString="<%$ ConnectionStrings:HalloweenConnection %>"
    SelectCommand="SELECT [ProductID], [Name], [ShortDescription],
        [LongDescription], [CategoryID], [ImageFile], [UnitPrice], [OnHand]
        FROM [Products]
        WHERE ([ProductID] = @ProductID)">
    <SelectParameters>
        <asp:ControlParameter ControlID="ddlProducts" Name="ProductID"
            PropertyName="SelectedValue" Type="String" />
    </SelectParameters>
</asp:SqlDataSource>
```

Description

- A *Master/Detail page* is a page that displays a list of items from a database along with the details of one item from the list. The DetailsView control is often used to display the details portion of a Master/Detail page.

- The list portion of a Master/Detail page can be displayed by any control that contains a list of data items, including a drop-down list or a GridView control.

- A Master/Detail page usually includes two data sources, one for the master list and the other for the DetailsView control.

Figure 15-4   How to create a Master/Detail page

How to update the data in a DetailsView control

Besides displaying data for a specific item from a data source, you can also use a DetailsView control to edit, insert, and delete items. You'll learn how to do that in the following topics.

An introduction to command buttons

Much like the GridView control, the DetailsView control uses command buttons to let the user edit and delete data. Thus, the DetailsView control provides Edit, Delete, Update, and Cancel buttons. In addition, the DetailsView control lets the user insert data, so it provides for two more buttons. The New button places the DetailsView control into Insert mode, and the Insert button accepts the data entered by the user and writes it to the data source. These command buttons are summarized in figure 15-5.

There are two ways to provide the command buttons for a DetailsView control. The easiest way is to use the AutoGenerate*xxx*Button attributes, which are listed in the second table and illustrated in the code example. However, when you use these attributes, you have no control over the appearance of the buttons. For that, you must use command fields as described in the next figure.

A DetailsView control with automatically generated command buttons

Product ID:	pow01
Name:	Austin Powers
Short Description:	Austin Powers costume
Long Description:	Be the most shagadelic guest at this year's party, baby.
Category ID:	costumes
Image File:	powers1.jpg
Unit Price:	79.9900
On Hand:	25
Edit Delete New	

Command buttons

Button	Description
Edit	Places the DetailsView control in Edit mode.
Delete	Deletes the current item and leaves the DetailsView control in ReadOnly mode.
New	Places the DetailsView control in Insert mode.
Update	Displayed only in Edit mode. Updates the data source, then returns to ReadOnly mode.
Insert	Displayed only in Insert mode. Inserts the data, then returns to ReadOnly mode.
Cancel	Displayed in Edit or Insert mode. Cancels the operation and returns to ReadOnly mode.

Attributes that generate command buttons

Attribute	Description
`AutoGenerateDeleteButton`	Generates a Delete button.
`AutoGenerateEditButton`	Generates an Edit button.
`AutoGenerateInsertButton`	Generates a New button.

A DetailsView element that automatically generates command buttons

```
<asp:DetailsView ID="DetailsView1" runat="server"
    DataSourceID="SqlDataSource2" DataKeyNames="ProductID"
    AutoGenerateRows="False"
    AutoGenerateDeleteButton="True"
    AutoGenerateEditButton="True"
    AutoGenerateInsertButton="True">
</asp:DetailsView>
```

Description

- The DetailsView control supports six different command buttons.
- You can use the AutoGenerateDeleteButton, AutoGenerateEditButton, and AutoGenerateInsertButton attributes to automatically generate command buttons.
- To customize command button appearance, use command fields instead of automatically generated buttons as described in the next figure.

Figure 15-5   An introduction to command buttons

How to add command buttons

Like the GridView control, the DetailsView control lets you use CommandField elements to specify the command buttons that should be displayed by the control. One way to do that is to use the Add Field dialog box shown in figure 15-6 to add a command field to a DetailsView control. Of course, you can also use the Edit Fields dialog box to add command fields, or you can use the HTML Editor to code the CommandField elements manually.

To create a command button using the Add Field dialog box, you select CommandField as the field type. When you do, four check boxes appear that let you select which command buttons you want to show in the command field. In addition, a drop-down list lets you choose whether the command buttons should be displayed as buttons or hyperlinks.

When you first display the Add Field dialog box for a command field, you'll notice that the Show Cancel Button check box is disabled. That's because this button can only be used in conjunction with the New/Insert and Edit/Update buttons. When you select one of these buttons, then, the Show Cancel Button check box is enabled and it's selected by default. That makes sense because you'll typically want to allow the user to cancel out of an insert or edit operation.

Note that the CommandField element includes attributes that let you specify the text or image to be displayed and whether the button causes validation. For more information about using these attributes, please refer back to chapter 14.

Before I go on, you should realize that you can use the Add Field dialog box to create any of the elements shown in the third table in figure 15-2. To do that, you just select the type of field you want to create from the drop-down list at the top of the dialog box. Then, the appropriate options for that field type are displayed. If you experiment with this, you shouldn't have any trouble figuring out how it works.

The Add Field dialog box for adding a command field

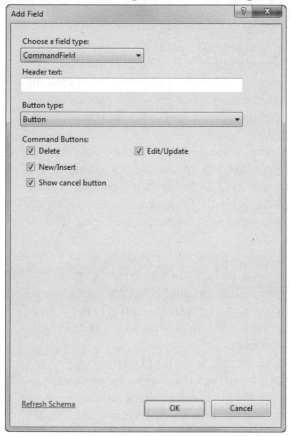

Code generated by the above dialog box

```
<asp:CommandField ButtonType="Button"
    ShowDeleteButton="True"
    ShowEditButton="True"
    ShowInsertButton="True" />
```

Description

- You can add command buttons to a DetailsView control to let the user update, insert, and delete data.

- The command buttons for a DetailsView control are similar to the command buttons for a GridView control. However, the DetailsView control doesn't provide a Select button, and it does provide New and Insert buttons. For more information about command buttons, please refer to figure 14-9 in chapter 14.

- To display the Add Field dialog box, choose Add New Field from the smart tag menu of the DetailsView control.

Figure 15-6   How to add command buttons

How to use events raised by the DetailsView control

Figure 15-7 lists the events that are raised by the DetailsView control. As you can see, these events are similar to the events raised by the GridView control. Most of these events come in pairs: one that's raised before an operation occurs, and another that's raised after the operation completes. For example, the ItemDeleting event is raised before an item is deleted, and the ItemDeleted event is raised after an item has been deleted.

As with the GridView control, the most common reason to handle the before events for the DetailsView control is to provide data validation. For example, when the user clicks the Update button, you can handle the ItemUpdating event to make sure the user has entered correct data. Then, you can set the e argument's Cancel property to True if the user hasn't entered correct data. This cancels the update.

The after-action events let you check that database operations have completed successfully. To do that, you need to check for two types of errors as illustrated in the example in this figure. First, you should check for database exceptions by testing the Exception property of the e argument. If it is not null, a database exception has occurred. Then, you should display an appropriate error message to let the user know about the problem.

If the data source uses optimistic concurrency, you should also check to make sure there hasn't been a concurrency error. You can do that by testing the AffectedRows property of the e argument. If a concurrency error has occurred, this property will be set to zero meaning that no rows have been changed. Then, you can display an appropriate error message.

If no errors occurred during the update operation, the ItemUpdated event shown in this figure ends by calling the DataBind method for the drop-down list control. This is necessary because view state is enabled for this control. As a result, this control will continue to display the old data unless you call its DataBind method to refresh its data. If view state were disabled for this control, the DataBind call wouldn't be necessary.

Events raised by the DetailsView control

Event	Description
ItemCommand	Raised when a button is clicked.
ItemCreated	Raised when an item is created.
DataBound	Raised when data binding completes for an item.
ItemDeleted	Raised when an item has been deleted.
ItemDeleting	Raised when an item is about to be deleted.
ItemInserted	Raised when an item has been inserted.
ItemInserting	Raised when an item is about to be inserted.
ItemUpdated	Raised when an item has been updated.
ItemUpdating	Raised when an item is about to be updated.
PageIndexChanged	Raised when the index of the displayed item has changed.
PageIndexChanging	Raised when the index of the displayed item is about to change.

An event handler for the ItemUpdated event

```
protected void DetailsView1_ItemUpdated(
    object sender, DetailsViewUpdatedEventArgs e)
{
    if (e.Exception != null)
    {
        lblError.Text = "A database error has occurred. " +
            "Message: " + e.Exception.Message;
        e.ExceptionHandled = true;
    }
    else if (e.AffectedRows == 0)
    {
        lblError.Text = "Another user may have updated that product. "
            + "Please try again.";
    }
    else
    {
        ddlProducts.DataBind();
    }
}
```

Description

- Like the GridView control, the DetailsView control raises events that you can use to test for database exceptions and concurrency errors.

- To determine if a SQL exception has occurred, test the Exception property of the e argument. If an exception has occurred, you can set the ExceptionHandled property to True to suppress the exception. You can also set the KeepInEditMode or KeepInInsertMode property to True to keep the control in Edit or Insert mode.

- If the AffectedRows property of the e argument is zero and an exception has not been thrown, a concurrency error has probably occurred.

- If the DetailsView control is used on a Master/Detail page, you should call the DataBind method of the master list control after a successful insert, update, or delete.

Figure 15-7   How to use events raised by the DetailsView control

How to create template fields

Like the GridView control, you can use template fields to control the appearance of the fields in a DetailsView control. You can do that to add validation controls or to use controls other than text boxes as described in the last chapter or to modify the text boxes that are displayed by default. Figure 15-8 illustrates how this works.

At the top of this figure, you can see two DetailsView controls displayed in Edit mode. The first control uses the default BoundField elements. Here, you can see that the text box for the long description isn't big enough to display all of the data in this column for the selected product, which makes it more difficult for the user to modify this field. In addition, to change the category, the user must enter the category ID. That makes it more likely that the user will enter a value that isn't valid.

The second DetailsView control illustrates how you can use templates to make it easier for the user to work with the data. Here, all of the text boxes have been resized so they're appropriate for the data they will display. In particular, the text box for the long description has been changed to a multi-line text box. In addition, the text box for the category ID has been replaced by a drop-down list that displays the category name. This control is bound to a separate data source that retrieves the category IDs and category names from the Categories table.

To create template fields for a DetailsView control, you use the same techniques you use to create template fields for a GridView control. That is, you convert bound fields to template fields, you switch to template-editing mode, and you select the template you want to edit. The table in this figure lists the five templates that are available for the template fields in a DetailsView control. In most cases, you'll define just the Item, EditItem, and InsertItem templates as shown in the code example in this figure.

The template field shown here is for the Name column of the Products table. Notice that in addition to setting the width of the text boxes for this column in the EditItem and InsertItem templates, I also set the MaxLength attribute. That way, the user can't enter more characters than are allowed by the Name column. As you'll see in the aspx code for the Product Maintenance application that's presented next, I used this same technique to restrict the number of characters that can be entered for the ProductID, ShortDescription, LongDescription, and ImageFile columns.

A DetailsView control in Edit mode without and with templates

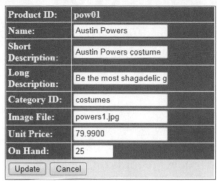 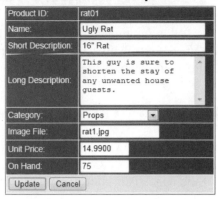

DetailsView template elements

Element	Description
ItemTemplate	The template used for an individual field.
AlternatingItemTemplate	The template used for alternating fields.
EditItemTemplate	The template used for a field in Edit mode.
InsertItemTemplate	The template used for a field in Insert mode.
HeaderTemplate	The template used for the header text for a field.

The aspx code for a custom template field

```
<asp:TemplateField HeaderText="Name:">
    <ItemTemplate>
        <asp:Label ID="Label8" runat="server" Text='<%# Bind("Name") %>'>
        </asp:Label>
    </ItemTemplate>
    <EditItemTemplate>
        <asp:TextBox ID="txtName" runat="server" Text='<%# Bind("Name") %>'
            Width="200px" MaxLength="50">
        </asp:TextBox>
    </EditItemTemplate>
    <InsertItemTemplate>
        <asp:TextBox ID="txtName" runat="server" Text='<%# Bind("Name") %>'
            Width="200px" MaxLength="50">
        </asp:TextBox>
    </InsertItemTemplate>
    <HeaderStyle HorizontalAlign="Left" Width="150px" />
    <ItemStyle Width="250px" />
</asp:TemplateField>
```

Description

- You can use template fields to control the appearance of the fields in a DetailsView control using the same techniques you use to work with template fields in a GridView control. See figure 14-15 in chapter 14 for more information.

Figure 15-8   How to create template fields

The Product Maintenance application

The following topics present an application that uses GridView and DetailsView controls in a Master/Detail page to maintain the Products table in the Halloween database.

The operation of the application

Figure 15-9 shows the operation of the Product Maintenance application. This application uses a GridView control to list the product records on the left side of the page. This control uses paging to allow the user to scroll through the entire Products table.

When the user clicks the Select button for a product, the details for that product are displayed in the DetailsView control on the right side of the page. Then, the user can use the Edit or Delete button to edit or delete the selected product. The user can also click the New button to insert a new product.

The aspx file

Figure 15-10 shows the Default.aspx file for the Product Maintenance application. In part 1, you can see the GridView control that displays the products as well as the data source for this control. Notice that the SelectedIndex attribute of the GridView control is set to 0. That way, the information for the first product will be displayed in the DetailsView control when the page is first displayed.

The DetailsView control is shown in parts 2 and 3 of the listing. Here, the DetailsView element includes the attributes that control the overall appearance of the control. I generated most of these attributes by applying a scheme to the DetailsView control, then editing the attributes to change the colors. You can also see that the scheme added RowStyle, EditRowStyle, and FooterStyle elements to the control. Since an InsertRowStyle element isn't included, this style will default to the EditRowStyle.

To make it easier for the user to work with the data in the DetailsView control, all of the bound fields have been converted to template fields. Then, the EditItem and InsertItem templates for these fields were modified so the fields are displayed as shown in the second DetailsView control in figure 15-8. In addition, required field validators were added for each field except for the category ID and image file fields, and compare validators were added for the unit price and on hand fields. Finally, a command field that provides for Edit, Delete, and New buttons was added.

The Product Maintenance application

Description

- The Product Maintenance application uses a GridView control and a DetailsView control to let the user update the data in the Products table.

- To select a product, the user locates the product in the GridView control and clicks the Select button. This displays the details for the product in the DetailsView control. Then, the user can click the Edit button to change the product data or the Delete button to delete the product.

- To add a new product to the database, the user clicks the New button in the DetailsView control. Then, the user can enter the data for the new product and click the Insert button.

Figure 15-9   The Product Maintenance application

The Default.aspx file   **Page 1**

```
<%@ Page Language="C#" AutoEventWireup="true" CodeFile="Default.aspx.cs"
Inherits="_Default" %>

<!DOCTYPE html>

<html xmlns="http://www.w3.org/1999/xhtml">
<head id="Head1" runat="server">
  <title>Chapter 15: Product Maintenance</title>
  <link href="Main.css" rel="stylesheet" type="text/css" />
</head>
<body>
    <header>
        <img src="Images/banner.jpg" alt="Halloween Store" />
    </header>
    <section>
    <form id="form1" runat="server">
      <div id="gridview">
        <asp:GridView ID="GridView1" runat="server" AllowPaging="True"
            DataKeyNames="ProductID" DataSourceID="SqlDataSource1"
            AutoGenerateColumns="False" SelectedIndex="0"
            CellPadding="4" GridLines="None" ForeColor="Black" Width="320px">
          <Columns>
            <asp:BoundField DataField="ProductID" HeaderText="ID"
                ReadOnly="True">
              <HeaderStyle HorizontalAlign="Left" />
              <ItemStyle Width="75px" />
            </asp:BoundField>
            <asp:BoundField DataField="Name" HeaderText="Name">
              <HeaderStyle HorizontalAlign="Left" />
              <ItemStyle Width="150px" />
            </asp:BoundField>
            <asp:BoundField DataField="CategoryID" HeaderText="Category">
              <HeaderStyle HorizontalAlign="Left" />
              <ItemStyle Width="95px" />
            </asp:BoundField>
            <asp:CommandField ButtonType="Button" ShowSelectButton="True" />
          </Columns>
          <HeaderStyle BackColor="#1C5E55" Font-Bold="True" ForeColor="White" />
          <RowStyle BackColor="White" ForeColor="Black" />
          <AlternatingRowStyle BackColor="#E3EAEB" ForeColor="Black" />
          <SelectedRowStyle BackColor="#F46D11" ForeColor="White" />
          <PagerStyle BackColor="#1C5E55" ForeColor="White"
              HorizontalAlign="Center" />
        </asp:GridView>
        <asp:SqlDataSource ID="SqlDataSource1" runat="server"
            ConnectionString="<%$ ConnectionStrings:HalloweenConnectionString %>"
            SelectCommand="SELECT [ProductID], [Name], [CategoryID]
                FROM [Products] ORDER BY [ProductID]">
        </asp:SqlDataSource>
      </div>
```

Figure 15-10   The aspx file for the Product Maintenance application (part 1 of 4)

The Default.aspx file   **Page 2**

```
<div id="detailsview">
  <asp:DetailsView ID="DetailsView1" runat="server"
      DataSourceID="SqlDataSource2"  DataKeyNames="ProductID"
      Height="50px" Width="350px" AutoGenerateRows="False"
      BackColor="White" BorderColor="White" BorderStyle="Ridge"
      BorderWidth="2px" CellPadding="3" CellSpacing="1"
      GridLines="None" OnItemDeleted="DetailsView1_ItemDeleted"
      OnItemDeleting="DetailsView1_ItemDeleting"
      OnItemInserted="DetailsView1_ItemInserted"
      OnItemUpdated="DetailsView1_ItemUpdated">
    <Fields>
      <asp:TemplateField HeaderText="Product ID:">
        <ItemTemplate>
          <asp:Label ID="Label4" runat="server"
              Text='<%# Bind("ProductID") %>'></asp:Label>
        </ItemTemplate>
        <EditItemTemplate>
          <asp:Label ID="Label1" runat="server"
              Text='<%# Eval("ProductID") %>'></asp:Label>
        </EditItemTemplate>
        <InsertItemTemplate>
          <asp:TextBox ID="txtID" runat="server"
              Text='<%# Bind("ProductID") %>' Width="100px"
              MaxLength="10">
          </asp:TextBox>
          <asp:RequiredFieldValidator
              ID="RequiredFieldValidator1" runat="server"
              ControlToValidate="txtID"
              ErrorMessage="Product ID is a required field.">*
          </asp:RequiredFieldValidator>
        </InsertItemTemplate>
        <HeaderStyle HorizontalAlign="Left" Width="130px" />
        <ItemStyle Width="220px" />
      </asp:TemplateField>
      .
      .
      .
      <asp:TemplateField HeaderText="Category:">
        <ItemTemplate>
          <asp:Label ID="Label3" runat="server"
              Text='<%# Bind("CategoryID") %>'></asp:Label>
        </ItemTemplate>
        <EditItemTemplate>
          <asp:DropDownList ID="ddlCategory" runat="server"
              DataSourceID="SqlDataSource3"
              DataTextField="LongName" DataValueField="CategoryID"
              SelectedValue='<%# Bind("CategoryID") %>' Width="130px">
          </asp:DropDownList>
        </EditItemTemplate>
        <InsertItemTemplate>
          <asp:DropDownList ID="ddlCategory" runat="server"
              DataSourceID="SqlDataSource3"
              DataTextField="LongName" DataValueField="CategoryID"
              SelectedValue='<%# Bind("CategoryID") %>' Width="130px">
          </asp:DropDownList>
        </InsertItemTemplate>
        <HeaderStyle HorizontalAlign="Left" Width="130px" />
        <ItemStyle Width="220px" />
        .
        .
```

Figure 15-10   The aspx file for the Product Maintenance application (part 2 of 4)

The Default.aspx file   **Page 3**

```
            <asp:CommandField ButtonType="Button"
                ShowDeleteButton="True"
                ShowEditButton="True"
                ShowInsertButton="True" />
        </Fields>
        <RowStyle BackColor="#E3EAEB" ForeColor="Black" />
        <EditRowStyle BackColor="#1C5E55" ForeColor="White" />
        <FooterStyle BackColor="#E3EAEB" />
    </asp:DetailsView>
    <asp:SqlDataSource ID="SqlDataSource2" runat="server"
        ConflictDetection="CompareAllValues"
        ConnectionString="<%$ ConnectionStrings:HalloweenConnectionString %>"
        OldValuesParameterFormatString="original_{0}"
        SelectCommand="SELECT [ProductID], [Name], [ShortDescription],
            [LongDescription], [CategoryID], [ImageFile],
            [UnitPrice], [OnHand]
          FROM [Products]
          WHERE ([ProductID] = @ProductID)"
        DeleteCommand="DELETE FROM [Products]
          WHERE [ProductID] = @original_ProductID
            AND [Name] = @original_Name
            AND [ShortDescription] = @original_ShortDescription
            AND [LongDescription] = @original_LongDescription
            AND [CategoryID] = @original_CategoryID
            AND (([ImageFile] = @original_ImageFile)
             OR (ImageFile IS NULL AND @original_ImageFile IS NULL))
            AND [UnitPrice] = @original_UnitPrice
            AND [OnHand] = @original_OnHand"
        InsertCommand="INSERT INTO [Products] ([ProductID], [Name],
            [ShortDescription], [LongDescription], [CategoryID],
            [ImageFile], [UnitPrice], [OnHand])
          VALUES (@ProductID, @Name, @ShortDescription,
            @LongDescription, @CategoryID, @ImageFile,
            @UnitPrice, @OnHand)"
        UpdateCommand="UPDATE [Products] SET [Name] = @Name,
            [ShortDescription] = @ShortDescription,
            [LongDescription] = @LongDescription,
            [CategoryID] = @CategoryID,
            [ImageFile] = @ImageFile,
            [UnitPrice] = @UnitPrice,
            [OnHand] = @OnHand
          WHERE [ProductID] = @original_ProductID
            AND [Name] = @original_Name
            AND [ShortDescription] = @original_ShortDescription
            AND [LongDescription] = @original_LongDescription
            AND [CategoryID] = @original_CategoryID
            AND (([ImageFile] = @original_ImageFile)
             OR (ImageFile IS NULL AND @original_ImageFile IS NULL))
            AND [UnitPrice] = @original_UnitPrice
            AND [OnHand] = @original_OnHand">
        <SelectParameters>
          <asp:ControlParameter ControlID="GridView1" Name="ProductID"
              PropertyName="SelectedValue" Type="String" />
        </SelectParameters>
```

Figure 15-10   The aspx file for the Product Maintenance application (part 3 of 4)

The Default.aspx file Page 4

```
            <DeleteParameters>
                <asp:Parameter Name="original_ProductID" Type="String" />
                <asp:Parameter Name="original_Name" Type="String" />
                <asp:Parameter Name="original_ShortDescription" Type="String" />
                <asp:Parameter Name="original_LongDescription" Type="String" />
                <asp:Parameter Name="original_CategoryID" Type="String" />
                <asp:Parameter Name="original_ImageFile" Type="String" />
                <asp:Parameter Name="original_UnitPrice" Type="Decimal" />
                <asp:Parameter Name="original_OnHand" Type="Int32" />
            </DeleteParameters>
            <UpdateParameters>
                <asp:Parameter Name="Name" Type="String" />
                <asp:Parameter Name="ShortDescription" Type="String" />
                <asp:Parameter Name="LongDescription" Type="String" />
                <asp:Parameter Name="CategoryID" Type="String" />
                <asp:Parameter Name="ImageFile" Type="String" />
                <asp:Parameter Name="UnitPrice" Type="Decimal" />
                <asp:Parameter Name="OnHand" Type="Int32" />
                <asp:Parameter Name="original_ProductID" Type="String" />
                <asp:Parameter Name="original_Name" Type="String" />
                <asp:Parameter Name="original_ShortDescription" Type="String" />
                <asp:Parameter Name="original_LongDescription" Type="String" />
                <asp:Parameter Name="original_CategoryID" Type="String" />
                <asp:Parameter Name="original_ImageFile" Type="String" />
                <asp:Parameter Name="original_UnitPrice" Type="Decimal" />
                <asp:Parameter Name="original_OnHand" Type="Int32" />
            </UpdateParameters>
            <InsertParameters>
                <asp:Parameter Name="ProductID" Type="String" />
                <asp:Parameter Name="Name" Type="String" />
                <asp:Parameter Name="ShortDescription" Type="String" />
                <asp:Parameter Name="LongDescription" Type="String" />
                <asp:Parameter Name="CategoryID" Type="String" />
                <asp:Parameter Name="ImageFile" Type="String" />
                <asp:Parameter Name="UnitPrice" Type="Decimal" />
                <asp:Parameter Name="OnHand" Type="Int32" />
            </InsertParameters>
        </asp:SqlDataSource>
        <asp:SqlDataSource ID="SqlDataSource3" runat="server"
            ConnectionString="<%$ ConnectionStrings:HalloweenConnectionString %>"
            SelectCommand="SELECT [CategoryID], [LongName] FROM [Categories]
                ORDER BY [LongName]">
        </asp:SqlDataSource>
        <p>
            <asp:ValidationSummary ID="ValidationSummary1" runat="server"
                HeaderText="Please correct the following errors:"
                CssClass="error" />
        </p>
        <p>
            <asp:Label ID = "lblError" runat="server" EnableViewState="False"
                CssClass="error"></asp:Label>
        </p>
        </div>
    </form>
    </section>
</body>
</html>
```

Figure 15-10   The aspx file for the Product Maintenance application (part 4 of 4)

In parts 3 and 4 of figure 15-10, you can see the aspx code for the data source that the DetailsView control is bound to. This data source includes Delete and Update statements that use optimistic concurrency.

A data source is also included for the drop-down lists that are used to display the categories in the EditItem and InsertItem templates for the CategoryID field. You can see this data source in part 4 of this figure. If you look back at the definitions of the drop-down lists, you'll see how they're bound to this data source.

The code-behind file

Figure 15-11 shows the code-behind file for the Default page of the Product Maintenance application. Even though this application provides complete maintenance for the Products table, only four methods are required. These methods respond to events raised by the DetailsView control. The first three handle database exceptions and concurrency errors for updates, deletions, and insertions.

Note that the error-handling code for the insert method is simpler than the error-handling code for the update and delete methods. That's because optimistic concurrency doesn't apply to insert operations. As a result, there's no need to check the AffectedRows property to see if a concurrency error has occurred.

The last method, DetailsView1_ItemDeleting, handles a problem that can occur when you apply a format to a control that's bound to the data source. In this case, the currency format is applied to the unit price field in the Item template. Because this application uses optimistic concurrency, the original values of each field are passed to the Delete statement as parameters to make sure that another user hasn't changed the product row since it was retrieved. Unfortunately, the DetailsView control sets the value of the unit price parameter to its formatted value, which includes the currency symbol. If you allow this value to be passed on to the Delete statement, an exception will be thrown because the parameter value is in the wrong format.

Before the Delete statement is executed, then, the DetailsView1_ItemDeleting method is called. This method removes the currency symbol from the parameter value so the value will be passed to the Delete statement in the correct format.

The Default.aspx.cs file

```
public partial class _Default : System.Web.UI.Page
{
    protected void DetailsView1_ItemUpdated(
        object sender, DetailsViewUpdatedEventArgs e)
    {
        if (e.Exception != null)
        {
            lblError.Text = "A database error has occurred. " +
                "Message: " + e.Exception.Message;
            e.ExceptionHandled = true;
            e.KeepInEditMode = true;
        }
        else if (e.AffectedRows == 0)
            lblError.Text = "Another user may have updated that product. " +
                "Please try again.";
        else
            GridView1.DataBind();
    }

    protected void DetailsView1_ItemDeleted(
        object sender, DetailsViewDeletedEventArgs e)
    {
        if (e.Exception != null)
        {
            lblError.Text = "A database error has occurred. " +
                "Message: " + e.Exception.Message;
            e.ExceptionHandled = true;
        }
        else if (e.AffectedRows == 0)
            lblError.Text = "Another user may have updated that product. " +
                "Please try again.";
        else
            GridView1.DataBind();
    }

    protected void DetailsView1_ItemInserted(
        object sender, DetailsViewInsertedEventArgs e)
    {
        if (e.Exception != null)
        {
            lblError.Text = "A database error has occurred. " +
                "Message: " + e.Exception.Message;
            e.ExceptionHandled = true;
            e.KeepInInsertMode = true;
        }
        else
            GridView1.DataBind();
    }

    protected void DetailsView1_ItemDeleting(
        object sender, DetailsViewDeleteEventArgs e)
    {
        e.Values["UnitPrice"]
            = e.Values["UnitPrice"].ToString().Substring(1);
    }
}
```

Figure 15-11   The code-behind file for the Product Maintenance application

How to use the FormView control

Besides the DetailsView control, ASP.NET also provides a FormView control. Like the DetailsView control, the FormView control is designed to display data for a single item from a data source. However, as you'll see in the following topics, the FormView control uses a different approach to displaying its data.

An introduction to the FormView control

Figure 15-12 presents an introduction to the FormView control. Although the FormView control is similar to the DetailsView control, it differs in several key ways. Most importantly, the FormView control isn't restricted by the HTML table layout of the DetailsView control, in which each field is rendered as a table row. Instead, the FormView control uses templates to render all of the fields as a single row by default. This gives you complete control over the layout of the fields within the row.

Because you have to use template fields with a FormView control, this control can be more difficult to work with than a DetailsView control that uses bound fields. As you learned earlier in this chapter, though, you can convert the bound fields used by a DetailsView control to template fields so you have more control over them. In that case, a FormView control is just as easy to work with.

When you create a FormView control and bind it to a data source, the Web Forms Designer will automatically create default templates for you, as shown in the first image in this figure. Then, you can edit the templates to achieve the layout you want. To do that, choose Edit Templates from the smart tag menu. This places the control in template-editing mode, as shown in the second image in this figure. Here, the drop-down list shows the various templates you can use with a FormView control. For most applications, you'll use just the Item, EditItem, and InsertItem templates.

A FormView control after a data source has been assigned

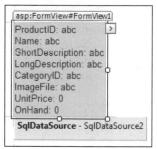

A FormView control in template-editing mode

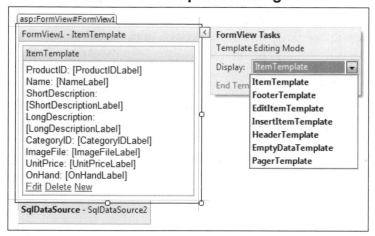

How the FormView control differs from the DetailsView control

- The DetailsView control can be easier to work with, but the FormView control provides more formatting and layout options.
- The DetailsView control can use BoundField elements or TemplateField elements with templates that use data binding expressions to define bound data fields. The FormView control can use only templates with data binding expressions to display bound data.
- The DetailsView control renders each field as a table row, but the FormView control renders all the fields in a template as a single table row.

Description

- A FormView control is similar to a DetailsView control, but its templates give you more control over how its data is displayed. To accomplish that, all the columns in the data source can be laid out within a single template.
- After you create a FormView control and assign a data source to it, you can edit the control's templates so the data is displayed the way you want.

Figure 15-12   An introduction to the FormView control

How to work with the Item template

When you use the Web Forms Designer to create a FormView control and bind it to a data source, the Web Forms Designer automatically generates basic templates for the FormView control. For instance, the code in figure 15-13 shows a typical Item template. This template is used to display the data from the data source in ReadOnly mode.

As you can see, the Item template consists of a literal header and a label control for each field in the data source. The Text attribute of each label control uses either the Bind or Eval method for data binding. The Eval method is used for columns that can't be modified. That's the case for the ProductID column in the Products table, since this is the key column.

To control the format and layout of the data that's displayed in ReadOnly mode, you can edit the Item template. To do that, it's common to use CSS as described in chapter 5. In particular, it's common to float the literal text to the left of the labels so the labels are left-aligned.

Note that if the data source includes Update, Delete, and Insert commands, the Item template will include command buttons that let the user edit, delete, or add new rows. Although these buttons are created as link buttons, you can easily change them to regular buttons or image buttons.

The Item template generated for a FormView control

```
<asp:FormView ID="FormView1" runat="server" DataKeyNames="ProductID"
    DataSourceID="SqlDataSource2">
    <ItemTemplate>
        ProductID:
        <asp:Label ID="ProductIDLabel" runat="server"
            Text='<%# Eval("ProductID") %>' /><br />
        Name:
        <asp:Label ID="NameLabel" runat="server"
            Text='<%# Bind("Name") %>' /><br />
        ShortDescription:
        <asp:Label ID="ShortDescriptionLabel" runat="server"
            Text='<%# Bind("ShortDescription") %>' /><br />
        LongDescription:
        <asp:Label ID="LongDescriptionLabel" runat="server"
            Text='<%# Bind("LongDescription") %>' /><br />
        CategoryID:
        <asp:Label ID="CategoryIDLabel" runat="server"
            Text='<%# Bind("CategoryID") %>' /><br />
        ImageFile:
        <asp:Label ID="ImageFileLabel" runat="server"
            Text='<%# Bind("ImageFile") %>' /><br />
        UnitPrice:
        <asp:Label ID="UnitPriceLabel" runat="server"
            Text='<%# Bind("UnitPrice") %>' /><br />
        OnHand:
        <asp:Label ID="OnHandLabel" runat="server"
            Text='<%# Bind("OnHand") %>' /><br />
    </ItemTemplate>
    .
    .
    .
</asp:FormView>
```

Description

- When you bind a FormView control to a data source, the Web Forms Designer generates an Item template that includes heading text and a bound label for each column in the data source.

- The Item template is rendered whenever the FormView control is displayed in ReadOnly mode.

- The Item template uses the Eval and Bind methods to create binding expressions for the columns in the data source (see figure 13-15 in chapter 13).

- If the data source includes Update, Delete, and Insert commands, the generated Item template will include Edit, Delete, and New buttons.

- The Web Forms Designer also generates an EditItem template and an InsertItem template, even if the data source doesn't include an Update or Insert command. For more information, see the next figure.

- You can modify a generated template so you can use CSS to control the format and layout of the data that's rendered for that template.

Figure 15-13   How to work with the Item template

How to work with the EditItem
and InsertItem templates

As figure 15-14 shows, the Web Forms Designer also generates EditItem and InsertItem templates when you bind a FormView control to a data source. These templates are used to display the fields in Edit and Insert mode, and they're generated even if the data source doesn't have an Update or Insert command. As a result, you can delete these templates if your application doesn't allow for edits and inserts. Although this figure only shows an EditItem template, the InsertItem template is similar.

One drawback to using the FormView control is that once you edit the Item template so the data is arranged the way you want, you'll usually want to provide similar layout code in both the EditItem template and the InsertItem template. That way, the layout in all three modes will be similar. One way to do that is to copy the code in one template and paste it into another. Then, you can make the necessary adjustments, such as replacing the labels that were generated for the Item template with the text boxes that were generated for the EditItem or InsertItem template.

Depending on the complexity of the layout, it may take considerable work to get the templates looking the way you want them. In addition, if you later decide to change that layout, you'll have to make the change to all three templates. Unfortunately, there's no escaping this duplication of effort.

A generated EditItem template as displayed in a browser window

```
ProductID: rat01
Name: Ugly Rat
ShortDescription: 16" Rat
LongDescription: This guy is sure to shorte
CategoryID: props
ImageFile: rat1.jpg
UnitPrice: 14.9900
OnHand: 75
Update Cancel
```

The aspx code for the EditItem template shown above

```
<EditItemTemplate>
    ProductID:
    <asp:Label ID="ProductIDLabel1" runat="server"
        Text='<%# Eval("ProductID") %>' />
    <br />
    Name:
    <asp:TextBox ID="NameTextBox" runat="server"
        Text='<%# Bind("Name") %>' />
    <br />
    ShortDescription:
    <asp:TextBox ID="ShortDescriptionTextBox" runat="server"
        Text='<%# Bind("ShortDescription") %>' />
    <br />
    .
    .                   The code generated for the LongDescription, CategoryID,
    .                   ImageFile, UnitPrice, and OnHand columns is similar to the
    .                   code generated for the ShortDescription column.
    .
    .
    <asp:LinkButton ID="UpdateButton" runat="server"
        CausesValidation="True" CommandName="Update" Text="Update" />
         
    <asp:LinkButton ID="UpdateCancelButton" runat="server"
        CausesValidation="False" CommandName="Cancel" Text="Cancel" />
</EditItemTemplate>
```

Description

- The EditItem template determines how the FormView control is rendered in Edit mode. It includes a text box for each editable bound column in the data source. The Text attribute for each text box uses a binding expression that binds the text box to its data source column.

- The EditItem template also includes Update and Cancel buttons.

- The InsertItem template is similar to the EditItem template. It determines how the FormView control is rendered in Insert mode.

Figure 15-14   How to work with the EditItem and InsertItem templates

A Shopping Cart application
that uses a FormView control

To show the versatility of the FormView control, the following topics present a version of the Order page in the Shopping Cart application that was originally presented in chapter 9. That version of the application used simple label and image controls to display the information for the product selected by the user. Because data binding didn't work for those controls, C# code was required in the Page_Load method to set the values of the label and image controls. In contrast, this new version of the application takes advantage of the data binding ability of the FormView control, so no Page_Load method is required.

The operation of the application

To refresh your memory, figure 15-15 shows the Order page displayed by the Shopping Cart application. As you can see, this page lets the user select a product from a drop-down list. When the user selects a product, the page displays the name, description, price, and an image of the selected product. Then, the user can order the product by entering a quantity and clicking the Add to Cart button.

This time, the product information is displayed within a FormView control, and the Item template is coded so CSS can be used to display the image to the right of the text. This demonstrates the layout flexibility of the FormView control. With a DetailsView control, it wouldn't be possible to display the image to the right of the text, because the DetailsView control displays each column of the data source in a separate table row.

The Order page of the Shopping Cart application

Description

- This is the Shopping Cart application that was originally presented in chapter 9, but this time it's implemented with a FormView control that displays the data for the selected product.

- The Item template for the FormView control includes labels that are bound to the columns in the data source. It also includes an Image control whose ImageUrl property is bound to the ImageFile column in the data source.

- The controls in the Item template of the FormView control are formatted using CSS.

Figure 15-15   The Shopping Cart application with a FormView control

The aspx file for the Order page

Figure 15-16 shows the aspx file for the Order page of the Shopping Cart application. Here, the FormView control includes an Item template that contains a division with four label controls that present the name, short description, long description, and price for the selected product. This division is followed by an image control that displays the product's image. A style sheet is used to format the image and labels so they appear as shown in the previous figure.

Note that although the Web Forms Designer generated the EditItem and InsertItem templates, this application doesn't use them. As a result, I deleted those templates so they wouldn't clutter the listing.

There are two interesting things to notice about the format strings used in the binding expressions on this page. First, the format string used to bind the image control is this: "Images/Products/{0}". Since the ImageFile column in the Products table contains just the name of the image file for each product, not its complete path, this formatting expression prefixes the file name with the path Images/Products/ so the image file can be located.

Second, the format string used in the binding expression that displays the unit price is this: "{0:c} each". As a result, the price is displayed in currency format, followed by the word "each."

The code-behind file for the Order page

Figure 15-17 shows the code-behind file for the Order page. This code is similar to the code for the original version of this program that was presented back in chapter 9. However, there are two substantial differences. First, this version doesn't include a Page_Load method because it doesn't need to do any data binding.

Second, the GetSelectedProduct method in this version is simpler than the one in the original version. That's because the data source for the DetailsView control retrieves a single row based on the item that's selected in the drop-down list. That means it's not necessary to filter the DataView object that's retrieved from the data source. Instead, the index value 0 is used to retrieve data from the first and only row of the data source.

The Order.aspx file

Page 1

```
<%@ Page Title="" Language="C#" MasterPageFile="~/Site.master"
AutoEventWireup="true" CodeFile="Order.aspx.cs" Inherits="Order" %>

<asp:Content ID="headContent" ContentPlaceHolderID="headPlaceHolder"
    Runat="Server">
    <link href="Styles/Order.css" rel="stylesheet" />
</asp:Content>

<asp:Content ID="formContent" ContentPlaceHolderID="formPlaceHolder"
    Runat="Server">
    <label>Please select a product: </label>
    <asp:DropDownList ID="ddlProducts" runat="server"
        AutoPostBack="True" DataSourceID="SqlDataSource1"
        DataTextField="Name" DataValueField="ProductID">
    </asp:DropDownList>
    <asp:SqlDataSource ID="SqlDataSource1" runat="server"
        ConnectionString="<%$ ConnectionStrings:HalloweenConnectionString %>"
        SelectCommand="SELECT [ProductID], [Name] FROM [Products]
            ORDER BY [Name]">
    </asp:SqlDataSource>
    <div id="productData">
      <asp:FormView ID="FormView1" runat="server"
        DataSourceID="SqlDataSource2">
        <ItemTemplate>
          <div id="product">
            <asp:Label ID="lblName" runat="server"
                Text='<%# Bind("Name") %>' >
            </asp:Label>
            <asp:Label ID="lblShortDescription" runat="server"
                Text='<%# Bind("ShortDescription") %>'>
            </asp:Label>
            <asp:Label ID="lblLongDescription" runat="server"
                Text='<%# Bind("LongDescription") %>'>
            </asp:Label>
            <asp:Label ID="lblUnitPrice" runat="server"
                Text='<%# Bind("UnitPrice", "{0:c} each") %>'>
            </asp:Label>
          </div>
          <asp:Image ID="imgProduct" runat="server" width="200px"
              ImageUrl='<%# Bind("ImageFile", "Images/Products/{0}") %>' />
        </ItemTemplate>
      </asp:FormView>
      <asp:SqlDataSource ID="SqlDataSource2" runat="server"
        ConnectionString="<%$ ConnectionStrings:HalloweenConnectionString %>"
        SelectCommand="SELECT [ProductID], [Name], [ShortDescription],
            [LongDescription], [ImageFile], [UnitPrice]
            FROM [Products]
            WHERE ([ProductID] = @ProductID)">
        <SelectParameters>
          <asp:ControlParameter ControlID="ddlProducts" Name="ProductID"
              PropertyName="SelectedValue" Type="String" />
        </SelectParameters>
      </asp:SqlDataSource>
    </div>
```

Figure 15-16   The aspx file for the Order page of the Shopping Cart application (part 1 of 2)

The Order.aspx file

```
    <div id="order">
        <p id="quantity">
            <asp:Label ID="Label2" runat="server" Text="Quantity:">
            </asp:Label>
            <asp:TextBox ID="txtQuantity" runat="server"></asp:TextBox>
            <asp:RequiredFieldValidator
                ID="RequiredFieldValidator1" runat="server"
                ControlToValidate="txtQuantity" Display="Dynamic"
                ErrorMessage="Quantity is a required field."
                CssClass="validator">
            </asp:RequiredFieldValidator>
            <asp:RangeValidator ID="RangeValidator1" runat="server"
                ControlToValidate="txtQuantity" Display="Dynamic"
                ErrorMessage="Quantity must range from 1 to 500."
                MaximumValue="500" MinimumValue="1" Type="Integer"
                CssClass="validator">
            </asp:RangeValidator>
        </p>
        <asp:Button ID="btnAdd" runat="server" Text="Add to Cart"
            OnClick="btnAdd_Click" />
        <asp:Button ID="Button1" runat="server"  Text="Go to Cart"
            CausesValidation="False" PostBackUrl="~/Cart.aspx" />
    </div>
</asp:Content>
```

Figure 15-16   The aspx file for the Order page of the Shopping Cart application (part 2 of 2)

The Order.aspx.cs file

```
using System;
using System.Collections.Generic;
using System.Linq;
using System.Web;
using System.Web.UI;
using System.Web.UI.WebControls;
using System.Data;

public partial class Order : System.Web.UI.Page
{
    protected void btnAdd_Click(object sender, EventArgs e)
    {
        if (Page.IsValid)
        {
            Product selectedProduct = this.GetSelectedProduct();
            CartItemList cart = CartItemList.GetCart();
            CartItem cartItem = cart[selectedProduct.ProductID];
            if (cartItem == null)
            {
                cart.AddItem(selectedProduct, Convert.ToInt32(txtQuantity.Text));
            }
            else
            {
                cartItem.AddQuantity(Convert.ToInt32(txtQuantity.Text));
            }
            Response.Redirect("Cart.aspx");
        }
    }

    private Product GetSelectedProduct()
    {
        DataView productsTable = (DataView)
            SqlDataSource2.Select(DataSourceSelectArguments.Empty);
        DataRowView row = (DataRowView)productsTable[0];
        Product p = new Product();
        p.ProductID = row["ProductID"].ToString();
        p.Name = row["Name"].ToString();
        p.ShortDescription = row["ShortDescription"].ToString();
        p.LongDescription = row["LongDescription"].ToString();
        p.UnitPrice = (decimal)row["UnitPrice"];
        p.ImageFile = row["ImageFile"].ToString();
        return p;
    }
}
```

Figure 15-17   The code-behind file for the Order page of the Shopping Cart application

Perspective

The DetailsView and FormView controls work well for any application that displays bound data one row at a time. The choice of which one to use depends mostly on how much control you want over the layout of the data. If you want to present a simple list of the fields in a row, the DetailsView control will automatically present data in that format. But if you need more control over the layout of the data, you'll want to use the FormView control.

Term

Master/Detail page

Summary

- The DetailsView control displays the data for a single row of a data source. Although this control supports paging, it is typically used in combination with a list or GridView control that lets the user select the item to be displayed.

- A *Master/Detail page* is a page that displays a list of items from a database along with the details for one item in the list. The DetailsView control is often used for the detail portion of the page.

- The DetailsView control provides for editing, updating, and inserting rows without requiring any C# code. To implement that, this control provides six different command buttons. But if you want to control the appearance of the buttons, you can use command fields instead of command buttons.

- To provide for data validation, database exceptions, and concurrency errors, you can write event handlers for the events of the DetailsView control.

- To control the appearance of the fields in a DetailsView control, you can use template fields.

- The FormView control is similar to the DetailsView control, but the templates for the FormView control give you more control over how the data is displayed.

Exercise 15-1   Develop an application that uses a DetailsView control

In this exercise, you'll develop an application that lets the user select a customer from a GridView control and maintain that customer in a DetailsView control. To make that easier, you'll start from an application with a page that contains a GridView control that lists customers and validation summary and label controls that will be used to display error messages.

Review the starting code for the application

1. Open the Ex15CustMaintDetailsView application in the aspnet45_cs directory.

2. Review the aspx code for the SQL data source, and notice that it retrieves the Email, LastName, and FirstName columns from the Customers table.

3. Display the page in Design view, and notice that only the LastName and FirstName columns are displayed in the GridView control. That's because the Visible property of the Email column has been set to False. This column must be included in the data source, though, because it's the primary key of the Customers table, and it will be used to display the selected customer in a DetailsView control.

4. Run the application to see that you can page through the customers, but you can't select a customer.

Add a select function to the GridView control

5. Add a command field to the GridView control that will let the user select a customer.

6. Run the application again and click the Select button for any customer. Notice how the formatting for the selected row changes. That's because a SelectedRowStyle element is included for the control.

Add a default DetailsView control

7. Add a DetailsView control at the beginning of the division that contains the validation summary control, and set its width to 350 pixels.

8. Create a data source for the DetailsView control that retrieves each of the columns from the Customers table for the customer that's selected in the GridView control. Be sure to generate Insert, Update, and Delete statements and use optimistic concurrency.

9. Use the Add Field dialog box to add a command field that lets the user Edit, Delete, and Add rows.

10. Run the application, display the last page of customers in the GridView control, and select customer "Barbara White". The data for that customer should be displayed in the DetailsView control.

11. Click the Edit button to see that the text boxes that let you edit the data for a customer are all the same size, and the text box for the address is too small to display the full address for this customer.

12. Click the Cancel button to exit from Edit mode, and close the browser window.

Create templates for the DetailsView control

13. Use the Fields dialog box to convert each of the bound fields in the DetailsView control to a template field.

14. Modify the EditItem template for each field except the Email and State fields so the width of the text box is appropriate for the data, and so the user can't enter more characters than are allowed by the database. (LastName, FirstName, and PhoneNumber: 20 characters; Address: 40 characters; City: 30 characters; and ZipCode: 9 characters.)

15. Assign a meaningful name to each text box you just modified. Then, add a required field validator to each of these fields that displays an asterisk to the right of the text box and displays an error message in the validation summary control if a value isn't entered in the field.

16. Add another data source to the page below the data source for the DetailsView control. This data source should retrieve the StateCode and StateName columns from the States table and sort the results by the StateName column.

17. Replace the text box in the EditItem template for the State field with a drop-down list, and bind the list to the data source you just created so the state name is displayed in the drop-down list and the state code is stored in the list. Then, use the DataBindings dialog box (see chapter 13) to bind the SelectedValue property of the drop-down list to the State field of the Customers table.

18. Run the application and click the Edit button in the DetailsView control to make sure you have the controls in the EditItem template formatted properly.

19. Copy the text boxes, validation controls, and drop-down list you created for the EditItem templates to the InsertItem templates of the same fields. In addition, add a required field validator to the InsertItem template for the Email field, and modify the text box so it's wider and accommodates a maximum of 25 characters.

20. Run the application again and click the New button. The InsertItem template should look just like the EditItem template except the email field is editable.

Add code to check for database and concurrency errors

21. Add event handlers for the ItemUpdated, ItemDeleted, and ItemInserted events of the DetailsView control. The ItemUpdated and ItemDeleted methods should check for both database and concurrency errors, but the ItemInserted method should check only for database errors. Display an appropriate error message in the label at the bottom of the page if an error is detected. Otherwise, bind the GridView control so it reflects the current data. If you need help, refer to figure 15-11.

22. Run the application and test it to make sure it works correctly.

16

How to use the ListView and DataPager controls

In this chapter, you'll learn how to use the ListView and DataPager controls. As you'll see, the ListView control works much like the GridView control you learned about in chapter 14. However, it provides features that make it more versatile than the GridView control. For example, you can use the ListView control to insert rows into a data source, and you can use it to display items from the data source in customized formats. You can also use the DataPager control in conjunction with the ListView control to implement paging.

How to use the ListView control

The ListView control is a highly customizable control that was introduced with ASP.NET 3.5. In the topics that follow, you'll learn the basic skills for defining the content and appearance of this control. In addition, you'll learn how to provide sorting, paging, and grouping for this control.

An introduction to the ListView control

Figure 16-1 presents a ListView control that provides for updating the data in the Categories table of the Halloween database. As you can see, this control presents the data in a row and column format just like the GridView control. In fact, if you compare this control to the GridView control shown in figure 14-1 of chapter 14, you'll see that these controls look quite similar. The main difference is that the ListView control includes an additional row for inserting a new row into the table.

The first table in this figure lists some of the basic attributes of the ListView control. In most cases, these attributes are set the way you want them by default. If you want to change the location of the row that provides for insert operations, though, you can do that by changing the value of the InsertItemPosition attribute.

To define the layout of a ListView control, you use the templates listed in the second table in this figure. At the least, a ListView control typically contains a Layout template and an Item template. You use the Layout template to define the overall layout of the control, and you use the Item template to define the layout that's used for each item in the data source. You'll see how these and many of the other templates can be used as you progress through this chapter.

A ListView control that provides for updating a table

		CategoryID	ShortName	LongName
Delete	Edit	costumes	Costumes	Costumes
Delete	Edit	fx	FX	Special Effects
Delete	Edit	masks	Masks	Masks
Delete	Edit	props	Props	Props
Insert	Clear			

Basic attributes of the ListView control

Attribute	Description
DataSourceID	The ID of the data source to bind to.
DataKeyNames	The names of the primary key fields separated by commas.
InsertItemPosition	The location within the ListView control where the InsertItem template is rendered. You can specify FirstItem, LastItem, or None.

Template elements used by the ListView control

Element	Description
LayoutTemplate	Defines the basic layout of the control.
ItemTemplate	The template used for each item in the data source.
ItemSeparatorTemplate	The template used to separate items in the data source.
AlternatingItemTemplate	The template used for alternating items in the data source.
EditItemTemplate	The template used when a row is being edited.
InsertItemTemplate	The template used for inserting a row.
EmptyDataTemplate	The template used when the data source is empty.
SelectedItemTemplate	The template used when a row is selected.
GroupTemplate	The template used to define a group layout.
GroupSeparatorTemplate	The template used to separate groups of items.
EmptyItemTemplate	The template used for empty items in a group.

Description

- The ListView control displays data from a data source using templates. It can be used to edit and delete data as well as insert data.

- The template elements define the formatting that's used to display data. These templates are generated automatically when you configure a ListView control. See figure 16-2 for information on configuring this control.

- The Layout template defines the overall layout of the control. This template includes an element that's used as a placeholder for the data. Then, the other templates are substituted for this placeholder as appropriate.

Figure 16-1   An introduction to the ListView control

How to configure a ListView control

The easiest way to configure a ListView control is to use the Configure ListView dialog box shown in figure 16-2. Before you do that, though, you have to add the ListView control to the page and bind it to a data source. Then, you can use the Configure ListView command in the control's smart tag menu to display this dialog box.

When you use the Configure ListView dialog box to configure a ListView control, Visual Studio generates templates based on the options you choose. If you want to generate templates that use a standard row and column format, for example, you can select the Grid layout as shown here. Then, if you want to add formatting to the templates, you can select a style. In this figure, for example, I selected the Blues style.

The other options in this dialog box let you enable editing, inserting, deleting, and paging. Note that if the data source isn't defined with Update, Insert, and Delete commands, the Enable Editing, Enable Inserting, and Enable Deleting options won't be available. Even so, EditItem and InsertItem templates are generated for the ListView control. If your application won't provide for updating and inserting data, then, you may want to delete these templates.

The Item template that's generated for a ListView control depends on the columns in the data source that the control is bound to and whether you enable editing and deleting. If you enable editing and deleting, Edit and Delete buttons are added to this template. You'll learn more about how these buttons and the other buttons used by the ListView control work later in this chapter.

If you select the Enable Paging option, a DataPager control is also added to the ListView control. The exact format of this control depends on the option you choose from the drop-down list. You'll learn more about this later in this chapter too.

As you select options in the Configure ListView dialog box, a preview of the control is displayed in the Preview window. That way, you can be sure that the ListView control is generated the way you want. And that will save you time later if you need to customize the control.

The Configure ListView dialog box

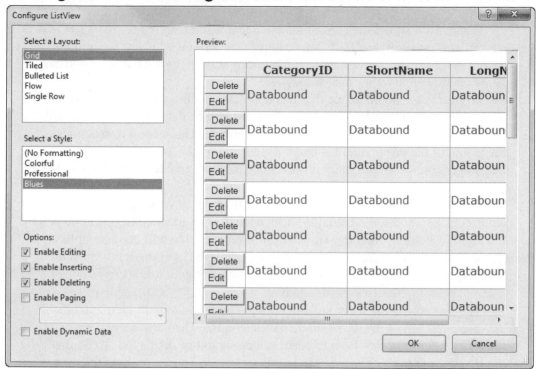

Description

- After you add a ListView control and bind it to a data source, you can configure it to generate many of the templates shown in figure 16-1. To do that, you use the Configure ListView dialog box.

- To display the Configure ListView dialog box, choose the Configure ListView command from the control's smart tag menu. Then, you can select a layout and style for the control, and you can enable editing, inserting, deleting, and paging.

- The EditItem and InsertItem templates are generated regardless of whether the data source provides for editing and inserting and whether editing and inserting are enabled for the ListView control.

- If you enable editing, an Edit button is added to the Item and AlternatingItem templates that lets the user switch to edit mode. If you enable deleting, a Delete button is added to the Item and AlternatingItem templates.

- If you enable inserting, the InsertItemPosition attribute is set to LastItem. This causes the InsertItem template to be displayed after the existing rows in the data source.

- If you enable paging, a DataPager control is added to the ListView control. See figures 16-6 and 16-7 for information on how to use this control.

Figure 16-2   How to configure a ListView control

How to work with the Layout template

Figure 16-3 shows the Layout template that was generated for the ListView control you saw in figure 16-1. This control was configured using the options shown in figure 16-2, except that no formatting was applied. That way, you can focus on the layout rather than the styles.

To start, you should notice that this template contains a table with two rows. The first row defines the layout of the data that will be displayed in the control. I'll have more to say about this row in just a minute. The second row defines the layout of the pager area. If I had enabled paging, this row would contain a DataPager control. In this case, however, paging isn't enabled, so the second row is empty.

The first row in the table within the Layout template contains a single column that contains another table. Notice that the ID attribute of this table is set to itemPlaceholderContainer. This indicates that the table will contain a place-holder where items from the data source are displayed. Although this attribute isn't required, it's included by default when you configure a ListView control using the Configure ListView dialog box.

The first row in the inner table defines the table headers (th elements) that are displayed across the top of the ListView control. Then, the second row identifies where the data from the data source should be displayed. To do that, the ID attribute of this row is set to itemPlaceholder. To specify how the data is displayed, you use the other templates of the ListView control. In the next figure, for example, you'll see the code for a basic Item template.

Before I go on, you should notice that each element within the Layout template has a Runat attribute set to "server". This is necessary for the table and tr elements that specify an id attribute since only server controls can include this attribute. Although the Runat attribute isn't required for the other elements, it's added by default when you configure the control.

If you use the Configure ListView dialog box as shown in the previous figure, the ListView control that's generated always contains a Layout template. If you're creating a simple layout, though, you should know that you can omit this template. For example, suppose you want to create a list of names and addresses formatted like this:

FirstName LastName
Address
City, State ZipCode

Since the Layout template for this list would contain only the item placeholder, it can be omitted. This feature was added with ASP.NET 4.

You should also realize that you can't modify the Layout template for a ListView control from Design view. Instead, you'll need to work with it in Source view. As you'll learn later in this chapter, though, you may be able to work with the other templates from Design view depending on what layout you use.

The Layout template for the ListView control in figure 16-1

```
<LayoutTemplate>
    <table runat="server">
        <tr runat="server">
            <td runat="server">
                <table id="itemPlaceholderContainer" runat="server"
                    border="0" style="">
                    <tr runat="server" style="">
                        <th runat="server"></th>
                        <th runat="server">CategoryID</th>
                        <th runat="server">ShortName</th>
                        <th runat="server">LongName</th>
                    </tr>
                    <tr id="itemPlaceholder" runat="server">
                    </tr>
                </table>
            </td>
        </tr>
        <tr runat="server">
            <td runat="server" style="">
            </td>
        </tr>
    </table>
</LayoutTemplate>
```

Description

- The Layout template that's generated for a ListView control that uses a grid layout consists of a table with two rows and one column. The first row defines the layout of the data that's displayed in the control, and the second row defines the layout of the DataPager control if paging is enabled.

- The column in the first row of the table for the Layout template contains another table with two rows. The first row defines the headers that are displayed for the columns of the data source as well as a header for any buttons that are displayed by the control. The second row defines a placeholder where the data defined by the other templates will be displayed.

- By default, the ID of the control that's used as a placeholder is set to itemPlaceholder. If you want to use a different name, you can set the ItemPlaceholderID attribute of the ListView control to the name you want to use.

- You can modify the Layout template any way you like. The only requirement is that it must contain a placeholder element that runs on the server.

- Design view doesn't support displaying the Layout template. Because of that, you must work with this template in Source view.

Figure 16-3   How to work with the Layout template

How to work with the Item template

You use the Item template to define how the items from a data source are displayed within a ListView control. To illustrate, figure 16-4 shows the Item template that was generated for the ListView control in figure 16-1. The first thing you should notice here is that this template contains a single tr element. That's necessary because the element that defines the item placeholder in the Layout template is a tr element. Then, at runtime, the tr element in the Item template is substituted for the tr element in the Layout template.

By default, the Item template for a ListView control with a grid layout contains one column for each column in the data source. As you can see, the data from each column is displayed in a label that's bound to the data source using the Eval method. In addition, if editing or deleting is enabled for the ListView control, an additional column is included in the Item template. This column contains the Edit and Delete buttons that can be used to perform edit and delete operations.

In addition to the Item template, an AlternatingItem template is generated for you when you configure a ListView control. Unless you apply a style to the control, though, this template is identical to the Item template, so each row in the control has the same appearance. If you want every other row to have a different appearance, you can modify the Item and AlternatingItem templates as appropriate. For example, you might want to set the background color for the AlternatingItem template so it's different from the background color for the Item template.

The Item template for the ListView control in figure 16-1

```
<ItemTemplate>
    <tr style="">
        <td>
            <asp:Button ID="DeleteButton" runat="server"
                CommandName="Delete" Text="Delete" />
            <asp:Button ID="EditButton" runat="server"
                CommandName="Edit" Text="Edit" />
        </td>
        <td>
            <asp:Label ID="CategoryIDLabel" runat="server"
                Text='<%# Eval("CategoryID") %>' />
        </td>
        <td>
            <asp:Label ID="ShortNameLabel" runat="server"
                Text='<%# Eval("ShortName") %>' />
        </td>
        <td>
            <asp:Label ID="LongNameLabel" runat="server"
                Text='<%# Eval("LongName") %>' />
        </td>
    </tr>
</ItemTemplate>
```

Description

- The Item template defines the layout of the data that's displayed in the ListView control. This template is substituted for the placeholder in the Layout template at runtime.

- The Item template that's generated for a ListView control with a grid layout consists of a single row with one column for each column in the data source. The data for each column is displayed in a label that's bound to the data source using the Eval method.

- If editing or deleting is enabled for the ListView control, an additional column that contains the buttons used to implement these operations is included in the Item template. See figure 16-11 for more information.

- You can modify the Item template any way you like to customize the layout that's used to display the data. To do that, you work in Source view since the Item template can't be displayed in Design view.

- The Item template is the only required template. If editing and inserting are enabled, however, you must also include EditItem and InsertItem templates. See figure 16-12 for more information.

Figure 16-4   How to work with the Item template

How to provide for sorting

Figure 16-5 shows how you provide sorting for a ListView control. To do that, you add a button to the Layout template for each column you want to sort by. The ListView control in this figure, for example, provides for sorting by using link buttons in the column headers for the first three columns.

To indicate that a button should be used for sorting, you set the CommandName attribute of the button to Sort. Then, you set the CommandArgument attribute of the button to the name of the column in the data source that you want to sort by. If the user clicks the Product ID button in the ListView control shown here, for example, the products will be sorted by the ProductID column. Similarly, if the user clicks the Name button, the products will be sorted by the Name column.

You can also sort by two or more columns in the data source. To do that, you separate the column names with commas. You can see how this works in the link button for the Category column in this figure. If you click this button, the products will be sorted by the Name column within the CategoryID column.

By the way, the sort sequence that's used for a ListView control is the same as the sequence that's used for a GridView control. That is, the first time you click a sort button, the column is sorted in ascending sequence. The second time you click the button, the column is sorted in descending sequence. If a sort button sorts by two or more columns, only the last column toggles between ascending and descending sequence. The other columns are always sorted in ascending sequence.

Also like the GridView control, the ListView control doesn't actually do the sorting. Instead, it relies on the underlying data source to sort the data. As a result, sorting will only work if the DataSourceMode attribute for the data source is set to DataSet.

A ListView control that provides for sorting

Product ID	Name	Category	Unit Price	On Hand
pow01	Austin Powers	costumes	$79.99	25
frankc01	Frankenstein	costumes	$39.99	100
hippie01	Hippie	costumes	$79.99	40
jar01	JarJar	costumes	$59.99	25
martian01	Martian	costumes	$69.99	100
super01	Superman	costumes	$39.99	100
bl01	Black Light	fx	$19.99	200
fogj01	Fog Juice (1qt)	fx	$9.99	500
fog01	Fog Machine	fx	$34.99	100
str01	Mini-strobe	fx	$13.99	200
skullfog01	Skull Fogger	fx	$39.95	50
tlm01	T&L Machine	fx	$99.99	10

The Layout template for the ListView control

```
<LayoutTemplate>
    <table id="itemPlaceholderContainer" runat="server"
        border="1" cellspacing="0" cellpadding="2">
        <tr id="head" runat="server">
            <th runat="server" class="left">
                <asp:LinkButton ID="LinkButton1" runat="server"
                    CommandName="Sort" CommandArgument="ProductID">
                    Product ID</asp:LinkButton></th>
            <th runat="server" class="left">
                <asp:LinkButton ID="LinkButton2" runat="server"
                    CommandName="Sort" CommandArgument="Name">
                    Name</asp:LinkButton></th>
            <th runat="server" class="left">
                <asp:LinkButton ID="LinkButton3" runat="server"
                    CommandName="Sort" CommandArgument="CategoryID, Name">
                    Category</asp:LinkButton></th>
            <th runat="server" class="right">Unit Price</th>
            <th runat="server" class="right">On Hand</th>
        </tr>
        <tr id="itemPlaceholder" runat="server">
        </tr>
    </table>
</LayoutTemplate>
```

Description

- To sort the data in a ListView control, you add a button to the Layout template, set the button's CommandName attribute to Sort, and set its CommandArgument attribute to the name of the column you want to sort by. To sort by two or more columns, separate the column names with commas.

- For sorting to work, the DataSourceMode attribute of the data source must be set to DataSet.

Figure 16-5   How to provide for sorting

How to provide for paging

To provide paging for a ListView control, you use the DataPager control. Figure 16-6 presents the basic skills for using this control. The easiest way to create this control is to select the Enable Paging option from the Configure ListView dialog box. When you do that, a drop-down list becomes available that lets you choose whether you want to add a *next/previous pager* or a *numeric pager*.

The ListView control at the top of this figure shows the default next/previous pager, and the first code example shows the aspx code for this pager. Notice that the DataPager control contains a Fields element. This element can contain one or more NextPreviousPagerField or NumericPagerField controls. In this case, the Fields element includes a single NextPreviousPagerField control. You'll learn more about the attributes that you can code on this control in the next figure.

The second pager in this figure is a simple numeric pager. In the aspx code for this pager, you can see that the PageSize property is set to 4 so only four items will be displayed on each page. Then, the pager contains a NumericPagerField control with no attributes. Because of that, the default settings for this control are used. That means that a maximum of five page buttons are displayed, along with an ellipsis button (…) if additional pages are available.

A ListView control that uses a next/previous pager

Product ID	Name	Category	Unit Price	On Hand
hippie01	Hippie	costumes	$79.99	40
jar01	JarJar	costumes	$59.99	25
martian01	Martian	costumes	$69.99	100
mum01	Mummy	masks	$39.99	30
pow01	Austin Powers	costumes	$79.99	25
rat01	Ugly Rat	props	$14.99	75
rat02	Uglier Rat	props	$19.99	50
skel01	Life-size Skeleton	props	$14.95	10
skullfog01	Skull Fogger	fx	$39.95	50
str01	Mini-strobe	fx	$13.99	200

First | Previous | Next | Last

The aspx code for the next/previous pager

```
<asp:DataPager ID="DataPager1" runat="server">
    <Fields>
        <asp:NextPreviousPagerField ButtonType="Button"
            ShowFirstPageButton="True"
            ShowLastPageButton="True" />
    </Fields>
</asp:DataPager>
```

A numeric pager

1 2 3 4 5 ...

The aspx code for the numeric pager

```
<asp:DataPager ID="DataPager1" runat="server" PageSize="4">
    <Fields>
        <asp:NumericPagerField />
    </Fields>
</asp:DataPager>
```

Description

- To provide paging for a ListView control, you use a DataPager control. To add a DataPager control to a ListView control, you can select the Enable Paging option in the Configure ListView dialog box and then select Next/Previous Pager or Numeric Pager from the drop-down list that's displayed.

- The DataPager control contains a Fields element that can contain two types of pager controls. The NextPreviousPagerField control can display first, previous, next, and last buttons. The NumericPagerField control can display page numbers as well as an ellipsis button if additional pages are available.

- You can customize the appearance of a DataPager control by adding two or more pager controls to it. See figure 16-7 for more information.

- You can also create a DataPager control by dragging it from the Toolbox. When you do that, however, you have to add the Fields element and the pager controls manually.

Figure 16-6   How to provide for paging

How to customize paging

Figure 16-7 shows how you can customize a DataPager control. To do that, you use the attributes of the DataPager control and the NextPreviousPagerField and NumericPagerField controls shown in this figure. For example, to change the number of items that are displayed on each page, you set the PageSize attribute of the DataPager control.

Because the DataPager is a separate control, you don't have to place it inside the ListView control. Instead, you can place it anywhere you want on the page. If you do that, however, you need to set the PagedControlID attribute of the control. This attribute identifies the ListView control that it provides paging for.

By the way, the DataPager control can be used only with controls that implement the IPageableItemContainer interface. Currently, the ListView control is the only control that meets that criterion. In the future, however, I would expect other data-bound controls to implement this interface so their paging can be done from outside the controls.

The attributes of the NextPreviousPagerField control shown in this figure determine the type of buttons that are used in the pager and which buttons are displayed. The default is to display Previous and Next link buttons. Similarly, the attributes of the NumericPagerField control determine the type of buttons that are used and the number of buttons that are displayed. The default is to display a maximum of five link buttons.

The code example in this figure shows a custom DataPager control that uses two next/previous pagers and one numeric pager. The resulting control is shown below this code. This should help you begin to see the flexibility that the DataPager control provides.

Attributes of the DataPager control

Attribute	Description
PageSize	Specifies the number of items to be displayed on each page. The default is 10.
PagedControlID	The ID of the ListView control that the DataPager control provides paging for. Used only if the DataPager control is placed outside the ListView control.

Attributes of the NextPreviousPagerField control

Attribute	Description
ButtonType	The type of buttons to be used. You can specify Button, Image, or Link.
ShowFirstPageButton	Determines whether the first page button is displayed. Default is False.
ShowPreviousPageButton	Determines whether the previous page button is displayed. Default is True.
ShowNextPageButton	Determines whether the next page button is displayed. Default is True.
ShowLastPageButton	Determines whether the last page button is displayed. Default is False.

Attributes of the NumericPagerField control

Attribute	Description
ButtonCount	The maximum number of buttons to be displayed.
ButtonType	The type of buttons to be used. You can specify Button, Image, or Link.

Aspx code for a DataPager control that uses both types of pagers

```
<asp:DataPager ID="DataPager1" runat="server" PageSize="4">
    <Fields>
        <asp:NextPreviousPagerField ButtonType="Button"
            ShowFirstPageButton="True" ShowNextPageButton="False"
            ShowPreviousPageButton="False" />
        <asp:NumericPagerField ButtonCount="3" />
        <asp:NextPreviousPagerField ButtonType="Button"
            ShowLastPageButton="True" ShowNextPageButton="False"
            ShowPreviousPageButton="False" />
    </Fields>
</asp:DataPager>
```

The resulting DataPager control

Description

- You can use the PageSize attribute of the DataPager control to specify the number of items to display on each page.

- You can place a DataPager control outside of the ListView control. Then, you must set the PagedControlID attribute of the DataPager control to the ID of the ListView control you want to use it with.

- The NextPreviousPagerField and NumericPagerField controls also have attributes that let you change the text or image for the buttons that are displayed.

Figure 16-7 How to customize paging

How to group ListView data

Another feature of the ListView control is its ability to group data so it's displayed in two or more columns. In figure 16-8, for example, you can see the beginning of a ListView control that groups product data into two columns.

The easiest way to create a control like this is to select the Tiled layout from the Configure ListView dialog box. When you do that, Layout and Group templates like the ones shown here are generated. In addition, the GroupItemCount attribute is included for the ListView control. This attribute determines the number of columns in the group, and it's set to 3 by default.

When you use Tiled layout, the Layout template includes a nested table just like it does for the Grid layout. In this case, though, the id attribute of the nested table is set to groupPlaceholderContainer to indicate that it will contain a placeholder where groups of data will be displayed. This placeholder is defined by the single row for the table, whose id attribute is set to groupPlaceholder. Then, the row that's defined by the Group template is substituted for this row at runtime.

The row in the Group template defines the placeholder for the items in the group. This row contains a single column with an id attribute that's set to itemPlaceholder. Just as it does when it's included in the Layout template, this id indicates where the data from the data source is displayed. Then, the other templates determine how the data is displayed. To do that, these templates must contain a single td element that's substituted for the td element in the Group template when the application is run.

The beginning of a ListView control with two columns

```
Name: Austin Powers                              Name: Black Light
ShortDescription: Austin Powers costume          ShortDescription: Black light with base
Category: Costumes                               Category: Special Effects
UnitPrice: 79.9900                               UnitPrice: 19.9900
OnHand: 25                                       OnHand: 200

Name: Darth Vader Mask                           Name: Deranged Cat
ShortDescription: The legendary Darth Vader      ShortDescription: 20" Ugly cat
Category: Masks                                  Category: Props
UnitPrice: 19.9900                               UnitPrice: 19.9900
OnHand: 100                                      OnHand: 45
```

The Layout and Group templates for the control

```asp
<asp:ListView ID="ListView1" runat="server" DataSourceID="SqlDataSource1"
    GroupItemCount="2">
    <LayoutTemplate>
        <table runat="server">
            <tr runat="server">
                <td runat="server">
                    <table id="groupPlaceholderContainer" runat="server"
                           border="0">
                        <tr id="groupPlaceholder" runat="server"></tr>
                    </table>
                </td>
            </tr>
            .
            .
        </table>
    </LayoutTemplate>
    <GroupTemplate>
        <tr id="itemPlaceholderContainer" runat="server">
            <td id="itemPlaceholder" runat="server">
            </td>
        </tr>
    </GroupTemplate>
    <ItemTemplate>
    .
    .
    </ItemTemplate>
</asp:ListView>
```

Description

- You can use the Group template to display items in two or more columns. Then, the Group template replaces the element in the Layout template that has the ID "group-Placeholder," and the Group template contains an element with the ID "itemPlace-holder" that's replaced by the Item template.

- To determine the number of columns in the group, you set the GroupItemCount attribute of the ListView control.

- The easiest way to create a Group template is to select the Tiled layout from the Configure ListView dialog box. Then, a group with three columns is created, and you can modify the aspx code to format the control any way you like.

Figure 16-8   How to group ListView data

A list application
that uses a ListView control

Now that you've learned the basic skills for working with a ListView control, the following topics present the design and code for an application that uses this control to display a list of products. If you compare this application with the list application in chapter 14 that uses a GridView control, you'll begin to see the flexibility that the ListView control provides.

The Product List application

Figure 16-9 presents the Product List application. Here, you can see that the first column in the ListView control contains the product name for each row in the Products table of the Halloween database. Then, the second column contains the headings for the other product columns that are included in the list, and the third column contains the data from each of the product columns. This type of layout wouldn't be possible with the GridView control.

You should also notice the DataPager control that's used with the ListView control. This control specifies that only four products should be displayed on each page. It's implemented using a next/previous pager with custom values for the text that's displayed on the buttons.

The Product List application

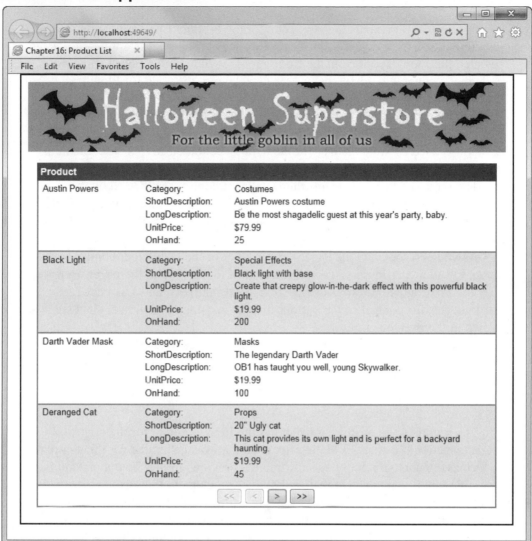

Description

- The ProductList application uses a ListView control to display a list of all the products in the Products table. The ListView control is bound to a SqlDataSource control that works in DataSet mode.

- The ListView control uses Item and AlternatingItem templates to display every other row with a different background color.

- A DataPager control is used within the ListView control to display four products on each page.

Figure 16-9   The Product List application

The aspx file

Figure 16-10 presents the aspx code for the Product List application. To generate the starting code for the ListView control used by this application, I selected the Flow layout from the Configure ListView dialog box. Unlike the code that's generated when you use the Grid layout, the code for Flow layout doesn't use tables. That makes it easy to apply styles using CSS.

The first page of this listing shows the Layout template for the ListView control. The two divisions in this template were generated by default. The first division is used as the container for the item placeholder. In this case, the item placeholder is coded within a span element.

The second division contains the DataPager control that's used by the ListView control. By default, this division was generated with a style attribute, but I deleted that attribute and included an id attribute instead. That way, I was able to format the data pager using CSS.

As you can see, I set the PageSize attribute for the DataPager control to 4. Then, I used a NextPreviousPagerField control to implement the pager. Here, I set the FirstPageText, PreviousPageText, NextPageText, and LastPageText attributes of this control so the buttons display less-than and greater-than signs as shown in the previous figure.

The only other change I made to this template was to add a paragraph before the two divisions. This paragraph contains the literal text that's displayed at the top of the ListView control. Like the division that contains the DataPager control, I included an id attribute for this paragraph so I could format it with CSS.

The second page of this listing shows the Item template for the control. I made considerable changes to the aspx code that was generated for this template to format the data so it looks as shown in the previous figure. To understand how this code works, you need to realize that the <p> element that displays the name of a product is floated to the left of the remaining product information using CSS. Similarly, the <p> element that identifies each of the remaining product columns is floated to the left of the <p> element that contains the label that displays the column value.

The third page of this listing shows the AlternatingItem template for the ListView control. This code is identical to the code for the Item template except that I gave the main division for this template a different value for the id attribute. That way, I was able to assign a different background color for alternate rows.

The SqlDataSource control is also shown on the third page of this listing. Notice here that the data source retrieves data from both the Products and Categories tables. The Categories table is included so the LongName column can be displayed instead of the CategoryID column from the Products table.

The Default.aspx file   **Page 1**

```
<%@ Page Language="C#" AutoEventWireup="true" CodeFile="Default.aspx.cs"
Inherits="_Default" %>

<!DOCTYPE html>

<html xmlns="http://www.w3.org/1999/xhtml">
<head id="Head1" runat="server">
    <title>Chapter 16: Product List</title>
    <link href="Main.css" rel="stylesheet" type="text/css" />
</head>
<body>
    <header>
        <img src="Images/banner.jpg" alt="Halloween Store" />
    </header>
    <section>
    <form id="form1" runat="server">
        <asp:ListView ID="ListView1" runat="server"
            DataKeyNames="ProductID" DataSourceID="SqlDataSource1">
            <LayoutTemplate>
                <p id="product">Product</p>
                <div id="itemPlaceholderContainer" runat="server">
                    <span runat="server" id="itemPlaceholder" />
                </div>
                <div id="pager">
                    <asp:DataPager ID="DataPager1" runat="server"
                        PageSize="4">
                        <Fields>
                            <asp:NextPreviousPagerField
                                ButtonType="Button"
                                ShowFirstPageButton="True"
                                ShowLastPageButton="True"
                                FirstPageText="&lt;&lt;"
                                PreviousPageText="&lt;"
                                NextPageText="&gt;"
                                LastPageText="&gt;&gt;" />
                        </Fields>
                    </asp:DataPager>
                </div>
            </LayoutTemplate>
```

Figure 16-10   The aspx file for the Product List application (part 1 of 3)

The Default.aspx file

```
<ItemTemplate>
    <div id="itemtemplate">
        <p class="name">
            <asp:Label ID="NameLabel" runat="server"
                Text='<%# Eval("Name") %>' />
        </p>
        <div class="info">
            <p class="label">Category:</p>
            <p class="control">
                <asp:Label ID="CategoryLabel" runat="server"
                    Text='<%# Eval("Category") %>' />
            </p>
            <p class="label">ShortDescription:</p>
            <p class="control">
                <asp:Label ID="ShortDescriptionLabel"
                    runat="server"
                    Text='<%# Eval("ShortDescription") %>' />
            </p>
            <p class="label"> LongDescription:</p>
            <p class="control">
                <asp:Label ID="LongDescriptionLabel"
                    runat="server"
                    Text='<%# Eval("LongDescription") %>' />
            </p>
            <p class="label">UnitPrice:</p>
            <p class="control">
                <asp:Label ID="UnitPriceLabel" runat="server"
                    Text='<%# Eval("UnitPrice", "{0:c}") %>' />
            </p>
            <p class="label">OnHand:</p>
            <p class="control">
                <asp:Label ID="OnHandLabel" runat="server"
                    Text='<%# Eval("OnHand") %>' />
            </p>
        </div>
    </div>
</ItemTemplate>
```

Figure 16-10   The aspx file for the Product List application (part 2 of 3)

The Default.aspx file   **Page 3**

```
            <AlternatingItemTemplate>
                <div id="alternatetemplate">
                    <p class="name">
                        <asp:Label ID="NameLabel" runat="server"
                            Text='<%# Eval("Name") %>' />
                    </p>
                    <div class="info">
                        <p class="label">Category:</p>
                        <p class="control">
                            <asp:Label ID="CategoryLabel" runat="server"
                                Text='<%# Eval("Category") %>' />
                        </p>
                        <p class="label">ShortDescription:</p>
                        <p class="control">
                            <asp:Label ID="ShortDescriptionLabel"
                                runat="server"
                                Text='<%# Eval("ShortDescription") %>' />
                        </p>
                        <p class="label"> LongDescription:</p>
                        <p class="control">
                            <asp:Label ID="LongDescriptionLabel"
                                runat="server"
                                Text='<%# Eval("LongDescription") %>' />
                        </p>
                        <p class="label">UnitPrice:</p>
                        <p class="control">
                            <asp:Label ID="UnitPriceLabel" runat="server"
                                Text='<%# Eval("UnitPrice", "{0:c}") %>' />
                        </p>
                        <p class="label">OnHand:</p>
                        <p class="control">
                            <asp:Label ID="OnHandLabel" runat="server"
                                Text='<%# Eval("OnHand") %>' />
                        </p>
                    </div>
                </div>
            </AlternatingItemTemplate>
        </asp:ListView>
        <asp:SqlDataSource ID="SqlDataSource1" runat="server"
            ConnectionString=
                "<%$ ConnectionStrings:HalloweenConnectionString %>"
            SelectCommand="SELECT Products.ProductID, Products.Name,
                Categories.LongName AS Category, Products.ShortDescription,
                Products.LongDescription, Products.UnitPrice, Products.OnHand
                FROM Products INNER JOIN Categories
                ON Products.CategoryID = Categories.CategoryID
                ORDER BY Products.Name">
        </asp:SqlDataSource>
    </form>
    </section>
</body>
</html>
```

Figure 16-10   The aspx file for the Product List application (part 3 of 3)

How to update ListView data

To update ListView data, you use the EditItem and InsertItem templates. I'll show you how to use these templates in just a minute. But first, I want to describe the various buttons you can use to work with data in a ListView control.

How to use buttons to perform update operations

You may recall that when you use a FormView control or a DetailsView control with templates to update data, the templates include buttons that let you insert, update, and delete data. You also use buttons to perform these operations using a ListView control. Although the buttons you need are generated automatically when you configure a ListView control, you will better understand how the ListView control works if you understand these buttons.

When the user clicks a button in a ListView control, the operation that's performed is determined by the value of the button's CommandName attribute. Figure 16-11 lists the predefined values for this attribute and describes their functions. For the most part, these values should be self-explanatory. For example, if the user clicks a button whose CommandName attribute is set to Edit, the row that contains that button is placed in edit mode. In that mode, the row is displayed using the EditItem template. As you'll see in a minute, the EditItem template contains buttons whose CommandName attributes are set to Update and Cancel. Then, if the user changes the data in that row and clicks the update button, the row in the database is updated. If the user clicks the cancel button instead, the original data is redisplayed using the Item template.

Notice that the ListView control can also contain a button whose CommandName attribute is set to Select. When this button is clicked, the selected row is displayed using the SelectedItem template. You can use a button like this to create a Master/Detail page like the one you saw in chapter 15 using a ListView control rather than a GridView control.

Buttons for working with the data in a ListView control

CommandName attribute	Description
Edit	Switches the ListView control to edit mode and displays the data using the EditItem template.
Update	In edit mode, saves the contents of the data-bound controls to the data source.
Cancel	Cancels the current operation. If a row is being edited, the original data is displayed using the Item template. If a row is being inserted, an empty InsertItem template is displayed.
Delete	Deletes the item from the data source.
Insert	Inserts the contents of the data-bound controls into the data source.
Select	Displays the contents of the data-bound controls using the Select-edItem template.

The aspx code for the Edit and Delete buttons in an Item template

```
<asp:Button ID="DeleteButton" runat="server"
    CommandName="Delete" Text="Delete" />
<asp:Button ID="EditButton" runat="server"
    CommandName="Edit" Text="Edit" />
```

Description

- To work with the data in a ListView control, you can use buttons whose CommandName attributes are set to predefined values. Then, when the user clicks these buttons, they perform the functions shown above.

- Although you must set the CommandName attribute to one of the values shown above to perform the associated function, you can set the Text attribute to anything you like.

- You can also create buttons that perform custom functions by setting the CommandName attribute to a custom value. Then, you can use the ItemCommand event of the ListView control to determine which button was clicked and perform the appropriate action.

Figure 16-11 How to use buttons to perform update operations

How to work with the EditItem and InsertItem templates

To help you understand how the EditItem and InsertItem templates work, figure 16-12 presents these templates for the ListView control you saw back in figure 16-1. This control was used to maintain the data in the Categories table of the Halloween database.

If you review the code for the EditItem template, you'll see that it includes two buttons whose CommandName attributes are set to Update and Cancel. Then, it includes a bound control for each of the three columns in the data source. The first column, CategoryID, is displayed in a label and is bound using the Eval method. That makes sense because this is the primary key for the table and shouldn't be changed. The other two columns, ShortName and LongName, are displayed in text boxes that are bound using the Bind method so they can be changed.

The InsertItem template is similar. Instead of update and cancel buttons, however, it includes insert and cancel buttons. Notice that although the CommandName attribute for the cancel button is set to Cancel just like it is for the cancel button in the EditItem template, the Text attribute is set to Clear instead of Cancel. That better describes what happens when this button is clicked. Also notice that all three columns in the data source are displayed in text boxes that are bound using the Bind method. That makes sense because all three values are required for a new category.

How to use events raised by the ListView control

The ListView control raises many of the same events as the DetailsView and FormView controls. For example, the ItemUpdating event is raised before an item is updated, and the ItemUpdated event is raised after an item has been updated. Similarly, the ItemInserting event is raised before an item is inserted, and the ItemInserted event is raised after an item has been inserted. And the ItemDeleting event is raised before an item is deleted, and the ItemDeleted event is raised after an item has been deleted.

You'll typically use the before events to provide data validation in the code-behind file, and you'll use the after events to provide error handling code if the operation wasn't successful. This works the same as in the maintenance applications of the last two chapters.

The EditItem template for the ListView control in figure 16-1

```
<EditItemTemplate>
    <tr style="">
        <td>
            <asp:Button ID="UpdateButton" runat="server"
                CommandName="Update" Text="Update" />
            <asp:Button ID="CancelButton" runat="server"
                CommandName="Cancel" Text="Cancel" /></td>
        <td>
            <asp:Label ID="CategoryIDLabel1" runat="server"
                Text='<%# Eval("CategoryID") %>' /></td>
        <td>
            <asp:TextBox ID="ShortNameTextBox" runat="server"
                Text='<%# Bind("ShortName") %>' /></td>
        <td>
            <asp:TextBox ID="LongNameTextBox" runat="server"
                Text='<%# Bind("LongName") %>' /></td>
    </tr>
</EditItemTemplate>
```

The InsertItem template for the ListView control in figure 16-1

```
<InsertItemTemplate>
    <tr style="">
        <td>
            <asp:Button ID="InsertButton" runat="server"
                CommandName="Insert" Text="Insert" />
            <asp:Button ID="CancelButton" runat="server"
                CommandName="Cancel" Text="Clear" /></td>
        <td>
            <asp:TextBox ID="CategoryIDTextBox" runat="server"
                Text='<%# Bind("CategoryID") %>' /></td>
        <td>
            <asp:TextBox ID="ShortNameTextBox" runat="server"
                Text='<%# Bind("ShortName") %>' /></td>
        <td>
            <asp:TextBox ID="LongNameTextBox" runat="server"
                Text='<%# Bind("LongName") %>' /></td>
    </tr>
</InsertItemTemplate>
```

Description

- The EditItem template determines how an item in the ListView control is rendered in edit mode. By default, it includes a label for each column in the data source that can't be modified and a text box for each column in the data source that can be modified. These controls are bound to the columns of the data source using the Eval and Bind methods.

- The InsertItem template is similar to the EditItem template. It determines the content that's rendered for a new item that's being inserted.

- The EditItem template also includes update and cancel buttons by default, and the InsertItem template includes insert and cancel buttons.

Figure 16-12   How to work with the EditItem and InsertItem templates

Perspective

In this chapter, you've seen how the templates of the ListView control provide for features that aren't available with the other data-bound controls. In particular, you saw how to use the Item and AlternatingItem templates in conjunction with the Layout template to display data. You saw how to use the Group template to display data in two or more columns. And you saw how to use the DataPager control to provide for paging.

You also saw how to use the EditItem and InsertItem templates along with the buttons that let you insert, update, and delete data. With this as background, you should now be able to use the ListView and DataPager controls in your own applications.

Terms

next/previous pager
numeric pager

Summary

- The ListView control works much like a GridView control but it provides features that make it more versatile, including automatic formatting, sorting, paging, grouping, editing, deleting, updating, and inserting.

- The ListView control displays the data from a data source using templates to format the data. These templates are generated automatically when you configure this control.

- To provide sorting for a ListView control, you add buttons at the top of the columns in the Layout template. Then, you set the CommandName attribute to Sort and the CommandArgument attribute to the name of the column you want to sort by.

- To provide paging for a ListView control, you use a DataPager control and configure it to work with the ListView control.

- To group the data for two or more items in a ListView control, you use the Group template.

- To edit, update, and insert data in a data source, you use buttons with their CommandName attributes set to predefined values like Edit, Update, Delete, and Insert. The Edit and Insert buttons automatically work with the EditItem and InsertItem templates.

- When you use the ListView control, the code-behind file only needs to provide data validation and error handling for database operations.

Exercise 16-1   Create a Customer List application

In this exercise, you'll use a ListView control to create a simple customer list that provides for sorting and paging.

1. Open the Ex16CustomerList application in the aspnet45_cs directory. This application contains the starting page and the database, image, and style sheet used by the page.

2. Add a ListView control to the main division of the page, and create a data source that retrieves the LastName, FirstName, State, City, and PhoneNumber columns from the Customers table, sorted by last name.

3. Display the Configure ListView dialog box, make sure Grid layout is selected, select the Blues style, enable paging, and select the Numeric Pager item from the drop-down list that becomes available.

4. Run the application to see how the ListView control looks, and experiment with the buttons in the DataPager control to see how they work.

5. Replace the literal text for the LastName, State, and City columns with link buttons. Add a CommandName attribute to each link button with the value "Sort", and add a CommandArgument attribute whose value is the name of the column to be sorted.

6. Run the application again, and make sure that the sorting works correctly.

7. Switch to Source view, and delete the EditItem, InsertItem, and SelectedItem templates since they aren't used by this application.

8. Locate the Layout template, and add a class attribute to each th element with the value "left". This will left-align the headers.

9. Locate the Item template, and add a class attribute to each td element with the values "lastname", "firstname", "state", "city", and "phone" respectively. Do the same for the AlternatingItem template. This will set the widths for the columns.

10. Run the application one more time to see how it looks.

17

How to use object data sources with ADO.NET

This chapter shows you how to use object data sources as an alternative to SQL data sources. The benefit of using object data sources is that they let you use a three-layer design in which the data access code is kept in data access classes. This lets you separate the presentation code from the data access code, but still lets you use the data binding features of ASP.NET.

To write the data access classes that are used with object data sources, you need to be able to use ADO.NET, which you'll be introduced to in this chapter. Then, if you decide you want to use object data sources in your applications, you'll want to learn more about using ADO.NET.

An introduction to object data sources

The following topics introduce you to object data sources, ADO.NET, and the 3-layer architecture that they let you implement.

How 3-layer applications work in ASP.NET

Today, a best practice for web development is to use a *3-layer architecture* that separates the presentation, business rules, and data access components of the application. The *presentation layer* includes the web pages that define the user interface. The *middle layer* includes the classes that manage the data access for those pages, and it may also include classes that implement *business rules* such as data validation requirements and discount policies. The *database layer* consists of the database itself.

In this chapter, you'll learn how to use *object data sources* to implement the 3-layer architecture. Figure 17-1 shows how this works. Here, you can see that the ObjectDataSource control serves as an interface between the data-bound controls in the presentation layer and the data access classes in the middle layer.

When you use an ObjectDataSource control, you must create a data access class to handle the data access for the control. This class provides at least one method that retrieves data from the database and returns it in a form that the ObjectDataSource control can handle. It can also provide methods to insert, update, and delete data. The data access class should be placed in the application's App_Code folder.

When you code a data access class, you can use any techniques you want to access the database. In this chapter, for example, you'll see data access classes that use ADO.NET. These classes can be used to get data from a SQL Server database, from other types of databases such as Oracle or MySQL databases, or from other sources such as XML or plain text files.

If you have already developed data access classes for the database used by your application, you may be able to use those classes with an object data source. Often, though, it's better to develop the data access classes specifically for the ObjectDataSource controls that you're going to use. That way, you can design each class so it works as efficiently as possible.

Incidentally, Microsoft uses both the term *business object class* and the term *data object class* to refer to a class that provides data access for an object data source. In this chapter, though, I used the term *data access class* for this type of class because if you use static methods to provide the data access functions, an object is never instantiated from the class.

Also, you may be accustomed to using the term *3-tier architecture* for the *3-layer architecture* that's described in figure 17-1. Because some people use *3-tier* to refer to an architecture that puts the three layers on three different physical devices, though, I've used the term *3-layer* in this chapter. Although you could put each of the three layers on three separate devices, you don't have to.

The 3-layer architecture in ASP.NET

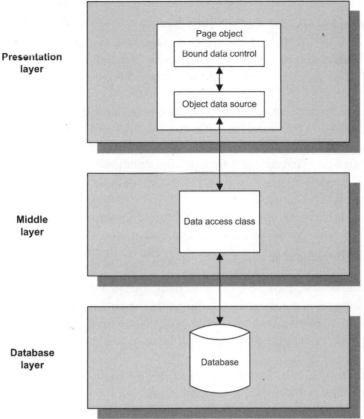

The three layers

- The **presentation layer** consists of the ASP.NET pages that manage the appearance of the application. This layer can include bound data controls and ObjectDataSource objects that bind the data controls to the data.

- The **middle layer** contains the *data access classes* that manage the data access for the application. This layer can also contain business objects that represent business entities such as customers, products, or employees and that implement business rules such as credit and discount policies.

- The **database layer** consists of the database that contains the data for the application. Ideally, the SQL statements that do the database access should be saved in stored procedures within the database, but the SQL statements are often stored in the data access classes.

Description

- An *object data source* is implemented by the ObjectDataSource control, which lets you use data binding with the *3-layer architecture* for a database application.

- An object data source is similar to a SQL data source. However, instead of directly accessing a database, the object data source gets its data through a data access class that handles the details of database access.

Figure 17-1   How 3-layer applications work in ASP.NET

How to create and work with ADO.NET classes

To code the data access classes that you use with object data sources and the 3-layer architecture, you use *ADO.NET* (*Active Data Objects*). Figure 17-2 presents the ADO.NET classes and members that are used by the applications in this chapter. Although there are other classes and members, these are the ones you'll use most often.

Before you can access the data in a database, you have to create a connection object that defines the connection to the database. On the constructor for this object, you can include a connection string that provides the information that's needed to connect to a database. That means it includes information such as the name of the database and the database server. It can also contain authentication information such as a user ID and password.

The two methods of this class that are shown in this figure let you open and close the connection. In general, you should leave a connection open only while data is being retrieved or updated. You'll see one way you can do that without using the Open and Close methods later in this chapter.

To execute a SQL statement against a SQL Server database, you create a SqlCommand object that contains the statement. Notice that the constructor for the object shown here accepts a string that contains the SQL statement to be executed, along with the SqlConnection object that will be used to connect to the database.

To execute a command object, you can use the two Execute methods shown in this figure. To execute a Select statement, for example, you use ExecuteReader method. Then, the results are returned as a SqlDataReader object. To execute an Insert, Update, or Delete statement, you use the ExecuteNonQuery method. This method returns an integer value that indicates the number of rows that were affected by the command. If, for example, the command deletes a single row, the ExecuteNonQuery method returns 1.

If the SQL statement you're executing includes one or more parameters, you can use the Parameters property of the SqlCommand object to work with the parameters of this object. This property returns a SqlParameterCollection object. Then, you can use the AddWithValue method of the SqlParameterCollection class to add parameters to the collection.

To work with the data reader that's returned by the ExecuteReader method of a command object, you can use the members of the SqlDataReader class. To start, you can use the Read method to read the next row of data. Then, you can use the indexer shown here to access individual columns in the current row by name. Finally, when you're done using the data reader, you can use the Close method to close it.

How to create and work with a connection
A constructor for the SqlConnection class
```
new SqlConnection(connectionString)
```

Two methods of the SqlConnection class

Method	Description
Open()	Opens a connection to a database.
Close()	Closes a connection to a database.

How to create and work with a command
A constructor for the SqlCommand class
```
new SqlCommand(commandText, connection)
```

Some of the members of the SqlCommand class

Property	Description
Parameters	The SqlParameterCollection object with the parameters used by the command.
Method	**Description**
ExecuteReader()	Executes a query and returns the result as a SqlDataReader object.
ExecuteNonQuery()	Executes the command and returns an integer representing the number of rows affected.

A method of the SqlParameterCollection class

Method	Description
AddWithValue(name, value)	Adds a parameter with the specified name and value to the collection.

How to create and work with a data reader
How to create a SqlDataReader object
```
sqlCommand.ExecuteReader()
```

Some of the members of the SqlDataReader class

Indexer	Description
[name]	Accesses the column with the specified name from the current row.
Method	**Description**
Read()	Reads the next row. Returns True if there are more rows. Otherwise, returns False.
Close()	Closes the data reader.

Description

- A SqlConnection object is required to establish a connection to a SQL Server database.

- A SqlCommand object is used to execute a SQL command against a SQL Server database. A SqlCommand object can contain one or more parameters.

- A SqlDataReader object provides read-only, forward-only access to the data in a database.

Figure 17-2   How to create and work with ADO.NET classes

How to use the ObjectDataSource control

Figure 17-3 presents the basics of working with the ObjectDataSource control. The image at the top of this figure shows how an ObjectDataSource control that's bound to a drop-down list appears in the Web Forms Designer. Then, the first code example shows the aspx code for the drop-down list and the object data source it's bound to. As with any other data source, you can add an object data source to a web page by dragging it from the Toolbox or by selecting the Choose Data Source command from a bindable control.

In the first code example, you can see that the drop-down list is bound to the object data source using the DataSourceID attribute just as it is for a SQL data source. You can also see that the code for the ObjectDataSource control has just two attributes besides the required ID and Runat attributes. The TypeName attribute provides the name of the data access class, and the SelectMethod attribute provides the name of the method within that class that's used to retrieve the data. In this case, the data access class is ProductDB and the select method is GetAllCategories.

You'll use the other attributes of the ObjectDataSource control shown here when you insert, update, and delete data. You'll learn more about these methods when I present the Category Maintenance application later in this chapter.

The second code example in this figure shows the GetAllCategories method of the ProductDB class. This method uses straightforward ADO.NET code to retrieve category rows from the Categories table and return a data reader that can be used to read the category rows. Notice, though, that the return type for this method is IEnumerable. Because the SqlDataReader class implements the IEnumerable interface, a data reader is a valid return object for this method. (You'll learn more about the return types that are acceptable for a select method in figure 17-9.)

A drop-down list bound to an ObjectDataSource control

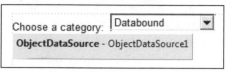

The code for the drop-down list and the ObjectDataSource control

```
<asp:DropDownList ID="ddlCategories" runat="server"
    AutoPostBack="True" DataSourceID="ObjectDataSource1"
    DataTextField="ShortName" DataValueField="CategoryID">
</asp:DropDownList>
<asp:ObjectDataSource ID="ObjectDataSource1" runat="server"
    TypeName="ProductDB"
    SelectMethod="GetAllCategories">
</asp:ObjectDataSource>
```

The GetAllCategories method of the ProductDB class

```
[DataObjectMethod(DataObjectMethodType.Select)]
public static IEnumerable GetAllCategories()
{
    SqlConnection con = new SqlConnection(GetConnectionString());
    string sel = "SELECT CategoryID, LongName "
        + "FROM Categories ORDER BY LongName";
    SqlCommand cmd = new SqlCommand(sel, con);
    con.Open();
    SqlDataReader dr = cmd.ExecuteReader();
    return dr;
}
```

Basic attributes of the ObjectDataSource control

Attribute	Description
TypeName	The name of the data access class.
SelectMethod	The name of the method that retrieves the data.
UpdateMethod	The name of the method that updates the data.
DeleteMethod	The name of the method that deletes the data.
InsertMethod	The name of the method that inserts the data.
DataObjectTypeName	The name of a class that provides properties that are used to pass parameter values.
ConflictDetection	Specifies how concurrency conflicts will be detected. CompareAllValues uses optimistic concurrency checking. OverwriteValues, which is the default, does no concurrency checking.

Description

- The ObjectDataSource control specifies the name of the data access class and the methods used to select, update, delete, and insert data.

Figure 17-3   How to use the ObjectDataSource control

How to configure an ObjectDataSource control

Figure 17-4 shows how you can use the Configure Data Source dialog boxes to configure an ObjectDataSource control. As you can see, the first dialog box lets you choose the business object that will be associated with this object data source. The selection you make here will be specified in the TypeName attribute of the ObjectDataSource control. (Notice that Microsoft refers to the data access class as a *business object* in this wizard. In other contexts, though, Microsoft refers to the data access class as a *data object* or a *data component*.)

The drop-down list in the first dialog box lists all of the classes that are available in the App_Code folder. If you check the "Show Only Data Components" box, only those classes that are identified as data components will be listed. In figure 17-11, you'll learn how to mark classes this way.

When you select a data access class and click Next, the second Configure Data Source dialog box is displayed. Here, you can select the method you want to use to retrieve data for the object data source. The one you select is specified in the SelectMethod attribute of the ObjectDataSource control. (In this step, the wizard uses a .NET feature called *reflection* to determine all of the available methods, and you'll learn more about reflection in a moment.)

If you select a select method that requires parameters, the Define Parameters step lets you specify the source for each of the required parameters. Then, Visual Studio generates the elements that define the parameters required by the ObjectDataSource control. This works the same as it does for a SQL data source.

As you can see in this figure, the second Configure Data Source dialog box also provides tabs that let you specify the methods for update, insert, and delete operations. Later in this chapter, you'll see an application that uses these methods. But for now, I'll just focus on how you can use an ObjectDataSource control to retrieve data.

How to work with bound controls

Although you can bind a control such as a drop-down list or GridView control to an object data source, you can't always use the designer to select individual fields like you can when you use a SQL data source. That's because the fields are defined in the data access class and not directly in the data source. When you bind a drop-down list, for example, you may have to manually enter the names of the fields you want to display and use for the value of the control. Similarly, when you bind a GridView control, you may have to manually enter the name of each field you want to bind and, if the control provides for sorting, you may have to enter the name of the field for each sort expression. In addition, you may have to enter the appropriate field name or names for the DataKeyNames attribute of the control.

To avoid having to enter the names of these fields, you can code the select method so it returns a strongly-typed collection. You'll see an example like that later in this chapter. For now, just realize that because select methods that return a strongly-typed collection can make an object data source easier to work with, you should use them whenever that makes sense.

The dialog boxes for configuring a data source

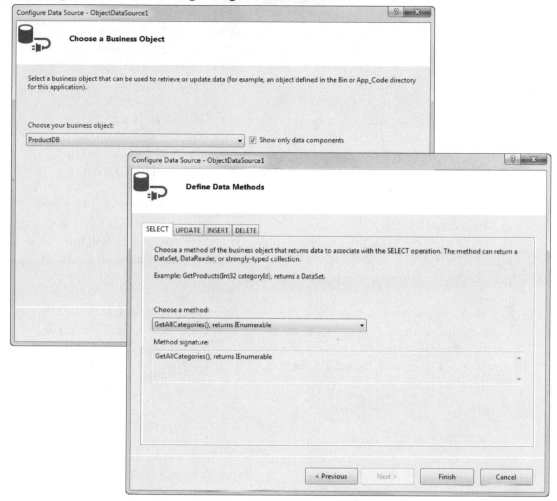

Description

- You can use the Configure Data Source dialog boxes to configure an ObjectDataSource control by choosing Configure Data Source from its smart tag menu.
- The Choose a Business Object step lets you select the data access class you want to use.
- The Define Data Methods step includes tabs that let you choose the methods you want to use for select, update, insert, and delete operations.
- If you choose a method that requires parameters, a Define Parameters step will appear. This step will let you choose the source of each parameter required by the method. For example, you can specify that a drop-down list should be used as the source for a parameter.
- If you create a new data source from a bound control, the Data Source Configuration Wizard asks you to choose a data source type. To create an object data source, select the Object option. Then, when you click the Next button, the first dialog box shown above is displayed.

Figure 17-4   How to configure an ObjectDataSource control

A Product List application

To illustrate the basics of working with the ObjectDataSource control, figure 17-5 presents a Product List application. This application is identical in appearance to the Product List application that was presented in chapter 13. However, instead of using SqlDataSource controls to retrieve the data, it uses ObjectDataSource controls.

This figure also lists the methods that are provided by the data access class named ProductDB that is used by this application. The first method, GetAllCategories, returns an IEnumerable object (actually, a data reader) that contains the data for all of the categories in the Categories table. This data includes just the category ID and long name for each category.

The second method, GetProductsByCategory, returns an IEnumerable object (again, a data reader) that includes all of the products in the Products table that have the category ID that's supplied by a parameter. This parameter will be bound to the SelectedValue property of the drop-down list. As a result, the ID of the category selected by the user will be passed to the GetProductsByCategory method.

This application illustrates how the use of object data sources lets you separate the presentation code from the data access code. As you will see, all of the presentation code is in the aspx file. And all of the data access code is in the data access class that's named ProductDB.

The Product List application

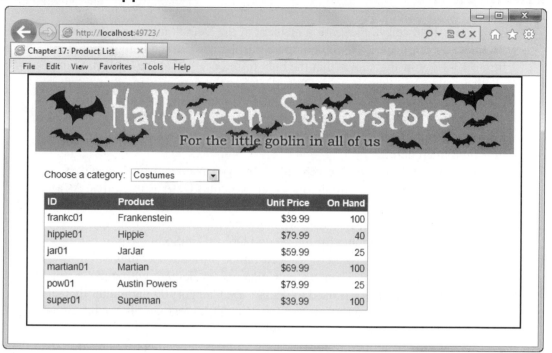

Methods of the ProductDB class

Method	Description
`GetAllCategories()`	Returns an IEnumerable object with the ID and long name of all the categories in the Categories table.
`GetProductsByCategory(categoryID)`	Returns an IEnumerable object with the ID, name, unit price, and on-hand quantity for all products in the Products table for the specified category.

Description

- The Category drop-down list is bound to an ObjectDataSource control that retrieves a list of categories from the Categories table.

- The DataList control is bound to a second ObjectDataSource control that uses a parameterized query to retrieve the products for a selected category. The CategoryID for the parameter is taken from the SelectedValue property of the drop-down list.

- Both ObjectDataSource controls use a data access class named ProductDB that contains the static methods that return a list of categories and the products for a specific category.

Figure 17-5   The Product List application

The aspx file

Figure 17-6 shows the section element of the Default.aspx page for the Product List application. If you compare this listing with the listing shown in figure 13-17, you'll discover that the only difference is that the SqlDataSource elements have been replaced by ObjectDataSource elements. In other words, the code for the drop-down list and DataList controls is identical whether the application uses a SQL data source or an object data source. (For this application, the formatting attributes for the data list have been stored in a skin, so you don't see them here.)

In the first ObjectDataSource control, the TypeName attribute specifies ProductDB, and the SelectMethod attribute specifies GetAllCategories. As a result, the GetAllCategories method in the ProductDB data access class will be called to retrieve the category data when the drop-down list is bound.

The TypeName attribute for the second ObjectDataSource control also specifies ProductDB, and the SelectMethod attribute specifies GetProductsByCategory. Then, a ControlParameter element within the SelectParameters element is used to declare the CategoryID parameter that's passed to the GetProductsByCategory method. This parameter is bound to the SelectedValue property of the drop-down list.

Because the data binding for this application is defined entirely in the aspx file, there is no code-behind file for this page. As a result, the only C# code for this application is in the ProductDB class, which is presented in the next figure.

The section element of the Default.aspx file

```
<section>
<form id="form1" runat="server">
    <label>Choose a category: </label>
    <asp:DropDownList ID="ddlCategory" runat="server"
        DataSourceID="ObjectDataSource1" DataTextField="LongName"
        DataValueField="CategoryID" AutoPostBack="True">
    </asp:DropDownList><br />
    <asp:ObjectDataSource ID="ObjectDataSource1" runat="server"
        SelectMethod="GetAllCategories" TypeName="ProductDB">
    </asp:ObjectDataSource>
    <asp:DataList ID="dlProducts" runat="server" DataKeyField="ProductID"
        DataSourceID="ObjectDataSource2">
        <HeaderTemplate>
            <table>
                <tr>
                    <td class="col1">ID</td>
                    <td class="col2">Product</td>
                    <td class="col3">Unit Price</td>
                    <td class="col4">On Hand</td>
                </tr>
            </table>
        </HeaderTemplate>
        <ItemTemplate>
            <table>
                <tr>
                    <td class="col1">
                        <asp:Label ID="lblID" runat="server"
                            Text='<%# Eval("ProductID") %>' />
                    </td>
                    <td class="col2">
                        <asp:Label ID="lblName" runat="server"
                            Text='<%# Eval("Name") %>' />
                    </td>
                    <td class="col3">
                        <asp:Label ID="lblUnitPrice" runat="server"
                            Text='<%# Eval("UnitPrice", "{0:C}") %>' />
                    </td>
                    <td class="col4">
                        <asp:Label ID="lblOnHand" runat="server"
                            Text='<%# Eval("OnHand") %>' />
                    </td>
                </tr>
            </table>
        </ItemTemplate>
    </asp:DataList>
    <asp:ObjectDataSource ID="ObjectDataSource2" runat="server"
        SelectMethod="GetProductsByCategory" TypeName="ProductDB">
        <SelectParameters>
            <asp:ControlParameter ControlID="ddlCategory" Name="CategoryID"
                PropertyName="SelectedValue" Type="String" />
        </SelectParameters>
    </asp:ObjectDataSource>
</form>
</section>
```

Figure 17-6   The aspx file for the Product List application

The ProductDB class

Figure 17-7 presents the C# code for the ProductDB class. To create this class, I used the WEBSITE→Add New Item command to add a class file to the App_Code folder. Then, I added the code for the public GetAllCategories and GetProductsByCategory methods. I also created a private method named GetConnectionString. This method is used by both of the public methods to retrieve the connection string for the Halloween database.

Before I explain the details of how these methods work, I want to point out the DataObject and DataObjectMethod attributes that appear in this class. These attributes are used to identify the class and methods as data objects, and you'll learn how to use them in figure 17-11. For now, just realize that they're used by the Configure Data Source wizard to determine which classes and methods to display when you configure an object data source.

The GetAllCategories method starts by creating a connection to the Halloween database. To get the connection for this database, it calls the GetConnectionString method. Next, this method creates a string variable that contains the Select statement that will be used to retrieve data from the Halloween database:

```
SELECT CategoryID, LongName
FROM Categories
ORDER BY LongName
```

Then, a SqlCommand object is created using the string variable that contains the Select statement and the connection object as parameters. Finally, the connection is opened, the ExecuteReader method of the command object is called to create a data reader object that contains the requested data, and the data reader is returned to the object data source.

The GetProductsByCategory method is slightly more complicated because it uses a parameter in its Select statement:

```
SELECT ProductID, Name, UnitPrice, OnHand
FROM Products
WHERE CategoryID = @CategoryID
ORDER BY ProductID
```

Here again, a SqlCommand object is created using this Select statement and the connection object. Then, a parameter named CategoryID is added to the command's Parameters collection before the connection is opened. This parameter is assigned the value of the CategoryID parameter that's passed to the method. Finally, the command is executed so it returns a data reader with the requested data.

The GetConnectionString method uses the ConfigurationManager class to retrieve the connection string named "HalloweenConnectionString" from the web.config file. As a result, the connection string for the Halloween database must be included in this file. Unlike when you create a SQL data source, though, you can't save the connection string in the web.config file when you create an object data source. Instead, you have to manually add this connection string to the web.config file. To refresh your memory about the syntax of a connection string in this file, please refer to figure 13-4 in chapter 13.

The ProductDB class

```
using System;
using System.Collections;
using System.Configuration;
using System.Data;
using System.Data.SqlClient;
using System.ComponentModel;

[DataObject(true)]
public static class ProductDB
{
    [DataObjectMethod(DataObjectMethodType.Select)]
    public static IEnumerable GetAllCategories()
    {
        SqlConnection con = new SqlConnection(GetConnectionString());
        string sel = "SELECT CategoryID, LongName "
            + "FROM Categories ORDER BY LongName";
        SqlCommand cmd = new SqlCommand(sel, con);
        con.Open();
        SqlDataReader dr = cmd.ExecuteReader();
        return dr;
    }

    [DataObjectMethod(DataObjectMethodType.Select)]
    public static IEnumerable GetProductsByCategory(string CategoryID)
    {
        SqlConnection con = new SqlConnection(GetConnectionString());
        string sel = "SELECT ProductID, Name, "
            + "UnitPrice, OnHand "
            + "FROM Products "
            + "WHERE CategoryID = @CategoryID "
            + "ORDER BY ProductID";
        SqlCommand cmd = new SqlCommand(sel, con);
        cmd.Parameters.AddWithValue("CategoryID", CategoryID);
        con.Open();
        SqlDataReader dr = cmd.ExecuteReader();
        return dr;
    }

    private static string GetConnectionString()
    {
        return ConfigurationManager.ConnectionStrings
            ["HalloweenConnectionString"].ConnectionString;
    }
}
```

Note

* The DataObject and DataObjectMethod attributes are described in figure 17-11.

Figure 17-7   The ProductDB class for the Product List application

How to create a data access class

The most challenging aspect of using object data sources is developing the data access classes that they require. So the topics that follow explain how to design and implement these classes.

How to design a data access class

As figure 17-8 shows, the data access class used by an ObjectDataSource control can have four different types of methods that are used to select, insert, update, and delete data. You can use any method names that you want for these methods, and you can design the class so it has more than one of each of these types of methods. For example, the ProductDB class used in the previous figure has two select methods that are named GetAllCategories and GetProductsByCategory.

The data access methods can be static methods or instance methods. If you define them as instance methods, the ObjectDataSource control will create an instance of the data access class before it calls the method, and then destroy the object after the method has been executed. For this to work, the data access class must provide a parameterless constructor. In C#, though, a parameterless constructor is provided by default if the class has no constructors.

Because creating and destroying a data access object can be time consuming, I suggest that you use static methods for the select, insert, update, and delete methods whenever possible. That way, the ObjectDataSource control won't have to create an instance of the data access class when it calls one of the data access methods.

Although you provide the names of the methods called by the ObjectDataSource control by using the SelectMethod, InsertMethod, UpdateMethod, and DeleteMethod attributes, the ObjectDataSource control doesn't generate the parameters that will be passed to these methods until runtime. Because of that, the ObjectDataSource control must use a .NET feature called *reflection* to determine if a method it calls contains the correct parameters. It also uses reflection to determine the return type of a select method. As you'll see in the next figure, this lets you design a select method that can return the selected data in a variety of forms.

In case you haven't encountered reflection before, it's a .NET feature that provides information about compiled classes at runtime. For example, reflection can determine what methods are provided by a particular class. In addition, it can determine what parameters each method requires and the type returned by the method.

Types of methods in a data access class

Method type	Description
Select	Retrieves data from a database and returns it as an IEnumerable object.
Insert	Inserts data for one row into the underlying database. The values for the new row are passed via one or more parameters.
Update	Updates the data for one row in the underlying database. The values for the updated row, along with any values that are used to implement optimistic concurrency, are passed via one or more parameters.
Delete	Deletes a row from the underlying database. The key or keys for the row to be deleted, along with any values that are used to implement optimistic concurrency, are passed via one or more parameters.

How an object data source determines which method to call

- The name of the method used for select, insert, update, and delete operations is specified by the SelectMethod, InsertMethod, UpdateMethod, or DeleteMethod attribute.

- The ObjectDataSource control determines what parameters need to be passed to the data access class methods based on the data fields to be inserted, updated, or deleted and whether or not optimistic concurrency is used.

- The ObjectDataSource control uses reflection to determine the parameter signatures for the insert, update, and delete methods provided by the data access class.

- At runtime, if the class doesn't provide a method with the correct name and parameters, an exception is thrown.

Description

- A data access class can declare public methods that select, insert, update, and delete data. These methods can be instance methods or static methods.

- You can use any method names you want for the select, insert, update, and delete methods.

- If the select, insert, update, and delete methods are static methods, the methods are used without creating an instance of the data access class.

- If the select, insert, update, and delete methods are instance methods, an instance of the data access class is created and destroyed for each data access operation. In this case, the data access class must provide a parameterless constructor.

- You can use parameters to pass selection criteria or other data to the select, insert, update, and delete methods. For more information on the parameters used with insert, update, and delete methods, see figure 17-10.

- *Reflection* is a .NET feature that provides information about compiled classes and methods at runtime.

Figure 17-8   How to design a data access class

How to create a select method

Figure 17-9 shows how to design and code a select method that can be used with an ObjectDataSource control. The table at the top of this figure lists the four different types of values that a select method can return. The simplest is the IEnumerable interface, which can return a data reader or a data view since the DataReader and DataView classes implement the IEnumerable interface.

The IEnumerable object can also be a strongly-typed collection that's created by using the generics feature of C#. This technique is illustrated in the example in this figure. Here, the select method starts by creating a List<> object that will store a list of Category objects. Then, a Category object is created for each row that's retrieved by the data reader. To do that, the values of the row are assigned to the properties of the object. Then, the Category object is added to the List<Category> object. Finally, the data reader and connection are closed and the List<Category> object is returned to the object data source.

The select method can also return a DataTable or DataSet object. Because a dataset can contain more than one table, the ObjectDataSource control simply uses the first table in the dataset. As a result, you must design the select method so the first table in the dataset contains the data you want to access.

The main advantage of returning a dataset is that the object data source can cache a dataset. Then, to enable caching, you can set the EnableCaching attribute to True for the ObjectDataSource control. In that case, the select method will be called only the first time the data is requested. For more information on caching, which works the same as it does for a SqlDataSource control, please refer back to chapter 13.

You can also pass parameters to the select method. In that case, the ObjectDataSource control must include a SelectParameters element. This element is added automatically if you use the Configure Data Source wizard to create the control. Then, you can create a ControlParameter element that binds a parameter to a control such as a drop-down list. You saw an example of this in figure 17-6.

Allowable return types for a select method

Return type	Description
IEnumerable	A collection such as an ArrayList, or a strongly-typed collection such as System.Collections.Generic.List. (Because the DataReader and DataView classes implement IEnumerable, the select method can also return a data reader or a data view.)
DataTable	If the select method returns a data table, the ObjectDataSource control automatically extracts a data view from the table and uses the view for data binding.
DataSet	If the select method returns a dataset, the ObjectDataSource control extracts a data view from the first data table in the dataset and uses the view for data binding.
Object	If the select method returns an object, the ObjectDataSource control wraps the object in an IEnumerable collection with just one item, then does the data binding as if the method returned an IEnumerable object.

A select method that returns a strongly-typed collection

```
public static List<Category> GetCategories()
{
    List<Category> categoryList = new List<Category>();
    string sel = "SELECT CategoryID, ShortName, LongName "
        + "FROM Categories ORDER BY ShortName";
    SqlConnection con = new SqlConnection(GetConnectionString());
    SqlCommand cmd = new SqlCommand(sel, con);
    con.Open();
    SqlDataReader dr = cmd.ExecuteReader();
    Category category;
    while (dr.Read())
    {
        category = new Category();
        category.CategoryID = dr["CategoryID"].ToString();
        category.ShortName = dr["ShortName"].ToString();
        category.LongName = dr["LongName"].ToString();
        categoryList.Add(category);
    }
    dr.Close();
    con.Close();
    return categoryList;
}
```

Description

- The select method returns data retrieved from the underlying database. It can return the data in several forms, including a data reader, dataset, or strongly-typed collection.

- If the select method returns a dataset, the object data source can cache the data.

- The select method can return a strongly-typed collection using C#'s generics feature. To use this feature, the application must include a business class that defines the objects in the collection. See figure 17-10 for more information.

- If the select method accepts parameters, the parameters must be declared within the SelectParameters element of the ObjectDataSource control.

Figure 17-9   How to create a select method

How to create update, delete, and insert methods

Besides select methods, the data access class used by an object data source can provide methods that update, delete, and insert data in the underlying database. Before you can code these methods, you need to determine what parameters are required. Figure 17-10 summarizes how an object data source generates these parameters.

Any insert or delete method you create requires a single business object as its parameter. This business object must contain all the values required by the method, and you can give it any name you choose. If an update method doesn't provide for optimistic concurrency checking, it too requires a single business object as its parameter.

If an update method provides for optimistic concurrency checking, it requires two parameters as shown in the code at the top of this figure. One of the parameters must be a business object that provides the original values for the row to be updated, and the other parameter must be a business object that provides the new values for the row. Note that the name of the parameter for the business object that contains the new values can have any name you choose. However, the name of the parameter for the business object that contains the original values must be the same as the name of the parameter for the business object with the new values, preceded by the value of the OldValuesParameterFormatString attribute. In this example, the value of this attribute is original_, which is the default.

Two parameters are also required if the key column for a table is updatable. In that case, though, the object data source won't automatically generate two parameters. Because of that, you will need to set the ConflictDetection property of the object data source to CompareAllValues even if the update method doesn't provide for optimistic concurrency checking, and you will need to set the OldValuesParameterFormatString property accordingly. Then, you can use the property that contains the value for the key column of the object that contains the original values to identify the row to be updated.

The business objects that you pass to update, delete, and insert methods are defined by the class that's identified on the DataObjectTypeName attribute of the object data source. This class must meet the requirements listed in this figure. First, the class must provide a parameterless constructor. Since C# provides a parameterless constructor by default if a class isn't defined with any constructors, you may be able to omit this constructor. However, I prefer to include it for completeness.

Second, the class must define a public property for each bound field that's passed from the bound control to the object data source. If the object data source is bound to a GridView or DetailsView control that uses BoundField elements, the names of these properties must be the same as the names specified for the DataField attributes of those elements. In contrast, if the object data source is bound to a GridView or DetailsView control that uses TemplateField elements, or if the object data source is bound to a FormView or ListView control, the names of these properties must be the same as the names in the Eval and Bind methods of the bound controls.

A typical update method

```
public static int UpdateCategory(Category original_Category,
    Category category)
{
    SqlConnection con = new SqlConnection(GetConnectionString());
    string up = "UPDATE Categories "
        + "SET ShortName = @ShortName, "
        + "LongName = @LongName "
        + "WHERE CategoryID = @original_CategoryID "
        + "AND ShortName = @original_ShortName "
        + "AND LongName = @original_LongName";
    SqlCommand cmd = new SqlCommand(up, con);
    cmd.Parameters.AddWithValue("ShortName", category.ShortName);
    cmd.Parameters.AddWithValue("LongName", category.LongName);
    cmd.Parameters.AddWithValue("original_CategoryID",
        original_Category.CategoryID);
    cmd.Parameters.AddWithValue("original_ShortName",
        original_Category.ShortName);
    cmd.Parameters.AddWithValue("original_LongName",
        original_Category.LongName);
    con.Open();
    int updateCount = cmd.ExecuteNonQuery();
    con.Close();
    return updateCount;
}
```

How parameters are generated

- When the insert or delete method is called, one parameter of the business class type is generated and passed to the method. The parameter that's declared in the method can have any name you choose.

- One parameter of the business class type is also generated and passed to the update method when this method is called if optimistic concurrency isn't used. The parameter that's declared in the method can have any name you choose.

- If optimistic concurrency is specified, two parameters are generated and passed to the update method. One contains the original values, and the other contains the new values. The name of the parameter that contains the original values must be the same as the name of the parameter that contains the new values, preceded by the string that's specified by the OldValuesParameterFormatString attribute.

Requirements for the business class

- The class must provide a parameterless constructor.

- The class must have public properties with names that match the names of the bound fields that are passed to the object data source from the bound control.

- The public properties must have both get and set accessors.

Description

- To properly design an update, delete, or insert method, you must be aware of how the ObjectDataSource control generates the parameters passed to these methods.

Figure 17-10   How to create update, delete, and insert methods

Third, the property for each bound field must include both get and set accessors. The object data source uses the set accessors to set the values of the properties based on the values passed to it from the bound control. And the insert, update, and delete methods in the data access class use the get accessors to assign the values of the properties to parameters of command objects.

Once the ObjectDataSource control has determined what parameters need to be passed, it uses reflection to determine whether the data access class has a method that accepts the required parameters. If so, the method is called using these parameters. If not, an exception is thrown.

Before I go on, I want to point out that you don't have to use business objects as the parameters of insert, update, and delete methods. Instead, you can use a parameter for each bound field that's required by a method. This technique can be cumbersome, though, if more than just a few fields are required. In addition, it's more difficult to determine what parameters the object data source will generate. It's also more difficult to work with bound controls like the GridView control because you have to manually enter the name of each field you want to bind. That's because the fields are defined in the data access class and not directly in the data source. (When you use business objects, the business class is identified in the data source, and the properties of that class are made available to bound controls.) For these reasons, I recommend that you use business objects whenever possible.

How to use attributes to mark a data access class

Figure 17-11 shows how you can use *C# attributes* to identify a data access class and its methods. In case you haven't worked with attributes before, they are simply a way to provide declarative information for classes, methods, properties, and so on. Although some of these attributes have meaning at runtime, the attributes in this figure are used at design time. In particular, the Configure Data Source wizard uses these attributes to determine which classes in the App_Code folder are data access classes and which methods in the data access class are select, insert, update, and delete methods.

Note, however, that you don't need to use these attributes. The only reason to use them is to help the Configure Data Source wizard recognize the data access classes and methods. If you haven't marked your data access classes with these attributes, you can still access them from the wizard by clearing the Show Only Data Components check box in the Choose a Business Object step of the wizard (see figure 17-4).

Attributes for marking data access classes

To mark an element as...	Use this attribute...
A data object class	`[DataObject(true)]`
A Select method	`[DataObjectMethod(DataObjectMethodType.Select)]`
An Insert method	`[DataObjectMethod(DataObjectMethodType.Insert)]`
An Update method	`[DataObjectMethod(DataObjectMethodType.Update)]`
A Delete method	`[DataObjectMethod(DataObjectMethodType.Delete)]`

A marked data access class

```
using System.Data;
using System.Collections.Generic;
using System.Data.SqlClient;
using System.Configuration;
using System.ComponentModel;

[DataObject(true)]
public static class CategoryDB
{
    [DataObjectMethod(DataObjectMethodType.Select)]
    public static List<Category> GetCategories()
    {
        List<Category> categoryList = new List<Category>();
        string sel = "SELECT CategoryID, ShortName, LongName "
            + "FROM Categories ORDER BY ShortName";
        SqlConnection con = new SqlConnection(GetConnectionString());
        SqlCommand cmd = new SqlCommand(sel, con);
        con.Open();
        SqlDataReader dr = cmd.ExecuteReader();
        Category category;
        while (dr.Read())
        {
            category = new Category();
            category.CategoryID = dr["CategoryID"].ToString();
            category.ShortName = dr["ShortName"].ToString();
            category.LongName = dr["LongName"].ToString();
            categoryList.Add(category);
        }
        dr.Close();
        con.Close();
        return categoryList;
    }
}
```

Description

- You can use DataObject and DataObjectMethod attributes to mark data access classes and methods. Visual Studio uses these attributes to determine which classes and methods to list in the drop-down lists of the Configure Data Source wizard.

- The DataObject and DataObjectMethod attributes are stored in the System.ComponentModel namespace.

Figure 17-11   How to use attributes to mark a data access class

A Category Maintenance application

To give you a better idea of how you can use an object data source to update, delete, and insert data, the following topics present an application that maintains the Categories table in the Halloween database. This application is a variation of the Category Maintenance application that was presented in chapter 14.

The design

Figure 17-12 presents the design for this version of the Category Maintenance application. It uses a GridView control to let the user update and delete category rows and a DetailsView control to insert new category rows. Both the GridView and DetailsView controls are bound to a single ObjectDataSource control. But the DetailsView control is used only in Insert mode, so it isn't used to display, update, or delete existing category rows.

The table in this figure shows the public methods that are provided by the CategoryDB class. These four methods provide the select, update, delete, and insert functions. Since all of these methods are defined as static, an instance of the CategoryDB class doesn't have to be created to access the database.

The aspx file

The two parts of figure 17-13 show the Default.aspx file for this application. In part 1, you can see the aspx code for the GridView control that displays the category rows. Its Columns collection includes three BoundField columns, named CategoryID, ShortName, and LongName. (I didn't use templates or validation controls for this application so it would be easier to focus on how the ObjectDataSource control is used.)

In part 2, you can see the aspx code for the ObjectDataSource control. It names CategoryDB as the data access class and Category as the business class. It also provides the names of the select, insert, update, and delete methods that will be used to access the data. Notice that the ConflictDetection attribute is set to CompareAllValues so optimistic concurrency will be used. You'll see one way to implement optimistic concurrency with an object data source when you see the C# code for this application.

Also notice that parameters are included only for the update method. These parameters are included because the update method requires two parameters: an object that contains the original values and an object that contains the new values. Because these parameters must be given appropriate names as explained earlier, the object data source must include parameters that specify these names. In contrast, the names of the parameters in the insert and delete methods can be anything you like, so they don't have to be defined by the object data source.

You can also see the aspx code for the DetailsView control in part 2. Here, I set the DefaultMode attribute to Insert so this control is always displayed in Insert mode.

The Category Maintenance application

Methods of the CategoryDB class

Method type	Signature
Select	`public static List<Category> GetCategories()`
Update	`public static int UpdateCategory(` `        Category original_category, Category category)`
Delete	`public static int DeleteCategory(Category category)`
Insert	`public static int InsertCategory(Category category)`

Description

- This version of the Category Maintenance application uses a GridView control to update and delete rows and a DetailsView control to insert rows. These controls are bound to an ObjectDataSource control that accesses the Categories table of the Halloween database.

- The data access class named CategoryDB provides the select, insert, update, and delete methods.

Figure 17-12   The Category Maintenance application

The Default.aspx file   **Page 1**

```
<%@ Page Language="C#" AutoEventWireup="true" CodeFile="Default.aspx.cs"
Inherits="_Default" Theme="Default" %>

<!DOCTYPE html>

<html xmlns="http://www.w3.org/1999/xhtml">
<head id="Head1" runat="server">
    <title>Chapter 17: Category Maintenance</title>
    <link href="App_Themes/Default/Main.css" rel="stylesheet"
        type="text/css" />
</head>
<body>
    <header>
        <img src="Images/banner.jpg" />
    </header>
    <section>
    <h1>Category Maintenance</h1>
    <form id="form1" runat="server">
        <asp:GridView ID="GridView1" runat="server"
            AutoGenerateColumns="False" DataKeyNames="CategoryID"
            DataSourceID="ObjectDataSource1"
            OnRowDeleted="GridView1_RowDeleted"
            OnRowUpdated="GridView1_RowUpdated">
            <Columns>
                <asp:BoundField DataField="CategoryID" HeaderText="ID"
                    ReadOnly="True" >
                <HeaderStyle HorizontalAlign="Left" />
                <ItemStyle Width="100px" />
                </asp:BoundField>
                <asp:BoundField DataField="ShortName"
                    HeaderText="Short Name">
                <HeaderStyle HorizontalAlign="Left" />
                <ItemStyle Width="150px" />
                </asp:BoundField>
                <asp:BoundField DataField="LongName"
                    HeaderText="Long Name">
                <HeaderStyle HorizontalAlign="Left" />
                <ItemStyle Width="200px" />
                </asp:BoundField>
                <asp:CommandField ButtonType="Button"
                    ShowEditButton="True" />
                <asp:CommandField ButtonType="Button"
                    ShowDeleteButton="True" />
            </Columns>
        </asp:GridView>
```

Figure 17-13   The aspx file of the Category Maintenance application (part 1 of 2)

The Default.aspx file   **Page 2**

```
<asp:ObjectDataSource ID="ObjectDataSource1" runat="server"
    DataObjectTypeName="Category" DeleteMethod="DeleteCategory"
    InsertMethod="InsertCategory"
    OldValuesParameterFormatString="original_{0}"
    SelectMethod="GetCategories" TypeName="CategoryDB"
    UpdateMethod="UpdateCategory"
    ConflictDetection="CompareAllValues"
    OnDeleted="ObjectDataSource1_Deleted"
    OnUpdated="ObjectDataSource1_Updated">
    <UpdateParameters>
        <asp:Parameter Name="original_Category" Type="Object" />
        <asp:Parameter Name="category" Type="Object" />
    </UpdateParameters>
</asp:ObjectDataSource>
<p id="new">To create a new category, enter the category information
    and click Insert.</p>
<p>
    <asp:Label ID="lblError" runat="server" EnableViewState="False">
    </asp:Label>
</p>
<asp:DetailsView ID="DetailsView1" runat="server"
    AutoGenerateRows="False" DataSourceID="ObjectDataSource1"
    DefaultMode="Insert" OnItemInserted="DetailsView1_ItemInserted">
    <Fields>
        <asp:BoundField DataField="CategoryID"
            HeaderText="Category ID:"
            SortExpression="CategoryID" />
        <asp:BoundField DataField="ShortName"
            HeaderText="Short Name:"
            SortExpression="ShortName" />
        <asp:BoundField DataField="LongName"
            HeaderText="Long Name:"
            SortExpression="LongName" />
        <asp:CommandField ButtonType="Button"
            ShowInsertButton="True" />
    </Fields>
</asp:DetailsView>
</form>
</section>
</body>
</html>
```

Figure 17-13   The aspx file of the Category Maintenance application (part 2 of 2)

The code-behind file

Figure 17-14 shows the code-behind file for the Default.aspx page of the Category Maintenance application. This file consists of five methods that handle the exceptions that might be raised and the concurrency errors that might occur when the object data source's update, delete, or insert methods are called.

The first method is executed after the data source is updated. This method retrieves the return value from the update method using the ReturnValue property of the e argument and assigns it to the AffectedRows property of the e argument. This is necessary because the AffectedRows property isn't set automatically like it is for a SQL data source. For this to work, of course, the update method must return the number of rows that were updated. You'll see the code that accomplishes that in figure 17-16.

The second method is executed after a row in the GridView control is updated, which happens after the data source is updated. This method checks the Exception property of the e argument to determine if an exception has been thrown. If it has, an error message is displayed, the ExceptionHandled property is set to True to suppress the exception, and the KeepInEditMode property is set to True to leave the GridView control in edit mode.

If an exception didn't occur, this method continues by checking the AffectedRows property of the e argument. The value of this property is passed forward from the AffectedRows property of the object data source's Updated event. If the value of this property is zero, the row was not updated, most likely due to the concurrency checking code that was added to the SQL Update statement. As a result, an appropriate error message is displayed.

The next two methods are similar, except they handle the Deleted event of the ObjectDataSource control and the RowDeleted event of the GridView control. Like the Updated event handler of the ObjectDataSource control, the Deleted event handler sets the AffectedRows property of the e argument. And, like the RowUpdated event handler of the GridView control, the RowDeleted event handler checks for exceptions and concurrency errors.

The last method is executed after a row is inserted using the DetailsView control. It checks whether an exception has occurred and responds accordingly. Note that currency checking isn't necessary here because a concurrency error can't occur for an insert operation.

By the way, this code illustrates just one way that you can provide for concurrency errors. Another way is to write the update and delete methods so they throw an exception if a concurrency error occurs. Then, the RowUpdated and RowDeleted event handlers can test the e.Exception property to determine if this exception has been thrown. I prefer the technique illustrated here, though, because the code for the RowUpdated and RowDeleted event handlers is nearly the same as it is when you use a SQL data source. The only difference is that you have to use the InnerException property of the current Exception object to get the exception that caused the error. That's because a system exception occurs when a database exception isn't caught by the CategoryDB class, and the system exception is the one that's passed to the event handlers.

The Default.aspx.cs file

```
using System;
using System.Web.UI.WebControls;

public partial class _Default : System.Web.UI.Page
{
    protected void ObjectDataSource1_Updated(object sender,
        ObjectDataSourceStatusEventArgs e)
    {
        e.AffectedRows = Convert.ToInt32(e.ReturnValue);
    }

    protected void GridView1_RowUpdated(Object sender, GridViewUpdatedEventArgs e)
    {
        if (e.Exception != null) {
            lblError.Text = "A database error has occurred.<br /><br />" +
                e.Exception.Message;
            if (e.Exception.InnerException != null)
                lblError.Text += "<br />Message: "
                    + e.Exception.InnerException.Message;
            e.ExceptionHandled = true;
            e.KeepInEditMode = true;
        }
        else if (e.AffectedRows == 0)
            lblError.Text = "Another user may have updated that category."
                + "<br />Please try again.";
    }

    protected void ObjectDataSource1_Deleted(object sender,
        ObjectDataSourceStatusEventArgs e)
    {
        e.AffectedRows = Convert.ToInt32(e.ReturnValue);
    }

    protected void GridView1_RowDeleted(object sender, GridViewDeletedEventArgs e)
    {
        if (e.Exception != null) {
            lblError.Text = "A database error has occurred.<br /><br />" +
                e.Exception.Message;
            if (e.Exception.InnerException != null)
                lblError.Text += "<br />Message: "
                    + e.Exception.InnerException.Message;
            e.ExceptionHandled = true;
        }
        else if (e.AffectedRows == 0)
            lblError.Text = "Another user may have updated that category. "
                + "<br />Please try again.";
    }

    protected void DetailsView1_ItemInserted(object sender,
        DetailsViewInsertedEventArgs e)
    {
        if (e.Exception != null) {
            lblError.Text = "A database error has occurred.<br /><br />" +
                e.Exception.Message;
            if (e.Exception.InnerException != null)
                lblError.Text += "<br />Message: "
                    + e.Exception.InnerException.Message;
            e.ExceptionHandled = true;
        }
    }
}
```

Figure 17-14   The code-behind file for the Category Maintenance application

The Category class

Figure 17-15 presents the Category business class that's used by the object data source for this application. If you've used business classes like this before, you shouldn't have any trouble understanding how it works. In this case, the class includes three public properties that correspond with the three columns of the Categories table. The values of these properties are stored in the three private fields declared by this class. As required for business classes that are used by an object data source, each property is defined with both a get and a set accessor. This class also includes a parameterless constructor that's called when the object data source creates an instance of the class.

The Category.cs file

```
public class Category
{
    private string categoryID;
    private string shortName;
    private string longName;

    public Category()
    {
    }

    public string CategoryID
    {
        get
        {
            return categoryID;
        }
        set
        {
            categoryID = value;
        }
    }

    public string ShortName
    {
        get
        {
            return shortName;
        }
        set
        {
            shortName = value;
        }
    }

    public string LongName
    {
        get
        {
            return longName;
        }
        set
        {
            longName = value;
        }
    }
}
```

Note

* Because auto-implemented properties automatically provide for both get and set accessors, you can use them in a business class instead of standard properties.

Figure 17-15   The Category class for the Category Maintenance application

The CategoryDB class

The two parts of figure 17-16 present the CategoryDB class that's used as the data access class for this application. This class uses the DataObject and DataObjectMethod attributes to mark the class as a data object class and to mark the methods as data object methods.

The four public methods in this class provide for the select, insert, delete, and update operations performed by this application. These methods use standard ADO.NET code to access the database. I'll describe this code briefly here so you have a general idea of how it works.

The GetCategories method retrieves all of the rows and columns from the Categories table in the Halloween database. Like the method you saw in figure 17-9, this data is stored in a List<Category> object. Then, this object is returned to the object data source, which uses it to populate the GridView control. Note that because List<Category> is a strongly-typed collection, the names of the properties that the Category class exposes were available from the Fields dialog box for the GridView control so I didn't have to enter them manually.

The only difference between this method and the method shown in figure 17-9 is that the connection and command objects in this method are created within using statements. Then, when the using blocks end, any resources associated with the objects are released. In addition, before the resources for the connection are released, the connection is closed. Because of that, it isn't necessary to explicitly close the connection.

To get a connection to the Halloween database, the GetCategories method calls the private GetConnectionString method. This method gets the connection string from the web.config file. The GetConnectionString method is also called by the other public methods.

When the user clicks the Insert button in the DetailsView control, the object data source executes the InsertCategory method. This method is declared with a single parameter for a Category object. When the object data source executes this method, it passes the values that the user entered into the DetailsView control to this object. Then, the method assigns the CategoryID, ShortName, and LongName properties of that object to the parameters that are defined in the Values clause of the Insert statement. When the Insert statement is executed, a new row with these values is inserted into the Categories table.

Before I go on, you should realize that if you run an application that uses an object data source with debugging and an unhandled exception occurs, Visual Studio will enter break mode. That's true even if the code-behind file checks for database errors as shown in figure 17-14. When this happens, you can simply click the Continue button to execute the code in the code-behind file.

The CategoryDB.cs file   Page 1

```csharp
using System.Data;
using System.Collections.Generic;
using System.Data.SqlClient;
using System.Configuration;
using System.ComponentModel;

[DataObject(true)]
public static class CategoryDB
{
    [DataObjectMethod(DataObjectMethodType.Select)]
    public static List<Category> GetCategories()
    {
        List<Category> categoryList = new List<Category>();
        string sel = "SELECT CategoryID, ShortName, LongName "
            + "FROM Categories ORDER BY ShortName";
        using (SqlConnection con = new SqlConnection(GetConnectionString())) {
            using (SqlCommand cmd = new SqlCommand(sel, con)) {
                con.Open();
                SqlDataReader dr = cmd.ExecuteReader();
                Category category;
                while (dr.Read())
                {
                    category = new Category();
                    category.CategoryID = dr["CategoryID"].ToString();
                    category.ShortName = dr["ShortName"].ToString();
                    category.LongName = dr["LongName"].ToString();
                    categoryList.Add(category);
                }
                dr.Close();
            }
        }
        return categoryList;
    }

    private static string GetConnectionString()
    {
        return ConfigurationManager.ConnectionStrings
            ["HalloweenConnectionString"].ConnectionString;
    }

    [DataObjectMethod(DataObjectMethodType.Insert)]
    public static void InsertCategory(Category category)
    {
        string ins = "INSERT INTO Categories "
            + " (CategoryID, ShortName, LongName) "
            + " VALUES(@CategoryID, @ShortName, @LongName)";
        using (SqlConnection con = new SqlConnection(GetConnectionString())) {
            using (SqlCommand cmd = new SqlCommand(ins, con)) {
                cmd.Parameters.AddWithValue("CategoryID", category.CategoryID);
                cmd.Parameters.AddWithValue("ShortName", category.ShortName);
                cmd.Parameters.AddWithValue("LongName", category.LongName);
                con.Open();
                cmd.ExecuteNonQuery();
            }
        }
    }
}
```

Figure 17-16   The CategoryDB class for the Category Maintenance application
(part 1 of 2)

When the user clicks the Delete button in the GridView control, the object data source executes the DeleteCategory method. This method also accepts a single parameter for a Category object. This object contains the values that were originally retrieved from the Categories table. The CategoryID, ShortName, and LongName properties of this object are assigned to the parameters that are defined in the Where clause of the Delete statement.

Notice that this method returns an integer value. Then, when the command that contains the Delete statement is executed, the result is stored in an integer variable, which is returned to the object data source. Because this value indicates the number of rows that were deleted, it can be used as shown in figure 17-14 to check for a concurrency error.

The last method, UpdateCategory, is executed when the user clicks the Update button in the GridView control. It accepts two parameters for Category objects. The first one contains the values that were originally retrieved from the Categories table, and the second one contains the new values for the row. The CategoryID, ShortName, and LongName properties of the first object are assigned to the parameters that are defined in the Where clause of the Update statement, and the ShortName and LongName properties of the second object are assigned to the properties that are defined in the Set clause of the Update statement.

Like the DeleteCategory method, the UpdateCategory method returns an integer value that indicates the number of rows that were affected by the update operation. Then, this value can be used to check for a concurrency error.

The CategoryDB.cs file   **Page 2**

```csharp
[DataObjectMethod(DataObjectMethodType.Delete)]
public static int DeleteCategory(Category category)
{
    int deleteCount = 0;
    string del = "DELETE FROM Categories "
        + "WHERE CategoryID = @CategoryID "
        + "AND ShortName = @ShortName "
        + "AND LongName = @LongName ";
    using (SqlConnection con = new SqlConnection(GetConnectionString())) {
        using (SqlCommand cmd = new SqlCommand(del, con)) {
            cmd.Parameters.AddWithValue("CategoryID", category.CategoryID);
            cmd.Parameters.AddWithValue("ShortName", category.ShortName);
            cmd.Parameters.AddWithValue("LongName", category.LongName);
            con.Open();
            deleteCount = cmd.ExecuteNonQuery();
        }
    }
    return deleteCount;
}

[DataObjectMethod(DataObjectMethodType.Update)]
public static int UpdateCategory(Category original_Category,
    Category category)
{
    int updateCount = 0;
    string up = "UPDATE Categories "
        + "SET ShortName = @ShortName, "
        + "LongName = @LongName "
        + "WHERE CategoryID = @original_CategoryID "
        + "AND ShortName = @original_ShortName "
        + "AND LongName = @original_LongName";
    using (SqlConnection con = new SqlConnection(GetConnectionString())) {
        using (SqlCommand cmd = new SqlCommand(up, con)) {
            cmd.Parameters.AddWithValue("ShortName", category.ShortName);
            cmd.Parameters.AddWithValue("LongName", category.LongName);
            cmd.Parameters.AddWithValue("original_CategoryID",
                original_Category.CategoryID);
            cmd.Parameters.AddWithValue("original_ShortName",
                original_Category.ShortName);
            cmd.Parameters.AddWithValue("original_LongName",
                original_Category.LongName);
            con.Open();
            updateCount = cmd.ExecuteNonQuery();
            con.Close();
        }
    }
    return updateCount;
}
}
```

Figure 17-16   The CategoryDB class for the Category Maintenance application
                (part 2 of 2)

How to use paging and sorting with object data sources

When you use an object data source, you should know that it doesn't automatically provide for paging or sorting with controls like the GridView control. Because of that, you have to set the attributes of the object data source that provide for paging and sorting, and you have to provide for paging and sorting in the data access class. If the data that's initially returned by the select method is sorted, you also have to provide for this in the code-behind file.

How to configure an ObjectDataSource control for paging and sorting

To create an ObjectDataSource control that provides for paging, you set the first four attributes shown in figure 17-17. When set to True, the EnablePaging attribute enables paging for the control. Then, the StartRowIndexParameterName and MaximumRowsParameterName attributes specify the names of parameters that will be used by the select method in the data access class to determine which rows are returned by the method. You'll see an example of how that works in figure 17-19. For now, just realize that when you use a pager control to display another page of data in a bound control, the bound control passes the values that will be assigned to these two parameters to the ObjectDataSource control.

The fourth attribute, SelectCountMethod, names a method in the data access class that returns a count of the total number of rows that are retrieved by the select method. The control that's bound to the object data source uses this value to determine what pager controls to display. For example, if the bound control uses first, previous, next, and last pager controls, it will be able to determine when the first or last page is displayed so it can omit the first and previous or next and last pager controls. This is illustrated by the GridView control shown at the top of this figure. In this case, the first page is displayed so the first and previous pager controls aren't included.

The last attribute in this figure, SortParameterName, provides the name of the parameter in the select method that will be used to sort the data. When the user clicks on the column header of a column in a bound control that provides for sorting, this control passes the sort sequence to the object data source. If the user clicks the ID header in the GridView control shown here, for example, the sort sequence "ProductID" is passed to the object data source. And if the user clicks this column header again, the sort sequence "ProductID DESC" is passed to the object data source. Then, the object data source passes the sort sequence on to the select method.

By the way, if you use the wizard to create an ObjectDataSource control from a data access class that provides for paging or sorting, you should know that the wizard will ask you to define the parameters used by the select method. Because these parameters are identified by attributes of the control, however, you can just click Finish when the Define Parameters step is displayed. Then, you'll need to delete the parameters that are generated by default.

A GridView control that provides for paging and sorting

ID	Name	Category	Unit Price	On Hand
pow01	Austin Powers	costumes	$79.99	25
bl01	Black Light	fx	$19.99	200
vader01	Darth Vader Mask	masks	$19.99	100
cat01	Deranged Cat	props	$19.99	45
bats01	Flying Bats	props	$69.99	25
fogj01	Fog Juice (1qt)	fx	$9.99	500
fog01	Fog Machine	fx	$34.99	100
frankc01	Frankenstein	costumes	$39.99	100

≥ ≥≥

Attributes of the ObjectDataSource control for paging and sorting

Attribute	Description
EnablePaging	True if the ObjectDataSource control supports paging.
StartRowIndexParameterName	The name of the parameter in the select method that receives the index of the first row to be retrieved.
MaximumRowsParameterName	The name of the parameter in the select method class that receives the maximum number of rows to be retrieved.
SelectCountMethod	The name of a public method that returns the total number of rows that are retrieved by the select method.
SortParameterName	The name of the parameter in the select method of the data access class that is used to sort the data.

How to configure a control for paging

- To use paging with a control like a GridView control that's bound to an object data source, you set the first four attributes of the ObjectDataSource control shown above.

- When a pager control on a bound control is clicked, the index of the starting row to be displayed and the maximum number of rows to be displayed are passed to the ObjectDataSource control. The ObjectDataSource control then passes these values to the parameters of the select method specified by the StartRowIndexParameterName and MaximumRowsParameterName attributes of the control.

- In addition to the select method that retrieves the rows to be displayed, the data access class must include a method that returns the total number of rows that are retrieved. This method is named on the SelectCountMethod attribute of the ObjectDataSource control, and it's used by the bound control to determine what pager controls to display.

How to configure a control for sorting

- To use sorting with a control that's bound to an object data source, you must set the SortParameterName attribute of the ObjectDataSource control.

- When the column header for a column that provides for sorting on a bound control is clicked, the value of the SortExpression attribute for that column is passed to the ObjectDataSource control, which passes it to the parameter of the select method specified by the SortParameterName attribute.

Figure 17-17   How to configure an ObjectDataSource control for paging and sorting

The aspx file that provides for paging and sorting

Figure 17-18 presents the aspx code for the GridView control you saw in the previous figure, along with the ObjectDataSource control it's bound to. Here, you can see that both the AllowPaging and AllowSorting attributes of the GridView control are set to True. In addition, the OnSorting attribute indicates that when the user clicks on the header for a column that provides for sorting, the grdProducts_Sorting event handler will be executed. You'll see why this is necessary in just a minute.

This GridView control also includes a SortExpression attribute for its product ID, name, and category ID columns. Notice that the sort expression for the category ID column includes the names of two columns. That way, this application will work just like the Product List application of chapter 14.

For the ObjectDataSource control to provide for paging, its EnablePaging attribute is set to True. In addition, its StartRowIndexParameterName, MaximumRowsParameterName, and SelectCountMethod attributes are set to appropriate values. To provide for sorting, its SortParameterName attribute is also set.

The code-behind file that provides for sorting

In many cases, the select method associated with an object data source will return the data in a sorted sequence. For example, the data that's retrieved by the GetProducts method of the ProductDB class that's used by the ObjectDataSource control in figure 17-18 sorts the data by name in ascending sequence, as shown in the GridView control in figure 17-17. Then, if the user clicks the column header for this column, the data should be sorted in descending sequence by this column.

Unfortunately, the GridView control has no way of knowing how the data is sorted. Because of that, the first time you click on a column header, it will assume that you want the column sorted in ascending sequence. To provide for sorting a column in descending sequence the first time the column header is clicked, you can add code like that shown in figure 17-18 to the code-behind file.

To start, the first time the page is loaded, the Page_Load event handler adds an item named InitialSort to view state and sets its value to True. This indicates that the data is sorted in its initial sequence. In other words, the data is sorted in the sequence specified by the select method.

Each time the user clicks a column header to sort the data, the grdProducts_ Sorting event handler is executed. This event handler starts by checking to see if the InitialSort item exists, which it will the first time a column header is clicked. Then, it removes this item from view state and checks if the SortExpression property of the e parameter is equal to the default sort column that's declared in the ProductDB class. If it is, it means that the user clicked the column header for the column that was initially used to sort the data. Then, the SortDirection property of the e parameter is set to indicate that the column should be sorted in descending sequence. Note that each subsequent time the user clicks a column header, the view state item will be null and no processing will be performed by this event handler.

The aspx code for the GridView and ObjectDataSource controls

```
<asp:GridView ID="grdProducts" runat="server"
    AutoGenerateColumns="False" DataKeyNames="ProductID"
    DataSourceID="ObjectDataSource1" AllowPaging="True" PageSize="8"
    AllowSorting="True" OnSorting="grdProducts_Sorting">
    <Columns>
        <asp:BoundField DataField="ProductID" HeaderText="ID"
            ReadOnly="True" SortExpression="ProductID">
            <HeaderStyle HorizontalAlign="Left" />
            <ItemStyle Width="75px" />
        </asp:BoundField>
        <asp:BoundField DataField="Name" HeaderText="Name"
            SortExpression="Name">
            <HeaderStyle HorizontalAlign="Left" />
            <ItemStyle Width="200px" />
        </asp:BoundField>
        <asp:BoundField DataField="CategoryID" HeaderText="Category"
            SortExpression="CategoryID, Name" />
        <asp:BoundField DataField="UnitPrice"
            HeaderText="Unit Price" DataFormatString="{0:c}">
            <ItemStyle HorizontalAlign="Right" />
        </asp:BoundField>
        <asp:BoundField DataField="OnHand" HeaderText="On Hand">
            <ItemStyle HorizontalAlign="Right" />
        </asp:BoundField>
    </Columns>
</asp:GridView>
<asp:ObjectDataSource ID="ObjectDataSource1" runat="server"
    SelectMethod="GetProducts" TypeName="ProductDB"
    EnablePaging="True" StartRowIndexParameterName="startIndex"
    SelectCountMethod="SelectCount" MaximumRowsParameterName="maxRows"
    SortParameterName="sortOrder">
</asp:ObjectDataSource>
```

The Default.aspx.cs file

```
public partial class _Default : System.Web.UI.Page
{
    protected void Page_Load(object sender, EventArgs e)
    {
        if (!IsPostBack)
            ViewState["InitialSort"] = true;
    }

    protected void grdProducts_Sorting(object sender, GridViewSortEventArgs e)
    {
        if (ViewState["InitialSort"] != null)
        {
            ViewState.Remove("InitialSort");
            if (e.SortExpression == ProductDB.DefaultSortColumn)
                e.SortDirection = SortDirection.Descending;
        }
    }
}
```

Figure 17-18   The aspx and code-behind files that provide for paging and sorting

How to create a data access class that provides for paging and sorting

Figure 17-19 shows the code for a data access class that's used by the object data source you saw in the last figure. This class includes three methods. GetProduct is a select method that returns the products for the requested page in the requested sequence. The method named LoadProductList, which isn't shown here, uses standard ADO.NET code to get all the products from the database and store them in the List<Product> object named productList that's declared at the class level. This method uses caching so the products only have to be retrieved from the database once. After that, they're retrieved from the cache. (Because the select method doesn't return a dataset, this can't be accomplished using the caching attributes of the object data source.) Finally, the method named SelectCount returns a count of the products in the product list.

Before I go on, you should notice the public constant that's coded at the class level. This is the constant that's used by the code-behind file that you saw in the last figure. It indicates that, by default, the products are sorted by the Name column in ascending sequence.

The body of the select method starts by calling the LoadProductList method. Then, it uses a switch statement to determine how the products should be sorted. To do that, the parameter that contains the sort expression, sortOrder, is used as the switch expression. Then, the case labels implement the six possible sort sequences: ascending and descending for each of the three sort columns.

Each case label uses LINQ extension methods to sort the products and return the products for the requested page. For example, if the user clicks the ID header in the GridView control when the web page is first displayed, the statement in the second case label is executed. This statement uses the OrderBy method to sort the products by the ProductID column. Then, it uses the Skip method to skip to the product that's specified by the startIndex parameter, and it uses the Take method to retrieve up to the number of products specified by the maxRows parameter. Finally, it uses the ToList method to convert the resulting IEnumerable object to a List<Product> object, and it returns the list to the object data source.

Note that the first time the select method is called, no value is passed to the sortOrder parameter. Because of that, the statement in the default label is executed, which sorts the products by name in ascending sequence.

Now, take a look at the statements for the fourth and fifth case labels, which are executed when the user clicks the Category header in the GridView control. The first time this header is clicked, the statement in the fourth label sorts the products by category ID in ascending sequence, then by product name in ascending sequence. The second time it's clicked, the statement in the fifth label sorts the products by category ID in ascending sequence, then by product name in descending sequence.

Note that if the application didn't provide for sorting, the switch statement wouldn't be needed. Instead, you could provide for paging using a single statement like this that returns the rows for the requested page:

```
return productList.Skip(startIndex).Take(maxRows).ToList();
```

The data access class used by the object data source

```
using System;
using System.Configuration;
using System.Data;
using System.Linq;
using System.Data.SqlClient;
using System.ComponentModel;
using System.Collections.Generic;

[DataObject(true)]
public static class ProductDB
{
    public const string DefaultSortColumn = "Name";
    private static List<Product> productList;

    [DataObjectMethodAttribute(DataObjectMethodType.Select)]
    public static List<Product> GetProducts(int startIndex, int maxRows,
        string sortOrder)
    {
        LoadProductList();

        switch (sortOrder)
        {
            case "Name DESC":
                return productList.OrderByDescending(p => p.Name)
                    .Skip(startIndex).Take(maxRows).ToList();
            case "ProductID":
                return productList.OrderBy(p => p.ProductID)
                    .Skip(startIndex).Take(maxRows).ToList();
            case "ProductID DESC":
                return productList.OrderByDescending(p => p.ProductID)
                    .Skip(startIndex).Take(maxRows).ToList();
            case "CategoryID, Name":
                return productList.OrderBy(p => p.CategoryID)
                    .ThenBy(p => p.Name)
                    .Skip(startIndex).Take(maxRows).ToList();
            case "CategoryID, Name DESC":
                return productList.OrderBy(p => p.CategoryID)
                    .ThenByDescending(p => p.Name)
                    .Skip(startIndex).Take(maxRows).ToList();
            default:
                return productList.OrderBy(p => p.Name)
                    .Skip(startIndex).Take(maxRows).ToList();
        }
    }

    public static int SelectCount()
    {
        return productList.Count;
    }
    .
    .
    .

}
```

Figure 17-19   A data access class that provides for paging and sorting

Perspective

In this chapter, you've learned how to use object data sources to build 3-layer web applications. As you've seen, object data sources take advantage of the data binding features of ASP.NET but still separate the presentation code from the data access code. Because of that, you may want to use object data sources instead of SQL data sources and thus build 3-layer applications.

If you decide that you do want to use object data sources in your applications, you will want to learn more about using ADO.NET code. For that, we recommend our ADO.NET book for C# programmers, which provides a complete course in ADO.NET database programming. When you finish it, you'll be able to use ADO.NET with or without data sources.

Terms

3-layer architecture	data object class
presentation layer	data access class
middle layer	business object
business rules	data object
database layer	data component
object data source	reflection
ADO.NET (Active Data Objects)	C# attribute
business object class	

Summary

- In a *3-layer architecture*, the *presentation layer* consists of the web pages that define the user interface. The *middle layer* consists of the classes that implement the *business rules* for the application and manage the data access for the web pages. And the *database layer* consists of the database itself.

- One way to build 3-layer applications is to use *object data sources*. With this approach, you use the classes and members of *ADO.NET* to develop the *data access classes* that enforce the business rules and work with the database.

- Three of the ADO.NET classes that you can use with object data sources are the SqlConnection, SqlCommand, and the SqlDataReader classes.

- The ObjectDataSource control specifies the name of the data access class and the names of the methods in the class that select, update, delete, and insert data. This control also determines the parameters that are passed to the methods.

- *Reflection* is a .NET feature that provides information about the compiled classes and methods at runtime.

- You can use the DataObject and DataObjectMethod *attributes* in the C# code for your data access classes to identify the classes and methods. These attributes determine what's in the drop-down lists in the Configure Data Source wizard.

- To provide paging and sorting for the data that's defined by an object data source, you have to configure the ObjectDataSource control and provide the C# in the code-behind file and data access class that implements the paging and sorting.

Exercise 17-1   Create a Customer List application

In this exercise, you'll develop an application that uses two object data sources to display a list of customers in a selected state. To make that easier, you'll start from an application that contains the data access class that will be used by the object data sources, along with the starting page, the database, image, and style sheet used by the page, and a web.config file that contains a connection string to the Halloween database.

Review the code in the data access class

1. Open the Ex17CustomerList application in the C:\aspnet45_cs directory.

2. Display the CustomerDB class in the App_Code folder, and notice that it contains three methods named GetAllStates, GetCustomersByState, and GetConnectionString. Also notice that the class is marked with a DataObject attribute and the GetAllStates and GetCustomersByState methods are marked with a DataObjectMethod attribute.

3. Review the code for the GetAllStates and GetCustomersByState methods to see that they both return an IEnumerable object. Specifically, the GetAllStates method returns a data reader object that contains the StateCode and StateName columns from the States table, and the GetCustomersByState method returns a data reader object that contains the LastName, FirstName, and PhoneNumber columns from the Customers table.

Add the drop-down list and its data source

4. Display the page in Design view, add a drop-down list to the form, and select the Choose Data Source command from the smart tag menu to display the first step of the Data Source Configuration Wizard.

5. Select the option for creating a new data source, select Object from the second step of the wizard, and click OK to display the first Configure Data Source dialog box.

6. Display the drop-down list in this dialog box to see that it contains only the CustomerDB class. Select this class and then click Next to display the second Configure Data Source dialog box.

7. Display the drop-down list in this dialog box to see that that it contains both of the methods that are marked as data object methods. Select the GetAllStates method and then click Finish to return to the first step of the Data Source Configuration Wizard.

8. Display the drop-down lists in the wizard to see that they're both empty. Then, enter "StateName" in the first drop-down list and "StateCode" in the second drop-down list.

9.   Enable auto postback for the drop-down list you just created, and change the
      ID attribute to an appropriate value.

Add the GridView control and its data source

10.   Add a GridView control below the ObjectDataSource control, and bind it to
      a new object data source that gets its data from the GetCustomersByState
      method of the CustomerDB class. This method should get the value of its
      parameter from the drop-down list.

11.   Run the application, display customers from different states, and notice that
      the widths of the columns in the GridView change depending on the data they
      contain.

12.   Return to Design view, display the Fields dialog box for the GridView control,
      and notice that the Auto-generate Fields option is selected.

13.   Remove the check mark from the Auto-generate Fields option, and then
      add three bound fields for the three columns that are returned by the
      GetCustomersByState method. To do that, you'll need to manually enter the
      column name for the DataField property, and you'll need to add a column
      header for the HeaderText property. In addition, set the width of each column
      to 150 pixels, and left-align the column headings.

14.   Run the application again to see how this looks. Then, close the browser
      window.

Section 4

Finishing an ASP.NET application

This section consists of four chapters that present ASP.NET skills that are often used in professional web applications. To start, chapter 18 shows you how to use a secure connection for an application, and chapter 19 shows you how to authenticate and authorize the users of an application using the Web Site Administration Tool and the login controls. These are essential skills for e-commerce applications.

Next, chapter 20 shows you how to use email and custom error pages as well as how to deal with the problems that can occur when users click the Back buttons in their browsers. These are useful skills for most professional applications. Then, chapter 21 shows you how to configure and deploy an application.

Because each of the chapters in this section is written as an independent module, you can read these chapters in whatever sequence you prefer. Eventually, though, you'll want to read all of these chapters because you should at least be aware of the capabilities that they offer.

18

How to secure a web site

Security is one of the most important concerns for any developer of ecommerce web sites. To secure a web site, you must make sure that the private data that's sent between the client and the server can't be deciphered. To accomplish that, this chapter shows you how to use an Internet protocol called SSL.

An introduction to SSL

To prevent others from reading data that's transmitted over the Internet, you can use the *Secure Sockets Layer*, or *SSL*. SSL is an Internet protocol that lets you transmit data over the Internet using data encryption. The topics that follow explain how SSL works and how you enable it for an application that uses IIS Express.

How secure connections work

Figure 18-1 shows a web page that uses SSL to transfer data between the server and the client over a *secure connection*. To determine if you're transmitting data over a secure connection, you can read the URL in the browser's address bar. If it starts with HTTPS rather than HTTP, then you're transmitting data over a secure connection.

With a regular HTTP connection, all data is sent as unencrypted text. As a result, if a hacker intercepts this data, it is easy to read. With a secure connection, though, all data that's transferred between the client and the server is encrypted. Although a hacker can still intercept this data, he won't be able to read it without breaking the encryption code.

Notice here that a message is displayed at the right end of the address bar indicating that a certificate error has occurred. That's because I used the test certificate that comes with IIS Express to test this application. You'll learn more about certificates in just a minute. But first, you need to know how to enable SSL when you use IIS Express.

A page that was requested with a secure connection

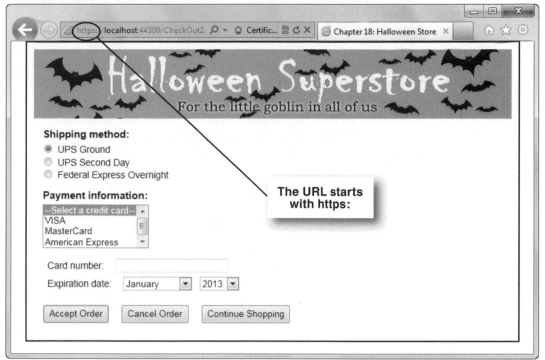

Description

- The *Secure Sockets* Layer, or *SSL*, is the protocol used by the World Wide Web that allows clients and servers to communicate over a *secure connection*.
- With SSL, the browser encrypts all data that's sent to the server and decrypts all data that's received from the server. Conversely, the server encrypts all data that's sent to the browser and decrypts all data that's received from the browser.
- SSL is able to determine if data has been tampered with during transit.
- SSL is also able to verify that a server or a client is who it claims to be.
- The URL for a secure connection starts with HTTPS instead of HTTP.

Notes

- To test an application that uses SSL, you must run the application under IIS or IIS Express.
- With some browsers, a lock icon is displayed when a secure connection is being used.

Figure 18-1   How secure connections work

How to enable SSL
for a project that uses IIS Express

When you create an application that runs under IIS Express, it's assigned a port number on the local server. You can see this port number in the address bar after the localhost keyword when you run the application. In figure 18-2, you can see that this port number is included in the URL property for the project. This property specifies the URL of the *binding* for the HTTP protocol.

To use SSL with an application that runs under IIS Express, you need to create a binding for the HTTPS protocol for the application. To do that, you simply set the SSL Enabled property of the project to True. Then, the binding is created and the URL for that binding is displayed in the SSL URL property. Here, you can see that this binding is assigned to port 44300, which is the standard port for the HTTPS binding when you use IIS Express.

A project with SSL enabled

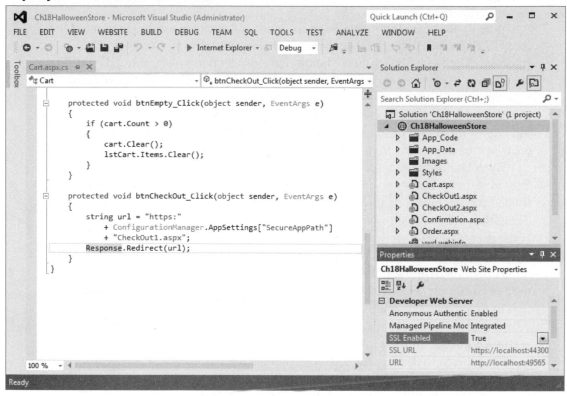

Description

- When you create a web site that uses IIS Express, a *binding* for the HTTP protocol is created, and you can see the URL for that binding in the URL property of the project.

- To use SSL with a web site that's running under IIS Express, you set the SSL Enabled property of the project to True. Then, a binding is created for the HTTPS protocol, and you can see the URL for that binding in the SSL URL property of the project.

Figure 18-2   How to enable SSL for a project that uses IIS Express

How digital secure certificates work

When you use SSL with IIS Express, a test certificate is used to authenticate IIS Express. This certificate is installed along with Visual Studio and IIS Express. When you deploy an application to a production server, though, you'll need to use a *digital secure certificate*. Figure 18-3 provides information about how these certificates work and where you get them.

Digital secure certificates serve two purposes. First, they establish the identity of the server or client. Second, they provide the information needed to encrypt data before it's transmitted.

By default, browsers are configured to accept certificates that come from trusted sources. If a browser doesn't recognize a certificate as coming from a trusted source, however, it informs the user and lets the user view the certificate. Then, the user can determine whether the certificate should be considered valid. If the user chooses to accept the certificate, the secure connection is established.

Sometimes, a server may want the client to authenticate itself with *SSL client authentication*. Although this isn't as common as *SSL server authentication*, it is used occasionally. For example, a bank might want to use SSL client authentication to make sure it's sending sensitive information such as account numbers and balances to the correct person. To implement this type of authentication, a digital secure certificate must be installed on the client.

If you want to develop an ASP.NET application that uses SSL to secure client connections, you must first obtain a digital secure certificate from a trusted source such as those listed in this figure. These *certification authorities*, or *CAs*, verify that the person or company requesting the certificate is a valid person or company by checking with a *registration authority*, or *RA*. To obtain a digital secure certificate, you'll need to provide a registration authority with information about yourself or your company. Once the registration authority approves the request, the certification authority can issue the digital secure certificate.

A digital secure certificate from a trusted source isn't free, and the cost of the certificate will depend on a variety of factors including the level of security. As a result, when you purchase a digital certificate, you'll want one that fits the needs of your web site. In particular, you'll need to decide what *SSL strength* you want the connection to support. SSL strength refers to the level of encryption that the secure connection uses when it transmits data.

Most certificates sold today provide for up to 128-bit SSL strength. It's nearly impossible to break the encryption code provided by this SSL strength, and most browsers support it. If a browser doesn't support it, however, the browser will use the maximum strength it does support, which is either 40-bit or 56-bit. Most CAs also sell certificates that provide for 256-bit SSL strength.

Types of digital secure certificates

Certificate	Description
Server certificate	Issued to trusted servers so client computers can connect to them using secure connections.
Client certificate	Issued to trusted clients so server computers can confirm their identity.

Common certification authorities that issue digital secure certificates

```
www.symantec.com
www.geotrust.com
www.entrust.com
www.thawte.com
www.digicert.com
```

Concepts

- *Authentication* determines whether a server or client is who it claims to be.
- When a browser makes an initial attempt to communicate with a server over a secure connection that uses SSL, the server authenticates itself by sending its *digital secure certificate* to the browser.
- In some instances, the server may also request that a browser authenticate itself by presenting its own digital secure certificate. This is uncommon, however.
- To use SSL in your web applications, you must first purchase a digital secure certificate from a trusted *certification authority*, or *CA*. Once you obtain the certificate, you send it to the people who host your web site so they can install it on the server.
- A certification authority is a company that issues and manages security credentials. To verify information provided by the requestor of the secure certificate, a CA must check with a *registration authority*, or *RA*. Once the registration authority verifies the requestor's information, the certification authority can issue a digital secure certificate.
- Since SSL is built into all major browsers and web servers, installing a digital secure certificate enables SSL.
- *SSL strength* refers to the length of the generated key that is created during the encryption process. The longer the key, the more difficult it is to break the encryption code.
- The SSL strength that's used depends on the strength provided by the certificate, the strength supported by the web server, and the strength supported by the browser. If a web server or browser isn't able to support the strength provided by the certificate, a lesser strength is used.

Note

- You can use the IIS Management Console to request and install certificates. To display this console, click the System and Security link in the Control Panel, followed by the Administrative Tools link. Then, double-click on Internet Information Services (IIS) Manager.

Figure 18-3   How digital secure certificates work

How to use a secure connection

In the topics that follow, you'll first learn how to request secure connections for the pages of your applications. Then, you'll learn how to force a page to use a secure connection when a user bypasses your navigation features.

How to request a secure connection

Figure 18-4 shows how to request a secure connection in an ASP.NET application. To do that, you execute a Response.Redirect method with the URL for the HTTPS protocol rather than the URL for the HTTP protocol. Then, depending on how the user's browser is configured, the user may see a dialog box similar to the one shown in this figure before the application enters the secure connection. In addition, if a test certificate is being used, the browser will display a page warning you that it may not be safe to continue to the web site. In that case, you can follow the directions on that page to display the requested page with a secure connection.

To request a secure connection using HTTPS, you must use an absolute URL. If you're using IIS Express, that means that the URL must include the domain name and the port number for the HTTPS binding. For example, the first URL in this figure specifies //localhost as the web server's domain name and 44300 for port number. This is followed by the name of the page to be displayed.

Rather than coding the domain name and port number into each URL, you may want to store this information in the web.config file as shown in the second example in this figure. This information is stored as an element within the appSettings section of this file. Then, you can use the AppSettings property of the ConfigurationManager class to retrieve the value of this element. This is illustrated in the third example.

Once your application has established a secure connection, it can navigate to other pages using relative URLs while maintaining the secure connection. To close the secure connection, the application must navigate to another page by specifying an absolute URL that uses the HTTP protocol rather than the HTTPS protocol. This is illustrated in the last example in this figure. This example uses the second element in the appSettings section of the web.config file, which specifies localhost for the domain name and 49565 for the port number. If you look back to figure 18-2, you'll see that this is the port number that was assigned to this application for the HTTP protocol.

Note that the technique for requesting a secure connection can be simplified if you're using a server other than IIS Express. If you're using IIS, for example, no port number is required. Instead, you include the localhost domain name, followed by the application path like this:

```
https://localhost/aspnet_45/Ch18HalloweenStore/
```

Because of that, you can code a single element in the web.config file with this value. Then, you can simply append HTTP or HTTPS to this value. If you use this technique, you'll only need to change the application path in the web.config file if you deploy the application to a different location.

A dialog box that may be displayed for secure connections

A URL that requests a secure connection for IIS Express

```
https://localhost:44300/CheckOut1.aspx
```

A web.config file that defines secure and unsecure path settings

```xml
<?xml version="1.0"?>
<configuration>
    <appSettings>
        <add key="SecureAppPath" value="//localhost:44300/" />
        <add key="UnsecureAppPath" value="//localhost:49565/" />
    </appSettings>
    .
    .
```

Code that retrieves the secure application path from the web.config file

```csharp
string url = "https:"
    + ConfigurationManager.AppSettings["SecureAppPath"] + "CheckOut1.aspx";
Response.Redirect(url);
```

Code that returns to an unsecured connection

```csharp
string url = "http:"
    + ConfigurationManager.AppSettings["UnSecureAppPath"] + "Order.aspx";
Response.Redirect(url);
```

Description

- To request a secure connection, you must use an absolute URL that specifies HTTPS as the protocol. Once you establish a secure connection, you can use relative URLs to continue using the secure connection.

- To return to an unsecured connection after using a secure connection, you must code an absolute URL that specifies the HTTP protocol.

- Instead of coding the application's path into each URL, you can store secure and unsecure paths in the appSettings section of the web.config file. That way, if the paths change, you can change them in just one location.

- You can use the AppSettings property of the ConfigurationManager class within the application to access the elements in the appSettings section of the web.config file.

- Depending on the security settings in your browser, a dialog box may be displayed before a secure connection is established or before a secure connection is closed.

- If your application is using a server other than IIS Express, you can use a single setting in the web.config file that includes the domain name and path for the application.

Figure 18-4   How to request a secure connection

How to force a page to use a secure connection

When you build a complete web application, you usually include navigation features such as menus or hyperlinks that guide the user from page to page. Unfortunately, users sometimes bypass your navigation features and access pages in your application directly. For example, a user might bookmark a page in your application and return to it later. Other users might simply type the URL of individual pages in your application into their browser's address bar. Some users do this innocently; others do it in an attempt to bypass your application's security features.

Because of that, a page that should use SSL to send or receive sensitive information shouldn't assume that a secure connection has been established. Instead, it should check for a secure connection and establish one if necessary. To do that, you can use the properties of the HttpRequest class shown in figure 18-5.

To check for a secure connection, you use the IsSecureConnection property. Then, if the connection isn't secure, you can switch to a secure connection as shown in the first example in this figure. This example uses the same technique that was shown in the previous figure, and it's appropriate if you're using IIS Express. Notice that you typically include this code at the beginning of the Load method for the page. That way, you can be sure that no other code is executed until a secure connection is established.

If you're using a server other than IIS Express, you can use the technique shown in the second example. Here, the Url property is used to retrieve the URL for the page. Then, this URL is modified so it uses the HTTPS protocol. After you do that, you can use the Redirect method to redirect the browser using the new URL.

Properties of the HttpRequest class for working with secure connections

Property	Description
IsSecureConnection	Returns True if the current connection is secure. Otherwise, returns False.
Url	The URL of the current request.

A Page_Load method that forces the page to use a secure connection

```
protected void Page_Load(object sender, EventArgs e)
{
    if (!Request.IsSecureConnection)
    {
        string url = "https:"
            + ConfigurationManager.AppSettings["SecureAppPath"]
            + "CheckOut2.aspx";
        Response.Redirect(url);
    }
}
```

A statement that replaces the HTTP protocol with the HTTPS protocol

```
string url = Request.Url.ToString().Replace("http:", "https:");
```

Description

- If a page requires the user to enter sensitive information, such as passwords or credit card data, it should make sure that it's operating on a secure connection. To do that, the page should check the IsSecureConnection property of the HttpRequest object in its Load event handler.

- If the page isn't using a secure connection, it should switch to a secure connection to protect the privacy of the user's data. To do that, it can replace the unsecure application path with a secure application path.

- If your application is using a server other than IIS Express, you can switch to a secure connection by replacing the HTTP protocol in the URL to HTTPS and then redirecting the browser to the new URL. To get the current URL, you can use the Url property of the HttpRequest object.

Figure 18-5   How to force a page to use a secure connection

A Halloween Store application that uses SSL

To show how secure connections are used in a typical application, the next two topics present a version of the Halloween Store application that uses SSL.

The operation of the Halloween Store application

Figure 18-6 shows the five pages of the Halloween Store application. As you can see, this application lets the user select products and display the shopping cart without establishing a secure connection. When the user clicks the Check Out button from the Cart page, however, a secure connection is established. The secure connection is then maintained while the two Check Out pages and the Confirmation page are displayed. When the user clicks the Return to Order Page button, however, the Order page is redisplayed with an unsecured connection.

The code for the Halloween Store application

Figure 18-7 presents the code for using SSL in the Halloween Store application. At the top of the first page of this figure, you can see the code for the Click event of the Check Out button on the Cart page. (The code for the Click event of the Check Out button on the Order page is identical.) This code creates a URL that uses the HTTPS protocol and the value of the element with the SecureAppPath key that's specified in the appSettings section of the web.config file. Then, it redirects the browser to the first Check Out page using a secure connection.

In the code for the first Check Out page, you can see that the Load event handler checks if a secure connection has been established. If not, a URL with the HTTPS protocol is created. Then, the browser is redirected to that URL, which uses a secure connection.

If the user clicks the Continue Checkout button, a relative URL is used to display the second Check Out page, which means that the secure connection is maintained. If the user clicks the Cancel or Continue Shopping button, however, the browser is redirected to the Order page with an unsecured connection.

The code for the second Check Out page is shown in part 2 of this figure. Like the first Check Out page, its Load event handler makes sure that a secure connection is established before proceeding. In addition, if the user clicks the Cancel or Continue Shopping button, the Order page is redisplayed with an unsecured connection. If the user clicks the Accept Order button, however, the secure connection is maintained and the Confirmation page is displayed.

Some of the code for the Confirmation page is also shown in this figure. As you can see, if the user clicks the Return to Order Page button on this page, the Order page is redisplayed with an unsecured connection.

How security is used by the Halloween Store application

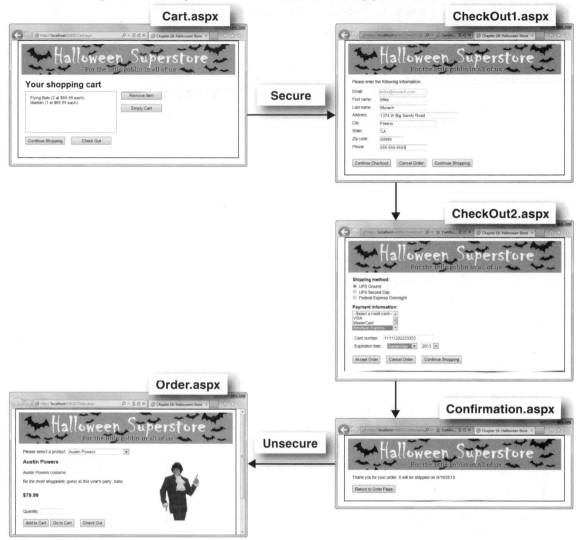

Description

- When the user clicks the Check Out button from the Cart page (or the Order page), the browser is redirected to the first Check Out page using a secure connection.

- When the user clicks the Continue Checkout button from the first Check Out page, the browser is redirected to the second Check Out page and remains in the secure connection.

- When the user clicks the Accept Order button from the second Check Out page, the browser is redirected to the Confirmation page and remains in the secure connection.

- When the user clicks the Return to Order Page button from the Confirmation page, the browser is redirected to the Order page in an unsecured connection.

Figure 18-6   The operation of the Halloween Store application with SSL

Some of the C# code for the Cart page

```
public partial class Cart : System.Web.UI.Page
{
    .
    .
    protected void btnCheckOut_Click(object sender, EventArgs e) {
        string url = "https:"
            + ConfigurationManager.AppSettings["SecureAppPath"]
            + "CheckOut1.aspx";
        Response.Redirect(url);
    }
}
```

Some of the C# code for the first Check Out page

```
public partial class CheckOut1 : System.Web.UI.Page
{
    .
    .
    protected void Page_Load(object sender, EventArgs e) {
        if (!Request.IsSecureConnection)
        {
            string url = "https:"
                + ConfigurationManager.AppSettings["SecureAppPath"]
                + "CheckOut1.aspx";
            Response.Redirect(url);
        }
    }

    protected void btnCheckOut_Click(object sender, EventArgs e) {
        if (Page.IsValid)
        {
            .
            .
            Response.Redirect("CheckOut2.aspx");
        }
    }

    protected void btnCancel_Click(object sender, EventArgs e) {
        Session.Remove("Cart");
        String url = "http:"
            + ConfigurationManager.AppSettings["UnsecureAppPath"]
            + "Order.aspx";
        Response.Redirect(url);
    }

    protected void btnContinue_Click(object sender, EventArgs e) {
        string url = "http:"
            + ConfigurationManager.AppSettings["UnsecureAppPath"]
            + "Order.aspx";
        Response.Redirect(url);
    }
}
```

Figure 18-7   The code for the Halloween Store application (part 1 of 2)

Some of the C# code for the second Check Out page

```
public partial class CheckOut2 : System.Web.UI.Page
{
    .
    .
    .
    protected void Page_Load(object sender, EventArgs e) {
        if (!Request.IsSecureConnection)
        {
            String url = "https:"
                + ConfigurationManager.AppSettings["SecureAppPath"]
                + "CheckOut2.aspx";
            Response.Redirect(url);
        }
    }

    protected void btnAccept_Click(object sender, EventArgs e) {
        if (Page.IsValid)
        {
            .
            .
            Response.Redirect("Confirmation.aspx");
        }
    }

    protected void btnCancel_Click(object sender, EventArgs e) {
        Session.Remove("Cart");
        String url = "http:"
            + ConfigurationManager.AppSettings["UnsecureAppPath"]
            + "Order.aspx";
        Response.Redirect(url);
    }

    protected void btnContinue_Click(object sender, EventArgs e) {
        String url = "http:"
            + ConfigurationManager.AppSettings["UnsecureAppPath"]
            + "Order.aspx";
        Response.Redirect(url);
    }
}
```

Some of the C# code for the Confirmation page

```
public partial class Confirmation : System.Web.UI.Page
{
    .
    .
    protected void btnReturn_Click(object sender, EventArgs e) {
        string url = "http:"
            + ConfigurationManager.AppSettings["UnsecureAppPath"]
            + "Order.aspx";
        Response.Redirect(url);
    }
}
```

Figure 18-7   The code for the Halloween Store application (part 2 of 2)

Perspective

Now that you've completed this chapter, you should be able to use SSL encryption to secure the data transmissions between client and server. That's one part of securing an application. The other part is making sure that only authorized users are able to use your application, and you'll learn how to provide for that in the next chapter.

By the way, if you're interested in seeing the rest of the code for the Halloween Store application in this chapter, you should know that you can download all of the applications in this book from our web site (www.murach.com). See appendix A for details.

Terms

Secure Sockets Layer (SSL)	client authentication
secure connection	digital secure certificate
binding	certification authority (CA)
authentication	registration authority (RA)
server authentication	SSL strength

Summary

- To communicate over a *secure connection*, you use the *Secure Sockets Layer*, or *SSL*. If you're using IIS Express, you can enable SSL by setting the SSL Enabled property of the project to Enabled. This creates a *binding* for the HTTPS protocol.

- When a browser uses SSL to communicate with a server, the server *authenticates* itself by sending its *digital secure certificate* to the browser. This is referred to as *SSL server authentication*.

- A client can also use a digital secure certificate to authenticate itself using *SSL client authentication*.

- You can obtain a digital secure certificate from a *certification authority* (*CA*), which checks with a *registration authority* (*RA*) to be sure that the request is from a valid person or company.

- When you purchase a digital certificate, you'll need to decide what *SSL strength* you need. The SSL strength determines the level of encryption that's used to transmit data over a secure connection.

- To request a secure connection, you use the absolute URL for the HTTPS protocol. Then, you can use relative URLs to maintain the secure connection. To close the secure connection, you use the absolute URL for the HTTP protocol.

- A page can use the IsSecureConnection property of the HttpRequest object to be sure that it's using a secure connection. It can also use the Url property of this object to get the URL of the current request.

19

How to authenticate and authorize users

In the last chapter, you learned how to secure the transmission of data between client and server. Now, you'll learn how to restrict access to some of the pages of an application, but let authorized users access those pages. To provide this functionality without writing a single line of code, you can use the Web Site Administration Tool and the login controls.

An introduction to authentication

If you want to limit access to all or part of your ASP.NET application to certain users, you can use *authentication* to verify each user's identity. Then, once you have authenticated the user, you can use *authorization* to check if the user has the appropriate privileges for accessing a page. That way, you can prevent unauthorized users from accessing pages that they shouldn't be able to access.

Three types of authentication

Figure 19-1 describes the three types of authentication you can use in ASP.NET applications. The first, called *Windows-based authentication*, requires that you set up a Windows user account for each user. Then, you use standard Windows security features to restrict access to all or part of the application. When a user attempts to access the application, Windows displays a login dialog box that asks the user to supply the user name and password of the Windows account. This type of authentication is most appropriate for a local setting like a company intranet.

To use *forms-based authentication*, you add a login page to your application that typically requires the user to enter a user name and password. Then, ASP.NET displays this page automatically when it needs to authenticate a user who's trying to access the application. ASP.NET automatically creates a database to store user data such as user names and passwords, and it includes login controls that automatically generate code that reads data from and writes data to this database. As a result, you can implement forms-based authentication without having to write a single line of code. That makes this type of authentication easy to use, and you'll see how this works as you progress through this chapter.

In recent years, authentication services offered by third parties such as Facebook or Google have become popular. If you want to experiment with one of these third-party services, you can install the NuGet package called DotNetOpenAuth.

Windows-based authentication

- Causes the browser to display a login dialog box when the user attempts to access a restricted page.
- Is supported by most browsers.
- Is configured through the IIS management console.
- Uses Windows user accounts and directory rights to grant access to restricted pages.
- Is most appropriate for an intranet application.

Forms-based authentication

- Allows developers to code a login form that gets the user name and password.
- The user name and password entered by the user are encrypted if the login page uses a secure connection.
- Doesn't rely on Windows user accounts. Instead, the application determines how to authenticate users.

Third-party authentication services

- Provided by third parties using technologies like OpenID and OAuth. The Facebook, Google, and Amazon services are the most popular, but Microsoft also offers this kind of service.
- Allows users to use their existing logins, and frees developers from having to worry about the secure storage of user credentials.
- For ASP.NET applications, a NuGet package called DotNetOpenAuth lets your application issue identities or accept identities from other web applications, and even access user data on other services.

Description

- *Authentication* refers to the process of validating the identity of a user so the user can be granted access to an application. A user must typically supply a user name and password to be authenticated.
- After a user is authenticated, the user must still be authorized to use the requested application. The process of granting user access to an application is called *authorization*.

Figure 19-1   Three types of authentication

How forms-based authentication works

To help you understand how forms-based authentication works, figure 19-2 shows a typical series of exchanges that occur between a web browser and a server when a user attempts to access a page that's protected by forms-based authentication. The authentication process begins when a user requests a page that is part of a protected application. When the server receives the request, it checks to see if the user has already been authenticated. To do that, it looks for a cookie that contains an *authentication ticket* in the request for the page. If it doesn't find the ticket, it redirects the browser to the login page.

Next, the user enters a user name and password and posts the login page back to the server. Then, if the user name and password are found in the database, which means they are valid, the server creates an authentication ticket and redirects the browser back to the original page. Note that the redirect from the server sends the authentication ticket to the browser as a cookie. As a result, when the browser requests the original page, it sends the cookie back to the server. This time, the server sees that the user has been authenticated and the requested page is sent back to the browser.

By default, the authentication ticket is sent as a session cookie. In that case, the user is authenticated only for that session. However, you also can specify that the ticket be sent as a persistent cookie. Then, the user will be authenticated automatically for future sessions, until the cookie expires.

HTTP requests and responses with forms-based authentication

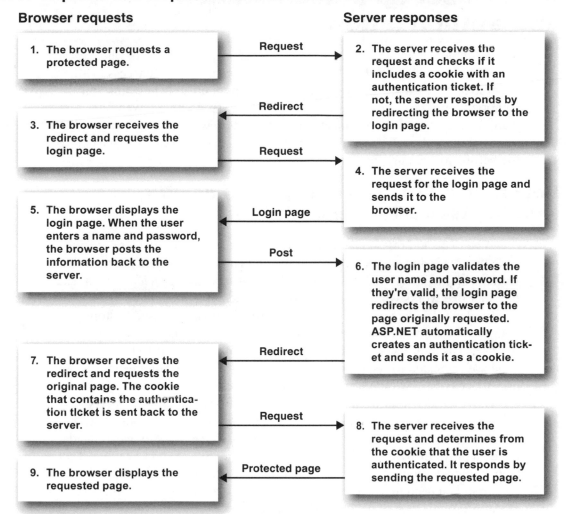

Browser requests

Server responses

1. The browser requests a protected page.

→ Request →

2. The server receives the request and checks if it includes a cookie with an authentication ticket. If not, the server responds by redirecting the browser to the login page.

← Redirect ←

3. The browser receives the redirect and requests the login page.

→ Request →

4. The server receives the request for the login page and sends it to the browser.

5. The browser displays the login page. When the user enters a name and password, the browser posts the information back to the server.

← Login page ←

→ Post →

6. The login page validates the user name and password. If they're valid, the login page redirects the browser to the page originally requested. ASP.NET automatically creates an authentication ticket and sends it as a cookie.

7. The browser receives the redirect and requests the original page. The cookie that contains the authentication ticket is sent back to the server.

← Redirect ←

→ Request →

8. The server receives the request and determines from the cookie that the user is authenticated. It responds by sending the requested page.

9. The browser displays the requested page.

← Protected page ←

Description

- When ASP.NET receives a request for a protected page from a user who has not been authenticated, the server redirects the user to the login page.

- To be authenticated, the user's computer must contain an *authentication ticket*. By default, this ticket is stored as a session cookie.

- ASP.NET automatically creates an authentication ticket when the application indicates that the user should be authenticated. ASP.NET checks for the presence of an authentication ticket any time it receives a request for a restricted page.

- The authentication ticket cookie can be made persistent. Then, the user will be authenticated automatically in future sessions, until the cookie expires.

Figure 19-2   How forms-based authentication works

How to set up authentication and authorization

By default, all pages of a web site can be accessed by all users whether or not they are authenticated. As a result, if you want to restrict access to all or some of the pages of the web site, you need to set up authentication and authorization. The easiest way to do that is to use the ASP.NET Web Site Administration Tool as shown in the topics that follow. But if you're using SQL Server Express LocalDB, you'll need to make some changes to the web.config file before you can use the Web Site Administration Tool.

How to use SQL Server Express LocalDB with the Web Site Administration Tool

When you add roles and users, a class known as a *data provider* contains the code that reads and writes the data for the users and roles. A data provider that works with membership data is often called a *membership provider*, and a data provider that works with roles data is often called a *role provider*.

By default, a data provider named AspNetSqlProvider is used to store both membership and role data in a SQL Server Express database named ASPNETDB.mdf that's stored in the App_Data folder of your web site. This database is created for you automatically and the Web Site Administration Tool uses this database without any configuration effort.

However, if you're working with the LocalDB version of SQL Server Express, you will need to add configuration settings to the web.config file before you can use the Web Site Administration Tool. Once these additions are made, the data provider will work the same as it does with SQL Server Express. The web.config additions that you need to make are highlighted in figure 19-3.

First, you need to add a connection string that points to the LocalDB version of the ASPNETDB.mdf database. Second, you need to add the roleManager and membership elements that use the connection string that you've just created. Once these settings are made, the database file will automatically be created when you start using the Web Site Administration Tool.

You may be interested to know that you can also create custom membership and role providers instead of using the default providers. To create a membership provider, you code a class that implements the abstract MembershipProvider class. To create a role provider, you code a class that implements the abstract RoleProvider class. After you implement all of the necessary properties and methods of these classes, you can add your providers to the list of available providers and use the Provider tab of the Web Site Administration Tool to select them.

You can also modify the attributes of the providers to change the way that they behave. For a membership provider, for example, you can relax the strict password requirements. Or, for the role provider, you can specify the cookie name and timeout period. If you want to use either of these advanced features, you can consult the MSDN documentation.

A web.config file that uses custom role and membership providers

```
<configuration>
  <connectionStrings>
    <add name="LocalDbProviderConnectionString"
      connectionString="Data Source=(LocalDB)\v11.0;AttachDbFilename=
        |DataDirectory|\ASPNETDB.mdf;Integrated Security=True"
      providerName="System.Data.SqlClient" />
  </connectionStrings>
  <system.web>
    ...
    <roleManager defaultProvider="AspNetSqlLocalDbProvider">
      <providers>
        <clear />
        <add name="AspNetSqlLocalDbProvider"
          connectionStringName="LocalDbProviderConnectionString"
          type="System.Web.Security.SqlRoleProvider"/>
      </providers>
    </roleManager>
    <membership defaultProvider="AspNetSqlLocalDbProvider">
      <providers>
        <clear />
        <add name="AspNetSqlLocalDbProvider"
          connectionStringName="LocalDbProviderConnectionString"
          type="System.Web.Security.SqlMembershipProvider" />
      </providers>
    </membership>
  </system.web>
</configuration>
```

Description

- If you're using SQL Server Express, you can use the Web Site Administration Tool out of the box with no configuration needed. This tool uses the ASPNETDB.mdf database file in the App_Data folder.

- If you're using SQL Server Express LocalDB, you need to modify the web.config file as shown above before you can use the Web Site Administration Tool. First, you must provide the connection string for the default *data provider*. Second, you must provide settings for the default *role* and *membership providers*, which use the connection string for the default data provider.

- Whether you're using SQL Server Express or the LocalDB version of SQL Server Express, you don't need to create the ASPNETDB.mdf database file. It will be created automatically when you start using the Web Site Administration Tool.

- If you want to create custom role and membership providers, you can do that. For more information, please refer to the MSDN documentation.

Note

- The connection string in the connectionStrings element above is shown on two lines due to space considerations. In your web.config file, it should be on one line.

Figure 19-3   How to use SQL Server Express LocalDB with the Administration Tool

How to start the Web Site Administration Tool

To start the ASP.NET Web Site Administration Tool, you use the
WEBSITE→ASP.NET Configuration command. This starts a web browser that
displays the home page for this tool. Then, you can click on the Security tab to
access a web page like the one in figure 19-4. This page lets you set up users,
create groups of users known as roles, and create access rules that control access
to parts of your application.

To set up authentication for the first time, you can click on the link that starts
the Security Setup Wizard. This wizard walks you through several steps that
allow you to set up the security for your application. Alternatively, you can use
the links at the bottom of the page to select the authentication type and manage
the users, roles, and access rules for your application.

How to enable forms-based authentication

By default, a web site is set up to use Windows authentication. If all users
will be accessing your web site through a private local Windows network (an
intranet), this option may be the easiest to implement because it uses built-in
Windows dialog boxes to allow users to log in.

However, if any of your users will access your web site from the Internet,
you'll need to switch to forms-based authentication. To do that, you can click
on the Select Authentication Type link from the Security tab of the Web Site
Administration Tool to display the page in figure 19-4. Then, you can select the
From the Internet option. When you use this option, you'll need to create a web
form that allows users to log in as shown later in this chapter.

The Security tab of the Web Site Administration Tool

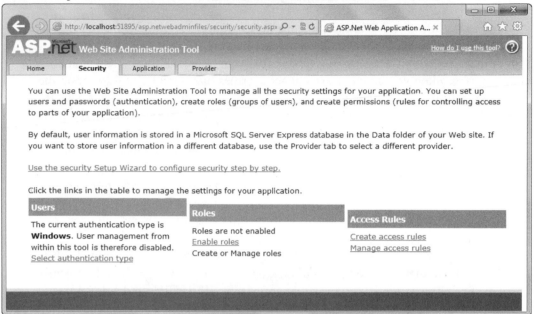

How to enable forms-based authentication

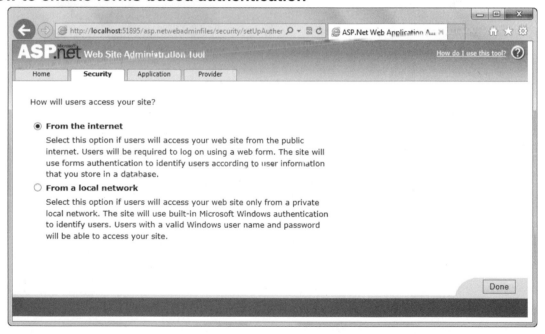

Description

- To start the ASP.NET Web Site Administration Tool, use the WEBSITE→ASP.NET Configuration command.

- To switch to forms-based authentication, select the From the Internet option. Then, Create User and Manage Users links become available on the main security page.

Figure 19-4   How start the Administration tool and enable forms-based authentication

How to create and manage roles

Roles allow you to apply the same access rules to a group of users. Although roles are optional and are disabled by default, they make it easy to manage authentication. As a result, you'll typically want to enable roles. Also, since you use roles when you create users and access rules, it's often helpful to set up the roles before you create the users and access rules. That way, you don't have to go back later and edit your users and access rules so they are associated with the correct roles.

To understand how roles work, let's say you create a role named admin for all employees that will be administrators for the web site, and you assign this role to multiple users. Later, if you want to give all users in the admin role additional permissions, you don't have to give the permissions to each user. Instead, you can just give the additional permissions to the admin role and all users in that role will get the new permissions.

Before you can work with roles using the Web Site Administration Tool, you must enable them. To do that, you click on the Enable Roles link in the Security tab. Then, you can click on the Create or Manage Roles link to display a page like the one in figure 19-5.

The first two controls on this page allow you to add roles. To do that, you just enter a name for the role and click on the Add Role button, and the role will appear in the table at the bottom of the page. Then, you can click on the Manage link for the role to add users to the role or to remove users from the role. Or, you can click the Delete link for the role to delete the role entirely.

User names and roles

User name	Roles
anne	admin
mary	admin, custserv
mike	custserv

How to create and manage roles

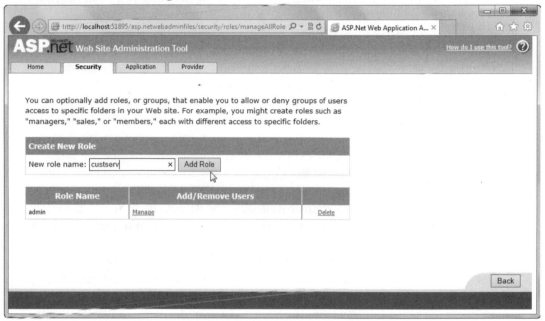

Description

- A *role* allows you to apply the same access rules to a group of users.

- Each user may be associated with one or more roles.

- By default, roles are disabled. To enable them, you need to click on the Enable Roles link in the Security tab.

- Once you enable roles, you can click on the Create or Manage Roles link in the Security tab to display the page shown above. This page lets you add roles, manage all users associated with a role, and delete roles.

Figure 19-5   How to create and manage roles

How to create and manage users

The first page displayed in figure 19-6 shows how to use the Web Site Administration Tool to create users. To do that, you start by entering all of the required information for a user. This information includes a user name, a password, an email address, and a security question and answer. The default password policy for an ASP.NET 4.5 application requires that you enter at least seven characters with one of them being a non-alphanumeric character.

If you want to associate the user with one or more roles, you can select the check box next to each role that you want to apply to the user. In this figure, for example, the user is associated with the admin role. When you're done, you can click on the Create User button to create the user.

Once you've created one or more users, you can use the second screen displayed in this figure to manage them. To edit a user's email address, enter or change the description for a user, change the roles assigned to a user, or change a user's status, you can click the Edit User link. You can also change the roles assigned to a user by clicking on the Edit Roles link for the user and then working with the check boxes that are displayed in the Roles column of the table. And you can change a user's status by clearing the Active check box to the left of the user's name. This prevents the user from logging into your application but retains his or her information in your database.

If your application contains many users, you may need to use the Search For Users controls to search for users. When you use these controls, you can search by user name or email address. For example, to search by email address, you can select the E-mail option from the Search By drop-down list, enter the email address in the For text box, and click on the Find User button. If necessary, you can use the asterisk (*) wildcard for multiple characters, and you can use the question mark (?) wildcard for a single character. Alternatively, you can click on the letters displayed on this page to display all users whose user name or email address begins with the specified letter. Either way, you should be able to quickly find the user that you're looking for.

How to create a user

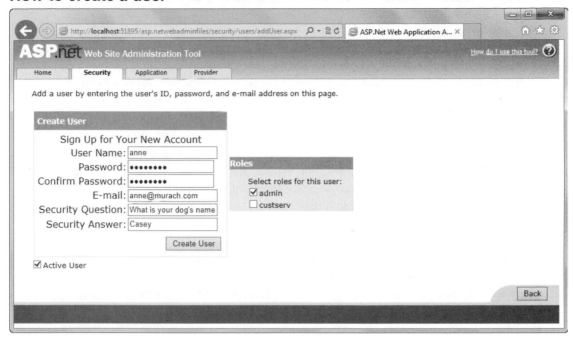

How to manage users

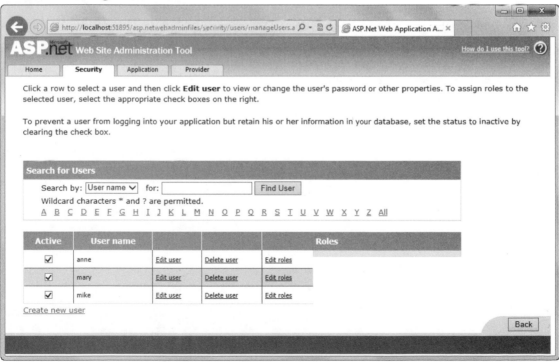

Figure 19-6   How to create and manage users

How to create and manage access rules

The first page in figure 19-7 shows how to create an *access rule* that restricts access to all or part of a web application. If you want to apply an access rule to the entire web application, you can select the root directory for the web application and apply the rule. Then, this rule will apply to all subfolders. For example, if you want to allow only authenticated users to access your web site, you can select the root directory, and create a rule that denies access to anonymous users.

However, it's more common to allow all users including anonymous users to access the pages in the root directory. That way, all users can view your home page and any other pages that you want to make available to the general public. Then, you can restrict access to the pages in your application that are stored in subfolders. For example, this screen shows how to create a rule for the Maintenance folder that denies access to all users.

The second page in this figure shows how to manage the access rules for a folder. To do that, you can select the folder to display all of the access rules for that folder. Then, you can move rules up or down, which is important since they're applied in the order in which they're displayed. Or, you can delete any rules that you no longer want to apply.

In this example, you can see the rules that restrict access to the Maintenance folder. Here, the bottom rule (which can't be deleted) is the rule that's automatically applied to all pages of a web site if you don't create new rules. This rule allows access to all users including anonymous users. Then, the middle rule overrides the bottom rule and denies access to all users including authenticated users. However, the top rule overrides the middle rule and allows access to users in the admin role. As a result, only authenticated users in the admin role are able to access the pages in the Maintenance folder.

How to create an access rule

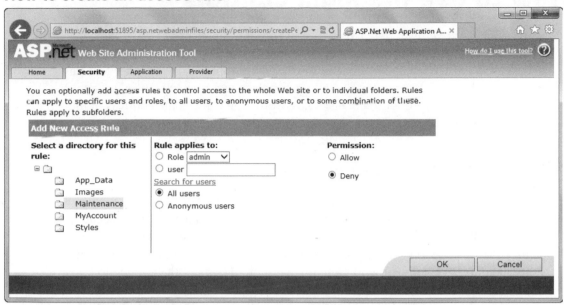

How to manage access rules

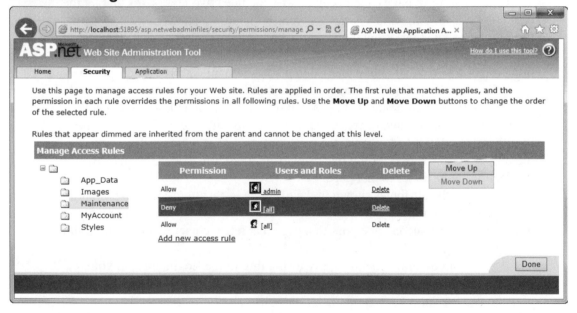

Description

- An *access rule* determines which users have access to portions of a web site.
- Each rule overrides the rules below it. As a result, for the Maintenance directory shown above, users in the admin role are allowed and all other users are denied.

Figure 19-7   How to create and manage access rules

How to use the login controls

Once you've restricted access to some or all of the pages of your web application, you need to allow users with the proper permissions to log in and access the restricted pages. In addition, you may want to provide other features such as allowing users to log out, to create an account by themselves, to recover a forgotten password, or to change a password. You can use the controls in the Login group of the Toolbox to automatically handle these tasks.

How to use the Login control

Figure 19-8 shows how to create a login page that contains a Login control. When you create a login page, you should name it Login.aspx. That's because ASP.NET looks for a page with this name when it attempts to authenticate a user. Also, since this page is used for the entire application, you usually want to use a simple format so it works equally well for all parts of the application.

Once you've created a page named Login.aspx, you can add all of the login functionality just by adding a Login control to the page. To do that, drag the Login control that's in the Login group of the Toolbox onto the page.

Like most login pages, the Login control includes two text boxes that let the user enter a user name and a password. It also includes a check box that lets the users indicate whether or not they want to be logged in automatically the next time the application is accessed. If the user selects this check box, the application creates a persistent cookie that contains the authentication ticket.

When the user clicks the Log In button within the Login control, the code for the control tries to authenticate the user. It does that by checking to see whether the user name and password are in the membership data store. Then, if the user is authenticated, the code checks the role provider to see whether the user has the proper authorization for the requested page. If so, this code continues by redirecting the browser to that page.

If you set the attributes shown in the example in this figure, the LogIn button is followed by two links. The first one goes to a page that lets the user create a new account. The second one goes to a page that lets the user recover a forgotten password.

If you want to automatically apply formatting to the Login control, you can select the Auto Format command from the control's smart tag menu. Then, you can use the Auto Format dialog box to select a scheme, like the Elegant scheme that's used in this example. To implement the formatting, Visual Studio adds formatting attributes to the aspx code for the control. This feature works similarly for the CreateUserWizard, PasswordRecovery, and ChangePassword controls that are described in the pages that follow.

Although it isn't shown in this figure, a login page should always force the page to use a secure connection. Then, if a hacker manages to intercept a user's user name and password, your application won't be compromised.

A Login control in the Web Forms Designer

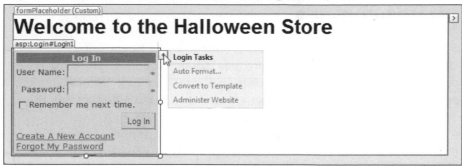

The aspx code for the Login control

```
<asp:Login ID="Login1" runat="server"
    CreateUserText="Create A New Account"
    CreateUserUrl="~/CreateUser.aspx"
    PasswordRecoveryText="Forgot My Password"
    PasswordRecoveryUrl="~/PasswordRecovery.aspx">
</asp:Login>
```

Common attributes of the Login control

Attribute	Description
DisplayRememberMe	Determines whether the Remember Me check box is displayed. By default, this is set to True.
RememberMeText	The text for the label of the RememberMe text box.
RememberMeSet	Determines whether a persistent cookie is sent to the user's computer, which is based on whether the RememberMe check box is selected.
FailureText	The text that's displayed when a login attempt fails.
CreateUserText	The text for the Create User link.
CreateUserUrl	The URL of the page to display when the user clicks the Create User link.
PasswordRecoveryText	The text for the Forgot Password link.
PasswordRecoveryURL	The URL of the page to display when the user clicks on the Forgot Password link.

Description

- When a user attempts to access a page that requires authentication, ASP.NET automatically redirects the user to the application's login page. This page must be named Login.aspx.

- To automatically apply formatting to the Login control, select the Auto Format command from the control's smart tag menu and then select a scheme from the dialog box.

Figure 19-8   How to use the Login control

How to use the LoginStatus and LoginName controls

Figure 19-9 shows how you can use the LoginStatus and LoginName controls. In the page at the top of this figure, you can see that the LoginName control provides the name of a logged in user. In contrast, the LoginStatus control provides a Login link if a user hasn't logged in yet, and a Logout link if the user has logged in.

To use these controls, you just drag them onto the form from the Login group of the Toolbox. Then, you can change the properties as needed. For instance, you can use the LoginText and LogoutText attributes of the LoginStatus control to change the text that's displayed by the links. And you can use the FormatString attribute of the LoginName control to add text before or after the placeholder for the user name.

When the user clicks on the Login link of a LoginStatus control, the user will be redirected to the login page and required to enter a user name and password. Then, after the user has been authenticated, the user will be redirected to the original page. Conversely, when the user clicks the Logout link, the user will be redirected to the login page (Login.aspx).

When a user has been authenticated, the LoginName control will display the user name. Otherwise, the control won't display the user name. However, it will display any other text that has been specified in the FormatString attribute.

The LoginName and LoginStatus controls displayed in a browser

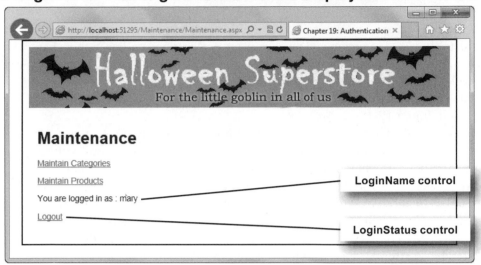

The LoginName and LoginStatus controls in the Web Forms Designer

The aspx code for the LoginName and LoginStatus controls

```
<asp:LoginName ID="LoginName1" runat="server"
    FormatString="You are logged in as: {0}" />

<asp:LoginStatus ID="LoginStatus1" runat="server" />
```

Common attribute of the LoginName control

Attribute	Description
FormatString	The text that's displayed with the user name. This string uses "{0}" to identify the User name parameter, and you can add text before or after this parameter.

Common attributes of the LoginStatus control

Attribute	Description
LoginText	The text that's displayed for the login link.
LogoutText	The text that's displayed for the logout link.

Figure 19-9   How to use the LoginStatus and LoginName controls

How to use the CreateUserWizard control

If you only have a few users for your application, you can use the Web Site Administration Tool to create and manage users as described earlier in this chapter. Then, you can use the Login, LoginStatus, and LoginName controls to allow users to log in and out. Often, though, you'll want to allow users to create user accounts for themselves. To do that, you can use the CreateUserWizard control as shown in figure 19-10.

By default, the CreateUserWizard control uses two steps to create a new user: the Create User step and the Complete step. To display these steps, you can use the drop-down list in the smart tag menu as shown in this figure. Usually, these steps work like you want them to. In that case, you can simply set the ContinueDestinationPageUrl property of the control to indicate what page the user is directed to when the Continue button in the Complete step is clicked.

If you need to modify the behavior of either of the steps, you can do that by selecting the Customize command for that step from the smart tag menu for the control. Then, you can customize that step by modifying the controls and properties of the step. If you modify the Complete step, you can specify the page that's displayed when the user clicks the Continue button by setting the PostBackUrl property of that button rather than by setting the ContinueDestinationPageUrl property of the CreateUserWizard control.

When you use the pages that result from the CreateUserWizard control, you should realize that the membership provider is being used to write the data to the appropriate data source. This works the same as it does for the Web Site Administration Tool.

The CreateUserWizard control with the smart tag menu shown

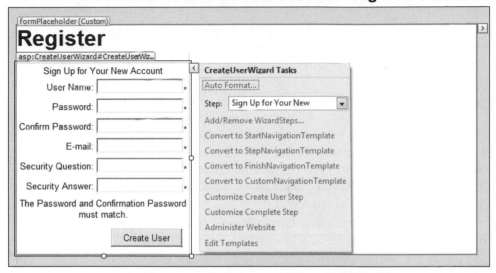

The two steps of a customized CreateUserWizard control in a browser

Description

- If you select the CreateUserWizard control in the Web Forms Designer, you can use the smart tag menu to switch between its two steps and customize or reset either step.

- To identify the page that the user is directed to when the Continue button in the Complete step is clicked, you can set the ContinueDestinationPageUrl property of the control. Or, if you've customized the Complete step, you can set the PostBackUrl property of the Continue button.

Figure 19-10   How to use the CreateUserWizard control

How to use the PasswordRecovery control

It's inevitable that some users will forget their passwords. Fortunately, the PasswordRecovery control makes it easy to automate the process of recovering forgotten passwords. This process is described in figure 19-11, and it's especially useful if you are managing a site with a large number of users.

When you use the PasswordRecovery control, the new password is sent to the user via email. As a result, you need to make sure that your system is set up so it can send email before you test this control. By default, an application will try to send email to an SMTP server set to localhost on port 25.

The most important element of the PasswordRecovery control is the MailDefinition element. In particular, you must set the From attribute of the MailDefinition element to the email address that's sending the email message or an error will occur when your system attempts to send the email. Typically, the From email address is set to the email address that's used by the web site administrator. If you set this attribute correctly, a standard message will be sent to the user. To customize the subject line and message body, you can edit the other attributes of the MailDefinition element.

The PasswordRecovery control uses three views. In the Web Forms Designer, you can switch between these three views by using the smart tag menu, and you can edit the properties for any of these views.

When you display this control in a browser, the first view asks the user to enter a user name. Then, the second view requires the user to answer the security question. If the answer to this question is correct, the new password is emailed to the address that's associated with the user name, and the third view is displayed. This view displays a message that indicates that the password recovery was successful and that a password has been sent to the user via email.

The PasswordRecovery control in the Web Forms Designer

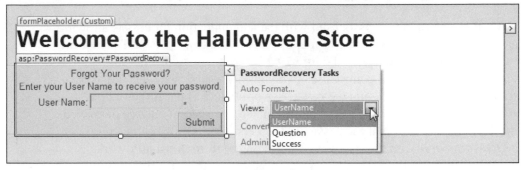

The first two views of the PasswordRecovery control

The aspx code for the PasswordRecovery control

```
<asp:PasswordRecovery ID="PasswordRecovery1" runat="server">
    <MailDefinition From="murachbooks@murach.com">
    </MailDefinition>
</asp:PasswordRecovery>
```

Description

- After the second view is completed, the password will be reset and the new password emailed to the user.

- For this to work, you need to edit the From attribute of the MailDefinition element to supply the from address for this email. In addition, the web server that you're using must be configured to work with an SMTP server.

- By default, an application will try to send email to an SMTP server set to localhost on port 25. For information on how to change these settings, see chapter 20.

Figure 19-11   How to use the PasswordRecovery control

How to use the ChangePassword control

Another common task associated with the authentication process is allowing users to change their passwords. To make that easy for you, ASP.NET provides the ChangePassword control, and figure 19-12 shows how to use it.

The ChangePassword control uses two views. The first view lets the user enter the current password and the new password twice. Then, if the old password is correct and the two new passwords match, the second view is displayed. This view tells the user that the password has been successfully changed.

Once you've placed the PasswordControl on the form, it usually works the way you want it to. However, you may need to edit the Url attributes so they point to the pages that you want to navigate to when the user clicks on the Cancel and Continue buttons.

The first view of the ChangePassword control in the Web Forms Designer

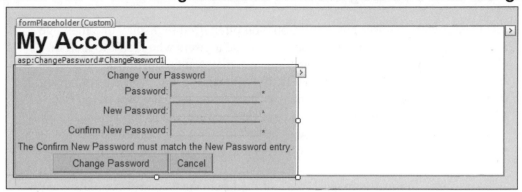

The second view of the ChangePassword control

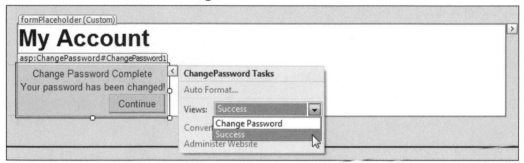

The aspx code for the ChangePassword control

```
<asp:ChangePassword ID="ChangePassword1" runat="server"
    CancelDestinationPageUrl="~/MyAccount.aspx"
    ContinueDestinationPageUrl="~/MyAccount.aspx">
</asp:ChangePassword>
```

Description

- The ChangePassword control uses two views to allow users to change their passwords. The first view lets the user change the password. The second view is displayed when the change has been successful.

- The CancelDestinationPageUrl and ContinueDestinationPageUrl attributes provide the URLs that are navigated to when the Cancel or Continue buttons are clicked.

Figure 19-12   How to use the ChangePassword control

How to use the LoginView control

If your web site uses authentication, you often need to display one message to users who are logged in and another message to users who aren't logged in. For example, when a user isn't logged in, you may want to display a message that asks the user to log in. Conversely, if a user is logged in, you may want to display a message that welcomes the user back and allows the user to log out. Figure 19-13 shows how to use the LoginView control to accomplish these tasks.

The LoginView control uses two views. The first view contains the controls that are displayed to users who aren't logged in (*anonymous users*). The second view contains the controls that are displayed to users who are logged in (*authenticated users*). In this figure, each view of the LoginView control contains some text followed by a LoginStatus control. This is a fairly typical use of the LoginView control. However, the LoginView control can contain additional content if that's necessary.

The LoginView control in the Web Forms Designer

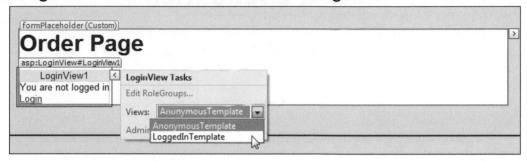

The aspx code for the LoginView control

```
<asp:LoginView ID="LoginView1" runat="server">
    <LoggedInTemplate>
        You are logged in<br />
        <asp:LoginStatus ID="LoginStatus1" runat="server" />
    </LoggedInTemplate>
    <AnonymousTemplate>
        You are not logged in<br />
        <asp:LoginStatus ID="LoginStatus2" runat="server" />
    </AnonymousTemplate>
</asp:LoginView>
```

The LoginView control displayed in a browser

Description

- The LoginView control lets you change what's on the web page depending on whether the user isn't logged in (an *anonymous user*) or is logged in (an *authenticated user*).

Figure 19-13   How to use the LoginView control

The Authentication application

To show how to use forms-based authentication to restrict access to a web application, this topic presents part of a Halloween Store application that we'll refer to as the Authentication application. This application restricts access to all pages in the Maintenance folder to users with admin privileges. In addition, it restricts access to all pages in the MyAccount folder to users who have created an account and logged in.

As you review this application, please keep in mind that the authentication and authorization features don't require any code. That's why the figures that follow show only the pages, the directory structure, the access rules, and the web.config files.

The pages

Figure 19-14 shows just four pages of the Authentication application, but you can also think of the pages in figures 19-10 through 19-12 as part of this application. For instance, the Forgot Your Password link on the Login page goes to the page in figure 19-11, and the Need to Create a New Account link goes to the page in figure 19-10.

To start this application, the Menu page in the figure contains three links that allow you to perform some tests to make sure that the authentication and authorization features are working correctly. The first link on this page lets the user access an Order page to begin placing an order. When the user clicks on this link, the system tries to authenticate the user by checking whether the user has a cookie with a valid authentication ticket. If so, the user will be authenticated automatically. If not, the user can view the Order page as an anonymous user. Either way, the Order page will be displayed. In other words, this page is available to both anonymous and authenticated users.

The second link on the Menu page lets the user access the MyAccount page where the user can edit settings for his personal account. To be able to access this page, the user must be authenticated. When the user clicks on this link, the system attempts to authenticate the user by checking if the browser has a cookie with a valid authentication ticket. If so, the user will be authenticated automatically and allowed to access the MyAccount page. If not, the user will be redirected to the Login page so he can log in. Once the user supplies a valid user name and password to the Login page, the browser will be redirected to the MyAccount page.

The third link on the Menu page lets users access the Maintenance page that can be used to manage data that's stored in the Categories and Products tables of the database for the web site. To be able to access this page, the user must be authenticated and the user must be associated with the admin role. When the user clicks on this link, the system attempts to authenticate the user by checking if the browser has a cookie with a valid authentication ticket. If so, the user will be authenticated automatically and allowed to access the Maintenance page. If

The Menu page

The Login page

Description

- The Menu page contains three links. The first lets anonymous users or authenticated users access the Order page. The second lets authenticated users access the MyAccount page. The third lets authenticated users in the admin role access the Maintenance page.

- The Login page is only displayed if the user clicks on the second or third link and the browser doesn't contain a cookie that authenticates the user.

- If the user clicks on the Create A New Account link on the Login page, the CreateUser page is displayed. If the user clicks on the Forgot My Password link on the Login page, the PasswordRecovery page is displayed.

Figure 19-14   The pages of the Authentication application (part 1 of 2)

not, the user will be redirected to the Login page so he can log in. Once the user supplies a valid user name and password for a user with admin privileges, the browser will be redirected to the Maintenance page.

On the MyAccount and Maintenance pages, the LoginStatus control lets users log out when they're done. This removes the authentication ticket from the browser. As a result, the application won't remember the user the next time the user attempts to access the application, even if the user has selected the Remember Me check box to store the authentication ticket in a persistent cookie.

The MyAccount page

The Maintenance page

Description

- The MyAccount page lets a user edit account data. The user must be authenticated, but need not be associated with any role.

- The Maintenance page lets a user maintain data in the Categories and Products tables. The user must be authenticated and must be associated with the admin role.

- The LoginStatus control on these pages lets the user log out when done. This removes the authentication ticket from the browser. As a result, the application won't be able to remember the user the next time the user attempts to access the application.

Figure 19-14   The pages of the Authentication application (part 2 of 2)

The directory structure

Figure 19-15 shows the directory structure for the Authentication application. This shows the App_Data folder that stores the database that's used to store the data about the web site's registered users and their roles. It also shows two directories that store web pages that have restricted access. First, it shows the Maintenance directory, which contains the Maintenance page shown in the previous figure. Second, it shows the MyAccount directory, which contains the MyAccount page shown in the previous figure, along with the ChangePassword page.

In addition, there are three web.config files for this application: one for the root directory, one for the Maintenance directory, and one for the MyAccount directory. The complete listings for these files are shown in figure 19-16.

The access rules

Figure 19-15 also shows the one access rule for the MyAccount directory. This rule denies access to anonymous users. As a result, only users who are authenticated can access the MyAccount directory.

The Maintenance directory, on the other hand, contains two access rules. The first rule denies access to all users. Then, the second rule allows access to authenticated users who are associated with the admin role. To refresh your memory about how this works, please refer back to figure 19-7.

The directory structure for the Authentication application

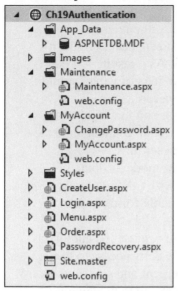

The access rules for the MyAccount directory

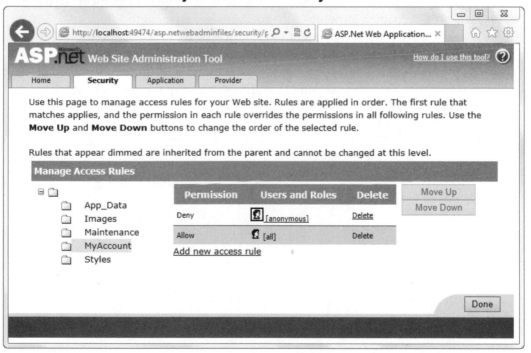

Description

- To access the MyAccount or ChangePassword page in the MyAccount directory, the user must be authenticated but doesn't need to be associated with any role.

Figure 19-15   The directory structure and access rules for the Authentication application

The web.config files

Figure 19-16 shows the three web.config files for the Authentication application. When you use the Web Site Administration Tool to create access rules, it automatically creates and modifies these web.config files. As a result, you don't have to edit them manually. However, it's good to have an idea of what's going on under the hood as you use the Web Site Administration Tool.

In addition, once you become familiar with these files, you may find that you prefer to edit or review them manually. But first, you need to understand the XML code that's used by these files to store configuration settings.

To enable forms-based authentication, you can use the mode attribute of the authentication element. This attribute is set to Windows by default to use Windows authentication, but you can set it to Forms to enable forms-based authentication.

Once you've enabled forms-based authentication, you can use the authorization element to deny or allow access to specified users. To deny access to users, you can code a deny element within the authorization element and set the users and roles attributes. To allow access to users, you can code an allow element within the authorization element and set the users and roles attributes. Note that before you can use the roles attribute, you must enable role management. To do that, you set the enabled attribute of the roleManager element to True.

If you want to apply access rules to the root directory for the application, you can code an authorization element within the web.config file in the root directory. However, it's more common to apply access rules to subdirectories of the root directory. In that case, you can code a web.config file for each directory as shown in this figure.

The web.config files for the Authentication application

For the root directory

```
<?xml version="1.0"?>
<configuration>
    <system.web>
        <authentication mode="Forms"/>
        <roleManager enabled="True" ... >
        ...
    </system.web>
</configuration>
```

For the MyAccount directory

```
<?xml version="1.0" encoding="utf-8"?>
<configuration>
    <system.web>
        <authorization>
            <deny users="?" />
        </authorization>
    </system.web>
</configuration>
```

For the Maintenance directory

```
<?xml version="1.0" encoding="utf-8"?>
<configuration>
    <system.web>
        <authorization>
            <allow roles="admin" />
            <deny users="*" />
        </authorization>
    </system.web>
</configuration>
```

Wildcard specifications in the users attribute

Wildcard	Description
*	All users, whether or not they have been authenticated.
?	All unauthenticated users.

Discussion

- When you use the Web Site Administration Tool, it automatically creates and modifies the web.config files for an application. If you prefer, you can manually edit these files and you can read them to review the settings for an application.

- To enable forms-based authentication, set the mode attribute of the authentication element to Forms. This attribute is set to Windows by default.

- To enable role management, set the enabled attribute of the roleManager element to True.

- To deny access to users, you can code a deny element within the authorization element. To allow access to users, you can code an allow element within the authorization element. Then, you can set the users and roles attributes of these elements.

Figure 19-16   The web.config files for the Authentication application

Perspective

This chapter has presented the skills that you need for using forms-based authentication to restrict access to a web application. When you combine these skills with those of the previous chapter, you should have all of the skills you need for providing the security that an e-commerce application needs.

Terms

authentication	membership provider
authorization	role provider
Windows-based authentication	role
forms-based authentication	access rule
authentication ticket	anonymous user
data provider	authenticated user

Summary

- *Authentication* is how you verify each user's identity. *Authorization* is how you determine what privileges a user has.

- *Forms-based authentication* works by adding an *authentication ticket* to a cookie when the user logs in, and then checking for the ticket on protected pages. If the ticket isn't found, the user is redirected to the login page.

- You can use the Web Site Administration Tool to set up authentication and authorization. If you're using SQL Server Express LocalDB, though, you'll need to add some configuration elements to the web.config file before you can use that tool.

- In the Security tab of the Web Site Administration Tool, you can enable forms-based authentication, create and manage *roles*, create and manage users, and create and manage *access rules*.

- ASP.NET provides several login controls to work with authentication and authorization. They are located in the Login group of the Toolbox.

- With the login controls, you can allow users to log in, log out, create an account, recover a forgotten password, or change a password. You can also display information such as the user's username or content specific to *anonymous users* and *authenticated users*.

- Changes made in the Web Site Administration Tool are stored in web.config files. The web.config file in the root directory stores settings such as authentication type and data providers. Access rules for specific directories are stored in web.config files within those directories.

20

How to use email, custom error pages, and back-button control

Once you've got an application working the way it's supposed to, you can add enhancements that make it work even better. In this chapter, you'll learn how to add three of the most useful enhancements. First, you'll learn how to send email from an ASP.NET application. Then, you'll learn how to create and use custom error pages. And last, you'll learn how to handle the problems that can occur when the user uses the Back button to access a page that has already been posted.

How to send email

When you create a web application, you often need to send email messages from the application. For instance, when a user makes a purchase from an e-commerce site, a web application usually sends the customer an email that confirms the order. Or, if a serious error occurs, the web application often sends the support staff an email message that documents the error. In the topics that follow, you'll learn how to send email from your ASP.NET applications.

An introduction to email

You're probably familiar with *mail client* software such as Microsoft Outlook or Outlook Express that allows you to send and retrieve email messages. This type of software communicates with a *mail server* that actually sends and retrieves your email messages. Most likely, your mail server software is provided by your Internet Service Provider (ISP) or through your company.

The diagram in figure 20-1 shows how this works. The two protocols that are commonly used to send email messages are *SMTP* and *POP*. When you send an email message, the message is first sent from the mail client software on your computer to your mail server using the SMTP protocol. Then, your mail server uses SMTP to send the mail to the recipient's mail server. Finally, the recipient's mail client uses the POP protocol to retrieve the mail from the recipient's mail server.

A third protocol you should know about is *MIME*, which stands for *Multipurpose Internet Mail Extension*. Unlike SMTP or POP, MIME isn't used to transfer email messages. Instead, it defines how the content of an email message and its attachments are formatted. In this chapter, you'll learn how to send messages that consist of simple text as well as messages that use HTML.

How email works

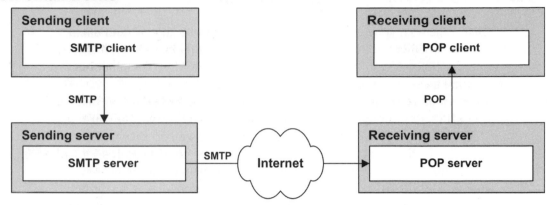

Three email protocols

Protocol	Description
SMTP	*Simple Mail Transfer Protocol* is used to send a message from one mail server to another.
POP	*Post Office Protocol* is used by mail clients to retrieve messages from mail servers. POP version 3, known as POP3, is the most widely-used version, but a specification for POP version 4 has been developed.
MIME	The *Multipurpose Internet Mail Extension* specifies the type of content that can be sent as a message or attachment.

Three common reasons for sending email from an ASP.NET application

- **To confirm receipt of an order.** When the user completes an order, the application can email a confirmation of the order to the user.
- **To remind a registered user of a forgotten password.** If the user forgets her password, the application can send an email that contains the user's password or a temporary new password to the email address that's on file for the user.
- **To notify support personnel of a problem.** If a problem like an unhandled exception occurs, the application can email a message that summarizes the problem to the appropriate support person.

Description

- When an email message is sent, it goes from the sender's *mail client* to the sender's *mail server* to the receiver's mail server to the receiver's mail client.
- *SMTP* and *POP* are the protocols that are commonly used for sending and retrieving email messages. *MIME* is the protocol for defining the format of an email message.

Figure 20-1   An introduction to email

How to use a third-party SMTP server

Out of the box, your ASP.NET applications won't be able to send email. This is true whether you're using IIS Express or the full version of IIS to host your applications. As a result, before you can test an ASP.NET application that sends email messages, you must install an SMTP server.

In previous versions of Windows, you could use the SMTP server that was built into IIS. Now, though, IIS doesn't include an SMTP server, so you'll need to get a separate one. Several SMTP servers can be downloaded for free from the Internet. One of these is called smtp4dev and is hosted on Microsoft's Codeplex web site. This SMTP server is designed for development environments.

Figure 20-2 describes how to download and use smtp4dev. It's a dummy SMTP server that works by intercepting emails sent from your application and displaying them in an inbox-like interface. No emails get sent, however, which means that you can send emails to and from any email address without worrying about cluttering up an actual inbox.

Once an email message is in the smtp4dev "inbox", you can look at it in two ways. You can click the View button, which will show the email message in your default mail client. This will give you an idea of how the email will look to a user who receives it. Or you can click the Inspect button, which will show you the parts of the email, such as text and attachments, and let you look at the source, header, and body for each part.

When you close or minimize the user interface, it will be minimized to the system tray. This means that it will still be running, and when your application sends an email, you will get a notification in the lower right corner of your screen, as shown in this figure. This is similar to the way that many mail clients work. Clicking on the notification will open the email message in your default mail client. This is the same as clicking the View button when the interface is open.

Like many free third-party utilities, stmp4dev can be a little temperamental. In particular, it will occasionally fail when you try to send an email. If this happens, it will usually work correctly on the next attempt. A side benefit of this is that it reminds you to write your code to take SMTP failures into account. Although that certainly wasn't the developer's intention, this is a good thing to be reminded of, since things like sending emails and accessing databases do sometimes fail, and you should code accordingly.

The third-party smtp4dev SMTP server application interface

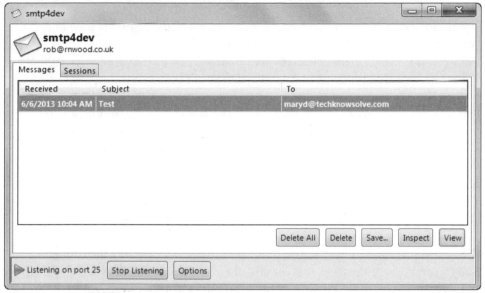

An email notification when smtp4dev is minimized in the system tray

How to install and work with smtp4dev

- At http://smtp4dev.codeplex.com, click on Downloads and choose the Standalone version. Save the downloaded .exe file to a convenient location, such as your desktop.

- Double-click the .exe file to open the user interface shown above. If you close or minimize the interface, it will be minimized to the system tray.

- To open the interface again, open the system tray by clicking on the up arrow in the lower right corner of the task bar. Then, right-click the smtp4dev icon and click View Messages.

- To completely exit smtp4dev, open the system tray, right-click the icon, and select Exit. To start smtp4dev again, double-click the .exe file.

Description

- Previous versions of Windows included an SMTP server with IIS, but now you must download a separate SMTP server even if you have the full version of IIS installed. A popular free third-party SMTP server for development is called smtp4dev.

Figure 20-2   How use a third-party SMTP server

How to create an email message

Figure 20-3 shows the constructors and properties of the MailMessage class that you use to create email messages. It also shows the constructors of the MailAddress class. This class is used to create the addresses that are stored in the From, To, CC, and Bcc properties of a mail message. These classes are part of the System.Net.Mail namespace.

The first example in this figure illustrates how you can use these classes to create a mail message that includes a carbon copy (cc). Here, all of the values needed to create the email message are passed to the method as arguments. Then, the first three statements of the method create MailAddress objects for the from, to, and cc addresses. Notice that the MailAddress object for the from address includes both an email address and a display name. When a display name is included, it's displayed in the mail client's email list instead of the email address.

The fourth statement in this method creates a MailMessage object using the to and from MailAddress objects. Then, the next two statements set the Subject and Body properties of the message. Finally, the last statement adds the cc MailAddress object to the collection of objects in the CC property.

The second example in this figure shows how to create the same email as in the first example without setting the display name for the sender. To do that, you create the MailMessage object using the from and to addresses and the subject and body. This example also illustrates how you can create a MailAddress object for the carbon copy and add it to the collection of objects using a single statement.

Although the examples in this figure create messages that will be sent to a single recipient, you should realize that you can send a message to any number of recipients. To do that, you need to use the first constructor for the MailMessage class shown here to create an empty mail message. Then, you can create a MailAddress object for the sender and assign it to the From property of the message. And you can create a MailAddress object for each recipient and add it to the collection of MailAddress objects returned by the To property of the mail message. For example, to create a message that will be sent to two people, your code will look something like this:

```
MailMessage msg = new MailMessage();
msg.From = new MailAddress("anne@murach.com");
msg.To.Add(new MailAddress("mike@murach.com"));
msg.To.Add(new MailAddress("maryd@techknowsolve.com"));
```

Constructors and properties of the MailMessage class

Constructor	Description
`MailMessage()`	Creates an empty mail message.
`MailMessage(from, to)`	Creates a mail message with the to and from addresses specified as strings or MailAddress objects.
`MailMessage(from, to, subject, body)`	Creates a mail message with the to address, from address, subject and body specified as strings.

Property	Description
`From`	A MailAddress object for the message sender.
`To`	A collection of MailAddress objects for the message recipients.
`CC`	A collection of MailAddress objects for the copy recipients.
`Bcc`	A collection of MailAddress objects for the blind copy recipients.
`Subject`	The subject line for the message.
`Body`	The body of the message.
`IsBodyHtml`	A Boolean value that indicates if the body of the message contains HTML. The default is False.
`Attachments`	A collection of Attachment objects.
`AlternateViews`	A collection of AlternateView objects for multipart emails.

Constructors of the MailAddress class

Constructor	Description
`MailAddress(address)`	Creates an email address with the specified address string.
`MailAddress(address, displayName)`	Creates an email address with the specified address and display strings.

Code that creates an email message with a carbon copy

```
private void SendTextMessageCC(string fromAddress, string fromName,
    string toAddress, string subject, string body, string ccAddress)
{
    MailAddress fromAdd = new MailAddress(fromAddress, fromName);
    MailAddress toAdd = new MailAddress(toAddress);
    MailAddress ccAdd = new MailAddress(ccAddress);
    MailMessage msg = new MailMessage(fromAdd, toAdd);
    msg.Subject = subject;
    msg.Body = body;
    msg.CC.Add(ccAdd);
}
```

Another way to create a message

```
MailMessage msg = new MailMessage(fromAddress, toAddress, subject, body);
msg.CC.Add(new MailAddress(ccAddress));
```

Figure 20-3   How to create an email message

How to send an email message

After you create an email message, you use the SmtpClient class shown in figure 20-4 to send the message. The technique you use to do that depends on the message you're sending and on whether you have set the SMTP configuration settings for the application. To set the SMTP configuration settings, you use the Web Site Administration Tool as shown in this figure. Then, these settings are saved in the web.config file.

Before I go on, you should realize that the server name shown here, local-host, doesn't necessarily refer to IIS. Instead, it refers to the SMTP server that's installed on your local machine.

The first example in this figure shows how to send a message using settings in the web.config file. When you use this technique, you don't have to specify the name or port for the SMTP server when you create the SmtpClient object. Instead, these settings are taken from the Smtp section of the web.config file.

The first example also illustrates how to send a message that's been stored in a MailMessage object. To do that, you simply name the MailMessage object on the Send method.

If you haven't set the SMTP configuration options, or if you want to override these options, you can specify the domain name of the server when you create the SmtpClient object. This is illustrated in the second example in this figure. Here, the name "localhost" is specified so the SMTP server on the local machine will be used. Notice that when you use the local server, you don't have to specify a port number. That's because the default port number is 25, which is also the default port for an SMTP server. If you use a server at a different port, though, you have to specify the port number.

The second example also illustrates how you can send a mail message without creating a MailMessage object. To do that, you just pass the from and to addresses and the subject and body text to the Send method. Then, the Send method creates the MailMessage object for you and sends it. You can use this format of the Send method if the message is in simple text format, you don't need to send the message to more than one person, you don't need to send copies of the message to anyone, and you don't need to send attachments with the message.

If you've read chapter 19, you know that another way to send an email is to use the PasswordRecovery control. This control sends an email to a user that includes the user's password. Because you don't specify the server that's used to send the message when you use this control, you must set the server name (and port if necessary) in the web.config file for it to work. In addition, you should set a from address to appear in the email that's sent by this control.

The ASP.NET Web Site Administration Tool

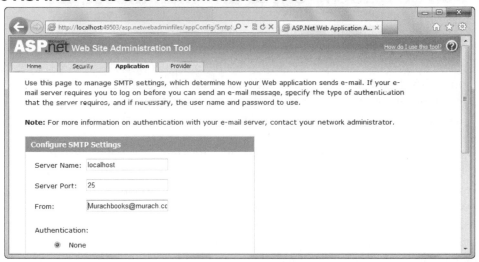

Constructors and methods of the SmtpClient class

Constructor	Description
SmtpClient()	Creates a client using the settings specified in the web.config file.
SmtpClient(name)	Creates a client that can send email to the specified SMTP server.
SmtpClient(name, port)	Creates a client that can send email to the specified SMTP server and port.

Method	Description
Send(message)	Sends the specified MailMessage object.
Send(from, to, subject, body)	Creates and sends an email message using the specified from, to, subject, and body strings.

Code that sends a message using settings in the web.config file

```
SmtpClient client = new SmtpClient();
client.Send(msg);
```

Code that creates and sends a message to a named server

```
SmtpClient client = new SmtpClient("localhost");
client.Send(fromAddress, toAddress, subject, body);
```

Description

- To send an email message, you use the SmtpClient class in the System.Net.Mail namespace.
- To use the Web Site Administration Tool to specify the settings that will be used to send email messages, select the WEBSITE→ASP.NET Configuration command, display the Application tab, click the Configure SMTP E-mail Settings link, and enter the values.

Figure 20-4   How to send an email message

How to add an attachment to an email message

An *attachment* is a file that's sent along with an email message. The most common types of attachments are text files, word processing documents, spreadsheets, photos, and other media files such as sound and video files.

Figure 20-5 shows how you can create an attachment and add it to an email message. After you create an attachment object using the Attachment class, you add the object to the mail message's Attachments collection. Then, you can send the message.

Note that the code examples in this figure use the MapPath method of the HttpServerUtility object to get the file path of the document to attach. This is a good way to get file paths because it means you won't have to adjust this code when you move from a development to a production server and the file paths change.

Since SMTP protocol is designed to send text messages, not binary files, any email attachment for a binary file must be converted to text format before it can be sent. Then, the text attachment must be converted back to a binary file when it's received. The most common format for converting attached binary files to text and back to binary is called *UUEncode*, and it's used by default. The other available format for converting binary files is called *Base64*.

The syntax for creating an attachment

```
new Attachment(fileName)
```

One way to create a new attachment and add it to a message

```
MailMessage msg = new MailMessage(fromAddress, toAddress, subject, body);
string fileName = Server.MapPath("Attachments/ReturnPolicy.doc");
Attachment attach = new Attachment(fileName);
msg.Attachments.Add(attach);
```

Another way to create a new attachment and add it to a message

```
MailMessage msg = new MailMessage(fromAddress, toAddress, subject, body);
string fileName = Server.MapPath("Attachments/ReturnPolicy.doc");
msg.Attachments.Add(new Attachment(fileName));
```

Description

- An *attachment* is a file that is sent along with an email message. When the recipient receives the email message, he can open or save the attachment.

- To add an attachment to an email message, you create the attachment using the Attachment class. Then, you add the attachment to the message using the Add method of the Attachments collection of the MailMessage class.

- If an email attachment contains a binary file, it must be converted to text before it can be sent, and it must be converted back to binary when it's received. By default, binary files are converted to a format called *UUEncode*. However, you can also use a format called *Base64*.

Figure 20-5   How to add an attachment to an email message

How to create an HTML message

By default, email messages consist of plain text with no formatting. However, you can also create a formatted message by using HTML. You should know, though, that it's a best practice to include a plain text message as well as an HTML message. You do this by creating a *multipart email message*.

The reason for sending multipart emails is that some people have their mail clients set to only show text, or to only show HTML from trusted senders and text from all others. Then, if you don't include a text version of your email, most mail clients will strip the HTML tags from your email message. This can cause words to run together and other formatting problems. Additionally, visually impaired people who use screen readers can have trouble with HTML messages.

Figure 20-6 shows a SendConfirmation method that creates a multipart email message. The method first creates a MailMessage object and adds a from address, a to address, and a subject. Then, it calls the GetConfirmationMessage method twice: once for the plain text version and once for the HTML version of the body of the message. The GetConfirmationMessage method uses basic HTML to create the HTML message, and carriage returns in the text message. Note that the messages include the customer's first and last names, which are retrieved from a customer object that contains the customer data.

An HTML email message can include links to your web site. However, you should avoid sending HTML that includes scripts or web form controls. Many mail servers will reject them because that kind of content is often malicious.

After loading the plain text message in the Body property of the MailMessage object and the HTML message in a local variable called html, the method creates an AlternateView object. The AlternateView class of the System.Net.Mail namespace allows you to specify copies of an email message in different formats. Usually you will use the static CreateAlternateViewFromString method of the AlternateView class to create the alternate message. The first parameter of this method is the html message, the second is the encoding type, and the third is the media type.

After creating the AlternateView object for the HTML message, the method adds it to the MailMessage object's AlternateViews collection. It then creates an SmtpClient object and sends the email. This figure shows how this email looks in a mail client as HTML and as text. Notice that in the text version, the HTML is presented as an attachment that the users can view if they choose to do that.

A multipart email message with both text and HTML

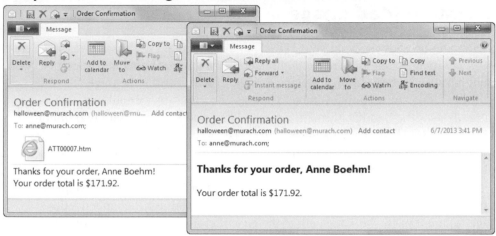

A method that sends a multipart email message

```
private void SendConfirmation(Customer customer, decimal total)
{
    MailMessage msg = new MailMessage(
        "halloween@murach.com", customer.EmailAddress);
    msg.Subject = "Order Confirmation";
    msg.Body = GetConfirmation(customer, total, false);

    //create an alternate HTML view
    string html = GetConfirmation(customer, total, true);
    AlternateView view = AlternateView
        .CreateAlternateViewFromString(html, null, "text/html");

    //add the HTML view to the message and send
    msg.AlternateViews.Add(view);
    SmtpClient client = new SmtpClient("localhost");
    client.Send(msg);
}

private string GetConfirmation(Customer c, decimal total, bool isHtml) {
    if (isHtml)
        return "<html><head><title>Order confirmation</title></head>"
            + "<body><h3>Thanks for your order, "
            + c.FirstName + " " + c.LastName + "!</h3>"
            + "<p>Your order total is " + total.ToString("c")
            + ".</p></body></html>";
    else
        return "Thanks for your order, "
            + c.FirstName + " " + c.LastName + "!\r\n"
            + "Your order total is " + total.ToString("c") + ".";
}
```

Description

- The AlternateView class of the System.Net.Mail namespace lets you include both text and HTML formats in an email, which is considered a best practice.

Figure 20-6   How to create an HTML message

How to create an HTML message with an embedded image

Sometimes you will want your HTML to include images. These are called *embedded* images, and they're different than images that are attached to an email, because embedded images appear in the HTML for the message.

Figure 20-7 shows how to embed an image in a multipart email message. This code uses the SendConfirmation method that you just saw, with two important differences. First, the LinkedResource class of the System.Net.Mail namespace is used to contain the image. This class represents an external resource that is embedded in an email.

In this figure, for example, the SendConfirmation method uses the MapPath method of the HttpServerUtility object to get the file path for the embedded image. Then, it passes this file path to the constructor of the LinkedResource object. This creates an object named img that represents the embedded image. Last, it sets the img object's ContentId property to "logoImage". This last step is a crucial one, since this is the name that you will use to add the image to your HTML.

The other change in the code is in the GetConfirmation method, where an image element is added to the HTML. The crucial step here is that the src attribute of the img element needs to point to the ContentID (cid) of the embedded image. In the example in this figure, the src attribute of the image tag is set to cid:logoImage, with no quotation marks.

An HTML email message with an embedded image

A method that sends a multipart email with an embedded image

```
private void SendConfirmation(Customer customer, decimal total)
{
    MailMessage msg = new MailMessage(
        "halloween@murach.com", customer.EmailAddress);
    msg.Subject = "Order Confirmation";
    msg.Body = GetConfirmation(customer, total, false);

    //create an alternate HTML view
    string html = GetConfirmation(customer, total, true);
    AlternateView view = AlternateView
        .CreateAlternateViewFromString(html, null, "text/html");

    //link and identify the image to embed
    string imgPath = Server.MapPath("Images/banner.jpg");
    LinkedResource img = new LinkedResource(imgPath);
    img.ContentId = "logoImage";

    //add the image to the HTML view, the view to the message, and send
    view.LinkedResources.Add(img);
    msg.AlternateViews.Add(view);
    SmtpClient client = new SmtpClient("localhost");
    client.Send(msg);
}
private string GetConfirmation(Customer customer, decimal total, bool isHtml){
    if (isHtml)
        return "<html><head><title>Order confirmation</title></head>"
            + "<body><img src=cid:logoImage>"
            + "<br /><br /><h3>Thanks for your order, "
            + customer.FirstName + " "
            + customer.LastName + "!</h3>"
            + "<p>Your order total is " + total.ToString("c")
            + ".</p></body></html>";
    ...
}
```

Description

- To embed an image as part of the HTML email, as opposed to including it as an attachment, you need to use the LinkedResource class of the System.Net.Mail namespace to hold the image and then refer to the image in the HTML code.

Figure 20-7   How to create an HTML message with an embedded image

How to use custom error handling

When an error occurs in an ASP.NET application, an exception is thrown. Then, if the exception isn't handled by the application, an ASP.NET Server Error page is displayed. This page includes an error message, a portion of the source code that threw the unhandled exception, and other debugging information. Since this type of error page usually isn't appropriate for the users of an application, you typically replace the generic error pages with your own custom error pages after you test the entire web site but before you go live with it.

An introduction to custom error handling

Figure 20-8 describes four techniques you can use to display your own custom error pages. Depending on your application, you may need to use one or more of these techniques.

The first technique is to enclose code that might generate exceptions in a try block of a try-catch statement. Then, you can redirect to a custom error page if an exception does occur.

The second technique is to code a Page_Error method in the code-behind file for a page. This method is called whenever an unhandled exception occurs on the page. Then, in the Page_Error method, you redirect the user to a custom error page.

The third technique is to code an Application_Error method in the global.asax file. This method is called whenever an unhandled exception occurs on a page that doesn't have a Page_Error method. Then, the Application_Error method can redirect the user to a custom error page.

The fourth technique is to use the customErrors element in the web.config file to designate custom error pages. This technique is used to display custom error pages when common HTTP errors such as a 404 – Not Found error occur.

A custom error page in a browser

Four ways to display a custom error page when an exception occurs

- Use try-catch statements to catch exceptions as they occur, then redirect or transfer to a custom error page.
- Use the Page_Error method in a code-behind file to catch unhandled exceptions at the page level, then redirect or transfer to a custom error page.
- Use the Application_Error method in the global.asax file to catch unhandled exceptions at the application level, then redirect or transfer to a custom error page.
- Use the customErrors element of the web.config file to specify custom error pages that are displayed for specific types of HTTP errors.

Description

- If an unrecoverable error occurs, most applications display a custom error page to inform the user that a problem has occurred.
- Before the custom error page is displayed, the C# code will often do other processing, like recording the error in an error log or sending an email message to the support staff that lets them know that a problem has occurred.

Figure 20-8   An introduction to custom error handling

How to get and use the Exception object for an error

Figure 20-9 shows how you can use the properties and methods of the Exception and HttpServerUtility classes to get and use the Exception object for an error. This is the object that contains information about the exception that has occurred. The examples in this figure show how this works.

The first example shows how you can use a try-catch statement to get the Exception object. Here, the catch block catches the Exception object if any of the statements in the try block throw an exception. You can use this technique in any method of a code-behind or class file.

The second example shows how to get the Exception object within the Page_Error method. This method is executed automatically if an exception isn't handled by the other methods of a code-behind file. Here, you use the GetLastError method of the Server object, which you access using the Server property of the page.

The third example shows how to get the Exception object within the Application_Error method of the global.asax file. This method is executed automatically if an exception isn't handled by any of the methods in the code-behind file including the Page_Error method. In the Application_Error method, however, the GetLastError method doesn't return the correct Exception object. That's because a second exception called HttpUnhandledException is thrown if an exception occurs and the exception isn't handled by a try-catch statement or a Page_Error method. As a result, the GetLastError method returns the HttpUnhandledException exception, not the exception that originally caused the error. To access the original exception, you must use the InnerException property of the Exception object that's returned by the GetLastError method.

Although you might think that you could use the ClearError method to clear the HttpUnhandledException exception and then use GetLastError to get the original exception, that won't work. That's because you can only use GetLastError to get the Exception object for the last exception that occurred. In this case, that's the HttpUnhandledException exception.

The fourth example shows how you might use the properties of an Exception object as you test an application. Here, the Write method of the HttpResponse object is used to display the Message and Source properties on the page. Notice that before this method is executed, the ClearError method of the Server object is used to clear the error. That way, the ASP.NET Server Error page won't be displayed.

Common properties of the Exception class

Property	Description
Message	A message that describes the error.
Source	The name of the application or object that caused the error.
InnerException	The Exception object that caused the exception at the application level.

Methods of the HttpServerUtility class for working with exceptions

Method	Description
GetLastError()	Gets the most recent exception.
ClearError()	Clears the most recent exception.

Code that gets the Exception object at the method level

```
try
{
    // statements that could throw an exception
}
catch (Exception ex)
{
    // statements that use the Exception object named ex
}
```

Code that gets the Exception object at the page level

```
Exception ex = Server.GetLastError();
```

Code that gets the Exception object at the application level

```
Exception ex = Server.GetLastError().InnerException;
```

Code that displays the error message and source of the Exception object

```
Server.ClearError();
Response.Write(ex.Message + "<br />" + ex.Source);
```

Description

- You can use a try-catch statement in any method of a code-behind or class file to get the Exception object for an error.

- The Page_Error method runs when an unhandled exception occurs. There, you can use the GetLastError method of the Server object to get the Exception object for the error.

- If you don't handle an exception with a try-catch statement or a Page_Error method, an HttpUnhandledException is thrown. Then, you can use the Application_Error method in the global.asax file to handle the exception. There, you can use the GetLastError method of the Server object to get the Exception object for the exception, and you can use the InnerException property of that exception to get the Exception object for the error.

- During testing, you may want to use the Write method of the HttpResponse object to write information about the exception to the page. Before you do that, you need to clear the error from the Server object so the ASP.NET Server Error page isn't displayed.

Figure 20-9   How to get and use the Exception object for an error

How to create a custom class for handling exceptions

As you just saw, code to handle exceptions can be used in many different places. Because of this, many developers write a custom error handling class that they can call from try-catch statements, page error handlers, and the global.asax file. Another reason to use a custom error handling class is so you can process the exception as soon as it occurs, since the GetLastError method will return null once you redirect to an error page.

Figure 20-10 shows a custom error class. It contains a private Exception object that is filled by the constructor when an instance of the class is created. The constructor uses the GetLastError object of the HttpServerUtility object to get the Exception object. However, because this code isn't in a code-behind or global.asax file, it uses the Current property of the HttpContext object to get the Server property.

After getting the Exception object, the constructor checks whether the InnerException property for the error is set to null. If it is, it means that the error was caught by a try-catch statement or a page-level error handler. If it isn't, it means that the error was caught at the application level. Either way, the correct object is stored in the Exception object, so this class works for handling errors that are caught at all three levels.

The error handling class has a method called SendEmail that uses the techniques you learned earlier in this chapter to send an email about the error to support staff. There are two things to note about this method. The first is that it places the code that sends the email in a try-catch statement. This is because code that sends emails can fail, so you should plan for it in your code. The second is that the try-catch statement returns string messages indicating the result of the send operation. This is so code that calls this method can be notified of the result and take appropriate action.

This figure also shows how the error handling class can be used in the Application_Error method in the global.asax file. Here, the code constructs a new ErrorHandler object from the ErrorHandler class, and that object has a property that contains the Exception object for the error. Next, the Application_Error method in the global.asax file calls the SendEmail method, stores the result of the SendEmail operation in a local variable, appends the result to the URL as a query string, and redirects to the error page. The error page can then use the information in the query string to take further action, such as notifying the user whether or not the support team has been informed of the problem.

The reason that the code sends information to the error page in the query string of the URL is that this is the most reliable way to do it. If the error occurs at the beginning of a page's life cycle, information stored in session state or cookies might be lost.

A custom error handling class

```
using System.Net.Mail;

public class ErrorHandler
{
    private Exception ex;
    public ErrorHandler() {
        Exception e = HttpContext.Current.Server.GetLastError();
        if (e.InnerException == null) ex = e;
        else ex = e.InnerException;
    }

    public string SendEmail() {
        string body = "An exception occurred at "
            + DateTime.Now.ToLongTimeString()
            + " on " + DateTime.Now.ToLongDateString()
            + "<br /> Error Message: " + ex.Message;
        MailMessage msg = new MailMessage(
            "halloween@murach.com", "support@murach.com");
        msg.Subject = "Exception in Halloween application";
        msg.Body = body;
        msg.IsBodyHtml = true;
        SmtpClient client = new SmtpClient("localhost");
        try {
            client.Send(msg);
            return "sent";
        }
        catch {
            return "notsent";
        }
    }
}
```

An Application_Error method in the global.asax file that uses the error handling class and then redirects to a custom error page

```
void Application_Error(object sender, EventArgs e)
{
    ErrorHandler handler = new ErrorHandler();
    string result = handler.SendEmail();
    Response.Redirect("ErrorPage.aspx?email=" + result);
}
```

Description

- You can use a custom error handling class in a try-catch statement, a Page_Error method, or an Application_Error method in the global.asax file.

- The error handling class should process the exception before transferring to an error page. This is because after redirecting, the GetLastError method will return null.

- If you run an application with debugging and an unhandled exception occurs, Visual Studio enters break mode and displays a dialog box that describes the error and provides links you can use to get additional information on the error. To continue program execution when this dialog box is displayed, click the Continue button.

Figure 20-10   How to create a custom class for handling exceptions

How to handle HTTP errors with the web.config file

Not all unrecoverable errors cause ASP.NET to throw an exception. As figure 20-11 shows, some error conditions result in HTTP errors that are handled by the web server itself. For these errors, you can use the customErrors element in the web.config file to specify custom error pages.

Although there are many different types of HTTP errors that can occur, the common types are listed in this figure. Of these, the most common is the 404 error. This error occurs when a user attempts to retrieve a page that doesn't exist. In some cases, a 404 error is caused by a missing page or a page that has been renamed. In other cases, a 404 error is caused by an error in your application's navigation controls, such as a hyperlink that uses an incorrect URL. Or the user may have typed an incorrect URL in to the browser's address bar.

As this figure shows, you include an error element in the web.config file for each HTTP error that you want to redirect to a custom error page. In the example, this is done for two types of errors. The first error element specifies that the page named E404.aspx should be displayed if a 404 error occurs. The second element specifies that the page named E500.aspx should be displayed if a 500 error occurs.

You can also specify a default error page that's displayed if an HTTP error that isn't specifically listed in an error element occurs. In the example in this figure, the defaultRedirect attribute specifies that a page named DefaultError.aspx should be displayed if an HTTP error other than 404 or 500 occurs.

A customErrors element in the web.config file for custom error pages

```
<system.web>
    .
    .
    <customErrors mode="On" defaultRedirect="DefaultError.aspx">
        <error statusCode="404" redirect="E404.aspx" />
        <error statusCode="500" redirect="E500.aspx" />
    </customErrors>
    .
    .
</system.web>
```

Common HTTP error codes

Code	Description
401	Unauthorized request. The client must be authorized to access the resource.
403	Forbidden request. The client is not allowed to access the resource.
404	File Not Found. The resource could not be located.
500	Internal Server Error. This is usually the result of an unhandled exception.

Description

- The customErrors element in the web.config file lets you designate custom error pages that are automatically displayed when unrecoverable HTTP errors occur. You don't have to write any code to redirect or transfer to these pages.

- To enable custom error pages, add a customErrors element to the system.web element of the web.config file. Then, set the mode attribute to On, and set the defaultRedirect attribute to the name of the generic error page.

- To associate a custom error page with an HTTP error, add an error element that specifies the HTTP error code in the statusCode attribute and the name of the custom error page in the redirect attribute.

- You can also add a customErrors element to the web.config file using the Web Site Administration Tool. To do that, select the WEBSITE→ASP.NET Configuration command, display the Application tab, click the Define Default Error Page link, and select the appropriate settings.

Note

- You shouldn't use a customErrors element if you use the Application_Error method to handle errors. If you do, the customErrors element will be ignored.

Figure 20-11   How to handle HTTP errors with the web.config file

How to handle the back-button problem

If the user clicks the Back button in the browser window to return to a previous ASP.NET form and then posts the form, the application's session state may not correspond to that form. In some cases, this can result in a problem that we refer to as the *back-button problem*. The topics that follow show you how to deal with this problem.

An introduction to the back-button problem

Figure 20-12 illustrates the back-button problem in a shopping cart application. Here, the contents of the user's shopping cart are stored in session state and displayed on the page. The user then deletes one of the two items, which changes the data in session state. At that point, the user changes her mind and clicks the Back button, which displays both items again, even though session state only includes one item.

If the user now proceeds to check out, the order is likely to show one item when the user thinks she has ordered two items. But that depends upon how the application is coded. In the worst cases, the back-button problem may cause an application to crash. In the best cases, clicking on the Back button won't cause a problem at all.

A similar problem occurs when the user clicks on the Refresh button for a page that has already been submitted. Although most browsers warn the user about resubmitting a page, this can still cause problems if the user ignores the warning.

In general, there are three ways to handle the back-button problem. The first is to try to prevent pages from being saved in the browser's cache by sending page cache settings with the HTTP response. Then, when the user clicks the Back button, the old page can't be retrieved and a new request for the page is sent to the server. There are several methods in ASP.NET for doing that, and you will find many examples online. However, these techniques don't work if the user's browser ignores the page cache settings that are sent with a response. Because of this, they aren't recommended and won't be covered in this chapter.

The second way is to use the *Post-Redirect-Get (PRG) pattern* to prevent pages that are posted to the server from being saved in the browser's cache. If the PRG pattern is used for the example in this figure, the user will be taken back to the Order page when she clicks the Back button. Then, when she navigates to the Cart page, she will see the correct cart information. As you will see, the PRG pattern is easy to use, has only minor drawbacks, and also fixes the Refresh problem.

The third way is to code web forms so they detect when the user attempts to post a page that isn't current. To do that, a form can use timestamps or random numbers to track the use of pages. If timestamps are used for the example in this figure, the user will still see the incorrect data when she clicks the Back button in step 3. But if she tries to resubmit the incorrect data, the application will detect that the data is incorrect and take appropriate action. This technique also fixes the Refresh problem.

A back-button problem in the Cart page of the Halloween Store application

1. The user adds two products to the shopping cart. The shopping cart data is stored in session state and contains two items: one Deranged Cat at $19.99 and one Flying Bats at $69.99. The shopping cart displayed in the browser window looks like this:

2. The user selects the Deranged Cat product and clicks the Remove Item button to delete it. The product is deleted from the shopping cart in session state and the updated page is sent to the browser:

3. The user decides that she wants to purchase the Deranged Cat after all and clicks the browser's Back button, thinking this will undo the Delete action. The browser retrieves the previous page from its local cache:

Because the browser redisplayed this page directly from its cache, the Deranged Cat was not added back to the shopping cart in session state. As a result, session state contains only one item even though the web page displays two items.

Three ways to handle the back-button problem

- Disable browser page caching for user input forms. Because this method is unreliable, it won't be covered in this chapter.
- Use the *Post-Redirect-Get (PRG) pattern* to keep the posted page from being saved in the browser's cache.
- Use timestamps or random numbers to track pages so you can detect when a page isn't current.

Description

- When a user clicks the browser's Back button, the browser retrieves a locally cached copy of the previous page without notifying the server. As a result, the information stored in session state can become out of sync with the data displayed in the browser window.
- Clicking the Refresh button can cause a similar problem, but the browser usually warns the user about re-submitting the page.

Figure 20-12   An introduction to the Back-button problem

How to use the Post-Redirect-Get pattern

Figure 20-13 shows how to use the PRG pattern to solve the back-button problem. To start, this figure summarizes the normal postback pattern for a page. That is, the browser sends a POST request, the server handles the request, and the server returns a 200 HTTP response code with the HTML for the page. Then, the page is stored in the browser's cache.

The first code example in this figure shows the normal postback pattern in the Cart page. When the user clicks the Remove Item button, the selected item is removed from the Cart object in session state, and the HTML for displaying the updated Cart page is sent back to the browser. The problem is that by sending the page as a response to a POST request, the page is added to the browser's cache. Then, if the user clicks the Back button or the Refresh button to reload and resubmit this page, it can have serious consequences.

In contrast, the PRG pattern solves the back-button problem by splitting the posting of data and the retrieval of updated data into two separate roundtrips. More specifically, when the PRG pattern receives a POST request, it handles it and returns a 302 HTTP response code that tells the browser to redirect to the URL that's included with the response. Then, since no HTML is returned with the response, there's nothing for the browser to cache. Instead, the browser sends a GET request for the page and caches the page it receives in response to this second request.

The second code example in this figure shows the PRG pattern in the Cart page. When the user clicks the Remove Item button, the selected item is removed from the Cart object in session state, and the response tells the browser to redirect to the same page. Then, if the user clicks the Back button or Refresh button to reload and resubmit the page, the browser will receive the updated data so the page in the cache won't be out of sync with the data on the server.

The normal postback pattern for a page

- The browser sends a POST request for a page.
- The server handles the request and returns a 200 HTTP response code (OK) and the HTML for the page, which is stored in the browser's cache.

The aspx code for a method that uses the normal postback pattern

```
protected void btnRemove_Click(object sender, EventArgs e) {
    if (cart.Count > 0)     {
        if (lstCart.SelectedIndex > -1) {
            cart.RemoveAt(lstCart.SelectedIndex);
            this.DisplayCart();
        }
        else {
            lblMessage.Text = "Please select the item you want to remove.";
        }
    }
}
```

The Post-Redirect-Get (PRG) pattern for a page

- The browser sends a POST request for a page.
- The server handles the request and returns a 302 HTTP response code (Found) that tells the browser to redirect to the URL that's included in the response. Then, since no HTML is returned with the response, the page isn't stored in the browser's cache.
- The browser sends a GET request for the URL that was returned.
- The server returns a 200 HTTP response code (OK) and the HTML for the page, which is stored in the browser's cache.

The aspx code for a method that uses the PRG pattern

```
protected void btnRemove_Click(object sender, EventArgs e) {
    if (cart.Count > 0)     {
        if (lstCart.SelectedIndex > -1) {
            cart.RemoveAt(lstCart.SelectedIndex);
            Response.Redirect("~/Cart.aspx");
        }
        else {
            lblMessage.Text = "Please select the item you want to remove.";
        }
    }
}
```

Description

- The PRG pattern works because a page isn't put into the browser's cache until after it has been updated.
- The PRG pattern is easy to implement, and it also fixes the Refresh button problem.
- The disadvantages of using the PRG pattern is that it requires two roundtrips instead of one and it doesn't preserve view state.

Figure 20-13   How to use the Post-Redirect-Get pattern

How to use timestamps

Figure 20-14 shows how to use timestamps, which is another reliable way to avoid the back-button problem. This technique also avoids the Refresh problem.

In this figure, you see the code for a web page that uses timestamps to determine whether the posted page is current. The basic technique is to record a timestamp in two places when a page is posted: view state and session state. Then, the view state stamp is sent back to the browser and cached along with the rest of the information on the page, while the session state stamp is saved on the server.

Later, when the user posts a page for the second time, the Page_Load method calls a private method named IsExpired. This method retrieves the timestamps from view state and session state and compares them. If they are identical, the page is current and IsExpired returns False. But if they are different, it indicates that the user has posted a page that was retrieved from the browser's cache via the Back button. In that case, the IsExpired method returns True. Then, the Page_Load method redirects to a page named Expired.aspx, which in turn displays a message indicating that the page is out of date and can't be posted.

Notice that before comparing the timestamp items in session state and view state, the IsExpired method checks that both of these items exist. If not, the method returns False so that current timestamps can be saved in both session state and view state.

For this to work, of course, the page must be posted back to the server. That means that you can't use the PostBackUrl property of a button to display another page if you first want to check that the current page hasn't expired. For example, suppose the user deletes an item from the cart and then uses the Back button to add it back as shown in figure 20-12. Then, if the user clicks either the Check Out button or the Continue Shopping button, you want the Expired page to be displayed so the user knows that the shopping cart isn't accurate. To do that, the Check Out and Continue Shopping buttons must post the Cart page back to the server, which doesn't happen if you use the PostBackUrl property.

A page that checks timestamps

```
public partial class Cart : System.Web.UI.Page
{
    private CartItemList cart;

    protected void Page_Load(object sender, EventArgs e)
    {
        if (IsExpired())
            Response.Redirect("Expired.aspx");
        else
            this.SaveTimeStamps();
        cart = CartItemList.GetCart();
        if (!IsPostBack)
            this.DisplayCart();
    }

    private bool IsExpired()
    {
        if (Session["Cart_TimeStamp"] == null)
            return false;
        else if (ViewState["TimeStamp"] == null)
            return false;
        else if (ViewState["TimeStamp"].ToString() ==
                    Session["Cart_TimeStamp"].ToString())
            return false;
        else
            return true;
    }

    private void SaveTimeStamps()
    {
        DateTime dtm = DateTime.Now;
        ViewState.Add("TimeStamp", dtm);
        Session.Add("Cart_TimeStamp", dtm);
    }
    .
    .
    .
}
```

Description

- When you use timestamps to solve the back-button problem, two copies of the timestamp for the page are saved: one in view state, the other in session state.

- The IsExpired method tests the view state and session state timestamps to make sure they are the same. If they aren't, the user has posted a page that has been retrieved from the browser's cache.

- This method also fixes the Refresh button problem.

- Some developers prefer to use random numbers rather than timestamps, but either technique will work.

Figure 20-14   How to use timestamps

Perspective

This chapter has presented three types of enhancements that you can add to an application after you have the basic functions working right. In practice, most applications use both email and custom error pages to make an application more user friendly and less error prone.

In contrast, many applications ignore the back-button problem on the theory that the users should be smart enough to avoid that problem themselves. As a result, clicking on the Back button and reposting a page will cause a problem on many e-commerce sites. That's why you may want to use the techniques in this chapter, especially the PRG pattern, to handle that problem on your web site.

Terms

mail client   attachment
mail server   multipart email message
Simple Mail Transfer Protocol   embedded image
   (SMTP)   back-button problem
Post Office Protocol (POP)   Post-Redirect-Get (PRG) pattern
Multipurpose Internet Mail Extension
   (MIME)

Summary

- You can use the classes of the System.Net.Mail namespace to send email from your ASP.NET applications. The members in these classes let you send emails to multiple recipients, add carbon copies and blind carbon copies, add attachments, and format your emails with HTML that includes *embedded images*.

- The *Simple Mail Transfer Protocol (SMTP)* and *Post Office Protocol (POP)* are the protocols commonly used to send and receive emails. The *Multipurpose Internet Mail Extension (MIME)* protocol defines how the content of an email message is formatted.

- You will need to use a third-party SMTP server to send email with IIS or IIS Express. Several free servers that you can use for development are available online, including smtp4dev at Microsoft's Codeplex web site.

- When an error occurs in an ASP.NET application, you can handle it in a try-catch statement, in the page-level Page_Error method, in the application-level Application_Error method, or with customError elements in the web.config file.

- When a user clicks the Back button in the browser window, it can cause the data in the browser's cache to become out of sync with the data on the server.

- The *Post-Redirect-Get (PRG) pattern* fixes the back-button problem by splitting the posting of data to the server and the retrieval of updated data from the server into two separate roundtrips to the server.

- The use of timestamps fixes the back-button problem by allowing the developer to detect when the user is posting a page from the browser's cache.

21

How to configure and deploy ASP.NET applications

This chapter presents the most common ways that ASP.NET applications can be configured and deployed. To start, it presents the Web Site Administration Tool. Then, it presents three general ways to deploy an application, and it presents three specific deployment techniques.

How to use
the Web Site Administration Tool

Before you deploy an application, you may need to change the configuration information in the web.config file. For example, you may need to modify the application settings so they're appropriate for the server where the application will be deployed. Although you can edit the web.config file for an application manually, this technique is error prone. Because of that, you'll want to use the Web Site Administration Tool instead.

When you use this tool, you should know that it has two limitations. First, it doesn't let you set all of the configuration options in the web.config file. For example, you can't use it to change the connection strings stored in the file or to specify custom error pages. Second, you can only use this tool from within Visual Studio. As a result, you can't use it for a web site that's been deployed to a production server unless you can open the web site in Visual Studio.

As figure 22-1 shows, the Web Site Administration Tool is a web-based editor. It uses a tabbed interface that lets you switch between the home page and the pages that configure security, application, and provider settings.

How to use the Security tab

The Security tab lets you configure the ASP.NET authentication feature. That includes configuring users, roles, and access rules. You learned how to use this tab in chapter 19, and you can refer to that chapter for more information.

How to use the Application tab

The Application tab lets you create custom application settings that appear in the appSettings element of the web.config file and can be accessed in code by using the System.Configuration.ConfigurationManager class. In chapter 18, for example, you saw how to add a setting that specifies the path for an application. To enter this information using the Web Site Administration Tool, you can click the Create Application Settings link on the Application tab. Then, you can use the page that's displayed to enter the key and value for the setting.

The Application tab also lets you configure a web site to work with an SMTP server so it can send and receive email. You saw how this works in chapter 20. It also lets you configure debugging options for the site. Before you deploy the final version of an application, for example, you'll want to disable debugging. Finally, it lets you start and stop the site.

How to use the Provider tab

The Provider tab lets you select different providers for membership and role data. ASP.NET provides four providers for you to choose from. You can also write your own custom providers.

The home page of the Web Site Administration Tool

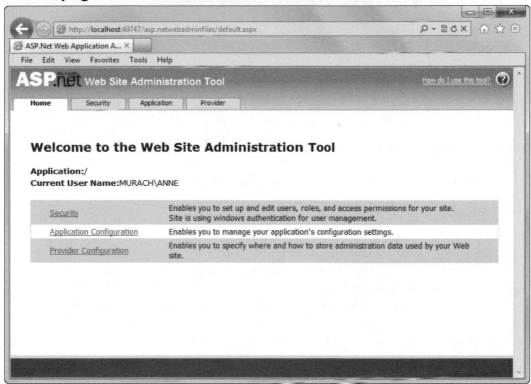

The four tabs of the Web Site Administration Tool

- **Home:** Displays the home page.
- **Security:** Lets you configure users, roles, and access rules. For more information, see chapter 19.
- **Application:** Lets you create custom application settings, configure SMTP email support (see chapter 20), control debugging and tracing settings, and start or stop the application.
- **Provider:** Lets you configure providers for features such as membership and roles.

Description

- The Web Site Administration Tool lets you configure certain web.config settings using a browser-based interface.
- To start the Web Site Administration Tool, open the project in Visual Studio and choose WEBSITE→ASP.NET Configuration.

Figure 21-1   How to use the Web Site Administration Tool to configure an ASP.NET application

An introduction to deployment

Deployment refers to the process of copying an ASP.NET web application from the development system to the production server on which the application will be run. ASP.NET provides several alternatives for deploying web applications. In the next two topics, you'll learn about the three basic ways to deploy an application, and you'll learn how to use the simplest deployment technique.

Three ways to deploy an ASP.NET application

Figure 21-2 lists the three basic approaches to deploying an ASP.NET application. The first is commonly called *XCopy deployment* because it simply copies the files required by the application to the production server. To do that, you can use the DOS XCopy command, or you can use the Copy Web Site command from within Visual Studio as described in figure 21-3.

The second way to deploy a web site is called *one-click deployment*, or *one-click publish*. This type of deployment lets you create one or more profiles that specify the deployment options you want to use for an application. Then, you can use the appropriate profile each time you deploy the application. To use one-click deployment, you can use the Publish Web Site command from within Visual Studio as shown in figures 21-4 and 21-5.

The third way to deploy a web application is to develop a setup project that creates a Windows *Setup program* for the application. Then, you can run this Setup program on the production server to install the application. This approach is described in figures 21-6 through 21-9.

Which of these deployment alternatives is the best choice depends on the needs of the application. XCopy deployment is the easiest, and it's often used during development to create copies of an application on different servers for testing purposes. For small applications, XCopy deployment may also be the best choice for production deployment.

One-click deployment has several advantages over XCopy deployment. For example, you can compile the pages of an application before deploying the application to the server. This provides better performance for the first users that access the site. In addition, it provides increased security because you don't have to copy the application's source files to the server. If the application uses a database, you can also deploy the database with the application, and you can change the connection string that's used by the application so it's appropriate for the deployed database.

For applications that are deployed to one or just a few servers, one-click deployment is usually the best choice. However, if you're distributing an application to many different servers, you should consider creating a Setup program for the application. When you use Visual Studio 2012, you create a Setup program using a product called InstallShield Limited Edition. Although creating a Setup program using InstallShield can involve considerable work, the effort will be repaid each time you use the program to install the application.

XCopy deployment

- To manually copy the files of an ASP.NET web site to a server, you can use the XCopy command from a command prompt. Then, you can use the IIS Management Console to create an IIS application that's mapped to the directory that you copied the web site to.
- To automate the deployment, you can create a batch file for the XCopy command. Then, you can run the batch file any time you make changes to the application and want to deploy the updated code.
- You can also do XCopy deployment from Visual Studio by using the Copy Web Site command (see figure 21-3).

One-click deployment

- Lets you create one or more profiles that specify deployment options.
- Lets you deploy precompiled assemblies to the specified server with or without the source files.
- Can be done from within Visual Studio using the Publish Web Site command (see figures 21-4 and 21-5).

Setup program deployment

- Uses a setup project to build a Windows Setup program that can be run to deploy a web application to a server (see figures 21-6 through 21-9).
- Useful if you want to distribute a web application to multiple servers.
- An application that's installed by a Setup program can be removed by using the Uninstall or Change a Program window that can be accessed from the Control Panel.
- In Visual Studio 2012, you create a Setup program using a product developed by Flexera Software called InstallShield Limited Edition.

Description

- Visual Studio 2012 provides three general methods for deploying ASP.NET applications: *XCopy deployment*, *one-click deployment*, and *Setup program deployment*.
- The method you use for deployment depends on how often the application will need to be deployed and whether you want to include the source code with the deployed application.

Notes

- The deployment features are installed by default but are optional and can be disabled. Additionally, some features were not included in Visual Studio 2012 and Visual Studio Express 2012 for Web when they were originally released.
- If you find that the feature you want to use isn't available, you can install the Web Publish Update. You can find this update by doing an Internet search for "Visual Studio Web Publish Update".

Figure 21-2   Three ways to deploy an ASP.NET application

How to use XCopy deployment

To implement XCopy deployment from within Visual Studio, you use the Copy Web Site command shown in figure 21-3. This command lets you copy a web site to a file system, local IIS, FTP, or remote IIS web site. In addition, it lets you copy all of the files in the web site or just selected files, and you can use it to synchronize web sites so that both sites have the most recently updated versions of each file.

To use this command, open the web site you want to copy and start the Copy Web Site command to display the window shown in this figure. Here, the Source Web Site section lists the files in the current web site. Next, click the Connect button to display an Open Web Site dialog box that lets you pick the location where you want to copy the web site. If you're copying to a local or remote IIS server, you can also use this dialog box to create a new IIS application on the server if the application doesn't already exist.

Once you select the remote web site, its files will appear in the Remote Web Site section of the dialog box. You can then select the files you want to copy in the Source Web Site list and click the right-arrow button that appears between the lists to copy the files from the source web site to the remote web site. You can use the other buttons to copy files from the remote web site to the source web site, to synchronize files in the web sites, or to stop a lengthy copy operation.

The Copy Web Site window

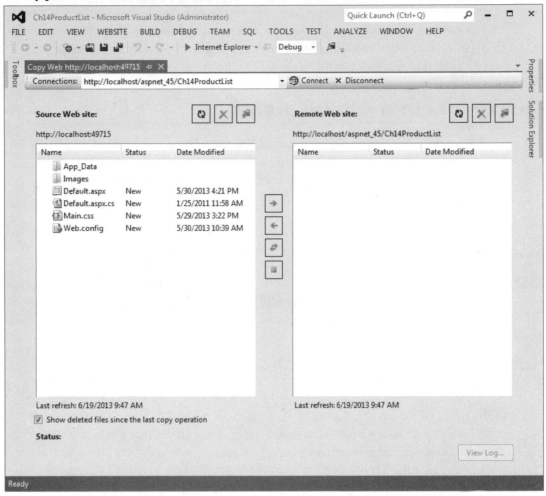

How to use the Copy Web Site command

1. In Visual Studio, open the web site you want to deploy and choose the WEBSITE→Copy Web Site command.

2. Click the Connect button to display an Open Web Site dialog box that lets you choose the destination for the copy operation.

3. Select the files you want to copy. (Press Ctrl+A to select all of the site's files.)

4. Click the → button to copy the files from the source web site to the remote web site.

Description

- You can use the Copy Web Site command to deploy an ASP.NET application with XCopy deployment.

Figure 21-3   How to use XCopy deployment

How to use one-click deployment

To use one-click deployment, you start by using the Publish Web dialog box to create a profile that contains the deployment options you want to use. Then, you can use that profile each time you deploy the application.

How to create a publish profile

To create a *publish profile*, you use the Profile tab of the Publish Web dialog box as shown in figure 21-4. Here, you can see that the <New Profile...> option is being selected from the drop-down list. When you select this option, the New Profile dialog box is displayed. Then, you can enter a name for the profile and click the OK button.

You can also create a profile by importing a .publishsettings file. This is often the case when you use a hosting provider, and it can simplify the process of creating a publish profile.

Once you create one or more profiles, you can use the Manage Profiles button to manage them. The dialog box that's displayed when you click this button lets you rename or remove profiles.

How to define the connection

To define the connection for a profile, you use the Connection tab of the Publish Web dialog box. This tab is also shown in figure 21-4.

To start, you select a publish method. Here, you can see that I selected Web Deploy. This is the recommended method because it's the most versatile. If it doesn't provide the deployment options you want, though, you can choose one of the other deployment methods. They include File System, FTP, FPSE, and Web Deploy Package.

Next, you enter the name of the server where the application will be deployed, along with the name of the site. In this case, I entered localhost for the server so the application will be deployed to the server on the local computer. You can also deploy to a server on your network or to a hosting company on the Internet.

For the site name, you enter the name of the IIS web site, the path to the IIS application, and the name of the application. In this example, the application will be deployed to the aspnet_45 directory of the default web site. (Here, Default Web Site is the actual name of the web site.) Note that the web site you specify must already exist. However, the directory and path will be created if they don't exist.

If a user name and password are required to deploy to the server, you can enter that information as well. In addition, if you want to display the application in your default browser after it's deployed, you can enter the URL in the Destination URL text box. Finally, you can make sure that the settings on the Connection tab are valid by clicking the Validate Connection button.

The Profile and Connection tabs of the Publish Web dialog box

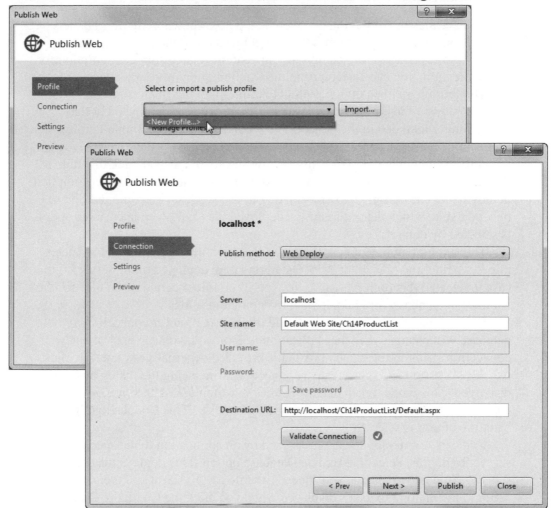

Description

- Select the BUILD→Publish Web Site command to display the Publish Web dialog box. In the Profile tab, select <New Profile...> from the drop-down list, and then enter a name for the profile in the New Profile dialog box.

- In the Connection tab, select a method from the Publish Method drop-down list and then enter the options for that method. For the Web Deploy method, you must enter a server and a site name. You can also enter a destination URL to display the web site when it's deployed. To be sure the connection is valid, click the Validate Connection button.

- The other publish methods let you deploy a web site using FTP or FPSE; deploy a web site to a folder that you specify so you can use your own FTP tool; and deploy a .zip file for the web site that can later be installed on the target server.

Figure 21-4   How to create a publish profile and define the connection for one-click deployment

How to set the file and database options

The Settings tab of the Publish Web dialog box, shown in figure 21-5, lets you set options related to the files that are published and the databases that are used by the application. In addition, if you've defined a custom configuration for the application, you can select it from the Configuration drop-down list.

The first file publish option, Remove Additional Files at Destination, lets you remove files from the server that were previously deployed but that are no longer included in the project. The second option, Precompile During Publishing, causes the application to be compiled before it's deployed. If you select this option, the Configure link becomes available. If you click this link, a dialog box is displayed that lets you set additional options related to precompiled deployment. The option you're most likely to use is Allow Precompiled Site to be Updatable, which determines if the deployed files can be updated. This option is selected by default.

The last file publish option, Exclude Files from the App_Data Folder, determines whether the files in the App_Data Folder are deployed to the server. In this case, I selected this option because the App_Data folder contains the files for the Halloween database, and I don't want to deploy those files.

If the application uses a database and the information for connecting to that database will change when the application is deployed, you can enter the new connection string in the combo box that's provided. Alternatively, you can click the ellipsis button and then create a connection string using the dialog box that's displayed. This works much like the Add Connection dialog box you saw in chapter 13. When you're done, make sure that the Use This Connection String at Runtime option is selected.

You can also deploy the database used by an application to the specified server. To do that, select the Update Database option. This deploys the database schema. To deploy the data, you'll need to write a SQL script and then add that script to the dialog box that's displayed when you click the Configure Database Updates link.

How to preview the files to be deployed

The Preview tab of the Publish Web dialog box lets you display a list of the files that will be deployed. To do that, you click the Start Preview button in this tab. Then, when the list is displayed, you can deselect the check box for any files you don't want to deploy.

How to publish the web site

At this point, you can click the Publish button to publish the web site and save the deployment options in the profile. Alternatively, you can click the Close button to save the profile without publishing the web site. Then, when you're ready to deploy it, you can select the profile from the Publish drop-down list in the Web One Click Publish toolbar and then click the Publish Web button.

The Settings tab of the Publish Web dialog box

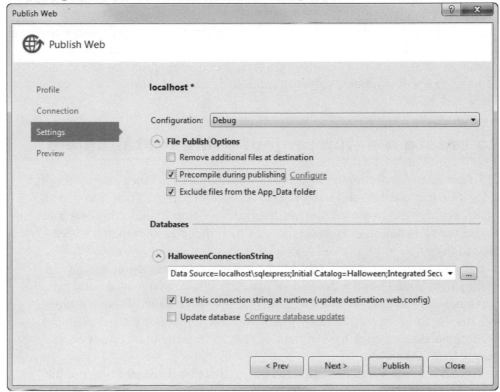

Description

- To remove files that were previously deployed and that are no longer included in the project, select the Remove Additional Files at Destination option.

- To compile an application before it's deployed, select the Precompile During Publishing option. You can also click the Configure link to set an option that determines if the deployed files are updateable.

- If you don't want to deploy files in the App_Data folder, such as databases used for testing, select the Exclude Files from the App_Data folder option.

- If the web.config file defines one or more connection strings, the names of these strings will be displayed in the Databases portion of the Settings tab. Then, if the application will use a different connection string when it's deployed, you can enter that string or click the button with the ellipsis on it to display a dialog box that you can use to create the string.

- If you enter or create a new connection string, be sure the Use This Connection String at Runtime option is selected so the connection string in the web.config file is updated.

- To create a database schema from a database that's used by the application, select the Update Database option. To add data to the database, create a custom SQL script, click the Configure Database Updates link, and add the script to the dialog box that's displayed.

Figure 21-5   How to set the file and database options for one-click deployment

How to create and use a Setup program

Another way to deploy a web application is to develop a *setup project* that creates a standard Windows Setup program that you can use to install the web application on an IIS server. To illustrate the use of a Setup program, the topics that follow use a free product called *InstallShield Limited Edition* that comes with Visual Studio.

How to create a setup project using InstallShield

To create an InstallShield project for a web application, you start by opening the solution that contains the web project you want to deploy. Then, you add an InstallShield project to the solution as described in figure 21-6. In this example, you can see an InstallShield project named Ch14ProductListSetup that's been added to the solution for the Ch14ProductList application.

Before I go on, you should realize that InstallShield isn't automatically installed with Visual Studio. Because of that, you'll have to download and install it separately. To do that, select the Enable InstallShield Limited Edition option that's displayed in the Add New Project dialog box in place of the InstallShield project template, and click the OK button. Then, follow the instructions on the web site that's displayed.

The easiest way to configure a setup project with InstallShield is to use the Project Assistant shown in this figure. This assistant consists of the seven pages summarized in the table. To display these pages, you can click the links at the bottom of the window, or you can click the right and left arrow buttons to move to the next and previous pages.

The Application Information page lets you specify general information like the company, application name, and application version. The Installation Requirements page lets you specify what operating systems the application can be installed on and any software that must be installed for the application to work correctly. If the application uses features of .NET Framework 4.5, for example, you can select it as a prerequisite. Note, however, that the only version of SQL Server that you can currently include as a prerequisite is SQL Server 2008 Express SP1. That's because SQL Server 2008 Express R2 and SQL Server 2012 Express can't be installed from a Setup program.

The Application Files pages lets you specify what files you want to deploy. You'll learn more about using this page in just a minute. The Application Shortcuts page lets you create shortcuts for the application, and the Application Registry page lets you specify entries to be added to the Windows Registry. You're not likely to use these pages for a web application, though.

Finally, the Installation Interview page lets you specify what dialog boxes are displayed when the application is installed. For example, you can display a dialog box with a license agreement, and you can display a dialog box that lets the user enter their name and company. You can also set an option that causes the application to be launched when the installation is complete.

The InstallShield Project Assistant

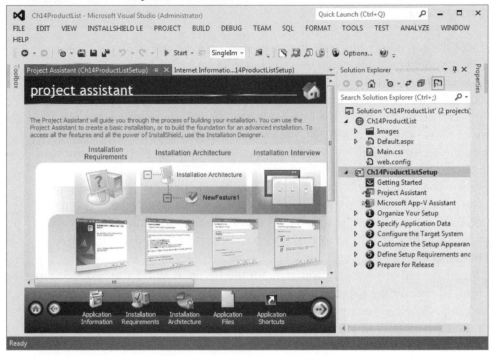

The seven pages of the Project Assistant

Page	Description
Application Information	Lets you specify general information about your application.
Installation Requirements	Lets you specify the required software and operating systems.
Installation Architecture	Not available in InstallShield LE.
Application Files	Lets you specify the application files you want to install.
Application Shortcuts	Lets you create shortcuts for the application.
Application Registry	Lets you specify entries that should be added to the Windows Registry.
Installation Interview	Lets you specify the dialog boxes that are displayed during installation.

Description

- To create a *setup project*, open the solution that contains the application you want to deploy, and choose the FILE→Add→New Project command to display the Add New Project dialog box. Then, expand the Other Project Types group, select Setup and Deployment, select the InstallShield Limited Edition Project template, enter a name for the project, and click OK.

- When you first create an *InstallShield* project, the Project Assistant is displayed. You can use the pages of this assistant to configure the project as described above. You can also use the nodes that are subordinate to the numbered nodes in the Solution Explorer to set configuration options that aren't available from the Project Assistant.

Figure 21-6   How to create a setup project using InstallShield

How to configure an InstallShield project for deployment to IIS

In addition to the configuration options that are available from the Project Assistant, you can use the nodes that are subordinate to the numbered nodes in the Solution Explorer to set additional options. To deploy a web application, for example, you have to use the Internet Information Services node. When I double-clicked on this node, the Internet Information Services tree shown in figure 21-7 was displayed with just the Web Sites folder subordinate to it. Then, I added nodes for the web site and IIS application where the web application will be deployed as described in this figure.

When you add the web site, a pane is displayed to the right of the tree that lets you set the properties for the site. At the least, you'll want to specify a name and ASP.NET version for the site. By default, if the web site you name already exists, the application will simply be added to that site. Otherwise, the web site will be created.

You also need to set some properties for the IIS application you add. To start, you need to specify the name you want to use for the application. You can also specify the ASP.NET version for the application, and you can specify the names of one or more default documents. You can see the settings for the Product list application in this figure. Notice here that the ASP.NET version is set to 4.0 instead of 4.5. That's because when you install .NET 4.5, its files effectively replace the files for .NET 4.0. In other words, .NET 4.0 is overwritten and the version number isn't updated.

The window for configuring an IIS application

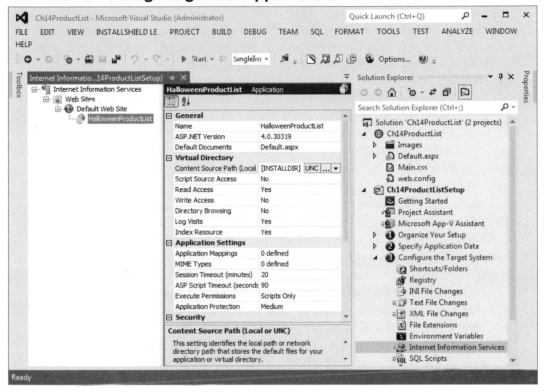

Description

- To deploy an ASP.NET application to IIS, you must define the web site and IIS application for the deployment. To do that, you double-click on the Internet Information Services node that's subordinate to the Configure the Target System node in the Solution Explorer to display the window shown above.

- To define the web site, right-click on the Web Sites node and select the Add Web Site command. Then, enter a name for the web site and select the ASP.NET version for the web site in the Properties pane that's displayed.

- To define the IIS application, right-click on the web site you created and select the New Application command. Then, enter a name and ASP.NET version for the application, and specify the names of one or more default documents.

- By default, the web site is created if it doesn't exist and the IIS application is created. If the web site already exists, the application is added to the existing web site.

Figure 21-7   How to configure an InstallShield project for deployment to IIS

How to add output files to an InstallShield project

Figure 21-8 shows the Application Files page of the Project Assistant. You can use this page to add any output files to the InstallShield project that you want the Setup program to deploy. For most web applications, you'll only add files to the Program Files folder.

In this example, the Program Files folder contains a subfolder with the company name that was entered on the Application Information page. Then, this folder contains another subfolder with the application name that was entered on the Application Information page. If you want to, you can change the name of either of these folders by right-clicking on it, selecting the Rename command from the shortcut menu that's displayed, and then entering the new name.

An InstallShield project must include at least the content files for the project. To add this content, select the folder where you want to add the files. Then, click the Add Project Outputs button, and use the Visual Studio Output Selector dialog box that's displayed to select the Content Files option. You can also add additional files and folders using the Add Files and Add Folders buttons.

By default, InstallShield includes files in the App_Data folder of the application that's being deployed, including local databases. If that's not what you want, you should delete these files before you add the application's content files to the setup project. In addition, you should modify the connection string for the database in the web.config file before you deploy the application so it will work with the production database.

The Application Files page of the Project Assistant

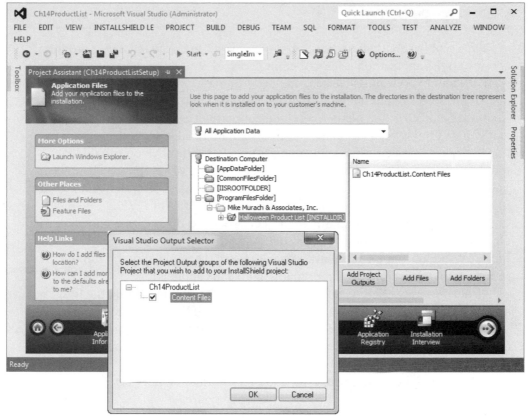

Description

- To add files to an InstallShield project, you use the Application Files page.

- To add project output, select the appropriate folder in the directory tree for the destination computer and click the Add Project Outputs button to display the Visual Studio Output Selector dialog box. Then, select the output you want to include (in most cases, just the content files), and click the OK button.

- To see what files will be added to the project for an option, right-click on the output item in the right pane of the Application Files page and select Resolve Project Output from the shortcut menu that's displayed.

- You can add additional files and folders using the Add Files and Add Folders buttons. You can also add a folder to an existing folder in the directory tree by right-clicking on the existing folder, selecting New Folder, and then entering a name for the folder.

Note

- If the project you're deploying includes a SQL Server Express LocalDB database, you'll want to delete that database and the App_Data folder from the project so they're not deployed with the other project files. You'll also want to change the connection string for the database in the web.config file.

Figure 21-8   How to add output files to an InstallShield project

How to create and use the installation files for a Setup program

Once you've configured the setup project, you can create the Setup program and install the application as described in figure 21-9. To start, you select the type of output you want to create from the Solution Configurations drop-down list. If you select SingleImage, a single file named setup.exe will be generated. Then, you can store that file in a central location such as on a network server, and you can run it from any computer to install it on that computer.

If you want to deploy an application from a CD or DVD, you can do that too. In that case, you need to select the CD_ROM or DVD-5 option. Then, when you build the project, the compiler will generate all of the files you need, including the setup.exe file, and you can burn those files to a CD or DVD.

Next, you build the InstallShield project. After you do that, you can click the Open Release Folder button in the InstallShield toolbar to display the generated files in Windows Explorer. Finally, you can install the application by running the setup.exe program from the server that will host the application.

When you run a Setup program to install the web application on the host server, it steps you through the installation process. In this figure, for example, you can see the screen for the Ready to Install step of a Setup program that was created using InstallShield. Here, the files for the web site will be copied to the destination folder that's shown. Then, the application will be deployed to IIS using the settings you specified in the Internet Information Services window.

The Ready to Install step of the InstallShield Wizard

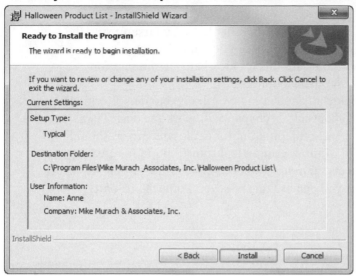

Description

- To create the installation files for a Setup program, right-click the setup project in the Solution Explorer and use the Build command. Then, to view the installation files in Windows Explorer, click on the Open Release Folder button in the InstallShield toolbar.

- The files that are generated depend on the option that's selected in the Solution Configurations drop-down list in the Standard toolbar. If you select SingleImage, a single file named setup.exe is created.

- If you want to install an application from a CD or DVD, you can select the CD_ROM or DVD-5 option from the Solution Configurations combo box. Then, several files including a setup.exe file arc generated, and you can burn those files to a CD or DVD.

- To install the application, run the setup.exe file on the server that will host the application. This displays a standard setup wizard.

- When you install the application, the content files are copied to the location you specified, an IIS web site is created, if necessary, and the IIS application is added to that web site.

Figure 21-9   How to create and use the installation files for a Setup program

Perspective

As you develop a web application, you'll probably find yourself using the Web Site Administration Tool to configure the application. Before you deploy an application, you may also need to use this tool to change configuration settings so they're appropriate for production.

When you're ready to deploy an application, you'll need to decide which of the techniques you learned about in this chapter will work the best. Then, if you decide that you want to use a Setup program for deployment, you should keep in mind that InstallShield Limited Edition is just one option for creating this type of program. You can also purchase other editions of InstallShield that provide more functionality, or you can use one of several other third-party products.

Terms

deployment	Setup program
XCopy deployment	publish profile
one-click deployment	setup project
one-click publish	InstallShield

Summary

- You can use the Web Site Administration Tool to configure a web application before you deploy it. That includes configuring users, roles, and access rules; creating custom application settings, configuring SMTP email support, and controlling debugging settings; and configuring membership and role providers.

- Visual Studio provides for three basic types of *deployment*: XCopy deployment, one-click deployment, and Setup program deployment.

- *XCopy deployment* lets you copy the files of a web application from one location, such as a local server, to another location, such as a production server.

- *One-click deployment* lets you create one or more publish profiles that specify deployment options. A *publish profile* specifies where the application will be deployed, what files will be deployed, whether the application will be precompiled, and what connection string will be used for any databases used by the application.

- *InstallShield* lets you create a setup project that compiles to a *Setup program*. Then, you can run the Setup program on a server to install the application.

- You can use the InstallShield Project Assistant to set the basic options for the sctup project. For a web application, you also need to specify the web site and IIS application where the files will be deployed.

Section 5

Going to the next level

This section consists of three chapters that present skills that will take you to the next level of professional web development. Chapter 22 shows you how to use ASP.NET Ajax in your applications. Chapter 23 shows you how to develop and use WCF and Web API services. And chapter 24 introduces you to ASP.NET MVC, which is an approach to web development that is dramatically different than using Web Forms. You can read these chapters in whatever sequence you prefer.

22

How to use ASP.NET Ajax

This chapter introduces you to the ASP.NET server controls that provide for building Ajax-enabled web pages. These controls let you develop web applications that are more responsive to users and that help reduce the load on the web server.

An introduction to Ajax

Over the years, web sites have changed from collections of static web pages to dynamic, data-driven web applications. As web applications started performing many of the same functions as traditional desktop applications, users wanted their web applications to behave like desktop applications, too. Today, a *rich Internet application* (*RIA*) is a web application that provides users with an enhanced user interface, advanced functionality, and quick response times like desktop applications.

To build a RIA, you use a framework like Java applets, Adobe Flash player, or Microsoft Silverlight. With most frameworks, though, the users must install plug-ins into their web browsers. The only framework that uses just the features that are built into all modern web browsers is *Asynchronous JavaScript and XML* (*Ajax*).

Examples of Ajax applications

Google's Auto Suggest feature, shown in figure 22-1, is a typical Ajax application. As you type the start of a search entry, Google uses Ajax to get the terms and links of items that match the characters that you have typed so far. Ajax does this without refreshing the page so the user doesn't experience any delays. This is sometimes called a "partial page refresh."

Because this Ajax technology is so powerful, it is used by many web sites and applications. When you post a comment to a friend's Facebook page, for example, the comment just appears. And when you move the cursor over a movie on NetFlix, information about the movie appears in a popup. In both cases, Ajax is used to get the required data from a data store and update the page without reloading it.

Google's Auto Suggest feature

Netflix's popup feature

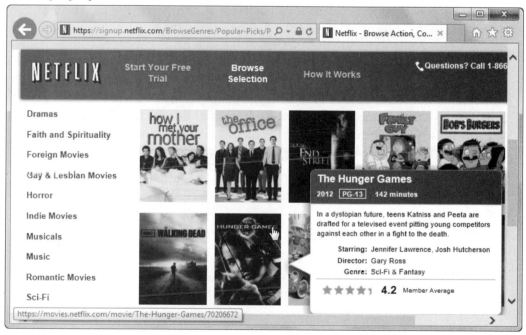

Description

- A *rich Internet application* (*RIA*) is an application that is displayed in a web browser, but has some of the features of a desktop application such as an enhanced user interface and quick response time.

- One way to build an RIA is to use *Asynchronous JavaScript and XML* (*Ajax*). Unlike normal HTTP requests, Ajax lets you receive data from a web server without reloading the page. This is sometimes known as a "partial page refresh."

Figure 22-1   Examples of Ajax applications

How Ajax works

When a web browser sends a normal HTTP request to a web server, the server returns an HTTP response that contains the content to be displayed for the page. Whether the page is static or dynamic, once the page is returned, the connection to the server is closed. Even if state is maintained with application variables, session variables, or cookies, a full HTTP request and response cycle must take place to update the web page. This is illustrated by the first diagram in figure 22-2.

In contrast, if portions of a web page are Ajax-enabled, Ajax can update the web page after it's loaded without having to perform a full HTTP request and response cycle. This is illustrated by the second diagram in this figure. Here, the browser initiates a request that sends just the data that's needed by the server to respond to the request. That can include information about what event triggered the request, as well as the contents of the relevant controls on the page. Then, when the server sends its response back to the browser, the browser can use the data in the response to update the contents of the web page without having to reload the entire page.

To make this work, all modern browsers provide an *XMLHttpRequest object* (or *XHR object*) that is used to send an asynchronous request to the web server and to receive the returned data from the server. In addition, JavaScript is used in the browser to issue the request, parse the returned data, and modify the page to reflect the returned data. In many cases, a request will include data that tells the server what data to return.

How a normal HTTP request is processed

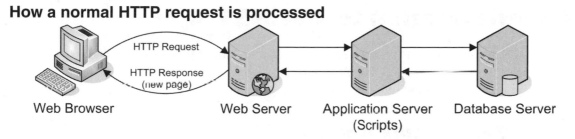

How an Ajax XMLHttpRequest is processed

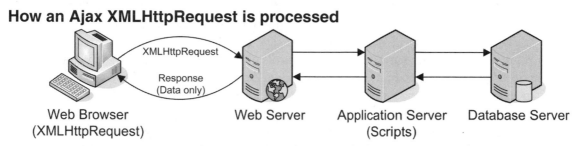

How Ajax updates the contents of a web page

1. An event happens on the web page, like moving the mouse, clicking a button, changing a field, or a timer going off. This event triggers the JavaScript code for the event.

2. JavaScript prepares a request and uses the XHR object to send it to the web server. This request contains information about the event and the current state of the controls on the web page.

3. The server receives the data, processes it, and sends a response back to the browser. The response contains the updated state of the controls on the web page.

4. JavaScript parses the response and uses the data it contains to update the contents of the web page. The browser then updates the user's screen.

Description

- Each time a standard HTTP request and response is performed, the entire page is returned from the server and the page is loaded into the browser. This type of request and response is required the first time a page is requested even if the page is Ajax-enabled.

- With an Ajax request, the browser can request just the information it needs to update the page. Then, the information that's returned from the server can be used to update the page without having to reload it.

- JavaScript is essential to the use of Ajax because JavaScript not only sends the requests but also processes the responses and updates the page with the new data.

- To send an Ajax request, JavaScript uses a browser object known as an *XMLHttpRequest object* (or just *XHR object*). This object can include data that tells the application server what data is being requested.

- An XHR object is often processed by server code that's written in PHP or C#. Then, the JavaScript has to be coordinated with the server code.

Figure 22-2   How Ajax works

An introduction to ASP.NET Ajax

Starting with ASP.NET 3.5 and Visual Studio 2008, Microsoft provided integrated support for building Ajax-enabled web applications using ASP.NET. The topics that follow introduce you to the components of *ASP.NET Ajax*.

How ASP.NET Ajax works

As you have seen, a standard HTTP request and response cycle that's triggered by an event in an ASP.NET web page is called a *postback*. When a postback occurs, the view state of the controls on the page is sent to the server as part of the request. Then, the server processes the request, updates the view state as necessary, and sends a response back to the browser that contains a new page with the new view state.

In contrast, ASP.NET Ajax enables a process known as an *asynchronous postback*. This is similar to a standard postback in that the view state of controls on the page is sent to the server in response to an event on the page. In an asynchronous postback, however, the XHR object is used to send the view state to the server. Then, the response that's returned by the server is used to update the controls on the page without having to reload the entire web page in the browser.

Figure 22-3 shows the three components of ASP.NET Ajax and illustrates how they work. The *ASP.NET Ajax client-side framework* is a JavaScript library that is loaded by the web browser when an Ajax-enabled ASP.NET page is displayed. It allows JavaScript code to interact with the ASP.NET application server through the XHR object it encapsulates.

ASP.NET Ajax also provides five server controls. They are used to Ajax-enable an ASP.NET web page so that other ASP.NET server controls can be updated in the web browser without having to reload the page. These controls render JavaScript code as part of the web page just as other controls render HTML and CSS. The code they render uses the ASP.NET Ajax client-side framework to process events in the web page, manage and update controls in the web page, and trigger an asynchronous postback to interact with the server.

The ASP.NET Ajax client-side framework and the ASP.NET Ajax server controls are built into ASP.NET and Visual Studio. In contrast, the *ASP.NET Ajax Control Toolkit* is not. Instead, it's available as a separate download for Visual Studio. This toolkit consists of components and server control extensions that provide a variety of effects, animations, and interactive features.

The architecture of ASP.NET Ajax

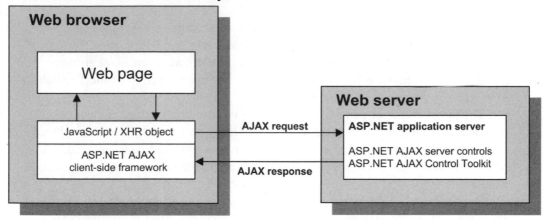

Components of ASP.NET Ajax

Component	Description
ASP.NET Ajax client-side framework	A JavaScript library that's loaded on the client to support the ASP.NET Ajax server controls.
ASP.NET Ajax server controls	Five server controls that encapsulate other ASP.NET controls on the web page to indicate that they will be controlled on the client by the ASP.NET Ajax client-side framework.
ASP.NET Ajax Control Toolkit	An open source project that provides more than 40 ASP.NET controls that you can use to build Ajax-enabled web applications.

Description

- An *asynchronous postback* is the process used by ASP.NET to perform a partial-page update. During an asynchronous postback, the view state of the web page is sent to the server, which processes the request and sends back the new view state of the controls being updated.

- The ASP.NET Ajax server controls enclose other ASP.NET server controls to make them Ajax-enabled. These controls can then be updated using an asynchronous postback.

- A single page can have one or more groups of Ajax-enabled controls that can be updated independently or simultaneously. Server controls that are not Ajax-enabled still trigger a full postback that causes the entire page to be reloaded.

- The *ASP.NET Ajax Control Toolkit* adds animation and effects to standard server controls. It is a joint effort between Microsoft and the ASP.NET Ajax community.

Figure 22-3   How ASP.NET Ajax works

The ASP.NET Ajax server controls

Figure 22-4 describes the five ASP.NET Ajax server controls that you can use to enable and manage asynchronous postbacks on a web page. These controls allow the other controls on the page to participate in an asynchronous postback. You'll find these controls in the Ajax Extensions group of the Toolbox in Visual Studio.

The ScriptManager control is the primary control that enables asynchronous postbacks, and it must be on a page for ASP.NET Ajax to work. It is often placed on a master page so all the pages that use the master page are Ajax-enabled. The other Ajax controls can then be placed on either the master page or content pages.

In addition to enabling asynchronous postbacks, the ScriptManager control provides for loading and managing additional JavaScript files. It also provides for registering *web services* so they can be accessed by JavaScript code on the client. Web services provide a way for one web site to communicate with another web site. You'll learn more about web services in the next chapter.

Note that you can have only one ScriptManager control on a page. If, for example, you add a ScriptManager control to a master page, you can't also add one to a content page that uses the master page. However, you can add a ScriptManagerProxy control to the content page. This control lets you load additional JavaScript files or register additional services needed by the content page but not by all the pages that use the master page.

In this context, a *proxy* is an object that's created on the client that you can use to access a service that's running on the server. When you use the ScriptManagerProxy control, it automatically creates the proxy for you.

After you add a ScriptManager control to a page, you can use the UpdatePanel control to enclose standard ASP.NET server controls. Then, the controls inside the UpdatePanel control are updated by Ajax when an asynchronous postback occurs. Note that you can have multiple UpdatePanel controls on a page. You can also have controls outside the UpdatePanel controls. If an event occurs on one of those controls, a full postback occurs on the web page, unless it has been designated as a trigger for an update panel.

Although an asynchronous postback is faster than a full postback, there may be times when an asynchronous postback takes more than a few seconds to perform. In that case, you may want to provide a visual indication that the postback is in progress. To do that, you can use the UpdateProgress control.

If you want to trigger an asynchronous postback at a set time interval, you can use the Timer control. This can be useful if you want to poll the server for any updates that need to be displayed. Keep in mind, however, that if an asynchronous postback is triggered too often, the load on the server can increase dramatically.

ASP.NET Ajax server controls

Control	Description
ScriptManager	Enables the use of the other ASP.NET Ajax controls, loads the ASP.NET Ajax client-side framework, and manages client-side JavaScript code.
ScriptManagerProxy	Extends the scripting services provided by a ScriptManager control.
UpdatePanel	Identifies a set of server controls to be updated using an asynchronous postback.
UpdateProgress	Provides visual feedback that an asynchronous postback is in progress.
Timer	Periodically triggers an asynchronous postback on an UpdatePanel control.

The ScriptManager control

- You can only have one ScriptManager control on a page. This includes master and content pages. If you put a ScriptManager control on a master page, you can't use one on a content page. If there is more than one ScriptManager control on a page, an Invalid Operation exception is generated.

- The ScriptManager control can also be used to load and manage additional JavaScript files and to register *web services* so they can be accessed by JavaScript code on the client. See figure 22-6 for details.

The ScriptManagerProxy control

- The ScriptManagerProxy control lets you load JavaScript files and register web services. It can be used in a content page if the master page contains a ScriptManager control.

The UpdatePanel control

- The UpdatePanel control is a container control that holds other server controls that will be updated during an asynchronous postback. All controls inside an UpdatePanel control will be updated at the same time. A page can contain multiple UpdatePanel controls, each with a different set of controls.

The UpdateProgress control

- The UpdateProgress control provides a visual indication that an asynchronous postback is in progress. Then, the user will know to wait until the postback completes before doing anything else on the page.

The Timer control

- When one or more UpdatePanel controls need to be updated automatically, you can use the Timer control to trigger partial-page updates at a set time interval.

Figure 22-4   The ASP.NET Ajax server controls

The ASP.NET Ajax Control Toolkit

The ASP.NET Ajax Control Toolkit provides more dynamic, visually appealing user interface controls. It is not a required component of ASP.NET Ajax and it is not built into Visual Studio. Instead, it's an open source project hosted at Microsoft's Codeplex web site that you can download and use for free. The easiest way to add the Ajax Control Toolkit to your web site is by using the NuGet Package Manager, as shown in figure 22-5.

The figure also lists some of the most common controls in the toolkit. Many of these controls extend the functions of existing ASP.NET controls. For example, the Calendar control extends the function of a TextBox control.

The toolkit currently contains over forty control extensions, and more are being added with every release. To view descriptions of these controls along with live examples, you can go to the web site listed in this figure.

The toolkit is not an official part of ASP.NET. It is an open source project developed as a joint effort between Microsoft and the community at Microsoft's Codeplex web site and is continually being updated. You should check the toolkit site often for new features, bug fixes, and security vulnerabilities.

The Manage NuGet Packages dialog box

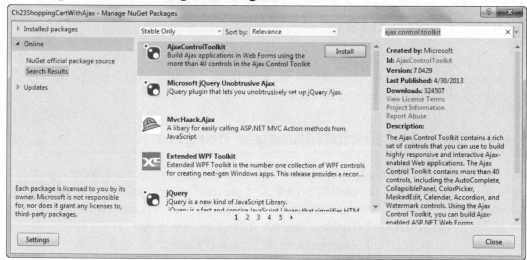

Common ASP.NET Ajax Control Toolkit controls

Control	Description
Accordion	Contains multiple panes of content, but only displays one at a time.
Animation	Adds methods to change the position, size, opacity, and color of a control. They can be combined to create many dynamic effects.
Calendar	Shows a calendar in a pop-up window for easy date entry.
CollapsiblePanel	Provides a one-click, hide/show effect for a control.
DragPanel	Lets the user move a panel of content around on the page.
HoverMenu	Displays a menu when the user hovers over a control.
ModalPopup	A pop-up control that hides the page until the user selects an option.
NumericUpDown	Adds up and down arrows to a text box for changing the value.
PopupControl	Hides a set of controls until they are displayed in a pop-up window.
RoundedCorners	Adds rounded corners to a control.
Slider	Lets the user enter a value by dragging a slider.
SlideShow	Shows multiple images in one image tag. The images can change automatically or the user can manually scroll back and forth.
Tabs	Shows multiple panes of content in a tabbed format.

How to get the NuGet package for the Ajax Control Toolkit

- Use the WEBSITE→Manage NuGet Packages command to open the Manage NuGet Packages dialog box. Type "Ajax control toolkit" in the search box in the upper right corner. When the package is displayed, click the Install button.

A web site that has live examples of the toolkit controls

http://www.asp.net/ajaxlibrary/AjaxControlToolkitSampleSite/

Figure 22-5   The ASP.NET Ajax Control Toolkit

How to use the ASP.NET Ajax server controls

The ASP.NET Ajax server controls can be added to almost any page to manage asynchronous postbacks. In the topics that follow, you'll learn the details of using each of the five controls.

How to use the ScriptManager control

As you have learned, you must add a ScriptManager control to a web page to enable asynchronous postbacks. Figure 22-6 presents some common attributes of this control along with some code examples. Note that this code must be added inside a Form element before any other ASP.NET Ajax controls.

By default, all the JavaScript code for a page is loaded before the user interface is displayed. This ensures that the user interface is fully functional when it's displayed. In some cases, though, loading the scripts first makes the user interface take too long to display. Then, you should consider setting the LoadScriptsBeforeUI attribute to False so the user interface is displayed before the JavaScript is loaded. If you do that, keep in mind that the user interface may not be fully functional when it's first displayed.

The AsyncPostBackTimeout attribute determines how long the ASP.NET Ajax client-side framework waits for a response after triggering an asynchronous postback. If a response isn't received within the specified time period, an exception is raised and the postback is cancelled. If the value of this attribute is set to a time interval that's too short, users will see a larger number of errors. If it's set to a time interval that's too long, users will wait too long to find out that there's a problem with the request.

The IsInAsyncPostBack attribute is a read-only Boolean value that is set to True while an asynchronous postback is in progress. This attribute can be examined by either client-side or server-side code. In most cases, you'll use it in the Load event handler for a web page. Because this event handler is executed for full postbacks as well as asynchronous postbacks, you can use the IsInAsyncPostBack attribute to execute code depending on which type of postback is being performed. For example, code that initializes a control would not run during an asynchronous postback.

In addition to setting attributes of the ScriptManager control, you can add Scripts and Services child elements. You use the Scripts element to load additional JavaScript code. Within this element, you code ScriptReference elements that identify the files that contain the code.

You use the Services element to create service proxies that allow the use of web services in client-side JavaScript code. Within this element, you code ServiceReference elements that specify the location of the svc file for each WCF service or the asmx file for each ASMX web service.

Common attributes of the ScriptManager control

Attribute	Description
`AsyncPostBackTimeout`	Sets the time in seconds before an asynchronous postback times out if there is no response. The default is 90.
`EnablePageMethods`	Determines if static methods on an ASP.NET page that are marked as web methods can be called from client scripts as if they're part of a service. The default is False.
`EnableScriptLocalization`	Determines if the server looks for localized versions of script files and uses them if they exist. The default is True.
`IsInAsyncPostBack`	A read-only Boolean value that is True if the page is currently processing an asynchronous postback.
`LoadScriptsBeforeUI`	Determines if scripts are loaded before or after user interface elements. If False, the user interface may load more quickly but not be functional at first. The default is True.

The aspx code for a ScriptManager control

```
<asp:ScriptManager ID="ScriptManager1" runat="server">
</asp:ScriptManager>
```

The aspx code for a ScriptManager control that registers scripts

```
<asp:ScriptManager ID="ScriptManager1" runat="server">
    <Scripts>
        <asp:ScriptReference Path="~/Scripts/SampleScript.js" />
        <asp:ScriptReference Assembly="SampleAssembly"
            Name="SampleAssembly.SampleScript.js" />
    </Scripts>
</asp:ScriptManager>
```

The aspx code for a ScriptManager control that registers two web services

```
<asp:ScriptManager ID="ScriptManager1" runat="server">
  <Services>
    <asp:ServiceReference
        Path="http://www.example.com/Services/SampleService.svc" />
        Path="~/Services/SampleService.asmx" />
  </Services>
</asp:ScriptManager>
```

Description

- The Scripts element of a ScriptManager control can contain ScriptReference elements that cause the ScriptManager control to load and manage additional scripts. The ScriptReference elements can load JavaScript code from a file using the Path attribute or from an assembly using the Assembly and Name attributes.

- The Services element of a ScriptManager control can contain ServiceReference elements that cause the ScriptManager to create service proxies. To create a WCF service proxy, code a Path attribute that points to the svc file for the service. To create an ASMX web service proxy, code a Path attribute that points to the asmx file for the web service.

Figure 22-6   How to use the ScriptManager control

How to use the ScriptManagerProxy control

The ScriptManagerProxy control is used to extend the capabilities of a ScriptManager control. The most common scenario for using a ScriptManagerProxy control is when you use a ScriptManager control on a master page and you want to add either JavaScript code or a service proxy to a content page that uses that master page. This is illustrated in figure 22-7. Here, you can see a content page that uses a master page that contains a ScriptManager control.

Unlike the ScriptManager control, you can have more than one ScriptManagerProxy control on a page. However, these controls can't be used to modify the properties of the ScriptManager control. They can only add additional ScriptReference and ServiceReference elements to a page. As you can see in the second and third examples in this figure, you code these elements just like you do for a ScriptManager control.

A content page with a ScriptManagerProxy control

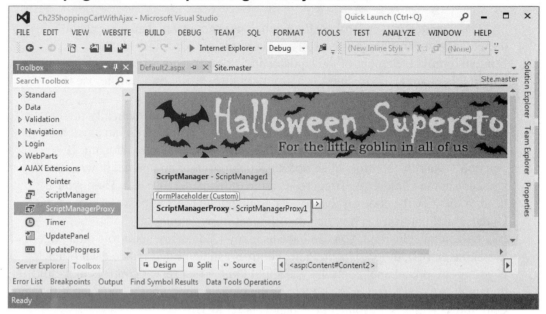

The aspx code for the ScriptManagerProxy control

```
<asp:ScriptManagerProxy ID="ScriptManagerProxy1" runat="server">
</asp:ScriptManagerProxy>
```

The aspx code for a ScriptManagerProxy control that registers scripts

```
<asp:ScriptManagerProxy ID="ScriptManager1" runat="server">
    <Scripts>
        <asp:ScriptReference Path="~/Scripts/SampleScript.js" />
        <asp:ScriptReference Assembly="SampleAssembly"
            Name="SampleAssembly.SampleScript.js" />
    </Scripts>
</asp:ScriptManagerProxy>
```

The aspx code for a ScriptManagerProxy control that registers a service

```
<asp:ScriptManagerProxy ID="ScriptManager1" runat="server">
    <Services>
        <asp:ServiceReference
            Path="http://www.example.com/Services/SampleService.svc" />
    </Services>
</asp:ScriptManagerProxy>
```

Description

- The ScriptManagerProxy control lets you extend the scripting services that are provided by a ScriptManager control. It's used most often on a content page whose master page contains a ScriptManager control.

- You can have multiple ScriptManagerProxy controls on a page. However, the ScriptManagerProxy controls can't override the properties of the ScriptManager control.

Figure 22-7   How to use the ScriptManagerProxy control

How to use the UpdatePanel control

The UpdatePanel control encloses other server controls that are updated during an asynchronous postback. These controls are placed inside the ContentTemplate element of the UpdatePanel control. Then, the controls within this element are updated as a group. Figure 22-8 shows how to use the UpdatePanel control.

When controls are added to an update panel, they are automatically made triggers for the panel. That means that if any of the controls cause an asynchronous postback, the panel is updated. In most cases, that's what you want. If you don't want the controls in an update panel to trigger an update, however, you can set the ChildrenAsTriggers attribute of the panel to False. Then, you'll need to identify the controls that trigger an update in the Triggers element of the UpdatePanel control. I'll describe this element in just a minute.

As you have learned, you can have as many UpdatePanel controls on a page as you need. In addition, UpdatePanel controls can be nested inside each other. If you nest UpdatePanel controls, you should know that server controls in a child update panel won't trigger the update of the parent panel. That's true even if the ChildrenAsTriggers attribute of the panels is set to True.

By default, a panel is updated any time an asynchronous postback occurs on the page. This behavior is controlled by the UpdateMode attribute of the UpdatePanel control, which is set to Always by default. If you want a panel to be updated only when an asynchronous postback is caused by one of the panel's triggers, you can set the UpdateMode attribute to Conditional. Note that if an UpdatePanel control is nested inside another UpdatePanel control, it is always updated when its parent UpdatePanel control is updated. Also note that if you set the ChildrenAsTriggers attribute to False, you must set the UpdateMode attribute to Conditional or an exception will occur.

You can specify the controls that cause a panel to be updated in the Triggers element of the control, as illustrated in the second example in this figure. Here, the Triggers element includes two asp elements. The AsyncPostBackTrigger element identifies a control that causes an asynchronous postback to occur. In this case, the control is defined outside the update panel. However, you can also use this element for a control that's defined within an update panel. If necessary, you can use the EventName attribute to name the event that causes the postback. If this attribute is omitted, the postback occurs for the default event of the control.

The second element, PostBackTrigger, names a control inside the update panel that causes a full postback to occur rather than an asynchronous postback. In other words, instead of causing just the panel to be updated, it causes the entire page to be reloaded.

This figure also lists some compatibility issues you may encounter when you use certain controls within an UpdatePanel control. You'll want to review this list before you use the UpdatePanel control so you're aware of any potential problems when you use these controls.

Two attributes of the UpdatePanel control

Attribute	Description
`ChildrenAsTriggers`	Determines if the controls in a panel trigger the content of the panel to be updated when a control causes a postback. The default is True.
`UpdateMode`	Determines when the content of a panel is updated. If set to Always, the panel is updated whenever a postback occurs. If set to Conditional, the panel is updated only when one if its own triggers causes a postback. A nested UpdatePanel control is always updated when its parent UpdatePanel control is updated. The default is Always.

The starting aspx code for an UpdatePanel control

```
<asp:UpdatePanel ID="UpdatePanel1" runat="server">
    <ContentTemplate>
    </ContentTemplate>
</asp:UpdatePanel>
```

The aspx code for an UpdatePanel control that specifies triggers

```
<asp:UpdatePanel ID="UpdatePanel1" runat="server">
    <ContentTemplate>
        <asp:Button ID="Button2" runat="server" Text="Add" />
    </ContentTemplate>
    <Triggers>
        <asp:AsyncPostBackTrigger ControlID="Button1" EventName="Click" />
        <asp:PostBackTrigger ControlID="Button2" />
    </Triggers>
</asp:UpdatePanel>
```

Compatibility issues with other controls

- The GridView and DetailsView controls can't be used in an update panel if you set their EnableSortingAndPagingCallbacks attributes to True.

- The TreeView control can't be used in an update panel if you enable callbacks that are not part of an asynchronous postback, set its styles directly as control attributes, or set the EnableClientScript attribute to False.

- The Menu control can't be used if you set its styles directly as control attributes.

- A FileUpload control can only be used as a postback trigger for an update panel.

- The Login, PasswordRecovery, ChangePassword, and CreateUserWizard controls can only be used if you convert their contents to editable templates.

Description

- The ContentTemplate element of an UpdatePanel control contains the controls that are updated during an asynchronous postback. UpdatePanel controls can be nested.

- You can use the Triggers element to specify controls that cause the panel to be updated. The AsyncPostBackTrigger element identifies a control inside or outside of the UpdatePanel control that triggers an asynchronous postback. The PostBackTrigger element identifies a control inside the UpdatePanel control that triggers a full postback.

Figure 22-8   How to use the UpdatePanel control

How to use the Timer control

The Timer control triggers a periodic asynchronous postback. This control is typically placed inside the ContentTemplate element of the UpdatePanel control that's updated when the postback occurs. If it isn't placed inside an UpdatePanel control, it triggers a full postback of the entire page.

Figure 22-9 illustrates how the Timer control works. To start, you can determine how often an asynchronous postback occurs by setting the Interval attribute of the control. This attribute is measured in milliseconds. In the example in this figure, the Interval attribute is set to 10,000, or 10 seconds.

When you set the Interval attribute, you should be careful not to specify a value that's too small. If you do, it can cause a severe load on the server, particularly when many people have the page displayed. A value of 5,000 to 10,000 milliseconds is probably the smallest value you would want to use under most circumstances.

Also, you shouldn't expect the timer to be too accurate. That's because it's controlled by the timing mechanisms available to JavaScript in the web browser, and these mechanisms can be off by several hundred milliseconds.

If you need to, you can have two or more Timer controls on the same page. In most cases, you'll place these controls in different update panels. Then, you'll typically set the UpdateMode attribute of the UpdatePanel controls to Conditional so the Timer in one panel won't trigger the update of another panel.

Although you can use two or more Timer controls in the same update panel, there's usually no need to do that. Instead, if you need an update panel to refresh at different rates depending on what's happening in the web page, you can use a single Timer control and change its Interval attribute. If you want to use two or more Timer controls with preset intervals, however, you can use the Enabled attribute of the controls to determine which control is used at any given time.

A Timer control in Design view

Two attributes of the Timer control

Attribute	Description
`Interval`	Determines how often in milliseconds the control triggers an asynchronous postback. The default value is 60,000 milliseconds (60 seconds).
`Enabled`	Determines whether a postback occurs when the time specified by the Interval attribute elapses. The default is True. You might set this attribute to False if you include more than one Timer control in the same panel, but you want only one to initiate a postback at any given time.

The aspx code for an UpdatePanel control with a Timer control

```
<asp:UpdatePanel ID="UpdatePanel1" runat="server">
    <ContentTemplate>
        <asp:Timer ID="Timer1" runat="server" Interval="10000">
        </asp:Timer>
    </ContentTemplate>
</asp:UpdatePanel>
```

Description

- The Timer control should be placed inside the ContentTemplate element of the UpdatePanel control that is updated when the timer triggers an asynchronous postback.

- Setting the value of the Interval attribute too small can cause an increase in the load on the web server and an increase in the amount of traffic to the web server.

- The accuracy of the Timer control is determined by the accuracy of the JavaScript implementation in the user's web browser.

Figure 22-9   How to use the Timer control

How to use the UpdateProgress control

The UpdateProgress control displays information to the user when an asynchronous postback is in progress. You code this information within the ProgressTemplate element of the control as shown in figure 22-10. Here, the information consists of text, but you can include images or controls as well. Note that this text is displayed only when an asynchronous postback is taking place. Otherwise, it's hidden.

The DynamicLayout attribute of the UpdateProgress control determines how space is allocated for the content of the control. By default, space is allocated only when the content is being displayed. That means that any elements on the page that appear after the UpdateProgress control are shifted down when the content is being displayed and shifted back up when the content is hidden again. If that's not what you want, you can allocate space for the content even when it isn't being displayed by setting the DynamicLayout attribute to False. It's up to the developer to determine which layout works best for the page.

In some cases, an asynchronous postback happens so quickly that the content of the UpdateProgress control flickers on the screen. To prevent that from happening, you can set the DisplayAfter attribute to determine how long the control should wait after the asynchronous postback starts to display its content. By default, this attribute is set to 0.5 seconds. Then, if the postback takes longer than that to complete, the content of the UpdateProgress control is displayed on the page.

In most cases, you'll code the UpdateProgress control within an UpdatePanel control as shown in this figure. Then, its content is displayed only when an asynchronous postback occurs on that panel. However, you can also code an UpdateProgress control outside an UpdatePanel control. Then, you can set its AssociatedUpdatePanelID attribute to the ID of the panel you want to use it with. Or, you can omit this attribute, in which case its content is displayed anytime an asynchronous postback occurs.

An UpdateProgress control in Design view

Three attributes of the UpdateProgress control

Attribute	Description
DynamicLayout	Determines whether space for the content of the control is dynamically allocated on the page when the content is displayed. The default is True. If set to False, space is allocated for the content even when it is hidden.
DisplayAfter	Determines how long in milliseconds after the asynchronous postback has started to display the content. The default is 500 milliseconds (0.5 seconds). This value can prevent the content from flickering when the postback happens quickly.
AssociatedUpdatePanelID	The ID of the UpdatePanel control that the control is associated with.

The aspx code for an UpdatePanel control with an UpdateProgress control

```
<asp:UpdatePanel ID="UpdatePanel1" runat="server">
    <ContentTemplate>
        <asp:UpdateProgress ID="UpdateProgress1" runat="server">
            <ProgressTemplate>Updating...Please wait.</ProgressTemplate>
        </asp:UpdateProgress>
    </ContentTemplate>
</asp:UpdatePanel>
```

Description

- An UpdateProgress control must contain a ProgressTemplate element that defines the content of the control. This content is displayed only while an asynchronous postback is in progress. It is hidden after the asynchronous postback is complete.

Figure 22-10   How to use the UpdateProgress control

An application that uses ASP.NET Ajax

To illustrate how an application that uses Ajax works, the topics that follow present a page in the Shopping Cart application that displays information about the Halloween Store products and keeps track of how many times each product has been viewed.

The View Products page

Figure 22-11 presents the View Products page of the Shopping Cart application. To start, this page displays the products in a selected category in a GridView control. This part of the web page works like the Product List application you saw in chapter 13, but it's Ajax-enabled. This means that when the user selects a category in the drop-down list, the products for that category will be displayed in the GridView control without reloading the whole page.

Below the GridView control is a DetailsView control that displays product details when a user clicks the View link for a product. To the right of both of these controls is another GridView control that displays how many times each product has been viewed, and below this GridView control is an update progress control.

These controls are placed inside two UpdatePanel controls. The first one includes the GridView control for the products and the DetailsView control for the selected product. The second panel includes the GridView control for the most viewed products and the update progress control. This update progress control contains an animated "spinner" image and a "Loading…" message.

Although the drop-down list and the Clear Selection button aren't inside an update panel, the drop-down list is set as a trigger for the first panel. This means that the drop-down list causes an asynchronous postback. In contrast, the button causes a regular postback.

As you will see, the data for the most viewed products is stored in application state. If you wanted to have a permanent record of this data, you would need to save it in a persistent data store such as a database.

The View Products page

Description

- The View Products page is a variation of the Product List application you saw in chapter 13. It lets users view more details of a product, and also keeps track of how many times each product has been viewed. The product view information is stored in an application state variable.

- This page uses two UpdatePanel controls. The first one contains the GridView control that displays the products and the DetailsView control that displays the selected product.

- The second UpdatePanel control contains the GridView control that displays the number of product views and an UpdateProgress control that displays an animated spinner image and a message while a selected product is being retrieved.

- The drop-down list and the Clear Selection button aren't coded inside an UpdatePanel control. However, the drop-down list is set as a trigger for the first panel, which causes an asynchronous postback. In contrast, the Clear Selection button causes a regular postback.

- The second update panel is triggered by a change in the index of the GridView control that's in the first panel.

Figure 22-11   The View Products page

The ProductView class

Figure 22-12 presents the two classes that are used by this application. The ProductView class represents the data for one line in the GridView control for the most viewed products. This class consists of just four properties: ProductID, ProductName, CategoryID, and ViewCount.

The ProductViewList class

The ProductViewList class represents a list of the ProductView objects. This class starts by declaring a private field named list that stores the list. Then, it includes two methods that are used to work with the list.

The public Add method uses the ProductID property of the ProductView object that's passed to it to see if that object is already in the list. It does this by attempting to retrieve an object with the same ProductID from the list. If the object it attempts to retrieve is null, the ProductView object isn't in the list yet, so the method adds it to the list. If the object isn't null, the method increments its ViewCount property by 1.

Note, however, that this method starts by executing the Sleep method of the current thread. This method is included just for testing purposes. It delays the Add method by two seconds to make sure that the update progress control is displayed. Otherwise, the page update may go so fast that the progress control is never displayed. You would of course remove this method after testing.

The other public method, the Display method, sorts the items in the list by the ViewCount property in descending order so the most viewed items will appear at the top of the grid when the list is displayed. Then, it sorts the items by the ProductName property so products with the same number of views will be displayed in alphabetical order.

The ProductView.cs file

```csharp
public class ProductView
{
    public string ProductID { get; set; }
    public string ProductName { get; set; }
    public string CategoryID { get; set; }
    public int ViewCount { get; set; }
}
```

The ProductViewList.cs file

```csharp
using System;
using System.Collections.Generic;
using System.Linq;
using System.Web;

public class ProductViewList
{
    private List<ProductView> list = new List<ProductView>();

    public void Add(ProductView newView) {
        System.Threading.Thread.Sleep(2000);
        string id = newView.ProductID;
        ProductView view = list.FirstOrDefault(v => v.ProductID == id);
        if (view == null) {
            list.Add(newView);
        }
        else {
            view.ViewCount += 1;
        }
    }

    public List<ProductView> Display() {
        return list.OrderByDescending(p => p.ViewCount).ThenBy(
                                      p => p.ProductName).ToList();
    }
}
```

Description

- The ProductView class is a data transfer object that holds information about the product and the number of times the product has been viewed.

- The ProductViewList class contains a private collection of ProductView objects, and exposes two methods.

- The Add method uses a LINQ query to check if the ProductView object that's passed to it is already in the collection. If it isn't, the object is added. If it is, the object's ViewCount property is incremented by one. This method also calls the Sleep method of the current Thread object to simulate a processing delay of two seconds.

- The Display method uses a LINQ query to return the collection of ProductView objects, sorted by the number of views in descending order and then by product name.

Figure 22-12   The ProductView and ProductViewList classes

The aspx file and the first UpdatePanel control

Figure 22-13 presents the form element in the aspx file for this application. This element starts with a ScriptManager control. It is followed by the drop-down list for product categories and the Clear Selection button. Neither of these controls is inside an update panel, and both call the Reset method when their default event occurs. The Reset method, as you'll see in the code-behind file, clears the selection from the GridView control for products. You'll come back to these controls in just a moment.

The drop-down list and button are followed by an update panel that contains the GridView control that displays the products and the DetailsView control that displays the data for the selected product. This update panel has a Trigger element that identifies the SelectedIndexChanged event of the categories drop-down list as the trigger for an asynchronous postback. This means that when the user selects an item in the drop-down list, an asynchronous postback of the update panel is started, even though the drop-down list isn't inside the update panel. In contrast, when the Clear Selection button is clicked, a regular postback occurs.

The form element in the Default.aspx file   **Page 1**

```
<form id="form1" runat="server">
  <asp:ScriptManager ID="ScriptManager1" runat="server">
  </asp:ScriptManager>
  <h1>View Our Products By Category</h1>
  <div id="products">
    Choose a category: 
    <asp:DropDownList ID="ddlCategory" runat="server" AutoPostBack="True"
        Width="130" DataSourceID="SqlDataSource1" DataTextField="LongName"
        DataValueField="CategoryID" OnSelectedIndexChanged="Reset">
    </asp:DropDownList>
    <asp:SqlDataSource ID="SqlDataSource1" runat="server"
        ConnectionString="<%$ ConnectionStrings:HalloweenConnectionString %>"
        SelectCommand="SELECT [CategoryID], [LongName]
                      FROM [Categories] ORDER BY [LongName]">
    </asp:SqlDataSource>
    <asp:Button ID="btnClear" runat="server" Text="Clear Selection"
        OnClick="Reset" />

    <asp:UpdatePanel ID="pnlProducts" runat="server">
      <Triggers>
        <asp:AsyncPostBackTrigger ControlID="ddlCategory"
          EventName="SelectedIndexChanged" />
      </Triggers>
      <ContentTemplate>
        <asp:GridView ID="grdProducts" runat="server"
          DataSourceID="SqlDataSource2" DataKeyNames="ProductID"
          AutoGenerateColumns="false" Width="400"
          OnSelectedIndexChanged="grdProducts_SelectedIndexChanged">
          <Columns>
            <asp:CommandField ShowSelectButton="true" SelectText="View" />
            <asp:BoundField DataField="ProductID" HeaderText="ID"
              ReadOnly="True" />
            <asp:BoundField DataField="Name" HeaderText="Name" />
            <asp:BoundField DataField="UnitPrice" HeaderText="Price"
              DataFormatString="{0:c}" />
            <asp:BoundField DataField="OnHand" HeaderText="On Hand" />
          </Columns>
        </asp:GridView>
        <asp:SqlDataSource ID="SqlDataSource2" runat="server"
          ConnectionString=
            "<%$ ConnectionStrings:HalloweenConnectionString %>"
          SelectCommand="SELECT [ProductID], [Name], [UnitPrice], [OnHand]
                        FROM [Products] WHERE ([CategoryID] = @CategoryID)
                        ORDER BY [ProductID]">
          <SelectParameters>
            <asp:ControlParameter Name="CategoryID" Type="String"
              ControlID="ddlCategory" PropertyName="SelectedValue" />
          </SelectParameters>
        </asp:SqlDataSource>
        <h2>Product Details</h2>
        <asp:DetailsView ID="dvwProduct" runat="server"
          AutoGenerateRows="False" DataKeyNames="ProductID"
          DataSourceID="SqlDataSource3" Width="400">
```

Figure 22-13   The aspx file for the View Products page (part 1 of 2)

The second UpdatePanel control

The second update panel contains the GridView control that displays the number of times each product has been viewed. This update panel doesn't contain any controls that cause a postback. Instead, the data source for the GridView control is reset in code every time a product is viewed. You'll see this in the code-behind file in just a minute.

This means that the panel needs to be refreshed every time the user clicks on any View link in the products grid. Because the UpdateMode attribute of the update panel has been left at its default of Always, this happens automatically. In case this attribute is ever changed, though, a Triggers element is included in the update panel. This element triggers an asynchronous postback when the SelectedIndexChanged event for the GridView control fires.

This update panel also contains an UpdateProgress control. Because the DynamicLayout attribute of this control has been left at its default value of True, space is allocated for it on the page only when it's displayed. The content of this control includes an animated gif file and a text comment.

The Default.aspx file   Page 2

```
      <Fields>
        <asp:BoundField DataField="ProductID" HeaderText="ID"
          ReadOnly="True" />
        <asp:BoundField DataField="Name" HeaderText="Name" />
        <asp:BoundField DataField="UnitPrice" HeaderText="Price"
          DataFormatString="{0:c}" />
        <asp:BoundField DataField="OnHand" HeaderText="On Hand" />
        <asp:BoundField DataField="ShortDescription" HeaderText="Short
          Description" />
        <asp:BoundField DataField="LongDescription" HeaderText="Long
          Description" />
        <asp:BoundField DataField="CategoryID" HeaderText="Category ID" />
      </Fields>
    </asp:DetailsView>
    <asp:SqlDataSource runat="server" ID="SqlDataSource3"
      ConnectionString=
        '<%$ ConnectionStrings:HalloweenConnectionString %>'
      SelectCommand="SELECT [ProductID], [Name], [ShortDescription],
        [LongDescription], [CategoryID], [UnitPrice], [OnHand]
        FROM [Products] WHERE ([ProductID] = @ProductID)">
      <SelectParameters>
        <asp:ControlParameter ControlID="grdProducts" Type="String"
          PropertyName="SelectedValue" Name="ProductID" />
      </SelectParameters>
    </asp:SqlDataSource>
  </ContentTemplate>
  </asp:UpdatePanel>
</div>

<div id="views">
  <h2>Most viewed</h2>
  <asp:UpdatePanel ID="pnlViews" runat="server">
    <Triggers>
      <asp:AsyncPostBackTrigger ControlID="grdProducts"
        EventName="SelectedIndexChanged" />
    </Triggers>
    <ContentTemplate>
      <asp:GridView ID="grdViews" runat="server"
        AutoGenerateColumns="false" Width="200">
        <Columns>
          <asp:BoundField DataField="ProductName" HeaderText="Product" />
          <asp:BoundField DataField="ViewCount" HeaderText="Views" />
          <asp:BoundField DataField="CategoryID" HeaderText="CatID" />
        </Columns>
      </asp:GridView>
      <asp:UpdateProgress ID="UpdateProgress1" runat="server">
        <ProgressTemplate>
          <div class="spinner"><img src="Images/spinner.gif"
            alt="Please Wait" />Loading...</div>
        </ProgressTemplate>
      </asp:UpdateProgress>
    </ContentTemplate>
  </asp:UpdatePanel>
</div>
</form>
```

Figure 22-13   The aspx file for the View Products page (part 2 of 2)

The code-behind file

Figure 22-14 presents the code-behind file for the page. This file consists of a private constant, a private helper method, and three event handlers.

The private constant is a string constant named APP_KEY. This will be used as the key value when working with the variable in application state that holds the ProductViewList object. Using a constant in this way, rather than typing out "viewlist" each time you use the key, is a good way to reduce the chance of errors.

The private helper method is called BindViewGrid, and it accepts a list of ProductView objects as a parameter. As its name implies, this method gets the list, sets it as the data source for the GridView control that displays the number of product views, and calls the GridView control's DataBind method. This causes the product view information to show on the page. The BindViewGrid method is called when the page loads, and whenever a user views a product.

The first event handler is the Page_Load event handler. It starts by declaring a ProductViewList object named viewlist. Then, it checks application state to see if it contains an item with the same name as the APP_KEY constant value. If it doesn't, a new object is created from the ProductViewList class, and this object is added to application state. Otherwise, the item in application state is cast as a ProductViewList object and assigned to the viewlist variable. After the viewlist variable is loaded, its Display method is called to send a list of ProductView objects to the BindViewGrid method.

The second event handler handleds the SelectedIndexChanged event of the products GridView control, which is fired whenever a user views a product. It starts by declaring a new ProductView object. Then, it loads the object's properties with data about the product that's been selected for viewing.

The ProductID property value comes from the SelectedValue property of the GridView control for the products. This is because the GridView control's DataKeys property is set to ProductID. In contrast, the ProductName property value has to come from the SelectedRow property of the GridView control. The CategoryID value comes from the SelectedValue property of the category drop-down list, and the ViewCount property value is set to a default value of 1.

Next, this method locks application state so another user can't modify it at the same time. Then, it gets a reference to the ProductViewList item in application state, stores it in a variable named viewlist, adds the viewed product to the viewlist variable, and unlocks application state. Last, the viewlist's Display method is called to sort the list of ProductView objects, and the list is passed to the BindViewGrid method.

The third event handler is called Reset, and as you saw in the aspx code, it is called by both the category drop-down list and the Clear Selection button. It sets the SelectedIndex property of the products GridView control to -1, which clears the selected item in the GridView control. This also clears the data from the DetailsView control, since it gets the parameter value for its select method from the GridView control's SelectedValue property.

The Default.aspx.cs file

```
using System;
using System.Collections.Generic;
using System.Linq;
using System.Web;
using System.Web.UI;
using System.Web.UI.WebControls;

public partial class _Default : System.Web.UI.Page
{
    private const string APP_KEY = "viewlist";

    protected void Page_Load(object sender, EventArgs e) {
        ProductViewList viewlist;
        if (Application[APP_KEY] == null) {
            viewlist = new ProductViewList();
            Application.Add(APP_KEY, viewlist);
        }
        else {
            viewlist = (ProductViewList)Application[APP_KEY];
            BindViewGrid(viewlist.Display());
        }
    }

    protected void grdProducts_SelectedIndexChanged(object sender,
                                                    EventArgs e) {
        ProductView view = new ProductView();
        view.ProductID = grdProducts.SelectedValue.ToString();
        view.ProductName = grdProducts.SelectedRow.Cells[2].Text;
        view.CategoryID = ddlCategory.SelectedValue.ToString();
        view.ViewCount = 1;

        Application.Lock();
        ProductViewList viewlist = (ProductViewList)Application[APP_KEY];
        viewlist.Add(view);
        Application.UnLock();

        BindViewGrid(viewlist.Display());
    }

    protected void Reset(object sender, EventArgs e) {
        grdProducts.SelectedIndex = -1;
    }

    private void BindViewGrid(List<ProductView> views) {
        grdViews.DataSource = views;
        grdViews.DataBind();
    }
}
```

Description

- The code-behind file uses a ProductViewList object stored in application state to display and update the number of times each product has been viewed.

Figure 22-14   The code-behind file for the View Products page

Perspective

Now that you've completed this chapter, you should be able to use the ASP.NET Ajax server controls to develop Ajax-enabled web applications of your own. Of course, there's a lot more to learn about ASP.NET Ajax than what's presented here. You may also want to take a different approach to using Ajax and learn how to use jQuery to implement Ajax applications. For that, we recommend *Murach's JavaScript and jQuery*.

Terms

rich Internet application (RIA)	ASP.NET Ajax client-side framework
Asynchronous JavaScript and XML (Ajax)	ASP.NET Ajax server controls
	ASP.NET Ajax Control Toolkit
XMLHttpRequest (XHR) object	web service
ASP.NET Ajax	proxy
asynchronous postback	

Summary

- *Asynchronous JavaScript and XML (Ajax)* is a framework that allows you to develop *rich Internet applications (RIA)*. These are web applications that provide advanced functionality and quick response times. Unlike other RIA frameworks, Ajax uses just the features that are built into modern browsers.

- With a traditional web request, the browser sends an HTTP request to the web server, receives an HTTP response back, and reloads the page. With an Ajax request, portions of the page can be updated without having to perform a full HTTP request and response cycle, so the page doesn't have to be reloaded.

- Ajax works by using JavaScript and the browser's *XMLHttpRequest (XHR) object* to send an asynchronous request to the server. The server processes the request and sends back only the data needed to update the page. JavaScript then parses the data in the response and updates the page.

- *ASP.NET Ajax* is a framework that lets you build RIAs with standard server controls that are combined with Ajax server controls.

- The *ASP.NET Ajax client-side framework* is a JavaScript library that interacts with the ASP.NET application server through the XHR object. The *ASP.NET Ajax server controls* are server controls that Ajax-enable a page. The optional *ASP.NET Ajax Control Toolkit* is a collection of components and server control extensions that add effects, animations, and interactive features to a page.

- The ScriptManager control enables *asynchronous postbacks* on a page. The UpdatePanel control encloses the standard server controls that are updated during an asynchronous postback.

- The Timer control triggers a periodic asynchronous postback. The UpdateProgress control displays information only while an asynchronous postback is in progress.

23

How to create and use WCF and Web API services

In earlier versions of ASP.NET, Microsoft offered ASMX web services. Then, Microsoft introduced WCF (Windows Communication Foundation) services, which provide more power and flexibility but are also more complex. Because of this complexity, many developers chose to remain with the simpler ASMX model. Now, with ASP.NET 4.5, WCF services have become almost as easy to use as ASMX services.

In addition, though, ASP.NET 4.5 introduces Web API services, which have the goal of developing services that can be easily consumed by browsers and mobile devices. In this chapter, you'll learn the basic concepts and skills that you need to create and use both WCF and Web API services.

An introduction to web services

A *web service* is a class that resides on a web server and can be accessed via the Internet or an intranet. Web services provide a way to make useful functions available to clients on other platforms. For example, the web site for the United States Postal Service offers web services that let you calculate shipping rates, correct addresses, and track packages.

Web services communicate with clients by using either SOAP or REST protocols. In general, WCF services use SOAP and Web API services use REST.

SOAP services

SOAP (*Simple Object Access Protocol*) uses XML to send data between host and client. SOAP can be used over many types of transport media and has many security options, but it can also be cumbersome to work with. Usually, some sort of proxy class is needed to work with a SOAP service. But, as you'll see later, WCF generates the proxy classes for you.

Figure 23-1 illustrates how WCF services work with SOAP. In this case, the service is offered by a web site that's hosted by IIS, but WCF services can also be hosted by a Windows Forms application, a Console application, or a Windows service. This chapter, though, will focus on WCF services that are hosted by IIS.

As this figure shows, a WCF service exposes one or more *endpoints*. Then, the WCF client uses SOAP over HTTP to communicate with one of these endpoints. For this to work, both the client and the server must be running a version of the .NET Framework that supports WCF.

REST services

REST (*Representational State Transfer*) uses HTTP and URLs, rather than XML, so it is less cumbersome than SOAP. For example, proxy classes aren't needed with REST services. In fact, because REST services often return *JSON* (*JavaScript Object Notation*), they can be consumed by JavaScript without any transformation at all. This makes REST services popular for Ajax applications.

Figure 23-1 illustrates how Web API services work with REST. In this case, the client sends an HTTP request to a specified URL and receives a JSON or XML response. Also, the clients that consume Web API services don't need to have the .NET Framework installed. Although you can also build REST services with WCF, it requires much more configuration than with Web API services.

A WCF service that uses SOAP

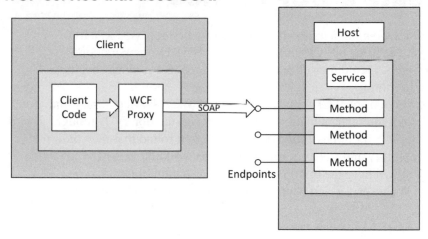

A Web API Service that uses REST

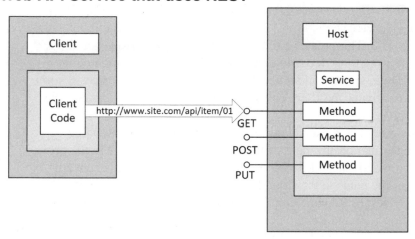

Advantages of SOAP
- Can be used over many transport media, such as TCP, MSMQ, and HTTP.
- Can create strict contracts between two parties and add security layers.

Advantages of REST
- Relies on the existing HTTP standard, so it's faster and easier to configure.
- Can return data in *JSON (JavaScript Object Notation)* or XML format.

Description
- A *web service* on a host server provides a service that can be *consumed* by clients on different platforms.
- Clients communicate with web services by using either *SOAP (Simple Object Access Protocol)* or *REST (Representational State Transfer)*.
- *WCF services* use SOAP to communicate with clients. *Web API services* always use REST.

Figure 23-1   An introduction to web services

How to create a WCF service

WCF (Windows Communication Foundation) was first released as part of .NET Framework 3.0. Today, WCF unifies all older .NET Framework communication technologies, including web services, advanced web service specifications, and .NET Remoting.

With earlier versions of WCF, you had to create a WCF service library and then create and configure an application to host your service library. Although that approach offered a lot of flexibility, developers often found that they didn't need the extra flexibility and were put off by the extra work. Now, with ASP.NET 4.5, you still have the option of creating a separate library, but you can also create a WCF service and host in one step by creating a *WCF service application.*

How to start a WCF service application

To start a WCF service application, you use the New Project dialog box as shown in figure 23-2. This creates a file named IService1.cs. However, the easiest way to start a WCF service is to delete this file and its accompanying Service1.svc file. Then, you can add a new WCF Service file. Nevertheless, some developers prefer to rename the IService1.cs and Service1.svc files and edit the starting code for those files.

If you choose to rename these default files, you should use the Rename command to change other occurrences of the interface or class name in the project. To use this command, place the mouse pointer over the bar that's beneath the last character of the name in the Code Editor, click the drop-down arrow that appears, and select the Rename command from the smart tag menu that's displayed. If you don't use the Rename command, you'll have to rename each occurrence manually or use search-and-replace to locate and change them.

The procedure in this figure shows how to adjust the starting files and folders for a WCF service named CategoryService that lets clients edit and update the data in the Categories table of the Halloween database. In brief, you delete the IService1.cs and Service1.svc files, and you add the folders and files that you need for the Category service. The Solution Explorer in this figure shows the folders and files of the service application after these adjustments are made.

In the DataAccess folder, you can see a file named CategoryDB.cs. This file is the same as the one used for the Category Maintenance application in the object data sources chapter (figure 17-16). Similarly, the Halloween.mdf file is the same database file that you've been using throughout this book.

The New Project dialog box and the files and folders after adjusting

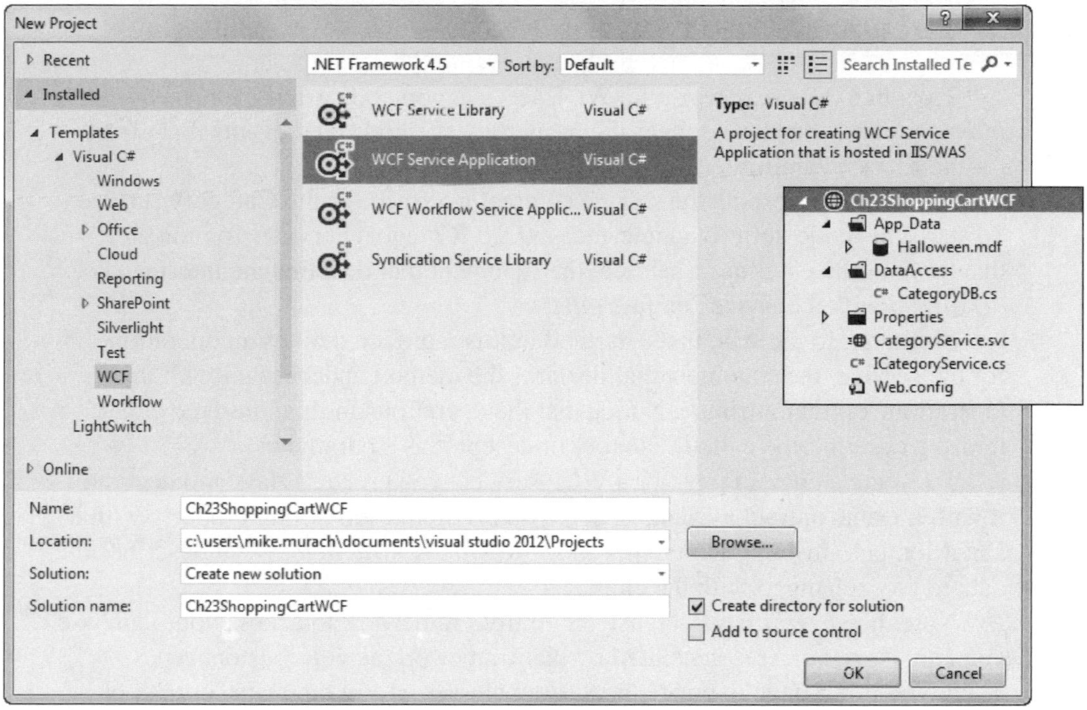

How to create a new WCF service application

- To start a *WCF service application*, select the FILE→New→Project command, select the WCF template group, and then select the WCF Service Application template.

- Enter a name and location for the service application and click OK.

How to set up the folders and files for a Category service

- Delete the files named IService1.cs and Service1.svc.

- Right click the project, select the Add→WCF Service command, name the new service CategoryService, and click OK. This will add files called CategoryService.svc and ICategoryService.cs to the root directory.

- Right-click the App_Data folder and add the Halloween.mdf file.

- Right-click the project and add a new folder named DataAccess. After adding the folder, right-click it and add a new class file named CategoryDB.cs. This is the data access class.

- Add a connection string for accessing the Halloween data base to the <configuration> element of the web.config file.

Description

- In this chapter, you'll learn how to create a Category service that lets a client get, edit, or update the records in the Categories table of the Halloween database.

- The procedure in this figure shows how to set up the folders and files for this service.

Figure 23-2   How to start a WCF service application

How to code a service contract interface and a data contract class

To define the *operations* of a WCF service, you code a *service contract interface*. This interface defines the properties, methods, and events that classes for the service can implement.

Figure 23-3 presents the service contract interface for the Category service. To start, this code defines an interface named ICategoryService. To indicate that this interface defines a service, the statement that declares the interface is *decorated* with a ServiceContract *attribute*.

Similarly, to indicate that a method in this interface defines an operation for the service, the statement that declares the method is decorated with the OperationContract attribute. Notice that the operations in this interface either return a custom type called Category or accept it as a parameter.

To create a custom type for a WCF service, you create a class and decorate it with a DataContract attribute. Then, you decorate each public property with a DataMember attribute. Doing this creates a *data contract class* that describes the data to be exchanged with the client.

Note, however, that if you use the Entity Framework to access your database, you can use the classes generated by that framework as your custom types. Then, you don't have to create the custom classes or add the DataContract or DataMember attributes yourself.

The ICategoryService interface

```
using System;
using System.Collections.Generic;
using System.Linq;
using System.Runtime.Serialization;
using System.ServiceModel;
using System.Text;

namespace Ch23ShoppingCartWCF
{
    [ServiceContract]
    public interface ICategoryService
    {
        [OperationContract]
        List<Category> GetCategories();

        [OperationContract]
        Category GetCategoryById(string id);

        [OperationContract]
        int InsertCategory(Category c);

        [OperationContract]
        int UpdateCategory(Category c);

        [OperationContract]
        int DeleteCategory(Category c);
    }

    [DataContract]
    public class Category
    {
        [DataMember]
        public string CategoryID { get; set; }

        [DataMember]
        public string ShortName { get; set; }

        [DataMember]
        public string LongName { get; set; }
    }
}
```

Description

- To define the operations of a service, you code a *service contract interface* with the ServiceContract attribute. Then, you can code one or more methods with the OperationContract attribute.

- To define the data that's used by a service, you code a *data contract class* with the DataContract attribute. Then, you code one or more properties that have the DataMember attribute. If you are using classes generated by Entity Framework, you can skip this step.

Figure 23-3   How to code a service contract interface and a data contract class

How to code a service contract class that implements the interface

Once you have a service contract interface in place, you write the *service contract class* that implements the interface's properties, methods, and events. Figure 23-4 presents the CategoryService.svc.cs file, which is the service contract class that implements the ICategoryService interface.

This CategoryService class starts by declaring a private CategoryDB object named data, which is initialized in the class's constructor method. This is the data access class that will be used to interact with the database, and it is like the data access class that provides the methods for the object data source in chapter 17. To make it easier to work with the data access class in the service contract class, a using statement adds the namespace of the data access class. The rest of the methods in the class implement the methods defined by the interface.

As the interface in the last figure specifies, the GetCategories method in the service contract class calls a method in the data access class (GetCategories) that returns a list of Category objects. Similarly, the GetCategoryById method in the contract class calls a method in the data access class that returns one Category object based on the category id that's passed to the method as a string.

In contrast, the InsertCategory, UpdateCategory, and DeleteCategory methods all return int types. This is because the data access class methods return the number of rows affected by the operation. By returning this value, these methods provide the clients that call these methods with a way of checking the results of the insert, update, and delete operations.

In some cases, you will also want to return information to the client if an error occurs. An easy way to do that is to return a specific value if the operation fails. In this figure, you can see that the InsertCategory method returns a value of -1 if the InsertCategory method of the data access class throws an exception. Although this has the benefit of being simple, the drawback is that the client will need to know what the return value means.

Another way to return error information to the client is through the use of *fault contracts*. To learn more, you can use the MSDN documentation.

The CategoryService class

```
using System;
using System.Collections.Generic;
using System.Linq;
using System.Runtime.Serialization;
using System.ServiceModel;
using System.Text;
using Ch23ShoppingCartWCF.DataAccess;

namespace Ch23ShoppingCartWCF
{
    public class CategoryService : ICategoryService
    {
        CategoryDB data;
        public CategoryService() {
            data = new CategoryDB();
        }

        public List<Category> GetCategories() {
            return data.GetCategories();
        }

        public Category GetCategoryById(string id) {
            return data.GetCategoryById(id);
        }

        public int InsertCategory(Category c) {
            try {
                return data.InsertCategory(c);
            }
            catch {
                return -1;
            }
        }

        public int UpdateCategory(Category c) {
            return data.UpdateCategory(c);
        }

        public int DeleteCategory(Category c) {
            return data.DeleteCategory(c);
        }
    }
}
```

Description

- To implement the operations of a service, you code a *service contract class* that implements the service contract interface.

- The service contract class can include properties, methods, and events that aren't a part of the service interface, like the constructor method and the CategoryDB object above. This object gets and updates data in the Categories table in the Halloween database.

- The service contract class can also include data validation or error handling, as in the InsertCategory method above.

Figure 23-4   How to write the service contract class that implements the interface

How to view and test a WCF service

Figure 23-5 shows how to test a WCF service. In this figure, the GetCategoryById method was double-clicked and a value of "costumes" was entered for the id parameter in the Request pane. In the Response pane, you can see that the WCF service returned a value of type Category. This is a custom type that was decorated with the DataContract attribute. The Response pane also displays the individual properties of the Category type.

Although the response from the service is formatted in the Response pane, you can also look at the raw SOAP request and response by clicking on the XML tab in the lower left corner of the bottom pane. This shows the SOAP format that's required by WCF services.

This figure also shows how to view information about a service in a Service page in the web browser. The Service page includes basic information about how to use the service, including some C# and Visual Basic code that you can use to consume the service from a client application. You'll learn more about consuming a service next.

The WCF Test Client window

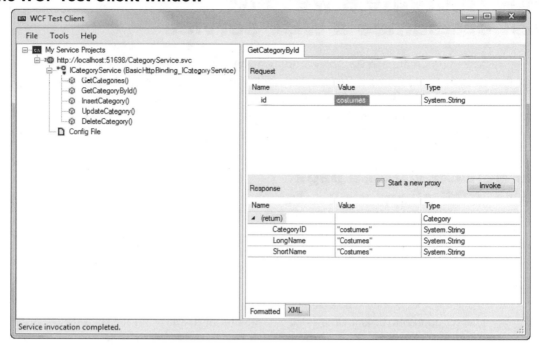

How to test a WCF service

- Start by setting the .svc file for the service as the start page for the web site. Then, click the browser name in the Standard toolbar or press F5. That causes Visual Studio to display the WCF Test Client window for the service.

- To test a service operation, double-click on the operation in the left pane of the window to display a tab for the operation in the right side of the window. Then, enter any required parameters for the operation in the Request section of the tab and click the Invoke button. If you get a security warning, click OK. The Response pane will then show the data that's returned by the operation.

- You can view the XML for the response by clicking on the XML tab in the lower left corner of the right pane of the WCF Test Client window.

How to view information about a WCF service in a browser

- Right-click the .svc file for the service and select View in Browser, or open a browser and type the URL shown at the top of the left pane of the Test Client window, just below My Service Projects. Either way, a Service page is displayed.

Figure 23-5 How to view and test a WCF service

How to create a web site that consumes a WCF service

After you create a WCF service application, you can create a client web site that consumes the service. Because any web site can be a client web site, you can use any of the skills you've learned in this book to develop it. Then, you can add a reference for the service you want to use to the client web site, and you can write code or use server controls that consume the service.

The Edit Categories page of the WCF client web site

Figure 23-6 shows two views of the Edit Categories page that will consume the WCF Category web service. This page consists of two server controls. The first one is a drop-down list that lists all the categories in the database. Since its AutoPostBack property is set to True, this page posts back to the server whenever the user selects a new category.

The second control is a DetailsView control that displays all the data for the category that's selected in the drop-down list. In the first screen in this figure, you can see that the Costumes category is selected and the CategoryID, LongName, and ShortName fields of that category are displayed.

However, this DetailsView control is configured to let a user edit and delete existing categories, and to insert new ones. As a result, link buttons that allow for these operations are shown in the bottom row of the control.

The second screen in this figure shows the DetailsView control when it's in Insert mode, which it goes into when the New link button is clicked. Then, the user can enter the data for a new category and click either the Insert or Cancel link button to finish the operation.

The Edit Categories page of the WCF client web site

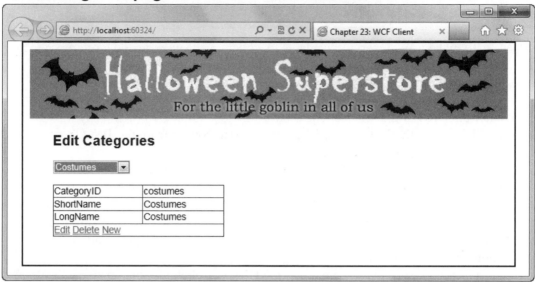

The Edit Categories page of the WCF client web site in Insert mode

Description

- The Edit Categories page consists of a drop-down list that displays the categories, and a DetailsView control that displays the details of the category selected by the drop-down list.
- In default mode, the DetailsView control displays the data in the selected category. But the links in the bottom row let the user edit, delete, and add a category.
- In Insert mode, the user can enter the data for a new category and then click on the Insert or Cancel link to complete the operation.

Figure 23-6   The Edit Categories page of the WCF client web site

How to add a WCF service reference to a client web site

To make a WCF service available to a client web site, you add a reference to the service in the client site by using the Add Service Reference dialog box, as shown in figure 23-7. If your client web site is in the same solution as your WCF web service, you can just click the Discover button. Otherwise, you'll need to enter the URL of the service. The easiest way to get that URL is to copy it from a web browser that's displaying the service, or to copy it from the Test Client window you saw in figure 23-5.

It's important to note that in order to add a reference like this, the host web site must be running. That's why this figure describes two ways that you can have your host and your client running at the same time. The easiest way is to put them both in the same solution. However, having each in its own solution is almost as easy, and it provides a more "real world" feel of the host and the client being in different places.

Once you click Discover or enter the URL and click Go, the service will be displayed in the Services list. Then, you can expand this service to see the service contract, service interface, and operations of the interface, although you don't need to do that to add the reference. Finally, you enter the name you want to use for the service's namespace and click the OK button. In this example, that name is CategoryService.

When you add a reference to a WCF service to a web site, Visual Studio creates a *proxy* class that provides access to the operations and data types that are defined by the service, and it creates a folder for the service reference under the App_WebReferences folder in the Solution Explorer. This folder has the name that you entered for the namespace in the Add Service Reference dialog box. If you expand this folder, you can see the configuration files for the service. Since these files are generated for you automatically, you don't need to understand the code that they contain. But if you're curious about how these files work, you can display them in the Text Editor.

Before I go on, you should realize that if the port number for the development server that's used to run the host web site is different from the port number that's used for the service reference, the client web site won't be able to locate the service. If, for example, you try to run the client web site for this chapter after you download it from our web site, it won't work. To fix that, you need to delete the folder for the service reference from the App_WebReferences folder. Then, you need to start the host web site and use its URL to add a service reference back to the client web site.

The Add Service Reference dialog box

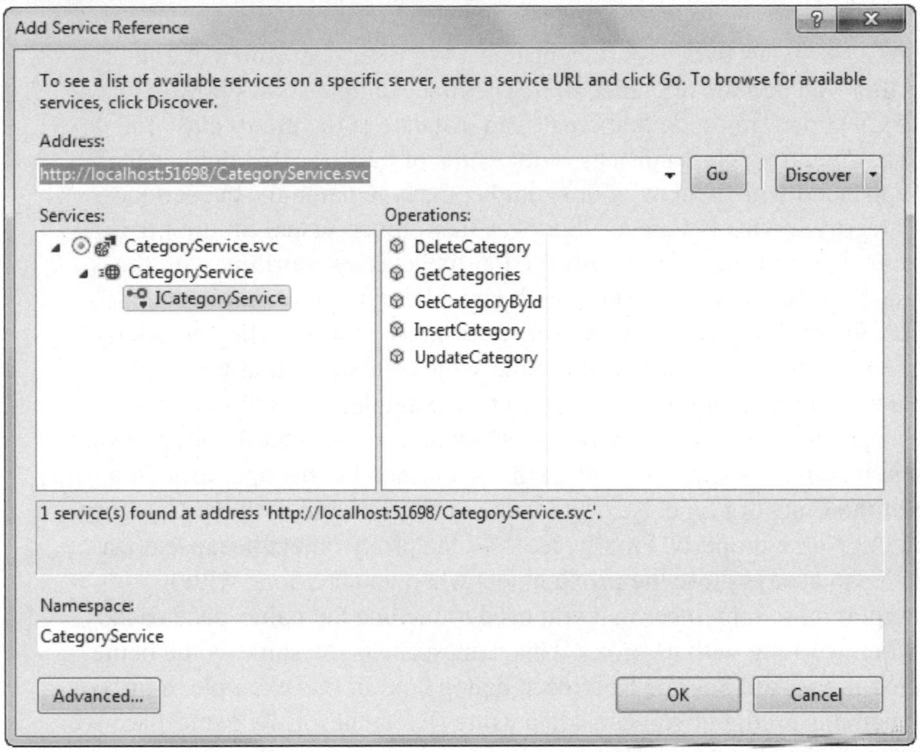

Two ways to have a client and service run simultaneously in IIS Express

- Add the client web site to the same solution using the FILE→Add→New Web Site command. Or, if the web site already exists, use the FILE→Add→Existing Web Site command to add it. After the web site is added, right-click it and select Set as StartUp Project.
- Open and run the service in Visual Studio. Then, open another instance of Visual Studio to create and run the client web site.

How to add a web service reference to a web site

- With the web service running, use the WEBSITE→Add Service Reference command, or right-click the project and select Add Service Reference. That displays the Add Service Reference dialog box.
- If the web site is in the same solution as the service, click the Discover button. Otherwise, paste the URL for the service into the Address text box and click the Go button. Then, enter a namespace for the service and click OK. Visual Studio will create a folder for the service reference under the App_WebReferences folder in the Solution Explorer.

Description

- When you add a service reference to a client, the service must be running. Then, Visual Studio creates a *proxy* class that provides access to the operations and data types that are defined by the service.

Figure 23-7   How to add a WCF service reference to a client web site

How to consume a WCF service

Figure 23-8 shows two ways to consume a WCF service from a client web site after you add the reference to it. The first example shows how to do it with C# code. This code first creates an instance of the proxy class for the service. The proxy class consists of the name of the class that defines the service, appended with "Client". For example, the type name for the service named CategoryService is CategoryServiceClient. Since Visual Studio provides IntelliSense support for working with WCF proxy classes, working with the proxy in code is the same as working with any other type of object in code.

Once you create a proxy class object, you can use it to call the operations the service provides. To do that, you use the same techniques that you use to execute a method of any other object. In this example, the code calls the GetCategoryById operation of the proxy object and passes a hard-coded id value to it. Then, it stores the Category object that's returned by this operation in a variable of the Category type. Next, it loads a string variable with the Category object's LongName property. Finally, it closes the proxy object because it's a best practice to always close the proxy object when you are done with it.

It's important to remember that you need to include the namespace of the service when working with its proxy. This namespace is the same as the name you entered in the Add Service Reference dialog box. In this example, a fully-qualified name is used, but you can add a using statement for the namespace so it's easier to refer to the proxy object.

The second way to consume a WCF service from a client web site is with data sources and data-bound controls. The second example in this figure shows the aspx code for the drop-down list and DetailsView controls of the Edit Categories page that you saw in figure 23-6. These server controls are bound to ObjectDataSource controls, and the data source controls use the same fully-qualified type name that is in the first example. Then, the data source controls use the operations, or methods, of the proxy for their select, insert, update, and delete methods.

You configure an ObjectDataSource control to work with a WCF proxy class in the same way that you do for any other data access object, by clicking on the smart tag and then choosing Configure Data Source. However, you may need to uncheck the Show Only Data Components check box to see the WCF proxy class in the drop-down list. Remember that you want to choose the object whose name ends with "Client".

In this example, the aspx code for the DetailsView control has event handlers set up for its OnItemDeleted, OnItemInserted, and OnItemUpdated events. This, however, isn't required for working with a WCF service, but is particular to this page. All three of these event handlers just call the DataBind() method of the drop-down list control to reload the data for the list. If, for example, a category is deleted, the dvCategory_ItemDeleted method of the code-behind file is called, which reloads the data for the drop-down list so the deleted category won't be in it any more.

C# code to use the WCF service

```
CategoryService.CategoryServiceClient svc = new
    CategoryService.CategoryServiceClient();
CategoryService.Category category = svc.GetCategoryById("fx");
string name = category.LongName;
svc.Close();
```

The data source and data-bound controls
from the Edit Categories aspx file

```
<asp:DropDownList ID="ddlCategories" runat="server" AutoPostBack="True"
    DataSourceID="ddlDataSource" DataTextField="LongName"
    DataValueField="CategoryID">
</asp:DropDownList>
<asp:ObjectDataSource runat="server" ID="ddlDataSource"
    SelectMethod="GetCategories"
    TypeName="CategoryService.CategoryServiceClient">
</asp:ObjectDataSource>

<asp:DetailsView ID="dvCategory" runat="server" DataKeyNames="CategoryID"
    Height="75px" Width="250px" AutoGenerateRows="False"
    DataSourceID="detailsDataSource"
    OnItemDeleted="dvCategory_ItemDeleted"
    OnItemInserted="dvCategory_ItemInserted"
    OnItemUpdated="dvCategory_ItemUpdated">
    <Fields>
        <asp:BoundField DataField="CategoryID" HeaderText="CategoryID"
            SortExpression="CategoryID"></asp:BoundField>
        <asp:BoundField DataField="ShortName" HeaderText="ShortName"
            SortExpression="ShortName"></asp:BoundField>
        <asp:BoundField DataField="LongName" HeaderText="LongName"
            SortExpression="LongName"></asp:BoundField>
        <asp:CommandField ShowInsertButton="True" ShowEditButton="True"
            ShowDeleteButton="True"></asp:CommandField>
    </Fields>
</asp:DetailsView>
<asp:ObjectDataSource runat="server" ID="detailsDataSource"
    DataObjectTypeName="CategoryService.Category"
    DeleteMethod="DeleteCategory" InsertMethod="InsertCategory"
    SelectMethod="GetCategoryById" UpdateMethod="UpdateCategory"
    TypeName="CategoryService.CategoryServiceClient">
    <SelectParameters>
        <asp:ControlParameter ControlID="ddlCategories"
            PropertyName="SelectedValue"
            Name="id" Type="String">
        </asp:ControlParameter>
    </SelectParameters>
</asp:ObjectDataSource>
```

Description

- You can work with the service proxy classes in code or with data source and data-bound controls.

- You can use the DataObjectTypeName attribute of the ObjectDataSource to set the name of the class the control uses for a parameter in update, insert, or delete operations.

Figure 23-8   How to consume a WCF service

How to create a Web API service

As more web sites and mobile devices use Ajax to communicate with web services, two main problems with SOAP-based web services have been exposed. First, SOAP requests and responses are verbose, leading to slower network speeds for large requests or responses. Second, the XML returned by a SOAP service must be parsed before it can be used.

REST-based web services address these concerns in two ways. First, because the requests are made using the HTTP protocol, the requests and data are in the URL and HTTP request body, just like any other HTTP request made by a browser. Second, the response to a REST service is usually in JSON format, which is more compact than XML. If, for example, you look at the XML of the SOAP response as described in figure 23-5, you'll see a response that is several lines long, even though the equivalent JSON response is one line. Beyond that, a JSON response is a JavaScript object, which means that it can be consumed by JavaScript without any parsing.

Now, with ASP.NET 4.5, you can use the Web API (Application Programming Interface) to create and consume *Web API services*. This feature uses the ASP.NET MVC framework to create REST web services that can return either JSON or XML to a client. In the next chapter, you'll learn more about ASP.NET MVC so what follows is just an introduction to how it can be used to develop Web API services.

How to start a Web API service

To start a Web API service, you use the procedure in figure 23-9. Note here that you are creating an MVC application that uses the Web API template. After you create the service application, the code for a file named ValuesController.cs is shown in the Code Editor. This file is located in the Controllers folder.

When you create a Web API service this way, numerous files and folders are created by default, but most of the time you'll only be working with the App_Data, Models, and Controllers folders. As a result, you will usually want to adjust the starting files and folders. This figure, for example, shows how to adjust the folders and files for a Categories service that's like the WCF service you just studied. After you add the database and C# files to the application, you will want to develop the *controller* in the Controller folder. This file will provide the methods for your service.

One way to start the controller is to use the Rename command to rename the ValuesController file so its name is more appropriate. The benefit of this is that you can use the default methods that it provides as a guide to coding your own methods. The drawback is that renaming a file tends to be error prone.

The other way to develop the controller is to delete the ValuesController file and add a new controller. This avoids renaming, but you lose the default methods. So, a good compromise is to add a new controller, copy and paste the default action methods from the ValuesController file into the new file, and then delete the ValuesController file.

The New Project dialog box

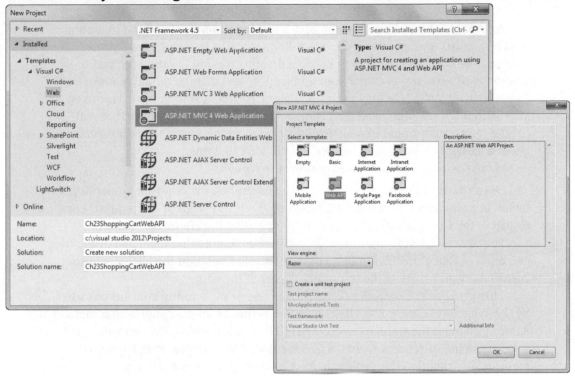

How to start a new Web API service

- Select the FILE→New→Project command, select the Web template group, and select the ASP.NET MVC 4 Web Application template. Then, enter a name and location for the service application, and click OK.

- In the New ASP.NET MVC 4 Project dialog box, select the Web API template and click OK.

How to adjust the initial files and folders for the Edit Categories page

- Right-click the App_Data folder and add the Halloween.mdf file.

- Right-click the Models folder and add class files named Category.cs and CategoryDB.cs. The Category class is similar to the Category class in the WCF example, but it doesn't need to have any DataContract or DataMember attributes. The CategoryDB class is the data access class.

- To add a new controller file to the Controllers folder, right-click the folder and select Add→Controller. In the Add Controller dialog box, name your controller, select Empty API controller in the Template drop-down list, and click Add.

Description

- The Web API template adds numerous files and folders to the project, but in most cases you will only work with the App_Data, Models, and Controllers folders.

- When adding a *controller*, be sure its name ends with the word "Controller".

Figure 23-9   How to start a Web API service

How to write a web service controller

An ASP.NET MVC application uses a *routing framework* to send incoming HTTP requests to the appropriate controller according to a predefined *route pattern*. For now, all you need to know is that this routing is set up for you automatically when you create your application, and that the default pattern is "api/{controller}/{id}". This means that any URL request to your service must start with the term "api", and then contain the name of the controller that will handle it and an optional id parameter. For example, a request to get information about a category whose id is "masks" would look like this:

`http://www.domain.com/api/categories/masks`

Once the HTTP request is routed to the controller, the controller determines which *action method* will handle it based on the HTTP verb of the request. For instance, the CategoriesController in figure 23-10 is the controller that will handle requests like the one above. It's important to note that the name of the file and class is CategoriesController, but the controller name in the URLs is lower case and doesn't include the "Controller" part of the name.

This CategoriesController demonstrates one of the naming conventions used by the Web API framework. The convention is that as long as your action method name starts with the same name as the HTTP verb it handles, the controller will route that kind of request to that action method. For example, POST (insert) requests are routed to the method named PostCategory, and PUT (update) requests are routed to the method named PutCategory. The comments above the methods in this figure show what action the HTTP verb is associated with and what a URL request for that method would look like.

Note that you can have more than one action method for a specific HTTP verb. For instance, the CategoriesController in this figure has three methods that handle GET requests. If there is more than one method for a verb, the controller uses the method signature and the default route pattern to select the correct one.

For example, the GetCategories method has no parameters, so GET requests with no URL parameter are routed there. In contrast, GET requests with a parameter get routed to the GetCategoryById or GetCategoriesByShortName method. The controller decides which one based on the name of the parameter in the URL. If the parameter name is specified, as in "categories/?name=Masks", the controller looks for a method with a parameter of the same name. If the parameter name isn't specified, as in "categories/masks", the controller looks for a method with a parameter with the default name of "id".

The Web API expects simple parameter types like ints or strings to be in the URL and complex parameter types like Category objects to be in the body of the HTTP request. These complex parameters must have the [FromBody] attribute, as shown in the PostCategory and PutCategory methods.

The controller in this figure also includes a commented-out call to the Sleep method of the current Thread. This can be a useful way to simulate service delays when you're testing the client web site that consumes the service.

The CategoriesController.cs file

```csharp
using Ch23ShoppingCartWebAPI.Models;

namespace Ch23ShoppingCartWebAPI.Controllers
{
    public class CategoriesController : ApiController
    {
        CategoryDB data;
        public CategoriesController() {
            this.data = new CategoryDB();
        }
        // GET: api/categories
        public IEnumerable<Category> GetCategories() {
            //System.Threading.Thread.Sleep(3000); //3 seconds
            return data.GetCategories();
        }
        // GET: api/categories/masks
        public Category GetCategoryById(string id) {
            return data.GetCategoryById(id);
        }
        // GET: api/categories/?name=Masks
        public IEnumerable<Category> GetCategoriesByShortName(string name)
        {
            return data.GetCategoriesByShortName(name);
        }
        // POST(Insert): api/categories
        public int PostCategory([FromBody]Category value) {
            return data.InsertCategory(value);
        }
        // PUT(Update): api/categories/masks
        public int PutCategory(string id, [FromBody]Category value) {
            Category c = GetCategoryById(id);
            c.ShortName = value.ShortName;
            c.LongName = value.LongName;
            return data.UpdateCategory(c);
        }
        // DELETE: api/categories/masks
        public int DeleteCategory(string id) {
            Category c = GetCategoryById(id);
            return data.DeleteCategory(c);
        }
    }
}
```

Description

- The controller for a service needs to end with the word "Controller" and be in the Controllers folder.

- As long as the names for the *action methods* in the controller begin with the right HTTP verbs, the *routing framework* will route HTTP requests to them correctly.

- You can use the System.Threading namespace to simulate service delays for testing.

Figure 23-10   How to write a web service controller

How to view and test a Web API service

Although Visual Studio doesn't provide a test mechanism for Web API services like it does for WCF services, remember that REST services are accessed by using regular HTTP requests. This means that you can test the GET methods by using a browser.

The table in figure 23-11 shows the HTTP verbs, action methods, and URLs for the Web API Categories service, as well as a procedure for testing the GET methods in a browser. Because the web service response is sent as JSON rather than HTML, the test won't automatically display the data in your browser. Rather, you'll get a message asking if you want to open or save the JSON file. For instance, this figure shows the response for this GET request

`http://localhost:<portnumber>/api/categories`

after clicking the Open button and opening the response in Notepad. This shows the JSON array of all the categories in the database.

You can also display information about a Web API service in a web browser, as described in this figure. Then, a Help page is displayed that displays the methods of the service. This Help page is actually a NuGet package called ASP.NET Web API Help Page, and its code files are located in the Areas/HelpPage folder.

By default, the Help page for a Web API service displays minimal information, but you can enhance that if you want to. To learn more about that, you can search for "ASP.NET Web API Help Page." Note, however, that the Help page uses ASP.NET MVC, so you'll probably want to read the MVC chapter in this book before trying to enhance the Help page.

You can also test the HTTP verbs for a Web API service by using a third-party proxy tool. For instance, Fiddler is a popular freeware tool, and Charles is a popular paid tool.

HTTP Verbs and corresponding methods and URIs in the Category service

Verb	Action Method	URL
GET	GetCategories()	/api/categories
GET	GetCategoryById(string id)	/api/categories/masks
GET	GetCategoriesByShortName(string name)	/api/categories/?name=Masks
POST	PostCategory(Category value)	/api/categories
PUT	PutCategory(string id, Category value)	/api/categories/masks
DELETE	DeleteCategory(string id)	/api/categories/masks

Testing the GET methods in a browser

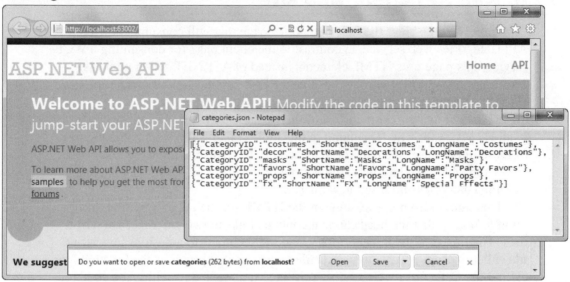

How to test the GET methods of a Web API service

- In Visual Studio, click the browser name in the Standard toolbar or press F5. Then, an ASP.NET Web API page like the one above is displayed in the browser.
- Add one of the GET URLs shown in the table above to the URL in the address bar of the browser and refresh the page. Then, click on the Open or Save button to see or save the response from the server.

How to view information about a Web API service

- Click the "API" link at the top right of the home page shown above. This will display a Help page that lists basic information about your service.

Figure 23-11   How to view and test a Web API service

How to create a web site
that consumes a Web API service

After you create a Web API service, you can create a client web site that consumes it. Since the client site is a regular web site, you can use any of the skills you've learned in this book to develop it. In contrast to the way you work with WCF services, though, you don't need to add any references or set up any proxy classes for Web API services.

The Edit Categories page
of the Web API client web site

Figure 23-12 shows the Edit Categories page that will consume the Web API Categories web service. In contrast to the client page for consuming a WCF service, this page uses HTML elements instead of ASP.NET server controls. That's because the best way to consume a REST service is with JavaScript, and HTML elements are better suited for working with JavaScript.

Instead of using a drop-down list, this page displays all the category data in an HTML table. The ID column in this table contains links, and clicking one of these links causes the data for that category to be displayed in the text boxes below the table. The buttons at the bottom of this page let a user edit and delete existing categories and insert new ones.

This figure also presents some of the HTML for the page. Here, the first thing to note is that the head element contains links to two external JavaScript files. The first is to the jQuery library, and the second is to a custom JavaScript file called webapi.js. This webapi.js file is the one that provides the functions for calling the Categories web service. You'll learn more about writing the code for this file in the next figure.

The HTML table that displays the category data has an id of "categories", and its tbody element will be dynamically loaded by JavaScript. Then, the input elements below the HTML table are for the text boxes that display the data items for a category, and each of these input elements has both an id and a name attribute. The id attribute is used for CSS styling and by the JavaScript code that works with each element. The name attribute is used by jQuery to retrieve the value from the element for POST and PUT requests.

When coding the name attributes, the values must be the same as the property names of the Category object. This is so the [FromBody] attributes you saw in figure 23-10 will work correctly. So, the name attribute must be "CategoryID" for the id text box, "ShortName" for the short name text box, and "LongName" for the long name text box. You can find the required property names on the Help page described in figure 23-11.

The input button elements below the text boxes each have an onclick attribute that identifies the JavaScript function that will be called when the button is clicked. Below the buttons is a message label that will display information about the current operation. For instance, when the page first loads, it says "Loading..." until the categories are loaded. This is a good idea since there are often network latencies when dealing with a web service.

A Categories page when jQuery is used to consume the Web API service

The head and body elements of the page

```
<head id="Head1" runat="server">
    ...
    <script src="Scripts/jquery-2.0.0.min.js"></script>
    <script src="Scripts/webapi.js"></script>
</head>
<body>
    <header><img src="/Images/banner.jpg" alt="Halloween Store" /></header>
    <form id="form1" runat="server">
        <section>
        <h1>Edit Categories</h1>
        <table id="categories">
            <thead><tr><th>ID</th><th>ShortName</th><th>LongName</th></tr>
            </thead>
            <tbody></tbody></table>
        <div>
            <label>ID:</label><input type="text" id="id" name="CategoryID" />
            <label>Short Name:</label><input type="text" id="short"
                name="ShortName" />
            <label>Long Name:</label><input type="text" id="long"
                name="LongName" /></div>
        <div>
            <input type="button" value="Insert" onclick="insertCat();" />
            <input type="button" value="Update" onclick="updateCat();" />
            <input type="button" value="Delete" onclick="deleteCat();" />
            <input type="button" value="Clear" onclick="clearFields();" />
            <span id="message">Loading...</span></div>
        </section>
    </form>
</body>
```

Figure 23-12   The Edit Categories page of the Web API client web site

How to consume a Web API service using jQuery

Most of the time, you'll want to use jQuery to consume a Web API service. That's because you can make asynchronous Ajax requests with jQuery, which can improve response times. To illustrate the use of jQuery, figure 23-13 presents some of the JavaScript and jQuery code that's in the webapi.js file for the web site that consumes the Web API service. This JavaScript code is loaded automatically when the page is requested by a browser, it runs in the browser without server calls, and it can respond to user events like clicking on a link.

If you know how to use jQuery, you should be able to follow most of this code. If you don't know how to use jQuery, this example shows how important JavaScript and jQuery have become to the modern web developer. In either case, here's a description of what's going on.

The first line of JavaScript code loads the base URL of the web service in a variable called api. This is a good practice because if the URL of the web service changes, you only have to change it in one place.

The first function in this figure is the jQuery ready function that runs as soon as the Document Object Model for the web page has been built and before the page has been displayed. This ready function calls a helper function named displayCategories that uses the jQuery $.getJSON function to retrieve the category data from the web service. Then, it uses the jQuery $.each function to put the JSON data into an array of rows, one row at a time, including a link for the ID column. The href attribute for each link is the value of the api variable plus the category's id. Last, this function clears the message at the bottom of the page and puts the rows of the array into the body of the table in the HTML for the form. At that point, the web page looks like the one in the previous figure.

The next line of code in the ready function wires an event handler to the click event of each of the links in the ID column that were created by the displayCategories function. This click event handler prevents the default redirect behavior of the link, and then calls the findCategory function and passes the value of the link's href attribute to it.

The findCategory function first provides information about what operation is occurring. Then, it uses the $.getJSON method to make a request to the web service. The first parameter to this method is the URL of the web service method, which was passed in from the link's href attribute. The second parameter is an embedded function whose data parameter contains the JSON response from the web service. Within the embedded function, the values of the text elements are loaded and the message label is cleared. Note that because the data variable is JSON, the JavaScript can work with it directly.

The next three functions are the insert, update, and delete functions, and they function similarly to each other. First, they provide information about the operation. Then, they call the jQuery $.ajax method. In the insertCat function, for example, the $.ajax method sets the request verb to POST, provides the URL for the web service, gets the form values by using the serialize function, sets the data type as JSON, and sets the functions to be called on success and on error.

This should give you some idea of how jQuery can be used to consume a Web API service. To learn more, please refer to our JavaScript and jQuery book.

The JavaScript and jQuery in the webapi.js file for the Edit Categories page

```
var api = "http://localhost:63002/api/categories/";

$(document).ready(function () {
    displayCategories();
    $(document.body).on('click', 'a', function (e) {
        e.preventDefault();
        findCategory($(this).attr("href"));
    });
});
function displayCategories() {
    $.getJSON(api, function (data) {
        var rows = "";
        $.each(data, function (key, val) {
            rows += "<tr><td><a href=" + api + val.CategoryID + ">"
                    + val.CategoryID + "</a></td>";
            rows += "<td>" + val.ShortName + "</td>";
            rows += "<td>" + val.LongName + "</td></tr>";
        });
        $('#message').text("");
        $("#categories > tbody tr").remove();
        $('#categories > tbody').append(rows);
    })
    .fail(showError);
}
function findCategory(href) {
    $('#message').html("Finding...");
    $.getJSON(href, function (data) {
        $('#id').val(data.CategoryID);
        $('#short').val(data.ShortName);
        $('#long').val(data.LongName);
        $('#message').text("");
    })
    .fail(showError);
}
function insertCat() {
    $('#message').text("Inserting...");
    $.ajax({
        type: 'POST',
        url: api,
        data: $('#form1').serialize(),
        dataType: "json",
        success: displayCategories,
        error: showError
    });
}
// this code continues with the updateCat, deleteCat, and other functions
```

Description

- When you use jQuery to consume a Web API service, Ajax is used to get and update the data with asynchronous requests. This is generally considered to be the best way to consume Web API services.

- This again shows how important JavaScript and jQuery are to the web developer. To learn more about how this page works, you can use *Murach's JavaScript and jQuery*.

Figure 23-13   How to consume a Web API service using jQuery

How to consume a Web API service using C# code

As you've just learned, you will usually want to use jQuery to consume Web API services because jQuery can make asynchronous Ajax requests from the browser. However, you can also consume a Web API service synchronously using C# code. In figure 23-14, for example, you can see a web page that uses a GridView control and a C# code-behind file to display the category data that's returned by the Categories web service.

When a web site consumes a Web API service, the data can be returned as JSON or XML data. Although there are native and third-party .NET classes for working with JSON, the .NET XML classes and the LINQ to XML functionality make XML a good choice when you're using C# code to consume a service.

To illustrate, the code in this figure uses the HttpWebRequest object of the System.Net namespace to make a GET request. Here, the ContentType property of the request object specifies XML as the return type. Next, the GetResponse method is used to load the response from the web service in a WebResponse object, and the data in that object is converted into a Stream object of the System.IO namespace.

Once the web service response has been serialized to a stream, it can be read into a DataSet object of the System.Data namespace. In this example, the categories data will be the only table in the dataset, so you set the first table in the dataset as the GridView's data source and then bind it to the GridView control.

The downside to using C# code rather than the asynchronous capabilities of jQuery is in how it handles service delays. In this example, if the service takes a few seconds to respond, the entire page will be blank until the response is received. Because of this, if you can't use jQuery, you should probably use some of the ASP.NET Ajax controls described in the previous chapter when you're working with web services.

Incidentally, the code in this figure will also work in a Windows Forms application. For that type of application, you can deal with service delays by using the async and await keywords that are new to the .NET Framework 4.5. To find out more about these keywords, you can refer to the MSDN documentation.

A Categories page when C# is used to consume the Web API service

The code-behind file for the page

```
...
using System.Net;
using System.IO;
using System.Data;

public partial class ServerSide : System.Web.UI.Page
{
    protected void Page_Load(object sender, EventArgs e)
    {
        //configure web request object
        string url = "http://localhost:63002/api/categories/";
        HttpWebRequest request = (HttpWebRequest)WebRequest.Create(url);
        request.Method = "GET";
        request.ContentType = "text/xml; encoding='utf-8'";

        //send request, get xml response and convert to stream
        WebResponse response = request.GetResponse();
        Stream stream = response.GetResponseStream();

        //read stream into a dataset
        DataSet ds = new DataSet();
        ds.ReadXml(stream);

        //bind data set to gridview
        grdCategories.DataSource = ds.Tables[0];
        grdCategories.DataBind();
    }
}
```

Description

- When you consume a Web API service with C#, normal HTTP requests are made, unless you use the ASP.NET Ajax controls presented in chapter 22.

Figure 23-14   How to consume a Web API service using C# code

Perspective

In this chapter, you've learned the basic skills for creating and consuming WCF services, and you've been introduced to Web API services. Of course, there's a lot more to learn, starting with the next chapter on ASP.NET MVC. We hope, however, that this chapter has given you the foundation that you need for learning more on your own.

Terms

web service	operation
consume a service	decorate with an attribute
SOAP (Simple Object Access Protocol)	service contract interface
	data contract class
endpoint	service contract class
REST (Representational State Transfer)	proxy
	Web API service
JSON (JavaScript Object Notation)	controller
WCF (Windows Communication Foundation) service	routing framework
	route pattern
WCF service application	action method

Summary

- A *web service* is a class that resides on a web server and can be *consumed* by clients. Web services communicate with clients using *SOAP* or *REST*.

- ASP.NET 4.5 provides two primary web service technologies: *WCF (Windows Communication Foundation)* and *Web API (Application Programming Interface)*. WCF services usually use SOAP, and Web API services always use REST.

- To create a *WCF service*, you write a *service contract interface* that defines the service's *operations*. This interface and its properties, methods, and events must be *decorated* with the correct *attributes*. Then, you write a *service contract class* that implements the operations defined in the interface.

- With some WCF services, you must also write a *data contract class* that describes the data to be exchanged between service and client. To do that, you write a class and decorate it and its properties with the correct data attributes.

- To consume a WCF service from a client, you first add a service reference, which generates a *proxy* class. Then, you work with the proxy class.

- To create a *Web API service*, you create an ASP.NET MVC application from the Web API template. Then, you write a *controller* that contains the *action methods* that handle HTTP requests.

- To consume a Web API service from a client, you usually use jQuery methods to communicate with the service and parse the JSON data that's returned from it. But you can also use ASP.NET server controls and C# to consume the service.

24

An introduction to ASP.NET MVC

In recent years ASP.NET MVC has gotten more attention as a web development tool. That's because it facilitates unit testing, uses naming and structure conventions for configuration, and works directly with HTTP requests. Sometimes, you'll even see ASP.NET MVC touted as a replacement for ASP.NET Web Forms, but that isn't the case.

Rather, you should see ASP.NET MVC as a complement to Web Forms, because each has its own strengths. Web Forms are typically used for intranet web applications and web sites that need to use state or complex server controls. MVC is typically used for websites with high traffic and a need for search engine optimization and good performance.

In this chapter, you'll learn the basic concepts and skills for working with ASP.NET MVC web applications. Then, you can decide whether ASP.NET MVC is something you want to learn more about.

An introduction to MVC

Web Forms applications often combine code that accesses databases with HTML code, as with SqlDataSource controls. Also, the code-behind files in Web Forms applications are tightly coupled with their aspx files, which makes it hard for one person to work on an aspx file while another works on its code-behind file. Shortcomings like that can make it difficult to code, test, debug, and maintain large applications. That's why the developers of large web sites commonly use the *MVC (Model-View-Controller) design pattern*.

The MVC design pattern

The MVC pattern works by breaking an application into component parts. Figure 24-1 presents a diagram that shows the components of the MVC pattern and how they work together.

The *model* is in charge of data. Specifically, it gets and updates the data in a data store. It applies business rules to the data. And it validates data entered by the user.

The *view* is in charge of the user interface. Specifically, it creates the HTML that the application will send to the browser in response to the browser's HTTP request.

The *controller* is in charge of coordinating the model and the view. Specifically, it receives the HTTP request from the browser, decides what data to get from the model, and then sends the data from the model to the appropriate view.

The *view model* is an optional component in charge of transferring the data retrieved by the controller to the view. View models usually consist only of properties, like the ones in data transfer objects. Although view models aren't required, they are widely used in ASP.NET MVC applications because they facilitate some of the data binding.

It's important to note that each component should stick to its own area of concern and be as independent as possible. For example, the model should retrieve and validate data but it shouldn't have anything to do with displaying it. Similarly, the controller should move data between the model and the view but it shouldn't apply any business rules to it. Setting up the components this way makes them more testable, and it makes it easier to change a component without affecting other components.

This figure also lists the main benefits of the MVC design pattern. In brief, breaking an application into separate parts makes it easier to have different team members work on different parts, to swap out parts, and to test individual components. MVC also produces applications that work better with the stateless HTTP protocol.

The MVC design pattern

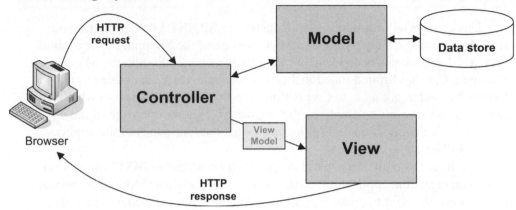

The MVC Components

- The *Model-View-Controller (MVC) design pattern* breaks web applications into their component parts so they are easier to code, test, and maintain.
- The *model* consists of the files that contain data access code, business logic code, and data validation code.
- The *view* consists of the files that create the HTML for the user interface and return a response to the user.
- The *controller* consists of the files that receive requests from the user, get the appropriate data from the model, and provide that data to the view.
- The *view model* is an optional component that consists of files whose only job is to transfer data from the controller to the view. Technically, this isn't part of the MVC pattern, but view models are often used with ASP.NET MVC.

The benefits of MVC

- The MVC structure leads to better *separation of concerns*. For instance, the designers can work with the views and the developers can work with the controllers.
- Even if you are both designer and developer, with MVC you can more easily make changes. For example, if you change your data store from SQL Server to Oracle, you only have to change the model.
- The MVC structure can be more complex, because everything is broken into pieces. But if you follow specific conventions regarding what to name the pieces and where to put them, MVC frameworks will hook everything up for you. This means less code to write, and fewer configuration files to edit.
- The HTML produced by MVC frameworks is concise, which makes it easier to integrate with JavaScript libraries and can also improve page load performance.
- MVC works with the stateless nature of the web. This means that there's less overhead trying to replicate state, which can also improve performance.

Figure 24-1   An introduction to MVC

The Shopping Cart as an MVC application

This chapter will introduce you to the basic ASP.NET MVC concepts and skills by showing examples from an MVC version of the Shopping Cart application that this book has been using. To keep things simple, though, the MVC Shopping Cart has limited functionality. For example, the Order page has an Add to Cart button but not a Go to Cart button. And the Cart page displays what's in the cart but doesn't do anything else. Figure 24-2 shows one page of the Shopping Cart application and summarizes what the four pages of the application will illustrate.

This figure also gives a general procedure for creating an MVC application. First, you create the application itself. Then, you add a model. After your model is in place, you use it to create a controller. And after the controller is in place, you use it to create your view.

You repeat steps 2 through 4 of this procedure many times as you build an MVC application. For instance, when working on the Contact Us page, you'll first create the model that provides the contact information for the page. Next, you'll create the controller that retrieves the contact information in response to an HTTP request. Then, you'll create the view that displays the contact information in the browser.

As you read this chapter, don't worry if you find yourself struggling to follow some of the examples. Since an ASP.NET MVC application is so different from a Web Forms application, it takes time to grasp the concepts. What you should have by the end of the chapter is some exposure to the basics, some code examples to refer to, and a jumping off point for further study.

The Shopping Cart as an MVC application

The pages in the Cart application and the concepts they illustrate

Page	Illustrates
Home	A simple controller and a simple view.
Contact Us	A controller that uses a view model, and a strongly-typed view.
Order	Controls in a view, controllers that handle both GET and POST requests, and how to work with the data posted to the server.
Cart	Models and view models, and how to work with model binding.

A procedure for creating an MVC application

1. Create the application.
2. Create the model.
3. Create the controller.
4. Create the views.

Description

- This chapter uses an MVC version of the Shopping Cart application to illustrate ASP.NET MVC. This is a simplified version of the Web Forms application that has been used throughout this book.

Figure 24-2   The Shopping Cart as an MVC application

An introduction to ASP.NET MVC

ASP.NET MVC is Microsoft's MVC framework. Since it is built on ASP.NET, many of the objects that you've worked with in Web Forms, such as the session state object and the response object, are also available in MVC. But how an MVC application is organized and how it handles HTTP requests is completely different.

In the topics that follow, you'll learn to start a new MVC application and work with its files and folders. You'll learn about view engines and routing. And you'll learn how to add models, views, and controllers to your project.

How to start an ASP.NET MVC application

Figure 24-3 shows how to start a new MVC web application. As with Web Forms, there are many templates available for MVC applications. Most of the time, you'll use the Basic template, so that's what is used in this chapter. It's a good idea, though, to experiment with some of the other templates, since they can be a good source of sample code.

When you start an MVC application, you should note the Create a Unit Test Project check box in the New ASP.NET MVC 4 Project dialog box. Since this is an introductory chapter, it doesn't cover the more advanced subject of unit testing. But unit testing is an important advantage of the MVC framework, so you'll want to learn more about it later. When you're ready, the MSDN documentation contains several tutorials about creating unit tests for ASP.NET MVC applications and is a good overall resource.

The dialog boxes for starting an ASP.NET MVC application

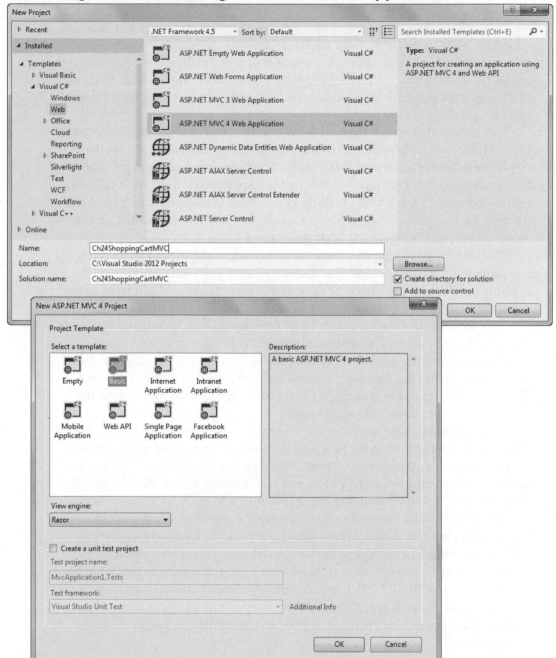

How to start an MVC application

- Use FILE→New→Project to open the New Project dialog box. Then, select Visual C#→Web→ASP.NET MVC 4 Web Application, name the project, and click OK.

- In the New ASP.NET MVC 4 Project dialog box, select Basic, leave the View engine set to Razor, and click OK.

Figure 24-3   How to start an ASP.NET MVC application

The folders and files for a new MVC application

Figure 24-4 shows the folders and files that are produced when you start an ASP.NET MVC application from the Basic template. Although the number of folders and files can seem overwhelming at first, you should realize that the large number of folders has to do with the structure of an MVC application. Since an MVC application is broken into components, there needs to be separate folders and files for these components.

You should also realize that you usually won't need to touch most of these files or folders. For example, the Global.asax file automatically contains the Application_Start code that an MVC application requires, and the App_Start folder automatically contains the code that the Application_Start code calls. So, unless you want to work with bundling as described below, you won't need to do anything here. Similarly, the various .config files are already set up, so you usually won't need to make any changes to them.

The table in this figure describes the main folders and files in more detail, including their default content. You'll spend most of your time working with the Models, Controllers, Views, Scripts, and Content folders. You'll learn more about the first three in a moment, and more about the last two right now.

The Scripts folder contains JavaScript files. By default, it contains the files used by the jQuery, knockout, and modernizr JavaScript libraries, and MVC uses a *bundling framework* to add these scripts to your application. This framework bundles the files together, and serves them to the browser as one file. The BundleConfig.cs file in the App_Start folder contains the instructions that specify which files to include in a bundle.

You'll probably want to put your own scripts in the Scripts folder too. Then, you can add your scripts to the bundling instructions, or you can use traditional script elements to identify your scripts. Although this chapter doesn't show how to work with the BundleConfig.cs file, you can probably figure out how to add your own scripts to it by studying the default instructions.

The Content folder contains style sheets and image files. By default, it contains a style sheet called Site.css with some basic styles for the application, and a folder called themes that contains the style sheets and images used by jQuery UI. You'll probably want to place your own style sheets in this folder too.

Here again, ASP.NET MVC bundles the style sheets and the bundling instructions are in the BundleConfig.cs file. So, you can add your own style sheets to the bundling instructions, or you can use traditional link elements to identify them.

The folders and files produced by the MVC Basic template

The main folders and files

Folder/File	Contains
App_Data folder	Data files such as database or XML files.
App_Start folder	The code called on application startup. By default, it contains code that initializes an error handling filter, bundles the default JavaScript and CSS files, and sets up default Web API and MVC routing.
Content folder	The style sheet files and images. By default, it contains a style sheet called Site.css and and a themes folder containing files used by jQuery UI.
Controllers folder	The controller files.
Models folder	The model files.
Scripts folder	The JavaScript files. By default, it contains files for several JavaScript libraries.
Views folder	The view files. By default, it contains a Shared folder with a layout and error view, a ViewStart view, and a web.config file.
Global.asax file	The application-level event handlers. By default, its Application_Start method calls code in the App_Start folder.
.config files	The configuration files for NuGet packages and the application.

Description

- Most of the time, you will only need to work with the folders containing models, views, controllers, scripts, and styles.

Figure 24-4   The folders and files produced by the MVC Basic template

The Razor view engine and syntax

When you're working with a dynamic web application, you need some way to combine dynamic data with the static HTML of the page and render it all to the browser. The mechanism that does this is called the view engine.

ASP.NET Web Forms applications use the *ASPX view engine*. This engine uses HTML, server controls, and inline data binding that looks like this:

```
<h3>Hello <%=name %>, the year is <%= DateTime.Now.Year %></h3>
```

The ASPX view engine then puts it all together and sends it to the browser as HTML.

When ASP.NET MVC first came out, it also used the ASPX view engine. In fact, this engine is still available from the View Engine drop-down list when you create a new MVC application. However, many developers found its inline data binding syntax cumbersome and hard to read.

In response, Microsoft came out with the *Razor view engine*, which has a simpler data binding syntax. For example, the Razor version of the ASPX data binding example above looks like this:

```
<h3>Hello @name, the year is @DateTime.Now.Year</h3>
```

Figure 24-5 contains several examples of the Razor data binding syntax.

How to work with routing

Figure 24-5 also presents the RegisterRoutes method of the RouteConfig.cs file. This file is located in the App_Start folder, and it is created by default when you start a new ASP.NET MVC web application. Usually, this is all that you need, so you won't have to create your own routes. But here's what's going on in the RegisterRoutes method.

The first line of the RegisterRoutes method tells the *routing framework* to ignore requests for .axd files. This is to keep routing from interfering with the features of ASP.NET that use .axd extensions.

The next line of the RegisterRoutes method calls the MapRoute method to set up the default route for the application. This method has three parameters, and the name parameter simply names the route.

The url parameter sets the *route pattern* of {controller}/{action}/{id}. This parameter tells the routing framework that when it sees a URL like http://halloweenstore.com/Order/Index/rat01, "Order" is the name of the controller, "Index" is the name of the controller's action method, and "rat01" is a URL parameter named "id". The routing framework will then look in the Controllers folder for a controller called OrderController, and pass it the request.

The defaults parameter sets default values for the route. The default values in this example mean that a URL of http://halloweenstore.com will be sent to the Index action method of the HomeController controller, and that the id parameter is optional.

ASP.NET MVC view engines

- *View engines* are modules that take the data sent by the controller, combine it with the HTML in the view, and render it to the browser. Since the view engine for ASP.NET MVC is designed to be easily replaced, third-party view engines are available, and some developers create custom view engines.

- The default view engine for ASP.NET MVC used to be the same as for ASP.NET Web Forms, and that view engine is still available when you create an MVC application.

The Razor view engine

- In 2010, Microsoft developed a new view engine called Razor, which is now the default view engine for ASP.NET MVC. The *Razor view engine* has a simple syntax that allows developers to easily *bind* data from the controller to the HTML in the view.

Razor syntax examples

```
<p id="copyright">&copy; @DateTime.Now.Year</p>

@*This is a comment in the markup*@
<p>@foreach (string url in Model.SocialMediaUrls) {
        <a href="@url" target="_blank">@url</a><br />
   }
</p>

@{
    //And this is a comment inside a code block
    ViewBag.Title = "Shopping Cart";
    string day = DateTime.Now.DayOfWeek.ToString();
}
```

The default RegisterRoutes method in the RouteConfig.cs file

```
public static void RegisterRoutes(RouteCollection routes)
{
    routes.IgnoreRoute("{resource}.axd/{*pathInfo}");

    routes.MapRoute(
        name: "Default",
        url: "{controller}/{action}/{id}",
        defaults: new { controller = "Home", action = "Index",
            id = UrlParameter.Optional }
    );
}
```

Description

- The Razor view engine and the default *routing* are available when you create an ASP.NET MVC application, with no configuration necessary.

- The Razor view engine provides IntelliSense support, and web files that use Razor have a .cshtml file extension, rather than .aspx.

Figure 24-5   The Razor view engine and routing in ASP.NET MVC

How to create a model

A *model* contains the code that deals with data. To illustrate, figure 24-6 shows the expanded Models folder for the Shopping Cart MVC application. It contains a DataAccess folder that contains an Entity Data Model that was created by using the Entity Framework, although the data access methods could have been created by regular C#. The Models folder also contains a ViewModels folder that contains several view model files.

The model for an application has three main tasks. First, it gets and updates the data in the data store. Second, it applies business rules to the data. Third, it applies validation rules to the data.

Because a model can do so much, model files can get large. Then, it can be a good idea to break the files into smaller areas of responsibility. For example, in the Cart model in this figure, you could move the data access methods to a separate file called CartData.cs in the DataAccess folder.

The model files themselves are regular class files that use regular C# code. In fact, most of the code in the Cart model (not shown here) is similar to the App_Code class files of the Web Forms version of the cart application.

The *view model* files in the ViewModels folder are light-weight objects used to transfer data to the view. As mentioned earlier, these aren't required, but they're a good idea because they make many MVC tasks easier. This figure shows the complete Cart view model object, which consists of two properties.

Keep in mind that you don't need to have a one-to-one relationship between models and view models. For example, the Cart and Order pages each have a model and a view model, but the Contact page has a view model but no model. You also don't need to have a one-to-one relationship between the models or view models and the pages in the application. For example, there is a Product view model but there isn't a Products page.

Instead, you set up the model files in a way that makes sense for the data you're working with. In this application, both the Cart page and the Order page work with products, so it makes sense to have a Products view model that can be sent to their respective views.

Conversely, the Contact Us page displays data that doesn't change over time, so the application doesn't keep the data in a data store. Rather, it hard codes the data in a view model that contains read-only properties like Email and Phone. Because there's no need to retrieve Contact data from a data store, there's no need for a Contact model.

The Models subdirectory

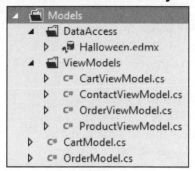

How to add a model

- Right-click the Models folder, select Add→Class, name the class, and click OK.

The Cart model

```
using Ch24ShoppingCartMVC.Models;

namespace Ch24ShoppingCartMVC.Models {
    public class CartModel {
        public CartViewModel GetCart(string id = "") {...}
        public bool AddToCart(CartViewModel model) {...}
        private ProductViewModel GetSelectedProduct(string id) {...}

        //Data Access methods
        private List<ProductViewModel> GetCartFromDataStore() {...}
        private bool AddItemToDataStore(CartViewModel model) {...}
    }
}
```

The Cart view model

```
using Ch24ShoppingCartMVC.Models;

namespace Ch24ShoppingCartMVC.Models {
    public class CartViewModel {
        public List<ProductViewModel> Cart { get; set; }
        public ProductViewModel AddedProduct { get; set; }
    }
}
```

Description

- The *model* contains the code that deals with data.
- A model is composed of regular class files. Generally, you'll follow some kind of naming convention for these files, as shown above, but this isn't required.
- You can use as many class files in your model as you need, and you can divide your model into smaller sections, such as sections for data access code and view models.
- View models aren't required, but if you use them, they should contain only what is needed by the view.

Figure 24-6   How to create a model

How to create a controller

A *controller* contains the code that handles HTTP requests from the browser. Figure 24-7 shows the Controllers folder for the Shopping Cart MVC application and the process for adding a new controller to it. The Controllers folder in this example contains three controller files.

The MVC framework expects a controller to be named in a specific way. It should start with the name you want to appear in the URL, like "Home" or "Cart", and it should end with "Controller". If you follow this naming convention, your controllers will be hooked up to the default routes shown in figure 24-5 without any further effort.

There are three main tasks that a controller does to handle an HTTP request: (1) identify the type of HTTP request it has received; (2) get the data needed for the request; and (3) send that data to the appropriate view. A controller does these tasks with *action methods*. For instance, the Home controller in this figure contains two action methods, Index and Contact. Each of these methods handles HTTP GET requests. The Index method loads hard-coded data, and the Contact method gets data from a view model.

Action methods are regular class methods that return ActionResult objects derived from the ActionResult base class. For example, the Index and Contact methods each return a ViewResult object. The MVC framework knows that an action method that returns a ViewResult object is going to send data to a view. Similarly, it knows that an action method that returns a RedirectToRouteResult object is going to redirect to another controller. The MVC framework uses the data in these objects to do the appropriate action.

It's important to note that you don't have to have a controller file for every page. In the Shopping Cart MVC application, for instance, there are four pages but only three controllers. This is because the Home controller handles requests for both the Home page and the Contact Us page. The Home page is handled by the Index action method, and the Contact Us page is handled by the Contact action method.

It's also common to have two action methods in a controller with the same name, such as two Index action methods. When this happens, you need to add ActionMethodSelectorAttributes, like [HttpGet] or [HttpPost]. This tells the controller which action method to use when the page loads for the first time, and which one to use when the page posts back. This is similar to a Page.IsPostBack test in Web Forms. Although you don't have to use ActionMethodSelectorAttributes on all action methods, it's a good idea to use them anyway to reduce the chance of error.

Last, it's important to know that controllers are only in charge of coordinating and transferring. They shouldn't apply any business or validation logic. A common phrase that can help you keep this in mind is that you should have "fat" models and "skinny" controllers.

The Controllers subdirectory and the Add Controller dialog box

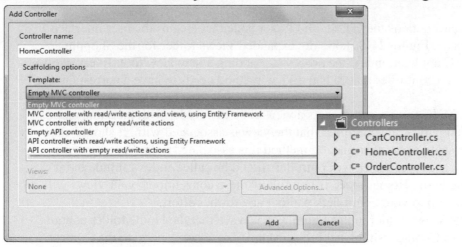

How to add a controller

- Right-click the Controllers folder and select Add→Controller. In the Add Controller dialog box, select a template and click Add.

The Home controller

```
namespace Ch24ShoppingCartMVC.Controllers {
    public class HomeController : Controller
    {
        [HttpGet]
        public ViewResult Index() {
            ViewBag.HeaderText = "Welcome to the Halloween Store";
            ViewData["FooterText"] = "Where every day is Halloween!";
            return View();
        }
        [HttpGet]
        public ViewResult Contact() {
            ContactViewModel model = new ContactViewModel();
            return View(model);
        }
    }
}
```

Description

- *Controllers* do follow a naming convention, so you must name them carefully. The part of the name before "Controller" is what will appear in your friendly URLs.
- Controllers contain *action methods* that perform actions in response to HTTP requests. The names of the actions also appear in your URLs.
- Action methods return objects derived from the ActionResult class, including ViewResult objects and RedirectToRouteResult objects. Controllers pass data to the view using the ViewData or ViewBag objects, or with the View method.

Figure 24-7   How to create a controller

How to create a view

A *view* contains the HTML and Razor code that creates the user interface for the page. Figure 24-8 shows the expanded Views folder for the Shopping Cart MVC application and the process for adding a new view to it. Every action method in a controller that calls the View method needs to have a corresponding view.

The MVC framework expects a view to be in a folder with the same name as the first part of the controller that the view is associated with. It should also have the same name as the action method it is associated with. So, a view for the Index action of the HomeController should be called Index.cshtml, and it should be in the Home folder. If you follow these conventions, your views will be hooked up to your controllers without any further effort.

In the Views folder in this figure, you can see that the Home folder contains files called Contact.cshtml and Index.cshtml. These correspond to the Contact and Index action methods of the HomeController that you saw in the last figure. Although there are several ways to add views to the Views folder, the easiest way to make sure your views follow the proper conventions is to use the procedure in this figure. This procedure was used to add the Cart, Home, and Order folders to the application.

In contrast, the Shared folder, _ViewStart.cshtml file, and Web.config file were added by default when the application was created. You'll learn more about working with the _ViewStart view and the contents of the Shared folder later. The Web.config file contains configuration information related to the MVC framework, and you probably won't need to edit it.

When you create a view, you can create a regular view or a strongly-typed view. Strongly-typed views let you take advantage of IntelliSense when working with data sent from the controller, and you'll learn more about them in a minute.

You can also choose a scaffold template or create a partial view. Although neither of these options is covered in this chapter, you might want to experiment with them, particularly the scaffolding options.

The Views subdirectory and the Add View dialog box

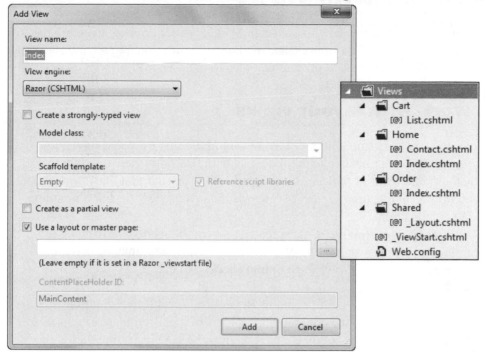

How to add a view to an application

- Right-click an action method in a controller, like the Index method in the previous figure, and select Add View.
- In the Add View dialog box, make sure that the view name matches the action method name, and that the Use a Layout or Master Page option is checked.
- If you want to create a strongly-typed view, check that option and select an object from the drop-down list. If the object you want isn't there, click Cancel, build the application using the BUILD→Build Solution command, and try again.
- Click Add. Then, Visual Studio will create a new view and place it in a subfolder of the Views folder that has the same name as the controller name.

Description

- You'll need to create a *view* for each controller action method that calls the View method. If you name the view correctly and put it in the right spot, the MVC framework will automatically hook it up to the action method. If you use the procedure above to create the view, Visual Studio takes care of this for you.
- The Scaffold template option in the AddView dialog box is a way to let Visual Studio create pre-designed views for specific purposes, like views that list items. This chapter doesn't cover the scaffolding options, but they're something you might want to experiment with.

Figure 24-8   How to create a view

How to work with views

At this point, you know how to create an MVC application, how to set up the model, view, and controller components, and how to retrieve data in a controller. The next step is to learn how to present that data to the user with views.

How to work with layout views

The *layout view* is stored in the _Layout.cshtml file that's created by default when you create an application using the Basic template. This view contains code that's shared by multiple views in an application, similar to a master page in a Web Forms application. Figure 24-9 shows the layout view for the Shopping Cart MVC application.

The _ViewStart.cshtml file is also created by default when you create an application. It contains a single line of code that tells any view that you create with the Use a Layout or Master Page option checked to use _Layout.cshtml as its layout view.

The layout view in this figure contains RenderBody and RenderSection methods that are similar to the content placeholders of a master page. The RenderBody method in the section element renders the HTML for the view.

The RenderSection method in the head element renders anything in the view that is within an @section css{} code block. The RenderSection methods in and below the footer element work the same way. You should know, though, that the view isn't required to have these code blocks, because the required parameter of each RenderSection method is set to false.

The layout view also contains several methods that link external style sheets and JavaScript files. The Styles.Render and Scripts.Render methods call the bundled scripts and styles that you learned about in figure 24-4. In addition, this layout view contains traditional script and link elements. This is how the Shopping Cart MVC application adds its own scripts and style sheets.

You'll notice that the Scripts.Render method appears at both the top of the page in the head element, and at the bottom of the page just after the closing footer tag. This is because it's good to place JavaScript files at the bottom of a page so they don't block rendering of the HTML. However, the modernizr library needs to be loaded in the head element in order for it to work properly with IE8 and earlier.

The layout view's menu links are rendered by HTML helpers. You'll learn about these shortly. Last, the viewport meta element at the top of the page isn't specific to ASP.NET MVC or Razor. Rather, this is a common way to make web sites work better with mobile devices.

The _Layout.cshtml file

```html
<!DOCTYPE html>
<html>
<head>
    <meta charset="utf-8" />
    <meta name="viewport" content="width=device-width" />
    <title>@ViewBag.Title</title>
    @Styles.Render("~/Content/css")
    @Scripts.Render("~/bundles/modernizr")
    <link href="~/Content/Main.css" rel="stylesheet" />
    @RenderSection("css", required: false)
</head>
<body>
    <header><img src="~/Content/Images/banner.jpg" alt="Store" /></header>
    <aside>
        <nav>
            <ul id="menu">
                <li>@Html.ActionLink("Home", "Index/", "Home")</li>
                <li>@Html.ActionLink("Order", "Index/", "Order")</li>
                <li>@Html.ActionLink("Cart", "List/", "Cart")</li>
                <li>@Html.ActionLink("Contact Us", "Contact/", "Home")</li>
            </ul>
        </nav>
    </aside>
    <section>
        @RenderBody()
    </section>
    <footer>
        @RenderSection("footer", required: false)
        <p id="copyright">
            &copy; @DateTime.Now.Year - My ASP.NET MVC Application</p>
    </footer>
    @Scripts.Render("~/bundles/jquery")
    <script src="~/Scripts/halloween.js" type="text/javascript"></script>
    @RenderSection("scripts", required: false)
</body>
</html>
```

Description

- The *layout view* is in the _Layout.cshtml file in the Shared view folder. This view is similar to a master page, and this file is automatically created when you use the Basic or Internet Application template.

- The _ViewStart.cshtml file in the Views folder is also created automatically, and it is similar to setting the master page for the application in the web.config file.

- The RenderBody and RenderSection Razor methods are similar to master page content placeholders.

- By default, the layout view contains several Styles.Render and Scripts.Render methods. These render the default styles and scripts in the Content and Scripts folders. You can also use traditional style and script elements in a layout view.

Figure 24-9   How to work with layout views

How to work with regular views

Figure 24-10 shows the Home page of the Shopping Cart MVC application, and the controller action method and view that produced it.

The Index action method in this figure returns a ViewResult object in response to an HTTP GET request. Because there are no other action methods named Index in the controller, you don't have to add the HttpGet attribute to the method. Including it, though, makes it clear when this action method will be called.

This action method loads string data into the ViewBag and ViewData objects. The ViewData object is a dictionary collection that stores data as key/value pairs. The key is a string data type and the value is stored as an object data type. The ViewBag object, by contrast, is a dynamic object. This means that you add properties to it on the fly, and it dynamically adds the properties and determines their data types. Under the covers, this object stores these properties in the ViewData dictionary and handles the type casting.

One thing to note about the Index action method is that it loads hard-coded strings as data. This is to keep the example simple, but in real life you wouldn't want to hard code data in a controller.

The Index.cshtml view file in this figure is located in the Home subfolder of the Views folder. That's because it's associated with the Index action method of the Home controller. As you learned earlier, naming the view this way and placing it in this location allows the MVC framework to hook it up with its controller.

This view starts with a block of Razor code that contains a ViewBag.Title property assignment. This code block and assignment are added by default when you create the view. You can also add any other code that you might use in your view to this code block. For instance, this example creates a string variable named day that holds the name of the current day of the week.

The view then adds a link to an external style sheet called Home.css that is located in the Content folder. It adds this link by using a Razor @section block. As you may recall from the last figure, anything within the @section code block will be rendered by the RenderSection method in the layout view that has the same name.

Next, the view works with the data sent by the action method of the controller. First, it adds the HeaderText property of the ViewBag object inside the h1 element. Then, it adds the FooterText property of the ViewData collection to the footer @section block. Note that the data from the ViewData needs to be cast, but the data from the ViewBag object doesn't. You should know, however, that you won't have IntelliSense support for either object.

This view also adds the day variable declared in the opening block to a div element. It does this using Razor's inline data binding.

A regular view: Home/Index

The HomeController Index action method

```
[HttpGet]
public ViewResult Index() {
    ViewBag.HeaderText = "Welcome to the Halloween Store";
    ViewData["FooterText"] = "Where every day is Halloween!";
    return View();
}
```

The Home/Index.cshtml view

```
@{
    ViewBag.Title = "Shopping Cart";
    string day = DateTime.Now.DayOfWeek.ToString();
}
@section css {
    <link href="~/Content/Home.css" rel="stylesheet" />
}
<h1>@ViewBag.HeaderText</h1>
<div>Thank you for visiting us this beautiful @day!</div>
@section footer {
    <p>@ViewData["FooterText"].ToString()</p>
}
```

Description

- The text you place in the ViewBag.Title object is added to the layout view's title element.

- Data in the ViewData object must be typecast. Data in the ViewBag object is dynamically typed and doesn't need to be cast. Neither has IntelliSense support.

- A Razor @section code block is rendered by a RenderSection method in the layout view that has the same name.

Figure 24-10   How to work with regular views

How to work with strongly-typed views

Figure 24-11 shows the Contact Us page of the Shopping Cart MVC application, and the controller action method and view that produced it. Like the Index action method in the previous figure, the Contact action method in this figure returns a ViewResult object in response to an HTTP GET request. Unlike the Index action method, the Contact action method doesn't use the ViewBag or ViewData objects to send data to the view.

Instead, the action method creates an instance of the ContactViewModel object. You may remember from the figure on models that the Contact view model contains contact information that's hard-coded in read-only properties like Email and Phone. If you need to work with hard-coded data like this, putting the data in a view model is better than hard coding it in the controller.

Once the action method has retrieved the data, it sends the data to the view by passing the Contact view model as a parameter to the View method. Objects that are passed in this way are available to the view through the view's Model property.

The Contact.cshtml view file in this figure is located in the Home subfolder of the Views folder because it is associated with the Contact action method of the Home controller. Again, this naming and placement is necessary for the MVC framework to hook the view up with its controller.

As mentioned above, the view's Model property contains the ContactViewModel object that is passed to the View method in the Contact action method. In a regular view, the Model property works like the ViewBag object in that you don't have to typecast its properties. However, you also don't get IntelliSense support.

What makes a *strongly-typed* view different from a regular view is the @model directive you see at the top of the view file in this figure. This directive identifies the type of the object in the Model property, which is what allows Visual Studio to provide IntelliSense support.

Most of the time, you'll make a view strongly-typed when you create it by checking the Create a Strongly-typed View option in the Add View dialog box. But you can also make a regular view strongly-typed by manually adding the @model directive. If you add the directive manually, though, be sure it is fully qualified as shown in this figure.

This view uses inline Razor data binding to add the properties of the ContactViewModel to the user interface. One of the read-only properties of the ContactViewModel is a collection of URLs for the Halloween store's social media sites. To display these, the view uses a block of Razor code and the foreach syntax to loop through the collection and display each URL within an anchor element.

A strongly-typed view: Home/Contact

The HomeController Contact action method

```
[HttpGet]
public ViewResult Contact() {
    ContactViewModel model = new ContactViewModel();
    return View(model);
}
```

The Home/Contact.cshtml view

```
@model Ch24ShoppingCartMVC.Models.ContactViewModel
@{
    ViewBag.Title = "Contact Us";
}
<h1>Contact Us</h1>
<p>Email: @Model.Email</p>
<p>Phone: @Model.Phone</p>
<p>Fax: @Model.Fax</p>
<p>Address: @Model.Address</p>
<p>@foreach (string url in Model.SocialMediaUrls) {
        <a href="@url" target="_blank">@url</a><br />
    }
</p>
```

Description

- The view's Model property contains the object that was passed as a parameter to the View method in the action method of the controller.

- The Model property is available to all views, and you can use it without typecasting the values. But you'll only get IntelliSense support with a *strongly-typed view*.

- The @model directive at the top of the page is what makes a view strongly-typed.

Figure 24-11   How to work with strongly-typed views

How to work with controls and postbacks

Now, you know how to send data from a controller to a view, and how to work with the data once it gets to the view. But the simple views you've seen so far only display data. In a real world MVC application, you also need to interact with users through controls on a form, and you need to be able to work with the form data once the page is posted to the server.

How to work with controls

In a Web Forms application, you use server controls to interact with users. But server controls aren't available in ASP.NET MVC. Instead, you can add HTML input and select elements to your view, as in the view shown in figure 24-12. This view produces the page you saw in figure 24-2.

The other alternative is to use some of the MVC *HTML helpers* that are summarized in the table in this figure. These helpers are similar to server controls, but they are lighter weight and there are fewer of them. They are easy to extend, though, so many developers create their own. Each of the helpers has several overloaded methods, and most have two versions, such as Html.Label and Html.LabelFor.

If you want the values entered in an HTML element to post back to the server, you need to place the element inside a form. But unlike Web Forms, you can have more than one form element on a page. For example, the view in this figure has two forms, one that posts to the Index action method of the Order controller, and one that posts to the List action method of the Cart controller. The first form is created with a traditional HTML form element, and the second one is created by using the Html.BeginForm helper. Here again, it's important to note that when you identify the controller to post to, you don't include the "Controller" part of the name.

You also need to make sure any element that is posting to the server has a name attribute. In this example, the select element in the first form has a name of "ddlProducts", the text box in the second form has a name of "txtQuantity", and the hidden input in the second form has a name of "hdnId". The first two elements also have an id property for working with CSS or JavaScript, but this attribute isn't necessary for posting.

In contrast, controls that aren't going to post to the server don't need to have a name attribute. For example, the label elements in this figure only display data, so they have ids for styling purposes but not names.

Many of the elements in this figure use Razor data binding to get their values. To facilitate that, a variable named product was added in the opening code block to make binding to the Model's SelectedProduct property easier.

Common HTML helpers

Html Helpers	Corresponding HTML
`Html.ActionLink`	`<a href="">Text</a>`
`Html.BeginForm`	`<form action="" method=""></form>`
`Html.Checkbox[For]`	`<input type="checkbox" />`
`Html.DropDownList[For]`	`<select></select>`
`Html.Hidden[For]`	`<input type="hidden" />`
`Html.Label[For]`	`<label for="" />`
`Html.Password[For]`	`<input type="password" />`
`Html.RadioButton[For]`	`<input type="radio" />`
`Html.TextArea[For]`	`<textarea></textarea>`
`Html.TextBox[For]`	`<input type="text" />`

Controls in the Order/Index.cshtml view

```
@model Ch24ShoppingCartMVC.Models.OrderViewModel
@{
    ViewBag.Title = "Order Page";
    var product = Model.SelectedProduct;
}
@section css {
    <link href="~/Content/Order.css" rel="stylesheet" />
}
<form id="frmDropDown" action="/Order/Index/" method="post">
    <h1>Halloween Store Order Page</h1>
    <label>Please select a product </label>
    <select id="ddlProducts" name="ddlProducts" class="autoPostBack">
        @foreach (var item in @Model.ProductsList) {
            <option value="@item.Value" selected="@item.Selected">
                    @item.Text</option>
        }
    </select>
</form>

@using (Html.BeginForm("List", "Cart", FormMethod.Post,
        new { id = "frmCart" })) {
    <div id="productData">
        <label id="lblName">@product.Name</label>
        @Html.Label("", @product.ShortDescription,
                    new { id = "lblShortDescription" })
        <label id="lblLongDescription">@product.LongDescription</label>
        <label id="lblUnitPrice">@product.UnitPrice.ToString("c2")
        </label>
        <label id="lblQuantity">Quantity </label>
        <input id="txtQuantity" name="txtQuantity" type="text"
            value="@product.Quantity" />
        <input type="hidden" name="hdnId" value="@product.ProductID" />
        <br />
        <input type="submit" id="btnAdd" value="Add to Cart" />
    </div>
    <img src="~/Content/Images/Products/@product.ImageFile" alt="" />
}
```

Figure 24-12   How to work with controls

How to work with redirection

If your web site has more than one page, you'll need to add navigation links to your pages. You'll also need to redirect in code, such as after processing a postback.

To provide navigation links, you can use traditional HTML anchor elements or the Html.ActionLink helper shown in figure 24-13. A benefit of using the helper is that you don't need to worry about getting the relative URL right. Instead, you provide the name of the controller and the name of the action method and the MVC routing framework takes care of the rest. This is also a benefit of using the Html.BeginForm helper.

This figure shows how to create a navigation link using the Html.ActionLink method, and it provides comments that explain each of the parameters sent to the method. The route arguments parameter is where you include any URL parameters. The parameter in this figure is adding a value for the id part of the default routing pattern.

The htmlArguments parameter is how you can add attributes to the anchor element that the Html.ActionLink helper produces. The parameter in this figure is adding a class="link" attribute.

To redirect in code, you use one of the Redirect methods shown in the table in this figure. This is similar to using the Response.Redirect method in a Web Forms application, and, in fact, the MVC methods use the Response.Redirect method under the covers. Each of the MVC methods has two versions. The Redirect version returns a response status code of 302 Found to the browser, and the RedirectPermanent version returns a status code of 301 Moved Permanently.

For redirecting between controllers, you'll use the RedirectToAction method most of the time. The parameter for the controller name is optional if you are redirecting to an action method in the same controller, but it's usually best to include it so it's clear what the code is doing.

When a form is submitted, ASP.NET MVC applications commonly use the *PRG (Post-Redirect-Get) pattern*. This is to avoid the back-button and refresh problems described in chapter 20, and to separate the POST responsibility of sending data to the server from the GET responsibility of retrieving data from the server.

This figure shows an example of the PRG pattern in the Cart controller. Here, the POST List action method adds an item to the cart and then redirects to the GET List action method to display the cart. Since the POST method retrieves the cart object as part of its processing, it sends it along to the GET method in the TempData object. This is similar to using session state, and the TempData object actually uses session state under the covers. The difference is that the data in the TempData object is only stored until the next request is received.

Redirection in a view using the Html.ActionLink helper method

```
@Html.ActionLink(Model.Name,        // link text
    "Index",                        // action method
    "Order",                        // controller name
    new { id = Model.ProductID },   // route arguments
    new { @class = "link" }         // htmlArguments...if none, use null
)
```

Redirection in a controller using the Redirect methods

Method	Description
Redirect[Permanent]()	Requires a full URL. Most often used for external URLs.
RedirectToRoute[Permanent]()	Requires a full RouteDictionary object.
RedirectToAction[Permanent]()	Requires an action method name. Has overloads.

Three examples of redirection in controllers

```
[HttpGet]
public RedirectResult Index() {
    return Redirect ("http://www.murach.com");
}
[HttpPost]
public RedirectToRouteResult Index(OrderViewModel order) {
    return RedirectToRoute(
        Url.RouteUrl(new { controller = "Order", action = "Index" }));
}
[HttpGet]
public ActionResult Index(string id) {
    if (id == null)
        return RedirectToAction("Index", "Order");
    else {
        //code to get product by id goes here
        return View(product);
    }
}
```

The Post-Redirect-Get pattern in a controller

```
[HttpGet]
public ViewResult List() {
    CartViewModel cart = (CartViewModel)TempData["cart"];
    Return View(cart);
}
[HttpPost]
public RedirectToRouteResult List(OrderViewModel order) {
    //code to add order and get cart goes here
    TempData["cart"] = cart;
    return RedirectToAction("List", "Cart");
}
```

Description

- The *PRG (Post-Redirect-Get) pattern* is recommended with ASP.NET MVC. You can pass data from the POST action to the GET action using the TempData object.

Figure 24-13   How to work with redirection

How to add AutoPostBack functionality with jQuery

A handy feature of ASP.NET Web Forms is that you can set the AutoPostBack attribute of controls like drop-down lists and check boxes to True. That makes those controls initiate a postback when their value changes. Although this functionality isn't available with ASP.NET MVC, you can easily add it using jQuery as shown in figure 24-14. With this code in place, all you need to do to add AutoPostBack functionality to your controls is add a class attribute with its value set to "autoPostBack".

How to work with the FormCollection object

To help you work with the data that's posted back to the server, ASP.NET MVC stores the data in a FormCollection object. This is a NameValueCollection object that stores values as key/value pairs. The key for each key/value pair is the element's name.

To illustrate, figure 24-14 shows the Order controller. This controller has two Index action methods, one that handles POST requests and one that handles GET requests. As you saw earlier, the corresponding Order view contains a form that posts to Order/Index. Within the form is a select element with a name attribute of "ddlProducts" and a class attribute of "autoPostBack". This means that the form posts to the server each time the value of the select element changes, and the selected value is included in the FormCollection object.

In this example, the POST Index action method retrieves the selected value from the FormCollection object, which is returned as a string. Then, it initiates the PRG pattern by redirecting to the GET Index action. To do that, it uses the RedirectToAction method and passes it the name of the action method, the name of the controller, and the select value as the id URL parameter.

Although it doesn't use the FormCollection object, it's worth taking a minute to look at how the GET Index action method works. First, it checks the TempData object for a SelectList object called products. If it's not there, it gets a list of products from the Order model and creates a new SelectList object by sending in the list, the name of the value field, the name of the display field, and the id of the selected product.

Then, it checks for the id URL parameter. If there isn't one, it gets the id of the first item in the SelectList object, saves the SelectList object in the TempData object so it doesn't have to build it again, and then redirects to itself using the RedirectToAction method and the first item's id. This is for situations when someone enters the URL in the browser but leaves out the parameter.

If there is an id parameter, it uses it to get product data from the Order model, sets a default value for the Quantity property, loads the products list, and sends it all to the view. Because the action method can return either a ViewResult or a RedirectToRouteResult, it is declared as returning the base ActionResult.

How to add AutoPostback functionality with jQuery

In your Javascript file

```
$(document).ready(function () {
    $('.autoPostBack').change(function () {
        $(this).closest('form').submit();
    });
});
```

In your view

```
<select id="ddlProducts" name="ddlProducts" class="autoPostBack">
```

Working with the FormCollection object in the Order controller

```
namespace Ch24ShoppingCartMVC.Controllers {
    public class OrderController : Controller
    {
        private OrderModel order = new OrderModel();
        [HttpGet]
        public ActionResult Index(string id) {
            //get list for drop down from temp data or order
            SelectList products = (SelectList)TempData["products"];
            if (products == null) {
                var list = order.GetProductsList();
                products = new SelectList(
                                list, "ProductId", "Name", id);
            }
            //if no URL parameter, get first product and refresh
            if (string.IsNullOrEmpty(id)) {
                id = products.ElementAt(0).Value;
                TempData["products"] = products;
                return RedirectToAction("Index", "Order", new { id });
            }
            else { //get selected product and return it to the view
                OrderViewModel model = order.GetOrderInfo(id);
                model.SelectedProduct.Quantity = 1; //default value
                model.ProductsList = products;
                return View(model);
            }
        }

        [HttpPost] //post back - get selected ddl value and refresh
        public RedirectToRouteResult Index(FormCollection collection) {
            string pID = collection["ddlProducts"];
            return RedirectToAction("Index", "Order", new { id = pID });
        }
    }
}
```

Description

- The FormCollection object is a name/value collection object. It contains the string values of the input and select elements of a form that has been posted to the server.

- To be in the FormCollection object, an element must have a name attribute.

Figure 24-14   How to add AutoPostBack functionality and work with the FormCollection object

How to work with model binding

In the last figure, you learned how to work with data posted to the server by retrieving it from the FormCollection object. But there are two problems with that approach. First, you have to remember the names of the controls in the view and manually type the names in the controller. This requires switching between the two files and can also introduce errors. Second, it means your controller needs to know details about your view, which makes them more tightly coupled than you want.

The solution to these problems is to use *model binding*. You can think of model binding as making your controller's POST action method strongly-typed. Here's how to set it up.

First, in your view, you bind the controls to the model using Html For helpers. For instance, figure 24-15 shows the Quantity text box and the ProductID hidden field of the Order/Index view, rewritten to use the Html.TextBoxFor and Html.HiddenFor helpers.

Unfortunately, the syntax for a For helper can be hard to follow because the first parameter is a Lambda expression. In the Lambda expressions in this example, "m" represents the view's Model property, so the expression is telling the helper which property of the model to bind to. This means that the Html.TextBoxFor helper is binding the textbox to the Quantity property of the Model's SelectedProduct property, and the Html.HiddenFor helper is binding the hidden field to the ProductID property of the SelectedProduct property.

Then, in the POST action method in the controller, you change the object passed to the method from the FormCollection object to the type of the view's Model property. In this example, the Cart controller uses the POST List action method to accept an OrderViewModel object rather than a FormCollection object.

Making these two adjustments means that when your form posts to the server, the action method is passed a strongly-typed object, and you can use IntelliSense to work with the data sent from the form.

Once again, it's worth taking the time to look at the rest of the Cart controller. Here, the POST List action method receives data posted from the form, uses it to add a product to the cart, and then implements the PRG pattern by redirecting to the GET List action method. But first, it stores the cart in the TempData object.

The GET List action method first checks the TempData object for a CartViewModel object called cart. If it isn't there, it uses the Cart model to retrieve the cart view model object. Then, it sends the cart view model to the view.

There is also a GET Index action method that does nothing but redirect to the GET List action method. This is because the main GET action method for this controller is called List instead of Index. Although this name was chosen to make the URL more descriptive (Cart/List), if users navigate to just Cart/, they will get 404 File Not Found errors. However, adding an Index action method that redirects to List fixes this problem.

The Quantity textbox and ProductID hidden field of the Order/Index view, after it has been revised for model binding

```
@Html.TextBoxFor(m => m.SelectedProduct.Quantity,
    new { id = "txtQuantity" })
@Html.HiddenFor(m => m.SelectedProduct.ProductID)
```

Working with model binding in the Cart controller

```
namespace Ch24ShoppingCartMVC.Controllers {
    public class CartController : Controller
    {
        private CartModel cart = new CartModel();

        [HttpGet]
        public RedirectToRouteResult Index() {
            return RedirectToAction("List", "Cart");
        }
        [HttpGet]
        public ViewResult List() {
            CartViewModel model = (CartViewModel)TempData["cart"];
            if (model == null) model = cart.GetCart();
            return View(model);
        }
        [HttpPost]
        public RedirectToRouteResult List(OrderViewModel order) {
            CartViewModel model = cart.GetCart(
                                order.SelectedProduct.ProductID);
            model.AddedProduct.Quantity =
                                order.SelectedProduct.Quantity;
            cart.AddToCart(model);
            TempData["cart"] = model;
            return RedirectToAction("List", "Cart");
        }
    }
}
```

Description

- When working with the FormCollection object, you need to remember the names of the view's controls. This can lead to typos and other errors.

- *Model binding* lets you post the view model of a strongly-typed view directly to the controller and then work with the view model instead.

- Model binding provides IntelliSense support when working with data posted from the view, and also keeps your controller from having to know anything about how your view is constructed.

- The easiest way to set up model binding is to use the Html For helpers in your view. In the example above, the Html.TextBoxFor and Html.HiddenFor helpers replace the html input elements shown in the second form in figure 24-12.

- Both the textbox and the hidden field will have the name attributes generated by the HTML helpers. You can view the page source code in the browser to see the HTML produced by these helpers.

Figure 24-15   How to work with model binding

Perspective

Now that you've completed this chapter, you can start to appreciate the striking differences between Web Forms and MVC development. If you experiment with the downloadable application for this chapter, you will get an even better idea of how MVC works. Then, you can decide whether you want to learn more about MVC and maybe use it for your own applications.

Terms

MVC (Model-View-Controller) design pattern	inline data binding
model	Razor view engine
view	routing framework
controller	route pattern
view model	action method
bundling framework	layout view
ASP.NET MVC	strongly-typed view
view engine	HTML helper
ASPX view engine	PRG (Post-Redirect-Get) pattern
	model binding

Summary

- The *MVC (Model-View-Controller) design pattern* provides a modular structure that makes applications easier to test and maintain.

- The *model* handles data, the *view* handles the user interface, and the *controller* handles HTTP requests and coordinates the model and the view. The optional *view model* transfers data from the controller to the view and is widely used in ASP.NET MVC applications.

- ASP.NET MVC uses the *Razor view engine* to add dynamic data to the static HMTL in a view, and a *routing framework* to direct HTTP requests to the correct controller.

- The files in the Models and Controllers folders are regular class files. The model files handle data, including applying business and validation rules. The controller files handle HTTP requests by using *action methods*. The goal is to have "fat" models and "skinny" controllers.

- The files in the Views folder produce the HTML for the pages. These files should have the same name as their associated action method, should be in a folder with the same name as their associated controller, and can be *strong-typed*. The *layout view* functions as a master page for other views.

- *HTML helpers* are used to add controls to a view. Controls must have a name attribute and be in a form element. You can work with data posted to the server through the FormCollection object or with *model binding*.

- ASP.NET MVC applications commonly implement the *PRG (Post-Redirect-Get) pattern* when handling postbacks.

Appendix A

How to install and use the software and downloadable files

To develop ASP.NET 4.5 applications, you need to have Visual Studio 2012 or Visual Studio Express 2012 for Web installed on your PC. Both of these products include a new edition of IIS called IIS Express that you can use to run and test your applications. They also include a new edition of SQL Server called SQL Server Express LocalDB that you can use with databases on your local computer.

This appendix describes how to install Visual Studio 2012 or Visual Studio Express 2012 for Web. In addition, it describes what you need to do to use the database for this book, and it describes how to set up IIS on your local computer in case you want to deploy your applications to that server. But first, it describes the files for this book that are available for download from our web site and shows you how to download, install, and use them.

Please note that if you just want to develop and test ASP.NET applications on your own computer, you only need to install Visual Studio 2012 or Visual Studio Express 2012 for Web, along with our downloadable files. You don't need to do separate installs for SQL Server Express or IIS.

How to download and install the files for this book

Throughout this book, you'll see complete applications that illustrate the material presented in each chapter. To help you understand how these applications work, you can download the source code and database for these applications from our web site at www.murach.com. Then, you can open and run them in Visual Studio. These files come in a single download, as summarized in figure A-1. This figure also describes how you download and install these files.

When you download the single install file and execute it, it will install all of the files for this book in the Murach\aspnet45_cs directory on your C drive. Within this directory, you'll find a directory named book_applications that contains all the applications in this book. You can open these applications in Visual Studio and run them using IIS Express as described in this figure.

The download also includes the files for the Halloween database that's used throughout the book. You can use these files with SQL Server 2012 Express LocalDB, which comes with Visual Studio 2012. If you want to use SQL Server 2012 Express instead of LocalDB, you'll need to install SQL Server Express on your computer, and you'll need to create the Halloween database. You'll learn how to do that in figure A-3.

To help you practice the skills you'll learn in this book, we've included exercises at the ends of most of the chapters. We also provide starting points for many of these exercises in the C:\Murach\aspnet45_cs\exercise_starts directory. When you execute the setup file, the contents of this directory are copied to the C:\aspnet45_cs directory (creating this directory if necessary). This makes it easy to locate the exercise starts as you work through the exercises.

What the downloadable files for this book contain

- The source code for all of the applications presented in this book
- The starting points for the exercises in this book
- The solutions for the exercises in this book
- The Halloween database used by the applications and exercises

How to download and install the files for this book

1. Go to www.murach.com, and go to the page for *Murach's ASP.NET 4.5 Web Programming with C# 2012*.
2. Click on the link for "FREE download of the book applications." Then, download "All book files." This will download one file named acs5_allfiles.exe to your C drive.
3. Use Windows Explorer to find the downloaded file on your C drive. Then, double-click on this file and respond to the dialog boxes that follow. This installs the files in directories that start with C:\Murach\aspnet45_cs.

How to use IIS Express to run a downloaded application

- Start Visual Studio and use the FILE→Open→Web Site command to display the Open Web Site dialog box.
- Click on File System, navigate to and select the folder for the web site, and click the Open button.
- In the Solution Explorer, right-click the project and choose Use IIS Express. Then, click Yes in the first dialog box that's displayed and OK in the second dialog box.
- Right-click the starting page for the application and select Set As Start Page.

How to prepare your system for using the SQL Server database

- If you will be using SQL Server 2012 Express LocalDB, no preparation is required. The files for the Halloween database are included in the App_Data folder of each application that uses the database.
- If you will be using SQL Server 2012 Express, you will need to install this product and then run the batch file we provide to create the database and attach it to the database server as described in figure A-3.

How your system is prepared for doing the exercises

- Some of the exercises have you start from existing applications. The source code for these applications is in the C:\Murach\aspnet45_cs\exercise_starts directory. After the setup file installs the files in the download, it runs a batch file named exercise_starts_setup.bat that copies the contents of the exercise_starts directory to the C:\aspnet45_cs directory. Then, you can find all of the starting points for the exercises in directories like C:\aspnet45_cs\Ex01FutureValue and C:\aspnet45_cs\Ex04Cart.

Figure A-1   How to download and install the files for this book

How to install Visual Studio 2012

If you've installed Windows applications before, you shouldn't have any trouble installing Visual Studio 2012. You simply insert the DVD and the setup program starts automatically. This setup program will lead you through the steps for installing Visual Studio as summarized in figure A-2.

After you accept the license terms and click the Next button on the first page of the setup program, the program lets you select the optional features you want to install. This includes features like Blend for Visual Studio, LightSwitch, and developer tools for Microsoft Office, Microsoft SharePoint, and Microsoft Web. If you're sure you won't need some of these features, you can uncheck them. Then, when you click the Install button, all the features you selected, along with the .NET Framework 4.5, IIS Express, and SQL Server 2012 Express LocalDB, are installed.

The procedure for installing Visual Studio Express 2012 for Web is similar. Before you can install this edition, though, you have to download the setup program from Microsoft's web site. Then, when you run the setup program, no optional features are installed.

The Visual Studio 2012 Setup program

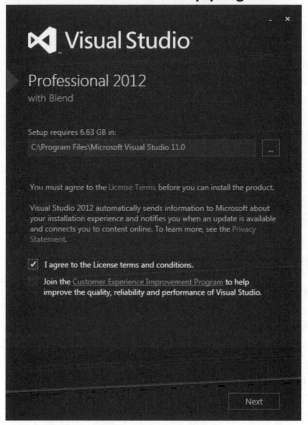

How to install Visual Studio 2012

1. Insert the DVD and the setup program will start automatically.

2. Review and then agree to the license terms by checking the appropriate box. Then, click the Next button.

3. When the Optional Features page is displayed, you can uncheck any features you don't need and then click the Install button.

4. When the Setup Success page is displayed, you can click the Restart Now button to restart your computer and finish the installation.

How to install Visual Studio Express 2012 for Web

1. Go to the page on Microsoft's web site for the download of the Visual Studio Express 2012 editions, and follow the directions to download the setup program for the Web edition.

2. Run the setup program. It works similarly to the setup program for Visual Studio 2012, but no optional features are available.

Note

- The Visual Studio 2012 setup programs install not only Visual Studio, but also .NET Framework 4.5, IIS Express, and SQL Server Express LocalDB.

Figure A-2   How to install Visual Studio 2012

How to use the Halloween database

In section 3 of this book, you will learn how to develop applications that work with the data in a database. The book applications in that section use a database named Halloween with an edition of SQL Server 2012 called SQL Server 2012 Express LocalDB. This edition of SQL Server is designed specifically for developers and doesn't require any management. It lets you create applications that automatically start the database engine and attach the database to the server when an application is run. In addition, it is automatically installed with Visual Studio 2012.

Figure A-3 summarizes the techniques for using the Halloween database with SQL Server Express LocalDB. To do that, you can simply add the Halloween.mdf file to the App_Data folder of a project. Then, you can create a SQL data source that uses this database as described in chapter 13. Alternatively, you can use an object data source with the database as described in chapter 20.

Of course, you can also use the Halloween database with other editions of SQL Server 2012. If you deploy an application to IIS on your local computer as described in chapter 21, for example, you won't be able to use SQL Server Express LocalDB with the application. In that case, you may want to install and use SQL Server 2012 Express as described in this figure. This edition of SQL Server 2012 is free, and it provides all of the features of the full editions of SQL Server 2012.

Although you don't need to know much about how SQL Server Express works to use it, you should know that when you run the setup program, it creates an instance of SQL Server with the same name as your computer appended with SQLEXPRESS. For example, the copy of SQL Server on my system is named Anne-PC\SQLEXPRESS. After this server is installed and started, you can create databases that are managed by the server. Then, you can connect to those databases from your C# applications using the generated server name or the name localhost\SqlExpress. Here, *localhost* indicates that the database server is running on the same computer as the application.

To create the Halloween database, you can run the batch file named create_database.bat that's stored in the C:\Murach\aspnet45_cs\Database directory when you download and install the files for this book as described in figure A-1. This batch file runs a SQL Server script named create_database.sql that creates the Halloween database and attaches it to the SQL Server Express database server that's running on your computer.

Note, however, that if the database server on your system has a name other than the computer name appended with SQLEXPRESS, the batch file we provide won't work. But you can easily change it so it will work. To do that, just open the file in a text editor such as NotePad. When you do, you'll see a single command with this server specification:

```
sqlcmd -S localhost\SqlExpress -E /i create_database.sql
```

Then, you can just change this specification to the name of your server.

How to use the database with SQL Server 2012 Express LocalDB

- The Halloween database files (Halloween.mdf and Halloween_Log.ldf) are included in the App_Data folder of each application for this book that uses this database.

- To use the Halloween database in your own applications, you can add the Halloween.mdf file to the App_Data folder of your project. This will automatically add the Halloween_Log.ldf file. Then, you can create a SQL data source from the database as described in chapter 13 or an object data source as described in chapter 20.

How to use the database with SQL Server 2012 Express

- To use the Halloween database with SQL Server Express, you must first create it. To do that, you can use Windows Explorer to navigate to the C:\Murach\aspnet45_cs\Database directory and double-click the create_database.bat file. This runs the create_database.sql file that creates the database objects and inserts the rows into each table.

- The create_database.sql file starts by deleting the Halloween database if it already exists. That way, you can use it to recreate the database and restore the original data if you ever need to do that.

- When you create the Halloween database, the Halloween.mdf and Halloween_Log.ldf files are created and stored in the default data directory for your instance of SQL Server. For SQL Server 2012, that directory is C:\Program files\ Microsoft SQL Server\MSSQL11.SQLEXPRESS\MSSQL\DATA.

- To define a connection to the Halloween database, you can use the server name localhost\SqlExpress or a name that consists of your computer name followed by \SqlExpress.

How to install and work with SQL Server 2012 Express

- To install SQL Server 2012 Express, you can download its setup file from Microsoft's web site for free and then run that file.

- After you install SQL Server Express, it will start automatically each time you start your PC. To start or stop this service or change its start mode, start the SQL Server Configuration Manager (Start→All Programs→Microsoft SQL Server 2012→Configuration Tools→SQL Server Configuration Manager), select the server in the right pane, and use the buttons in the toolbar.

Note

- SQL Server 2012 Express LocalDB is automatically installed with Visual Studio 2012, so no setup is required to use it.

Figure A-3   How to use the Halloween database

How to set up IIS on your local computer

In addition to IIS Express, which comes with Visual Studio 2012, Windows comes with the full edition of IIS. In most cases, you won't need to use the full edition of IIS to run and test your ASP.NET web applications. Instead, you can use IIS Express. The exception is if you want to deploy an application to IIS on your local computer. Then, you'll need to know how to set up IIS. Figure A-4 shows you how.

To start, you need to install IIS. To do that, you display the Windows Features dialog box as described here. This dialog box lists all the available Windows features. If all of the features of a component are installed, the check box in front of the component will have a check mark in it. If only some of the features are installed, the check box will be shaded.

To install the default features of IIS, you simply check its box and then click the OK button. If you want to install features other than the defaults, you can expand the Internet Information Services node and any of its subordinate nodes to select the features you want. By default, the features listed in step 2 of this figure should be selected. However, in some cases they aren't, so you need to select them.

If you know that you're going to deploy your applications to IIS, you should install IIS before you install Visual Studio. That way, Visual Studio can register ASP.NET with IIS. Otherwise, you'll need to use the aspnet_regiis program to do that as described in this figure.

To find the latest build number of .NET that you need to run this program, you can first enter a cd\ command at a command prompt to return to the root directory of the C drive. Then, you can run this command to identify the Windows root directory:

```
C:\>cd %systemroot%\Microsoft.NET\Framework
C:\Windows\Microsoft.NET\Framework>
```

This shows you what the root directory is so you can use Windows Explorer to find the latest build number in the Framework directory. To complete the registration, you can run these commands (assuming the build number is 30319):

```
C:\Windows\Microsoft.NET\Framework>cd v4.0.30319
C:\Windows\Microsoft.NET\Framework\v4.0.30319>aspnet_regiis -i
```

If the web application you're deploying uses the Halloween database, you'll also need to grant ASP.NET access to that database. To do that, you can use the grant_access.bat file as described in this figure. This file runs a script named grant_access.sql, which actually grants access to the ASP.NET 4 application pool. Application pools are used by IIS to separate the processing of various applications. The ASP.NET 4 application pool is the one that your ASP.NET 4.5 applications will run in by default if you run them under IIS.

The Windows Features dialog box

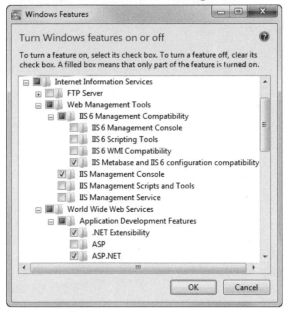

How to install IIS

1. Display the Control Panel and click the Programs link. Then, click the Turn Windows Features On or Off link in the Programs and Features category to display the Windows Features dialog box.

2. Select Internet Information Services from the list of features that are displayed, then expand this node and make sure that these features are selected:
   - Web Management Tools→IIS 6 Management Compatibility → IIS Metabase and IIS 6 configuration compatibility
   - Web Management Tools→IIS Management Console
   - World Wide Web Services→Application Development Features→ASP.NET

3. Click the OK button to complete the installation.

How to register ASP.NET with IIS

- If you know that you're going to use IIS, you should install it before you install Visual Studio. Otherwise, you'll need to register ASP.NET with IIS.

- To register ASP.NET with IIS, open a command prompt and use the cd command to change the directory to %systemroot%Microsoft.NET\Framework\v4.0.xxxxx, where %systemroot% is the root directory for Windows and xxxxx is the latest .NET build number. Then, enter the command aspnet_regiis -i.

How to grant ASP.NET access to the Halloween database

- Run the grant_access.bat file in the C:\Murach\apsnet45_cs\Database directory, which runs the grant_access.sql file.

Figure A-4   How to set up IIS on your local computer

Index

J

For more on Murach products, visit us at
www.murach.com

Books for .NET developers

Murach's ASP.NET 4.5 Web Programming with C# 2012	$57.50
Murach's C# 2012	54.50
Murach's ASP.NET 4.5 Web Programming with VB 2012	$57.50
Murach's Visual Basic 2012	54.50

Books for open-source web developers

Murach's HTML5 and CSS3	$54.50
Murach's JavaScript and jQuery	54.50
Murach's JavaScript and DOM Scripting	54.50
Murach's PHP and MySQL	54.50

Books for Java programmers

Murach's Java Programming	$57.50
Murach's Java Servlets and JSP (2nd Ed.)	52.50
Murach's Android Programming	57.50

Books for database programmers

Murach's SQL Server 2012 for Developers	$54.50
Murach's MySQL	54.50
Murach's Oracle SQL and PL/SQL	52.50

Prices and availability are subject to change. Please visit our web site or call for current information.

Our unlimited guarantee...when you order directly from us

You must be satisfied with our books. If they aren't better than any other programming books you've ever used...both for training and reference...you can send them back within 90 days for a full refund. No questions asked!

Your opinions count

If you have any comments on this book, I'm eager to get them. Thanks for your feedback!

To comment by

E-mail:	murachbooks@murach.com
Web:	www.murach.com
Postal mail:	Mike Murach & Associates, Inc.
	4340 N. Knoll
	Fresno, California 93722-7825

To order now,

 Web: www.murach.com

 Call toll-free:
1-800-221-5528
(Weekdays, 8 am to 4 pm Pacific Time)

 Fax: 1-559-440-0963

 Mike Murach & Associates, Inc.
Professional programming books

What software you need for this book

- Any of the full editions of Microsoft Visual Studio 2012 or Visual Studio Express 2012 for Web.
- These editions include everything you need for developing ASP.NET 4.5 applications, including .NET Framework 4.5, ASP.NET 4.5, C# 2012, a scaled-back version of IIS called IIS Express, and a scaled-back version of SQL Server called SQL Server Express LocalDB.
- If you want to store databases on your own PC and you don't want to use SQL Server 2012 Express LocalDB, you can install SQL Server 2012 Express.
- If you want to use IIS (Internet Information Services) on your own computer to test the deployment of an application, you'll need to be sure it's installed and set up properly.
- For information about installing these products, please see appendix A.

The downloadable files for this book

- The source code for all of the applications presented in this book.
- Starting points for the exercises in this book so you can get more practice in less time.
- Solutions for all of the exercises in this book so you can check your work on the exercises.
- The files for the Halloween database that's used by this book, along with files for creating this database if you're using an edition of SQL Server 2012 other than SQL Server 2012 Express LocalDB.
- Files for granting ASP.NET access to the Halloween database if you're running an application under IIS instead of IIS Express.
- For information about downloading and installing these applications and files, please see appendix A.

The VB edition of this book

- If this book looks interesting but you're a Visual Basic developer, please see *Murach's ASP.NET 4.5 Web Programming with VB 2012*. It covers all of the same features but uses Visual Basic coding examples.

www.murach.com